Gerontological Nursing

Gerontological Nursing

Second Edition

Mickey Stanley, RN, PhD, CS
Associate Professor
Southern Illinois University at Edwardsville
Edwardsville, Illinois

Patricia Gauntlett Beare, RN, PhD
Professor
Louisiana State University Medical Center
School of Nursing
New Orleans, Louisiana

F. A. DAVIS COMPANY • Philadelphia

F. A. Davis Company
1915 Arch Street
Philadelphia, PA 19103

Printed in the United States of America

Last digit indicates print number: 10 9 8 7 6 5 4 3 2 1

Acquisitions Editor: Alan Sorkowitz
Designer: Bill Donnelly
Cover Designer: Alicia Baronsky
Cover Photography: Doug Rickards

As new scientific information becomes available through basic and clinical research, recommended treatments and drug therapies undergo changes. The author(s) and publisher have done everything possible to make this book accurate, up to date, and in accord with accepted standards at the time of publication. The authors, editors, and publisher are not responsible for errors or omissions or for consequences from application of the book, and make no warranty, expressed or implied, in regard to the contents of the book. Any practice described in this book should be applied by the reader in accordance with professional standards of care used in regard to the unique circumstances that may apply in each situation. The reader is advised always to check product information (package inserts) for changes and new information regarding dose and contraindications before administering any drug. Caution is especially urged when using new or infrequently ordered drugs.

Library of Congress Cataloging in Publication Data

Gerontological nursing / [edited by] Mickey Stanley, Patricia
    Gauntlett Beare. — 2nd ed.
        p. cm.
    Includes bibliographical references and index.
    ISBN 0-8036-0369-X
    1. Geriatric nursing.   I. Stanley, Mickey.   II. Beare, Patricia
Gauntlett.
    [DNLM: 1. Nursing Assessment. WY 152 G3771 1999]
RC954.G4737 1999
610.73'65—dc21
DNLM/DLC
for Library of Congress   98-45217
                                                           CIP

Preface

By the year 2020, 20 percent of the population will be aged 65 years or older, with the greatest growth of our older population among those age 85 years or older. Where individuals age at an inevitable and steady pace from birth to death, the number of unhealthy older persons has increased. As a nation, we have largely failed to achieve healthful aging.

The purpose of this book is to promote a healthful lifestyle approach for older adults rather than a gloomy image of an aging population of sedentary, chronically ill adults. New concepts of successful aging through adaptation to the process of aging; the use of the classifications of primary, secondary, and tertiary prevention; and the concept of health promotion are the organizing frameworks for the delivery of nursing care and education. Health promotion for older adults focuses not on the disease or disability of older adults, but on maximizing potential and minimizing the effects of aging.

Features

The features that have been integrated into this text will facilitate its use as a textbook for nursing students and as a reference manual for the practicing nurse. The content is comprehensive, covering the full range of issues and problems of concern to older adults. Theoretical concepts have been integrated with the principles of nursing practice to provide a framework for the delivery of nursing care. Sufficient depth in the discussion of physiological changes associated with aging and the pathophysiological changes that accompany the major disease processes provides an excellent foundation upon which to develop the nursing plan of care. Care plans that illustrate major problem areas are provided, as are teaching guides to be used with older adults and their significant others. Coverage for dementias, theories of aging, and transcultural considerations has been expanded. Research briefs that illustrate the ongoing work to develop a research base for gerontological nursing practice have also been included. Current addresses of both local and national resources are presented to give readers access to additional information for themselves and clients and their families. Patient teaching guides are also included.

Section I provides a broad theoretical foundation for the practice of gerontological nursing, with an introduction to the concept of health promotion and health protection for this population and the standards of practice for gerontological nursing. The areas of public policy, cultural dimensions, legal and ethical issues, teaching and compliance, polypharmacy, and settings of care are explored to allow the reader to consider each of the remaining chapters from a multidimensional perspective. Section II begins a thorough discussion of each of the body systems, and Section III examines those problems that involve multisystem alterations. Section IV highlights those issues that involve both individual and family psychodynamics. Section V details the nursing management of older adults with disorders of mental processing, and Section VI provides an epilogue on the future of gerontological nursing.

In addition, we have added samples of critical pathways and MDS/RAP forms. A list of suggested student learning activities is included for each chapter in the book.

This edition now offers a full instructor's guide, with case studies (complete with answers) for classroom use or testing purposes, teaching tips (with special emphasis on incorporating the book's content into programs that integrate gerontology into broader nursing subject areas), and a testbank of approximately 200 multiple-choice questions.

Acknowledgments

We would like to take this opportunity to thank all those individuals who contributed their time and talents to the production of this text. These include the many contributors who willingly shared their expertise in gerontological nursing, those talented people who performed the multiple manuscript reviews, and the host of individuals at F. A. Davis who made it all come together into a finished product. To Alan Sorkowitz, the individual who has provided guidance throughout the entire process, goes a very special thanks. And last but not least, we wish to acknowledge all those older adults who teach us daily about their special needs and strengths.

Mickey Stanley
Patricia Gauntlett Beare

Contributors

Tanya Dandry Aiken, RN, BSN, JD
President and Chief Executive Officer
Aiken Development Group
New Orleans, Louisiana

Donna Angelucci, RN, MA
Assistant Director of Nursing, Education and Research
Bayshore Community Hospital
Holmdel, New Jersey

Sister Rose Therese Bahr, ASC, PhD, FAAN
Adorers of the Blood of Christ
Provincial House
Wichita, Kansas

Patricia Gauntlett Beare, RN, PhD
Professor
Louisiana State University Medical Center
School of Nursing
New Orleans, Louisiana

Kathryn A. Blair, RN, C, PhD
Assistant Professor
University of Northern Colorado
School of Nursing
Greeley, Colorado

Mary Bliesmer, RN, C, MPH
Associate Professor
Mankato State University
School of Nursing
Mankato, Minnesota

Kathleen C. Buckwalter, RN, PhD, FAAN
Associate Provost, Health Sciences
The University of Iowa
Iowa City, Iowa

Shirley Damrosch, RN, PhD
Associate Professor
University of Maryland
School of Nursing
Baltimore, Maryland

Cheryl Dellasega, RN, PhD, GNP
Assistant Professor
School of Nursing
Pennsylvania State University
State College, Pennsylvania

Barbara Cole Donlon, RN, MPH, EdD
Associate Professor
Primary Care Nurse Practitioner Program
Louisiana State University
New Orleans, Louisiana

Jan Dodge Dougherty, RN, MS
Case Management, Advanced Home Health
Chandler, Arizona

Lucie S. Elfervig, RN, DNS, CRNO, CS
Independent Ophthalmological Consultant, Clinical
    Specialist
Vitreo-Retinal Foundation
Memphis, Tennessee

Terry Fulmer, RN, PhD, FAAN
Professor
New York University School of Education
Division of Nursing
New York, New York

R. LaVerne Gallman, RN, PhD
Professor Emeritus
The University of Texas at Austin
School of Nursing
Austin, Texas

Joelle A. Graham, RN, MSN
Family Nurse Practitioner
Charleston, South Carolina

Barbara K. Haight, RN, C, DrPh, FAAN
Professor of Nursing
Chairperson, Department of Health Promotion and
    Community Oriented Care
Medical University of South Carolina
College of Nursing
Charleston, South Carolina

Helen L. Halstead, RN, PhD
Assistant Professor (Retired)
Wichita State University
Wichita, Kansas

Cathy S. Heriot, RN, PhD
Formerly Assistant Professor
Medical University of South Carolina
School of Nursing
Charleston, South Carolina

Mildred O. Hogstel, RN, C, PhD
Abell-Hanger Professor of Gerontological Nursing
Harris College of Nursing
Texas Christian University
Fort Worth, Texas

Beverley E. Holland, RN, PhD
Assistant Professor
Bellarmine College
Louisville, Kentucky

Nancy S. Jecker, PhD
Associate Professor
University of Washington
School of Medicine
Department of Medical History and Ethics
Department of Philosophy
School of Law
Seattle, Washington

Beverly K. Johnson, RN, PhD
Assistant Professor
Pacific Lutheran University
School of Nursing
Tacoma, Washington

Arthur (Don) Johnson, RN, PhD
Associate Professor
University of Texas Health Science Center San Antonio
School of Nursing
San Antonio, Texas

Rebecca Johnson, RN, PhD
Assistant Professor
University of Northern Illinois at DeKalb
School of Nursing
DeKalb, Illinois

Carolyn Kee, RN, PhD
Associate Professor
Department of Adult Health Nursing
School of Nursing
Georgia State University
Atlanta, Georgia

Patricia Knutesen, RN, MS
Public Health Consultant
Arizona Department of Health Services
Phoenix, Arizona

Christine R. Kovach, RN, PhD
Associate Professor
Marquette University
Milwaukee, Wisconsin

Molly Lawrence, RN, CS, MSN
Nurse Practitioner
St. Mary Hospital
Hoboken, New Jersey

Kelly H. Leech, RN, BSN
Captain, Army Nurse Corps
Walter Reed Army Medical Center
Washington, DC

Lora McGuire, RN, MSN
Pain Consultant and Instructor
Department of Nursing
Joliet Junior College
Joliet, Illinois

Joanne M. Miller, RN, PhD
Practitioner/Teacher Gerontological Nursing
Rush University
College of Nursing
Chicago, Illinois

Marilyn M. Pattillo, RN, CN, PhD
Director, Continuing Education
The University of Texas at Austin
School of Nursing
Austin, Texas

Demetrius Porche, RN, DNS
Associate Professor, Program Director Baccalaureate
  Program
Nicholls State University
Houma, Louisiana

Linda A. Roussel, RN, DSN, CRRN
Assistant Professor
School of Nursing
Louisiana State University
New Orleans, Louisiana

Mary Sapp
Executive Director
Texas Department on Aging
Austin, Texas

Linda Sarna, RN, DNSc, FAAN
American Cancer Society Professor of Oncology Nursing
Associate Professor, School of Nursing
University of California—Los Angeles
Los Angeles, California

Bernard Sorofman, PhD
Associate Professor
The University of Iowa
College of Pharmacy
Iowa City, Iowa

Mickey Stanley, RN, PhD, CS
Associate Professor
Southern Illinois University at Edwardsville
Edwardsville, Illinois

Gary P. Stoehr, PharmD
Associate Professor
Department of Pharmacy and Therapeutics
Associate Dean, Student and Academic Affairs
University of Pittsburgh, School of Pharmacy
Pittsburgh, Pennsylvania

Judith A. Strasser, RN, DNSc
Associate Professor
University of Maryland
School of Nursing
Baltimore, Maryland

Toni Tripp-Reimer, RN, PhD, FAAN
Professor and Director
Office for Nursing Research Development and
  Utilization
College of Nursing
The University of Iowa
Iowa City, Iowa

Laurel A. Wiersema, RN, MSN
Clinical Nurse Specialist
Barnes Hospital
Washington University Medical Center
St. Louis, Missouri

Sarah A. Wilson, RN, PhD
Associate Professor
Marquette University
Milwaukee, Wisconsin

Mary Ellen Hill Yonushonis, RN, MS
Assistant Professor
Pennsylvania State University
School of Nursing
State College, Pennsylvania

Contents

Introduction to Health Promotion/Protection in the Care of Older Adults

CHAPTER 1

Promoting Health through Public Policy and Standards of Care

Mary Sapp / Mary Bliesmer

OBJECTIVES

Upon completion of this chapter, the reader will be able to:

- Describe the changing demographics of the United States and its effects on the health-care system
- Discuss the nurse's role in health promotion and health protection for older adults
- Define public policy and describe the policy-making process
- Provide an overview of some of the major pieces of aging-specific legislation with particular relevance to health-care professionals
- Discuss some of the emerging issues in health-care policy
- Describe methods for nursing involvement in the policy-making process
- Address the moral imperative for nursing's involvement in the policy-making process
- Discuss the eight purposes of standards
- Explain how standards define nursing practice

The Aging Population

Whereas individuals age at an inevitable and steady pace from birth to death, the aging of society is neither inevitable nor uniform. Populations age when the proportion of older people relative to younger people increases.[1] Although America's population has been aging almost steadily since 1800, the pace of population aging has increased abruptly and dramatically in recent years. From 1960 to 1982, the number of children age 15 and under in the United States declined by about 7 percent and the proportion of the population under age 15 has declined by 28 percent. At the other end of the age scale, very different forces are at work. Since 1950, the ranks of America's older adults, age 65 and older, has more than doubled, and those of frail adults over age 85 has more than quadrupled. By the year 2035, one-fifth, and possibly one-fourth, of all Americans will be 65 years of age or older.[2] Approximately 75 million Americans were born between 1946 and 1964, and these "baby boomers" represent nearly one-third of our population. The first baby boomers turned 50 in 1996 and will turn 65 in 2011. By the year 2050, 1 in 3 Americans will be over 55 years old and 1 in 5 will be over 65. The fastest-growing demographic group in the United States is those older than age 85; this group will reach nearly 5 million by 2000.

Because of the exceptionally low birthrate from 1964 to the late 1970s and the loss of the traditional multiple generations of families living in the same neighborhoods, our aging population does not have sufficient family support.

The female majority in the United States continues to grow. American women can be expected to live until age 78.3, whereas men can expect to live only until age 71.4. This feminization has four implications for nursing: (1) the female majority is concentrated in the upper age ranges; (2) most older women do not have a spouse to care for them; (3) most older women live alone; and (4) most older women are in poorer health than men.[3]

Hispanic whites will be the largest ethnic group in the future because of their high birthrates and younger women. Census data for 1990 estimate the population makeup as 77 percent non-Hispanic whites, 12 percent blacks, 3 percent Asians, and 8 percent Hispanic. At present, the growthrate for whites is 8 percent, for blacks 16 percent, for Asians 65 percent, and for Hispanics 44 percent.[4]

The sudden appearance of large numbers of older persons has special implications for nursing and health care. First, compared with other age groups, older adults are by far the heaviest users of health services, and their growing numbers mean that they will be even more disproportionately represented in the health-care sector. Second, because life expectancy for women is on average 7.5 years longer than that for men, women will be disproportionately represented among the oldest and fastest-growing age groups.[5] Moreover, as a group, women use health services more than men, and they seek professional health care earlier than men do, even for more minor conditions.[6] Nurses of diverse cultural and ethnic background and specialties will need to build and improve skills in caring for older and predominantly female patients. Finally, per capita, health-care expenditures on persons over age 65 are nearly four times those of the rest of the population.[7]

The "graying" of the population has been noticed by the Public Health Service and the Institute of Medicine. In the Surgeon General's latest report, *Healthy People 2000: Citizens Chart the Course,* major attention is given to the health promotion and disease prevention needs of older people.[8] The federal initiative to fund Medicare Community Nursing Organization (CNO) demonstration projects designed to plan, authorize, and deliver health promotion and other nursing services by nurses is a positive sign that policy makers are acknowledging the value of health promotion and the significant role that nurses can have in this area.[9]

The Nurse's Role in Health Promotion for Older Adults

The aging of our society is the dominant demographic phenomenon of our time.[10] Three of the four most common causes of death among older adults—heart disease, cancer, and stroke—are the result of an unhealthy lifestyle.[11] However, the gloomy image of an aging nation of sedentary, chronically ill older adults is gradually being replaced by new concepts such as successful aging (i.e., an individual's ability to adapt to the process of aging)[12] and compression of morbidity (i.e., the delay of onset of chronic, debilitating illness until later in life).[10] Health protection and health promotion are emerging as appropriate frameworks for care of older adults. Professionals caring for older people are recognizing that prevention for a 65-year-old person, who can be expected to live another 20 years, is a necessary component of health care.

WHO ARE OLDER ADULTS?

Development of this approach requires consideration of who older adults are and what constitutes health promotion and prevention for this segment of the population. We know that older adults are a heterogeneous group. Each older adult represents a unique set of goals, experiences, values, and attitudes.[13] The late John Heinz, former chairman of the U.S. Senate Special Committee on Aging, noted:

> Growing old, while an inevitable process for all of us, has no common denominator when it comes to health. The image of a grayed and crippled, frail older American is just as much a stereotype as that of a robust and active one; neither captures the range of health status found in this segment of our Nation's population.[14]

Although chronic disease and aging are not synonymous, studies reveal an increased incidence of chronic disease occurring as people age. The 1989 census data revealed that by age 65, 70 percent of men and 77 percent of women surveyed had one or more chronic conditions. By age 80, these numbers increased to 81 percent for men and 90 percent for women.[15]

Because women outlive men, studies reveal that only 40 percent of older women compared with 77 percent of older men are living with a spouse.[16] Most older adults reside in the community, with less than 1 percent living in institutional settings. With advanced age, the statistics increase to approximately 22 percent of frail adults (those age 85 or older) living in institutional settings.[17] This clearly shows that most older adults live alone or have some form of assisted living arrangements, emphasizing the importance of health promotion and health protection as a focus of nursing intervention for all older adults.

WHAT IS HEALTH?

Age alone is an inadequate predictor of health status, primarily because one's definition of health changes with age. The traditional definition of health as the absence of disease or disability is clearly inappropriate for many older adults for whom chronic disease has become a way of life. Instead, more emphasis in this age group is placed on health as a state of mind, even in situations of a failing body.[17] Self-ratings of health among older adults often reflect such qualities as feeling good, being able to do things that are important, coping with life's demands, and achieving one's potential. One definition of health for older adults is "the ability to live and function effectively in society and to exercise self-reliance and autonomy to the maximum extent feasible, but not necessarily as total freedom from disease."[18] Health for older adults is a complex interaction of physical, functional, and psychosocial factors.[19] Health promotion for this segment of the population must also incorporate these parameters.

WHAT ARE HEALTH PROMOTION AND HEALTH PROTECTION?

Recent studies find that older adults are interested in health promotion and that many older adults currently practice more health-promoting behaviors than their younger counterparts.[19,20] When asked what behaviors they engaged in to maintain or improve their health, older adults listed staying active and maintaining a positive outlook on life; exercise, nutrition, rest, and relaxation; blood pressure monitoring and health checkups; and the self-discipline to do things in moderation.[20] This list actually represents a combination of health-promoting and health-protecting (preventive) behaviors.

According to Pender,[21] health promotion is a "multidimensional pattern of self-initiated actions and perceptions that serve to maintain or enhance the level of wellness, self-actualization and fulfillment of the individual." Such behaviors as engaging in regular physical and mental activity; getting adequate nutrition, rest, and relaxation; and maintaining social support networks are all health-promotion behaviors because they maintain or enhance one's level of wellness.

Health promotion for older adults then, is not focused on disease or disability but rather on the strengths and abilities of older adults. Health promotion seeks to maximize the older person's potential and minimize the effects of aging. The major health promotion activities deemed appropriate for older adults are regular physical, mental, and social activity; adequate nutrition and weight control; and stress management.[22]

These findings pose unique opportunities for the nursing profession. Nurses have the potential to improve the quality of life for a significant portion of the population by using a health-promotion framework to organize and deliver nursing care to older adults. This approach encourages nurses to view older adults positively—to identify and build on strengths rather than focus on limitations and problems. Health-protection behaviors are activities directed toward reducing the individual's risk of developing a specific disease. For example, regular health checkups and appropriate drug use are health-protecting behaviors. Some behaviors are both health-promoting and health-protecting. For example, regular physical exercise is a health-protecting behavior when it is undertaken to reduce one's risk of cardiovascular disease, depression, adult-onset diabetes from obesity, and osteoporosis. Following specific dietary restrictions such as low-cholesterol or high-fiber diets is a health-protecting behavior against cardiovascular disease and some forms of cancer. A thorough review of health protection for the commonly occurring problems of older adults can be found in Sections II through V.

Public Policy Development

The escalation of public and private expenditures for health care is causing major changes in the financing and delivery of health care. A system previously oriented to acute care is shifting to a system that emphasizes wellness, health promotion, and disease prevention. Employers seeking relief from the strain of increasing health insurance premiums have been driving the system to managed care models that replace incentives to use expensive health-care services with incentives to maintain wellness and consequently health promotion and disease prevention.

With public dollars covering a large portion of health-care expenditures for older adults, policy makers are faced with major concerns. The Clinton administration's efforts at health-care reform increased the level of attention to these issues and heightened the awareness of policy makers and the general public to the need to address them. The baby boom demographics add a sense of urgency to these considerations.

With the emphasis on wellness, health promotion, and cost containment, the role of the nurse will be focused more on these areas. With fewer and briefer inpatient stays and more emphasis on primary care and wellness through managed care arrangements, nurses are more often working in primary care and home health settings.

Although reform is occurring in the structure and form of health-care delivery, the needs of an aging population will require special attention, especially in terms of long-term care. Models of long-term care that provide a full array of services for persons in their homes or in community settings have been developed, but major public policy decisions in such areas as level of payment, coverage, state versus federal responsibility, and individual and family responsibility continue to be debated. Public policies established during the Great Society years of the 1960s, which created such programs for older adults as Medicare, Medicaid, and Older Americans Act services through the Administration on Aging, are being re-examined to consider their equity and fiscal implications in a rapidly aging society.

The decisions made by policy makers about the future of these programs and services will have tremendous implications for the overall well-being of older adults, their families, and the health-care professionals who serve them. Neither as citizens nor as professionals can nurses afford to ignore the public policy arena. The nature of services that will be available and accessible to seniors and the role of nurses in their delivery will be greatly affected by public policy.

Public Policy and Aging: The Nurse's Role

The nurse shares with other citizens the responsibility for initiating and supporting action to meet the health and social needs of the public. This responsibility is addressed in the International Council of Nurses Code for Nurses, which suggests that the nurse collaborates with members of the professions and other citizens in promoting community and national efforts to meet the health needs of the public.

AMERICAN NURSES' ASSOCIATION CODE FOR NURSES PUBLIC POLICY DEFINED

Public policy is the laws and ordinances or the interpretation of law by courts or public agencies. Nurses are increasingly recognizing that their ability to promote the health and well-being of the young and old, of families and communities, is determined largely by the activities of policy makers. Decisions made in our public policy arenas define the structural and philosophical under-pinning of the health-care delivery system and define the roles of nurses in that system.[23–25]

NURSING'S INVOLVEMENT WITH PUBLIC POLICY

Although nursing history textbooks proudly recount the well-known advocacy efforts of such notable nurses as Florence Nightingale, Lillian Wald, and Lavinia Dock, nurses have generally been reticent about being involved in public policy.[22] By stepping into the political arena, nurses have the opportunity to extend their care for the overall well-being of older persons into policies that will have an impact on the lives of millions of older persons and their families.

The Imperative for Involvement

As Thomas Jefferson said, "The individual citizen in a democracy is the highest official."[26] As individuals with the rights and responsibilities of citizens and as professionals committed to promoting a healthy community, nurses have a double imperative to participate in the political process.

In 1988, 1 in every 44 registered female voters was a nurse.[23] The power represented by that statistic is impressive. However, that statistic is merely an indictment for lost opportunity if nurses are not influencing the outcomes at the voting machines. Do candidates care what nurses think? Are they aware of nurses' positions on matters affecting older adults? If this awareness is lacking, then a significant means of influencing policy lies dormant. A simple but extremely important instrument for affecting policy is unquestionably the power of the vote, the power of the constituent.

Opportunities for Involvement

Beyond nurses' voting power, the opportunities today for nurses' involvement in the policy-making arena are many.

- Nurses can provide expertise in assisting candidates to develop their health-care platforms and can continue to provide expertise to them after their election to office.
- Nurses can join organizations that analyze issues and educate voters.
- Nurses can provide testimony at legislative and public hearings on health-care matters. This forum provides an excellent medium for public education regarding health-care issues in which nurses can be seen as true experts.
- Nurses may serve as members of legislative committees charged with studying health-care issues. These committees develop positions and strategies for the political activities of organizations such as the Texas Nurses' Association.

The power of the media to influence voters is tremendous, and response to positions taken and articles printed is also effective for communicating values and beliefs.

With the support of state nursing associations, nurses are being appointed to the state boards of health and other state agencies and boards. In this capacity, they can influence public health policy for the entire state and also ensure that the nursing viewpoint is well represented in policy design.

State agencies are extensively involved in policy interpretation, implementation, development, and revision. These agencies implement federal rules and regulations and are responsible for formulating state-level approaches to maintaining compliance with federal regulations, such as those that pertain to Medicare, Medicaid, and the Older Americans Act. The importance of nursing involvement with these agencies cannot be overstated.

Well-informed legislative aides and legislators are also in strategic positions to bring the nursing agenda to the public debate. For legislators who have no health-care background and lack the time required to research health policy positions adequately, a nurse can be a valuable member of the legislative staff. These positions provide a direct channel and opportunity for nursing values to influence policy deliberations and outcomes. Nurses in these positions also make it easier for nurses and nursing organizations to bring forward policy initiatives and input on current or proposed legislation.

Older persons should be encouraged to participate in policy discussions themselves, to express their hopes and desire for aging-friendly legislative initiatives. Older nurses are invaluable in "gray" consumer advocacy groups as policy positions are developed and the expertise of a nursing professional is needed.

The Moral Imperative

The nurse serves as a patient advocate, both within the health-care system and outside of it, in the area of policy. The nursing emphasis on health promotion, on care of the whole person, on community-based care accessible to the consumer, and on recognition of the older person and the family as the unit of care should be heard in health policy discussions and reflected in health policy decisions. Perhaps these concepts seem obvious, but they have not been addressed adequately. A strong voice needs to speak to these issues, concerns, and values.

It must also be recognized that the advocacy agenda for our aging population is an agenda for our entire population. Maternal and child health policies ultimately are an aging issue, as are all health policies. We are all affected by the health or disease of the community. The infant of today becomes the older adult of tomorrow, and a healthy infant has a better chance of facing old age with less morbidity than does a malnourished, ill child. Considering the special needs of older persons is appropriate and necessary to good social policy; however, considering these needs apart from the overall needs of all age groups and other competing demands is not.

Nurses can wield significant political power and can use it to enhance the overall well-being of older persons and their families. Participation, if only as an informed voter, is not optional; it is a moral imperative.

Standards of Practice for Gerontological Nursing

With the growing need for provision of health care for older adults also comes the question, "How can we provide high-quality nursing care for this population?" LeSage[27] suggests that to have a future impact on the health care that many of these persons will require: "nurses must identify scientific evidence for relationships of the care process to outcomes. Implementation and communication of such measures enhance nursing contributions to quality care." In this way, older persons will realize that their positive outcomes often are a result of nursing care specifically, especially care provided or directed by professional nurses.

Professional nurses play a major role in developing, implementing, and evaluating nursing practice standards, as well as providing a leadership role in quality assurance, for which these standards are useful. In 1987, the American Nurses' Association (ANA) Standards of Gerontological Nursing Practice were substantially revised from the original 1976 standards by an ANA task force, with assistance from the executive Committee of the Council on Gerontological Nursing. Subsequently, these standards were adopted by the ANA Cabinet on Nursing Practice and serve as a model for practice toward which gerontological nurses can strive in their various practice settings (Table 1–1).

As the gerontological specialty in nursing grows and thrives to meet the needs of an aging population, the 1987 ANA Standards of Gerontological Nursing Practice will continue to describe and prescribe professional nursing practice. These standards demonstrate the accountability of professional nurses as they provide nursing care to older people. Legally, practice standards may be used

TABLE 1–1   STANDARDS OF GERONTOLOGICAL NURSING PRACTICE: 1987 AND 1976

1987	1976
1 All gerontological nursing services are planned, organized, and directed by a nurse executive. The nurse executive has baccalaureate or master's preparation and has experience in gerontological nursing and administration of long-term care services or acute-care services for older adults.	1 Data are systematically and continuously collected about the health status of the older adult. The data are accessible, communicated, and recorded.
2 The nurse participates in the generation and testing of theory as a basis for clinical decisions. The nurse uses theoretical concepts to guide the effective practice of gerontological nursing.	2 Nursing diagnoses are derived from the identified normal responses of the individual to aging and the data collected about the health status of the older adult.
3 The health status of the older person is regularly assessed in a comprehensive, accurate, and systematic manner. The information obtained during the health assessment is accessible to and shared with appropriate members of the interdisciplinary healthcare team, including the older person and family.	3 A nursing plan of care is developed in conjunction with the older adult and/or significant others that includes goals derived from the nursing diagnosis.
4 The nurse uses health assessment data to determine nursing diagnoses.	4 The nursing care plan includes priorities and prescribed nursing approaches and measures to achieve the goals derived from the nursing diagnosis.
5 The nurse develops the plan of care in conjunction with the older person and appropriate others. Mutual goals, priorities, nursing approaches, and measures in the care plan address the therapeutic, preventive, restorative, and rehabilitative needs of the older person. The care plan helps the older person attain and maintain the highest level of health, well-being, and quality of life achievable, as well as a peaceful death. The plan of care facilitates continuity of care over time as the client moves to various care settings, and is revised as necessary.	5 The plan of care is implemented using appropriate nursing actions.
6 The nurse, guided by the plan of care, intervenes to provide care to restore the older person's functional capabilities and to prevent complications and excess disability. Nursing interventions are derived from nursing diagnoses and are based on gerontological nursing theory.	6 The older adult and/or significant other(s) participate in determining the progress attained in the achievement of established goals.
7 The nurse continually evaluates the client's and family's responses to interventions in order to determine progress toward goal attainment and to revise the data base, nursing diagnoses, and plan of care.	7 The older adult and/or significant other(s) participate in the ongoing process of assessment, the setting of new goals, the reordering of priorities, the revision of plans for nursing care, and the initiation of new nursing actions.
8 The nurse collaborates with other members of the health care team in the various settings in which care is given to the older person. The team meets regularly to evaluate the effectiveness of the care plan for the client and family and to adjust the plan of care to accommodate changing needs.	
9 The nurse participates in research designed to generate an organized body of gerontological nursing knowledge, disseminates research findings, and uses them in practice.	
10 The nurse uses the code for nurses established by the American Nurses Association as a guide for ethical decision making in practice.	
11 The nurse assumes responsibility for professional development and contributes to the professional growth of interdisciplinary team members. The nurse participates in peer review and other means of evaluation to ensure the quality of nursing practice.	

Source: *Standards and Scope of Gerontological Nursing Practice.* ©1987 American Nurses Association, Kansas City, Mo. Reprinted with permission.

as a guideline for identifying the prudent response of a nurse in a specific situation. The standards are a framework that provides an image of what gerontological nurses are about, what they can do, and what their unique contributions are.

Practice standards focus on the content of practice. "They provide a value orientation—what is essential or important for the practice to be judged at a specified level of quality, such as safe, good or excellent."[28] Beckman[28] tells us that standards are most useful as guides to nurses in their development until at least the proficiency level of practice as defined by Benner. Most experienced nurses may consciously refer to written standards only as practice changes are reflected in them because they have internalized the standards. Nursing standards can be used in assisting nurses in evaluating and improving their own practice, commending nurses when they provide excellent nursing care, providing objective criteria for the assessment of nurses' performance, determining the staffing needs of a clinical unit, identifying the need for and content of orientation and staff development programs, delineating the content of curricula and the criteria for evaluation of students, improving health-care delivery, and identifying foci of research.

Each standard is further described with structure, process, and outcome criteria.[29]

Beckman[28] states:

> Structure standards describe desirable conditions that allow or provide for quality of care. Process standards describe the desirable practices that should take place in the care process. Outcome standards describe the desirable end results: the health status, knowledge, performance, or other characteristic of the client that is expected as a result of care.

Summary

As our population continues to age, the need exists for nurses to examine older adults' needs, to influence health policy, and to evaluate today's standards of gerontology practice and to plan for the future. Nurses in our changing health-care environment are challenged to provide high-quality nursing care to a population that has more chronic disease, uses more health-care services, and in the near future, will consist more of minorities, the disadvantaged, and the financially vulnerable. As a profession, nursing must direct its energies, resources, and skills to influence public policy and to provide high-quality nursing care to older adults.

Student Learning Activities

1 Scan the local newspapers and lay publications for current issues that affect the health and safety of older adults in your community.

2 As a class, prepare a letter to your state representative that outlines the major points he or she needs to consider when addressing gerontological health-care issues.

3 Compare the ANA Standards of Nursing Practice with the Gerontological Standards for Nursing Practice.

4 Discuss the specific ways in which these standards guide nursing practice with older adults.

REFERENCES

1 Clement, P: History of US ageds' poverty shows welfare program changes. Perspect Aging 2:20, 1985.
2 US House of Representatives, 101st Congress, First Session: Developments in Aging. A Report of the Special Committee on Aging. US Government Printing Office, Washington, DC, 1988.
3 Healthcare's changing face: The demographics of the hospitals: 21st century. Hospitals 65(7):36, 1991.
4 Moora, M: Future trends in patient education. Semin Oncol Nurs 7(2):143, 1991.
5 Estes, C: Healthcare policy in the later twentieth century. Generations 12(3):44, 1988.
6 Atkins, GL: The politics of financing long term care. Generations 14:19, 1990.
7 US House of Representatives, 100th Congress, Second Session: Older Americans Act: A Staff Summary by the Select Committee on Aging (Senate Committee Pub no 100-683). US Government Printing Office, Washington, DC, 1987.
8 Institute of Medicine: Healthy People 2000—Citizens Chart the Course. National Academy of Sciences, Washington, DC, 1990.
9 Mittelstadt, P: HCFA solicits CNO sponsors. Am Nurse 41:2, 1991.
10 Omenn, GS: Prevention and the elderly: Appropriate policies. Health Aff (Millwood) Summer 9:80, 1990.
11 Dychtwald, K (ed): Wellness and Health Promotion for the Elderly. Aspen, Rockville, Md, 1986.
12 Atchley, RC: Social Forces and Aging, ed 5. Wadsworth, Belmont, Calif, 1988, p 245.
13 Boynton, P: Health maintenance alteration: A nursing diagnosis of the elderly. Clin Nurse Specialist 3(1):5, 1989.
14 US Senate Special Committee on Aging; The Health Status and Health Care Needs of Older Americans (Senate Committee Pub no 87-6635). US Government Printing Office, Washington, DC, 1986.
15 Burke, MM, and Walsh, MB: Gerontologic Nursing: Care of the Frail Elderly. CV Mosby, St Louis, 1992.
16 US Senate Special Committee on Aging: Aging America: Trends and Projections. US Dept of Health and Human Services, Washington, DC, 1988.
17 Miller, CA: Nursing Care of Older Adults. Scott, Foresman/Little, Brown Higher Education, Glenview, Ill, 1992.
18 Filner, B, and Williams, R: Health promotion for the elderly: Reducing functional dependency. In Healthy People 2000. US Government Printing Office, Washington, DC, 1979.
19 Walker, SN, et al: Health-promoting life styles of older adults: Comparisons with young and middle-aged adults, correlates and patterns. ANS 11:76, 1988.
20 Schafer, SL: Aggressive approach to promoting health responsibility. J Gerontol Nurse 15:22, 1989.
21 Pender, NJ: Health Promotion in Nursing Practice, ed 2. Appleton & Lange, Norwalk, Conn, 1987.
22 Nelson, L: Advocacy in nursing. Nurs Outlook 36(3):136, 1988.
23 Goldwater, M, and Zusy, MJL: Prescription for Nurses: Effective Political Action. CV Mosby, St Louis, 1990.
24 Stevens, BJ: Nursing, politics and policy formulation. In Wieczorek, RR (ed): Power, Politics and Policy in Nursing. Springer, New York, 1985.
25 Harrington, C: The political economy of health: A new imperative for nursing. Nurs Health Care 9(3):124, 1988.
26 Josephson, M: Ethics in government. Commonwealth 62:406, 1991.
27 LeSage, J: Quality care for nursing home residents. Chart Illinois Nurses' Assoc 21:4, 1987.
28 Beckman, JS: What is a standard of practice? J Nurs Qual Assur 1:2, 1987.
29 American Nurses' Association: Standards and Scope of Gerontological Nursing Practice. ANA, Kansas City, Mo, 1987.

CHAPTER 2

Theories of Aging

Barbara Cole Donlon

OBJECTIVES

Upon completion of this chapter, the reader will be able to:

- Identify the current biological and psychosocial theories of aging
- Describe the relevance of selected theories to nursing practice with older adults
- Discuss how nursing management for a selected client would be altered based on the selection of a theoretical frame of reference
- Describe health promotion behaviors that support successful aging for selected older adults

Gerontology, the scientific study of the effects of aging and age-related diseases on humans, includes the biological, physiological, psychosocial, and spiritual aspects of aging. Nurses who plan and deliver care to people in their later years draw on theory to establish a foundation for nursing care during this final phase of life.

Almost from the beginning of time, people have attempted to explain how and why aging occurs; however, no single theory explains the aging process.[1] Everyone ages, but individuals do so differently based on their hereditary makeup, environmental stressors, and a host of other factors. Although no theory alone can explain the complex physical, psychological, and social events that occur over time, an understanding of the research and resulting theories is essential for nurses to help older adults maintain physical health and robust psyches.

Aging is normal, with predictable physical and behavioral changes that occur in all people as they achieve certain chronological milestones. It is a complex, multidimensional phenomenon that is observable within a single cell and progresses through the entire system. Although it occurs at different rates, within fairly narrow parameters, the process is unsparing.

The theories that explain how and why aging occurs are generally grouped into two broad categories: biological and psychosocial (Table 2–1). The research involved with biological pathways has focused on discernible indicators of the aging process, many at the cellular level, while the psychosocial theorists have attempted to explain how the process is viewed in terms of behavior and personality.

Biological Theories

Biological theories attempt to explain the physical process of aging, including the alterations in structure and function, development, longevity, and death.[2] Changes in the body include molecular and cellular changes in the major organ systems and the body's ability to function adequately and resist disease. As our ability to investigate smaller and smaller compounds grows, an understanding of previously unrecognized linkages that either affect aging or cause aging increases. Although not a definition of aging, five characteristics of aging have been identified (Table 2–2). Biological theory also attempts to explain why people age differently over time and what factors affect longevity, resistance to organisms, and cellular alterations or death. An understanding of the biological perspective can provide the nurse with knowledge about specific risk factors associated with aging and about how people can be helped to minimize or avoid risk and maximize health.

GENETIC THEORY

Causal theories explain that aging is influenced primarily by gene formation and the impact of environment on genetic coding. According to genetic theory, aging is an involuntarily inherited process that operates over time to alter cellular or tissue structures.[2] In other words, life span and longevity changes are predetermined. Genetic theories include deoxyribonucleic acid (DNA) theory, error and fidelity theory, somatic mu-

TABLE 2–1 THEORIES OF AGING

Biological Theories	Level of Change
Genetic	Inherited gene pool and environmental impact
Wear and tear	Free radical insult
Environment	Increasing exposure to hazards
Immunity	Integrity of system to fight back
Neuroendocrine	Overproduction or underproduction of hormones

Psychological Theories	Level of Process
Personality	Introverts versus extroverts
Development tasks	Maturation across life span
Disengagement	Anticipated withdrawal
Activity	Fostering new endeavors
Continuity	Individuality of development
Nonequilibrium system	Compensation through self-organization

tation, and glycogen theory. These theories posit that the replication process at the cellular level becomes deranged by inappropriate information provided from the cell nucleus. The DNA molecule becomes crosslinked with another substance that alters the genetic information. This crosslinking results in errors at the cellular level that eventually cause the body's organs and systems to fail. Evidence to support these theories includes the development of free radicals, collagen, and lipofuscin.[3] In addition, the increased frequency of cancers and autoimmune disease disorders associated with advanced age suggests that error or mutation occurs at the molecular and cellular level.

WEAR-AND-TEAR THEORY

The wear-and-tear theory[3] proposes that accumulation of metabolic waste products or nutrient deprivation damages DNA synthesis, leading to molecular and eventually organ malfunction. Proponents of this theory believe that the body wears out on a scheduled basis.

Free radicals are examples of the metabolic waste products that cause damage when accumulation occurs. Free radicals are atoms or molecules with an unpaired

TABLE 2–2 BIOLOGICAL CHARACTERISTICS OF AGING

- Life expectancy increases, but mortality is inevitable.
- Aging is evident in cells, molecules, tissue, and bone mass.
- Deterioration is progressive and unsparing and affects all life systems.
- Prolonged time required to rebound from periods of assault, exhaustion, and stress.
- Vulnerability to infections, cancer, and other age-related diseases increases.

Source: Adapted from Cristofalo, VJ: Biological mechanism of aging. In Cristofalo, VJ (ed): Annual Review of Gerontology and Geriatrics, vol 10. Springer, New York, 1990.

electron. These highly reactive species are generated in reactions during metabolism. Free radicals are rapidly destroyed by protective enzyme systems under normal conditions. Some free radicals escape destruction and accumulate in important biological structures, where damage occurs.[1]

Because metabolic rate is related directly to free-radical generation, scientists hypothesize that the rate of free-radical production is in some way related to life-span determination. Caloric restriction and its effects on life-span extension may be based in this theory. However, others believe that caloric restriction may exert its effect through the neuroendocrine system.[4] Caloric restriction, which is briefly discussed at the end of this chapter, has been credited with increasing the life span of laboratory rats. Along with life span, the rats have decreased functional decline and experience fewer age-related disease states, decreased functional decline, and a decreased incidence of age-related disease. The relevance of these findings is still suspect for humans, primarily because of the lack of human research.[4]

ENVIRONMENTAL HISTORY

According to this theory, factors in the environment (e.g., industrial carcinogens, sunlight, trauma, and infection) bring about changes in the aging process.[5] Although these factors are known to accelerate aging, the impact of the environment is a secondary rather than a primary factor in aging. Nurses can have a profound impact on this aspect of aging by educating all age groups about the relationship between environmental factors and accelerated aging. Science is only beginning to uncover the many environmental factors that affect aging.

IMMUNITY THEORY

The immunity theory describes an age-related decline in the immune system. As people age, their defense to foreign organisms decreases, resulting in susceptibility to diseases such as cancer and infection.[6] Along with the diminished immune function, a rise in the body's autoimmune response occurs. As people age, they may develop autoimmune diseases such as rheumatoid arthritis and allergies to food and environmental factors. Proponents of this theory often focus on the role of the thymus gland. The weight and size of the thymus gland decrease with age, as does the body's capability for T-cell differentiation. Because of the loss of this T-cell differentiation process, the body mistakes old, irregular cells as foreign bodies and attacks them. In addition, the body loses its ability to mount a response to foreign cells, especially in the face of infections. The importance of a health maintenance, disease prevention, and health promotion approach to health care, especially as aging occurs, cannot be overstated. Although all people need routine screenings to ensure early detection and prompt treatment, in older adults, failure to protect an aging immune system through health screenings can lead to an early, unexpected death. In addition, nationwide immunization programs to prevent the occurrence and spread of epidemics, such as influenza and pneumonia among older adults also support this theoretical basis of nursing practice.

NEUROENDOCRINE THEORY

Biological theories of aging, dealing as they do with structure and change at the molecular and cellular level, seem amazingly similar in some situations. For example, the previous discussion on the thymus gland and the immune system and the interaction of the nervous and endocrine systems bear remarkable similarities. In the latter case, it is thought that aging occurs because of a slowing of the secretion of certain hormones that have an impact on reactions regulated by the nervous system. This is most clearly demonstrated in the pituitary gland, thyroid, adrenals, and the glands of reproduction. Recent research[7] suggests that although credence has been given to a predictable biological clock that controls fertility, there is much more to be learned from the study of the neuroendocrine system in relation to a systemic aging process that is controlled by a "clock."

One neurological area that is universally impaired with age is the reaction time required to accept, process, and react to commands. Known as behavioral slowing, this response is sometimes interpreted as belligerence, deafness, or lack of knowledge. Generally, it is none of those things, but older adults are often made to feel as if they are being uncooperative or noncompliant. Nurses can facilitate the caregiving process by slowing their instructions and expectations.

Psychosociological Theories

Psychosocial theories focus on behavior and attitude changes that accompany advancing age, as opposed to the biological implications of anatomic deterioration. For the purposes of this discussion, the sociological or nonphysical changes are combined with psychological changes.

Each individual, young, middle-aged, or old, is unique and has experienced, through the course of a life, a multitude of events. During the last 40 years, several theories have been put forth in an attempt to describe how attitudes and behavior in the early phases of life affect people's reactions during the late phase. This work is called the process of "successful aging." Examples of these theories include personality theory.

PERSONALITY THEORY

The human personality is a fertile area of growth in the later years and has stimulated considerable research. Personality theories address aspects of psychological growth without delineating specific tasks or expectations of older adults. Jung[8] developed a theory of adult personality development that viewed personalities as extroverted or introverted. He theorized that a balance between the two was necessary for good health. With decreasing demands and responsibilities of family and social ties, common in old age, Jung believed that people become more introverted. In Jung's concept of interiority, the second half of life is described as having purpose of its own: to develop self-awareness through reflective activity.

Jung saw the last stage of life as a time when people take an inventory of their lives, a time of looking backward rather than forward. During this process of reflection, the older adult must come to terms with the reality of his or her life retrospectively. The older adult often discovers that life has provided a series of options that, once chosen, lead the person in a direction that cannot be changed. Although regret over certain aspects of life are common, many older adults express a sense of satisfaction with what they have accomplished.

Neugarten et al.[9] noted that increased interiority is characteristic of aged persons and identified eight patterns of adjustment to aging. They found that healthy aging depended not on the amount of social activity a person has, but on how satisfied the person is with that social activity. For nurses working with this age group, helping the older adult identify opportunities for meaningful social activity is an important aspect of facilitating successful aging. Well-meaning friends, family, and professionals often feel compelled to encourage older adults to engage in socially accepted activities, such as participation in a Senior Center. If these activities are viewed by the older adult as frivolous or without merit, he or she is not likely to respond favorably to the encouragement. Conversely, many older adults actively seek the companionship of another person. When this occurs among older adults who have experienced the loss of a spouse, adult children are often offended. They see it as an attempt to replace a lost parent with a new relationship, creating a strain on existing family relationship.

DEVELOPMENTAL TASK THEORY

Several well-known theorists have described the process of maturation in terms of the tasks to be mastered at various stages throughout the life span. Erickson's[10] work is probably the best known in this field. Developmental tasks are the activities and challenges that one must accomplish at specific stages in life to achieve successful aging. Erickson described the primary task of old age as being able to see one's life as having been lived with integrity. In the absence of achieving that sense of having lived well, the older adult is at risk for becoming preoccupied with feelings of regret or despair. Renewed interest in this concept is occurring as gerontologists and gerontological nurses reexamine the tasks of old age. (See Chapter 25 for a thorough discussion of this concept.)

DISENGAGEMENT THEORY

Disengagement theory, first developed in the early 1960s, describes the process of withdrawal by older adults from societal roles and responsibilities.[11] According to the theorist, this withdrawal process is predictable, systematic, inevitable, and necessary for the proper functioning of a growing society. Older adults were said to be happy when social contacts diminished and responsibilities were assumed by a younger generation. The benefit to the older adult is in providing time for reflecting on life's accomplishments and for coming to terms with unfulfilled expectations. The benefit to society is an orderly transfer of power from old to young.

This theory sparked a great deal of controversy, partially because the research was viewed as flawed[12] and because many elders challenged the "postulats" generated by the theory to explain what happens in disengagement. For example, under this theoretical framework, mandatory retirement became an accepted social policy. As the natural life span has increased, retirement at 65 means that a healthy older adult can expect to live another 20 years. For many healthy, productive individuals, the prospect of a slower pace and fewer responsibilities is undesirable. Clearly, many older adults continue to be productive members of society well into their 80s and 90s.

ACTIVITY THEORY

In direct opposition to the disengagement theory is the activity theory of aging, which holds that the way to age successfully is to stay active.[5] Havighurst[13] first wrote about the importance of remaining socially active as a means to a healthy adjustment to old age in 1952. Since then, multiple studies have validated the positive relationship between maintaining meaningful interaction with others and physical and mental well-being. The notion of having one's needs met must be balanced with the importance of feeling needed by others. The opportunity to contribute in a meaningful way in the lives of one's significant others is an essential component of well-being for an older adult. Studies show that loss of role function in old age negatively affects life satisfaction. In addition, more recent work demonstrates the importance of continued physical and mental activity to the prevention of loss and the maintenance of health throughout the life span.[5]

CONTINUITY THEORY

The continuity theory, also known as a developmental theory, is a follow-up to the previous two theories and tries to explain the impact of personality on the need to remain active or disengage to be happy and fulfilled in old age.[14] This theory emphasizes the individual's previously established coping abilities and personality as a basis for predicting how the person will adjust to the changes of aging. Basic personality traits are said to remain unchanged as a person ages. Furthermore, personality traits typically become more pronounced as a person ages. A person who enjoys the company of others and an active social life will continue to enjoy this lifestyle into old age. One who prefers solitude and a limited number of activities will probably find satisfaction in a continuation of this lifestyle. Older adults who are accustomed to being in control of making their own decisions will not easily give up this role simply as a re-

sult of advancing years. In addition, the individual who has been manipulative or abrasive in their interpersonal interactions during younger years will not suddenly develop a different approach in late life.

When lifestyle changes are imposed on an older adult by changing socioeconomic or health factors, problems may arise. Personality traits that went unnoticed during brief encounters or episodic visits may become focal and the source of irritation when the situation necessitates a change in living arrangements. Families who are faced with the difficult decisions about changing living arrangements for an older adult often require a great deal of support. An understanding of the older adult's previous personality patterns can provide much-needed insight into this decision-making process. The reader is referred to Chapter 26 for a thorough discussion of these issues.

NEW HORIZONS IN AGING RESEARCH

Although there has been a profound interest in the aging process for centuries, theories of aging based on empirical evidence were first put forth as recently as the 1940s. This is true for both biological theories and psychosocial theories. Cristofalo[2] writes that although we have learned a great deal during the past 40 to 50 years about how cells work, we have learned little about the processes that bring about age. Schroots,[15] in summarizing the work of psychology in furthering our understanding of aging, finds that scholars have yet to uncover a definitive theory that fully explains how aging happens.

The search for the "fountain of youth" has become more technological in the 1990s. The theories that are generated in the new millennium will be derived from the areas of molecular genetics, cellular anatomy, and nutrition. For example, Sinclair and Guarentel,[16] while studying Werner's disease (a rare disorder of premature aging), reported that a simple mistake in cell division can produce the onset of signs of aging. The "mistake," as they call it, causes circular bits of redundant DNA to accumulate within the nuclei of the cell, thereby causing a clogging effect in the cell machinery. This knowledge will spur scientists to determine why it occurs and ultimately to identify ways to prevent this mistake from occurring.

Cell biologists, on the other hand, are reporting that they are on the frontier of discovering an "immortality gene."[17] On the basis of work at Baylor University, researchers have demonstrated that a specific gene called MORF4 (for mortality factor from chromosome 4) can be harvested from an individual, mutated to other genes, and then returned to the donor. They speculate that this process will produce a tumor suppressor and serve as an effective adjunct to the battle against many types of cancer. Still in the very early stage of development, the investigators hope they have the beginning tools to learn how cells can become "immortal."

The role of nutrition in the prolongation of life has received attention in the past and seems to be an area in which future research will prove interesting. Comparing cultural differences and longevity has stimulated many of the newest studies. Most of this research is still limited to animal studies, as evidenced by the work of Verdery et al.[4] They have found in small animals, and more recently in primates, that calorie restriction has considerable potential for prolonging life. Thirty rhesus monkeys in three age cohorts were given diets that were restricted to 70 percent of the controls for 6 to 7 years. Their health was considerably improved by the beneficial effect on body composition and glucose metabolism and a decreasing incidence of atherosclerosis.

New theories of aging will be continually generated by the scientific community. The question that remains unanswered is whether we will find ways to stop aging altogether or simply slow down the process. That question poses challenges for health-care providers and the future of life in an aging society.

Student Learning Activities

Identify an older adult in your community. Discuss the following topics and be prepared to share your observations with the class.

1 How do you view life now and how does that compare to your view of life when you were 20 or 30 years old?

2 Do you believe mandatory retirement at age 65 is good for the country or for you personally? Please explain.

3 How would you define health and successful aging?

4 What do you do to keep yourself healthy?

REFERENCES

1 Brookbank, JW: The Biology of Aging. Harper & Row, New York, 1990.

2 Cristofalo, VJ: Ten years later: What have we learned about human aging from studies of cell cultures. Gerontologist 36(6), 1996.

3 Elliopoulos, C: Gerontological Nursing, ed 3. JB Lippincott, Philadelphia, 1993.

4 Verdery, RB, et al: Caloric restriction increases HDL2 levels in rhesus monkeys. Am J Physiol 273(4 Pt 1):E714–9, October 1997.

5 Birren, JE, and Bengtson, VL (eds): Emergent Theories of Aging. Springer, New York, 1998.

6 Burnet, FM: An immunological approach to aging. Lancet 2, 1970.

7 Wise, PM, et al: Menopause: The aging of multiple pacemakers. Science 273(5721):67, July 5, 1996.

8 Jung, C: The stages of life. In Jung, C: Collected Works, vol 8, The Structure and Dynamics of the Psyche. Pantheon, New York, 1960.

9 Neugarten, BL, et al: Personality and patterns of aging. In Neugarten, BL (ed): Middle Age and Aging. University of Chicago Press, Chicago, 1968.

10 Erickson, EH, et al: Vital Involvement in Old Age. Norton, New York, 1986.

11 Comming, E, and Henry, WE: Growing Old: The Process of Disengagement. Basic Books, New York, 1961.

12 Achenbaum, WA, and Bengtson, VL: Re-engaging the disengagement theory of aging: On the history and assessment of theory development in gerontology. Gerontologist 34(6), 1994.

13 Havighurst, RJ: Development Tasks of Later Maturity. David McKay, New York, 1952.

14 Atchley, RC: A continuity theory of normal aging. Gerontologist 29(2):68, 1989.

15 Schroots, JJ: Theoretical developments in the psychology of aging. Gerontologist 36(6):742–748, 1996.

16 Sinclair, DA, and Guarentel, L: Extrachromosomal & DNA circles: A cause of aging in yeast. Cell 91(7):1033–1042, 1997.

17 Ehrenstein, D: Immortality gene discovered. Science 279, January 9, 1998.

CHAPTER 3

Mental Health Wellness Strategies for Successful Aging

Mildred O. Hogstel

OBJECTIVES

Upon completion of this chapter, the reader will be able to:

- Explore the components of successful aging
- Discuss how physical health and physical, mental, and social activity contribute to successful aging
- Evaluate how a multidrug regimen can affect mental health in older adults
- Evaluate possible effects of retirement on mental health
- Discuss how contributing to society through part-time employment, volunteer work, and political activity can help maintain mental wellness in older adults
- Evaluate the concept of social support
- Identify common sources of social support for older adults
- Identify the most common reversible and treatable mental and emotional problems in older adults
- Evaluate multiple nursing interventions that can help maintain mental wellness in older adults
- Explore specific nursing interventions in the home, hospital, and nursing facility that contribute to client feelings of self-worth and self-esteem

Mental Health Promotion

The activity social theory of aging is thought to contribute most to successful aging. This theory proposes that "older people who are aging optimally stay active and resist shrinkage in their social world. They maintain activities of middle age as long as possible and then find substitutes for activities that must be given up."[1] Some of the important strategies for successful aging are listed in Table 3–1. These strategies include physical, psychosocial, and environmental factors. Older adults who continue to be physically and mentally active seem to be the healthiest and happiest. As one older man said, "I'd rather wear out than rust out."

In a study of 2943 persons aged 65 to 84, from 1971 to 1983, it was determined that people who age successfully "express more satisfaction with their lives and incur substantially fewer health expenditures than other

elderly."[2] The same study also found that those who were at risk for not aging successfully were "those with poor self-assessed health, whose spouse has died, whose mental status is somewhat compromised, who develop cancer, and those who are forced to retire or retire because of poor health."[2] Some of the most important factors related to mental health wellness are:

- Physical health
- Physical activity
- Mental activity
- Social activity
- Social support

PHYSICAL HEALTH

Two major factors that affect mental health are physical health and financial resources. They are related because optimum physical health is often related to the

TABLE 3–1   STRATEGIES FOR SUCCESSFUL AGING

- Maintaining health by living a healthy lifestyle
- Continuing to be physically and mentally active
- Having a strong support system such as family, friends, and neighbors
- Being able to adjust or adapt to change
- Developing new interests
- Participating in personally rewarding activities such as employment or volunteering
- Having an adequate income to meet basic needs
- Avoiding stress-producing situations when possible
- Being autonomous and independent
- Doing what the person wants to do and not what family members or friends think he or she should do
- Planning a structured day and having something to look forward to

amount of money one has to spend on health care. For example, although most people over age 65 have Medicare health insurance, it does not provide comprehensive health-care coverage because of deductible and coinsurance expenses.[3] Also, Medicare does not pay for more preventive care or eye, hearing, and dental needs. If older adults cannot afford to purchase new eyeglasses (changes are needed more often as the eyes age), hearing devices, or properly fitting dentures (gums change over time), they are less likely to be involved in and enjoy mental activities and social activities in the community or to eat well-balanced meals, both of which ultimately contribute to successful aging and mental wellness. See Table 3–2 for 10 tips for healthy aging.

Older adults should take as few medications as possible and only for the treatment of specific medical conditions. Psychotropic medications, such as hypnotics and tranquilizers, are greatly overprescribed. The medications cause "addiction, daytime sedation, confusion, memory loss, increased risk of an injurious auto accident, poor coordination causing falls and hip fractures, impaired learning ability, slurred speech, and even death," thus interfering with physical and mental health.[4] However, clients should be warned not to stop medications suddenly because of possible adverse effects, and to

TABLE 3–2   10 TIPS FOR HEALTHY AGING

- Eat a balanced diet.
- Exercise regularly.
- Get regular checkups.
- Do not smoke. It is never too late to quit.
- Practice safety habits at home to prevent falls and fractures. Always wear a seat belt when traveling by car.
- Maintain contacts with family and friends, and stay active through work, recreation, and community.
- Avoid overexposure to sun and cold.
- Drink in moderation, if at all, and do not drive after drinking.
- Keep personal and financial records to simplify budgeting and investing. Plan long-term housing and financial needs.
- Keep a positive attitude toward life and have fun.

Source: National Institute of Aging, National Institutes of Health, Rockville, Md.

check with their primary care physicians before adding or stopping any medications.

Health Assessment

Nurses should encourage their older clients to have regular physical examinations by a family physician or gerontological nurse practitioner. Older adults and their families often need assistance in locating physicians who specialize in or are experienced in geriatric medicine. If health insurance and other financial resources are limited, nurses should refer clients to community programs that may provide health assessment or health care for free or on a sliding scale. Examples are free geriatric clinics sponsored by local health departments, hospitals, or medical schools; screening for cataracts and glaucoma by local ophthalmologists or community organizations; and hypertension and diabetes screening by volunteers in senior centers. Other community clinics staffed by gerontological nurse practitioners are also an ideal source for screening, support, and referral to help older adults maintain wellness in the community.

Older adults also need to be informed about the availability and accuracy of home screening devices, such as glucose monitors and fecal guaiac tests, and technology services in pharmacies, supermarkets, and malls that monitor blood pressure. Home testing technology is increasing the availability of health screening, but clients should be informed about the purposes and limits of such screening.

Nurses should also encourage their older clients to be more assertive in seeking and obtaining high-quality health care by asking specific questions about their medications, treatments, and care. Clients who are knowledgeable and fully informed about their health care are likely to be less anxious or depressed.

Appearance

Appearance often affects self-image and self-esteem. People usually feel better if they know they look better. Basic nursing interventions related to cleanliness, hygiene, and grooming are important in helping older adults maintain feelings of self-worth. Older men should be encouraged to shave daily and have a regular haircut and trim of excess hair on earlobes, nostrils, and eyebrows as needed. Older women should be assisted with a hairstyle they prefer and application of cosmetics appropriate for older skin. Commenting on a person's good appearance is almost always helpful, whether the person is 20 or 100 years old.

PHYSICAL ACTIVITY

One of the most beneficial components of a mental health program is exercise. By performing some form of aerobic activity for at least 20 minutes three or four times a week, with warm-up and cool-down periods, older adults can look forward to the greater possibility of years of good health. It is amazing how even a very small amount of physical activity, especially outdoors, can improve attitude, reduce stress and loneliness, improve sleep, and prevent feelings of depression. Senior Centers should have planned exercise activities, and nursing homes should have protected outside areas where residents can walk. Sunlight (a source of vitamin D) not only aids in the absorption of calcium (very important in helping prevent osteoporosis and fractures) but also has been shown to help prevent depression. If the weather prevents exposure to sunlight, appropriate lighting, without glare, should be provided indoors.

Almost everyone who is able to walk can participate in some kind of physical activity, even if only for a few minutes a day. Walking outside around the house two or three times a day is much better than sitting in the house all day. There are also fun and helpful exercises for older adults in wheelchairs and beds. Wandering, often seen in older adults with various types of dementia (e.g., Alzheimer's disease), should not be discouraged if a safe environment inside and outside is available. Wandering provides exercise, which decreases boredom, agitation, and anxiety and increases appetite, relaxation, and sleep. The benefits of some kind of physical exercise cannot be overestimated in maintaining physical and mental wellness.

MENTAL ACTIVITY

Mental activity is just as important as physical activity in successful aging. Many activities that older people can do will help their minds remain active and allow them to develop further intellectually. In fact, evidence suggests that older adults who have more education and mental stimulation are less likely to develop dementia of the Alzheimer's type, or at least the development of dementia may be delayed.

Active, healthy older adults continue to learn and can be encouraged to complete a college degree or begin a new one. With the average age of college students increasing every year, a 50-, 60-, or 70-year-old student should not feel out of place on a college campus. Some colleges and universities offer reduced tuition and fees for students 55 and older. Elderhostel programs at colleges and universities offer summer housing and short courses at minimal cost for older adults who like to travel to different parts of the country in the summer.

Another trend is multiple careers during a lifetime. A person may retire from one career at age 40 after 20 years and retire from a second career at age 60 after another 20 years. This person could easily spend another 20 years in a third career. Other older adults like to spend time reading new books, learning foreign languages, or taking music lessons. Learning these technical skills may not be as easy at age 70 as at age 10, but it is certainly possible for the motivated, active older adult.

Retirement

Retirement after many years of employment can be happy and fulfilling, or it can cause physical and mental health problems. After retirement some people never seem to adjust to the free time and seemingly long days.

Some older adults are not motivated to maintain their appearance when they have little or no contact with others outside the home. People who drank socially before retirement may start drinking throughout the day. Retirement is difficult for many people, especially those who have spent decades of energy and time on their careers. Because most of their personal rewards, such as money, respect, feelings of self-worth, and power, have come from their occupations for 40 years or more, these people feel the loss of all of these assets and rewards on retirement. They measure the quality and satisfaction of life by what they accomplish each day. If they do not believe they have accomplished anything, they feel worthless and depressed. Also, because they often did not take the time from their careers to develop hobbies or enjoy leisure-time activities, they begin to feel less worthy and ultimately depressed. According to Havighurst,[5] one of the developmental tasks of middle adulthood is to "develop adult leisure time activities," but successful, extremely busy, active people often never find the time or motivation to do so. They consider work fun and do not particularly enjoy social or recreational activities that they could continue into retirement. See Chapter 25 for a more thorough discussion of successful retirement.

Part-Time Employment

Although some people have the option of retiring early (in their 50s), this may not be a wise choice for those who have been involved in an active and rewarding career. With an uncertain economy and the possibility of increasing inflation, the pension received may not be adequate for another 30 to 40 years. One option is part-time employment in either the same career or another one that provides fulfilling experiences at a somewhat slower pace, as well as additional income. Part-time employment after retirement is an excellent way to slow down gradually and maintain contact with colleagues and peers during the transition period. Occasionally, educational institutions offer this choice, which benefits the institution and the employee. Some industries create part-time consulting positions after retirement for valuable employees.

SOCIAL ACTIVITY

Loss of a spouse is a common problem in late adulthood. Most women became widows in their 60s because their husbands are usually older in the first place and have about 7 years less life expectancy. Widowhood can cause severe depression for the older adult who has relied on his or her spouse to help make financial decisions or maintain a home, or whose primary social support group was the spouse's friends. The nurse should refer a recently widowed client to a local widowed persons' support group, which could help prevent feelings of loneliness and depression. These are very active social and support groups in the community.

Volunteer Activities

Some of the most involved and apparently happy retired people are those who are actively involved in community, political, legislative, and government activities. They may belong to the American Association of Retired Persons (AARP), the Gray Panthers, Senior Alliance, or Silver-Haired Legislature. They often have the time, ability, experience, and sometimes personal finances to become involved in activities related to the formation of public policy helpful to older adults at the local, state, or federal level. Many of these retired people have the specialized knowledge and professional experience to influence public policy. Such activities can produce personal rewards and enhance self-esteem, as well as provide a valuable service to the community and nation. The AARP is now considered one of the most powerful lobbying groups in Washington, DC. Some members of AARP fly to Washington frequently to testify before congressional committees discussing issues of concern to older people.

Other types of volunteer work exist in the local community that can keep older people involved in worthwhile activities. Some older adults volunteer in hospitals, nursing homes, churches, and private and public schools (where they help disadvantaged children learn to read and write). If the volunteer services of older adults were sought more vigorously in the community, society would benefit from their experience and expertise and older people would benefit by feeling needed, useful, and wanted, thus enhancing their self-esteem.

Sexual Relationships

Sexual activity is possible, pleasurable, and not to be considered unusual or abnormal for men and women into their 90s if they do not have health problems that prevent such activity and if an acceptable partner and environment exist. Adjustments may need to be made because of physical changes,[6] although sometimes just touching and being held close may be the most important part of the relationship. Chapter 30 provides a more thorough discussion of sexuality in older adults.

SOCIAL SUPPORT

Another important component of successful aging and mental health is an available and effective support system. The first source of support is usually a family member, such as a spouse, son, daughter, sibling, grandson, or granddaughter. However, family structure changes as some members die, move to other parts of the country, or become ill. Therefore, other sources of support are important. Some of these are neighbors, close friends, previous colleagues from work or organizations, and members of the older person's church.

Active religious participation may decrease with increasing age, but many older adults who have previously been active in a church usually want to continue religious activities.[7] In fact, the church may become the primary source of social support for some older adults who have no or few family members nearby. Support may be provided by clergy, trained volunteers such as those in the Stephens Ministry or the Church Eldercare Program,[8] or a staff or volunteer parish nurse. In addition to teaching, advocacy, coordinating volunteers, and referring to community agencies, one of the primary functions of the parish nurse is counseling when the church cannot meet an individual member's needs. The parish nurse may detect concerns about possible mental health problems so that they can be prevented or at least treated early. The parish nurse must be a good listener with excellent communication skills.[9] Spiritual beliefs and practices that continue into late adulthood are often extremely important to many people and help to contribute to their mental wellness.

Prevention of Mental Illness

Mental and emotional problems are not a normal part of aging. Just like physical problems, if mental, emotional, or behavioral problems occur in older people, they should be evaluated, diagnosed, and treated. Abnormal or unusual behavior should not be attributed to aging.

Health-care providers, family members, friends of older adults, and older people themselves can focus on preventing mental and emotional problems. Part of the problem is the ageism that persists in our society, based on lack of knowledge about aging and reflected in a lack of respect for older people. Sometimes older adults themselves begin to feel a decreased sense of worth and attractiveness and fear becoming a burden on family and society. These feelings of worthlessness, loneliness, and depression may be manifested in various physical symptoms. For example, complaints about multiple minor physical problems may be a symptom of depression. Frequent visits to the physician with diffuse somatic complaints should alert the family and physician to a greater need. Depression should be diagnosed and vigorously treated in older adults, as in any other age group. See Chapter 28 for more information on depression in older adults. Older adults may experience some physical, mental, and emotional changes as they age, but with the help and support of family, friends, and health-care providers, most severe mental and emotional problems can be prevented.

NURSING ACTIONS

One of the most important aspects of maintaining mental wellness in older adults is the nurse-client relationship and the use of therapeutic communication skills. Through the use of self, the nurse can demonstrate caring, warmth, concern, love, support, and respect for the older person. The value of personal time that a nurse takes to listen to and talk with an older person cannot be overemphasized. See Table 3–3 for general nursing interventions to help maintain mental wellness in older adults in all settings.

TABLE 3–3 GENERAL NURSING INTERVENTIONS TO HELP MAINTAIN MENTAL WELLNESS IN OLDER ADULTS IN ALL SETTINGS

Encourage feelings of self-worth and self-esteem.
  Call client by his or her last name (not an endearing term such as "Honey").
  Demonstrate respect for each person, regardless of age, condition, or status.
  Encourage independence.
  Avoid comments or actions that reflect ageism (e.g., references to "diapers").
  Allow as much control of care and environment as possible.
  Assist with hygiene and appearance as needed.
Use effective communication skills.
  Listen attentively.
  Speak slowly and clearly, in a low tone.
  Use appropriate eye contact.
  Encourage questions.
  Wait a little longer than usual for answers.
  Use therapeutic touch, if appropriate.
Discourage misuse of medications.
  Administer as few medications as possible to prevent possible delirium (confusion) and other complications such as falls, often caused by hypotension.
  Encourage a nutritious diet.
  Advise exercise and high-bulk foods instead of laxatives.
  Provide and encourage social activities instead of antidepressants.
  Encourage exercise and activities with others instead of sedatives, hypnotics, antianxiety agents, and alcohol.
Lead socialization, reminiscence, and remotivation groups.
  Provide a comfortable physical and psychological environment.
  Encourage all to participate.
  Value past life experiences of participants.
  Arrange for individual or group pet or music therapy.

Home

The home health-care nurse has a special opportunity and responsibility to help prevent loneliness, depression, phobias, and paranoid behaviors in older adults who live at home, especially those who are isolated and have a limited or no support system. Many older people often are very lonely and develop severe depression because of their limited contact with others. These people often develop deep fears about becoming ill and being unable to get assistance or about experiencing criminal attacks. Because of the lack of social contact with others or perhaps because of decreased sight or hearing, they may develop hallucinations or delusions such as the belief that neighbors or others are going to harm them or their home. The older person who exhibits such behavior may be brought to the attention of health-care providers by worried neighbors, especially if no close family members exist.

The home health-care nurse must also watch for signs and symptoms of elder abuse by family members or other caregivers. An older adult who is unusually quiet and withdrawn may be afraid or ashamed to tell the nurse about abuse that has occurred for fear of retaliation by the caregiver, fear of losing a place to live, or feeling ashamed to admit that a loved family member is causing the abuse. The family may not understand the process of aging and may financially, physically, or psychologically abuse the older person who exhibits what they consider abnormal behavior. In Chapter 27 the subject of elder mistreatment is discussed more fully.

One 100-year-old woman felt very secure and comfortable living in her own home alone because someone from a telephone reassurance program called her every morning, a Meals on Wheels volunteer visited briefly at lunchtime, and neighbors knew that, if her front porch light did not turn on at a certain time every night and go off at a certain time every morning, something was wrong, and they would call her. The woman had an amplifying device on her telephone so that she could hear better during phone calls. She also had frequent visits from several family members and a periodic visit from a home health-care nurse. She was happy and content living in her own home with her own belongings and might have deteriorated physically and mentally in an institutional setting, which would prevent this familiar lifestyle. Her support system was obviously strong and involved family, neighbors, and a variety of community resources.

Hospital

Hospital nurses have a unique responsibility in the discharge planning and teaching of older clients and their families. Older clients who do not completely understand instructions for home care may not ask for clarification for fear of being thought confused or unable to learn because of their age. Consequently, these clients may feel anxious and worthless. They want to go home, but after they get home and have problems because they did not understand the discharge instructions, they become fearful or depressed, and complications may result. Clear, specific, large-print written instructions are essential, especially when related to medications and treatments, so that repeat hospitalization will not be needed.

Nursing Facility

Staff members in a nursing facility (nursing home) have a special responsibility to help maintain the mental wellness of their residents. Perhaps this staff has the most difficult and challenging task of all because of the atmosphere of the typical nursing home and the nature of the long-term care given there. Long-term communal living with other people who are strangers requires a great deal of adjustment. Feelings of lack of control over self or environment can contribute to mental and emotional problems in older adults, especially in the nursing home setting. An early effective introduction and orientation program is essential so that new residents will know what to expect and so that they can begin making necessary adaptations. Many new resi-

Figure 3–1   Pet therapy programs reduce loneliness and offer nursing home residents the chance to give and receive love and affection. Interacting with a gentle animal provides residents with both mental health and physiological benefits, such as reduced blood pressure. (Photo courtesy of Masonic Home of New Jersey, Burlington, NJ.)

dents do not know what to expect in a nursing home and may fear the worst. Special encouragement and support during the first 24 to 48 hours will relieve some of their concerns and possibly prevent problems from occurring later.

Older adults, even those with multiple chronic health problems, should be encouraged to maintain as much control over their life and care as possible. Examples of activities that nursing home residents could have some control over are:

- Participation in development of the plan of care
- Choice of foods, if possible
- Type and time of bath
- Groups or individual social activities
- Whether to take medications ordered as needed

Some of the dissatisfaction, anger, and hostility felt among nursing home residents is caused by inadequate communication with the staff. Residents who desire the information should be informed about their specific care (e.g., name and purpose of medications and reasons for specific treatments).

Loneliness and depression are also common problems for many nursing home residents, especially those with some degree of immobility and those with few visitors and no other support system. Reminiscence, remotivation, music, pet therapy (Fig. 3–1), exercise, and other group activities are helpful, but people can feel lonely even in a group without some one-to-one contact and communication. Supportive and effective communication should be a primary goal of all nursing home staff. Depending on nursing home policy and family concerns, sexual activities between alert consenting adults should not be discouraged and should not be ridiculed by staff members.

Summary

Many factors contribute to successful aging, including the continuation of physical health, physical activity, mental activity, social activity, and social support. The activity theory proposes that people who continue the normal activities of middle age into late adulthood probably age the most successfully.

Nurses who care for older adults in all settings have a special responsibility and opportunity to help prevent mental health problems and promote mental wellness. Nursing interventions that enhance feelings of self-worth and self-esteem are important in relationships with older adults, especially those who live alone in the community, those who are hospitalized for an acute illness, and those who require long-term care in a nursing facility. Effective caring communication, especially attentive listening, is probably one of the most important skills a nurse can use with older patients in any setting.

Student Learning Activities

1 As you observe people in your community, identify four strategies you see that promote successful aging.

2 Interview two recently retired people regarding their interests, activities, and plans for the future.

3 Ask an older adult to discuss the effect that retirement has had on his or her life.

4 Discuss the nursing interventions for mental wellness from the chapter to determine whether these strategies are being used by the older adult.

REFERENCES

1 Atchley, RC: Social Forces and Aging, ed 7. Wadsworth, Belmont, Calif, 1994, p 367.
2 Roos, NP, and Havens, B: Predictors of successful aging: A twelve-year study of Manitoba elderly. Am J Public Health 81:63, 1991.
3 Knickman, JR, and Thorpe, KE: Financing health care. In Kovner, AR (ed): Health Care Delivery in the United States. Springer, New York, 1995, p 270.
4 Wolfe, SM, et al: Worst Pills Best Pills II. Public Citizen Health Research Group, Washington, DC, 1993, pp 201–202.
5 Havighurst, RJ: Developmental Tasks and Education, ed 3. McKay, New York, 1974.
6 Jones, A: Developmental changes. In Hogstel, MO (ed): Nursing Care of the Older Adult. Wiley, New York, 1988, pp 44–47.
7 Atchley, RC: Social Forces and Aging, ed 7. Wadsworth, Belmont, Calif, 1994, p 168.
8 Hogstel, MO, and Smith, HN: Eldercare/faith in action. Volunteer Training Manual, ed 2. Tarrant Area Community of Churches, Fort Worth, TX, 1995.
9 Solari-Twadell, PA, Djupe, AM, and McDermott, MA: Parish Nursing: The Developing Practice. National Parish Nurse Resource Center, Park Ridge, Ill, 1990, p 80.

CHAPTER 4

Cultural Dimensions in Gerontological Nursing*

Toni Tripp-Reimer / Rebecca Johnson / Bernard Sorofman

OBJECTIVES

Upon completion of this chapter, the reader will be able to:

- Discuss the concepts of culture, ethnicity, and race
- Describe problems with stereotyping ethnic groups
- Discuss the ways in which aging is defined cross-culturally
- Illustrate cultural variation in the status of older adults
- Identify demographic characteristics of American ethnic older adults
- Discuss the importance of family and religion as social support systems for ethnic older adults
- Describe ways in which ethnicity influences health beliefs and behaviors
- Identify strategies for gerontological nurses working with ethnic older adults

Despite more than half a century of research that has demonstrated that patterns of aging vary dramatically across different cultures, only recently has serious attention been given to the ways in which cultural factors influence the experience of aging for older adults in the United States. In part, this inattention was the result of the American myth of the "melting pot." This myth emerged from a cultural ideal of equality coupled with a European ethnocentric perspective. The myth promoted the notion that all Americans are alike (i.e., like middle-class persons of European descent). For many years, the notion that ethnicity should be discounted was prominent in the delivery of health care, including nursing. However, this misguided notion precludes a sensitive understanding of the patient, family, and community, and obscures important issues in gerontological nursing. Because America is a multicultural society, nurses need to be prepared to work with clients from a variety of cultural groups and to understand the ways in which cultural factors influence health behaviors. To be accepted, health care should be presented in ways that are appropriate to each patient. Nurses who understand and accept differences that arise from cultural variations are in a better position to meet the health needs of ethnic older adults. Cultural affiliation provides a contextual background from which nurses may anticipate differences in values, religions, lines of authority, family life patterns, language and communication processes, and patterns of beliefs and practices related to health and illness. Knowledge of cultural diversity provides clues to the meaning of behaviors that otherwise might be judged in a negative way or at least be misunderstood. Culture includes shared beliefs, values, and customs of a group of people. Understanding cultural variables is crucial for the practice of nursing for two major reasons. First, it leads to a better understanding of the behavior of patients and their families. Because culture patterns the ways in which illness is defined, it influences the perception of the ill person by the group and identifies appropriate illness and health-seeking behaviors. Consequently, understanding and incorporating cultural variables leads to a more realistic treatment plan. Second, through understanding cultural factors we come to a more complete understanding of ourselves and our relationships with colleagues. We begin to see that culture does not just belong to others but that we, too, are shaped by culture. Table 4–1 presents information on the major cultural groups found in the United States.

*The preparation of this chapter was partially supported by the NIH, NINR Grant NU RO1-1101. Some positions in this chapter were previously developed in the following: Tripp-Reimer, T, and Sorofman, B: Minority Elderly: Health Care and Policy Issues. Ethnicity and Public Policy 7:156, 1988. Tripp-Reimer, T: Cultural perspectives on aging. In Schrock, M (ed): Holistic Assessment of the Healthy Aged. Wiley, New York, 1979. p 18.

Text continued on p. 30.

TABLE 4–1   PREVAILING GERONTOLOGICAL ATTITUDES OF SELECTED CULTURAL GROUPS

Communication	Family Roles	High-Risk Health Behaviors	Nutrition
African-Americans			
Most are highly articulate, highly verbal, and openly express their feelings to trusted family or friends.	Family decision making may be patriarchal, matriarchal, or egalitarian. Shared roles are common.	High prevalence of smoking, but those who smoke do not smoke as much as most other groups.	Food, a symbol of health and wealth, is usually offered when entering a home. One is expected to accept the offer of food; to reject it is to reject the giver of the food.
Voice volume may be high and should not be mistaken as anger.	Older adults are valued and treated with respect.	Are at greater risk for lung cancer than European-Americans, probably because of past or present work environment.	Because many believe in witchcraft, some may be hesitant in accepting food because it may be a vehicle for poisoning.
Most are comfortable with touch and close personal space.	Older adults may play a critical role in caring for grandchildren and extended family.	High prevalence of alcohol consumption and cirrhosis.	Obesity may be seen as positive because one needs to have "meat" on his or her bones for when there is illness and one might lose weight.
Facial expressions tend to be expressive.			"High blood" is treated by eating vinegar, lemon, and garlic.
Maintaining direct eye contact may be interpreted by some as aggressive behavior.			"Low blood" is treated by eating rare meats, liver, greens, eggs, fruits, and vegetables.
May speak a dialect of black English in which *th* is pronounced as *d*, resulting in the word these being pronounced as *dese*.			Foods tend to be high in fat and sodium, particularly "soul food."
Some from Sea Islands off Georgia and South Carolina may speak Gullah, a Creole dialect derived from West African languages.			Muslims do not eat pork.
Many are present oriented and more relaxed with clock time.			Diet among lower socioeconomic groups may be low in thiamin, riboflavin, vitamins A and C, and iron.
Most prefer to be greeted formally as *Mr., Mrs.,* or *Miss.*			
Appalachians			
Pronunciations of many words date to sixteenth century, resulting in *allus* for *always, fit* for *fight, swelled* for *swollen, drug* for *dragged,* and deleting the *g* from words ending in *ing,* such as *readin, writin,* and *spellin.* This is especially common among rural older adults.	Traditional families are patriarchal, although women have significant say in household matters. Older women have a significant say in health-related matters.	Appalachian region has a high prevalence of smoking.	Wealth means having plenty of food for family, friends, and social gatherings.
Their ethic of neutrality avoids aggression, not interfering with others' lives, avoiding dominance over others, avoiding arguments, and seeking consent.	Most take great pride in doing things for themselves.	Exercise may not take a priority in maintaining health.	Rural traditional people have a diet that includes wild game.
Most are private people and do not share feelings easily with "outsiders."	Grandparents play a primary role in helping raise grandchildren.	Self-medication to the exclusion of biomedical care may be a high risk.	Many foods are prepared with lard, high-fat sauces, and high sodium (from preserving in salt).
The concept of family is extended to distant blood relatives and close friends.			Many in lower socioeconomic levels may lack calcium and vitamins A and C in their diet.
The more traditional older adults do not complain, control their anger, and may be sensitive to personal questions.			
Some may distrust people in hierarchical positions because of past inequities.			
To establish trust, one must be prepared to engage in small talk first before obtaining health-related data.			
Most older adults like personal space and may stand at a distance when communicating.			
Many may perceive direct eye contact as hostility or aggression.			
The traditional culture is one of *being* rather than *doing.*			

Death Rituals	Spirituality	Health-Care Practices	Health-Care Practitioners
For many, death does not end the connections between people, and relatives may communicate with the deceased's spirit. Voodoo death (root work) is a belief that death may come to a person by supernatural forces. Many believe that the body should be buried whole and thus are averse to autopsy. Some do not express grief openly until the funeral, at which time a catharsis may occur. Upon hearing of a death, some may "fall out," becoming unable to see or speak but able to hear. This is a culturally accepted condition that is not a medical emergency.	Religion is taken seriously and is an integral part of most African-Americans' lives. Religious involvement has been found to have a positive effect on mental health. Although most are Baptist, African-Americans are affiliated with all major religions. Some practice "laying on of hand" and "speak in tongues," a language understood only by the person reciting the prayer. Having faith in God is a major source of strength.	Natural illnesses occur in response to normal forces from which the person has not protected himself or herself. Unnatural illnesses are caused by a person or spirit and are treated by clergy, folk healer (root doctor), or praying to God. Many use home remedies, folk healers, and biomedical care simultaneously. Many take prescription medicine only when they are symptomatic, resulting in ineffective control of chronic conditions such as hypertension. Many believe that pain and suffering are something to be endured.	Folk practitioners may be spiritual leaders, grandparents, community elders, or voodoo doctors and priests. Some may have a distrust of the medical system and health-care practitioners based on discrimination from the era of slavery and unethical medical experimentation in the past. Most older adults do not have a problem receiving direct care from opposite-gender caregiver.
Family may sit vigil over the bed of the dying. Although funeral services are usually simple, they are an important occasion. Services for older adults are longer than services for younger people. The body may be displayed for hours in the home or at the church. A common practice is to bury the body with custom-made clothes and favorite possessions of the deceased. Elaborate meals may be served after funeral services. Giving flowers in honor of the dead is more important than donations to charity.	Although all religions exist in Appalachia, the predominant religions are Fundamentalist, Protestant, and Episcopalian denominations. A few still practice snake handling, talking in tongues, and having visions. Prayer is a primary source of strength for many, especially older adults. Many are fatalistic, believing that whatever happens is "God's will."	Many do not seek biomedical health care until after self-medication and folk practices have failed. May delay seeking formal health care until the problem is a crisis. May distrust the bureaucracy of the health-care system. Folk medicine practices are numerous among Appalachians; many practices are handed down through the family. Many believe that disability is natural with aging; thus, attempts at rehabilitation may be initially rejected. Many are stoic with pain. For some traditional rural individuals, a knife is placed under the bed to "cut the pain."	Biomedical practitioners known to the recipient are preferred over outsiders. Granny folk practitioners (usually women) are common among the traditional, especially rural older adults. Herbal and folk practitioners are highly respected, especially if known to the person.

TABLE 4–1   PREVAILING GERONTOLOGICAL ATTITUDES OF SELECTED CULTURAL GROUPS *(Continued)*

Communication	Family Roles	High-Risk Health Behaviors	Nutrition
Chinese-Americans			
Official language of China is Mandarin or *pu tong hua*; however, there are 10 other major languages and 45 minor languages; thus, a dialect specific interpreter may be necessary. Talking loudly may be interpreted as anger. May be reluctant to admit not knowing specific directions to save face. Thus, it is best to have the person repeat instructions or demonstrate their understanding. Most are open and demonstrative with close friends only. Touch by opposite sex may be unacceptable or uncomfortable, even in the health-care setting. More traditional Chinese-Americans do not maintain contact with people in hierarchical positions such as the health-care provider. Most think in terms of relationships rather than linearly, giving the impression that they are disorganized. Most, especially older adults, prefer to be addressed formally. The surname comes first, followed by the given name. Chinese language does not have the variety of tenses as the English language; thus, the Chinese may say "I go to doctor yesterday" or "I go to doctor tomorrow."	Traditional families are organized around the male lineage. The recognized male head of the extended family has great authority. The family unit is more important than the individual, so personal independence is not valued. Older adults are respected for their wisdom and longevity. Most traditional live in extended family units and are comfortable with close personal space.	Smoking remains a high-risk behavior, especially among men.	Food is of major importance for maintaining health, preventing illness, and maintaining social relationships. Traditional diet is highly varied depending on the region of the country from which they come. People from northern China eat more noodles, whereas people from southern China eat more rice. Beans, meats of all kinds, and tofu are common to most diets. Most older adults do not like ice in their drinks, believing that ice is bad for the body. Most vegetables and many fruits are cooked or lightly sautéed in oil. Salt and oil are important parts of the Chinese diet, which may increase the tendency for the high rates of hypertension. Foods are used to balance the yin and yang forces in the body. Many have lactose intolerance and must get calcium from leafy green vegetables.
Korean-Americans			
Korean language has four levels of speech that reflect inequalities in social status. Thus, if possible, the interpreters should come from same background as the client. The group is valued over the individual, men over women, and age over youth. Those holding the dominant position are usually the decision makers. High value is placed on harmony and the maintenance of a peaceful environment. Koreans are comfortable with silence and believe that silence is golden. Thus, there is little room for small talk. Most are very comfortable with close personal space and thus are comfortable with physical touch in the health-care environment. Otherwise, touch should be initiated by the one in the dominant status position.	Traditional older adults may still see women as appendages of males rather than as competent human beings. Female role is to protect the family. Rigid traditional gender roles may be responsible for the high degree of spousal abuse among Korean-Americans. Children are obligated to care for older parents, which is written into civil code in Korea. The oldest son has this primary responsibility. Old age and expected retirement begins at the age of 60, according to the lunar calendar.	Koreans have the highest rate of alcoholism in the world and this pattern may continue with Korean-Americans. The prevalence of smoking among men remains high.	Breakfast is considered the most important meal. Most traditional Korean foods are spicy and high in sodium. Most meals have rice and vegetables served in varying ways. Many vegetables are served with a spicy fermented cabbage. Meals are often taken in silence to enjoy the food. Many older adults have diets low in protein and vitamins A and C. Many have lactose intolerance and need to get calcium from sources other than milk and milk products.

Death Rituals	Spirituality	Health-Care Practices	Health-Care Practitioners
Chinese tradition in death and bereavement is centered on ancestor worship. Most fear death and avoid reference to it. Many older adults believe in ghosts and spirits and may fear them as they fear death. More traditional do not openly express grief, although grief is deeply felt. Mourners are recognized by a black band around the arm and white strips of cloth tied around their heads.	Chinese religions include Buddhism, Taoism, and Islam, with Christian religions gaining in popularity among those in the United States. Prayer is generally a source of comfort. Other major sources of strength include meditation, exercise, and massage.	Most in the United States use Western biomedical care in conjunction with Chinese medicine, such as acupressure, acumassage, acupuncture, moxibustion therapy, and herbal remedies. Most believe in a healthy mind, body, and spirit, which are balanced using the yin and yang forces. Many see no harm in sharing prescription medicines with others. Many, especially older adults, associate hospitals with death. Health insurance may be an unknown concept for many because it is uncommon in their country. Most are stoic with pain and describe it as diffuse and dull. Family readily cares for the sick at home.	Traditional Chinese medicine practitioners are highly respected. Western biomedical practitioners may be distrusted because of the pain and invasiveness of their procedures.
Many, especially older adults, consider it bad luck to die in the hospital. Oldest son is expected to sit by the body of the deceased parent during the viewing. The body should be placed in the ground facing either north or south. Cremation is usually practiced only for those who do not have a family. Moaning rituals over the deceased signify respect for the dead.	Chundo Kyo, a combination of Confucianism, Buddhism, and Daoism is the national religion of Korea. Many Korean-Americans practice this religion, but more than 65% affiliate with Christian churches. These churches in America are a major source of emotional support, practical information, language instruction, and health information for all age groups. Prayer practices vary, depending on the degree of westernization and generation. Many believe in shamanism.	Most believe in holistic health, emphasizing both emotional and physical health. Prevention may not be part of the belief system, especially among older adults because prevention, breast examination, and annual physical examinations have not been stressed in Korea. Many may not be aware of the concept of health insurance, especially among older adults and lower socioeconomic groups. Liberal self-medication and self-treatment are not unusual including intravenous infusions. Ginseng is used as a cure all. Seaweed soup and Chinese herbs are taken for prevention of illness and restoration of health. Many combine complementary and alternative therapies with biomedical care.	Most combine biomedical care with a shaman, who has supernatural healing powers associated with the spirits. Some associate shamanism with the lower socioeconomic classes only. Health-care professionals are respected, especially if they are older, but many Koreans may not be familiar with the concepts of physical therapist and technical support staff. Tend to carry out medical prescriptions precisely as directed.

TABLE 4–1 PREVAILING GERONTOLOGICAL ATTITUDES OF SELECTED CULTURAL GROUPS *(Continued)*

Communication	Family Roles	High-Risk Health Behaviors	Nutrition
Korean-Americans *(Continued)*			
Respect is shown to older adults and those in higher social position by not maintaining eye contact. However, health-care providers are in a hierarchical position and can maintain eye contact, but some older adults may not maintain eye contact with the health-care provider. Feelings are rarely displayed in facial expressions, and among older adults, smiling a lot shows a lack of intellect or disrespect. Most are punctual for health-care appointments if the importance is told to them ahead of time. Otherwise, most have a relaxed view of time in social engagements. The surname always comes first and adults should be addressed by their surname and the title *Mr., Mrs.,* or *Miss.*			
Mexican-Americans			
Mexico has 54 different languages and more than 500 different dialects; thus, one cannot assume that all Mexicans speak Spanish. Most speak rapidly, at a high pitch and volume, making it difficult for the untrained ear. Many, especially older adults, may avoid eye contact for fear of getting the "evil eye." Personalism, inquiring about family members and small talk, are valued before obtaining health information. Demonstrating respect is of utmost importance in establishing open and trusting relationships. Greet men first and greet each person with the appropriate title (*Mr., Mrs.,* or *Miss*) and a handshake. Time is relative rather than categorically imperative; thus, the health-care provider must stress the importance of timeliness for appointments. More traditional may have several last names, which include not only the husband's last name for a married woman, but also her maiden name followed by *y* and her mother's maiden name.	Typical family dominance pattern is patriarchal, but women have a significant voice in matters related to the home. The machismo of Mexican culture sees men as having strength, valor, and self-confidence. Women are expected to be devoted mothers. Family takes precedence over all other things in life. Blended communal families are the norm. When older adults are unable to live on their own, they generally move in with their children. The extended family system obligates family and friends to visit the ill when in the hospital. Good manners confer high status on the family and connote a good education.	Alcohol plays an important role in the Mexican culture, resulting in high rates of alcohol consumption, especially for men. Smoking is prevalent but the pack years are less than for other groups. Many do not see the importance of seat belt use when riding in automobiles. Obesity may be a significant problem, especially among older women.	Traditional diet varies widely according to degree of acculturation and region of origin in the mother country. Many believe in the balance of hot and cold food substances in the body. Hot and cold foods vary among families and region of origin; thus, the health-care provider must specifically ask each individual about food choices. Because food is a primary form of socialization, it may be difficult to maintain compliance with dietary prescriptions. For many, the main meal is taken in the late afternoon with a late dinner eaten after 8 or 9 PM. Many have a lactose intolerance and must get calcium from food sources other than milk and milk products. Corn tortillas, treated with calcium carbonate, are a good source of calcium for many.

Death Rituals	Spirituality	Health-Care Practices	Health-Care Practitioners
		Many tend to be stoic when in pain, although there is a wide variation in pain expression. Mental illness may carry a stigma. Most are familiar with the concept of home care and willingly care for older adults with chronic illnesses.	
May view death with stoic acceptance as a natural part of life. Among the traditional, family members may take turns sitting vigil over the dying. After a death has occurred, family and friends gather for a *velorio,* a festive watch over the deceased. Acceptable mourning practices include *ataque de nervios,* a hyperkinetic shaking and seizurelike activity that releases strong emotions of grief. This culture-bound syndrome is not an emergency and requires no medical intervention.	Most Mexicans and Mexican-Americans affiliate with Catholicism, although all major religions are represented. Family is foremost among this group and individuals get strength from family ties and relationships. In addition, they may have an intense pride for their country of origin. Most older adults enjoy talking about their soul or spirit. especially in times of illness.	The family is viewed as the most credible source of health information. May be reluctant to complain of health problems because they are "God's will." For many, good health means being free of pain. May liberally use over-the-counter medications and other medication (medicine that would require a prescription in the United States) brought into the United States from Mexico. Many subscribe to the hot and cold theory of diseases. New older immigrants may not be aware of the concept of health insurance. Many view pain as a necessary part of life and tend to be stoic with the expression of pain. There is no stigma attached to the sick role. Herbal therapy is commonly practiced, especially among older adults.	

TABLE 4–1   PREVAILING GERONTOLOGICAL ATTITUDES OF SELECTED CULTURAL GROUPS *(Continued)*

Communication	Family Roles	High-Risk Health Behaviors	Nutrition
Native-Americans			
Each Native-American tribe has its own language.	Most Native-American tribes are matrilineal in nature, but some are patrilineal or egalitarian.	Most tribes exhibit high rate of alcohol abuse.	Food is the center of all celebrations and may be used to feed higher powers.
Many older adults speak only their native language and a few are illiterate.	Among the more traditional, the relationship between siblings may be more important than between husband and wife.	Alcohol use is more prevalent than other kinds of chemical use. Alcohol use may account for the high rate of spousal abuse among many Native-American tribes.	Lack of fresh fruits and vegetables may be a significant problem for some.
Among many, talking loudly is considered rude.			Lamb is a major source of meat, although beef, pork, poultry, and fish are eaten in lesser quantities, depending on the geographic location of the tribe.
May be suspicious about sharing feelings based on past inequities.		Tobacco is commonly used for tribal rituals and ceremonies, but abuse is not common with older adults.	
Most are comfortable with long periods of silence. Failing to wait for a response may result in inaccurate or no information. Not allowing sufficient time to respond is considered rude.	Extended family is the norm and family goals are a priority, with older adults looked on with clear deference.		Corn and fry bread, cooked in lard, are dietary staples for many. The high-fat diet, contributing to obesity, is responsible for the high incidence of diabetes mellitus in some groups. Some tribes have more than a 50% incidence of diabetes mellitus.
Touch is considered unacceptable, especially among older adults; thus, touch should be held to a minimum and only for health examination purposes.	Younger family members generally take care of older adults when self-care becomes a concern.		Food is generally not seen as an item for promoting health, especially among older adults.
Approach older adults with a handshake; however, their handshake may be a light passing of the hands rather than a firm handshake.	Status among the traditional is not having more than someone else and not standing out from the clan.		Many have lactose intolerance and may have difficulty meeting calcium needs, especially in areas where fresh vegetables are difficult to obtain.
Pointing with the finger is considered rude. Giving directions is accomplished by a shifting of the lips.			
Among older adults, direct eye contact may be confrontational.			
Most are present- and past-oriented, with little planning for the future, which may be considered foolish.			
Time is viewed as something that one cannot control.			
The health-care provider can call an older adult "grandmother" or "grandfather" as a sign of respect.			
Vietnamese-Americans			
The Vietnamese language resembles Chinese, with each word having only one syllable. The word for "yes," rather than denoting a positive response, may simply reflect an avoidance of confrontation or a desire to please the other person.	The traditional Vietnamese family is strictly patriarchal and usually extended.	Hepatitis B is endemic among Vietnamese refugees. Many have drug-resistant tuberculosis.	Mealtime is an important family activity.
Although most immigrants speak English, many do not have the skills to express abstract ideas or psychiatric or mental health concerns.	Roles are gender-related, with men responsible for activities outside the home and decision making and women caring for the family, preparing meals, and raising children.	Mammograms are a foreign concept for many older adults.	Foods are specific to each holiday.
Most are uncomfortable with discussing feelings, resulting in mental difficulties being disguised in physical complaints.	Women, especially older women, usually make health-care decisions for the family.	Gastrointestinal cancer is high among Vietnamese, probably because asbestos is used in polishing rice in some parts of Vietnam.	Rice is a dietary staple. Other common foods are fish, shellfish, chicken, pork, soybean curd, noodles, leafy green vegetables, and other vegetables and fruits.
Beckoning with an upturned finger is considered rude; likewise, showing the soles of one's feet is rude. The head is considered sacred and therefore should not be touched.		Depression and suicide are major threats among many refugees.	Many have lactose intolerance and must get calcium from stews with bones cooked to a fine puree.
			Stir-frying, steaming, roasting, and boiling are common preparation practices.
			Older adults eat first. More traditional Vietnamese practice the *am* (cold) and *dong* (hot) balances of foods. Illnesses can be avoided with the proper balance of hot and cold foods.

Death Rituals	Spirituality	Health-Care Practices	Health-Care Practitioners
For most tribes, the body should go into the afterlife whole; thus, amputated limbs should be given to the family for a separate burial. The limbs are later exhumed and buried with the body. After death, a cleansing ceremony may be performed; otherwise, the spirit of the dead person may try to assume control of someone else's spirit. A death taboo involves talking with clients about a fatal illness; thus, discussions must be presented in the third person. Otherwise, they imply that the provider wished the client dead. Excessive display of emotions is not looked on favorably by some tribes; however, among other tribes, grief is expressed openly.	Native-American traditional religions remain dominant, although there continues to be a gradual increase in Christian religions. Many have traditional healing ceremonies that are held and sanctioned in Native-American health-care facilities. Spirituality for most Native-Americans is based on harmony with nature. Individual sources of strength are based on internal harmony and harmony with nature.	Most older adults combine bio-medical care with folk healers. Many older adults may have a problem relating to the germ theory of disease; forcing the issue may foster distrust. Most see health services as curative in nature, with little attention given to pre-vention. Wellness is as a state of harmony with nature; when one is out of harmony with one's surroundings, a healing ceremony may be performed. Pain may be seen as something to be endured; thus, many do not ask for analgesics. Among traditional older adults, herbal medicines may be used for pain control and their use not shared with the health-care provider. Rehabilitation is a new concept for many. Physical and mental handicaps do not generally carry a stigma. The sick role is not entered into easily, resulting in difficulties getting many to have adequate rest when ill. Organ donation, organ transplantation, and autopsy are unacceptable practices for most Native-Americans; forcing the issues may create a major cultural dilemma.	Most Native-Americans use biomedical care with folk healers, sometimes without the knowledge of health-care providers. Some folk practitioners are endowed with supernatural powers. Others use herbal medicines, massage, and amulets.
Most older adults accept death as part of life. The more traditional may be stoic and prefer to die at home. Most do not want to extend life and suffering. Most are reluctant to agree to an autopsy. Traditional mourning practices include gathering around the dying. After death family and close friends wear black armbands (men) and white headbands (women). Clergy visitation is associated with last rites; thus, the health-care provider should call the priest only on request by the family.	Major religious affiliations include Buddhism, Taoism, and Confucianism, with about 5% being Christian, most of whom are Catholic. Family remains a dominant spiritual force among most, especially the more traditional.	Health is maintained by balancing the hot and cold forces of nature and foods. Traditional Chinese medicine and herbs are commonly combined with biomedical care. The belief that life is predetermined may be a barrier to seeking health care. The invasiveness of biomedical care (drawing blood and other painful procedures) are inconsistent with traditional Vietnamese medical practices. The family is the primary provider of health care. Seeking outside care is crisis-driven for the more traditional.	Traditional healers include people who use herbal medicine, acupuncture, and spiritual healing; magicians and sorcerers; and traditional Chinese medicine practitioners. Traditional female Vietnamese may refuse to have a male touch their body; thus, a doll may be used to point out areas of concern on the body. Traditional women may want their husbands present for intimate care and examinations.

TABLE 4–1 PREVAILING GERONTOLOGICAL ATTITUDES OF SELECTED CULTURAL GROUPS *(Continued)*

Communication	Family Roles	High-Risk Health Behaviors	Nutrition
Vietnamese-Americans (Continued)			
Men should not touch women in public. However, it is acceptable for two people to touch and hold hands without a sexual connotation. Maintaining direct eye contact may be interpreted as disrespectful. Traditional older adults may be less concerned about the present and concentrate on the future, although clock imperative time may not be part of the lifestyle. Women keep their full three-part maiden name when they marry. The less traditional in America may take on the husband's surname.	Older adults are honored and have a key role in most family activities. Older adults are usually consulted for important decisions.		Rice gruel is eaten in increased quantities during illness. The Vietnamese diet is usually low in fat and sugar but high in sodium.

This table was prepared by Dr. Larry D. Purnell using data from Purnell, LD, and Paulanka, BJ: Transcultural Health Care: A Culturally Competent Approach. Philadelphia, FA Davis, 1998.

Definitions Related to Cultural Terms

Before discussing the relationships among culture, aging, and health behaviors, it is important to clarify the meanings of culture and related terms.

Culture (sometimes called a "blueprint for living") may be defined as the values, beliefs, and customs that are shared by members of an interacting social group. It may also be viewed as a set of behavioral standards and ways of thinking that are learned through enculturation.

Race is a classification system based on biophysiological characteristics. Petersen[1] defines race as a population group that differs from others in the frequency of one or more genes, with the significant genetic variables being defined according to the specific context.

A minority group statistically is any group (e.g., according to race, religion, gender) that constitutes less than a numerical majority of the population. However, as Mindel and Habenstein[2] point out, "minority" in the sociological sense refers to lack of power or subordination. Minority groups have less access to resources and authority and may be stigmatized by outsiders who erroneously presume that they are in some way inferior. Because the term is often used in a pejorative sense, it will not be used in this chapter.

Ethnicity is a broader term that implies cultural difference based on race (e.g., black), national origin (e.g., Haitian), religion (e.g., Jewish), or language (e.g., Hispanic).[3]

Guarding against Overgeneralization

Before beginning a discussion of specific issues related to ethnicity and gerontological nursing, a cautionary note is necessary. Although the patient's cultural heritage provides a significant context for planning nursing care, it is not predictive at the level of the individual. Ethnic affiliation should serve only as a background because each older adult's care must be made on an individualized basis. It is essential not to overgeneralize or stereotype on the basis of ethnic or cultural affiliation.

Usually, stereotyping is done unconsciously simply because the behaviors of others are interpreted from the perspective of our own value system. Most often, stereotypes are negative, pointing to imagined flaws of a group of people based on an ethnocentric or judgmental perspective. However, even stereotypes that highlight features believed to be strengths of particular ethnic groups may hinder effective care. For example, the way older African Americans are treated by their kin has had a more positive stereotype than is actually warranted.[4] Similarly, investigations of older adults in San Francisco's Chinatown have revealed a serious erosion of Chinese patterns of kinship occurring in the urban United States.[5,6] As a result of these positive but erroneous stereotypes, many actual problems of older African-Americans and Chinese-Americans and their families may be overlooked.

With regard to actual information concerning the relationship between aging and culture, critical informa-

Death Rituals	Spirituality	Health-Care Practices	Health-Care Practitioners
Sending flowers may be startling because flowers are usually reserved for the rites of the dead.		Many do not see the importance of following prescriptive advice and will discontinue medicines when symptoms subside. Most are stoic with pain, requiring astute observations and interventions. The word *psychiatrist* has no direct translation in the Vietnamese language. Mental illness may carry a significant stigma. Many believe that divulging health information may jeopardize their legal rights.	

tion now can be gleaned from the new subspecialty ethnogerontology, which is the study of causes, processes, and consequences of race, national origin, and culture on individual and population aging.[7] There are several important reasons why an older adult's ethnicity should be one of the most important aspects considered in gerontological nursing. First, cultural factors largely determine the definition and status of older adults. Second, the older adult's fundamental values, beliefs, and customs (including those related to health and illness) have been established through a cultural lens. Older adults often are the most traditionalist age-set in any ethnic group; as a consequence, the cultural factor holds particular salience for them. Finally, older adults in the United States have different degrees of eligibility, access, and use of health-care services from those of their younger counterparts. These points are expanded on in the sections that follow.

Aging in Cross-Cultural Context

DEFINING OLDER ADULTS

Just as all societies classify individuals by socially important characteristics (e.g., gender and kinship status), all societies also classify people according to age. For all current cultures for which data are available, each has at least one category of "old." However, the specific chronological time at which a person enters this category varies widely among different cultures, ranging from about 45 to 75 years of age.[8]

In part, differences in the age at which people are considered old results from variations in criteria used by societies. Four major dimensions are used either singly or, more often, in combination for classifying persons as older adults. These are physical, functional, symbolic, and temporal criteria.

Physical Criteria

Occasionally, a society considers people old when they manifest common physical traits related to aging, such as gray hair, wrinkles, or tooth loss. However, these physical criteria usually are used in combination with other criteria.

Functional Criteria

In some societies, people are considered old when they can no longer perform their normal adult role functions. Generally, this occurs in men when they can no longer engage in productive economic activity; women are so categorized when they can no longer accomplish household tasks.

Symbolic Criteria

A person may be defined as old after the occurrence of some socially symbolic event. Among several groups, a person is considered old when the first grandchild is born. In many African and Pacific Island societies, a man may be considered old when he assumes the head of his family's lineage.

Temporal Criteria

This classification is based on actual chronological age or, in age-graded societies, on the chronology of one's age-set.

Thus, a number of different methods exist for assessing age. Analyzing criteria from 57 societies around the world, Glascock and Feinman[9] determined that the most common criterion was change in social role (in combination with chronological age), followed by change in functional status (in combination with social role).

It is important to note that these criteria are not static. For example, in 1962, Samoans considered persons to be old when they were unable to care for themselves or contribute to the welfare of the household. However, by 1976, many Samoans had become more chronologically oriented, indicating that old age begins at age 60 or 65.[10] As societies change, so do the criteria for classifying persons as old.

STATUS AND TREATMENT OF OLDER ADULTS

Just as there are no universal methods of classifying older adults, there are no universals concerning the status and treatment of older adults. Although individual variations always exist, there are wide differences in the way older adults as a group are perceived and treated in different societies. In some societies, old age is a time of high prestige and power; in others, a time of alienation and insecurity.

The status of older adults tends to be higher in societies in which the older adult maintains control over family or community property, social resources, supernatural resources, or information.[11] For example, in societies whose primary economic activity is herding, horticulture, or agriculture, the older adult's control over resources is usually determined through religious prescriptions or established inheritance patterns. In these settings, the oldest member of a family or lineage may be responsible for virtually all the family wealth. Even when they become too weak to engage in strenuous activity, the older adults may be responsible for access to and allocation of the resources.[12] Similarly, in cultures without written traditions, such as the Republic of Mali in Northeast Africa, knowledge is passed verbally. In these societies, older adults are seen as the repositories of knowledge and are held in high esteem.[13]

Religious systems also can affect the ways in which the older adult is perceived. In societies in which ancestor worship is practiced, the status of older adults is almost uniformly high. As the closest living relative to the revered ancestors, the oldest family member maintains a high status because he or she is soon to join the ancestors. The lineage or clan elder also often serves as an intermediary between the ancestors and the rest of the family. Similarly, in many societies, religious knowledge and rituals are secret to all but the oldest members. Among the Highland Druze in the Middle East, for example, older adults keep the religion secret from both women and younger men.[14] Sokolovsky and Vesperi[15] summarize the cross-cultural literature and indicate that the status and treatment of older people are usually associated with four interrelated clusters of cultural phenomena:

- Available roles that emphasize continuity and significant responsibilities within the group
- Integration into a multigenerational domestic kin network
- Control of important material or information
- A value system emphasizing the community over individual ego development

Aging and Ethnicity in the United States

DEMOGRAPHIC CHARACTERISTICS

Population Trends

The study of older adults is increasingly important to nurses because of the projected growth of this group in the population. Older people constitute the fastest-growing age segment of the American population; ethnic diversity among older adults is increasing at even higher rates.

Geographic Dispersion

In the United States, the geographic configuration of older adults is complex; however, patterns of concentration by ethnicity can be identified.

Older black, Asian, Native-American, and Hispanic adults are concentrated in the West and South. Although older black adults are more dispersed than other groups, more than half live in southern states. Older Asian adults are concentrated in the western states (California, Hawaii, and Washington) and in New York. Specific population groups within these broader ethnic categories show even greater diversity. For example, among the Hispanic populations, a proportionately greater number of Puerto Ricans reside in urban areas in the Northeast, Cubans reside in suburban areas in the Southeast, and Mexican-Americans reside in rural areas of the Southwest.[16]

An additional important component regarding ethnic diversity among older adults concerns the nearly 8 million older adults of European descent classified as white. Although their ethnicity may not be as visible as that of older adults of color, it remains just as salient a factor in planning and delivering nursing care. However, as a group, older adults of European descent remain the least studied and perhaps the least understood of all.

Clearly, the demographic trends indicate that as a group, older adults are now very heterogeneous and they are becoming more diverse. This diversity has not received sufficient attention in the planning and delivery of health care.

Health Status

Despite the last decade's general trends for healthier lifestyles and decreased morbidity rates for older persons, nonwhite older adults continue to demonstrate worse levels of health and well-being than their white counterparts.[17]

Epidemiological research is sparse regarding the ethnic distribution of mental disorders among older adults. The lack of comparable data makes generalizations about mental disorders and functioning among older adults difficult. However, the data suggest that African-American older adults have high rates of depression and severe cognitive impairment, older Hispanic men have high rates of alcohol abuse and Hispanic women have higher rates of affective disorders, Native-Americans demonstrate increased rates of depression and alcohol abuse, and Asian-Americans demonstrate higher rates of organic brain disorders.[18]

Considerable ambiguity exists in these epidemiological data. For example, the higher prevalence rates of severe cognitive impairment among older African-Americans may stem from diagnostic or testing errors. For example, because the Mini-Mental State Examination (MMSE) scores tend to correlate with social status and educational level, one reason for low MMSE scores among African-Americans is their lower levels of education. However, other research indicates that the higher rates of cognitive impairment result from higher rates of multi-infarct dementia caused by a higher incidence of hypertension in the African-American population.[19] Furthermore, there is considerable within-group diversity regarding level and type of distress. For example, a study of older Hispanic immigrants from Mexico, Cuba, and Puerto Rico found that levels of psychological distress varied considerably across these three subgroups and that these differences were probably attributable to the complex interplay between educational attainment, language acculturation, financial strain, and social isolation.[20]

Furthermore, there is substantial evidence that physical illness is highly predictive of emotional distress and depression. For example, blacks are more likely than older whites to be ill and have ongoing chronic disorders; they have twice the rate of hypertension and diabetes and are much more likely to have arthritis and circulatory problems.[21] The physical comorbidity, which is generally higher among nonwhite older adults, corresponds to higher levels of mental distress.

SUPPORT SYSTEMS

Family

Although particular features vary among different ethnic groups, the concept of family is universal. For every ethnic group, the family usually is the most important support system for the older adult. Furthermore, the family provides the social context with which illness occurs and is resolved; consequently, it serves as a primary unit in health care. Although the family systems of American ethnic groups have been subject to erroneous characterization and overgeneralization,[22,23] it is important for gerontological nurses to understand the range of diversity in family structure and normative behavior.

Family structure and organization vary widely among American ethnic groups. Nuclear families, isolated individuals, and extended families exist in all ethnic groups, as do male-dominated, female-dominated, and egalitarian family units. Although an ideal or model family type may be identifiable for a portion of a particular ethnic group, there is likely to be a high proportion of families who do not conform to these characteristics. However, given these caveats, two different patterns of ethnic families will be described to illustrate diversity in structure and organization.

Mexican-American Families

The Mexican-American family is very heterogeneous with respect to class, urbanization, and degree of acculturation. Although the multigenerational household has never been the norm for Mexican-Americans, the older Mexican-American is substantially more likely than the older Anglo to live with relatives, and many fewer reside alone. However, this pattern predominantly depicts widowed or single older women and does not hold for older couples. In traditional rural Mexican-American families, three structural characteristics have been identified as having particular salience.[22]

The first characteristic is familism, an ethic in which the family collective supersedes the needs of any individual family member. Embedded in this concept are the ideals that mutual support (financial, material, caregiving, and social) are available within the extended kin network. The second characteristic is machismo, which stresses the importance of a man in ensuring the security of the family. Although this characteristic has primarily received a negative portrayal, it more accurately depicts an ethic of courage, honor, and respect for the family. The ethic of machismo does not mean that women are unimportant; in fact, they often hold the key role with regard to household matters and are the foundation of their families' internal support system. The final characteristic is jerarquismo (hierarchy), in which the younger family members are subordinate to the older family members, to whom they owe respecto (respect). Not only are older adults supposed to be more highly respected than younger family members, but even older siblings have higher authority than younger ones. Mindel[22] concludes that although a substantial amount of authority and respect are maintained for older adults, with time and increasing modernization, these aspects of Mexican-American culture are declining. However, Mexican-Americans still rely on family rather than friends or formal support sources more than Anglos or blacks.[24]

Korean-American Families

In Korea, the ethic of filial piety serves as a keystone of social support for older adults. This norm dictates that older adults should be respected and cared for because of their past contributions and sacrifices for the family. Components of filial piety include respect for one's parents, filial responsibility and sacrifice, and maintenance of harmony within the family. Although the enactment of filial piety has diminished somewhat in other East Asian countries such as Japan and China, it is still a salient norm in Korea.[25] In the United States, older Korean adults tend to be newer immigrants, generally arriving here under the sponsorship of one of their children who achieved American citizenship. The traditional emphasis on filial piety has diminished greatly in the United States. When residing with an older adult, older Korean-Americans usually receive supportive care; however, formal support services are often used when older adults and their children reside separately. In New York, about 20 percent of older Koreans reside alone and another 25 percent live with only a spouse; in contrast, in South Korea more than 80 percent of older adults are estimated to reside with children. However, even though separate households are more common in the United States, the pattern of assistance provided by children here is still considerable.[26]

Religious Support Systems

For many older adults, religion and a sense of spirituality serve as major supports in daily living as well as in times of adversity. Overwhelmingly, for older black adults, religion is an integral component of their lives. Being black is a positive predictor of frequency of prayer and church attendance, strength of religious affiliation, and the importance of religious beliefs.[27] Compared with their white counterparts, older black adults have a more intrinsic religious orientation to spirituality. They have been characterized as "living their religion," having it play a more important role in their daily experience of living.[28] Furthermore, local churches provide important nonreligious social services to older black adults. Churches promote a social milieu for the interaction of participants. Older persons who had been highly involved in church matters were likely to receive high-quality committed care from members of the church. Older black adults in the north-central area of the United States are reported to receive more assistance (social and material) from the church. Older black adults may have a larger informal network of family and friends in the South than in other regions of the country.[29,30] Similar systems of churches and synagogues serving as mechanisms of social support have also been reported for Mexican-Americans[31] and Jews.[32]

These sources of social support—the family, friends, and religious institutions—are significant, particularly for older adults. As such, they merit inclusion in the planning and delivery of care to gerontological patients.

Health and Illness Behaviors of Older Adults

DEFINING HEALTH AND ILLNESS

Whether an older adult believes that he or she is well or ill is determined largely by cultural factors, including the range of normal conditions and the classifications of illness available. Among many older adults, chronic conditions (e.g., low back pain) and signs of physical deterioration (e.g., loss of teeth) are considered normal signs of aging. As a consequence, biomedical treatment for these conditions may not be sought.

Another reason that professional health treatments are delayed or deemed inappropriate is that some illnesses fall into the classification of emic or folk illnesses. All cultures have indigenous health-care systems that include methods of prevention, diagnosis, and treatment of health problems not recognized by biomedicine. When an illness is attributed to a nonscientific cause, lay treatments or indigenous specialists (e.g., a curandero among Mexican-Americans or a medicine man among Native-Americans) may be used, at least initially. There are many common examples of folk illnesses and their corresponding treatments. One of the most pervasive and complex traditional health belief systems is that found throughout East Asia. This system, which has roots in China, holds the belief that illness results when the body's equilibrium is disrupted. Health is based on a balance of complementary yin and yang forces. An excess of yang causes symptoms such as constipation, fevers, and sore throats. Deficiency states that are considered to be yin conditions include diarrhea, dizziness, and indigestion. Each category of symptoms (yin or yang) is treated by the principle of opposition. Yang treatments are used for yin states, yin treatments for yang states. Examples of yang (or "hot") treatments include foods rich in fats or protein or highly spiced foods. Antibiotics and most Western prescription medications are also considered yang treatments. Yin (or "cold") treatments include acupuncture, many herbal teas, and fruits and vegetables.

These beliefs may have important clinical implications. Older Chinese-Americans have been found to modify their biomedically prescribed regimens based on their traditional health beliefs in the following ways: They may take only half the prescribed dosage of a medication because they believe it to be "too strong or hot," or they may not take prescribed pills with cold water because they think the coldness of the water will counteract the "hot" effects of the medication.[33] In addition, folk remedies may be used (either alone or in conjunction with a prescribed therapy) to treat illnesses that have been diagnosed by a physician. For example, older Puerto Rican diabetic adults may use sour or bitter drinks to reduce their blood sugar, or they may use herbs purchased at a botanica for the same purpose, even as they take their prescribed insulin. These illustrations are in no way meant to be comprehensive. The practical answer is not to learn in detail the infinite variety of cultural traits but rather to understand the range of variation within a particular clinical setting.

HEALTH SERVICE USE BY OLDER ADULTS

Older adults are underserved, throughout the continuum of acute to long-term care settings, for both physical and mental health problems.[34–37] This stands in striking contrast to their documented need for such services.

There is a tendency to invoke a stereotypic notion to explain these discordant data. Health professionals may think that older adults want to be treated only in traditional ways by traditional healers. However, this belief is often exaggerated; the identified preference for traditional healers may actually reflect lack of financial or physical accessibility or suitability. Older adults are often overcharacterized as being traditionalists; they are therefore assumed not to want to participate in mainstream health programs. This tendency has been called the cultural aversion hypothesis.[4] Assuming that older adults do not want to use the continuum of health services available is often erroneous and may place an undue burden on older adults and their families.

Clinical Implications for Working with Older Adults

A variety of nursing models have been devised for cultural assessment[38,39] and intervention.[40] To assess the likelihood of culture playing a major role in the treatment plan of the older adult, nurses may want to ascertain the patient's preferred language, generation of immigration, family composition, significant support persons, socioeconomic status, and location of residence (within or outside an ethnic enclave). Furthermore, because traditional beliefs may be held even when outward appearances indicate otherwise, the following guidelines, called the LEARN model, may be useful in developing a culturally appropriate care plan[41]:

L: Listen with understanding to the patient's perception of the problem and to his or her notions of the best way to treat it.

E: Explain your perception of the problem.

A: Acknowledge and discuss the differences and similarities between your viewpoints.

R: Recommend a treatment plan within the constraints of your ideas and those of the patient.

N: Negotiate an agreement (that may not be the first choice of either party).

In addition to the incorporation of the cultural component in the nursing assessment and treatment plan, it is also important to consider broader cultural issues, including ethnic factors in staffing (particularly if many patients prefer to speak in a language other than English), ethnic factors in the location of health or service sites (e.g., congregate meals located in an area that is accessible and safe for older adults), and consumer input and ethnic representation in program planning. The incorporation of these recommendations is likely to increase the participation and satisfaction of older adults in health and social service programs.

Student Learning Activities

1 Identify the major religious or cultural groups in your community. Identify a community leader from a group different from your own. Interview the leader to determine how the older person is viewed from their perspective, what families do when an older person becomes infirm or incapacitated, and what are the special needs of older adults in this group. Reflect on how this compares to your cultural group.

2 From your local university or college library, obtain newspapers published by three different ethnic groups in the United States. Identify themes related to older people in these publications. What features do the groups seem to have in common? What differences do you find?

3 Interview an administrator at a local nursing home. Determine the nursing home's number of residents of color and the admission policies of the nursing home. Compare this number with the proportion of people of color in your community. Also, compare the proportion of health providers of color to the proportion in your community. Investigate why the proportions may differ considerably.

REFERENCES

1 Petersen, W: Concepts of ethnicity. In Thernstrom, S, et al (eds): Harvard Encyclopedia of Ethnic Groups. Harvard University Press, Cambridge, Mass, 1981, p 234.

2 Mindel, CH, and Habenstein, RW: Ethnic Families in America: Patterns and Variations. Elsevier, New York, 1998.

3 Rempusheski, VF: Ethnic elderly: Care issues. In Swanson, E, and Tripp-Reimer, T (eds): Advances in Gerontological Nursing: Issues for the 21st Century. Springer, New York, 1996, pp 157–176.

4 Morrison, B: Sociocultural dimensions: Nursing homes and the minority aged. J Gerontol Social Work 5:127, 1982.

5 Douglas, K, and Fujimoto, D: Asian Pacific elders: Implications for health care providers. Clin Geriatr Med 11(1):69–82.

6 Carp, E, and Kataoka, E: Health care problems of the elderly of San Francisco's Chinatown. Gerontologist 16:30, 1967.

7 Jackson, JJ: Race, national origin, ethnicity, and aging. In Binstock, RH, and Shanas, E (eds): Handbook of Aging and the Social Sciences. Van Nostrand Reinhold, New York, 1985, p 264.

8 Cowgill, DO: Aging Around the World. Wadsworth, Belmont, Calif, 1986.

9 Glascock, AP, and Feinman, SL: Social asset or social burden: Treatment of the aged in non-industrialized societies. In Fry, CL (ed): Dimensions: Aging, Culture, and Health. Praeger, New York, 1981.

10 Holmes, L, and Rhoads, E: Aging and change in Samoa. In Sokolovsky, J (ed): Growing Old in Different Societies: Cross-Cultural Perspectives. Wadsworth, Belmont, Calif, 1983.

11 Fry, C: Cross-cultural comparisons of aging. In Ferraro, KF (ed): Gerontology: Perspectives and Issues. Springer, New York, 1990, p 129.

12 Sokolovsky, J: The Cultural Context of Aging: Worldwide Perspectives. Bergin Garvey, New York, 1990.

13 Rosenmayr, L: The position of the old in tribal society. In Bergener, N, et al (eds): Challenges in Aging. Academic Press, San Diego, 1990.

14 Gutman, D: Alternatives to disengagement: The old men of the Highland Druze. In Levine, R (ed): Culture and Personality. Aldine, Chicago, 1974, p 232.

15 Sokolovsky, J, and Vesperi, MD: The cultural context of well being in old age. Generations 15:21, 1991.

16 Bureau of the Census: Profiles of America's Elderly: Racial and Ethnic Diversity of America's Elderly Population. Pub no POP/93-1. Washington, DC: 1993.

17 US Department of Health and Human Services: Healthy People 2000: National Health Promotion and Disease Prevention Objectives. PHS 91-50213. Washington, DC: Author, 1990.

18 Baker, FM: Dementing illness and black Americans. In Jackson, JS, et al (eds): The Black American Elderly: Research on Physical and Psychosocial Health. Springer, New York, 1988, p 215.

19 Jackson, JS, et al: Ethnic and cultural factors in research on aging and mental health: A life-course perspective. In Padgett, D (ed): Handbook on Ethnicity, Aging and Mental Health. Greenwood, London, 1995, p 21.

20 Krause, N, and Goldenhar, LM: Acculturation and psychological distress in three groups of elderly Hispanics. J Gerontol Social Sci 47:S279, 1992.

21 Johnson, HR, et al: Health and social characteristics: Implications for services. In Harel, Z, et al (eds): Black Aged: Understanding Diversity and Service Needs. Sage, Newbury Park, Calif, 1990, p 69.

22 Mindel, CH: The elderly in minority families. In Hess, BB, and Markson, EW (eds): Growing Old in America: New Perspectives on Old Age. Transaction Books, New Brunswick, NJ, 1985, p 369.

23 Rosenthal, CJ: Family supports in later life: Does ethnicity make a difference? Gerontologist 26:19, 1986.

24 Lubben, JE, and Becerra, RM: Social support among black, Mexican, and Chinese elderly. In Gelfand, DE, and Barresi, CM (eds): Ethnic Dimensions of Aging. Springer, New York, 1987, p 130.

25 Sung, K: A new look at filial piety: Ideals and practice of family-centered parent care in Korea. Gerontologist 30:610, 1990.

26 Koh, JY, and Bell, WG: Korean elders in the United States: Intergenerational relations and living arrangements. Gerontologist 27:66, 1987.

27 Chatters, LM, and Taylor, RJ: Age differences in religious participation among black adults. J Gerontol 44:S183, 1989.

28 Nelson, PB: Ethnic differences in intrinsic/extrinsic religious orientation and depression in the elderly. Arch Psychiatr Nurs 3:199, 1989.

29 Taylor, RJ, and Chatters, LM: Church-based informal support among elderly blacks. Gerontologist 26:637, 1986.

30 Walls, CT, and Zarit, SH: Informal support from Black churches and the well-being of elderly Blacks. Gerontologist 31:490, 1991.

31 Kugelmass, JM: The miracle of Intervale Avenue. Natural History 89:27, 1980.

32 Levin, JS, and Markides, KS: Religious attendance and psychological well-being in middle-aged and older Mexican Americans. Sociological Analysis 49:66, 1988.

33 Yeo, G: Ethnogeriatric education: Need and content. J Cross-Cultural Gerontol 6:229, 1991.

34 Mui, AC, and Burnette, D: Long-term care service use by frail elders: Is ethnicity a factor? Gerontologist 34(2):190, 1994.

35 Boult, L, and Boult, C: Underuse of physician services by older Asian-Americans. J Am Geriatr Soc 43:408, 1995.

36 Padgett, DK, et al: Use of mental health services by black and white elderly. In Padgett, D (ed): Handbook on Ethnicity, Aging, and Mental Health, Greenwood, London, 1995, p 145.

37 Yeatts, D, et al: Service use among low-income minority elderly: Strategies for overcoming barriers. Gerontologist 32(1):24, 1992.

38 Tripp-Reimer, T, and Brink, PJ: Cultural assessment: Content and process. Nurs Outlook 32:78, 1984.

39 Tripp-Reimer, T: Cultural assessment. In Bellack, J, and Bamford, P (eds): Nursing Assessment: A Multidimensional Approach. Wadsworth, Monterey, Calif, 1984, p 226.

40 Tripp-Reimer, T, and Brink, PJ: Cultural brokerage. In Bulechek, G, and McCloskey, JC (eds): Nursing Interventions: Treatments for Nursing Diagnoses. WB Saunders, Philadelphia, 1985, p 352.

41 Berlin, EA, and Fowkes, WC, Jr: A teaching framework for cross-cultural health care: Applications in family practice. West J Med 139:934, 1983.

CHAPTER 5

Legal Issues Affecting Older Adults

Tonia Dandry Aiken

OBJECTIVES

Upon completion of this chapter, the reader will be able to:

- Define basic legal terminology
- Discuss the elements of negligence
- Relate common areas of nursing liability and legal exposure to the care of older adults
- Explain the elements of informed consent
- Define advance directives and discuss the differences between a living will and a medical durable power of attorney
- Explain the requirements for a "Do Not Resuscitate" order or "No Code" order
- Discuss Omnibus Budget Reconciliation Act guidelines
- Define the rights of older adults
- Identify common documentation problems and guidelines to improve documentation
- Discuss issues in home health nursing for older adults
- Define elder abuse

Legal issues affecting older adults are increasingly prevalent in today's courts. With the increasing number of people living to the age of 65 or older, legal issues are surfacing in the areas of competency, negligence, the rights of older adults, and patient care delivery.

Nursing and Medical Malpractice

One of the major areas of legal action is negligence in patient care delivery for older adults. Many older patients die or are injured as a result of failure of the health-care team to deliver appropriate care. Medical malpractice claims are numerous in the care of older adults. Such claims are civil wrongs called torts, which cause harm or damage to a person or party. A tort can be intentional or unintentional. Malpractice is professional misconduct, negligent care or treatment, or failure to meet the standards of care, resulting in harm to a person. In a malpractice claim, the patient, person, or party who is injured and files a lawsuit is the plaintiff. The person or party (i.e., the health-care provider) who is sued by the plaintiff is the defendant.

To determine whether the injury sustained by the plaintiff is caused by negligence, the care and treatment rendered to the patient are compared with acceptable standards of care. The standard of care is a measuring scale used to determine whether the health-care provider's conduct was acceptable (see Chapter 1). The nurse is held to the standard in effect at the time of the incident. An attorney or expert witness reviews the various sources of standards to determine whether any standards were breached and to discuss the cause of the plaintiff's damages. The courts look at whether the health-care provider acted as an ordinary prudent person or average nurse would under similar circumstances with the same knowledge, experience, and training. Some sources for nursing standards of care are listed in Table 5–1.

After the appropriate standards have been obtained, the attorney or expert retained reviews the medical

TABLE 5–1 SOURCES OF NURSING STANDARDS

- American Nurses' Association (ANA)
- National League for Nursing (NLN)
- State and federal statutes and regulations
- Nurse practice acts
- Nursing home regulations, surveys, and certifications
- Joint Commission on Accreditation for Healthcare Organizations (JCAHO)
- National specialty nursing organizations
- Hospital, unit, and office policies and procedures
- Nursing journal articles
- Nursing textbooks
- Expert witnesses
- Job descriptions

records to determine whether the four elements of negligence are present to substantiate the malpractice claim:

- *Duty.* A duty is owed to the person or party once the nurse accepts him or her as a patient. The nurse is required to provide the necessary care and treatment based on the national standards of care.
- *Breach of duty or standard of care.* An example of deviation and breach of duty or standard of care is a nurse who gives an injection in the patient's left inner lower quadrant and causes sciatic nerve injury.
- *Proximate cause or causal connection.* The court must find a causal connection between the breach and the damages, if any, to substantiate the claim. In the previous example, the breach is the injection into the left inner lower quadrant.
- *Damages.* The damage in the preceding example is the injury to the sciatic nerve of the patient. Plaintiffs are compensated for damages or injuries by monetary rewards. The award of money is an attempt to make the patient "whole" again by reimbursement of lost wages, past and future medical expenses, loss of love and affection, loss of consortium, pain and suffering, emotional distress, or loss of nurturing and guidance. In some states, punitive damages are awarded to punish the defendant for such reckless or grossly negligent conduct. The monetary award for punitive damages can be extremely high and is given to discourage any future behavior that can cause such harm.

RESPONDEAT SUPERIOR

Hospitals, nursing homes, and long-term care facilities can be held liable based on the legal doctrine of *respondeat superior,* or "Let the master answer." Under this theory, the facility is held responsible for the negligent acts or omissions of its employees even if the facility itself is not negligent.

In Caruso v. Pine Manor Nursing Center, a settlement was made with the estate of the patient who suffered from malnutrition and dehydration while in the nursing home.[1] The nursing home was held liable for its employees' breaches of the standard of care: failure of the staff to provide the patient with adequate food, failure of the staff to notify the physician of the patient's deteriorating condition, and failure of the staff to administer the patient's medication properly.

RES IPSA LOQUITUR

If the doctrine of *res ipsa loquitur,* or "The thing speaks for itself," is allowed by the court, there is an automatic inference of negligence. The burden of proof shifts to the defendant, who must prove that negligence did not occur. Examples of how it is used include burn cases resulting from thermal pads or heat lamps, and cases in which injuries result from instruments or sponges left in a patient during surgery.

The following elements are required in a *res ipsa loquitur* case.

- The patient did not contribute to his or her injury.
- The instrumentality, object, procedure, or treatment was under the exclusive control of the health-care provider.
- The injury or damage does not normally occur unless there is negligence.

In Keyes v. Tallahassee Memorial Regional Medical Center, a 77-year-old woman fell out of bed and broke a hip.[2] She was described as confused and disoriented. The Florida District Court of Appeal held that the plaintiff was entitled to use the *res ipsa loquitur* theory because the three aforementioned elements were evident. Testimony given established that the plaintiff would not ordinarily be able to escape if the restraint were properly tied. There was also little evidence presented on how the restraint was tied and none presented on how the patient fell to the floor.

STATUTE OF LIMITATIONS

If evidence is insufficient to support a malpractice claim, the attorney must file the claim with the appropriate court or medical malpractice tribunal. To protect the patient's claim, he or she must file it within the time allowed by the state or federal statute of limitation. The statute of limitations is the legal time limit allowed to file a claim and is usually measured from the time the alleged wrong occurred or is or should have been discovered. Federal and state laws differ on the specific length of time for filing malpractice claims.

QUASI-INTENTIONAL AND INTENTIONAL TORTS

Quasi-intentional torts are voluntary acts by a person that cause injury to someone. The person causing the injury may not have the intent required in intentional torts. Examples of quasi-intentional torts are defamation, invasion of privacy, and breach of confidentiality.

Defamation is untrue oral or written communication to a third party. The information tends to injure the person's character or reputation; decrease the person's self-esteem or the respect, confidence, or goodwill the person inspires; or cause adverse or derogatory feelings or opinions against the person. Libel is defamation in written form, whereas slander is oral defamation.

Invasion of privacy is a tort that concerns a person's peace of mind and the right to be left alone without being subjected to unwarranted and undesired publicity.

Breach of confidentiality is related to invasion of privacy. In the health-care setting, the major concern is confidential patient information and the misuse of such information by health-care providers. The nursing code of ethics requires that no confidential information be divulged.

Intentional torts are civil acts that are purposefully done to cause an injury or interfere with a person's rights. Examples of intentional torts are false imprisonment and medical assault and battery.

False imprisonment is an unlawful confinement by chemical, physical, or emotional restraints resulting in the person being conscious of the confinement or harmed by it.

Assault is the threat of an unpermitted touching or contact with a person.

Battery is the intentional touching of one person by another without consent.[3]

DOCUMENTATION

Documentation has many uses in the care of older adults. It is one of the best methods of defense in a malpractice suit if the charting is accurate, thorough, and timely. In addition to malpractice defense, documentation has many other uses:

- Records ongoing patient care
- Provides records for Medicare and Medicaid reimbursement
- Records untoward events such as falls
- Facilitates inpatient billing
- Enables quality ensurance and risk management
- Decreases the potential areas of legal exposure
- Tracks changes in nursing care (i.e., more staffing, changes in policies and procedures)
- Describes patient education and discharge instructions
- Relates physician conversations, family comments, and patient concerns and feelings
- Records patient's condition when entering or transferring to the facility
- Records patient's condition and instructions given to patient, family, or friends
- Provides legal records for malpractice, personal injury, or worker's compensation claims
- Records patient wishes for treatment and ongoing care, including information on advance directives
- Provides data for continuing education and research
- Provides a record of nursing care, which is the basis of a Joint Commission on Accreditation for Healthcare Organizations (JCAHO) evaluation

DOCUMENTATION RECOMMENDATIONS

Nurses are sued not because of their documentation or the lack of it but rather for negligent acts of omission or commission. However, the most effective method of defending a suit is thorough and accurate charting. Alterations, obliterations, use of liquid correction fluid, scratch outs, and different handwritings in the same entry are red flags alerting the attorney to possible negligence that may have caused the plaintiff's injury.

PATIENT CONFIDENTIALITY

The health-care record remains the property of the health-care provider. However, the information contained in the record belongs to the patient. In most states, patients can obtain copies of their medical records. Records must also be preserved and maintained for a certain period.

States designate different time period requirements for the following: health-care records, minor records, fetal monitor strips, Medicare records, radiological image reports, nursing home records, alcohol and drug treatment, mental illness records, and records of developmental disabilities. The health-care provider must develop policies for maintaining such documents.[4]

INCIDENT REPORTS

Incident reports are important tools used by nurses, attorneys, risk managers, health-care administrators, and insurance carriers. These reports are a source for assessing problem areas, assessing subjects for in-service teaching, minimizing patient risks, evaluating individual health-care providers, and assessing needs for policy and procedure revisions.[5]

Discoverability and confidentiality of incident reports depend on specific state and federal laws. In some states, the incident report cannot be obtained by the plaintiff's attorney. In others, it can be discovered and used by the attorney. Because of the potential of discoverability, nurses must chart with the idea that the incident report may be used at trial.

COMPUTERS

The use of computers in health-care facilities leads to additional problems in maintaining confidentiality. Policies and procedures must be developed to limit access points, limit use through designated security codes or passwords, and monitor information accessed by individuals.

Proper disclosure forms signed by patients must be obtained before health-care records are printed. Access logs and computer security logs must be maintained to protect data against unauthorized use, alteration, or loss.

Common Areas of Nursing Liability and Legal Exposure

In medical malpractice claims involving older adults, the following are recurrent breaches of the standard of care:

- Failure to adapt a care plan to the specific needs of older adults
- Failure to assess and implement nursing care adequately
- Failure to evaluate the patient's condition and modify care to prevent deterioration and maintain health
- Failure to administer medications in a timely and proper manner
- Failure to observe and detect multiple interactions of drug therapy (polypharmacy)
- Failure to document in a timely and proper manner the patient's condition, care and treatment rendered to the patient, and the patient's response to treatment
- Failure to follow the facility's policies and procedures
- Failure to document appropriate teaching, including patient responses and evidence of patient's understanding, what to do in an emergency, and the pamphlets or audiovisual aids used in teaching
- Failure to protect adequately the patient who is sedated, confused, or disoriented
- Failure to go through the hierarchy to get the appropriate and timely treatment needed by the patient
- Failure to document the need for restraints, failure to follow the facility's restraint policies and procedures, and failure to monitor and document the patient's condition properly (strangulation, skin breakdown, and death can result from improper monitoring)
- Failure to provide timely and proper skin care to prevent decubitus ulcers, which can lead to amputation, sepsis, or death
- Failure to properly assess, monitor, and take safety measures to prevent falls and injury to patients
- Failure to protect patients from burns
- Abandonment of a patient

CHARTING ON THE OLDER ADULT: DECUBITUS ULCERS

In older adults, skin breakdown and decubitus ulcers are of primary concern. For an in-depth discussion of this topic, see Chapter 11. Problems arise when decubitus ulcers go undetected or untreated by the healthcare provider. Such failures can result in gangrene, amputations, sepsis, and even death. If the nurse detects a breakdown, prompt treatment must be given and documented. It is difficult to defend a medical record that has a single notation of skin breakdown on day 1 and nothing further charted about the breakdown until day 7, when the patient is septic from the necrotic tissue noted on the heel and calf. The patient's skin integrity, skin care given (i.e., massages), skin breakdowns noted (described in detail), and care and treatment given should be documented.

FALLS

Falls are common among older adults. To underscore the importance of falls in this population, Chapter 21 presents a thorough discussion of this topic. The most important preventive measures are assessing for fall potential and implementing measures to prevent falls. There must be documentation that the patient was instructed to remain in bed or a family member was told and voiced understanding and that side rails were up and the call signal was at the bedside. The courts will consider whether medical orders were written requiring the nursing staff to use precautions and will look at the expert testimony on proper nursing practice under the circumstances. It is difficult to defend a claim if there is not frequent documentation of the patient.[6]

If a fall-warning mechanical device or alarm is used, its use must be recorded in the chart. This will show a judge or jury that the nurse was aware of the potential problem and attempted to prevent any injuries and provide a safe environment.

If a patient falls, information in the chart and in an incident report must include evaluation of the patient's physical and mental condition (including the integumentary, respiratory, cardiovascular, musculoskeletal, and neurological systems). Most cases are lost because of the lack of documentation of the circumstances before the fall rather than after the incident.

RESTRAINTS

Although restraining vests and jackets are intended to protect patients by securing them to the bed or chair, many broken bones, bruises, skin breakdowns, strangulations, and deaths result from the use of such devices. Chemical restraints may be used in cases of physical illness, drug toxicity, catastrophic reactions, cognitive impairment, delusions, hallucinations, and depression. However, as a result of chemical restraints, the patient may suffer from sedation, constipation, tardive dyskinesia, dystonia, pneumonia, anemia, low blood pressure, urinary retention, agitation, and decreased mental or physical activity.[7] See Chapter 21 for more in-depth information.

If a patient is restrained, the following items must be charted:

- Alternatives used before restraints
- Reason for restraints (including description of the patient's specific behavior and the type of restraint used)
- Verbal or written orders for restraints

INFORMED CONSENT ISSUES

Older adults have the right to make informed decisions about their care and treatment unless they have been determined by the courts to be incompetent or unable to make such decisions. To obtain informed consent, the health-care provider must discuss the following elements with the patient:

- Type of procedure to be performed
- Material risks and hazards inherent in the procedure
- Outcome hoped for
- Available alternatives, if any
- Consequences of no treatment[8]

ADVANCE DIRECTIVES

In 1990, the United States Supreme Court rendered an opinion in the Nancy Cruzan case.[9] The issue before the Court was whether a guardian could decide for an incompetent patient (Nancy Cruzan) whether she would want to exercise her right to die. The Court found that clear and convincing evidence of what the patient would decide must be presented unless there is an advance directive such as a living will.

Congress passed the Patient Self-Determination Act of 1990 in an effort to ensure that the patient's wishes are carried out if the patient becomes incompetent and cannot make informed decisions about future health care. A patient's wishes can be recorded by using advance directives. There are two types of advance directives: a living will and a medical durable power of attorney for health care, or health-care proxy.

The living will (Fig. 5–1) is a written declaration of the type of future treatment and care the patient will accept or refuse. It is made when the patient is competent. A medical durable power of attorney for health care designates a person (who does not have to be the spouse or next of kin) to make health-care decisions if the patient becomes unable to do so. The living will, which is based on the doctrine of informed consent, is a document that states the intent of the patient and instructs the physician on the patient's wishes to accept or refuse life-prolonging treatment. However, some argue that it is impossible to base living wills on this doctrine because the patient will not truly have knowledge of all treatment options available years later. However, living wills can be revoked very easily verbally, in writing, or by destroying the living will. In many states, terms are identified and defined for the person obtaining a living will. For example, in Louisiana, a life-sustaining procedure is any medical procedure or intervention that, within reasonable medical judgment, would only prolong the dying process for a person diagnosed with a terminal and irreversible condition.[10] In Louisiana, this includes invasive nutrition and hydration. Because of the differences from state to state, the health-care provider and patient must be aware of the state's specific definitions and legal requirements for a living will and medical durable power of attorney to come into play. It is important that the advance directives be given to the next of kin, physician, and patient's attorney. This way, the patient ensures that his or her wishes will be carried out.

MEDICARE AND MEDICAID PATIENTS

The Patient Self-Determination Act, implemented on December 1, 1991, requires health-care facilities that receive Medicare or Medicaid funding to make living wills available to patients on admission.

INCOMPETENT PATIENTS AND THE PATIENT'S RIGHT TO REFUSE TREATMENT

Incompetence does not necessarily mean that the patient must be unconscious, as seen in the Cruzan case. For example, In Re: Milton, a patient diagnosed with cancer was admitted to an Ohio hospital under a mental illness and mental health statute. The patient believed that she would be spiritually cured and refused treatment on the basis of religious beliefs. The patient's physician claimed she was delusional and was incompetent because she was admitted on the basis of a mental illness statute. The physician requested that the court order cancer therapy. The court found that the patient was competent and had a constitutional right to refuse oncology treatment.[11]

"DO NOT RESUSCITATE" ORDERS

Patients may also exercise their right to refuse treatment in the form of a "Do Not Resuscitate" (DNR) order. The attending physician must write a DNR order on the chart to legally protect the health-care providers. If the DNR order is not written, the patient should be resuscitated; otherwise, severe legal exposure could result. The DNR order is separate from an advance directive. The nurse must be familiar with the hospital's DNR policy. The physician is required to note in the medical record that the patient's decision was made after discussion and consultation regarding his or her condition and prognosis. If the family members make the decision for the patient, this information also must be documented in the medical record. It is also recommended that the physician obtain the signature of the patient or a family member in the medical record or on a hospital form agreeing to the DNR order. Policies regarding DNR and "No Code" orders should be periodically reviewed and updated. If the health-care provider has a question about who has the legal right to consent, state statutes and laws must be checked. Also, the patient must be given the opportunity to consent. In Payne v. Marion General Hospital, an Indiana court found that the patient was competent and should have been consulted by the physician before a "No Code" order was issued.[12]

To preserve the patient's wishes and protect the health-care providers, the following should be documented or included in the chart:

- DNR orders must be written in the patient's chart. It is extremely dangerous to accept verbal or telephone orders.
- Discussions with the patient and family should be documented. Also, the patient or family member must sign and date in the chart or on a hospital form that the patient's medical condition, types of treatment, and circumstances have been dis-

FLORIDA LIVING WILL

INSTRUCTIONS

PRINT THE DATE

PRINT YOUR NAME

Declaration made this _____ day of _____, 19_____.

I, _____, willfully and voluntarily make known my desire that my dying not be artificially prolonged under the circumstances set forth below, and I do hereby declare:

If at any time I have a terminal condition and if my attending or treating physician and another consulting physician have determined that there is no medical probability of my recovery from such condition, I direct that life-prolonging procedures be withheld or withdrawn when the application of such procedures would serve only to prolong artificially the process of dying, and that I be permitted to die naturally with only the administration of medication or the performance of any medical procedure deemed necessary to provide me with comfort care or to alleviate pain.

It is my intention that this declaration be honored by my family and physician as the final expression of my legal right to refuse medical or surgical treatment and to accept the consequences for such refusal.

In the event that I have been determined to be unable to provide express and informed consent regarding the withholding, withdrawal, or continuation of life-prolonging procedures, I wish to designate, as my surrogate to carry out the provisions of this declaration:

PRINT THE NAME, HOME ADDRESS AND TELEPHONE NUMBER OF YOUR SURROGATE

Name: _____

Address: _____

_____ Zip Code: _____

Phone: _____

©1996
CHOICE IN DYING, INC.

Figure 5–1 Sample of living will. Note that it is strongly advised that documents specific to the state in which one resides be used. (Reprinted by permission of Choice in Dying, Inc., 1035 30th Street, NW, Washington, DC 20007; 800-989-9455.)

cussed and the patient (or family member) has consented to a DNR order.
- Copies of the living will and medical durable power of attorney should be included in the patient's chart.
- "Slow code" orders must not be accepted as they are not legal and have ethical implications.

HOME HEALTH CARE AND OLDER ADULTS

An increasing area of exposure for liability for nurses is home health care. Many older patients are be-

ing treated at home rather than in the hospital. Nurses must be familiar with home health-care standards such as those from the American Nurses' Association (ANA), Standards of Community Health and Home Health Nursing Practice, the National Association for Home Care (NAHC), state and local licensing and accrediting laws, the JCAHO, the National League for Nursing Accreditation Standards for Community Home Health Agencies, and Medicaid contract provisions.[13]

Because this is an area of increased exposure and liability, more lawsuits are being filed against home health-care facilities and staff. For example, a New York woman

FLORIDA LIVING WILL — page 2 of 2

PRINT NAME, HOME ADDRESS AND TELEPHONE NUMBER OF YOUR ALTERNATE SURROGATE

I wish to designate the following as my alternate surrogate, to carry out the provisions of this declaration should my surrogate be unwilling or unable to act on my behalf:

Name: _____

Address: _____

_____ Zip Code: _____

Phone: _____

ADD PERSONAL INSTRUCTIONS (IF ANY)

Additional instructions (optional):

I understand the full import of this declaration, and I am emotionally and mentally competent to make this declaration.

SIGN THE DOCUMENT

Signed: _____

WITNESSING PROCEDURE

Witness 1:

    Signed: _____

    Address: _____

TWO WITNESSES MUST SIGN AND PRINT THEIR ADDRESSES

Witness 2:

    Signed: _____

    Address: _____

©1996
CHOICE IN DYING, INC.

Courtesy of Choice In Dying, Inc.   6/96
200 Varick Street, New York, NY 10014 212-366-5540

Figure 5–1 Continued.

settled with a home health agency for damages from a fall that caused a broken hip and left her bedridden. The patient sued the nursing agency for failure to hire competent personnel and failure to train and supervise its staff properly.[14] Other areas of concern include the failure to communicate findings to the physician and failure to take appropriate actions.

Documentation

Documentation is the most important method of legal protection in the home health setting. Several areas of home health documentation must be emphasized

in the patient's chart: assessment, nursing diagnoses, nursing care plan, intervention, and evaluation. Discharge plans and instructions must also be thoroughly documented and must include patient status, progress, follow-up care plans, unresolved diagnoses, the specific date when home health care will end, and other community resources the patient will need.[4]

Fax Machines

A potential area of liability is a home health-care agency's fax referral policy. If the agency receives fax referrals after hours, arguably it is presumed to have accepted the patient. If there is a delay in services that results in patient injury, the agency could be held liable. Time limitations must be specified in the agency's policies, and referring hospitals or physicians must be notified of such restrictions.

Acquired Immunodeficiency Syndrome Home Care

Policies and procedures must be developed by the agency in caring for older patients with human immunodeficiency virus (HIV) or acquired immunodeficiency syndrome (AIDS). An area of concern is confidentiality and HIV status. Does the nurse have an ethical obligation or duty to the older patient's spouse, family members, or lover to divulge the status and diagnosis if the third party could be harmed when the patient refuses to disclose his or her status? How far does this duty extend? This question of duty to warn is not easily answered but must be considered by the health-care provider. The nurse should also check state laws to determine whether the subject of notification of a third party has been addressed.

Regardless of the patient's decision to inform others of his or her diagnosis, the nurse has the obligation to teach all caregivers good infection control techniques and universal precautions. Nurses may share their concerns with patients who do not want to warn others and

should inform them that, in various states, it is a felony to be involved sexually while having a positive HIV status or AIDS without informing the other person of the status.

Omnibus Budget Reconciliation Act

The Omnibus Budget Reconciliation Act (OBRA) was signed into law on December 22, 1987. The Nursing Home Reform Amendments (NHRA) were passed by Congress as part of the OBRA legislation. As of October 1, 1990, nursing homes are held to a higher standard that focuses on the residents' "highest practical physical, mental and psychosocial well-being." The standard also directs nursing homes to support "individual needs and preferences" and "to promote maintenance or enhancement of the quality of life of each resident."[15] The NHRA within OBRA are cited in Table 5–2.

RIGHTS OF OLDER ADULTS

The Federal Older Americans Act of 1987 requires every state and the District of Columbia to establish and operate long-term ombudsmen programs. These programs provide people who act as advocates and investigate complaints made by residents or others about the actions or inactions of facilities, public and social service agencies, or health-care providers that adversely affect older adults. Long-term ombudsmen programs are authorized to pursue legal and administrative remedies for long-term care residents.

The rights of older adults are numerous (Table 5–3). Many programs have been instituted to maintain and uphold older adults' rights, which relate to many aspects of life, including medical treatment, employment, finances, private life, community activities, political arenas, legal proceedings, and religion. A list of national legal organizations for older adults appears in Table 5–4.

TABLE 5–2   OBRA: NURSING HOME REFORM AMENDMENTS

- FCFS and SNFS held to a single standard of care, called "nursing facilities."
- Comprehensive assessment of each resident annually and when significant changes in the patient's physical and mental status occur; assessment forms the basis of patient's care plan.
- Licensed nurses: 24 hours, including registered nurses every day for at least one shift (under Medicaid and Medicare; exceptions possible).
- Nurse aides: must complete a training and competency evaluation program or must be listed on the state's registry; must receive regular in-service education and performance review from the facility. State required to maintain a registry of qualified aides and information about confirmed incidents of neglect, abuse, or misappropriation of residents' property by aides.
- Increased social service requirements.
- Maintenance quality assessment and ensurance committees.
- Rehabilitative services available.
- Independent consultant monitoring of psychopharmacologic drugs.
- Physician (physician assistant or nurse practitioner) to visit every 30 days for 3 months, then every 90 days.
- Provisions to outlaw and discourage Medicaid patient discrimination.
- Recognition of residents' rights and promotion to enhance the quality of life of each resident.
- Development of standard and extended survey protocols to measure patient care and outcomes.
- Use of sanctions by the states to enforce nursing home regulations.

TABLE 5–3   RIGHTS OF OLDER ADULTS

- Right to individualized care
- Right to be free from neglect and abuse
- Right to be free from restraints (chemical and physical)
- Right to privacy
- Right to be free from discrimination
- Right to control funds
- Right to freedom
- Right to be involved in decision making for transfers and discharge planning
- Right to raise grievances
- Right to participate in facility and family activities and forums
- Right to visit and freely associate
- Right to have access to community services
- Right to vote
- Right to sue
- Right to enter into contracts
- Right to dispose of personal property
- Right to obtain a will
- Right to practice religion of choice
- Right to marry

TABLE 5–4 NATIONAL LEGAL ORGANIZATIONS FOR OLDER ADULTS

American Bar Association Commission on Legal Problems
  of the Elderly
1800 M Street, NW
Suite 200
Washington, DC 20036
202-331-2297

Center for Social Gerontology
117 N First Street
Suite 204
Ann Arbor, MI 48104
313-665-1126

Legal Counsel for the Elderly (LCE)
601 E Street, NW
Washington, DC 20049
202-662-4933

National Health Law Program
2639 S La Cienega Boulevard
Los Angeles, CA 90034
213-204-6010
or
1815 H Street, NW
Suite 705
Washington, DC 20035
202-887-5310

National Senior Citizens Law Center (NSCLC)
1052 W Sixth Street
Suite 700
Los Angeles, CA 90017
213-482-3550
or
1815 H Street, NW
Suite 700
Washington, DC 20006
202-887-5280

Summary

Older adults must be treated with care and dignity. Unfortunately, nurses see medical malpractice, tort claims, elder abuse, and loss of rights occurring over and over again. As nurses and patient advocates, we can make a difference for older patients.

Student Learning Activities

1 Contact Choice in Dying and obtain a copy of the living will and durable power of attorney for health care that is in use for your state.

2 Discuss the importance of completing these documents with all members of your immediate family.

3 Share with the class the feelings generated by this activity.

REFERENCES

1 Caruso v. Pine Manor Nursing Center, Ill., Cook County Circuit, no. 89L 12001, March 20, 1991.
2 Keyes v. Tallahassee Memorial Regional Medical Center, 579 So. 2d 201, Fla. App. 1 Dist., 1991.
3 Northrop, CE, and Kelley, ME: Legal Issues in Nursing. CV Mosby, St Louis, 1987, p 272.
4 Fishbach, F: Documenting Care Communication: The Nursing Process and Documentation Standards. FA Davis, Philadelphia, 1991.
5 Iyer, P, and Camp, N: Nursing Documentation: A Nursing Process Approach. CV Mosby, St Louis, 1991.
6 Cushing, M: Finding fault when patients fall. AJN 89(6):808, 1989.
7 Burger, SG: Eliminating inappropriate use of chemical restraints. J Longterm Care Admin 20(2):31, 1992.
8 Rozausky, F: Consent to Treatment: A Practical Guide, ed 2. Little, Brown, Boston, 1990.
9 Cruzan v. Director, Missouri Department of Health, 100 S.Ct. 2841, 1990.
10 Louisiana R.S. 40:1299.58.1–40:1299.58.10.
11 In Re: Milton, 29 Ohio St. 3rd 20, 505 N.E. 2d 255, 1987.
12 Payne v. Marion General Hospital, 549 N.E. 2d 1043, Ind. App. 2 Dist., 1990.
13 Brent, N: Quality assurance and the home health care nurse: Taking an active role. Home Healthcare Nurse 6:6, 1988.
14 Dickman v. City of New York, N.Y., Queens County Supreme Court, No. 2005/90, Apr. 24, 1991.
15 Omnibus Budget Reconciliation Act of 1990.

CHAPTER 6

Ethical Issues Affecting Older Adults

Nancy S. Jecker

OBJECTIVES

Upon completion of this chapter, the reader will be able to:

- Define ageism and identify examples of negative stereotypes about older adults
- Describe nurses' ethical responsibilities according to the models of caring and advocacy
- Critically analyze ethical issues that arise in nursing by appealing to concepts of care and advocacy
- Explain the ethical principles of autonomy, beneficence, nonmaleficence, and justice and understand the relevance of these principles to particular cases

As discussed in Chapter 1, the U.S. population has been aging at a dramatic pace over the last century, with more and more people in developed nations of the world joining the ranks of older adults. Nursing, and health care in general, are greatly influenced by this phenomenon.[1] Nurses who care for older patients encounter ethical issues unique to this population. One set of questions arises at the individual level and has to do with problems of aging and human meaning. What is the meaning of death in old age? How do negative stereotypes about aging affect the older person? How do cultural myths about ideal aging frustrate individual's efforts to fashion realistic goals and plans for the last stage of life?

A second group of questions has to do with the subjective experience of disease and disability as it is felt and interpreted by the older adult and responded to by the nurse, physician, or other health professional. How should the harms and benefits associated with various treatment options be weighed? How do illness or disability affect the individual's perception of quality of life? Do older or ill persons rate quality of life differently than healthy or young persons?

A third set of issues focuses on the process of medical decision making involving patients, family members, health professionals, courts, and hospital administrators. What authority should family members have in medical decision making? Can a competent older person ethically delegate decision-making authority to others?

Should competency be evaluated in terms of what a reasonable person would do or in terms of what is consistent with a person's past values and goals?

Finally, ethical issues related to older adults as a group arise in the context of the larger society. The aging of society prompts questions such as: What is a fair or just allocation of limited resources to the old? Is age rationing discriminatory or just? Related to these are questions regarding the role of the older person in society, the meaning of aging in the culture, and the public's commitment to secure the health and welfare of older adults.

Such questions are among the ethical topics this chapter addresses. The approach is to present a range of responses and to discuss critically the ethical principles underlying each. Because knowing one's subject matter is central to the endeavor of practical ethics, this chapter first considers social perceptions of older men and women and the relevance of these to the medical encounter. It then introduces a model of ethical reasoning and uses this model to discuss ethical cases in gerontological nursing.

Perceptions of Older Men and Women

Ageism may be one of the chief obstacles to securing high-quality and just health care for older adults.

Ageism[2] is bigotry and discrimination by one age group toward another age group. Directed toward older adults, ageism is defined as follows:

> A systematic stereotyping of and discrimination against people because they are old, just as racism and sexism accomplish this with skin color and gender. Old people are categorized as senile, rigid in thought and manner, old-fashioned in morality and skills. . . . Ageism allows the younger generation to see older people as different from themselves; thus they subtly cease to identify with their elders as human beings.[3]

Whereas some[4-6] doubt the prevalence of discriminatory negative attitudes toward older people, others maintain that ageism is manifest in a wide range of phenomena and is deeply rooted in the society. A growing body of literature suggests that attitudes toward old age in modern times are ambiguous and that positive and negative stereotypes coexist and interact tenuously.[7,8]

A major study of terms used to represent older people, aging, and the effects of aging found that terms applied to old age reflect a duality of positive and negative associations.[9] On one hand, old age has been looked on as a reversal of earlier growth stages, and the terminology of old age has focused on negative characteristics of older people. With urbanization and industrialization, there has been greater emphasis on the debilitative effects of old age, and older people increasingly have been regarded as useless and incapable of functioning in a rapidly changing society. On the other hand, terms of veneration and respect are interspersed with derogatory terminology. The unique and positive qualities associated with older adults include maturation, experience, knowledge of tradition, and wisdom.[10] Cultural and religious teachings often emphasize respecting and honoring the old, and social and economic factors such as wealth, property, and experience furnish sources of power for older citizens.

Ageist assumptions are not applied uniformly or equally. For example, such assumptions can be more onerous for older women than for men. In the English language, terms used to characterize older women have a much longer history of negative association for women than for men.[7] Words associating older women with evil and spiritual forces trace back to the thirteenth century and continue in the present use of language and in images of older women as the archetype for witches. Older men, by contrast, have been associated with sexual incompetence, physical decline, and miserliness since the sixteenth century. In contemporary society, ageist assumptions may be particularly burdensome for older women because a woman's youthful beauty and physical appearance are highly prized and her self-worth and self-esteem may come to rest on these.[11]

The Influence of Age and Gender on the Medical Encounter

Ageist assumptions infiltrate medical decision making when the older patient's medical problems are deemed inevitable and not treatable, simply a natural part of growing old.[12] Senility, memory loss, incontinence, sexual dysfunction, or preoccupation with death may be considered in this light.[13] Declining physiological functions that are statistically concomitant with aging may be assumed to be present in each aging individual. For example, because many nursing home residents are cognitively impaired, every resident is assumed to be.[14,15] Some have gone so far as to call ageism an occupational hazard of health-care practice[16] because in their work, health professionals see ill, frail, confused, and hospitalized older adults, whereas robust and healthy older people do not need their service. In addition, the scant amount of research or publication on health in aging enables myths and stereotypes about growing older to be sustained.[17] Others have pointed out that medical ageism may be contracted in professional training, when negative slang terms such as *gomer, vegetable, gork,* and *crock* are used to refer to older patients.[3] Professional education also may foster attitudes and practices that focus attention on the patient's body or organ systems and discount the patient's subjective experiences. This makes it easier for health professionals to stereotype and to distance themselves from older patients.

In a study at a major urban teaching hospital,[9] health professionals were found to be significantly more egalitarian, patient, engaged, and respectful with younger patients than with older ones. Although ageism was not present in an overt or blatant form, older patients were less successful than younger patients in capturing the attention of health professionals and hence less successful in having their concerns addressed.

Because more women than men are over the age of 65, sexist attitudes also can pose difficulties in older patient-physician relationships. Historically, women were socialized to be dependent and to let others make decisions for them. Evidence exists that women's choices about medical treatment continue to be delegated to others, such as family members, or in the absence of family, medical decisions may be expropriated to sentimental or politicized ideals of caregiving. One recent study[18] finds that courts are more likely to view a man's opinion as rational and a woman's as unreflective, emotional, or immature; women's moral agency in medical decisions is often not recognized; courts apply evidentiary standards differently to evidence about men's and women's preferences; and life support–dependent men are seen as subjected to medical assault, whereas women are seen as vulnerable to medical neglect.

Just as aging has been regarded as a disease process, normal aspects of women's biology have been equated with illness or regarded as otherwise deficient. In the nineteenth century, scientific medicine viewed the process of menstruation as pathological and stressed its accompanying pain, debilitating nature, and adverse impact on women's lives and activities.[19] Illness behavior and femininity became intertwined during this period, and the more pale, delicate, and sickly one became, the greater the perception that one was desirably feminine.[20] During the latter part of the nineteenth century, craniologists regarded women's smaller brains as evidence of inferior intelligence,[21] and psychotherapists at the turn of the twentieth century interpreted women's developmental differences as developmental deficiencies.[22]

Cultural values and stereotypes about women continue to infect medical practice and color relationships between patients and health professionals. Because older and female patients are doubly at risk for discriminatory treatment, it is not surprising that scarce medical resources are less likely to be distributed to older or female patients who are equally medically needy[23-26] and that age is a risk factor for inadequate treatment.[27] As caring for large numbers of older women becomes a central responsibility of nurses and other health professionals, it is crucial to recognize and avoid negative stereotypes that interfere with providing a high standard of health care.

The Nurse's Ethical Role

NURSING OLDER PATIENTS

What are the special ethical responsibilities of nurses who care for older women? Some have argued that society and its members bear special responsibilities to respond to the needs of vulnerable populations. According to one view,[28] a duty to protect those under the threat of harm applies not only to those whose material welfare is endangered, but also to groups whose feelings, self-images, or self-respect are especially susceptible to injury. Extending this argument to the health-care setting, it could be argued that nurses and other health professionals have a stronger obligation to older patients. Whereas all patients are vulnerable by virtue of their illness, older patients are in double jeopardy. They are vulnerable not only by virtue of being ill, but also by virtue of being older in a society that devalues and discriminates against the older person. Older women are even more vulnerable because the negative stereotypes of aging may be more harshly applied to them and may be more harmful when applied. Such patients are subjected to gender discrimination in the larger society and in the health-care setting.

In light of these considerations, some[9] urge that gerontological nurses and others who provide care for the older patient have a responsibility to do the following:

- Challenge myths and stereotypes associated with aging
- Distinguish the process of healthy aging from disease
- Examine social psychological and biological factors influencing healthy aging
- Develop strategies with older women to protect, promote, and maintain health
- Refine a functional conception of health which acknowledges personal as well as environmental resources and emphasize the growth potential of aging women at all levels of health

NURSING AS CARING

The more general ethical responsibilities of nurses have been described in terms of caring and advocacy. Reverby traces the history of nursing to its domestic roots in early-nineteenth-century America. During this time, almost every woman spent part of her life caring for the infirmities and illnesses of relatives and friends. When nursing was recognized as a professional occupation and the locus of nursing moved from home to hospital, the duty to care was interpreted to mean obedience to doctors' orders. According to Reverby,[29] the definition of caring has recently undergone a transformation. Now, more than previously, nurses claim a right to determine how a duty to care will be met. Today nurses aspire to a model of caring that incorporates rights to autonomy with traditional ideals of connectedness and altruism.

Modern nursing theorists who continue to identify caring as primary to nursing also stress that nursing theory must be built from nursing practice rather than from idealized images of nursing. Benner and Wrubel,[30] for example, develop their interpretive theory of caring from empirical observations of nursing practice. They define caring as a condition in which other people, events, projects, and things matter. So understood, caring is enabling for nursing because it fuses thought, feeling, and action and provides motivation and direction for nurses.

Swanson[31] also puts forward an inductive model of caring. According to this model, caring calls for acting in a way that preserves human dignity, restores humanity, and avoids reducing people to the moral status of objects. Caring, according to Swanson, involves five components: knowing, or striving to understand an event as it has meaning in the life of the other; being with, or being emotionally present to the other; doing for, or doing that which the other would do for himself or herself if it were possible; enabling, or facilitating the other's passage through life transitions and unfamiliar events; and maintaining belief, which implies sustaining faith in the other's capacity to get through an event or transition and to face a future of fulfillment.

Although nursing often is associated with the care function, both nurses *and* physicians care for and about patients[32] and caring is central to the ethical goals of health care. In addition, caring skills are medically and technically complex. Nursing practice has evolved from simpler domestic caring in the home to surgery and anesthesia in the modern intensive care unit (ICU). Finally, caring encompasses not only doing for others, but also refraining from using various forms of therapy and treatment.

NURSING AS ADVOCACY

In contrast to those who view caring as central to nursing, Annas argues that a new metaphor of nursing as advocacy should replace traditional models. Whereas the model of care emphasizes compassionate response to pain and suffering, advocacy emphasizes respect for patients and defense of their legal rights.[33] On this model, nurses ideally possess knowledge of patients' rights and stand ready to enter disputes for the purpose of safeguarding and protecting patients against rights abuses. Specifically, the rights that nurses are enlisted to defend might include those set forth in the 1973 American Hospital Association's Bill of Rights[34]:

Patient Bill of Rights

1 The patient has the right to considerate and respectful care.
2 The patient has the right to obtain from his physician complete current information concerning his diagnosis, treatment, and prognosis in terms the patient can be reasonably expected to understand.
3 The patient has the right to receive from his physician information necessary to give informed consent prior to the start of any procedure and/or treatment.
4 The patient has the right to refuse treatment to the extent permitted by the law and to be informed of the medical consequences of his action.
5 The patient has the right to every consideration of his privacy concerning his own medical care program.
6 The patient has the right to expect that all communications and records pertaining to his care should be treated as confidential.
7 The patient has the right to expect that within its capacity the hospital must make reasonable response to the request of the patient for services.
8 The patient has the right to obtain information as to any relationship of his hospital to other health care and educational institutions insofar as his care is concerned.
9 The patient has the right to be advised if the hospital proposes to engage in or perform human experimentation affecting his care or treatment.
10 The patient has the right to expect reasonable continuity of care.
11 The patient has the right to examine and receive an explanation of his bill regardless of source of payment.
12 The patient has the right to know what hospital rules and regulations apply to his conduct as a patient.

In keeping with the model of nurse as patient advocate, revisions in the International Council of Nurses Code of Ethics (1973) emphasize that "the nurse's primary responsibility is to those people who require nursing care" and "the nurse takes appropriate action to safeguard the individual when his care is endangered by a co-worker or any other person."[35]

Recent assessments of the advocacy model for nursing concentrate on the need to revise state laws to support nurses' advocacy and the need to expand public ed-

ucation to enable nurses to carry out an advocacy role more effectively.[36] Other assessments[37] argue that advocacy should be interpreted to mean helping others to exercise their freedom of self-determination authentically. So understood, advocacy differs both from paternalistic practices that limit individual liberty and from consumer protection, which implies merely technical advising to provide necessary information for the patient's selection among available courses of action.

Professional Codes and Their Limits

To meet the ethical challenges of nursing, the American Nurses' Association (ANA) has put forth a Code for Nurses.[38] The code affirms that the recipients and providers of nursing services are viewed as individuals and groups who possess basic rights and responsibilities and whose values and circumstances command respect at all times. Specifically, it provides the following guidance for conduct and relationships in nursing practice:

Code for Nurses

1 The nurse provides services with respect for human dignity and the uniqueness of the client unrestricted by considerations of social or economic status, personal attributes, or the nature of health problems.
2 The nurse safeguards the client's right to privacy by judiciously protecting information of a confidential nature.
3 The nurse acts to safeguard the client and the public when health care and safety are affected by the incompetent, unethical, or illegal practice of any person.
4 The nurse assumes responsibility and accountability for individual nursing judgments and actions.
5 The nurse maintains competence in nursing.
6 The nurse exercises informed judgment and uses individual competence and qualifications as criteria in seeking consultation, accepting responsibilities, and delegating nursing activities to others.
7 The nurse participates in activities that contribute to ongoing development of the profession's body of knowledge.
8 The nurse participates in the profession's efforts to implement and improve standards of nursing.
9 The nurse participates in the profession's effort to establish and maintain conditions of employment conductive to high-quality nursing care.
10 The nurse collaborates with members of health professions and other citizens in promoting community and national efforts to meet the health needs of the public.

In addition to the Code for Nurses, the ANA has issued Standards of Gerontological Nursing Practice.[39]

These standards emphasize autonomy and the role of older patients in medical decision making. For example, they require designing a plan of nursing care in conjunction with the older adult or significant others and implementing and assessing the care plan's goals and priorities in conjunction with the patient or significant others. To help counter stereotypes about aging and health, the ANA standards call for using systematic and continuous health status data on the older adult in treatment and diagnosis.

Together, these standards articulate nurses' minimum obligations and clarify reasonable expectations on the part of clients and others. Although these rules furnish valuable guidance, the full complexity of ethical issues in nursing can hardly be reduced to the rules promulgated by a professional organization. In the final analysis, nurses themselves must develop and apply their own critical reasoning skills to interpret and judge the ethical problems they face.

A Model of Ethical Reasoning

What ethical reasoning skills should nurses hone and use in dealing with practical ethical problems? One model of ethical argument sees the formation and defense of moral convictions in terms of various levels or tiers of moral justification.[40] At an initial level, a person expresses a concrete ethical judgment about a particular action, by a particular person, at a particular time and place. When pressed, this judgment might be defended by appealing to another level of ethical reasoning, the level of ethical rules. Ethical rules are general types or categories of actions. Ethical rules themselves might be connected, perhaps in an inchoate and not fully articulate way, to more fundamental ethical principles and theories. Consider the following example.[41]

> **CASE 1** A 79-year-old single woman living alone, somewhat isolated, and with minimal paranoia had previously stable angina that began to change. The doctor suggested cardiac catheterization. The patient refused, stating that she did not want to undergo that. One month later, the patient reported increased chest pain. She called an ambulance and was admitted to the medical ICU. Within 2 days, the patient's condition declined and she required resuscitation. Nursing staff began to ask, "Should we do all of this?" The patient's attending physician was out of town. The patient was intubated and resuscitated. The question arose, "What do we do now?" Her sister was consulted and responded, "I can't let my sister die. Do whatever you have to do to keep her alive." The patient had angiography, which disclosed four-vessel disease, and the patient was operated on.

In this example, members of the nursing staff might have reasoned that the decision to perform surgery was not ethically justified. Their judgment might be supported at one level by invoking moral rules, such as the rule assigning to competent patients a right to refuse medical treatment. The patient's refusal of cardiac catheterization to address her angina might be interpreted as evidence that she did not want any aggressive medical intervention used to treat her angina. This rule itself might be supported at the level of ethical principles by a principle of autonomy requiring noninterference with the autonomous choices and actions of others. Finally, such a principle might be embedded in an ethical theory, or coherent set of interconnected principles and rules. Kantian ethical theory, for example, has as its most fundamental ethical requirement a duty to treat persons as ends and never as means only.

Principles of Health-Care Ethics and the Older Patient

To clarify the application of this model of ethical reasoning to health care, it is useful to review some of the central principles of biomedical ethics. In the course of this review, the implications of these principles for the circumstances of older patients and nurses are discussed.

AUTONOMY

As previously noted, the principle of autonomy expresses the idea that the choices and actions of autonomous people should not be interfered with by others. This principle stresses the ethical significance of people as centers of values, decisions, and choices. Health professionals are required by this principle to disclose information about treatment options, evaluate whether patients understand the options and the harms and benefits of each, refrain from pressuring or coercing patients, determine whether patients are competent to give or withhold consent, and clarify patients' consent to or dissent from treatment options. Together, the requirements of disclosure, understanding, voluntariness, competence, and consent make up the central elements of informed consent as they have emerged in institutional policies and social regulations.[42] Because autonomous authorization of treatment is impossible in the absence of informed consent, the principle of autonomy and the requirement of informed consent are crucially linked.

A substantial body of literature on autonomy and the older patient has emerged in recent years. This literature addresses topics such as surrogate decision making for older adults,[43] informed consent for withholding and withdrawing treatment from older adults in the nursing home[44-46] and home health-care[47-49] settings, developing systems that promote autonomy in health care[50] and in the nursing home in particular,[51] obtaining informed consent for medical research,[52-55] euthanasia[56-58] and suicide[59] in old age, and the role of family in medical decisions for older patients.[60-62]

The following case exemplifies some of the issues that autonomy and medical decision making raise for the older adult.[63]

CASE 2   Mrs. J is 67 years old and has just learned she has a cancerous, rapidly growing brain tumor. She is already blind and knows that people with her condition usually die within 6 months; none have survived a year. She knows she will become increasingly disabled, both mentally and physically. She refuses to agree to any procedure that would prolong her life and says she wants to take her own life. Her physician seeks a psychiatric consultation. The psychiatrist said her choice was neither impaired nor the product of mental illness, but the nurses and her physician persist in thinking that she is depressed.

Among the ethical questions this case raises are whether the desire to commit suicide is always wrong or always should be prevented. The ethical principle of autonomy can be variously interpreted in this case. On one hand, a principle of autonomy may be understood as restricting the extent to which third parties can limit Mrs. J's liberty to end her life. On the other hand, it could be argued that a principle of autonomy does not apply at all because the patient lacks the capacity to make an autonomous choice about treatment. In this case, it is important to note that capacity is always decision-specific: It refers to a specific person's ability to make a specific choice, at a specific time, and under specific circumstances. Thus, Mrs. J may lack the capacity to conduct certain aspects of her financial affairs, yet retain the capacity to make many other choices. If Mrs. J is depressed, her ability to make decisions about medical treatments may improve once her depression is treated effectively. Some argue that a sliding scale should be applied to judgments about a patient's capacity to give or withhold consent.[43] On this model, where the possible harms are greater, the requirements for competence should be stricter. With respect to very minor decisions, a less stringent standard of patients' capacity may be used.

BENEFICENCE/NONMALEFICENCE

The principles of beneficence and nonmaleficence require promoting others' good and avoiding actions that might harm others. These principles stress the ethical significance of people as centers of conscious experience, with the ability to experience both pleasure and pain. Benefit and harm for older patients have been discussed in the literature in terms of caring for the dying incompetent patient,[64–66] suffering and quality of life in old age,[67–70] and the meaning of death in old age.[71]

The following case displays the complexity of beneficence and nonmaleficence in geriatric patient care.[72]

CASE 3   You are treating an 80-year-old widow who has diabetes and advanced arteriosclerosis. She has been in a nursing home for the past 2 years and has recently been admitted to the hospital with diabetic gangrenous infection of one foot. You can solve the present problem by doing an above-the-ankle amputation. However, you know that this cannot be a life-saving procedure, that there is no chance of the patient ever walking again, and that, as often happens in diabetic patients, the same infection may recur above the amputation site later. By doing the operation, you might give the woman another 1 or 2 years of life.

Crucial to interpreting the application of principles of beneficence and nonmaleficence in this case is the meaning of harm and benefit to the patient. Here it is useful to distinguish between the individual's subjective experience of quality of life and the evaluation of quality of life by a third party onlooker.[73] A nurse caring for this patient might place himself or herself in the patient's place and determine that the quality of life she enjoys is or is not worth prolonging. Yet this evaluation, however thoughtfully reached, does not necessarily match the evaluation that the patient herself would make under the circumstances. This patient might feel prepared to die and might place a small value on prolonging life by 1 or 2 years. For her, the pain and suffering associated with treatment and the disability that would follow may tip the balance in favor of not treating. Alternatively, the patient in this situation might want very badly to live a year or more to restore harmony in a family relationship or reach other goals. She may not lead a very active life, and so she may rate the negative effects of not being able to walk less significantly.

SOCIAL JUSTICE

A final principle of biomedical ethics requires treating people who are equal in an equal manner. This formal principle of justice applies to situations in which medical resources are scarce and there are insufficient resources to provide them to all patients who could benefit. Rationing can occur in both implicit and explicit ways. Implicit rationing takes place when scarce medical treatments are withheld in an unsystematic and implicit fashion. For example, when patients are placed at a disadvantage for receiving beneficial medical care because of their race or gender, rationing typically occurs in a covert and implicit manner rather than as part of a publicly stated policy.[74–76] Rationing decisions are also made unwittingly, and without explicit policies, when services are distributed on the basis of political contacts or according to criteria such as first come, first served, public or media pressure, and risk of legal or financial liability. Implicit rationing also occurs in certain settings when the use of or payment for services is controlled or slowed. Thus, rationing can be the result of bureaucratic obstacles that impede, inconvenience, and confuse health-care providers and consumers.[77] Finally, implicit rationing of medical services to patients who are poor and uninsured occurs when these patients are transferred (or "dumped") for purely economic reasons to public hospitals, or when overcrowding in the emergency departments of public hospitals restricts access to needed ambulatory medical care for the poor and uninsured.[78,79]

By contrast, explicit rationing is denying treatments based on a publicly stated policy. Such a policy may explicitly invoke substantive principles of justice, specifying when people are equal and when they are different in morally relevant respects. Thus, explicit rationing policies might call for distributing scarce resources based on a patient's medical need, social contributions, likelihood of benefit, quality of benefit, or ability to pay. An example of public and explicit rationing is the Oregon Basic Health Services Act of 1989, which sought to establish universal access to basic medical care for uninsured Oregonians by rationing "nonbasic" services based on factors such as the likelihood, length, and quality of medical benefit associated with using a medical treatment for a particular type of medical condition.[80,81] Explicit rationing also occurs in the context of managed care organizations that explicitly limit patients' access to health-care providers and explicitly deny reimbursement for certain kinds of medical conditions.[82]

Social justice discussions concerning older adults sometimes focus attention on the proposal to ration health care explicitly based on a patient's age[71,83–87] and have called attention to disparities in the quality of health care for older versus younger patients.[1] Arguments supporting rationing based on age can be divided into three general categories.[85] First, productivity arguments emphasize maximizing achievement of some end or goal, such as increasing productive work or contribution to the social order, reducing health-care expenditures, or maximizing return on life years saved by treatment.

Person-centered arguments, by contrast, hold that an age criterion is justified independent of the good that using this criterion would bring about. For example, Callahan[71] recently argued that denial of health care to older patients may be consistent with respect for the patient because in old age, death is not necessarily an evil to the one whose death it is. According to Callahan, the withholding of publicly supported life-extending care is tolerable once a "natural life span" has been lived, provided that the individual has discharged filial duties and his or her dying process does not involve tormenting or degrading pain.

A final form of argument in support of age-based rationing emphasizes the equality of all people. The thrust of this approach is that ageism is not objectionable in the way it is usually thought to be because unlike sexism or racism, differential treatment by age is compatible with treating people equally. As Daniels notes, if we treat the young one way and the old another, then over time, each person is treated both ways. In other words, each of us will experience both the advantages and disadvantages of age-based policies once we have lived through each stage of life.[83]

Arguments against age-based rationing emphasize need, special duties, or invidious discrimination.[85] Need-based arguments underscore the fact that older patients experience a greater incidence of disease and disability than other age groups. If society is responsible for meeting the essential needs of its members, then providing more medical care to older people is perfectly just.

Arguments invoking special duties hold that special duties to provide medical care to older patients are based on the relationship of the older individual to the community and the network of interpersonal relationships within which the person is embedded.[88] Alternatively, special duties might be thought to arise from the fact that older people as a group have made important contributions to science, technology, art, and culture. For example, Jonsen holds that simply by virtue of having lived a life, older adults in our society deserve respect and are entitled to certain benefit from the society.[89]

Finally, arguments against age rationing sometimes charge that age rationing is invidious because it is buttressed by negative attitudes toward older people or because it will inevitably engender such attitudes. Age-based rationing of health care would be interpreted by many as signaling that older people are less worthy human beings and so can be legitimately disenfranchised from other essential goods, such as housing and employment. By contrast, enfranchising older people in the area of health care would impress on people the importance of according respect to all, regardless of age.[90,91] Critics also charge that age-based rationing leads unwittingly to invidious discrimination against women because women's greater life expectancy means that more women than men fill the ranks of older age groups.[92]

The following case reveals the intricacies and difficulties associated with choosing patients to receive scarce, life-saving treatments.[93]

CASE 4 At the age of 70, Mrs. A has been admitted to the hospital for the fifth time in as many years for treatment of respiratory difficulty. The last time she was in the hospital, she nearly died. She has severe emphysema, and when she developed a cold, her deterioration was so rapid that only artificial respiration in the emergency room saved her life. It proved difficult to wean her from the respirator, and she spent 4 weeks in the ICU requiring constant care from medical staff, principally from Nurse B. After discharge, Mrs. A remained short of breath.

Now Mrs. A has contracted another cold. It is 2 AM and Nurse B is again called to see Mrs. A. It is obvious that Mrs. A is in respiratory failure and will probably die before morning if she is not given a respirator. However, hospital policy requires that respirators be used only in the ICU, where the required supporting staff and facilities are available. There is only one bed open in the ICU. The residents like to save one bed for an emergency. What should the nurse do? On what basis should she make her decision?

Would Mrs. A have a stronger or equal claim to the last bed in the ICU if she were 17 rather than 70? Should Mrs. A's ability to benefit from treatment matter? Should the quality of benefit she will receive matter? Should the length of benefit she will gain matter? Suppose a younger patient presents at the emergency room and requires the last bed in the ICU. What would you need to know about the other patient to decide whether that patient or Mrs. A should receive the last bed? Why are these factors relevant?

Summary

This chapter has discussed the phenomenon of an aging society and the perceptions of aged men and women in our society. The influence of these perceptions on the medical encounter places older and female patients at risk for unethical and inadequate care. Gerontological nurses and others who care for this population must cast aside negative stereotypes and base treatment decisions on current medical knowledge. In making ethical choices affecting the older adult, gerontological nurses should consider the alternative courses of action open to them and the justification for each in terms of ethical rules and principles. Only by careful and critical ethical reflection can health professionals rise to the challenge of caring for growing numbers of older patients in the next century.

Student Learning Activities

1 Identify a situation in your clinical setting that involves an ethical issue.

2 Discuss the situation with staff members who are familiar with this situation.

3 Classify the various viewpoints held by the different staff members.

4 Apply the model of ethical reasoning presented in this chapter to the situation.

5 Form two teams and debate the issue of whether soft restraints should be used on an older hospitalized patient who becomes disoriented to place and time at night.

REFERENCES

1 Jecker, NS: Ethical implications of societal aging. In Reich, WT (ed): Encyclopedia of Bioethics, ed 2. Macmillan, New York, 1995, pp 91–94.

2 Butler, RN: Age-ism: Another form of bigotry. Gerontologist 9:243–246, 1969.

3 Butler, RN: Dispelling ageism. Ann Am Acad Pol Soc Sci 503:138–147, 1989.

4 Green, SK: Attitudes and perceptions about the elderly: Current and future perspectives. Int J Aging Hum Dev 13:99–119, 1981.

5 Kogan, N: Beliefs, attitudes and stereotypes about old people: A new look at some old issues. Res Aging 1:11–36, 1979.

6 Lutsky, NS: Attitudes toward old age and elderly persons. In Eisdorfer, C (ed): Annual Review of Gerontology and Geriatrics, vol 1. Springer, New York, 1980, pp 287–336.

7 Cole, TR: The "enlightened" view of aging. Hastings Cent Rep 13:34–40, 1983.

8 Cole, TR: The Journey of Life: A Cultural History of Aging in America. Cambridge University Press, New York, 1992.

9 Covey, HC: Historical terminology used to represent older people. Gerontologist 28:291–297, 1988.

10 Jecker, NS: Adult moral development: Ancient, medieval and modern paths. Generations 14:19–24, 1990.

11 Sontag, S: The double standard of aging. Occas Pap Gerontol 31–39, 1975.

12 Caplan, AL: The "unnaturalness" of aging: A sickness unto death? In Caplan, AL, et al (eds): Concepts of Health and Disease. Addison-Wesley, Reading, Mass, 1981, pp 725–738.

13 Jecker, NS, and Jonsen, AR: Ethical issues in the care of the geriatric patient. In Stenchnever, MA, and Aagaard, G (eds): Caring for the Older Woman. Elsevier, New York, 1991, pp 7–20.

14 Crockett, W, and Hummert, ML: Perceptions of aging and the elderly. Annu Rev Gerontol Geriatr 7:217–239, 1987.

15 Leslie, LA: Changing factors and changing needs in women's health care. Nurs Clin North Am 21:111–123, 1986.

16 Greene, MG, et al: Ageism in the medical encounter: An exploratory study of the doctor-elderly patient relationship. Lang Communication 6:113–124, 1986.

17 Gelein, JL: Aged women and health. Nurs Clin North Am 17:179–185, 1982.

18 Miles, S: Courts, gender and the "right to die." Law Med Health Care 18:85–95, 1990.

19 Martin, E: The Woman in the Body, Beacon Press, Boston, 1987.

20 Collier, P: Health behaviors of women. Nurs Clin North Am 17:121–126, 1982.

21 Gould, SJ: The Mismeasure of Man. WW Norton, New York, 1981.

22 Gilligan, C: In a Different Voice. Harvard University Press, Cambridge, Mass, 1982.

23 Eggers, PW: Effect of transplantation on the medicare end-stage renal disease program. N Engl J Med 318:223–229, 1988.

24 Held, PJ, et al: Access to kidney transplantation: Has the United States eliminated income and racial differences? Arch Intern Med 148:2594–2600, 1988.

25 Kjellstrand, CM: Age, sex, and race inequality in renal transplantation. Arch Intern Med 148:1305–1309, 1988.

26 Kilner, JF: Selecting patients when resources are limited: A study of U.S. medical directors of kidney dialysis and transplantation facilities. Am J Public Health 78:144–147, 1988.

27 Wetle, T: Age as a risk factor for inadequate treatment. JAMA 258:516, 1987.

28 Goodin, RE: Protecting the Vulnerable. University of Chicago Press, Chicago, 1985.

29 Reverby, SM: Ordered to Care: The Dilemma of American Nursing, 1850–1945. Cambridge University Press, New York, 1987.

30 Benner, P, and Wrubel, J: The Primacy of Caring. Addison-Wesley, Menlo Park, Calif, 1989.

31 Swanson, KM: Providing care in the NICU: Sometimes an act of love. Adv Nurs Sci 13:60–73, 1990.

32 Jecker, NS, and Self, DJ: Separating care and cure: An analysis of historical and contemporary images of nursing and medicine. J Med Philos 16:285–306, 1991.

33 Annas, G The patient rights advocate: Can nurses effectively fill the role? Superv Nurse 5:21–25, 1974.

34 American Hospital Association: A patient's bill of rights: American Hospital Association, 1973. In Jameton, A (ed): Nursing Practice: The Ethical Issues. Prentice-Hall, Englewood Cliffs, NJ, 1984, pp 316–317.

35 International Council of Nurses: Code for nurses: Ethical concepts applied to nursing, 1973. In Benjamin, M, and Curtis, J (eds): Ethics in Nursing, ed 2. Oxford University Press, New York, 1981, pp 177–178.

36 Winslow, GR: From loyalty to advocacy: A new metaphor for nursing. Hastings Cent Rep 14:32–40, 1984.

37 Gadow, S: Existential advocacy: Philosophical foundations of nursing. In Spicker, SF, and Gadow, S (eds): Nursing: Images and Ideals: Opening Dialogue with the Humanities. Springer, New York, 1980, pp 79–99.

38 American Nurses' Association: American Nurses' Association code for nurses. In Callahan, JC (ed): Ethical Issues in Professional Life. Oxford University Press, New York, 1988, pp 451–452.

39 American Nurses' Association: Standards of gerontological nursing practice. American Nurses' Association, Kansas City, 1976.

40 Beauchamp, TL, and Childress, JF: Principles of Biomedical Ethics, ed 4. Oxford University Press, New York, 1994.

41 Bard, TR: Medical Ethics in Practice. Hemisphere, New York, 1990.

42 Faden, RR, and Beauchamp, TL: A History and Theory of Informed Consent. Oxford University Press, New York, 1986.

43 Brock, D, and Buchanan, A: Deciding for Others. Cambridge University Press, New York, 1989, ch 6.

44 Horan, M: Difficult choices in treating and feeding the debilitated elderly. In Gormally, L (ed): The Dependent Elderly. Cambridge University Press, New York, 1992, pp 11–27.

45 Cassel, CK: Deciding to forego life-sustaining treatment. Cardoza Law Rev 6:287–302, 1985.

46 Collopy, B, et al: New directions in nursing home ethics. Hastings Cent Rep (suppl)21:1–16, 1991.

47 Haddad, AM, and Kapp, MB: Withholding and withdrawing treatment. In Haddad, AM, and Kapp, MB (eds): Ethical and Legal Issues in Home Health Care. Appleton & Lange, San Mateo, Calif, 1991, pp 79–100.

48 Pousada L: High-tech home care for elderly persons. In Arras, J (ed): Bringing the Hospital Home. Johns Hopkins University Press, Baltimore, 1995, pp 107–128.

49 Collopy, B, et al: The ethics of home care: Autonomy and accommodation. Hastings Cent Rep (suppl)20:1–16, 1990.

50 Jecker, NS, and Self, DJ: Medical ethics in the twenty-first century: Respect for autonomy in care of the elderly patient. J Crit Care 6:46–51, 1991.

51 Freeman, IC: Developing systems that promote autonomy: Policy considerations. In Kane, RA, and Caplan, AL (eds): Everyday Ethics: Resolving Dilemmas in Nursing Home Life. Springer, New York, 1990, pp 291–305.

52 Dubler, NN: Some legal and moral issues surrounding informed consent for treatment and research involving the cognitively impaired elderly. In Kapp, MB, et al (eds): Legal and Ethical Aspects of Health Care for the Elderly. Health Administration Press, Ann Arbor, Mich, 1985, pp 247–257.

53 Stanley, B, et al: The elderly patient and informed consent. J Am Med Assoc 252:1302–1306, 1984.

54 Ratzan, RM: Being old makes you different: The ethics of research with elderly subjects. Hastings Cent Rep, 10:32–34, 1980.

55 Davis, A: Ethical considerations in gerontological nursing research. Geriatr Nurs July/August:269–272, 1981.

56 Jecker, NS: Giving death a hand: When the dying and the doctor stand in a special relationship. J Am Geriatr Soc 39, 1991.

57 Battin, MP: Euthanasia in Alzheimer's disease. In Binstock, RH, et al (ed): Dementia and Aging: Ethics, Values, and Policy Choices. Johns Hopkins University Press, Baltimore, 1992, pp 118–140.

58 Thomasma, DC: Mercy killing of elderly people with dementia. In Binstock, RH, et al (ed): Dementia and Aging: Ethics, Values, and Policy Choices. Johns Hopkins University Press, Baltimore, 1992, pp 101–117.

59 Bromberg, S, and Cassel, CK: Suicide in the elderly. J Am Geriatr Soc 31:698–703, 1983.

60 Jecker, NS: The role of intimate others in medical decision making. Gerontologist 30:65–71, 1990.

61 Younger, SL, et al: Family wishes and patient autonomy. Hastings Cent Rep 10:21–22, 1980.

62 Jecker, NS: What do husbands and wives owe each other in old age? In McCullough, L, and Wilson, N (eds): Long-Term Care Decisions. Johns Hopkins University Press, Baltimore, 1995, pp 155–180.

63 Veatch, RM: Medical Ethics. Jones & Bartlett, Boston, 1989, p 266.

64 Dyck, AJ: Ethical aspects of caring for the dying incompetent. J Am Geriatr Soc 32:661–664, 1984.

65 Hilficker, N: Allowing the debilitated to die. N Engl J Med 308:716–719, 1983.

66 Stollerman, GH: Loveable decisions: Rehumanizing medicine. J Am Geriatr Soc 34:172–174, 1986.

67 Cassell, EJ: The nature of suffering and the goals of medicine. N Engl J Med 306:639–645, 1982.

68 Pearlman, RA, and Jonsen, AR: The use of quality-of-life considerations in medical decision making. J Am Geriatr Soc 33:344–352, 1985.

69 Pearlman, RA, and Speer, JB: Quality of life considerations in geriatric care. J Am Geriatr Soc 31:113–119, 1983.

70 Thomasma, DC: Ethical judgments of quality of life in the aged. J Am Geriatr Soc 32:525, 1984.

71 Callahan, D: Setting Limits: Medical Goals in an Aging Society. Simon & Schuster, New York, 1987.

72 Brody, H: Ethical Decisions in Medicine, ed 2. Little, Brown, Boston, 1981, p 97.

73 Jonsen, AR, et al: Clinical Ethics, ed 3. Macmillan, New York, 1991.

74 Jecker, NS: Caring for "socially undesirable" patients. Cambridge Q Healthcare Ethics 5(3), 1996.

75 Olbrisch, ME, and Levenson, JL: Psychosocial evaluation of heart transplant candidates. J Heart Lung Transplant 10: 948–955, 1991.

76 Levenson, JL, and Olbrisch, ME: Psychosocial evaluation of organ transplant candidates. Psychosomatics 34:314–323, 1993.

77 Grumet, GW: Health care rationing through inconvenience. N Engl J Med 321:607–611, 1989.

78 Bindman, AB, et al: Consequences of queuing for care at the public hospital emergency department. JAMA 266:1091–1096, 1991.

79 Baker, DW, et al: Patients who leave a public hospital emergency department without being seen by a physician. JAMA 266:1085–1089, 1991.

80 Nelson, RM, and Drought, T: Justice and the moral acceptability of rationing medical care. J Med Philos 17:97–117, 1992.

81 Hadorn, DC: Setting health care priorities in Oregon. JAMA 265:2218–2225, 1991.

82 Jecker, NS: Managed competition and managed care: What are the ethical issues? In Sach, GA, and Cassel, CK (eds): Geriatric Clinics of North America. WB Saunders, Philadelphia, pp 527–540.

83 Daniels, N: Am I My Parents' Keeper? Oxford University Press, New York, 1988.

84 Avron, J: Benefit and cost analysis in geriatric care: Turning age discrimination into health policy. N Engl J Med 310: 1294–1301, 1984.

85 Jecker, NS, and Pearlman, AR: Ethical constraints on rationing medical care by age. J Am Geriatr Soc 37:1067–1075, 1989.

86 Jecker, NS: Disenfranchising the elderly from life-extending medical care. In Homer, P, and Holstein, M (eds): A Good Old Age? Simon & Schuster, New York, 1990, pp 157–169.

87 Jecker, NS: Towards a theory of age group justice. J Med Philos 14:655–676, 1989.

88 Kilner, J: Age as a basis for allocating lifesaving medical resources. J Health Polit Policy Law 13:405, 1988.

89 Jonsen, AR: Resentment and the rights of the elderly. In Jecker, NS (ed): Aging and Ethics. Humana Press, Clifton, NJ, 1991, pp 341–352.

90 Jecker, NS, and Pearlman, RA: Designing ethical alternatives to age-based rationing. In Hackler, C (ed): Health Care for an Aging Population. State University of New York Press, Albany, 1994, pp 121–144.

91 Cassel, CK, and Neugarten, BL: The goals of medicine in an aging society. In Binstock, RH, and Post, SG (eds): Too Old for Health Care? Johns Hopkins University Press, Baltimore, 1991, pp 75–91.

92 Jecker, NS: Age-based rationing and women. JAMA 266: 3012–3015, 1991.

93 Levine, C: Cases in Bioethics. St Martin's Press, New York, 1989, p 227.

CHAPTER 7

Health Teaching and Compliance

Patricia Gauntlett Beare

OBJECTIVES

Upon completion of this chapter, the reader will be able to:

- Describe the focus and purpose of health teaching
- Describe the effect of health problems on older adults' learning and adaptive measures to enhance learning
- Identify six factors in which health promotion can help older adults reduce risks and lead more productive lives
- Use the nursing process as a strategy for health teaching
- Compare various teaching strategies
- Describe documentation in terms of legal implications
- Describe the difficulty in determining compliance
- Describe five general factors the nurse should consider when working with a patient with a prescriptive regimen
- Describe four primary prevention teaching strategies to avoid noncompliance
- Describe measures the nurse can implement to improve compliance
- Identify factors that may affect compliance
- Identify factors affecting the ethics of patient education

Health Teaching

Health teaching is an essential component of gerontological nursing. The focus and purpose of health teaching is to define the problem, suggest coping behaviors, and facilitate client mastery and control.[1] For older adults, this may be to help the chronically ill adapt to illness, deal with problems, and understand the processes related to aging. It may also mean to help older persons maintain good health and independent functioning and live longer, healthier lives. Health promotion education efforts should emphasize preventing disease, maintaining existing abilities, and preventing impairments that can result in disability.[2] Clinical teaching of older adults recognizes that they bring to the learning experience an increase in knowledge gained through formal and informal channels of education. Older people are much less likely to have completed high school (about 49 percent) than the entire population aged 25 and older (75 percent). Fewer than 1 in 5 people in the older, nonwhite U.S. population has graduated from high school; most have no more than an elementary school education.[3]

Older Americans are likely to have chronic health problems such as cancer, diabetes, heart disease, arthritis, decreasing eyesight and hearing, and Alzheimer's disease. However, most older adults continue to live in the community, are mentally alert, and have a positive view of their health. Only about 5 percent of older people live in nursing homes.[3] Older people are the heaviest users of health care, accounting for 30 percent of all hospital discharges, 20 percent of all physician visits, and one-third of the personal health-care expenditures. People age 75 and older are most likely to be frail and to have a number of chronic diseases.[4]

The Department of Health and Human Services has instituted a national public education program called Healthy Older People that seeks to educate older people about health practices that can reduce risks of disabling illness and increase their prospects for more productive and active lives. Their program emphasizes the following six areas in which health promotion education can make a difference.

- Exercise and fitness help people look and feel better. Only 43 percent of people over age 65 exercise regularly. Education can help older adults to understand the benefits of exercise and assist them in selecting the right kind of exercise.
- A nutritious diet is essential for good health, yet education is needed to remind older people how to eat a healthful diet, counterbalancing the foods they are told to avoid.
- Older people use more than 25 percent of all prescribed medications and large amounts of over-the-counter medications. Because of the way they metabolize drugs, often with a reduction in drug excretion, older people are more susceptible to side effects and interactions involving foods and other drugs.
- Because smoking cessation is the single most important step toward improving one's health, teaching in this area can lead to behavior changes that can make a significant difference.
- Injuries from automobile or pedestrian accidents and falls account for 16,000 deaths per year among people age 65 and older. Education geared toward learning safety habits (e.g., using seat belts) or toward making changes in their environment (e.g., getting rid of scatter rugs on floors) can reduce older adults' risk of injury.
- Older people must also be educated regarding the need to use preventive health services. Older people should have regular physical examinations, including hearing, vision, and blood pressure screenings; dental checkups; immunizations; and checks of certain cancer sites.[5]

Research indicates that older people receive most of their health information from print media such as health magazines and medical columns, medical books, and encyclopedias. Television, family members, friends, physicians, nurses, and pharmacists were the next most common sources.[6,7] Participants in studies indicated a need for more health-care information, especially in the areas of health-care costs, diseases of old age, nutrition, exercise, and medication. Older people tend to seek information that helps them remain healthy rather than information that focuses on their health problems.

EDUCATIONAL STRATEGIES TO ACCOMMODATE THE PHYSICAL EFFECTS OF AGING

Respondents of a research study identified the following barriers to learning among older adults: memory impairment (66 percent), vision and hearing impairment (43 percent), fatigue (70 percent), and slower ability to learn (27 percent). Only 40 percent reported that they enjoyed learning in groups rather than individually.[8]

Visual changes include a decreased pupil size, causing less light to reach the retina and resulting in decreased visual acuity. Peripheral vision is reduced, color discrimination (blue-green) and fine visual detail are decreased, and sensitivity to glare is increased. To create printed materials for older adults, a large easy-to-read typeface, contrasting colors of black and white, and nonglare paper should be used, and material should be broken into simple, short paragraphs with large margins.

The older person takes more time to process and respond to information and environmental clues. The most important information should be given first, and clarified with the use of examples. Instruction for motor skills should be given one step at a time, waiting for each step to be mastered before teaching the next. If the older person's physical or cognitive skills inhibit learning, the significant caregiver may have to be taught the skill.[9]

Because of presbycusis, older adults have an inability to hear high-pitched sounds such as *f, s, k,* and *sh.* Male voices or whispers may be heard better because of their low pitches. Increasing the loudness of the sound does not help hearing because the pitch (cycles per second) differs from loudness (decibels). The educator should speak slowly and enunciate clearly. Background noise should be eliminated and nonverbal communication encouraged. The educator should face the older person, observe for nonverbal indicators that the older person has not heard the material, and rephrase the material until understanding occurs.

Because energy and stamina decrease with aging, fatigue occurs sooner in older adults. Lungs may not expand adequately because of posture changes, muscle weakness, and a smaller, more rounded ribcage. Age-associated memory decline includes a definite reduction in initial learning and retention of material, especially with transfer of information from primary (short-term) to secondary (long-term) memory and with retrieval of information from secondary memory.[10] See Table 7–1 for a teaching guide offering strategies to offset age-associated memory decline. Older patients can learn if they set the pace of learning to suit their current ability and develop memory aids, and content is delivered at a reasonable pace.[11]

Other factors that may interfere with learning include attitudes and feelings, illness, depression, self-esteem, and culture.[12] Sociological and psychological factors such as loss of loved ones, retirement, econom-

TABLE 7–1 TEACHING GUIDE: STRATEGIES TO OFFSET AGE-ASSOCIATED MEMORY DECLINE

- Encourage association between items.
- Increase time for teaching, especially psychomotor skills.
- Eliminate environmental distractions, such as projectors, and promote physical comfort.
- Make sure glasses are clean and in place.
- Encourage verbal responses.
- Set easily achievable goals.
- Allow time for the person to respond.
- Use soft white light to decrease glare.
- Correct wrong answers immediately and reinforce correct answers frequently.
- Sum up at the end and review all major points.
- Offer liquid nourishment and allow bathroom breaks.
- Clarify with examples that the older adult can relate to in everyday life.

ics, and loss of cognitive ability may affect learning.[13] Low self-esteem, which often accompanies chronic illness, may interfere with the learning process by promoting anxiety or fear of failure. Feelings of worthlessness, hopelessness, or pessimism may be organic in cause or may follow a loss of family, friends, or job. If the depression is moderate or severe, it may interfere with the motivation to learn.

Older adults come from many cultures. By the year 2050, nonwhites are expected to increase to 30 percent of the older population. Particular learning needs will be especially important in the Hispanic population. Older women outnumber older men 3 to 2, are often widowed, are over age 75, and often live alone. Religious beliefs are important to many older clients. Learning needs also vary depending on whether the older adult lives in a rural or urban area, in a retirement community, with a relative, or in a nursing home.[14]

ASSESSMENT

The process of older adult education begins with assessment and formulation of nursing diagnoses, problem list, and objectives. Knowledge deficits should be identified by both the nurse and the older adult. If the older adult does not understand that the knowledge deficit exists, he or she will not be motivated to learn.

Physical assessment includes observing the changes associated with the normal aging process and their impact on health status of functioning. Vision, perception, tactile sensation, musculoskeletal changes, and sensory deficits must be evaluated to set goals and to teach cognitive and psychomotor skills.[12]

Attitudes and feelings may affect the older adults' ability to follow a care plan. The nurse assesses for this inability by interviewing the patient and observing behavior such as compliance with treatment plan and medication regimen and keeping appointments.

The cognitive domain involves assessment of the patient's orientation to person, time, and place, as well as assessment of his or her ability to carry on a conversation and follow simple instructions. Evaluating confusion is important in determining whether the older adult can comply with instruction consistently. Cognitive impairment can be measured by the mini-mental state exam. It measures orientation, attention, registration, calculation, recall ability to follow a three-part command, and the use of language.[15,16]

Assessing Learning Styles and Needs

Questionnaires are a common way to elicit information. They may be used in structured interviews to elicit written information on general or specific learning needs. Questionnaires should include the older adult's concept of the illness, understanding of the treatment plan, goals, environmental conditions, learning needs, and concerns.

Written tests usually are not used in a needs assessment because they tend to cause anxiety and increase the older adult's fear of failing. Labeling the test as a questionnaire and presenting it as a tool to help you and the client discover learning needs may remove the threat. Educators should check with other health-care personnel (social worker, nurse, physician) to gain insight. Observation of older adults performing skills and checking hospital records are two other sources of information.

GOAL SETTING AND OUTCOMES

Goals provide the framework for measuring the success of teaching.[17] The older adult and the nurse must identify goals and outcomes that:
- Can be accomplished in a given timeframe
- Consider the older adult's resources such as money, transportation, and housing
- Can be accomplished if a support system is available
- Are congruent with physical, mental, and psychomotor status
- Can be of immediate value and importance to learning
- Are timely, practical, and realistic

INSTRUCTIONAL SETTING AND PROCESS

Timing of the instruction is important. Patient teaching should not be done at the time of discharge but as soon as the older adult is physically capable, has the energy and stamina, and has minimal anxiety over the illness or control over that anxiety. If the educational need is for teaching about a procedure, it should be done as close as possible to the date of the procedure. Educational teaching can be incorporated into the nurse's care plan. When performing treatments, the nurse can explain the procedure and involve the patient by having him or her hold something. The nurse can ask the patient how he or she will manage at home and other similar questions.

Family members can be involved in the actual care of the older adult. Families need explanations of the procedure as well as potential problems, when to call the physician, and sources of help. Remember, the nurse must also assess the responsible family member or significant other to determine learning needs. Identifying potential or active family problems is an ongoing part of need assessment.

ADULT LEARNING

The most important concept to remember in adult learning is practicality. The older adult will be motivated to learn if there is some reason to learn. Adult learners are goal-oriented. If the information is factually relevant and geared to staying well or maintaining independence, older adults will be motivated to learn. The older adult comes to the learning experience with previous knowledge and past experiences, which should be used, if possible, as a basis on which to build new knowledge. The nurse must pay constant attention to how the information will be used by the learner and should show the learner how this information can be used in everyday life.

Encourage learners to play an active role in their learning. Creative teaching strategies, including visual aids and mechanisms to ensure repetition while saving energy, are important. How the client has learned in the past will influence how he or she learns now. Although learning can occur in groups, individual teaching is more effective. The older adult must be ready and motivated to learn. Assessing his or her knowledge of the subject is important so that new information can be provided or inaccurate information corrected. Community support groups help the older person to share experiences and help build self-esteem.

TEACHING TECHNIQUES

Teaching techniques include lecture, demonstration and return demonstration, contracts, programmed study or self-study, group role-playing, and games. Table 7–2 provides suggestions for patient teaching with patients who have low literacy skills.

The lecture is the most common form of instruction. To be effective with older adults, a lecture must be short and factual, give useful information, and be presented in an appropriate way. Because positive reinforcement enhances learning, this should be used to indicate what he or she has done right or to support compliance.

Demonstration and return demonstration is a method used to teach procedures and is effective when the older adult practices the steps. Self-study involves simple texts that deliver information in a concise manner. These may be in the form of pamphlets, videotapes, or self-instruction packets.

Contracts involve setting a goal, identifying expected outcomes, and building in a reward when the goal is accomplished. This teaching technique is effective when used in an outpatient setting because the client and nurse can see changes with each return visit. It also involves the older adult making a commitment to goals and becoming actively involved in self-care.

Role-playing and games enable participants to review and work through simulated situations. These activities can be fun and involve active participation. Support groups can use role-playing and games as well as provide opportunities for older adults to discuss feelings, resources, and experiences.

EVALUATION

The evaluation process focuses on the learner and the extent to which the learning goals were accomplished. Evaluation techniques include observation of the learner to see whether a skill has been attained, written tests, or structured interviews. Self-reports can be used to record information by the older adult and evaluated by the nurse to plan future teaching interventions.

DOCUMENTATION AND LEGAL IMPLICATIONS

Individual patient teaching must be documented on a form in the patient's chart or medical record. Documentation should include the learning needs, teaching

TABLE 7–2 TEACHING GUIDE: SUGGESTIONS FOR TEACHING THE LOW-LITERACY PATIENT

- Assess the reading level of teaching material with a SMOG or Fry formula.
- Present the nuts and bolts of the information.
- Present no more than three new points at a time.
- Give the most important information points first and last: This is the how-to knowledge.
- Sequence information in the way the patient will use it and present in a logical, straightforward manner.
- Give information the patient can use immediately. For example, have the patient complete a medication chart.
- Repeat and summarize the main points of the message at the end of each session.
- Ask the patient to repeat the information or demonstrate the skill.
- Always use the same terms when referring to something with the same meaning (e.g., "your medicine" or "your drug"; do not use terms interchangeably).
- Use the smallest, simplest words when presenting information. Keep sentences short.
- Use technical words sparingly and never introduce more than five new words in each session.
- Present written information at a fifth-grade level or lower.
- Be concrete and time specific (e.g., "Take one tablet at 6 AM").
- Keep the information interesting and relevant to the patient's situation or lifestyle (e.g., diabetic exchange lists for a Mexican-American patient should include beans, tacos, tortilla, and other culturally relevant foods).
- Use written material that gets the reader involved (e.g., "How can you use this information in your own situation?").
- Speak and write in a nonthreatening conversational style.
- Avoid long explanations.
- Do anything you can to decrease anxiety.
- Reward frequently, even for small accomplishments.

content, learning progress or response to teaching, materials used, and results of the teaching, including verbal understanding and demonstration of learning. It is a legal duty of the nurse to educate the patient.

ETHICS OF PATIENT EDUCATION

In 1991, the Patient Self-Determination Act took effect. This act requires hospitals, home health-care agencies, nursing homes, and hospitals to tell patients of their right to accept or refuse medical care and to execute an advance directive. High-tech home care, choices in health-care, managed care delivery, advance directives, all require information from the health educator. Information must be provided that is unbiased, accurate, and sensitive to the health-care needs of the older patient; information that gives learners reasons and evidence to make sound choices for their health and health care.

SPECIAL LEARNING

Medication

Medication nonadherence among older adults is a major national health concern. Noncompliance with a prescribed medical regimen has been identified as a major contributing factor to therapeutic failure with older outpatients.[14] Researchers also report that less than 50 percent of older adults take medication as prescribed, with more than 90 percent of the nonadherence caused by taking less medication than prescribed.[18] In the United States, it has been estimated that 10 percent of hospital readmissions and 23 percent of nursing home admissions are related to patients' inability to take medicines correctly.[19] Researchers agree that older adults must understand and remember prescription information to comply with instructions. Systematic teaching about medications before discharge has been shown to increase understanding of medicines and change postdischarge behavior.[20,21] Prescription labeling is often poorly organized, complicated, and subject to misinterpretation. Even physically active and cognitively alert older adults have significant problems related to forgetting.[22] A number of studies indicate that compliance with tablet taking may be as low as 40 percent, with compliance decreasing as the number of tablets increases.[23] Factors cited as determinants of compliance include patient over 70 years (lower), perception of illness as severe (higher), prescribed treatment to be efficacious (higher), satisfaction with physician (higher), complexity of regimen (lower), adverse effects of medications (lower), type of container (childproof), and type of medication.[18]

Compliance

Compliance is the extent to which a patient's behavior agrees with the guidance or instructions given for any form of prescriptive therapy, whether it be diet, exercise, medication, or keeping an appointment with the physician.[24] Noncompliance, or not following instructions or guidelines, is a significant public health problem and the most serious problem facing medical practice today.[25]

Despite a vast amount of compliance research, no single pattern of factors has emerged to detect the potentially noncompliant person. The difficulty lies in the number of variables involved, as each person brings to an encounter with a health professional his or her own culture and unique set of values and past experiences. In addition, compliance seems also to be related to the complex interactions between these values and experiences and family support, personality of the health professional doing the teaching, and complexity of the regimen. Unfortunately, the health professional doing the teaching and the complexity of the regimen may be different each time the patient seeks professional health care, so the continuity of care is lost. This is especially true for hospitalization or clinic visits. When a patient fails to follow a regimen because of inadequate teaching, it should be called unintentional noncompliance because it is not the patient's fault. The nurse may need to spend several teaching sessions with the patient to see whether the patient has any difficulty such as opening containers or reading labels.[26]

An evolving concept in the compliance field concerns the interaction of behavior with a person's health beliefs. The health belief model (HBM) began in the

1950s with the Lewinian field theory,[27] which hypothesized that an individual's behavior depends on two variables: "(1) the value placed by an individual on a particular outcome and (2) the individual's estimate of the likelihood that a given action will result in that outcome."[28] The HBM, using these concepts, was developed in an effort to explain why people resisted routines for disease prevention and screening in an attempt to diagnose asymptomatic disease.[29] Becker et al.[30] revised the tool to explain compliance to prescribed therapeutic regimens, and Kasl[31] and Kirscht[32] revised it further for responses to symptoms. HBM research, although initially promising, has suffered from the lack of development of reliable and valid scales and of developing scales for each condition studied.[33]

From the health belief research, insight was gained into intentional noncompliance in which a patient does not follow a prescribed regimen because of preexisting beliefs, which may be unknown to the health professional, or because of feelings that the illness is not serious enough to require following a regimen.

Another theory used to evaluate compliance behaviors is the health locus of control.[34] This theory refers to the degree to which individuals believe that their behavior influences their well-being (locus of control), that others control their well-being, or that chance determines their well-being. Hallal[35] reported that this concept had some predictive value for some compliance behaviors. Others have not found it predictive of compliance with patients 65 years of age and older with multiple drug regimens. Like the HBM, this tool must be disease-specific.

It is difficult to determine whether a patient is complying with a regimen. Both patients and physicians overestimate compliance. Laboratory tests show that serum level can be altered if the patient takes a medication as prescribed a day or two before the test, even if that patient takes the medication sporadically the remainder of the time. Pill counts can be misleading. For example, to appear compliant, a patient who does not take his or her pills regularly may discard a number of them on the day they are to be counted. Clinical signs also may not be a reliable indicator. Craig[36] reported that 20 percent of 20 subjects verified by urine hydrochlorothiazide assay as being compliant had a diastolic blood pressure greater than 95 mm Hg. Considering the blood pressure reading alone, these patients would have been unfairly labeled as noncompliant. Kass et al.[37] reported the unreliability of clinical assessment (intraocular pressure, pupillary diameter, and pupillary reaction to light, either alone or in combination) to indicate the patient's compliance with pilocarpine treatment.

The integration of microelectronics into blister packs or the cap of a medication bottle is the newest method of determining compliance.[38–40] These devices record the time and date every time the medication container is opened. Later, the data are downloaded to a computer, analyzed, and printed. At present, although microelectronic monitoring is the most reliable method of determining medication compliance, because of its cost it is not practical for use with the general population. However, the results of clinical trial studies using this new system have provided additional data for patient medication-taking behavior.

Urquhart[41] described a new phenomenon, the drug holiday. The data showed episodes during a month when the medication was taken, omitted, started again, and omitted (this timing of medication ingestion is impossible to detect by pill count). The data were useful in determining not only whether therapeutic levels were maintained but also the correlation of clinical events (the sudden reappearance of untoward symptoms, the emergence of drug-resistant organisms) with drug holidays.

IMPACT OF NONCOMPLIANCE IN OLDER ADULTS

For those over age 65, the chances of having one or more medical problems rise.[42] The Office of Technology Assessment (OTA)[43] reported on two surveys in which the average number of chronic medical conditions ranged from three to five per ambulatory older person. A variety of therapies, therefore, may be used in their treatment. Patient noncompliance to any regimen may diminish the benefits of the therapy and may lead to unnecessary diagnostic studies or prolonged treatment.[44,45]

The OTA[43] reported that 30 percent of all prescription medications were for people 65 years of age and older, yet these individuals constitute only 12 percent of our population. Since 1962, the estimates of medication noncompliance have ranged from 15 to 93 percent.[46–48] Prescription medications are the fastest-rising element of health-care costs (the average cost of a prescription drug in 1987 was $15.32, a 156 percent increase from 1977).[49] The OTA[43] reported that, in the years ahead, the expenditures for prescription medications are likely to be equal to or higher than $9 billion. Therefore, the economic impact on certain segments of the older population can be devastating. The economically disadvantaged may actually have to choose between food and medication in their monthly budgets.

In 1988, the cost of a single drug holiday resulting in the patient with a breakthrough syndrome (sudden withdrawal of a medication followed by an exaggeration of the consequences of the absent drug effect) was estimated to be $1000.[50] The authors report that although the incidence figures are not available, drug holidays also play a role in other medical fields.

In the United States, it has been estimated that 10 percent of hospital readmissions and 23 percent of nursing home admissions are related to patients' inability to take medicines correctly.[51] Several studies conclude that readmissions could have been avoided in 40 to 59 percent of the patients if there had been better assessments, if rehabilitation had been more adequate, if discharge had been more carefully planned, if potential noncompliance problems with medications and diet had been identified, and if patients had been instructed to seek medical attention when symptoms occurred.[7–9] Yet despite a well-structured multidisciplinary approach and careful discharge planning, it is estimated that at least 8 percent of patients still will be readmitted within 3 months.[10,52]

Benson and Pharmaceutical Data Services, Inc.,[53] reports that up to one-half of all prescriptions do not produce their intended results because patients use them improperly. Other researchers[54–57] find that compliance decreases proportionally with increases in the number of medications, the complexity of the regimen, and the duration of the regimen.[54,57]

CLINICAL MANIFESTATIONS

Several studies confirm that patients with poor compliance have no readily observable characteristics.[58,59] Generally, the health-care professional considers the patient to be compliant if the treatment goal is achieved (the patient gets well or feels better). However, sometimes the patient is compliant by laboratory testing and yet does not have the desired outcome.[36] This is possible if the wrong diagnosis is made or the prescribed therapy is inadequate or inappropriate. In contrast, some patients who are not compliant with a regimen still experience the desired outcome. In these cases, the person's own defense system may have been sufficient or the lower medication dosage may have been adequate, as occurs in many older patients.

MANAGEMENT

Any person with a prescribed therapeutic regimen is considered at risk for noncompliance. From the time of the initial contact, unless the patient is critically ill, it is the nurse's responsibility to begin helping the patient move toward understanding and compliance. Although there are no definitive methods for solving the problem of noncompliance, there is enough practical knowledge from previous studies to guide practice in this area. The ensuring cues should be incorporated into primary and secondary teaching strategies.

Information Giver

A nurse has greater interaction with a patient than any other health-care professional and can have a significant influence on compliance. McCallum[60] reports that nurses, because of their education in communication skills, may have the best opportunity to determine whether a patient is having difficulty with a medication regimen. If a nurse appears hurried or unfriendly or does not give the patient a chance to ask questions, it will almost certainly lead to unintentional noncompliance.[61]

The nurse's initial interview with the hospitalized or ambulatory patient is an important component of care. The nurse should explore how the patient feels about health, whether he or she agrees with the diagnosis, whether he or she feels that the recommendations and treatment will help, whether he or she has any fears about side effects of medication, and whether the patient feels the regimen can be followed.[25]

Knowledge

Once beliefs and fears are known, actual information may be given to correct erroneous information.

RESEARCH BRIEF

Graveley, EA, and Oseasohn, CS: Multiple drug regimens: Medication compliance among veterans 65 years and older. Res Nurs Health 14:51, 1991.

It was found that veterans with regular appointments in an outpatient clinic were taking 1 to 10 prescribed oral pill medications daily (average 4), and 1 to 42 pills per day (average 11). The compliance rate was 27 percent. Of the 69 veterans who were dropped from the study, 27 percent had suffered morbidity or mortality within 21 days of their clinic visit. The most common problems with compliance were forgetting doses, not taking medication when feeling better, taking different dosages of the same medication, and medication dosage times that did not coincide with patients' daily routines.

Schwartz et al.[62] show that 21 percent of patients who made serious errors in compliance did so because of inaccurate knowledge. Knowledge about disease and treatments influences patient decisions. The use of visual aids is essential in helping the patient understand the relationship between the disease process and the prescribed regimen. Peck[63] finds that medication-taking behavior improved consistently with focused patient education. McCallum[60] reports that educational messages for hypertensive patients with a treatment regimen were more likely to elicit compliant behavior when they were realistic, believable, and judged by the patients to have personal relevance. Patients wanted to know about their disease and how the regimen would affect that process.

Patients also want to know the consequences of noncompliance.[60] However, judgement must be used in describing the risks. Creating fear and anxiety in the patient is not good teaching. In a classic study by Epstein and Lasagna,[64] subjects were told all possible side effects of a medication for reducing fever and headache pain. Many subjects refused to use the medication until they were told it was aspirin.

Family or Significant Other Support

Support from family and friends may play an important role in long-term compliance. Schatz[65] finds that one component of compliance in diabetic patients is support from family and friends. Family support has also been found to be significant in compliance with long-term medication regimens.[66,67] However, the differences in how family, friends, or significant others demonstrate support play a role in determining whether it is an indispensable contributor to compliance. A person who continuously reminds another to follow the physician's orders, makes another dependent on his or her instructions, or tells the patient he or she does not believe in the physician's instructions will promote compliance less effectively than one who is supportive and understanding.

Complexity of the Regimen

A complicated regimen, side effects of medications, and long-term treatment all predispose a patient to noncompliance.[25] Marston[68] reports that when more than one medical recommendation is made, patients are unlikely to follow all of them, and that when both drugs and other recommendations were made simultaneously, compliance decreased.

The more medications the patient takes, the greater the risk of noncompliance. The average number of medications taken by a person over age 65 is four. In one study, patients were taking up to 11 different medications per day and from 1 to 42 pills per day (see "Research Brief").

Research shows that when older outpatients take three or more medications, unit-of-use packaging and twice-daily dosing improves medication compliance over conventional packaging.[69]

Nursing Interventions

The patient interview will help the nurse determine the patient's readiness to learn. When the patient is ready, goals should be made with the patient participating in the decision-making process. Times for taking medication should be grouped and planned to coincide with the patient's daily routine to help introduce the routine into the patient's lifestyle. "The doctor wants you to take this every 6 hours" has no meaning for many people.[70] However, asking when the patient goes to bed at night and gets up in the morning and specifically planning medication to be taken around those times does have meaning. Otherwise, the patient will probably miss the night and morning doses. Telling the patient, "The doctor wants you to take this medication three times a day with your meals" has no meaning for the patient who eats only two meals a day. Often patients have a snack during the day, which could be substituted for what a younger person might consider a meal.

To promote compliance, patient education should focus on devoting time to instructions. Labels on prescription drugs must be simple, clear, and accompanied by well-organized verbal instruction.[71] Special instructions may be needed for the hearing-impaired or sight-impaired patient. A sample of a weekly medication chart is shown in Figure 7–1. In addition, general medication instructions, as shown in Table 7–3, should be provided.

TABLE 7–3 GENERAL MEDICATION INSTRUCTIONS

Name
Emergency telephone number
Warnings about food and drugs to avoid
Taken with food?
Instructions on storage
Physician's name and telephone number
Medication name and purpose
Dosage: How often and what time of day?
Date of issue
Side effects

Patient's name:

List all prescription medications the patient is currently taking (include those taken as needed).

Medication dose, frequency	Know purpose? Yes/No	Know side effects? Yes/No	Need help with medication? Yes/No	Problems taking (cost, side effects, difficulty getting to pharmacy, interferes with lifestyle)
1.				
2.				

List all the over-the-counter medication and other remedies the patient takes (pain, headache, stomach, nerves, constipation).

Medicine, remedy	How much taken?	How often taken?	Reason for taking this medicine
1.			
2.			

Figure 7–1 Weekly medication chart.

Research on mnemonics indicates that computer-assisted instruction, although expensive, may be useful and may significantly reduce forgetting.[71] A patient with a memory aid is more likely to follow the regimen prescribed. The health behavior should be attached to an established routine. The patient must be instructed regarding the large personal and social cost of nonadherence, including the undesirable drug reactions that may occur from nonadherence. Instruction should be written in simple (preferably four-grade-level) sentences and medical jargon should be avoided. Instructions should state explicitly how much medicine to take, when to take it, and for how long.

Many hospitalized patients are already following a medication regimen at home, continue with the same regimen during hospitalization, and have it reordered at time of discharge. A medication log (Fig. 7–2) may be considered in the hospital to help the patient continue with the already established routine. If a medication is added that will be continued after discharge, this should be added to the log, with the patient and nurse doing the time planning. Using the log, the patient can be taught to ask for the medications instead of depending on the nurse for administration. The patient can then cross out the appropriate time for the medication on the log after administration. In this way, errors in choosing the correct medication, dosage, and timing could be recognized and any questions answered before the patient is discharged. This daily active involvement in carrying out the regimen is an immediate and continued use of knowledge the patient has learned and is a strong reinforcer. Table 7–4 provides a list of red flags for poor compliance. Table 7–5 gives sample instructions to patients on taking medication wisely.

A patient who is put on a dietary regimen that will continue at home could also have the same type of log instituted in the hospital. With assistance, the patient could be responsible for recording his or her own intake during the day. Again, a routine is established that will help the patient be compliant when returning home.

Many patients send their prescriptions to a mail-order pharmacy. The American Association of Retired Persons and the Veterans' Administration have such a service. Patients who use such agencies need to have special instructions. Mail-order pharmacies take 10 to 15

Name of drug/Directions	Sun	Mon	Tue	Wed	Thu	Fri	Sat	Call physician if you have these symptoms
Drug A 3 times a day	8 AM 5 PM 9 PM	8 AM 5 PM 9 PM	8 AM 5 PM 9 PM					
Drug B 1 time a day	8 AM	8 AM	8 AM					
Drug C 2 times a day	8 AM 9 PM	8 AM 9 PM	8 AM 9 PM					

Figure 7–2 Medicine log.

TABLE 7–4   RED FLAGS FOR POOR COMPLIANCE

Action	Nursing Intervention
Physician discontinues a medication Physician changes the dosage or frequency of a drug, or both	Make sure patient knows and understands why. Cross out old routine on log and write new entry. Encourage patient to discard unused pills.
Different dosages of the same medication to be taken during the day	*Alert the patient.* Label one medication "A" on both bottle and log; label the other bottle "B."
Medication to be taken every other day	*Alert the patient.* Mark log "not today" on appropriate dates
Dosage of a medication to be decreased over time	*Alert the patient.* Make a specific calendar for this medication.

TABLE 7–5   TAKING MEDICATION WISELY

Do not increase the dosage ("if one is good, two must be better") of any medication just because you feel better.

Do not decrease your medication just because you feel better without calling **Dr. Jones**. Phone: **224-2231**.

Do not stop taking any medication without calling **Dr. Jones**. Phone: **224-2231**.

Do not double your dosage if you forget to take one dose of your medication.

Do not share your medication with family or friends or take *their* medication.

Do not mix alcohol with medication without first asking your pharmacist. Phone: **220-2014**.

If you physician stops a drug, throw the remaining pills away.

FOR ANY QUESTIONS CONCERNING YOUR
MEDICATIONS,
CALL:
DR. JONES
224-2231

days to return the medication, which poses potential risks to patients. A patient will have to reorder with a minimum of 30 pills remaining for a twice-a-day medication, 40 pills for a four-times-a-day medication, and so forth. Special care must be taken to ensure that patients understand when and how to follow the pharmacy's procedures.

Remind patients to bring all prescribed medications to each office or clinic visit. The medications can then be checked against the list made at the original interview and updated. If a patient forgets a medication on the list or brings in a new one, the reasons for the change can be explained. The medication or dietary log should also be reviewed and the patient's questions answered. The nurse should inquire about any signs of potentially dangerous medication side effects of difficulty in following the regimen. At the same time, the nurse should reinforce previous teaching, give support and encouragement, respect the patient's questions, and answer them in understandable terms.

Hall[72] reports, "The failure of an elderly patient to respond appropriately to an effective drug is nearly always due to the patient's failure to take the drug correctly rather than absorb it." Urquhart and Chevalley's[50] finding of drug holidays should alert the nurse to the possibility of noncompliance if a patient suddenly exhibits a sign that something in the regimen is not being followed. Examples include a patient who gains weight and is taking a diuretic, one who has a sudden irregular heart rate and is taking a medication to prevent this, a hypertensive patient who is taking an antihypertensive agent, one who does not lose weight while following a weight reduction diet, or a patient who is not gaining strength in a muscle while performing daily strengthening exercises.

Laboratory tests and clinical findings, although not entirely predictive of compliance or noncompliance, should be discussed with the patient. Indications that the patient is not following the regimen can be discussed in a nonthreatening manner, and appropriate changes can be made. If the patient is unable to under-

stand the plan of care, the nurse should ask permission to include the spouse, a family member, or significant other in the teaching.

A patient who indicates a willingness to follow a regimen but has difficulty doing so should be considered at risk. This patient may be telephoned and asked about the medications in conjunction with reinforcement of teaching, support, and encouragement. The use of sensory or visual aids should be investigated. Pill-alert alarms that can be timed to coincide with medication times are available. Some patients may benefit from an open egg carton, clearly marked with the hours to take the medicine, into which the patient puts medication each day, or a family member or neighbor can come each day and put the medications by time in the container for the patient. The nurse needs to be alert for any aid that might help a particular patient with compliance.

There may be times when the patient, despite all interventions, is unable to cope with a prescribed regimen. At this time, it is up to the primary health-care provider, nurse, and patient to discuss alternatives available in a particular community to assist the patient. Several resources are cited in Table 7–6.

TABLE 7–6   RESOURCES FOR PATIENT TEACHING

National Council on Patient Information and Education
666 Eleventh Street, NW
Suite 810
Washington, DC 20001

SRx Regional Program
1182 Market Street
Suite 204
San Francisco, CA 94101

Offerings for purchase include:
Medication fact sheets in English, Chinese, Spanish, and Vietnamese
Mini-class curriculum guides
Compliance aids including a personal medication record

Student Learning Activities

1 Identify samples of patient education materials that are given to older adults. Examine these materials for reading level and cultural sensitivity.

2 Survey a group of community-living older adults on the health issues they are most interested in.

3 As a class, prepare a poster presentation to be placed at local retirement centers, Senior Centers, and acute-care facility lobbies on the topic of highest interest from your survey.

REFERENCES

1 Hasselkabus, B: Patient education and the elderly: Physical and occupational therapy. Geriatrics 2(3):55, 1983.
2 Carter, WB, et al: Health education: Special issues for older adults. Patient Education Counseling 13(2):117, 1989.
3 Aging in America: Trends and Projections. US Senate Special Committee on Aging in conjunction with the American Association of Retired Persons, the Federal Council on Aging, and the US Administration on Aging, Washington, DC, 1987–1988.
4 Pocinki, K: Writing for an older audience: Ways to maximize understanding and acceptance. AMWA J 3(5):6, 1990.
5 Larson, E: Health promotion and disease prevention in the older adult. Geriatrics 43:31, 1988.
6 Aging and Health Promotion: Marketing Research for Public Education. Office of Disease Prevention and Health Promotion Administration on Aging, National Institute on Aging, National Cancer Institute, May 1984.
7 Connell, CM, and Crawford, CO: How people obtain their health information—a survey of two Pennsylvania counties. Public Health Rep 103(2):189, 1988.
8 Check, J, and Wurzbach, M: How elders view learning. Geriatr Nurs 5(1):37, 1984.
9 Kick, E: Patient teaching for elders. Nurs Clin North Am 24(3):681, 1989.
10 Arenberg, D, and Robertson-Tchabo, E: Learning and aging. In Birren, J, and Schare, K (eds): Handbook of the Psychology of Aging. Van Nostrand, New York, 1977, p 421.
11 Babcock, D, and Miller, M: Client Education Theory and Practice. CV Mosby, St Louis, 1994, pp 103–120.
12 Alywahby, N: Principles of teaching for individual learning of older adults. Rehab Nurs 14(6):330, 1989.
13 Weinrich, A, et al: Continuing education: Adapting strategies to teach the elderly. Gerontol Nurs 15(11):17, 1989.
14 Jernigan, A: Update on drugs and the elder. Am Fam Physician 29:238, 1984.
15 Folstein, M, et al: The meaning of cognitive impairment in the elderly. Am Geriatr Soc 228–235, 1985.
16 Folstein, M, et al: Mini mental state: A practical method for grading the cognitive state of patients for the clinician. J Psychiatr Res 12:188–194, 1975.
17 Beare, P, and Meyers, J: Principles and Practice of Adult Health Nursing. CV Mosby, St Louis, 1994.
18 Stewart, B, and Caranasos, G: Medication compliance in the elderly. Med Clin North Am 73(6):1551, 1989.
19 Merkatz, R, and Coneg, M: Helping America to take its medicine. Am J Med 93:6, 56–62, 1992.
20 Felo, S, and Warren, S: Medication usage by the elderly. Geriatr Nurs 14:1, 45–57, 1993.
21 Weinrich, A, et al: Continuing education: Adapting strategies to teach the elderly. J Gerontol Nurs 15:11, 17–32, 1989.
22 Leirer, VO, et al: Elders' non-adherence, its assessment and computerized assisted instruction for medication recall training. J Am Geriatr Soc 36(10):887, 1988.
23 Morgan, T, et al: Compliance and the elderly hypertensive. Drugs (suppl 4)31:174–183, 1986.

24 McDonald, M, and Grimm, RH: Compliance with hypertension treatment: Strategies for improving patient cooperation. Postgrad Med 77:233, 1985.
25 Eraker, SA, et al: Understanding and improving patient compliance. Ann Intern Med 100:258, 1984.
26 Edwards, P: Teaching older patients about their medication. Professional Nurse 11:3, 165–6, 1995.
27 Lewin, K: Field theory and learning. In Cartwright, D (ed): Field Theory in Social Science. Harper & Row, New York, 1951, p 60.
28 Maiman, LA, and Becker, MH (ed): The Health Belief Model and Personal Health Behavior. Slack, Thorofare, NJ, 1974, p 9.
29 Rosenstock, IM: Historical origins of the health belief model. In Becker, MH (ed): The Health Belief Model and Personal Health Behavior. Slack, Thorofare, NJ, 1974, p 1.
30 Becker, MH, et al: A new approach to explaining sick-role behavior in low income populations. Am J Public Health 64:205, 1974.
31 Kasl, S: The health belief model and behavior related to chronic illness. In Becker, MH (ed): The Health Belief Model and Personal Health Behavior. Slack, Thorofare, NJ, 1974, p 106.
32 Kirscht, JP: The health belief model and illness behavior. In Becker, MH (ed): The Health Belief Model and Personal Health Behavior. Slack, Thorofare, NJ, 1974, p 60.
33 Redeker, NS: Health beliefs and adherence in chronic illness. Image 20;31, 1988.
34 Wallston, KA, et al: Development of the multidimensional health locus of control scales. Health Educ Monogr 6:160, 1978.
35 Hallal, JC: The relationship of health beliefs, health locus of control, and self concept to the practice of breast self-examination in adult women. Nurs Res 31:137, 1982.
36 Craig, HM: Accuracy of indirect measures of medication compliance in hypertension. RINAH 8:61, 1985.
37 Kass, AK, et al: Can ophthalmologists correctly identify patients defaulting from pilocarpine therapy? Am J Ophthalmol 101:524, 1986.
38 Kass, MA, et al: Compliance with topical pilocarpine treatment. Am J Ophthalmol 101:515, 1986.
39 Averbuch, M, et al: Compliance monitoring in clinical trials: The MEMS device. Clin Pharmacol Ther 43:185, 1988.
40 Cramer, JA: Antiepileptic drug medication monitoring. Control Clin Trials 9:257, 1988.
41 Urquhart, J: Noncompliance: The ultimate absorption barrier. In Prescott, LF, and Nimmo, WS (eds): Novel Drug Delivery and Its Therapeutic Application. Wiley, New York, 1989.
42 Cassel, C: Geriatric Medicine: Medical, Psychiatric, and Pharmacological Topics. Springer-Verlag, New York, 1984.
43 Office of Technology Assessment, US Congress: Technology and Aging in America. Washington, DC, June 1985.
44 Becker, MH: Patient adherence to prescribed therapies. Med Care 23:382, 1985.
45 Carey, RL: Compliance and related nursing action. Nurs Forum 21:157, 1984.
46 Brand, FN, and Smith, RT: Medical care and compliance among the elderly after hospitalization. Int J Aging Hum Dev 5:331, 1974.
47 Robertson, WH: The problem of patient compliance. Am J Obstet Gynecol 152:948, 1985.
48 Graveley, EA, and Oseasohn, CS: Adherence to multiple drug regimens: Medication compliance among veterans 65 years and older. Res Nurs Health 14:51, 1991.
49 Scripps Howard Service: Cost hike for drugs continues. Express News, San Antonio, TX, July 3, 1988, p 7-C.
50 Urquhart, J, and Chevalley, C: Impact of unrecognized dosing errors on the cost and effectiveness of pharmaceuticals. Drug Information J 22:3613, 1988.
51 Vinson, M, et al: Early readmission of elderly patients with congestive heart failure. J Am Geriatr Soc 38:1290–1295, 1990.
52 Jaarsma, T, et al: Readmission of older heart failure patients. Prog Cardiovasc Nurs 11(1):15–20, 1996.

53 Benson, J, and Pharmaceutical Data Services Inc: Utilization Patterns in Geriatric Drugs in the United States, 1986. Presentation at a conference titled Current Issues in Geriatric Drugs, sponsored by the National Institute on Aging, Food and Drug Administration, and Georgetown University Center for the Aging, Washington, DC, May 4–5, 1987.

54 Baum, C, et al: Drug use and expenditures in 1982. JAMA 253:283, 1985.

55 Graveley, EA, and Oseasohn, CS: Multiple drug regimens: Medication compliance among veterans 65 years and older. Res Nurs Health 14:51, 1991.

56 Baum, C, et al: Drug use and expenditures in 1982. JAMA 253:382, 1985.

57 Murray, MD, et al: Factors contributing to medication noncompliance in elderly public housing tenants. Drug Intell Clin Pharmacol 20:146, 1986.

58 Haynes, RB: Determinants of compliance: The disease and the mechanics of treatment. In Haynes, RB, et al (eds): Compliance and Health Care. Johns Hopkins University Press, Baltimore, 1979, p 49.

59 Caron, HS, and Roth, HP: Patients' cooperation with a medical regimen: Difficulties in identifying the noncooperator. JAMA 203:922, 361.

60 McCallum, DB. Communicating the Benefits and Risks of Prescription Drugs. The Institute for Health Policy Analysis, Georgetown University Medical Center, Washington, DC, 1989.

61 Korsch, BM, and Negrete, VF: The doctor-patient communication. Sci Am 227:66, 1972.

62 Schwartz, D, et al: Medication errors made by elderly chronically ill patients. Am J Public Health 52:2018, 1962.

63 Peck, K: Increasing patient compliance with proscriptions. JAMA 248:2974, 1982.

64 Epstein, LC, and Lasagna, L: Obtaining informed consent: Form or substance. Arch Intern Med 123:682, 1979.

65 Schatz, PE: An evaluation of the components of compliance in patients with diabetes. J Am Diet Assoc 88:708, 1988.

66 Miller, P, et al: Health beliefs of and adherence to the medical regimen by patients with ischemic heart disease. Heart Lung 11:332, 1982.

67 Doherty, WM, et al: Effect of spouse support and health beliefs on medication adherence. J Fam Pract 17:837, 1983.

68 Marston, MV: Compliance with medical regimens: A review of the literature. Nurs Res 19:312, 1970.

69 Murray, M, et al: Medication compliance in elderly outpatients using twice-daily dosing and unit-of-use packaging. Ann Pharmacother 5:27, 616–620, 1993.

70 Mazzullo, J: Methods of improving patient compliance. In Lasagna, L (ed): Patient Compliance. Futura, New York, 1976.

71 Morrow, D, et al: Adherence and medication instruction. J Am Geriatr Soc 36:1147, 1988.

72 Hall, MRP: Drug therapy in the elderly. BMJ 3:582, 1973.

CHAPTER 8

Pharmacology and Older Adults: The Problem of Polypharmacy

Gary P. Stoehr

OBJECTIVES

Upon completion of this chapter, the reader will be able to:

- List the factors that contribute to multiple drug use in older adults
- List the most common categories of drugs used in older adults
- Describe how multiple drug use can lead to adverse drug reactions, drug interactions, and noncompliance
- Describe how the physiological changes of aging affect drug absorption, distribution, metabolism, and elimination
- Describe how some patient behaviors contribute to multiple drug use
- Understand the importance of setting a specific therapeutic goal for each medication prescribed
- Identify the elements of a good drug history
- Describe strategies to prevent polypharmacy in older adults

Older adults consume more drugs than any other age group. Nearly one-third of all of the prescription drugs dispensed in the United States are dispensed to people over the age of 65, and nearly two-thirds of all older adults use an over-the-counter (OTC) drug product regularly.[1]

Drug therapy is a cost-effective means for managing age-related health problems. Unfortunately, the response to drugs among older adults is sometimes unpredictable because of variations in sensitivity to the therapeutic and toxic effects of drugs. Because many drugs have narrow therapeutic indices, practitioners must constantly be on the alert for the unwanted effects.

Drugs play an integral role in the overall management of many of the health problems associated with aging. When realistic goals are established, drugs may enhance independence and the quality of life. Although setting realistic therapeutic goals does not guarantee success, failure to establish goals permits drug therapy to continue indefinitely, even after failure occurs. In an effort to correct the situation, new drugs are sometimes added to the regimen. The result may be an unwanted drug effect, a drug interaction, or noncompliance. For some patients, drug therapy actually compromises quality of life.

Demographics of Drug Use in Older Adults

The number of drugs taken by older adults varies, depending on local prescribing practices and the health of the population under study. Rural older adults report taking between 1.7 and 2.7 prescribed medications regularly, in addition to at least 1 nonprescription drug.[2-5] Those living in urban high-rise apartments report taking four to five prescription medications and three to four nonprescription products simultaneously. Residents of long-term care facilities often take seven or more medications simultaneously.[6] Prescription drug use in all of these populations increases with advancing age but declines after age 80, most likely as a result of death of the most chronically ill patients. The most commonly prescribed drug classes for people 65 years of age and older reflect the chronic diseases that affect this population.

Most older adults supplement their prescription regimens with nonprescription, or OTC, drugs. Although OTC drugs are used by most older adults, few volunteer this information to their physicians. The most commonly used products are internal analgesics (aspirin, acetaminophen, and ibuprofen), vitamins and minerals, laxatives, and cough and cold preparations.[1,3]

Analgesic drugs (primarily aspirin, acetaminophen, and ibuprofen) are used by 30 to 40 percent of older men and women, many of whom take more than one analgesic product simultaneously.[3,7] Vitamins and dietary supplements are used by 1 of every 3 people over age 65. Older women are less likely to use vitamins or nutritional supplements than are older men, and vitamin use is more prevalent in whites than in African-Americans or Hispanics.[3,8] Older adults are also frequent users of laxatives. Nearly 10 percent of people over the age of 65 years admit to using laxatives regularly and use increases with age. Unfortunately, some seniors become dependent on laxatives for bowel regulation.[3]

Polypharmacy

The term *polypharmacy* was originally coined as a descriptive term to characterize multiple drug use. However, important clinical outcomes may occur when multiple drugs are used, so a functional definition of *polypharmacy* is more clinically relevant. For this chapter, polypharmacy is present when medications are used with no apparent indication, medications are duplicated, interacting medications are concurrently used, contraindicated medications are used, drugs are used to treat adverse drug reactions, or there is improvement after discontinuation of medications.

A number of factors have been reported to contribute to multiple drug use in older adults. Drug therapy is the cornerstone of treatment for arthritis, hypertension, coronary artery disease, diabetes, and many of the other chronic medical problems seen in older adults. Because 4 of every 5 people over the age of 65 have one or more chronic disease, it is not surprising that this age group is the largest user of prescription drugs. The presence of a number of medical problems may lead patients to seek help from several physicians. A prescription is generated for 60 percent of office visits,[9] and because older adults visit the physician more than any other age group, they receive more prescription drugs. The availability of prescription entitlement programs and third-party payment plans is another factor that apparently contributes to multiple drug use in older adults.[2]

IMPACT OF THE PROBLEM ON OLDER ADULTS

Multiple drug use increases the potential for noncompliance and contributes to adverse drug reactions, drug interactions, and cost of health care. The addition of a new drug to the treatment regimen may require a change in the patient's lifestyle. The change may be minor (e.g., having to remember to take a single tablet in the morning) or more significant (e.g., having to take six or eight capsules daily, adjust to a controlled diet, restrict physical activity, supply blood periodically for laboratory monitoring of their drug therapy, or take additional drugs to offset anticipated drug side effects). Nonadherence to complex drug regimens is common, and the failure of health-care providers to coordinate medication regimens only compounds the problems.

Drug costs are often paid out of pocket, making prescription drugs one of the major health expenditures for older adults. To save money on prescription drugs, some older patients never have prescriptions filled, take less than the prescribed dosage, or use their medicine only when symptoms arise.

The psychosocial consequences of medication use are also an important consideration when establishing expectations for drug therapy. Unless they are involved in planning and implementing the therapeutic plan, patients may relinquish control and responsibility for their health to the provider. Dependent behavior may then lead to noncompliance, treatment failure, or overdependence on medication. These patients may actively seek medications, seemingly enjoying the attention and sympathy that accompanies being ill. Drug-seeking behavior of this type may lead to overuse of medications and physician shopping.

ADVERSE DRUG REACTIONS

The probability of adverse drug reactions increases with each drug prescribed,[10] so polypharmacy is one of the major contributing factors. Other risk factors include small stature (especially in women), history of allergic illness, previous adverse drug reactions, multiple chronic illnesses, renal failure, multiple physicians, abnormal mental status, living alone, financial problems, noncompliance, and visual or audiological problems. Many of these risk factors may be present simultaneously in older adults.[11]

Adverse reaction to drugs may cause minor inconvenience or necessitate a change in drug dosage. More serious adverse reactions may be severe enough to result in hospitalization. One study[12] reports that 1 of every 5 admissions of older patients to an acute-care hospital was the result of an adverse drug reaction (Table 8–1).

Many of the adverse effects of drugs are dose- or concentration-related. Serious adverse affects are more likely to occur in older adults not only because they often take more drugs than younger people, but also be-

TABLE 8–1 DRUGS RESPONSIBLE FOR HOSPITALIZATION BECAUSE OF ADVERSE REACTIONS

Analgesics	Insulin
Aspirin	Prednisone
Chemotherapy	Theophylline
Digoxin	Warfarin

cause drugs are more likely to accumulate in older adults. To prevent adverse reactions caused by exaggerated pharmacological effects, practitioners must understand how physiological, age-related changes affect drug disposition.

PHYSIOLOGY AND DRUG DISPOSITION IN OLDER ADULTS

Drugs undergo a four-step process before leaving the body: absorption, distribution, metabolism, and elimination. This process is known as the drug's pharmacokinetics. Each of these steps is affected to some extent by the patient's age.

Absorption

Drug absorption occurs by simple diffusion through the small intestine, a process that is concentration-dependent, requires no energy, and is unaffected by age. However, the rate of absorption and the peak effect of some drugs may be slowed in older adults because of an age-related decline in gastrointestinal blood flow and motility. Thus, age-related changes in drug absorption are unlikely to increase the risk of drug toxicity. However, the changes in gastrointestinal blood flow and motility may delay the peak effects of oral drugs. Because absorption of drugs in older adults may be delayed, drug toxicity that occurs in older patients may occur later and be more prolonged than drug toxicity in younger patients.[13]

Distribution

Once absorbed, most drugs distribute throughout the body in concentrations that depend on the drug's ability to penetrate both aqueous and lipid compartments. Because total body water is reduced by 10 to 15 percent between the ages of 20 and 80 years, older adults are likely to experience elevated plasma concentrations when drugs that distribute into plasma water are given unless dosage adjustments are made.[13] For example, older subjects given a standard intravenous dose of ethanol experienced higher peak alcohol concentrations than did younger subjects given the same dose.[14]

Body composition is also modified by age: Lean muscle mass declines and relative body fat increases. The age-related decline in lean body mass may result in higher than expected peak plasma concentrations of digoxin, gentamicin, and other drugs that distribute to lean tissues. In young adults, adipose tissue accounts for an average of 18 percent and 36 percent of the total weight of men and women, respectively. By age 65, adipose tissue accounts for 36 percent of the weight of men and 45 percent of the weight of women. Body fat serves as a reservoir for lipid-soluble drugs, helping lower plasma concentrations but increasing the duration of action. Increases in the duration of action of such fat-soluble drugs as flurazepam,[15] diazepam,[16] chlorpromazine,[17] and the tricyclic antidepressants[18] have been observed in older adults. These changes are at least par-

tially caused by an increase in the proportion of fat in older adults.[13]

Metabolism and Elimination

The kidney and liver are responsible for eliminating most drugs by biotransformation in the liver to a less active or inactive metabolite or elimination of the drug or its metabolites by the kidney. Both of these processes decline with aging. The rate of drug clearance through the liver may be affected by liver blood flow or the activity of drug-metabolizing enzymes. When adjusted for weight, liver blood flow decreases by 47 percent by age 65,[13] resulting partly from a concomitant decline in cardiac output. Liver blood flow, which is a major factor in the clearance of a number of drugs (Table 8–2), may be further compromised by cardiac and circulatory failure, fever, and dehydration. Dosages of some drugs may need to be reduced in older adults.

Changes in hepatic metabolism resulting from aging are highly variable and unpredictable. Researchers have shown that some drugs may accumulate in older users, but whether changes in the liver's metabolizing capacity are responsible remains to be demonstrated.[13]

Kidney function also plays a key role in eliminating drugs from the body. Like liver blood flow, kidney blood flow declines with age. Kidney mass also declines, with a loss in the number and size of nephrons. These age-related kidney function changes may be exaggerated in patients whose cardiac output has been impaired because of long-standing diabetes or hypertension and subsequent cardiac failure. Dosages of drugs that are eliminated by the kidney must be decreased in the older patient. (A partial list of drugs that may require such dosage adjustments is given in Table 8–3.)[19]

The pharmacokinetic changes that occur with aging may alter the absorption, distribution, metabolism, and elimination of drugs. Because some of these pharmacokinetic changes are difficult to predict, the clinician must begin therapy with the lowest effective dosage. Careful dosage titration, with small incremental increases in drug dosage, may be needed to achieve the therapeutic goal. Conservative dosing may help prevent dose-related toxicity and spare the patient the added cost of unnecessary drugs.

Sometimes adverse reactions are not caused by a single drug but instead result from the cumulative effects of several drugs with overlapping toxicities. Many drugs can cause cognitive impairment in older adults

TABLE 8–2   EXAMPLES OF DRUGS WITH REDUCED METABOLISM IN OLDER ADULTS FROM DIMINISHED LIVER BLOOD FLOW

Amitriptyline	Morphine
Desipramine	Nortriptyline
Imipramine	Propoxyphene
Isoniazid	Propranolol
Lidocaine	Verapamil
Meperidine	

TABLE 8–3 EXAMPLES OF DRUGS WITH REDUCED ELIMINATION IN OLDER ADULTS FROM DIMINISHED KIDNEY FUNCTION

Amantadine	Disopyramide
Amiloride	Ethambutol
Aminoglycoside antibiotics	Lithium
	Methotrexate
Atenolol	Methyldopa
Captopril	Metoclopramide
Chlorpropamide	Procainamide
Cimetidine	Pyridostigmine
Clonidine	Vancomycin
Digoxin	

(Table 8–4), and the likelihood that two or more of these will be prescribed together is high. Several studies of falls in older adults have linked drug use with an increased risk of falling and drugs that cause such adverse effects as orthostatic hypotension, drowsiness, dizziness, blurred vision, or confusion are particular hazards.[13] (See Chapter 21 for a complete discussion of the risk factors leading to falls.)

Unfortunately, many adverse drug reactions go unrecognized. New signs or symptoms may be attributed to acute or chronic illness rather than to a change in drug therapy. If troublesome, the symptoms of the adverse drug reaction may be treated with addition of another drug, which only compounds the problem of multiple drug use.

CASE 1 Mrs. R, a 78-year-old woman with Alzheimer's dementia, is given diphenhydramine to help her sleep. She experiences a paradoxical reaction to the antihistamine and becomes delirious. Her physician does not consider the possibility that diphenhydramine may have caused Mrs. R to become delirious, and prescribes haloperidol to treat the delirium.

CASE 2 Mr. J, an 86-year-old resident of a long-term care facility, experiences a fever, chills, cough, shortness of breath, and an increased production of sputum, which has turned yellowish brown. His physician admits him to the local hospital and prescribes erythromycin, the drug of choice for community-acquired pneumonia. Within 24 hours, Mr. J becomes nauseated and unable to eat. Rather than substituting a different antibiotic for the erythromycin, Mr. J's physician treats the nausea by adding prochlorperazine (Compazine) to

TABLE 8–4 SOME DRUGS CAUSING COGNITIVE IMPAIRMENT

Amantadine	Flurazepam
Aspirin	Haloperidol
Chlorpromazine	Meperidine
Cimetidine	Methyldopa
Diazepam	Reserpine
Diphenhydramine	Triazolam

the drug treatment plan. Mr. J's condition soon deteriorates. He becomes uncommunicative and confused, and his family complains that he is "out of it." During a routine check of vital signs, Mr. J's nurse observes that his eyes have "rolled back" and notes this observation in the chart. Two days later, Mr. J's physician realizes the Mr. J has experienced a dystonic reaction to prochlorperazine, and discontinues it. Cultures confirm that Mr. J has pneumococcal pneumonia. Mr. J's physician changes the antibiotic to procaine penicillin G, 1 million units every 6 hours. Mr. J's mental status improves quickly once the prochlorperazine is discontinued, and the nausea disappears within 24 hours of discontinuing erythromycin.

In both of these cases, failure to recognize adverse drug effects led to ordering more drugs. In Mrs. R's case, the additional drug was unnecessary, and in Mr. J's case, the additional drug caused a second adverse effect.

DRUG INTERACTIONS

The same factors that make older adults susceptible to adverse drug effects also make them susceptible to drug interactions. Multiple medication use, multiple physicians, and nonprescription drug use all contribute to drug interactions. Age-related declines in liver and kidney function make the consequences of drug interactions likely to be more serious in older adults.[20]

Drug interactions that might have trivial consequences in a young adult can have devastating consequences in an older person. For example, young people would undoubtedly be sedated by the combination of diphenhydramine and a phenothiazine such as chlorpromazine. In an older person, this combination could contribute to a fall, either by oversedation or by an effect on postural blood pressure. Drug interactions can be detected only if a complete and current list of medications is maintained. The medication profile should include a complete list of prescription and nonprescription medications written by all of the patient's physicians.

The most significant drug interactions in older adults involve drugs with narrow therapeutic indices or central nervous system effects. Nurses should screen medication profiles for drug interactions for patients taking drugs such as warfarin, phenytoin, carbamazepine, phenobarbital, digoxin, quinidine, procainamide, antidepressants, or benzodiazepines. Patients should be counseled to ask the pharmacist and their physician about drug interactions whenever a new drug is added to their regimen.

Management

1 Primary Prevention

The goal of primary prevention efforts is to decrease the rate at which new cases of polypharmacy appear in older adults by counteracting the circumstances that lead to multiple drug use. The outcome of these efforts should be a decrease in the number of drugs taken or a decline in the harmful consequences of multiple drug use (adverse drug effects, drug interactions, and non-adherence).

Several patient behaviors and beliefs contribute to multiple drug use. Perhaps the most obvious is the belief that medication offers the solution to every health problem. Convincing older clients that drugs are not a panacea for every complaint is not easy when television and radio advertisements promise immediate relief with nonprescription painkillers, vitamins, and cough and cold preparations. For a number of problems, nondrug measures are clearly preferred over prescription drug use. Primary prevention efforts may help reduce polypharmacy by offering simple nondrug solutions to common complaints of older adults. Some common complaints such as sleeplessness, constipation, and anxiety can be managed without medication. (See related chapters for an in-depth discussion of these topics.)

Community Educational Programs

Community programs designed to inform the public about problems with drug use could be scheduled for Senior Centers, places of worship, or meetings of retired citizens. Caregivers and adult day-care workers may also benefit from such programs. Pamphlets, flyers, and radio and television public service messages could also be useful to focus the community's attention on the problem of prescription drug misuse among older adults. Sponsors might include local medical, nursing, and pharmacy associations, insurance carriers, pharmacy chains, home health agencies, and hospital associations.

Many older adults are unaware of behaviors that lead to problems with prescription drug use. Today's older adults may have been taught the importance of frugality and thrift as children growing up during the Great Depression. Hoarding unused medication may be habitual for these people, many of whom have medicine cabinets filled with old prescriptions. Educational programs and media advertisements to promote cleaning of the medicine cabinet may provide useful reminders to older adults and their caregivers to dispose of old prescriptions and keep a list of current medications.

The desire to remain independent or to help a friend may lead older adults to swap medications. Nearly 10 percent of older adults surveyed in one study admitted to taking a prescription drug that was prescribed for someone else.[21] Swapping medications is a common practice that should be strongly discouraged.

In a large telephone survey[22] of adults who had recently obtained a new prescription, only about 60 percent reported that their physician or pharmacist provided directions for use. Most patients said that they received little or no information about side effects or contraindications from their physician or pharmacist, and few requested this information. The nurse can teach patients to request information from physicians and pharmacists. The patient should never leave the physician's office or the pharmacy without a clear under-

standing of the directions for use, the purpose, duration, and important side effects of new prescribed medications. Table 8–5 lists questions to ask the physician or pharmacist about each prescription drug.

"Brown Bag" Sessions for Older Adults

"Brown bag" sessions are conducted by pharmacists, physicians, and nurses as part of a community-wide educational effort to teach about the problems and risks of multiple drug use among older adults. Patients are asked to bring all of their medications with them to a central location, often a Senior Center or another location where senior citizens meet. Pharmacists and nurses review the medications, answer questions, and identify problems with medications.

Brown bag sessions are useful in revealing drug duplication, detecting drug interactions, and reinforcing the need to take medications as prescribed. Health-care providers who participate in these programs must be careful not to compromise the relationship between the patient and physician. Some questions and any drug problems discovered during these sessions are referred to the patient's physician.

Multiple Physicians

Patients and clients who want a quick solution to health problems or who have unrealistic expectations for resolution of their problems are likely to shop around for physicians. These patients are at risk for receiving redundant or interacting medications. Patients who change physicians or see a variety of physicians simultaneously may be reluctant to reveal their indiscretion, believing that somehow they have "cheated on" their physician. In some of these cases, the primary care physician can help reduce some of the consequences of multiple drug use by keeping all of their physicians informed of the drugs they are taking.

TABLE 8–5 TEACHING GUIDE: QUESTIONS TO ASK YOUR PHYSICIAN AND PHARMACIST ABOUT YOUR PRESCRIPTIONS

- What is the name of this medication?
- How will this medicine help me?
- How should I take this medicine? How much should I take at one time? When and how often should I take it?
- For how long should I take this medicine? How many refills do I have?
- Are there any foods I should avoid while taking this medicine?
- Will this medicine interfere with any of the other prescription or nonprescription drugs I am taking?
- Should I restrict any of my activities while taking this medicine?
- What side effects should I expect and what should I do if they occur?
- How and where should I store this medicine? Is there an expiration date?
- How much will this medicine cost? Is it available in a generic brand?

2 Secondary Prevention

Early detection and resolution of the problems associated with multiple drug use are the goals of secondary prevention. These efforts are often handicapped by inadequate data. A good drug history is the foundation for and an effective means of detecting drug problems.

Assessment: The Drug History

The medication history provides health practitioners with a record of current and past drug use. This history should outline a well-developed therapeutic plan that is clear to all who review the patient record. It can be used to determine the patient's understanding of medication directions and compliance, also possibly serving as legal proof in cases of malpractice or claims of injury or poisoning.

Various explanations exist for the inaccuracies found in drug histories. The person taking the history may feel rushed and not have the time to obtain a complete medication history. The hospitalized patient may be too ill or too confused at the time of admission to provide accurate information. Some patients may believe that OTC medications are insignificant and not even mention them. Others may not want to inform the admitting physician that someone else has prescribed drugs for them. Many health practitioners obtain medication histories by recording the directions from the patient's prescription vials. Although standard medical references recommend this technique,[23] it is certain to result in errors. Physicians often alter directions for taking medications without changing the label, and label directions are often misinterpreted by the patient.[24,25] The purpose of taking the medication history is to determine the client's actual medication-taking practices, which can be obtained reliably only from the client, and then only if he or she is willing to reveal noncompliance.

A suggested procedure for obtaining a good medication history is included in Table 8–6. The drug history should include more than just a list of medications. The nurse should use the medication interview as part of an assessment process that evaluates the client's knowledge of his or her health problems and medications. During the interview, the nurse may also assess some of the psychosocial aspects of drug therapy by asking pertinent questions, such as, "How do you feel about the drugs that have been prescribed?" and "How do you cope with a complex drug regimen?" One of the more revealing questions to ask is, "How do you manage to remember to take your medications?" The answers to these questions provide insight to the client's support system and motivation for following directions.

Most clients will develop a system for managing medication, which is a positive sign indicating the desire to be compliant. The system may be as simple as laying out all of the medications for the day on the dresser or as sophisticated as a daily calendar or an electronic pillbox. Some older clients rely on a spouse or another

TABLE 8–6 OBTAINING A DRUG HISTORY

Before the Patient Visit
  1 Determine the information you want to obtain.
  2 Review all of the records available to you.
The Interview
  1 Introduce yourself and the purpose for this interview.
  2 What medications has your physician prescribed for you? For each medication, ask the following:
    a Why are you taking this medication (purpose)?
    b How do you take this medication? (Include dosage or number of tablets taken and times taken.)
    c How long have you been taking this medication? If not long, what did you take before for this problem?
    d How does this medicine help your problem? (Try to get an understanding of the client's perception of the drug's effectiveness.)
  3 Do you use any over-the-counter medicines (cough and cold remedies, aspirin, antacids, and so on); that is, any medicines that do not require a prescription? For each of these medications, ask the following:
    a How often do you use the medicine?
    b Why do you take the medicine?
    c How does this medicine help you?
  4 Assess the following:
    a Client's knowledge of drug regimen: he or she should know the name and purpose of all medications prescribed.
    b Compliance with the prescribed regimen: he or she should be able to explain the directions for using all of the medications. Ask the patient to demonstrate the use of inhalers, insulin, or other drugs requiring complex administration techniques.
    c Client's ability to open childproof containers.
    d Client's ability to read and interpret prescription labels and medication directions.
    e Problems caused by the medication (adverse effects, financial problems, treatment failure).
  5 Documentation
    a List the current prescribed medications, their dosages, and their administration schedules.
    b List any over-the-counter medications, their dosages, and their administration schedules.
    c Summarize the patient's medication management system.
    d Summarize the patient's understanding of the purpose of the medications.
    e Summarize the patient's ability to follow directions and assess his or her level of compliance.
  6 Develop a plan to correct any problems uncovered during the interview. Provide directions for follow-up.

family member to help them manage medications. As long as the system is working, the nurse need not intervene. However, problems with medication use may arise when the spouse or caregiver is hospitalized, dies, or moves away. In these cases, the nurse should be prepared to suggest an alternative system for managing medications. See Chapter 7 for a discussion of medication noncompliance.

Older patients seldom volunteer information about OTC drugs they take. Some do not consider eyedrops, eardrops, inhalers, or topical creams to be actual medicines and so may neglect to mention them voluntarily during the interview. Therefore, the nurse should ask the patient specifically whether he or she uses any of these nonprescription drugs. Because alcohol is an important contributor to many drug interactions, nurses should summarize the patient's consumption of alcohol in the medication history as well.

Using the Drug History

Once the drug history is obtained, how can it be used? Whether practicing in the community or in a long-term care facility, the nurse can use the medication history to detect and, in conjunction with the patient's physician, resolve problems stemming from multiple drug use.

First, the nurse should examine the list of medications and determine whether a medical problem currently exists necessitating drug treatment. For each medical problem, the nurse must have a clear understanding of the goal of therapy. The nurse should never assume that patients taking antidepressant drugs have been diagnosed with depression or that those taking digoxin have congestive heart failure. Drugs are often prescribed for unclear reasons, and a healthy skepticism of prescribing rationales is needed when reviewing medication records. When no therapeutic goal is apparent, it may be necessary to question the patient's physician about the need for the drug.

The nurse should also search the medication list for duplicate drugs or drug classes. The same drug may be prescribed by trade name and by generic name by two different physicians. Likewise, patients may inadvertently receive prescriptions for two drugs from the same class, (e.g., nifedipine and diltiazem, both calcium channel blockers to treat angina). Prescriptions may be duplicated when a patient transfers from an acute-care to a long-term care facility.

Drug-drug and drug-food interactions can also be assessed using the medication profile. Drug-drug interactions should be suspected when a change in symptoms occurs after a new drug is added to the treatment regimen. The nurse should also consider interactions that may occur when prescription and nonprescription drugs are taken together and the problems that may arise when two or more drugs with similar side effects are simultaneously prescribed. Knowing what drugs are prescribed and when they are taken enables one to asses drug-food interactions. Some drugs should be taken on an empty stomach, and others should not be taken in conjunction with certain foods.

Access to the complete medical record is needed to assess whether there are any medical contraindications for any of the drugs prescribed. The nurse should assess whether the dosage form prescribed for the patient is appropriate. For example, can the patient demonstrate the technique required to manipulate aerosol inhalers? If not, perhaps a spacer device should be recommended. Can the patient demonstrate the proper method for drawing up and administering insulin? If not, perhaps the patient may require the assistance of a caregiver or home health care agency. Can the patient administer eyedrops properly? If not, then more education may be helpful.

Adverse drug effects should be clearly documented in the patient record. The nurse should report what happened, when the reaction occurred, and who observed it. This is a requirement for anyone practicing in a long-term care facility but should also be a part of community nursing practice.

When a new drug is added to a patient's treatment regimen, the nurse should assess whether it was prescribed to relieve a symptom caused by an adverse drug reaction. If so, the patient would be better served by discontinuing the offending agent rather than adding new medications. Sometimes the addition of new drugs only complicates the issue, as illustrated in the following case.

> **CASE 3**   Mrs. J, a 74-year-old woman with osteoarthritis, takes the following medications: ibuprofen, 800 mg three times daily; magnesium-aluminum hydroxide gel, 1 tsp four times daily; multivitamin, 1 tablet daily; and hydrocortisone cream 0.5 percent, used as needed for a rash. Mrs. J complains to her physician of gastric burning, which is attributed to her ibuprofen. Misoprostol, a gastric protective agent, is added to her regimen. Two days later she complains of diarrhea, a well-known side effect of misoprostol.

At this point, rather than adding yet another drug to treat the diarrhea, the prescriber should stop and assess the choice of drugs used to treat the patient's osteoarthritis. If the patient's complaints are mostly related to pain, then a change to salsalate may relieve the pain while alleviating the gastric irritation experienced. Another option would be to try a lower dosage of ibuprofen. As shown in this example, adding drugs to treat side effects complicates the regimen.

Summary

Prescription and OTC drugs are a major expense for older adults. Multiple drug use can impair the quality of life unless health-care providers monitor all of the drugs their patients are taking. The likelihood of experiencing an adverse drug reaction or drug interaction is increased when multiple drugs are prescribed. Therapeutic failures may occur if the older patient cannot successfully manage medication regimens. Many of the complications of multiple drug use can be prevented if patients understand the potential problems of polypharmacy and ask questions of their health-care providers. Nurses can help reduce the number of drugs used in this population by counseling patients about simple nondrug measures that may help alleviate common health complaints and by carefully reviewing the drugs taken by older patients. Problems can be prevented by reviewing patient records and screening drug profiles to determine whether the therapeutic plan is clearly outlined and whether any of the drugs prescribed are contraindicated, to detect unnecessary or duplicate drugs, and to find evidence of an adverse drug reaction or drug interaction. Accurate and complete medication histories are an important part of every patient's medical record.

Student Learning Activities

1 Identify an older adult in your clinical setting who is at risk for polypharmacy. What factors contribute to this risk? Which of these factors are preventable?

2 Select an older patient who is receiving multiple medications. Prepare a chart that displays the classification of the drug, its intended effects, known or suspected side effects, and drug interactions. Can you identify any medications that may be contributing to the patient's condition?

3 From your review of the drugs in this situation, how do the physiologic changes that occur with age affect drug distribution or action?

4 Outline some primary and secondary prevention strategies for this patient to reduce the number of medications needed.

REFERENCES

1 Chrischilles, EA, et al: Use of medications by persons 65 and over: Data from the Established Populations for Epidemiologic Studies of the Elderly. J Gerontol 47:M137, 1992.

2 Lassila, HC, et al: Factors associated with the use of prescription medications in an elderly rural population: The MoVIES Project. Ann Pharmacother 30:589, 1996.

3 Stoehr, GP, et al: Over-the-counter medication use in a rural community population: The MoVIES Project. J Am Geriatr Soc 45(2):158–165, 1997.

4 Helling, DK, et al: Medication use characteristics in the elderly: The Iowa 65+ Rural Health Study. J Am Geriatr Soc 35:4, 1987.

5 Hale, WE, et al: Drug use in an ambulatory elderly population: A five-year update. Drug Intell Clin Pharmacol 21:530, 1987.

6 Darnell, JC, et al: Medication use by ambulatory elderly: An in-home survey. J Am Geriatr Soc 34:1, 1986.

7 Chrischilles, EA, et al: Prevalence and characteristics of multiple drug use in an elderly study group. J Am Geriatr Soc 38:979, 1990.

8 Kim, I, et al: Vitamin and mineral supplement use and mortality in a US cohort. Am J Public Health 83:546, 1993.

9 Soumerai, SB, et al: Payment restrictions for prescription drugs under Medicaid. N Engl J Med 317:550, 1987.

10 Jue, SG: Adverse drug reactions in the elderly. In Vestal, RE (ed): Drug Treatment in the Elderly. ADIS Health Science Press, Sydney, Australia, 1984.

11 Pulliam, CC, and Stewart, RB: Adverse drug reactions in the elderly. In Pharmacy Practice for the Geriatric Patient. Health Sciences Consortium, Carrboro, NC, 1985.

12 Col, N, et al: The role of medication noncompliance and adverse drug reactions in hospitalization of the elderly. Arch Intern Med 150:841, 1990.

13 Nagle, BA, and Erwin, WG: Geriatrics. In Pharmacotherapy: A Pathophysiologic Approach. Elsevier, New York, 1996.

14 Vestal, RE, et al: Aging and alcohol metabolism. Clin Pharmacol Ther 21:343, 1977.

15 Carskadon, MA, et al: Daytime carryover of triazolam and flurazepam in elderly insomniacs. Sleep 5:361, 1982.

16 Klotz, U, et al: The effects of age and liver disease on the disposition and elimination of diazepam in adult man. J Clin Invest 55:347, 1975.

17 Rivera-Calimlin, L, et al: Plasma levels of chlorpromazine: Effect of age, chronicity of disease, and duration of treatment (abstract). Clin Pharmacol Ther 21:115, 1977.

18 Salzman, C: Clinical guidelines for the use of antidepressant drugs in geriatric patients. J Clin Psychiatry 46:38, 1985.

19 Goodman and Gilman's The Pharmacological Basis of Therapeutics. McGraw-Hill, New York, 1996.

20 Covington, TR, and Walker, JI: Current Geriatric Therapy. WB Saunders, Philadelphia, 1984.

21 Lundin, DV: Medication taking behavior and the elderly: A pilot study. Drug Intell Clin Pharmacol 12:518, 1978.

22 Morris, LA, et al: A survey of patient sources of prescription drug information. Am J Public Health 74:1161, 1984.

23 DeGowin, RL: DeGowin and DeGowin's Bedside Diagnostic Examination. Macmillan, New York, 1987, p 26.

24 Hermann, F: The outpatient prescription label as a source of medication errors. Am J Hosp Pharmacol 30:155, 1973.

25 Zuccollo, G, and Liddell, E: The elderly and the medication label: Doing it better. Age Ageing 14:371, 1985.

CHAPTER 9

Settings of Care

Mickey Stanley

OBJECTIVES
Upon completion of this chapter, the reader will be able to:

- Describe the various settings where nurses provide care to older adults
- Compare the services that are provided across the continuum of care for older adults
- Identify the importance of the concept of continuity of care for older adults
- Discuss the traditional and current model of case management in gerontological nursing

Nurses' Role with Older Adults Across Care Settings

The challenges of today's dynamic health-care environment offer nurses with a knowledge of gerontology exciting opportunities to make a real difference in the lives of older adults. Older adults are the primary users of health-care services along the continuum of care from the tertiary care center to home health or long-term care. Movement between the various settings of care is rapid and necessitates coordination of services by skilled and knowledgeable practitioners. An ability to assess current and potential needs, match those needs with appropriate services, and secure the necessary funding to ensure that all needs are met in a timely and seamless way requires ongoing communication and collaboration among all health-care providers. Older adults are the population in greatest need of care that is continuous and allows movement between service settings without gaps in care or duplication of services. This concept is known as a seamless web of care and is becoming the major emphasis in the world of managed care. This chapter examines the nurse's role with older adults in this dynamic health-care environment. The unique aspects of caring for older people in acute care, subacute care, rehabilitation, continued care communities, long-term care, and in the community are presented. The role of case manager for older adults is also discussed.

Use of Acute-Care Facilities by Older Adults

Older people are admitted to acute-care facilities with a number of complaints and problems but for primarily one purpose: to receive nursing care. The chief complaint may be the onset of a new acute condition such as chest pain or the exacerbation of a chronic condition such as foot ulcer in the diabetic patient. In addition to the presenting problem, most older adults have one or more nonacute chronic conditions that require ongoing management. These chronic conditions are often overlooked by health-care providers and contribute to the increased length of stay for older adults.

Older adults are the majority of patients cared for in many areas of acute care, including the emergency department (ED), operating room, critical care unit, and medical/surgical nursing unit. For the older person who enters the acute-care setting, the quality of nursing care can mean the difference between a return to his or her previous level of independence and lifestyle or the loss of independence and need for nursing home placement. High-quality nursing care that prevents iatrogenic and nosocomial problems and maximizes well-being requires an understanding of the unique needs of older adults and a commitment to professional gerontological nursing practice.

EMERGENCY DEPARTMENT

Older adults present to the ED for a variety of reasons. Nurses who work in this area note the large number of people who use the ED as a primary health-care clinic and the nonacute nature of their presenting signs and symptoms. However, studies[1] show that older adults do not abuse the ED; rather, their use of the ED reflects the proportion of older people in the geographical area and the availability of health-care options in the community. Newbern and Burnside[2] found that older adults who use the ED are likely to have an emergency diagnosis and are much more likely than the general population to be admitted to the hospital with a medical problem. A study at Yale–New Haven Hospital[1] found that cardiopulmonary problems were the most common complaint among older adults in the ED, followed by weakness, changes in mental status, and abdominal pain.

The presenting signs and symptoms of disease in older adults are often atypical and nonspecific compared with the presentation of younger patients. For example, the older adult with thyrotoxicosis presents with apathy rather than the hypermetabolic picture typically found in young adults.[3] The incidence of silent myocardial infarction increases with age and is characterized in older persons by fatigue and shortness of breath instead of chest pain.[4] Acute confusion, severe dehydration, and hypothermia are examples of clinical emergencies that may be mistakenly attributed to aging and therefore overlooked by emergency personnel.[1] Many ED personnel do not recognize the importance of such subtle or atypical signs and thus may characterize older people as abusers of the system.

The primary emphasis for the gerontological nurse in the ED is in recognizing the differences between aging and disease to avoid errors in diagnosis and treatment. The triage nurse must carefully elicit a history from the older adult with a high index of suspicion for such vague symptoms as mental status changes or shortness of breath. Most important, the ED nurse must assume the role of advocate to ensure that no further harm comes to the patient, either through neglect resulting from ageism or through unwanted or overaggressive therapy.[1]

An example of an age-appropriate program for older adults in the ED is the Quick Response Program.[5] This nurse-driven program provides immediate assessment, counseling, and applicable referrals within an ED. The program has been successful in identifying and preventing inappropriate hospital admissions by ensuring timely intervention into preventable problems and coordinating community resource use. Additional examples that are becoming more common across the country are nurse-run clinics that provide continued care after discharge with such diagnoses as congestive heart failure or diabetes. These nurse-run clinics provide ongoing support and teaching to keep older adults in their own homes by providing prompt intervention when symptoms begin to worsen.

INPATIENT CARE

The admission of an older adult to an acute-care bed may be traumatic for the patient and family. Many older persons do not report the early signs and symptoms of disease to their primary health-care providers or are unable to access appropriate care until late in the course of the illness. This practice may stem from a lack of understanding of the symptoms (e.g., nocturnal dyspnea as a symptom of congestive heart failure) or from a fear of hospitalization and potential loss of independence. The condition may have also been neglected because of ageism (e.g., "I'm too old for surgery" or "He or she is not a good surgical risk"). Thus, the condition is often serious when the patient reaches the acute-care setting. The patient may have sat in the ED or physician's office for hours awaiting treatment, a fatiguing experience even for the strong and healthy. Once the diagnosis is made, the patient is abruptly transported to the critical care or medical/surgical nursing unit.

Critical Care

Not all older adults perceive admission to a critical care unit as stressful. For many, the admission gives a sense of relief. "Someone is going to take care of me now." For most people, especially those experiencing their first critical care admission, however, the technology and pace of the intensive care unit are overwhelming. Families may need to be isolated in a waiting area. Sensory aids (i.e., glasses and hearing aids) are usually removed. Little time is spent orienting the patient to the new environment until the admission procedures have been completed and the patient's hemodynamic state stabilized. Exposure of body parts is common to allow extensive assessment and invasive treatment, with little regard for modesty. It is not surprising that most people consider this process traumatic.

The critical care nurse can do much to lessen the impact of such a traumatic experience. The use of eye contact, therapeutic touch, and a calm approach tells patients that they are in the hands of a competent and caring practitioner. In addition, respect for the patient's need for modesty and warmth requires little effort from the nurse and helps the patient maintain a sense of dignity in this threatening environment. The critical care nurse must also be a strong patient advocate, ensuring that the care provided reflects the person's desires and expectations.

Operating Room

Increasing numbers of older adults are admitted to acute-care facilities each year for elective or emergency surgery. In fact, one-third of all surgeries are performed on patients over the age of 65. Age alone does not predict outcomes. Studies[6] show mortality rates of 7.8 percent for elective surgery in those over age 70 and mortality rates of 36.8 percent for emergency surgery. The leading cause of postoperative morbidity and mortality is respiratory and cardiac complications. The major risk factors are underlying respiratory dysfunction or cardiac disease and an incision site near the diaphragm.[6]

Management of concomitant chronic conditions such as arthritis, diabetes mellitus, and hypertension preoperatively as well as postoperatively is a key factor in the success of surgical procedures for older adults. Efforts to support arthritic joints and provide padding on operating room tables for older adults who have spinal degeneration help ensure a successful recovery. The negative consequences of hypothermia postoperatively can be prevented by the use of head covers and warmed intravenous solutions intraoperatively. In addition, efforts to maintain mobility, nutrition, and hydration both preoperatively and postoperatively help ensure a successful postoperative course.

Older patients often report high levels of preoperative anxiety. Increased nurse-patient communication, sensitive use of touch, and arrangements for a family member or friend to be with the patient preoperatively decrease disabling anxiety in most older patients. Special considerations for the older adult undergoing surgery can be found in Table 9–1.[7]

Subacute Care

In a managed care environment, with its emphasis on rapid resolution of problems and prompt discharge, the older patient with confounding chronic conditions in addition to an acute problem often is classified as an outlier or delayed discharge.[8] These categories describe the client who continues to have complex needs for ongoing nursing care or who requires complex psychosocial discharge planning. To treat these clients, many acute-care and long-term facilities have developed a new type of environment known as subacute care or transitional care.

TABLE 9–1   SPECIAL CONSIDERATIONS FOR THE OLDER ADULT UNDERGOING SURGERY

- Unstable or complicated medical problems increase the risk of mortality.
- Medications taken to manage chronic problems make anesthesia and postoperative care more difficult.
- Age-related changes in the cardiovascular system make it difficult for older adults to adjust to stresses of surgery such as fluid depletion, volume overload, and hypoxia.
- Silent myocardial ischemia should be suspected in older people with risk factors such as diabetes, hypertension, and cigarette smoking.
- Increased age requires a decrease in anesthetic dosage, including inhalation anesthetic agents, intravenous anesthetic induction agents, and narcotics.
- Decreased clearance by an older adult's kidneys and liver results in a prolonged half-life of anesthetic agents, narcotics, muscle relaxants, and sedatives.
- Age greater than 70 years is an independent risk factor for a perioperative cardiac event.
- Regional anesthesia is an acceptable alternative to general anesthesia if the patient is alert and cooperative.

The philosophy of this new type of unit reflects the importance of a multidisciplinary approach, client and family involvement in goal setting, and a focus on the restorative needs of the older adult.[8] A major emphasis is placed on increasing levels of independence and preventing complications. Because of the differences in funding requirements, the older adult is provided additional time for healing, with the potential for a return to independent living rather than admission to a nursing home.[9]

An emerging trend in health care is the use of research-based protocols to ensure that the care for patients with specific diseases is timely and comprehensive. The Center for Health Education in Arvada, Colorado, has developed a series of research-based critical pathways called STATpaths that are age-specific for both subacute and long-term care. Figure 9–1 shows a STATpath for an older adult with an exacerbation of chronic obstructive pulmonary disease (COPD) in a subacute unit.

Acute-Care Nurses' Role in Health Protection

The nurse in an acute-care setting plays a primary role in protecting the health of older adults. To accomplish this end, the nurse must shift from a focus on episodic illness to one of primary, secondary, and tertiary prevention. This focus must begin before the person's admission as the nursing care is conceptualized and must be maintained throughout the patient's stay. For example, the nurse who is focused on episodic illness is concerned mainly with the extent of myocardial damage and the development of dysrhythmias for the older adult who is admitted with an acute myocardial infarction. The nursing care will be viewed as successful if the patient is transferred from the unit without evidence of congestive heart failure or serious rhythm disturbances.

In contrast, the nurse who is focused on prevention assumes the role of advocate and ensures that the patient's sleep patterns are not disturbed unnecessarily, that all invasive lines are removed as soon as hemodynamic stability is achieved, and that concomitant chronic conditions are addressed adequately in the medical and nursing care plans. The nursing care will be viewed as successful if the patient is returned to his or her usual environment with as many functional abilities intact as possible.

Figure 9–1   Research-based clinical protocol (critical path) for exacerbation of COPD. (Permission to reprint obtained from Center for Health Education, 11350 W. 72nd Place, Arvada, CO 80005, telephone 800-872-6166. STATpath Critical Paths for Sub-acute and Long Term Care are available upon order.)

COPD - Exacerbation (Pg. 3 of 4)

LOS: 12 days

⊠ Check when completed
* = if indicated

Admit Date _____   Transferred from _____   Resuscitation Status _____

Pathway	Day 8 _____	Day 9 _____	Day 10 _____	Day 11 _____
Consults	☐ PCP/Pulmonologist ☐ Respiratory Therapy ☐ PT/OT	☐ _____ ☐ _____ ☐ _____	☐ _____ ☐ _____ ☐ _____	☐ _____ ☐ _____ ☐ _____
Diagnostic Studies	☐ Abnormal labs reported to physician ☐ _____ ☐ _____	☐ _____ ☐ _____ ☐ _____	☐ _____ ☐ _____ ☐ _____	☐ *Repeat lab ☐ *Repeat chest X-ray ☐ _____ ☐ _____

Treatments	☐ Pulse ox daily
	☐ Wean O2 as toleratec
	☐ Titrate O2 to sat. @
	  > 90% or baseline
	☐ Resp. Tx PRN
	☐ I & O q̄ 8 hrs
	☐ PT: _____
	☐ OT: _____
	☐ _____
	☐ _____
		☐ Pulse ox daily
		☐ Wean O2 as tolerated
		☐ Titrate O2 to sat. @
		  > 90% or baseline
		☐ Resp. Tx PRN
		☐ I & O q̄ 8 hrs
		☐ PT: _____
		☐ OT: _____
		☐ _____
		☐ _____
			☐ Pulse ox daily
			☐ Wean O2 as tolerated
			☐ Titrate O2 to sat. @
			  > 90% or baseline
			☐ Resp. Tx PRN
			☐ I & O q̄ 8 hrs
			☐ PT: _____
			☐ OT: _____
			☐ _____
			☐ _____
				☐ Pulse ox daily
				☐ Wean O2 as tolerated
				☐ Titrate O2 to sat. @
				  > 90% or baseline
				☐ Resp. Tx PRN
				☐ I & O q̄ 8 hrs
				☐ PT: _____
				☐ OT: _____
				☐ _____
				☐ _____

Key Medications/ Diagnoses Allergies: _____ _____	Medication · Diagnosis ☐ Theophylline · COPD ☐ Antibiotic · Infection ☐ Steroids · COPD ☐ Inhalers · COPD ☐ Diuretic · COPD ☐ _____ ☐ _____ ☐ _____ ☐ _____	Medication · Diagnosis ☐ Theophylline ☐ *Antibiotic ☐ Corticosteroids ☐ Inhalers ☐ Diuretic ☐ _____ ☐ _____ ☐ _____ ☐ _____	Medication · Diagnosis ☐ Theophylline ☐ *Antibiotic ☐ Corticosteroids ☐ Inhalers ☐ Diuretic ☐ _____ ☐ _____ ☐ _____ ☐ _____	Medication · Diagnosis ☐ Theophylline ☐ Corticosteroids ☐ Inhalers ☐ Diuretic ☐ _____ ☐ _____ ☐ _____ ☐ _____
Diet	☐ DAT ☐ Monitor % meal intake ☐ _____ ☐ _____	☐ DAT ☐ Monitor % meal intake ☐ _____ ☐ _____	☐ DAT ☐ Monitor % meal intake ☐ _____ ☐ _____	☐ DAT ☐ Monitor % meal intake ☐ _____ ☐ _____

Therapeutic Activities	☐ Reinforce use of
	  energy conservation
	☐ Activity Profile
	  completed
		☐ Assess for decreased
		  functional strength
		☐ Uses adaptive
		  equipment as needed
			☐ Ambulate X 50' bid
			☐ Exercise program to
			  build energy
			☐ _____
				☐ Ambulate X 75' bid
				☐ Home exercise
				  program if appropriate
				☐ Review equip. for home

Safety	☐ *Restraint review
	Side Rails: ☐ Y ☐ N
	☐ _____
	☐ _____
	☐ _____
		☐ Up c̄ assistance
		☐ _____
		☐ _____
		☐ _____
			☐ Up in room ad lib
			☐ Home safety needs
			  assessed
			☐ _____
			☐ _____
				☐ Up ad lib
				☐ Home safety needs
				  ordered and in place
				  prior to discharge
				☐ _____

Discharge Planning	☐ Review psychosocial
	  needs
	☐ Assess educational
	  needs
	☐ Facilitate physician/
	  family conference PRN
	☐ _____
	☐ _____
		☐ Discuss signs and
		  symptoms of respira-
		  tory infection and when
		  to contact physician
		☐ Discuss need to avoid
		  smog, smoke and
		  pollutants
		☐ _____
			☐ Home referrals initiated
			  as needed
			☐ Assess home O2
			  needs and *order
			  equipment
			☐ _____
			☐ _____
				☐ If referrals initiated,
				  resources in place prior
				  to discharge
				☐ Finalize discharge plan
				☐ Review discharge
				  meds, dose, side
				  effects and frequency
				☐ _____

Critical Path Implemented Initial/Signature:	_____	_____	_____	_____

Addressograph:

1 *Primary Prevention*

Primary prevention in the acute-care setting consists of preventing disease or disability that results from hospitalization. These include iatrogenic or therapy-related problems (including malnutrition and sleep pattern disturbances) and nosocomial infections. Many older adults enter the hospital with borderline protein and calorie malnutrition resulting from loss of taste sensation, a diminished thirst drive, and poor dietary habits. When these people are subjected to extensive bowel preparation and not allowed anything by mouth (NPO) for several days, the result may be dehydration and malnutrition. The nurse with a philosophy of prevention will ensure that adequate fluid volume and calories are contained in the patient's clear or full-liquid diet before and during this diagnostic period or during the preoperative and postoperative course. Collaboration among the physician, nurse, and dietitian is essential to ensure that all acutely ill older people receive appropriate nutrition to meet the metabolic demands of the illness or surgery. A thorough discussion of the nutritional needs of older adults can be found in Chapter 18.

Many nursing units organize their routines around the convenience of the nursing staff rather than around individual needs. Patients are often awakened at midnight for a full assessment, perhaps only an hour or two after settling in for a night's sleep. This same patient may be awakened for a morning bath, daily weight check, and laboratory work at 4:30 AM. The intervening hours may be filled with interruptions for medications, vital signs, and around-the-clock breathing treatments. Alternatives to this type of unit routine include scheduling routine assessments for 7 AM and 7 PM and using the day and evening shifts for daily baths. Additional iatrogenic problems that nurses can be instrumental in preventing are falls, social isolation from restricted visiting hours, and fatigue and low self-esteem because of the lack of respect from caregivers.

2 *Secondary Prevention*

Secondary prevention in the acute-care setting involves the early detection and treatment of disease and disability. While providing care for the primary problem, the nurse must be alert to the subtle signs and symptoms of additional undiagnosed problems. After developing a therapeutic relationship with an older adult, the nurse may discover that the patient is depressed or having suicidal thoughts after a diagnosis of cancer or the death of a spouse or other loved one. The nurse may also observe maladaptive family-coping behaviors and uncover evidence of elder abuse.

Additional social problems that are receiving more attention in this population are drug and alcohol abuse. Vision and hearing problems may have also gone unnoticed or untreated in older adults who mistakenly consider these changes a normal part of aging. The astute nurse can identify and initiate a referral through the attending physician to ensure that these problems receive the necessary attention. For a thorough discussion of each of these problems, see the related chapters in this text.

Nosocomial infections are a serious threat to all older adults in acute-care settings. Infections are more common in older adults as a result of a decline in the immune system and loss of protective mechanisms, such as active cilia in the bronchial tree. In addition, diagnosis and treatment of infection in this age group are often delayed because of its atypical presentation. Fever is often absent, even in the presence of sepsis.[10] Pneumonia from aspiration or from the lack of effective pulmonary hygiene is a preventable problem that could result in death for the acutely or critically ill older adult.[10] Urinary tract infections resulting from indwelling Foley catheters are an equally serious and potentially preventable problem.[10] A conscientious turn, cough, and deep-breathe program and a bladder retraining program are standard precautions for all older adults.

3 *Tertiary Prevention*

Tertiary prevention involves the early management of problems to prevent further deterioration or complications. Excellent examples of tertiary prevention in the acute-care setting include frequent turning to avoid decubitus ulcer formation and early and continued ambulation to avoid the complications of immobility. Careful administration of medications to prevent side effects and drug interactions is also appropriate.

ADMISSION ASSESSMENT

Eliciting a complete and accurate history and physical examination from a person who has lived 60 years or longer is no small task. During the admission period, the patient is examined by multiple caregivers, often seeking the same information. Fatigue experienced by an acutely ill older person during a lengthy admission can intensify presenting symptoms such as pain or shortness of breath. The total admission assessment can be obtained in segments over the first 24 hours. In addition, collaboration among the various levels of health-care providers to ensure that the assessment is comprehensive but not repetitive is essential.

Data reflective of nursing's approach to health protection must be obtained for the development of a comprehensive care plan (Table 9–2). Included in the nursing data base is an assessment of the patient's current functional status. Reasons for assessing functional status in the older adults[11] include the following:

- Functional limitations may be a manifestation of disease.
- Knowledge of functional abilities before an acute illness helps the nurse set appropriate and realistic discharge goals.
- Assessment of functional deficits will clarify the need for specific services (e.g., physical therapy).
- Functional status assists in determining the need for placement.
- Difficulties in performing activities of daily living (ADLs) are predictive of readmission rates.

A variety of instruments are available through which the nurse may obtain information regarding the functional status of the older adult.[12] The functional

TABLE 9–2 ELEMENTS OF THE NURSING DATABASE

Previous level of independence with ADLs
  Functional ADLs (feeding, bathing, dressing, continence, toileting, ambulation)
  IADLs (transportation, shopping, preparing meals, use of telephone, housekeeping, laundry)
Nutrition and hydration history
  Recent weight loss or gain
  Difficulty swallowing, oral health
  Dietary patterns (foods consumed, with whom, where, and how much)
Medication use habits (prescribed and over-the-counter drugs)
  Reasons for difficulty following prescribed regimen
  Side effects or toxic effects
Current and previous cognitive states
Emotional well-being and history of recent loss
Concerns regarding new or subtle symptoms
Methods used to manage chronic conditions (including folk medicine practices)
Expectations of the health-care system

ADLs are activities necessary for self-care (i.e., bathing, toileting, dressing, and transferring). Instrumental activities of daily living (IADLs) include those that facilitate or enhance the performance of ADLs (i.e., shopping, transportation, and meal preparation). Assessment of functional ADLs only is inadequate for older people who live independently in the community, whether in their own homes or in retirement communities. A person may be able to live independently if adequate transportation (an IADL) is provided. Therefore, for older adults living in the community, an assessment of IADLs should also be done to ensure that adequate services are available to empower them to function independently. Two instruments that accomplish this assessment are the Index of Independence in Activities of Daily Living and the Instrumental Activities of Daily Living Scale. Both of these instruments are self-explanatory and can be administered through observation or self-report. In the Index of Independence in ADLs, the lower the score, the more functional the person. The value of these tools is in assessing the need for services in the community, planning care in the acute and long-term care facilities, and measuring outcomes. See Table 9–3 for the Index of Independence in Activities of Daily Living and Table 9–4 for the Instrumental Activities of Daily Living Scale.

TABLE 9–3 INDEX OF INDEPENDENCE IN ACTIVITIES OF DAILY LIVING

Based on an evaluation of the functional independence or dependence of people in bathing, dressing, toileting, transferring, continence, and feeding.
Specific definitions of functional independence and dependence:
  0 = Independent in all six functions (bathing, dressing, toileting, transferring, continence, and feeding)
  1 = Independent in five functions and dependent in one function
  2 = Independent in four functions and dependent in two functions
  3 = Independent in three functions and dependent in three functions
  4 = Independent in two functions and dependent in four functions
  5 = Independent in one function and dependent in five functions
  6 = Dependent in all six functions

Independence means without supervision, direction, or active personal assistance, except as specifically noted subsequently. This is based on current status and not on previous ability. A person who refuses to perform a function is recorded as not performing the function, even though he or she is deemed able.

Bathing (sponge, shower, or tub)
  Independent: Needs assistance only in bathing a single body part (e.g., back or disabled extremity) or bathes self completely
  Dependent: Needs assistance in bathing more than one body part; *body* needs assistance in getting in or out of tub or does not bathe self

Dressing
  Independent: Gets clothes from closets and drawers; puts on clothes, outer garments, braces; manages fasteners, excluding act of tying shoes
  Dependent: Does not dress self or remains partly undressed
Going to Toilet
  Independent: Gets to toilet; gets on and off toilet; arranges clothes; cleans organs of excretion (may manage own bedpan used at night only and may or may not be using mechanical supports)
  Dependent: Uses bedpan or commode or receives assistance in getting to and using toilet
Transfer
  Independent: Moves in and out of bed independently and moves in and out of chair independently (may or may not use mechanical supports)
  Dependent: Needs assistance in moving in or out of bed or chair or both; does not perform one or more transfers
Continence
  Independent: Urination and defecation entirely self-controlled
  Dependent: Partial or total incontinence in urination or defecation; partial or total control by enemas, catheters, or regulated use of urinals or bedpans or both
Feeding
  Independent: Gets food from plate or its equivalent into mouth (precutting of meat and preparing food, such as buttering bread, excluded from evaluation)
  Dependent: Needs assistance in act of feeding (see earlier); does not eat all or needs parenteral feeding

Source: Adapted from Katz, S, and Akpom, A: A measure of primary sociobiological functions. Int J Health Sci 6:493, 1976.

TABLE 9–4 INSTRUMENTAL ACTIVITIES OF DAILY LIVING SCALE

Action	Score
A. Ability to use telephone	
1. Operates telephone on own initiative; looks up and dials numbers, and so on	1
2. Dials a few well-known numbers	1
3. Answers telephone but does not dial	1
4. Does not use telephone at all	0
B. Shopping	
1. Takes care of all shopping needs independently	1
2. Shops independently for small purchases	0
3. Needs to be accompanied on any shopping trip	0
4. Completely unable to shop	0
C. Food preparation	
1. Plans, prepares, and serves adequate meals independently	1
2. Prepares adequate meals if supplied with ingredients	0
3. Heats and serves prepared meals, or prepares meals but does not maintain adequate diet	0
4. Needs to have meals prepared and served	0
D. Housekeeping	
1. Maintains house alone or with occasional assistance (e.g., "heavy work—domestic help")	1
2. Performs light daily tasks such as dishwashing and bedmaking	1
3. Performs light daily tasks but cannot maintain acceptable level of cleanliness	1
4. Needs help with all home maintenance tasks	1
5. Does not participate in any housekeeping tasks	0
E. Laundry	
1. Does personal laundry completely	1
2. Launders small items—rinses out socks, stockings, and so on	1
3. Requires all laundry to be done by others	0
F. Mode of transportation	
1. Travels independently on public transportation or drives own car	1
2. Arranges own travel via taxi but does not otherwise use public transportation	1
3. Travels on public transportation when assisted or accompanied by another	1
4. Travel limited to taxi or automobile with assistance of another	0
5. Does not travel at all	0
G. Responsibility for own medications	
1. Is responsible for taking medication in correct dosages at correct times	1
2. Takes responsibility if medication is prepared in advance in separate dosages	0
3. Is incapable of dispensing own medication	0
H. Ability to handle finances	
1. Manages financial matters independently (budgets, writes checks, pays rent and other bills, goes to bank), collects and keeps track of income	1
2. Manages day-to-day purchases but needs help with banking, major purchases, and so on	1
3. Incapable of handling money	0

Source: Adapted from Lawton, M, and Brody, EM: Assessment of older people: Self-maintaining and instrumental activities of daily living. Gerontologist 9:179, 1969.

PLANNING FOR CONTINUITY OF CARE

The success or failure of any discharge plan rests with one key player: the client. Many older adults have been labeled as noncompliant by health-care professionals because their desires and perceived needs for health care were not considered when plans were being made. Discharge planning is a systematic process beginning with the initial assessment, looking at acute and chronic problems as well as potential problems to be avoided, and the setting of realistic goals with the client and his or her family to maximize health and strengths.

The ideal approach to discharge planning is through a multidisciplinary team that includes physicians, nurses, dietitians, and social workers with geriatric experience, and rehabilitation services such as physical and occupational therapy. Geriatric nurses as case managers for at-risk older adults are in an ideal position to ensure that all needs are met through this process and that the risk of an unnecessary repeat hospitalization is avoided. A telephone follow-up program has been shown to be effective in screening for potential complications (to provide early intervention through referrals), as well as in encouraging health promotion and disease prevention for at-risk older adults who have been discharged from an acute-care facility or home health agency.[13]

Use of Rehabilitation Facilities by Older Adults

by Jessie Drew-Cates

Many older adults benefit from a structured rehabilitation program. Rehabilitation nursing in gerontology can be defined as a dynamic process of physical restoration that facilitates physical independence in all ADLs. This process includes the physical, emotional, psychological, social, and vocational potential of the older person. In the face of chronic illness, the goals of rehabilitation are to maintain physical independence and to facilitate psychological, social, vocational, and avocational well-being for the client.

Rehabilitation Team Members

Rehabilitation requires a health team approach. The team concept is an important element in rehabilitation. No single member of the team can do everything necessary to help a disabled client begin to function as fully as possible. The traditional inpatient rehabilitation team consists of physiatrists, psychologists, rehabilitation nurses, physical therapists, occupational therapists, speech therapists or speech pathologists, social workers, and recreational therapists. Members of the team can carry out their specialized therapy in an outpatient setting such as day care or in the client's home, free-standing adult day-care setting, or inpatient health-care facility. The team can also include vocational counselors, audiologists, physical therapy assistants, occupational therapy assistants, dietitians, and insurance nurses.

Gerontology nurses trained in rehabilitation gain knowledge of each specialized area formally claimed by other therapies. The greatest advantage for the nurse is the ability to observe the client in his or her personal setting. By observing clients in their own settings over many hours, the nurse can develop individualized interventions to facilitate choice and independence in activities. Gerontology nurses trained in rehabilitation can coordinate therapy and help older adults achieve daily goals. This means monitoring health care, assisting with ADLs, and facilitating the psychosocial adjustment to a disability.

Like other nurses, rehabilitation nurses in gerontology are both teachers and reinforcers of teaching done by other members of the team. Their role is often one of health-care coordination and management. At times, these nurses are counselors for older adults and their families.

Specific roles of the rehabilitation nursing staff might include determining the extent of bowel or bladder dysfunction, determining appropriate interventions, and evaluating the outcome of the plan to promote continence or control incontinence. Another role is the prevention and treatment of pressure ulcers. Particularly in gerontology rehabilitation, it is critical that the nurse be skilled in dementia disorders, cardiac disorders, and respiratory disorders associated with aging. See related chapters in this text for more in-depth information on these problems.

Rehabilitation Goals

Although rehabilitation goals may appear straightforward, each older adult is unique and requires an individual approach. The meaning of the disability and of particular life events determines the importance of functioning in various activities. Rehabilitation helps older adults determine what physical activities have inherent meaning and what choices the client may make to meet his or her own priorities.

For example, an older woman who can walk only with assistance may choose to give up walking if she must leave her home. She may decide it is more important for her to stay in her home with her husband and use a wheelchair than to live in another setting that permits daily assistance in walking.

Older people must also be helped to make choices about bladder training so that they feel they are accomplishing their goals. For some clients, this may mean using a urinary care product to protect against incontinence when outside the home rather than seeking assistance to the bathroom from friends during a social gathering. For others, it may mean obtaining physical assistance with daily bathing and dressing to conserve enough energy to attend religious services. The meaning of the disability and of particular life events is an important parameter in the goals of functioning for each client in his or her ADLs.

Gerontology nurses in community settings can help clarify an older adult's decision to seek an alternative living situation and give up his or her own residence. Some people who are living with debilitating cardiac or pulmonary disease, and possibly with some cognitive changes, may feel relieved to leave a situation in which they are alone. They may prefer to have others around them to help manage complex medication regimens, prepare meals for them, and provide activities that are within their physical capacity.

Psychosocial Adjustment to Physical Disability

Understanding and intervening in the psychosocial aspects of physical disability, both for the client and for the family, is another skill that is integral to rehabilitation and gerontology nursing. Helping older adults adjust to a physical disability means encouraging them to modify, adapt, or alter their behavior pattern so that they can discover and use new strategies in coping with the disability. Seeking previous coping strategies and adaptations to life stressors is often necessary to determine coping strategies in a current crisis.

Coping with a disability typically begins with a focus on the physical self, and then a shift in focus to the relational and goal-oriented self. The initial response to a physical disability is usually marked by a period of buffering. Clients, families, and nurses have said, "I can't believe this has happened," a response that is normal and necessary to cope with the disability. The older adult and family may focus initially on returning to the prior level of ability. Clients talk about wanting to play golf again, fix dinner again, or walk again. Although seemingly realistic to the client, these goals may be interpreted as a denial of the disability by health-care providers rather than as part of a process that can lead to reorganization and acceptance of the disability.

This behavior of expressing unrealistic goals represents a way to buffer the losses incurred by the disability. In the weeks and months that follow, as the physical disability becomes more apparent, these clients may begin to feel "like a baby again" as they relearn ADLs, a task that can result in such normal responses as frustration and anger.

Over weeks, months, and sometimes even years, older adults who initially expressed such seemingly unrealistic goals may begin to express more realistic goals as the extent of their physical losses becomes apparent. When older adults must face a new physical disability, alternative methods of caregiving include furnishing household help, moving the client in with a family member, or placing the client in a health-related facility.

Part of the role of a gerontology nurse is to help decide objectively the level of care and safety needed by older adults, given their ability to perform ADLs. The gerontology nurse must therefore be fully knowledgeable about assessing physical and cognitive deficits of an older adult and evaluating the amount of support, both tangible and emotional, that families and friends can offer. In addition, the gerontological nurse must know the community and residential resources to adequately facilitate proper care, according to the client's disability, personality, and financial situation.

An excellent tool to assist the nurse in determining the care and safety needs of an older adult being considered for rehabilitation is the ADL Rehabilitation Potential STATpath shown in Figure 9–2.

The roles of tangible social support (offered by people who may shop or drive for a physically disabled person) and emotional support are important to understand when assisting people to make life choices based on transitions caused by physical disability. Exploring all options can ease the process of returning to a home setting or being placed in another facility.

In addition to the physical losses of a new disability, emotional losses can occur. The physical dependency may mean delaying a return to home or never returning home. It may mean relinquishing a long-standing marital relationship and financial control. Socializing with old friends may now be difficult. Older adults with physical disability may become more lonely and more anxious about how they will manage as they grow older.

Despite physical disability, most older people seem to want to get on with their lives. They may use a combination of problem-focused and emotion-focused coping strategies to find ways around their physical disability and integrating a new self and body image from the pieces of the old self that continue to function. These people have an optimistic outlook on life, looking forward to social events, using diversion tactics, planning their lives to incorporate their new physical disability, and displaying a humorous and often joyous sense of being alive and functional.

Use of Long-Term Care by Older Adults

by Pamela Millsap

The concept of long-term care covers a broad spectrum of comprehensive health and wellness and support services to provide the physical, psychological, social, spiritual, and economic needs of people with chronic illness or disabilities. A chronic illness is a condition that is permanent, leaves a residual disability, results from an irreversible disability, requires a long period of supportive supervised care, or requires special education and training of the patient for rehabilitation.[14] The goal of long-term care services is to attain and maintain optimal wellness and functional independence. Long-term care does not provide a cure but rather an adjustment and support for long-term chronic care problems.[15] These services are provided in community and institutional settings and can range in scope from informal support to formal medical, nursing, or rehabilitative care.

Figure 9–2 Research-based clinical protocol (critical path) for determining ADL rehabilitation potential. (Permission to reprint obtained from Center for Health Education, 11350 W. 72nd Place, Arvada, CO 80005, telephone 800-872-6166. STATpath Critical Paths for Sub-acute and Long Term Care are available upon order.)

ADL Rehabilitation Potential (Pg. 1 of 5)

☒ Check when completed
* = if indicated

Days 1-3 of plan

☐ No change ☐ Continue
☐ Improved ☐ Resolved   Resuscitation Status _____

Date plan initiated _____   Date plan reviewed _____

Criteria	Staging/Acuity	Clinical Path	Intervention	Expected Outcomes
☐ Change in ADLs in last 90 days **Areas of change: 2 or >** ☐ Consciousness ☐ Communication ☐ Ambulation ☐ Toileting ☐ Dressing/grooming ☐ Feeding **ADL Rehab if:** ☐ Res. believes is capable of ↑ ADLs ☐ Staff believes res. capable of ↑ ADLs ☐ Performs activities but is slow **Key Problems** 1. ●⁵ **Impaired mobility** R/T disease process AEB ↓ ROM, pain, paralysis, weakness or dizziness 2. ▲⁵ **Alteration in comfort** R/T disease process or trauma AEB pain, discomfort, swelling or stiffness 3. ●⁵ **Altered self care** R/T disturbance of consciousness AEB difficulty in bathing, dressing, eating, or slow in activities 4. ▲⁷ **Altered self-esteem or self-concept** R/T feelings of helplessness AEB changes in life-style & relationships; language disturbance, changes in cognition & level of independence	☒ **best answer for each group** **ADL self performance:** ●⁵ ☐ Stage 0: Independent ☐ Stage 1: Requires cues 1 or 2 X/day, no physical assistance needed ☐ Stage 2: Requires cues > 3 X/day or physical assist c̄ mobility, meals, toileting ☐ Stage 3: Requires mod. assistance in mobility, eating, dressing & bathing ☐ Stage 4: Requires total ADL assistance, coma **Short term memory:** ●⁵ ☐ Stage 1: recalls current event >1 day but < 1 wk ☐ Stage 2: recalls current event > 4 hrs but < 1 day ☐ Stage 3: recalls current event > 1 hr but < 4 hrs ☐ Stage 4: recalls < 5 min **Activity support:** ▲¹⁰ ☐ Stage 0: Independent ☐ Stage 1: Mild-Supervision only, prepares activity ☐ Stage 2: Moderate-Help only to transfer ☐ Stage 3: Advanced-Help in part of activity ☐ Stage 4: Severe-Totally dependent **Cognitive skills for ADLs:** ●⁵ ☐ Stage 0: No deficit noted ☐ Stage 1: Mild-Copes c̄ routine care, handles new situations c̄ cues ☐ Stage 2: Moderate-Correct decisions 70-90%, difficulty c̄ new situations even c̄ cues ☐ Stage 3: Advanced-Correct decisions 60-70%, needs monitoring ☐ Stage 4: Severe-Correct decisions < 60%, needs constant supervision **Risk for falls:** ▲¹¹ ☐ Stage 0: At risk only ☐ Stage 1: Mild-No history of falls, c/o dizziness, weakness or confusion ☐ Stage 2: Moderate-No hx of falls, rates 3-5 on "Fall Risk Scale", depressed ☐ Stage 3: Advanced-c̄ or s̄ history of falls, rates 4-6, disoriented, ↓ mobility, uses adaptive devices, c/o urinary frequency ☐ Stage 4: Severe-Rates > 6, incontinence, nocturia, hx of CVA or CA **Assistive device:** ☐ Y ☐ N If yes, list: _____ Smoker: ☐ Y ☐ N	**Diagnostic Studies:** ☐ *X-ray _____ ☐ *EKG ☐ *EEG ☐ *CBC ☐ *Lytes ☐ *UA ☐ *Chem 22 ☐ *Thyroid profile ☐ *Drug level: _____ ☐ Monitor labs and report abnormalities to phys **Treatment:** ●⁵ ☐ Monthly weight ☐ *PROM or AROM ☐ Assess comprehension ☐ Assess communication ☐ Give clear, concise directions ☐ PT ☐ OT ☐ ST ☐ RT **Medication Diagnosis** ☐ Reevaluate all meds ☐ _____ ☐ _____ **Diet:** ☐ DAT ☐ High fiber diet ☐ Determine texture of food res. able to swallow ☐ Supplements ordered ☐ Nutritional assessment ☐ Monitor % meal intake **Therapeutic Recreation:** ☐ Initiate activity history ☐ ▲¹⁰ Promote release of energy & diversional activities as tolerated ☐ Activities spaced at intervals to allow rest **Activities & Safety:** ▲¹¹ ☐ Orient to environment ☐ Reorient PRN ☐ Set limits PRN ☐ Daily activities posted in clear view ☐ ▲¹⁸ Appropriateness of restraints documented: ☐ Chemical ☐ Physical ☐ Side rails **Social Services/ Discharge Plan:** ☐ Advance Directives reviewed ☐ Review social history ☐ Assess need for family meeting	**Nursing Assessment:** ☐ Assess q̄ 24 hrs by RN ☐ Reassess by RN/LPN c̄ shift PRN ☐ Impact of condition on life-style/implications for future ☐ Effects of meds ☐ Learning needs/capacity ☐ Resp rate and depth ☐ Mental status ☐ Skin/oral assessment **Nursing Interventions:** ☐ *VS c̄ orthostatics ☐ Observe feeding skills ☐ ●⁵ Assist c̄ mobility & ADLs as necessary ☐ *Pain management ☐ Set limits using calm, firm & reassuring manner ☐ Reinforce safety PRN ☐ Reorient frequently ☐ CNA Flowsheet completed and doc. ☐ _____ **Respiratory Therapy:** ●⁵ ☐ Evaluation initiated ☐ Pulse ox PRN ☐ O2 as ordered ☐ Teach breathing tech. ☐ _____ **PT/OT/ST:** ●⁵ ☐ Screen ☐ Request eval. & orders ☐ Initiate evaluation ☐ *Clarification of orders ☐ Assist c̄ ADLs PRN ☐ ST-eval swallow ability ☐ _____ **Resident/Family Teaching:** ☐ Describe disease process ☐ Explain procedures, diet, tests, meds, activity ☐ How to rate pain on 10 point scale ☐ Teach limit setting ☐ *Describe need to maintain alignment and reposition q̄ 2 hrs ☐ Explain the initial goal is to identify cause and to rehabilitate to highest practical self sufficiency	1. ●⁵ **Impaired mobility** ☐ May have ↓ ROM or mobility causing difficulty in ambulation ☐ May have difficulty c̄ transfers from bed to chair, chair to toilet, etc. ☐ Unsteady gait, may need assistance ☐ _____ 2. ▲⁵ **Alteration in comfort** ☐ Instructed to rate discomfort on 10 point scale c̄ 1 as mild & 10 as worst pain ever ☐ History of pain obtained ☐ Activities that ↓ or ↑ pain determined ☐ Pain documented and relief of pain noted ☐ _____ ☐ _____ 3. ●⁵ **Altered self care** ☐ ↓ energy even for minimal tasks ☐ Physical condition may require pacing of activities for energy conservation ☐ ↓ ability to concentrate or sequencing problem in accomplishing ADLs ☐ May need limit setting ☐ _____ ☐ _____ 4. ▲⁷ **Altered self-esteem or self-concept** ☐ Difficulty accepting need for dependence ☐ Withdrawal from others ☐ Irritable, angry, nervous, & feelings of hopelessness ☐ Refusal to look at oneself or affected area ☐ Excessive guilt and unrealistic self-expectations ☐ Becomes over-dependent & anxious ☐ _____

Critical Path Implemented Initial/Signature:	RN _____ LPN _____ RT _____	Dietary _____ Activities _____ SS _____	PT _____ OT _____ ST _____	Other _____

● = Automatic trigger plan of care	3 = Visual function	7 = Psychosocial well-being	11 = Falls	15 = Dental care
▲ = Potential trigger plan of care	4 = Communication	8 = Mood state	12 = Nutritional status	16 = Pressure ulcers
1 = Delirium	5 = ADL function/rehab potential	9 = Behavior problems	13 = Feeding tubes	17 = Psychotropic drug use
2 = Cognitive loss/dementia	6 = Urinary incontinence & indwelling catheter	10 = Activities	14 = Dehydration/fluid maintenance	18 = Physical restraints

Addressograph:

Critical Path: ADL Rehabilitation Potential (Pg. 1 of 5)

Characteristics of the Long-Term Care Facility Resident

There is currently a 50 percent chance that a woman over the age of 65 will spend time in a long-term care facility at some point in her life.[16] The chance for men of the same age is 30 percent.[16] The risk difference between men and women is based on current life span data: The likelihood of admission to a long-term care setting increases with age. Although statistically only about 5 percent of the population over age 65 resides in a long-term care facility, it is estimated that 25 to 40 percent of this population group will spend some time in this type of facility.[16]

Families currently provide 80 percent of the care required by older adults and others with chronic long-term care needs in the community setting.[16] Families and older adults decide to relocate to long-term care facilities when the burden of care exceeds the caregiver's ability. The decision to relocate is a difficult one that often is based on the loss of financial support, social support, health, emotional strength, or functional ability.[17] See Chapter 26 for an in-depth discussion of family dynamics.

Two types of residents are described in the literature based on their length of stay in the long-term facility.[18] The short-term resident usually leaves the facility in 3 to 6 months, is younger, has more physical problems, and is admitted from the hospital or rehabilitation facility. The person who has suffered a fracture, stroke, or acute illness with ongoing chronic problems or who has an ill caregiver might be admitted for a short stay. Ideally, the resident receives care necessary to regain maximal function and independence and then returns to the community.

The long-term resident usually is older, is admitted from home, and has more functional and cognitive impairments.[18] Long-term residents often remain at the facility until they die or are transferred to an acute-care setting. Recent changes in funding from federal to state budgets have increased the number of long-term residents who are chronically mentally ill, who are terminally ill, or who are suffering from head injuries, developmental disabilities, or acquired immunodeficiency syndrome (AIDS).[17] The ratio of long-term to short-term residents is currently about 9 to 1.[18]

Many long-term care residents have one or more chronic illnesses. In order of prevalence, the most common chronic illnesses are heart disease, cognitive impairment (dementia), arthritis, hypertension, and diabetes. Sensory impairment (hearing and vision loss) is present to varying degrees in 85 to 90 percent of long-term care residents.[16]

Currently, the greatest number of long-term care residents are admitted from home rather than from the hospital or other settings; however, this trend may change with changing societal needs.[16] The average stay for the long-term care resident is 2.4 years.[16] Eighty percent of the residents die in the facility or at the acute-care setting when transferred; the remaining 20 percent are discharged back to the community.[19]

Environment in the Long-Term Care Facility

The environment of the long-term care facility has an important effect on the general well-being of the residents and on the quality of life they experience. The physical and psychosocial environments of the facility are interdependent and constantly interacting with one another.

PSYCHOSOCIAL ENVIRONMENT AND THE ROLE OF THE NURSE

The structure of the long-term care facility provides the basis of survival: environmental safety, food, health services, and assistance with personal care. The social aspects of life, health, and well-being are intricately intertwined. The social needs of meaningful interpersonal contacts, relationships, self-esteem, autonomy, self-determination, personal space, and privacy are also necessary to meet the challenge of providing an environment that supports functional independence and growth.

Residents and their families should be encouraged to personalize the living space. Personal possessions will help the space seem "owned" by the resident. This also gives the staff a sense of the resident's identity; thus, the resident is less likely to be labeled as "sick." Biographical data and pictures of family and life interests displayed in the living space of the cognitively impaired resident give a sense of personal identity for both resident and staff.

Privacy is essential in the social environment of the long-term care facility. Flexibility in allowing residents to set personal space boundaries will increase their sense of autonomy and self-determination. The nurse should knock on closed doors, announce before entering, and ask permission to enter the resident's personal space. Belongings of the resident should not be rearranged or organized without permission. A cupboard or trunk that can be locked should be made available to the resident. Opportunity for choice and decision making, two important aspects of the social environment, are often neglected. In a long-term care facility, where conformity is mandated, basic decisions most people take for granted such as when to eat or bathe and where to sit in the dining room are removed from the residents. Flexibility in the routine is essential to establish an environment that fosters well-being.

Supportive staff attitudes foster functional independence and prevent learned helplessness. Many times the staff members "baby" the resident instead of encouraging independence. The staff fosters the resident's sick role. The health promotion and health protection model fosters the idea of rehabilitation, maximal function, and prevention of disabling complications of the chronic illness.

Family and community involvement can help establish a social environment conducive to maximizing growth, health potential, and function. Maintenance of social roles is important to well-being. Providing an environment that is welcoming encourages visiting and socializing with family and friends. Building ties with community churches, Senior Centers, foster grandparent programs, and other community agencies promotes activity and socialization with those living outside the facility and maintains social roles.

PHYSICAL ENVIRONMENT AND THE ROLE OF THE NURSE

Bright, warm, sensory-stimulating physical surroundings are important to the long-term care setting. The physical spaces accessible to the resident are the bedroom, toileting and bathing facilities, corridors, lounges, dining areas, and outside spaces identified for resident use. Bathrooms and bathing facilities should have grab bars, extended toilet seats, and good lighting to provide safety and promote independence. The nurse should be involved in assisting architects and other designers of the physical environment to meet the special needs of the resident. Nurses can also advocate changes in existing environments and can help personalize the physical space and make it homelike through creative intervention.

The debate regarding bedroom space is whether a single room, double room, or open ward is best. The single room promotes privacy and a sense of ownership in the environment. An open ward allows for increased sensory and psychosocial interactions, a sense of a small community, and a sense of comfort and security because the older adult is able to see the caregiver. A double room has potential for an incompatible roommate and often increases the residents' sense of territory and possessiveness of space. Many long-term care settings currently have double rooms. Room selection by the nurse is an important part of the initial assessment.

Corridors and hallways should be light and painted in contrasting colors to provide discernible boundaries between walls and floor. Ample hallway width is needed for functional aids that residents may use. Handrails and areas to sit and rest are important hallway features. Too often, the lounge/dining area is a large multipurpose room that is not conducive to relaxation and social visits. These rooms may be noisy and may lack intimacy. Smaller congregate rooms, television rooms, and reading rooms tend to decrease noise and confusion, as well as promote socialization and relaxation. A large room may be resectioned into smaller areas using strategic furniture arrangement and placement of plants or other types of structural devices.

The facility's dining area environment has a direct effect on nutrition. A dining area that is noisy or confusing tends to decrease the appetite. Food that is unappetizingly presented or served in a rush often goes uneaten. Having to eat with others who behave disruptively during the meal is also unpleasant. Nurses must intervene to make the dining area and mealtime pleasant. Residents should be seated according to social preference. Food appearance and service style should be discussed with the dietary service or nutritionist. Meal service times for residents with behavioral problems should be staggered or a therapeutic dining room provided for assistance and supervision of feeding residents and for careful monitoring of those with cognitive impairment.

Relocation

The move from one living environment to another is more than a change in physical space; it also has many social and emotional consequences. The decision to relocate is difficult. Relocating from one's own home to the hospital or to a long-term care facility can have a significant impact on the person's well-being. Older adults in this situation experience separation from their home, family, and possessions, as well as from their community and customs. Depression, anxiety, frustration, and regression are but a few of the emotions experienced upon relocation to a long-term care facility.

The negative impact on older adults' health during the relocation is most significant in those with sensory and cognitive impairments.[20] These residents are less able to interact actively with the environment, and they adapt more slowly to the relocation. Acute confusion, falls, depression, and decreased appetite may occur during the orientation phase of relocation. The nurse must assess and intervene to prevent or reduce these complications of relocation.[20]

Ideally, the older person should decide to move to a long-term carefacility out of choice rather than being forced to do so because of a crisis. The older person should be actively involved in the decision. Orientation sessions should be held before the admission. However, the ideal is not always reality. In the event that preparation is impossible, honesty is essential in the nurse's first encounter with the resident.[20] Nurses should listen empathetically to the resident and orient him or her to surroundings, routine, and staff expectations to help allay fears and anxiety. The long-term care facility will not be just like home; consequently, during the early phases of relocation, the new resident may need assistance validating the experience of relocation. The nurse should take extra time to listen and provide emotional support. It is helpful to introduce the resident to other residents with similar backgrounds and interests. Well-adjusted residents can be encouraged to seek the new resident and accompany him or her to the dining area for meals or other daily activities.

Role of the Nurse in Direct Resident Services

Holder[21] states "The needs of the residents cannot be met without professional caring nursing personnel to provide direct service and leadership." Nursing care in the long-term care facility is directed by the nursing process, with attention to the special needs of the long-term care residents and their families. Nursing care in this setting focuses on self-care that promotes independence and function. The "whole person" must receive care to attain the highest health potential. Table 9–5 lists the goals of nursing care for older adults in a long-term care facility.

TABLE 9–5 GOALS OF NURSING HOME CARE

- Provide a safe and supportive environment for the chronically ill and disabled resident.
- Improve and maintain the highest possible level of function and independence.
- Manage and delay progression of chronic illness, if possible.
- Prevent iatrogenic complications; identify and intervene promptly.
- Provide dignity, comfort, and peace for the terminally ill and their families.
- Preserve individual autonomy.
- Maximize and enhance quality of life, well-being, and life satisfaction.

ASSESSMENT

The Omnibus Reconciliation Act (OBRA) 1987 regulation, implemented by OBRA 1989, mandates the use of a minimum data set (MDS) assessment tool for all long-term care residents.[22] This assessment tool, which began to be used in October 1990, is a standardized, reproducible, comprehensive assessment tool that the nurse is responsible for completing with the assistance of the physician, social worker (designee), and dietitian. As part of the OBRA 1987 framework to improve and standardize care in the long-term setting, this tool provides comprehensive assessment of cognition, communication, vision, hearing, performance of ADLs, function, range of motion, rehabilitation potential, continence, psychosocial well-being, mood and behavior, activity preferences, terminal prognosis, medical problem list, allergies, physical concerns (e.g., constipation, dyspnea, edema, fecal impaction, joint pain, and recurrent pain), dental status, nutritional status, skin assessment, medication list, need for special treatments or procedures, abnormal laboratory work, and need for and use of restraints. (See Appendix A for a copy of the MDS.) This assessment must be completed upon admission and a reassessment completed every 90 days or if the resident's status changes.

Additional factors are essential for a complete assessment. A formal mental status examination provides valuable reproducible baseline information to evaluate any change in cognition.[23] Often a subtle change in an older adult's mental status is the first discernible change in a resident's condition. Nursing assessment of the resident's perceived health status and the resident's definition of health or wellness will help plan appropriate nursing intervention.[23] Previous health promotion activities should also be assessed. Legal issues to assess include right-to-die issues, determination of next of kin, patient self-determination act, and determination of a legal power of attorney or guardian.[23]

Developing and Implementing Plans of Care

Following a thorough assessment using the MDS and any additional tools or processes, a comprehensive prob-lem list that includes both actual and potential problems is generated. The MDS triggers the inclusion of potential problems based on the data entered. For example, if the resident is assessed to have periods of altered perception under Section B: Cognitive Patterns, a potential problem of falls is identified. Once a problem or potential problem is identified, the use of a resident assessment protocol is specified. This additional assessment tool facilitates a more comprehensive evaluation of the potential problem and the development of a specific plan of care.

An important aspect of the care plan is potential for and planned date of discharge. The health-care team and the resident and family should identify the goals that are to be met for discharge planning.

Teaching needs of the long-term care resident may include changing the definition of health and wellness to include chronic disease states. High-level wellness in the presence of chronic disease can be achieved. Another important intervention is to teach the older adult and family how to manage chronic illness or recover from a disability before being discharged to the community. The nurse should inform the resident and family about other community long-term care services that are available and should promote residents' self-care and independence. Health care promotion activities in the long-term care setting may involve exercise and body movement programs, development of individually meaningful activities within the facility or community, stress reduction, health maintenance needs, nutrition counseling, identification and reduction of lifestyle risk factors, and restorative or rehabilitative activities.[24]

Another important intervention is to develop protocols to identify and prevent potential problems that the resident may encounter in the long-term care setting. Common preventable iatrogenic problems in the long-term care setting include urinary tract and upper respiratory infections, skin breakdown, polypharmacy, falls, and deformities (contractures).[23] These problems are discussed in detail elsewhere in this text.

OBRA 1987 mandates ongoing interdisciplinary care planning involving the resident and family.[22] core professional team members include the nurse, physician, dietitian, and social worker or activity director. Other team members that may be included as resident needs dictate are a pharmacist and a rehabilitation therapist. This team meets with the common goal of planning care for the resident, with involvement of the resident and family. Assessment results and professional expertise are shared and goals of care established.

The nurse can play an important role in providing the leadership for this team. Besides being knowledgeable about the other disciplines, community resources, and group processes, the nurse is also responsible for the direct nursing services provided 24 hours a day. This knowledge base makes the nurse the logical leader of the group. Such a responsibility entails coordinating care, evaluating the need for team meetings between assigned times, and acting as the liaison among disciplines.

Use of Community Services by Older Adults

by Sheryl Soderlind Nokolassy

Nurses provide community care for the elderly in many settings, including the home, clinic, assisted living/retirement center, and adult day-care center. In these natural settings, assessment can include the size and diversity of the older person's social support system, the availability of economic resources, the use of community resources, and the community's health-care structure. These data facilitate holistic care for the community-living older adult.

The nurse must assess the community at large for the health roles that are provided by various community individuals, groups, and environmental and government organizations. The current health roles, communication styles, social interaction patterns, and perceived boundaries of each contributor are important to understand to determine the community's level of development and its ability to promote the highest level of health possible for older adults.

Older adults often need to take advantage of community resources to prevent crises. As people age, their ability to handle stress diminishes. Using the community assessment, nurses working with older adults can facilitate their use of community health and fiscal resources. The nurse's role in the community is based on establishing safety, teaching the older adult to maintain safety, and facilitating maximum individual and family independence and health. The nurse attempts to match each of the older persons's needs with the appropriate available community resources to foster independence and maintain quality of life.

Community Care Settings

HOME HEALTH

Home health care is the fastest-growing sector of the health-care system. Home health-care services are either episodic or ongoing, according to the older adult's need for services. These services are provided by private for-profit agencies or by nonprofit visiting nurse agencies or district organizations. Services provided include nursing, physical therapy, occupational therapy, speech therapy, social work, and home health-aid services. Some older people may use all services, and some only one service.

Recent studies[25,26] demonstrate the importance of home health services for older adults to prevent hospital readmissions. The ability of the home health nurse to assess the client on an ongoing basis and identify any symptoms of exacerbation of the presenting problem allows prompt intervention before symptoms worsen. The home health nurse is in an ideal position to assess the older adult's needs holistically and to coordinate the necessary services.

All forms of nursing care can be provided in the home setting. Many procedures previously considered high-tech are becoming common in home care (e.g., central line and Port-a-Cath care). Intravenous therapy and hyperalimentation are done routinely in the home. Many high-tech treatments are done with specialty companies and home care agencies working together on cases. The specialty company nurse covers a large geographic area, sometimes several states. The equipment needed for the older person's care is provided and maintained by this specialty company, which also provides initial training and backup problem solving help to the local home care nurse. The local home care agency provides the daily care to the client.

CLINICS

Nurse-run clinics that focus on the management of chronic diseases such as diabetes, congestive heart failure, and chronic obstructive lung diseases are demonstrating the importance of continuous monitoring and prompt intervention in keeping older people out of acute-care institutions and improving quality of life.[27] Many of these clinics are being offered through health maintenance organizations (HMOs) as a response to the spiraling costs of repeated hospitalizations for acute exacerbations of these chronic conditions. With aggressive follow-up, including telephone or in-home contact within a week of discharge, easy access to nurses with advanced assessment skills who can detect subtle changes in the client's condition, and standing orders or home-based care maps to allow medication adjustment as needed, older adults can be discharged earlier and readmission rates are being reduced.[27]

ASSISTED LIVING/RETIREMENT CENTER

Most older adults prefer to remain in their own homes, where family roots are established and memories provide a sense of comfort into old age. For some people, however, the family home where they have lived most of their adult lives and raised their children becomes a burden that exceeds the older adult's capabilities. Safety and security issues may trouble the older person. To meet these challenges, the model of the assisted living center or retirement center is becoming a popular option with many seniors. The Assisted

Living Association of America defines this new environment as

> a special combination of housing and personalized health care designed to respond to the individual needs of those who need help with activities of daily living. Care is provided in a way that promotes maximum independence and dignity for each resident and involves the resident's family, neighbors and friends.[28]

Many assisted living or retirement centers offer multiple levels of privacy, from single-dwelling homes, apartment-style facilities, or luxurious single-room accommodations. These centers offer increased security, socialization activities, well-balanced meals, and access to on-site nursing or health care.

ADULT DAY CARE

An additional community setting in which older people receive care is adult day care. Adult day care has two levels: social day care and adult day health. In social day care, the older adult does not need hands-on care by a nurse. In adult day health, the level of nursing care provided depends on the center's resources. Care is based on medical orders and nursing care plans. Progress notes are submitted to the physician. Some common nursing services provided are medication administration, medication and insulin prepouring, wound dressing, bathing, cardiopulmonary assessment, and range-of-motion exercises. These nursing services are not reimbursed by Medicare.

Traditional Perspectives on Case Management

by Ann S. Reban

Functioning as a case manager is not new to community health nurses. Coordinating resources to benefit homebound older adults has been an important part of the duties of public health and visiting nurses since the inception of community nursing agencies in the early 1900s.[29] Case management consists principally of client assessment and the provision, coordination, and monitoring of services.

The new context for viewing the role of a case manager is as part of a community-wide system to address the fragmentation and costliness of the present provision of health care for at-risk older adults. The characteristics of such a system include a population (i.e., community) focus; a coordination of services; a comprehensive, periodic assessment with an element of measurement; and a framework of information systems that will permit the judicious allocation of resources for the population served.[30]

In 1988, the National Council on Aging published standards to serve as voluntary guidelines for case management reflective of the new context and scope just described. These guidelines, prepared by the National Institute on Community-Based Long-Term Care, use the term *care management* rather than *case management* because the former conveys that the process is the management of care as opposed to the management of the case or person.[31] This suggests that the person receiving care retains the right of self-determination. Care (or case) management lends itself to promoting independence by encouraging clients and their caregivers to assume responsibility for their own care to the greatest extent possible.

Community-based long-term care operates under the assumptions that older adults should have one case manager, that case management should occur only when needed rather than whenever the person enters each community service, and that case management should target older adults with multiple needs who require skilled multidisciplinary assessment to define those needs.[30]

Case management for at-risk older adults at the community-based care level generally excludes hands-on care.[31] In rural areas with shortages of nurses and social workers, nurse case managers may be more comprehensive and provide case management as well as direct care.[30] Case management is viewed as a process, whether considered from the perspective of individual service provider agencies, health-care institutions, or long-term (community-based) programs. The particular focus of case management for nurses is on interaction with clients, their family caregivers, and other service providers; assessment and planning; implementing care; and evaluation. The intensity of this interaction with the patient or client may vary in degree depending on the setting in which the nurse practices.

The Influence of Practice Settings

The use of nurses in case management roles in acute-care hospitals began with the advent of diagnosis-related groups (DRGs) as the basis for Medicare reimbursement. This method uses DRG case types to identify critical events or pathways in the usual hospital episode that facilitate desired patient outcomes within allotted time frames. The introduction of DRGs highlighted the fact that older patients had lengthened hospital stays because of multisystem involvement. The goals of managed care (case management in this setting) are cost containment and continuity of care. This setting is characterized by interaction among the nurse case manager, the staff, and third-party payor, rather than involving the patient.[32]

Growing numbers of families and older adults are paying privately for geriatric case management services delivered primarily by social workers and nurses with an entrepreneurial spirit. The attractions for the professional nurse who functions in this role are the opportunities to establish long-term relationships with clients and their families, to be independent and self-managed, and to experience the satisfaction of developing individualized care plans. On the other hand, round-the-clock availability to clients may prove stressful. At the request of some clients, the private case manager may even assume the surrogate role of an absent adult daughter or son. Another stressor for private case managers is risky financial security.[33,34]

THE CASE FOR NURSES AS CASE MANAGERS

Registered nurses are moving increasingly into the full-time practice of case management for older adults and their caregivers.[34] The nature of the case manager's background is important from the at-risk older adult's standpoint. Interrelated and complex needs place these clients at risk of losing their independence. Many have physical health problems. "Nurses are particularly suited to provide case management for clients with multiple health problems that have a health-related component."[35]

In 1980, the American Nurses' Association (ANA) highlighted three characteristics of nursing that are critical in case management for high-risk clients: Nursing is highly interactive, complex, and nurturing.[35] In addition, nurses possess the physical assessment skills to detect acute and chronic health-care needs, knowledge of diagnoses and causes of diseases, and knowledge of treatments including medications. They are experienced in health promotion and disease prevention and are prepared to assess knowledge deficits in those areas. The case management process closely approximates the nursing process (i.e., assessment, planning, implementation, and evaluation). Other advantages are nurses' ability to collaborate with physicians and their knowledge of the world of health-care institutions.

From a community-based perspective, nurse case managers can move with their older clients into and out of the hospital system. They can influence discharge planning, offer support for hospitalized clients and monitor their care, recommend appropriate level of care and placement at discharge, take advantage of the benefits of hospitalization (e.g., encourage necessary diagnostic workups for other suspected problems), and work toward early client discharge.[35]

THE NURSE'S ROLE IN THE CASE MANAGEMENT PROCESS

There are four generally agreed-on roles enacted by the case manager:

Gatekeeper: Case management and other services are reserved for appropriate clients.

Counselor: Clients and families are assisted in identifying the strengths, problems, and needs in their situation; taught how to be savvy consumers of services; and encouraged in self-help to the greatest extent possible.

Advocate: In planning care and intervening as necessary, the case manager acts on behalf of the client, caregiver, or both to ensure the receipt of appropriate, responsive, high-quality services.

Service coordinator: Appropriate services are identified and their delivery coordinated on the client's behalf.[31]

Key elements of the case management process are:

- Case finding; case targeting
- Intake and screening
- Assessment
- Care planning
- Service arrangement and coordination
- Monitoring
- Ongoing reassessment
- Inactivation or termination

For the nurse case manager, these elements are woven together with the nursing process to achieve desired goals. These mutual goals and planned interventions are established through interaction among the case manager, the client, the client's significant others, and community and institutional service providers.

Student Learning Activities

1 Form small groups of three of four. Select a type of service setting from those listed here. Interview a member of the agency's administration regarding:
   a Type of services provided
   b Eligibility for these services
   c Common forms of reimbursement for these services
   d Future need for increased or decreased availability of the services

Type of service settings

Skilled nursing facility	Long-term care	Adult day care
Alzheimer's special care unit	Hospice/home health	Geriatric assessment clinic
Senior health center	Area agency on aging	Public transportation

2 Share the information learned with the class.

3 Evaluate the information to determine gaps in services or overlap of services available in your area.

REFERENCES

1 Fulmer, T, and Degutis, LC: Elders in the emergency department. Clin Issues Crit Care 3(1):89, 1992.
2 Newbern, VB, and Burnside, I: Needs of older persons in the emergency department. J Gerontol Nurs 20(7):53, 1994.
3 McMorrow, ME: Thyrotoxicosis in the elderly: Clinical presentation and nursing management. Clin Issues Crit Care 3(1):114, 1992.
4 Stanley, M: Elders in critical care: An overview. Clin Issues Crit Care 3(1):120, 1992.

5 Rajacich, DL, and Cameron, S: Preventing admissions of seniors into the emergency department. J Gerontol Nurs 21(10):36, 1995.

6 Chalfin, DB, and Nasraway, SA: Preoperative evaluation and postoperative care of the elderly patient undergoing major surgery. Clin Geriat Med 10(1):51, 1994.

7 Kelly, M: Surgery, anesthesia, and the geriatric patient. Geriatr Nurs 16(5):213, 1995.

8 Arford, PH, et al: Quality and cost outcomes of transitional care. Nurs Econ 14(5):266, 1996.

9 Mickota, S: A hospital-based skilled nursing facility: A special place to care for the elderly. Geriatr Nurs 16(2):64, 1995.

10 Fraser, D: Patient assessment: Infection in the elderly. J Gerontol Nurs 19(7):11, 1993.

11 Sehy, YA, and Williams, MP: Functional assessment. In Chenitz, C, et al (eds): Clinical Gerontological Nursing. WB Saunders, Philadelphia, 1991, p 119.

12 Heath, JM: Comprehensive functional assessment of the elderly. Prim Care 16:305, 1989.

13 Shu, E, and Mirmina, Z: Telephone reassurance program for elderly home care clients. Home Healthcare Nurse 14(3):155, 1996.

14 Burnside, I: Chronicity and long-term care. In Burnside, I (ed): Nursing and the Aged: A Self-Care Approach, ed 3. McGraw-Hill, New York, 1988, p 918.

15 Maraldo, PJ: Foreword. In Strategies for Long-Term Care. NLN Publication 20-2231:3, 1988.

16 Kaeser, L: Unpublished material, 1991.

17 Lusk, P: Who's knocking now? New clientele for nursing homes. J Gerontol Nurs 16:8, 1990.

18 Stevens, R: The nursing profession and reform of service for the elderly. In Mezey, MD, et al (eds): Nursing Homes and Nursing Care Lessons from the Teaching Nursing Home. Springer, New York, 1989, p 102.

19 Kane, RL: Long-term care resources. In Kane, RL, et al (eds): Essentials of Clinical Geriatrics, ed 2. McGraw-Hill, New York, 1989, p 397.

20 Lekan-Rutledge, D: Gerontological nursing in long-term care facilities. In Matteson, MA, and McConnell, ES (eds): Gerontological Nursing Concepts and Practice. WB Saunders, Philadelphia, 1988, p 793.

21 Holder, EL: The new national nursing facility reform law: A challenge providing new opportunities for nursing. NLN Publications 41-2381:1, 1991.

22 Beyers, M: Response to "The new national facility reform law: A challenge proving new opportunities for nursing." NLN Publications 41-2382:21, 1991.

23 Harrington, AM, and Waltman, RE: 8 Steps for evaluating a new long-term care patient. Nursing 19(5):74, 1989.

24 Robertson, JF: Promoting health among the institutionalized elderly. J Gerontol Nurs 17(6):15, 1991.

25 Dennis, LI, et al: The relationship between hospital readmissions of medicare beneficiaries with chronic illnesses and home care nursing interventions. Home Healthcare Nurse 14(4):303, 1996.

26 Bull, MJ: Use of formal community services by elders and their family caregivers two weeks following hospital discharge. J Adv Nurs 19:503, 1994.

27 Lasater, M: The effect of a nurse-managed CHF clinic on patient readmission and length of stay. Home Healthcare Nurse 14(5):351, 1996.

28 Just, G: Assisted living: Challenges for nursing practice. Geriatr Nurs 16(4):165, 1995.

29 Knollmueller, R: Case management: What's in a name? Nurs Management 20:38, 1989.

30 Kane, R: What is case management anyway? In Kane, R (ed): Case Management: What Is It Anyway? University of Minnesota DECISIONS Resource Center, Minneapolis, 1990, p 4.

31 National Institute on Community-Based Long-Term Care: Care Management Standards. National Council on Aging, Washington, DC, 1988, p 7.

32 Pierog, LJ: Case management: A product line. Nurs Admin Q 15:16, 1991.

33 Parker, M, and Secord, LJ: Private case management for older persons and their families: Where do nurses fit in? Aspen's Advisor for Nurse Executives 4:4, 1989.

34 Parker, M, and Secord, LJ: Guiding the elderly through the health care maze. Am J Nurs 88:1674, 1988.

35 Bower, KA: Case Management by Nurses. American Nurses Publishing, Washington, DC, 1992, p 14.

SECTION II

Health Protection from a
Body Systems Approach

CHAPTER 10

The Aging Sensory System

R. LaVerne Gallman / Lucie S. Elfervig

OBJECTIVES

Upon completion of this chapter, the reader will be able to:

- Discuss normal alterations in sensory responses with implications for care
- Use the nursing process to explore needs and plan nursing interventions for older clients experiencing alterations in sensory responses
- Discuss psychosocial implications for older clients with sensory changes
- Teach families about the individual needs of older clients with changes in sensory responses

Many older adults have sensory problems related to normal age-related changes. These changes do not occur at the same rate or at the same time for all people and may not always be dramatic or obvious. Sensory changes and resulting problems may be the strongest contributing factor in a change of lifestyle moving toward greater dependency and a negative perception of life.

Sensory perceptions influence one's ability to interact with others and to maintain or establish new relationships, respond to danger, and interpret sensory input in activities of daily living (ADLs). Isolation may result from changes in vision and hearing. Older adults with vision or hearing problems may be unwilling to venture out of the home because of their inability to distinguish once-easy-to-read signs or negotiate rough terrain. An older adult with a hearing impairment may respond inappropriately during a conversation, resulting in embarrassment and avoidance of verbal communication. Changes in vision and hearing may also cause misinterpretation of sensory stimuli in the environment.

Sensory perceptions allow one to appreciate and respond to the environment, which includes interesting and changing sights, beautiful music, interesting debates and discussions, indoor and outdoor entertainment, good-tasting food, a variety of wonderful fragrances, and the touch of a loved one. They also provide defenses in response to the environment. They act as one's security system, and an impaired security system can result in problems.

Taste and smell are important senses, but changes in these senses do not result in pronounced differences in response to the environment. However, the sensory perceptions in taste and smell facilitate one's response to enjoyable situations as well as to danger. For example, an older adult may be unable to detect spoiled food, leading to ingestion of toxins.

All of the senses play a role in one's perceptual response to the environment. They enable people to adapt to complex and changing situations in ADLs.

Vision

CHANGES IN AGING

Sensory deficits (e.g., vision changes) can be some of the continual adjustments that come with living into advanced age. Visual changes affect the performance of ADLs. The changes in visual and eye functioning that are considered normal in the aging process include decrease in the ability to accommodate, senile constricting of the pupil, and color changes and opacity of the lens (cataracts).

Vision changes are initially appreciated with the onset of presbyopia, the loss of accommodative ability. This change in accommodative ability usually starts in the fourth decade of life, when people have trouble reading small print. Impairment of accommodation occurs because the ciliary muscle becomes weaker and more relaxed and the crystalline lens becomes sclerotic, with the loss of elasticity and ability to focus up close (near vision).[1,2] This condition can be corrected with lenses such as bifocals.

The pupil size decreases (pupil miosis) with age because of pupil sphincter sclerosis.[1,3] Pupil miosis can narrow one's visual field, affecting peripheral vision to some degree,[1,3] but does not appear to interfere with everyday life in a remarkable way.

The color changes (e.g., yellowing) and increasing opacity of the crystalline lens occur over time, creating cataracts.[4,5] Cataracts create many aging signs and symptoms that interfere with vision and everyday activities. Blurred vision is a common symptom and is like having a film over the eye, which results in difficulty focusing and reading. This difficulty can be corrected temporarily with lenses. In addition, the older adult should be encouraged to use bright nonglare lamps. Sensitivity to light often occurs, causing the older adult to squint with bright lights or when outside on a sunny day. Light sensitivity may result in a tendency to stay indoors or use tinted sunglasses. Glare or halos, caused by a scattering of light, affect driving, especially at night when facing high-beam automobile headlights. This situation can be dangerous and may cause a decline in evening social activities if the older adult is reluctant to ask for assistance in driving. A decrease in night vision results in difficulty with driving and ambulating. Older adults require the use of night-lights in the home and additional time for vision to adjust to the change in illumination when going from a well-lighted to a dimly lighted environment. Cataracts also result in trouble with depth perception or stereopsis, which causes problems in judging height. Older adults should be taught to use their hands as a guide on stair rails and to use bright colors painted on the edge of steps. Alterations in color perception occur with cataract formation and result in colors appearing dull and muted, especially low-tone colors such as blues, greens, and violets.[1,4] The use of bright colors such as yellows, oranges, and reds is recommended to facilitate color discrimination. Eye pain or discomfort may be experienced by some older adults because as the cataracts grow they can temporarily increase intraocular pressure (IOP).[6] It is important to have regular vision and eye pressure checks and to have cataracts removed when they are ready.

Normal sensory system aging changes are summarized in Table 10–1.

TABLE 10–1 NORMAL SENSORY SYSTEM AGING CHANGES

Normal Age-Related Changes	Clinical Implications
VISION	
Decreased ability to accommodate	Difficulty reading small print
Senile constriction of pupil	Narrowing of field of vision
Increased opacity of lens with yellowing	Blurring of vision Sensitivity to light Decreased night vision Difficulty with depth perception
HEARING	
Slow decline in sensorineural function	Gradual loss of hearing

MANAGEMENT OF VISUAL CHANGES

Everyone experiences visual changes with aging, and these changes may be of great concern to many older people because perceptual responses to the environment are related to a feeling of security. Most people adapt remarkably well to the changes occurring in the aging process.[2] Using bright colors in dress, using appropriate eyeglasses or contact lenses in response to decreased accommodation, using safety features such as handrails and contrasting colors to compensate for decreased depth perception, and having an opaque lens surgically removed when the opacity is great enough are ways many older people adapt to their normal vision changes.

Assessment, Defining Characteristics, and Interventions

The nurse may obtain information about changes in vision from a number of sources. Initially, an assessment of visual sensory alteration should include a history of eye health and any disorders. People who are not wearing eyeglasses or contact lenses should be asked whether these are usually worn daily. Near focus ability may be checked by having the client read print at close range, about 16 inches (40 cm) away from the client's eye or comfortable reading distance, using a near-point card with his or her present corrections. Pupil size and reaction may be assessed by using a flashlight and shining a light into each eye and observing the reaction of the pupil.

The nurse should observe for ptosis (drooping) of the eyelid to determine whether there is interference with the line of vision and check the eyes for moisture and excessive tearing. The older adult should be asked about dryness of the eyes and whether lubricating eye drops are used. Peripheral vision may be checked by moving a pencil from each side of the head (up, down, right, and left) toward the center, while the patient looks straight ahead. The patient is asked to state when the pencil is first noticed. Ocular movements may be checked by having the patient follow the movement of a pencil through the field of vision. It is important to ascertain whether the patient has experienced pain in either eye. The assessment also includes information about blurring of vision, difficulty with glare, nighttime driving patterns, previous eye surgery, or vision changes that interfere with ADLs.

The defining characteristics may occur gradually and vary among individuals. Some may report that they have difficulty looking at near and far objects and discriminating between objects or letters. Others may say that their "arms got too short" to accommodate reading material. Still others may complain of seeing a halo around lights or having a dry, itchy, gritty feeling in their eyes. A change in the ability to discriminate between colors may be very disturbing to people who may sometimes mismatch colors or have difficulty locating doors in a room with little color contrast.

Surgical Removal of Cataracts

Cataracts can be helped with corrective lenses during the period of maturation. There is a "limbo period" when the vision is not quite decreased enough for surgery and corrective lenses are no longer beneficial. This time is frustrating to older adults because they cannot see clearly. Additional moral support may be helpful, especially if the client is still in the work force. After the cataract matures, surgical removal and intraocular lens (IOL) implantation is indicated. Aphakic eyeglasses or contact lenses are used if no lens implants are inserted, but only after both eyes have had cataracts removed. When a person is ready for cataract surgery, the following procedures are carried out in the clinic or office:

- Best-corrected visual acuity (BVA) refraction to determine whether the patient is ready for cataract surgery (According to government guidelines, the patient has to have a BVA of 20/50 or worse [this can vary among states].)
- Tonometry reading, measuring IOP to check for glaucoma
- Potential acuity meter to approximate visual acuity after cataract surgery
- Glare test to measure the degree of sensitivity to bright lights, which interferes with vision and ADLs
- Medical necessity questionnaire to determine how the cataract affects ADLs according to the patient
- Keratometry readings (K-readings, which measure cornea curvatures) and alpha ultrasound (A-scan) to determine axial length and IOL calibrations to obtain the correct size and power of the IOL implant (After the usual preoperative ocular, medical, social, and family history, laboratory test, chest x-ray, electrocardiogram [ECG], and physical examination, the patient is ready for surgery.)

Cataract surgery is an outpatient procedure. Cataract surgery can be performed under local or topical anesthesia. Postoperatively, the eye will be patched after surgery. The eye patch is removed the next day by the doctor during the first postoperative visit. The patient is asked to refrain from any activities that would increase IOP (no heavy lifting, no bending over, and no straining for approximately 2 to 3 weeks). An eye patch and metal or plastic shield over the operative eye will be worn when taking a nap or at night when asleep to keep fingers or hands from injuring the operative eye. When the patient has an eye patched, he or she must be instructed to be careful when ambulating or placing objects down because depth perception is temporarily impaired. The patient can wear eyeglasses over an eye patch, just the eyeglasses, or just the eye shield while awake. The patient will apply antibiotic/anti-inflammatory eyedrops four times a day (e.g., at breakfast, lunch, dinner, and bedtime) in the operative eye for about 2 weeks. The patient will have a second postoperative visit a week after surgery if there are no complications, then at regular intervals until the eye is healed.

The second cataract surgery, if the eye is ready, is usually done 2 months or longer after the first surgery.

The patient can usually obtain eyeglasses or contact lenses a month or more after cataract surgery to fine-tune his or her vision, if indicated.

After several weeks to years following cataract surgery, the patient may say that his or her vision is blurry or that there seems to be a film over the pseudophakic or aphakic eye. This is usually caused by the posterior capsule of the natural lens becoming cloudy or fibrotic over time.[7] This can usually be easily corrected with a YAG (yttrium aluminum garnet crystalline) laser during an office visit.[7] The main complication after YAG laser correction can be an increase in IOP, which is corrected with temporary use of glaucoma eyedrops.

Hearing

Palumbo[8] states that "hearing is a silent and often overlooked disability that can dramatically affect the quality of one's life" (p. 26). Hearing loss is the second most common health problem affecting older adults.[9] Some say that it has ripple effects that influence certain basic areas of human performance, decreasing enjoyment of life and reducing interaction with others and excursions outside the home.[10]

In people over 65 years of age, between 28 and 55 percent may have some degree of hearing impairment.[11] Among those older than age 80, 66 percent may have impaired hearing.[11] An estimated 90 percent of institutionalized people have hearing problems.[8]

CHANGES IN AGING

Hearing loss in older adults is described as presbycusis. Mhoon[5] defines the phenomenon as "a slowly progressive bilaterally symmetric disease in hearing that primarily affects high tones and is associated with aging" (p. 408). The cause is unknown, but various factors have been studied: nutrition, genetic factors, noise, hypertension, emotional stress, and arteriosclerosis.[9] Hearing loss is primarily sensorineural, but there may also be a conductive component associated with presbycusis. Sensorineural hearing loss occurs when the inner ear and nerve components (auditory nerve, brain stem, or cortical auditory pathways) are not functioning properly.[10] The cause of the conductive change is not understood, but it may be related to changes in the bones in the middle ear, in the cochlear partition, or in properties of the mastoid bone.[10]

In presbycusis, high-pitched consonant sounds are the first to be affected, and the change may occur gradually. Because the change is slow, the client may not immediately seek assistance, which is important because the earlier the hearing loss is identified and aid is implemented, the greater the possibility of success. Because hearing loss is usually gradual, a person may be unaware of the change until told by a friend or family member that he or she is becoming "hard of hearing."

The two most common functional hearing problems in the older population are inability to detect the volume of sound and the inability to detect high-frequency tones such as certain consonants (e.g., *f, s, sk, sh,* and *l*). The changes may occur in one or both ears. Various means are available to test for hearing disorders, such as otoscopy with histological, microbiological, and biochemical examination and radiological studies. Thorough otological and audiological examinations are essential.

MANAGEMENT OF HEARING LOSS

Assessment, Defining Characteristics, and Interventions

A valuable source of information for the diagnosis of hearing disorders is the case history. Through history taking, the nurse can learn when the client began having a hearing problem as well as other symptoms associated with it (e.g., accumulation of cerumen, pain in the ear, change in word perception, inappropriate response in conversation, tinnitus, or vertigo). Information can be gained from a functional assessment of the living environment as well as from assessment by the use of a tuning fork, a watch tick, and a whisper. The nurse should be alert for other clues that indicate hearing loss, such as the older adult asking people to repeat statements, moving the head to the right or left in an attempt to better understand what is being said, withdrawing from social activities, giving inappropriate responses in conversations, and turning up the radio or television volume to hear it.

The assessment includes information about previous ear infections (otitis media), discharge from either ear, current or past environmental exposure to noise, frequent upper respiratory infections, previous surgical procedures of the ear, difference in hearing high or low sounds, pain associated with hearing loss, and any previous hearing tests. It is also important to determine whether a family member or the client first noticed a change in his or her hearing. The following may be used to assist in determining the older adult's hearing status:

- Stand behind the client, clap hands loudly, and observe whether the client responds to a sudden noise.
- Speak a few words that have high-frequency consonant sounds and ask the client to repeat (e.g., *fair, sunny, skies, shout, fun*).
- Observe to determine whether the client is reading lips.
- Watch for misinterpretation of words.
- Listen for failure to respond to questions asked.
- Observe withdrawal behavior.
- Determine whether the client can hear a watch tick (bilaterally). Hold the watch a few inches above the head, posteriorly, and several inches from each ear. Note the distance at which the client indicates the watch tick is heard.

The assessment of hearing loss in older adults is complicated by several factors. Inappropriate responses may be misinterpreted as confusion, or the client may not be able to understand speech and follow instructions.[12]

The defining characteristics associated with a change in hearing vary among individuals. The characteristics may include a change in hearing perception, ringing in the ears (tinnitus), pain in one or both ears, change in the ability to hear high-frequency sounds, withdrawal, anxiety, inappropriate response in conversation, and clinical evidence of impaired hearing.[12]

Regardless of the cause of hearing loss, older adults have similar reactions to this impairment: anger, frustration, and withdrawal. Inability to participate effectively because of impaired hearing influences self-esteem. The sense of loss may be very keen when the impairment affects some ADLs. It is important for nurses and family members to understand the implications of a hearing impairment. Examples of the influence on ADLs include reluctance to participate in group activities, lack of response when spoken to, decrease in religious activities, increase in volume on radio or television, slow response to impending danger such as an approaching car, or noncompliance with a medication regimen. Early identification and rehabilitation may improve the client's self-perception and willingness to participate in family and other activities.

The use of a hearing aid facilitates communication, diminishes feelings of loneliness and social isolation, and returns a sense of control to the client. Some older adults may be helped by a hearing aid, and others may not. The person who demonstrates an improvement in speech discrimination with increased amplification is usually a good candidate for a hearing aid.[9]

Most older adults receive their information about the use and benefits of a hearing aid from television, newspaper, or radio advertisements; friends; or other members of the family.[10] However, the client should talk with an audiologist to learn more about hearing aids from a person who can provide detailed, accurate information. Different styles of hearing aids are available, and the style selected should depend on the person's ability to operate the device.[10] Consideration must be given to the client's dexterity (to control the volume) and to her or his vision (to see the controls). Current styles include in-the-ear, body-type, and postauricular aids. The in-the-ear aid has a small, raised volume control; the postauricular and body-type devices have larger volume controls that are easier to feel and adjust.[10] It is important to be guided by the client's specific needs and to explain options clearly so that the client can make an informed decision. The client and family may also need to consider the cost of the hearing aid; a short time is usually allowed to permit the client to adjust to the instrument selected and learn how to use it before making a final purchase.[10] Some problems may be associated with using a hearing aid. Because the instrument includes an amplifier, it amplifies background noise as well as the words spoken in a conversation; the background noise may be loud enough to cause a misinterpretation of words or to cause pain. Therefore, older adults may buy a hearing aid but use it little.

Adjusting to a deficit in hearing after a lifetime of normal hearing is difficult. The biopsychosocial wholeness of the person is threatened by this formidable change. The nurse's intervention should focus on facili-

TABLE 10–2 NURSING CARE PLAN

Nursing Diagnosis: Alteration in sensory/perceptual function: hearing	
Expected Outcomes	*Nursing Actions*
Patient is able to hear conversation.	Speak in a tone that does not include shouting (shouting increases the pitch of the voice).
	Face the patient when speaking.
	Speak slowly and distinctly.
	Use touch to get the patient's attention if standing behind him or her.
	Use simple sentences.
	Lower the pitch of the voice.
	Be aware of nonverbal communication (e.g., facial expression).

tating the client's movement toward optimum functioning in a fast-paced society. See Table 10–2 for a nursing care plan for an alteration in hearing.

Touch

Touch is defined by Weiss[13] as "any event of interbody contact, starting with its initiation by one individual and ending with cessation of contact with either person" (p. 82). Some nurses consider touch multidimensional, involving more than skin-to-skin contact.[14] Others describe it as a phenomenon that expresses pleasure, reassurance, and comfort.[15]

The daily activities of nurses in responding to older adults' needs provide the basis for touching. Society has given nurses permission to deviate from its norms and to touch others intimately while carrying out routine tasks in nursing care.[16] Nurses must recognize that touch involves the client's sensitivity to touch and is an effective means of communication. Different types of touch are associated with various meanings.

NEED FOR TOUCH

The need for affective touch continues throughout life and increases with age.[17] Many older people are more interested in touching and tactile sensations because (1) they have lost loved ones, (2) their appearance may not be as attractive as it once was and does not invite touching, and (3) the attitude of the public toward older adults does not encourage physical contact with them. Touch can be a means of providing sensory stimuli or relief from psychological and physical pain.[17] Cutaneous stimulation is thought to stimulate the production of endorphins, which cause a decrease in pain. For example, a slow-stroke back massage, a common procedure used in nursing, has not only physiological effects but also psychological effects.[17] The stroking stimulates circulation and promotes relaxation, and the desired effects may be achieved without having to use tranquilizers, sedatives, or pain medications. Some authors[16] point out that if a person is socially isolated, is lonely, or lacks self-esteem, he or she needs more touching.

There is a difference in touching by men and women. In some cultures, men may not have had as much freedom to touch. Women may have been given more opportunity to touch (with social approval) when providing health care. Touch is an effective tool to use with older clients, but the nurse must consider the client's wishes related to this type of intervention. The culturally related rules are important to know, and the nurse must be aware of who will permit touch, as well as where, when, and how. Some cultures use touch more in interactions than other cultures. For example, Eskimos, Hispanics, the French, and Jews often use touch in their contact with others. Other cultures also use touch, but perhaps in a less emphatic way. In some cultures, a handshake may be the recognized greeting of friendship; in others, an embrace may be the appropriate greeting. Both handshakes and embraces use touch and express caring or concern. The nurse must assess the client to determine whether touch is perceived as a positive therapeutic intervention.

Zones of intimacy or sensuality in human touch are the intimate zone (genitals), vulnerable zone (face, neck, and front of body), consent zone (mouth, wrist, feet), and social zone (hands, arms, shoulders, and back).[16] The nurse must be aware of these zones when entering the client's personal space to provide nursing care. In a study of the sensory qualities in tactile interaction, Weiss[16] identified 19 categories of touch on the body and 28 action categories (e.g., stroking, kissing, pinching, squeezing). "The meaning of touch varies among patients, and it may not always be positive."[13] It may be influenced by the context of the situation and the people in the interaction.[13]

The nurse's previous life experiences and values also influence his or her use of therapeutic touch. For example, some nurses may have had bad experiences with touch involving abuse or may have grown up in a family that did little touching. The touching style of the nurse is learned within his or her family and culture, in nursing school, and within the practice setting.[14] Therefore, in considering the client and the nurse, the rule should be to touch only if it is comfortable for both.

Another factor to be considered in providing touch is the intensity level of the contact, meaning the degree of pressure applied to the body surface: deep, strong, moderate, or light.[16] For example, deep pressure may be applied in a crisis situation to stop bleeding. Strong or moderate pressure may be used to restrain a person's arm, and light pressure may be used when the nurse places a hand on a client's shoulder to get the person's attention. All of these intensity levels have meaning for the provider and receiver of touch. The intensity may vary also because the sense of touch is decreased in an older person, and a firmer touch may be needed to elicit a response.[18]

When other senses become impaired, tactile stimulation becomes more important to older adults as a means of communication. Nurses must recognize this change and include it as part of the nursing care plan.

An important question that the nurse must ask as part of the assessment is whether the older person is being deprived of touch. Touch is the first sensory system to become functional. The skin is like a cloak that fits and envelops a person as he or she ages; then when the person reaches the seventh or eighth decade of life, the skin does not fit as well. It may sag and be noticeably looser in various parts of the body. However, throughout life, touch provides emotional and sensual knowledge about others.

Assessment, Defining Characteristics, and Interventions

The nursing assessment should include an observation of changes in the skin such as color, texture, dryness, scaliness, keratoses, turbidity, responses to cold and heat, responses to dullness and sharpness, and ability to handle familiar objects (e.g., coins or material). Turbidity may be checked by pinching the skin on the posterior aspect of the hand and observing the time of its return to its former state when released. Tactile response may be assessed by using a cotton ball and touching various spots on the arms, legs, and hands. The response to sharpness and dullness may be checked by touching the skin on the anterior forearm with the point of a needle and then with the head of the needle. The nurse should determine whether the client has lost significant others and friends because this may result in a decrease in touching received by the client. Again, the cultural background is important.

The defining characteristics related to tactile changes and stimulation may include a decreased sensitivity to touch, with a resultant change in response. The client may change his or her behavior and may even seek touch.

If deprived of touch, the older person may seek comfort through another means. In his initial studies of the human skin, Montague[19] noted that rocking is a means of stimulating the skin and that a person may receive comfort from this motion. Nurses should encourage the use of rocking chairs in long-term facilities as well as in other environments in which the client may use this simple activity to receive comfort.

For older persons who have other sensory impairments (e.g., vision and hearing), touch is particularly important. It is the means to maintain contact with the environment. For example, touching a stair rail or a piece of furniture may assist a client in remaining oriented and independent.

In Graves's research,[18] baby animals snuggle and cuddle against the body of their mother or sibling or any other introduced animal, which suggests that touch is important for physical and behavioral development. This supports Montague's findings[19] of the significance of touch and the human skin. Lack of physical contact may create a "skin hunger" or the need to be in contact with another.[15]

The nurse should be aware of cues that the client may be giving in response to touch.[14] For example, the client may draw away from a touch or move out of a close-contact situation or may frown in response to someone entering his or her personal space. The tenseness of the client's body may also be a sign that he or she does not want to be touched. Positive cues are evident when the client seeks touch through such means as hugging or shaking hands.

Taste

The emphasis on food is evident throughout life in our society. Food is needed not only for physical growth and development, but also for interaction with others that is pleasant and stimulating. A loss of food enjoyment as one ages may be perceived as loss of one of the major enjoyments in life.[20]

CHANGES IN AGING

As a person ages, "the total number of taste buds declines and the taste buds themselves deteriorate, which decreases taste sensitivity. Smoking, vitamin D deficiency, decreased saliva production, dentures, and certain medications also dull the sense of taste."[21] Taste buds regenerate throughout life, but older adults have a decreased sensitivity to sweet, sour, salty, and bitter tastes.[22] The changes are more noticeable for some than for others.

MANAGEMENT OF TASTE SENSORY CHANGES

Assessment, Defining Characteristics, and Interventions

The nursing diagnosis for impaired sensory response to taste is *sensory alteration: taste*. In the assessment of taste changes, the nurse should inspect the mouth and determine the color and moisture of the lips; the color, coating, and presence of any fissures of the tongue; presence and condition of the teeth or whether the dentures fit; condition of the gums (color, retraction, bleeding); amount of salivation; condition of the mucous membranes (color, moisture, any lesions); or malodor.[23] Taste sensitivity may be assessed by having the client taste liquids that have varying concentrations of sweetness, saltiness, sourness, and bitterness; these liquids might include sugar water, lemon juice, saline, and quinine. A cotton swab should be dipped into each solution, one at a time, and its tip rubbed on the lateral, anterior, and posterior areas of the client's tongue. The client should rinse his or her mouth with water after each taste test and wait 2 to 3 minutes between tests.

Studies[20] suggest that enjoyment of and preferences for different concentrations of stimuli change over the life span. This is particularly noticeable in older adults' preferences for higher concentrations of sugar, salt, or both in a variety of foods.

As people age, they tend to retain preferences for foods that they perceived as pleasant when young, even though taste acuity changes. Many older adults retain their taste for sweets, and they eat large amounts of carbohydrates because these foods taste good to them, are easy to chew, and may not be too expensive—a factor that may influence the amount of sweet cereals, potatoes, and bread consumed by older adults.

The nurse should also ask the client about any medications he or she is taking because of their possible influence on the appetite. The drug name, dosage, administration schedule, and length of time the client has been taking the drug are important in the case history.

The defining characteristics for the sensory alteration in taste may occur gradually. The client's family may observe that he or she likes to use a lot of sugar, salt, and spices. The client may complain about how food tastes and a lack of appetite, with a decrease in the desire for food. The nurse should encourage the family to use foods of different texture and different colors in an effort to make the meal more enticing for the client.[22] For example, if carrots, green beans, broccoli, and a meat were used to provide a pleasant color base to the food, the client may respond in a positive manner. Herbs are also used to enhance the flavor of food.

The taste buds are located primarily in the papillae of the tongue, and people who have a coated tongue or poor oral hygiene associated with dental problems may have a bad mouth odor that may affect taste. The malodor may be the cause of a poor appetite because of the close relationship between the olfactory and taste sensations. In a study at Duke University,[23] researchers supported the connection between a decrease in taste acuity and smell and anorexia in older adults, even in the absence of contributing disease and environmental factors.

When food tastes are related to happy events such as a holiday, the tastes are enhanced. Observation of older people in an institutional dining room as well as in a home setting shows that people have better eating behaviors if the meal is a pleasant occasion. In addition, most older people like to have a designated place to sit during a meal. The sensory pleasure of food, a nurturing environment, and a feeling that one has enough food are important factors in helping the older person feel secure. Furthermore, if older people have good memories of mealtime as being a time of communication and pleasant exchange rather than one of conflict, the food may be remembered as always tasting good. Other aspects of a food are equally as important as its taste. It is important not to provide the older person with only bland, spiceless, soft foods. Nurses should teach members of the family that older adults like a variety of familiar foods with enough taste and chewing requirements to make eating pleasant. Older people should be encouraged to chew their food thoroughly and to switch from one food to another when eating. For example, a client who has meat, broccoli, and corn as a meal should be encouraged to eat some meat, then some broccoli, and then some corn and to rotate the foods eaten so that he or she will not adapt to the taste of each food, with a decline in its taste sensation.

Another important fact that the nurse must consider when assessing the client's taste perception is what medications he or she takes. The most common cause of taste loss is drug therapy, and polypharmacy is common among older adults. Some medications (e.g., antirheumatic and antihypertensive drugs) depress the appetite. The nurse should work in collaboration with the physician by sharing information to determine whether the type or dosage of a medication may be changed. In addition, the nurse should review the schedule for administering the medications with the family and make any needed changes. If a medication must be taken with a meal, the nurse should determine whether there is a way to disguise the taste of a drug if the client complains that the medicine leaves a bad taste in his or her mouth. The client may rinse his or her mouth with water to remove the bad taste.

Threshold sensitivity for taste decreases with age, but with consideration given to such things as a pleasant environment and texture, color, variety, and seasoning of food, an older person may continue to enjoy meals.

Smell

The sense of smell is brought about through stimulation of olfactory receptors by volatile chemical substances. The smell enters the nasal cavity and travels up to the cilia of millions of microscopic olfactory nerve cells, and from these cells, the stimulus is transmitted to the olfactory cortex in the brain.[24] The olfactory and gustatory senses are closely related, and the loss of the olfactory sense has a profound effect on perceptions of taste. The loss of the ability to smell is known as anosmia.

CHANGES IN AGING

The sharpest decline in the sense of smell occurs during middle age, and for some people, it continues to diminish. The rate of decline varies. People respond to odors differently, and a person's response may be influenced by age, gender, ethnicity, and previous experience with that odor.

Olfactory nerves are complex, not completely understood, and thought to be capable of regenerating.[25] The sense of smell is not seriously affected by age alone but probably by other factors associated with age. Other causes also cited as contributors to a diminished sense of smell include colds, influenza, smoking, nasal obstruction, nasal discharges, chronic sinusitis, odor habituation, epistaxis, allergies, aging, and environmental factors.

MANAGEMENT OF SMELL SENSORY CHANGES

Assessment, Defining Characteristics, and Interventions

In assessment of the client, the nurse should inspect the nose carefully for septal deviation or nasal obstruction. An otoscope is used to examine the nasal cavity. The mucous membranes are examined to determine whether they are moist or if there is evidence of irritation. The client is asked to occlude each nostril (one at a time), close his or her mouth, and breathe through the unoccluded nostril to determine patency of the nostrils.[25] To assess the acuity of smell, the client is asked to close his or her eyes and identify odors of various substances (e.g., cinnamon, vinegar, coffee). Older people have more difficulty identifying odors than younger people.[20] The sinuses should be palpated to determine whether there is any pain or swelling.

The nurse should ask questions about a history of upper respiratory infections (including sinuses), allergies, smoking habits, current and past medications, epistaxis, and accidents that resulted in a head injury.

The defining characteristics may be gradual if the changes are related to aging, but sudden if related to a head injury. The client may complain of an inability to smell good odors, such as favorite foods cooking (e.g., apple pie, cinnamon cookies, barbecue). In addition, the anosmia may have had a negative effect on the client's appetite, and he or she may show little interest in eating.

The client may have an unpleasant body odor, which may result in social isolation. Family members should be encouraged to remind the client of the necessity of personal hygiene. The client may notice a diminished response to odors such as gas or spoiled food. This deficit has inherent dangers, and arrangements should be made to avoid possible consequences. Family or friends should be asked to check the client's residence for gas leaks regularly. Food should be dated so that the client will know when it should be discarded.

Alterations in the sense of smell can have a profound effect on perceptions of some of the joys in living. Impaired odor perceptions affect the quality of life by diminishing smell as a warning signal for danger and by reducing enjoyment of positive things such as smelling food cooking, roses in bloom, good perfume, or new-mown hay.[20] See Table 10–3 for a teaching guide covering interventions for alterations in smell.

Summary

This chapter has focused on normal sensory changes in vision, hearing, touch, taste, and smell in older adults. The biological changes associated with aging in each of these areas have been identified. Some pathophysiological problems were also discussed. Even though these changes require adaptation in ADLs, the emphasis is on what the client, family, and nurse can do to make the sensory alterations less stressful. The biological alterations have implications for psychosocial interactions in daily living. When older adults do not see or hear as well, have a decreased tactile response, or have a loss of taste and smell sensitivity, their inability to interact with others, to enjoy the foods eaten, to recognize the beauty of colors and sounds, and to respond to some dangers affects the quality of life.

Student Learning Activities

1 Review local newspapers and the lay literature for advertisements targeted to older adults with sensory loss, such as hearing loss or visual decline. What message do these advertisements present?

2 Collect information to be shared with the class regarding the types of hearing aids available and the cost of the assistive device. How is funding for the aids addressed? Are resources available in the community through charity or religious groups to assist those with financial need?

3 Visit a local outpatient surgery clinic that specializes in cataract removal. What special services are offered to older adults who are having this surgery?

REFERENCES

1 Hunt, L: Aging and the visual system. Insight 18:3, 1993.
2 Koretz, JF: Accommodation and presbyopia. In Albert, DM, and Jakobiec, FA (eds): Principles and Practice of Ophthalmology: Basic Sciences. WB Saunders, Philadelphia, 1994, pp 270–282.
3 Oates, DC, and Belcher, D: Aging changes in trabecular meshwork, iris, and ciliary body. In Albert, DM, and Jakobiec, FA (eds): Principles and Practice of Ophthalmology: Basic Sciences. WB Saunders, Philadelphia, 1994, pp 697–701.
4 Chylack, LT: Aging changes in the crystalline lens and zonules. In Albert, DM, and Jakobiec, FA (eds): Principles and Practice of Ophthalmology: Basic Sciences. WB Saunders, Philadelphia, 1994, pp 702–710.
5 Cotlier, E: The lens. In Moses, RA, and Hart, WM (eds): Adler's Physiology of the Eye: Clinical Application, ed 8. CV Mosby, St Louis, 1987, pp 268–290.
6 Kanski, JJ, and McAllister, JA: Glaucoma: A Colour Manual of Diagnosis and Treatment. Butterworths, London, 1989.
7 Kratz, RP, and Shammas, HJ: Color Atlas of Ophthalmic Surgery. JB Lippincott, Philadelphia, 1991.
8 Palumbo, M: Hearing access 2000: Increasing awareness of the hearing impaired. J Gerontol Nurs 16:26, 1990.
9 Mhoon, E: Otology. In Cassel, C, et al (eds): Geriatric Medicine, ed 2. Springer-Verlag, New York, 1990, pp 405–419.
10 Bess, FH, et al: Audiologic assessment of the elderly. In Rintelman, WF (ed): Hearing Assessment, ed 2. Pro-ed, Austin, Texas, 1991.
11 Christian, E, et al: Sounds of silence: Coping with hearing loss. J Gerontol Nurs 15:4, 1989.
12 Newman, D: Assessment of hearing loss in elderly people: The feasibility of a nurse-administered screening test. J Adv Nurs 15:400, 1990.
13 Weiss, S: Touch. Annu Rev Nurs Res 6:3, 1988.
14 Estabrooks, CA, and Morse, JM: Toward a theory of touch: The touching process and acquiring a touching style. J Adv Nurs 17:448, 1992.

TABLE 10–3   TEACHING GUIDE: INTERVENTIONS FOR ALTERATION IN SMELL

Instruct the patient or family to:
- Smell food before eating it and try to recall how it smelled. This may facilitate being able to smell a particular odor.
- Make meals enticing through color, texture, and variety.
- Emphasize personal hygiene in planning activities.
- Encourage the client to recall earlier pleasant smells that he or she enjoyed.
- Check for gas leaks at the client's residence regularly.
- Date foods and discard them by a designated date.

15 Vortherms, RC: Clinically improving communication through touch. J Gerontol Nurs 17:6, 1991.

16 Weiss, S: Measurement of the sensory qualities in tactile interaction. Nurs Res 41:82, 1992.

17 Fakouri, C, and Jones, P: Relaxation Rx: Slow stroke back rub. J Gerontol Nurs 13:32, 1989.

18 Graves, M: Physiological change and major diseases in the elderly. In Hogstel, M (ed): Nursing Care of the Older Adult. Wiley, New York, 1981.

19 Montague, A: Touching: Human Significance of the Skin. Columbia University Press, New York, 1971.

20 Murphy, C, and Davidson, T: Geriatric issues: Special considerations. J Head Trauma Rehab 7:76, 1992.

21 Newman, D, and Smith, D: Geriatric Care Plans. Springhouse Corp, Springhouse, Penn, 1991.

22 Blair, K: Aging: Physiological aspects and clinical implications. Nurse Pract 15:14, 1990.

23 Schiffman, SS: Taste and smell in disease. N Engl J Med 308:1275 1983.

24 Smith, D, and Shipley, M: Anatomy and physiology of taste and smell. J Head Trauma Rehab 7:1, 1992.

25 Knapp, M: A rose is still a rose. Geriatr Nurs 10:290, 1989.

CHAPTER 11

The Aging Integumentary System

Laurel A. Wiersema / Mickey Stanley

OBJECTIVES

Upon completion of this chapter, the reader will be able to:

- Describe the physiological changes of the skin with aging
- Recognize the impact of photoaging on the skin
- Describe lesions of the skin resulting from actinic exposure
- List two risks to the skin from trauma
- Describe two reasons for delayed wound healing in older adults
- Describe the process of skin assessment and demonstrate appropriate documentation
- Develop a care plan for maintenance of skin integrity

The skin is the largest organ of the body, representing approximately 16 percent of an adult's body weight. It is the only organ that can be touched, stroked, massaged, stretched, and sniffed. The skin is flexible and forgiving of distortion encountered through daily living. Without this flexibility, a simple handshake would result in the sloughing of skin from pressure and stretch. Because the skin is highly visible, it serves as a window to a person's own mortality. Although it is true that no one dies of old skin or carries skin failure as a diagnosis, understanding the physiological changes evident in the skin with increasing age provides the nurse with a plethora of information about the older client.

Architecturally, the skin is a complex organ consisting of the epidermis, dermis, and subcutis. Typically associated with aging are the visible changes in the skin such as atrophy, wrinkling, and sagging, These visible changes are highly variable, however, principally because of the relationship between intrinsic (natural) aging and extrinsic (environmental) aging.

Functionally, the skin is versatile, and its presence is critical for overall survival. Because it is capable of sensation, the skin protects the body from environmental assault and injury. An intact skin further protects the individual immunologically by preventing the entrance of bacteria into the body. The skin plays a principal role in thermoregulation and adaptation to the environment. It acts as an organ of excretion, secretion, absorption, and accumulation. Finally, the skin represents the individual's first contact with others socially and sexually. How we look to ourselves tends to determine how we feel about ourselves and is an essential component of our self-esteem and self-concept.

Normal Aging

STRATUM CORNEUM

The outermost layer of the epidermis, the stratum corneum, is composed principally of heaped-up corneocytes. With increasing age, the overall number of cells and cell layers remains essentially unchanged, but cellular cohesion is reduced. Renewal time of the cell layer is slower, resulting in a longer healing time. Decreased cell cohesiveness in conjunction with this decrease in cell replacement places the older adult at risk. The moisture content of the stratum corneum is diminished, but the water barrier status appears to be maintained, resulting in the appearance of rough, dry skin.[1] The roughness causes uneven light scatter, which causes skin to loose the glow often associated with youth and good health.

EPIDERMIS

The epidermis changes very little in thickness as people age. However, there is slower cell renewal, fewer basal cells, and a decrease in the number and depth of

TABLE 11–1   CHANGES IN THE EPIDERMIS

Changes	Clinical Consequence
Cellular replacement time increased	Delayed wound healing
Decreased melanocytes	Less protection from ultraviolet light
Decreased Langerhans's cells	Diminished response to skin testing
Flattened rete ridges	Easy separation, skin tears
Disarray of keratinocyte nuclei	Tendency toward abnormal growths such as seborrheic keratosis and skin tags

TABLE 11–2   CHANGES IN THE DERMIS

Change	Clinical Consequence
Decreased elasticity	Increased strength; less "give" under stress
Collagen less organized	Laxity; loss of turgor
Diminished vascularity	Pallor; loss of thermoregulation
Decreased cellular elements: macrophages, fibroblasts, mast cells	Poor immune response

the rete ridges. The rete ridges are formed by the epidermal protrusions from the basal layer that point downward into the dermis. The flattening of the rete ridges reduces the area of contact between the epidermis and the dermis, causing easy separation of these skin layers.[2] The resultant skin tears are slow to heal and predispose the individual to infection. Skin may blister with the use of tape or other substances that create friction. It is important to use an adhesive that is no stronger than the epidermal-dermal junction itself to prevent or minimize tape-induced injury.

The melanocytes show some decline in number with aging, and the remaining cells may not function normally. The hair may turn gray, the skin may become unevenly pigmented, and pigment protection from ultraviolet (UV) light may decrease.[3,4]

A decrease in immune competence is the result of the overall decline in the number of Langerhans' cells as people age. As their immunity is reduced, older adults' response to skin testing with presumed allergens diminishes, often exhibiting delayed skin test reactions.[5] The reaction may also be subtle, requiring astute assessment.

Architectural disarray of the keratinocyte nuclei can also be seen in older skin. This disorder may reflect an altered rate of cell proliferation and may contribute to excessive cellular growth, which may explain the tendency of older adults to develop neoplasias and cutaneous growths such as seborrheic keratosis and skin tags (Table 11–1).[6]

DERMIS

As an individual ages, dermal bulk decreases, the dermis thins, and the number of cells generally decreases. The physiological consequences of these changes include delayed or suppressed presentation of cutaneous diseases, delayed wound closure and healing, decreased thermoregulation, decreased inflammatory response, and decreased cutaneous absorption of topical agents (Table 11–2).

Degenerative changes in elastic tissue begin at about 30 years of age. Elastic fibers and collagenous tissue are gradually dissolved by enzymes, resulting in the visual changes of sagging and wrinkling. As elasticity decreases, the dermis increases in tensile strength; the result is less "give" when the skin is subjected to stress.

Collagen organization becomes haphazard, and the skin loses its turgor.[7]

Vascularity also decreases, with fewer small vessels present in the usually highly vascular dermis. The dermis contains fewer fibroblasts, macrophages, and mast cells. Visually, the skin may appear pale and may be less capable of thermoregulation. Older adults are therefore at increased risk of hyperthermia or hypothermia.

SUBCUTIS

In general, the subcutaneous tissue layer thins with increasing age. This contributes further to laxity of the skin and the appearance of sagging skin draped over the bony skeleton. The decreased fat layer is especially noticeable on the face, hands, feet, and shins, where veins become more visible and pronounced and the tissue becomes more prone to trauma. Fat deposits tend to increase in the abdomen of both men and women, as well as in the thighs of women. The redistribution and decrease in body fat further compromise the protective insulating function of the skin (Table 11–3).[8]

APPENDAGES

Skin appendages include hair, nails, pacinian corpuscles, Meissner's corpuscles, sweat glands, and sebaceous glands.[9] Each of these is discussed in brief here and summarized in Table 11–4.

The hair in the aging individual usually becomes increasingly more gray, with thinning of scalp hair caused by the decreased number of hair follicles. Compounding the issue is the increased number of hair follicles in the resting phase of the growth cycle. Women tend to have an increase in facial hair, especially above the upper lip and on the chin. In men, hair in the ears and nose becomes more prominent and bristly.

TABLE 11–3   CHANGES IN THE SUBCUTIS

Changes	Clinical Consequence
Resorption of body fat	Increased risk of hypothermia
Redistribution of body fat from extremities to abdomen	Increased risk of injury; altered body image

TABLE 11–4 CHANGES IN THE APPENDAGES

Change	Clinical Consequence
Loss of melanocytes	Graying hair
Loss of hair follicles	Thinning of scalp hair
Changes in hair type and distribution	*Men:* Decreased facial hair but increased hair in ears and nose
	Women: Increased facial hair above upper lip and on chin
Nail growth diminishes	Soft, fragile, lusterless nails
Meissner's corpuscles decrease	Decreased sense of touch
Pacinian corpuscles decrease	Decreased sense of pressure
Decrease in sweat glands	Dry skin, decreased thermoregulation
Decrease in apocrine glands	Decreased body odor

Nail growth diminishes with increased age, and the nails become soft, fragile, lusterless, and readily damaged. Longitudinal striations and ridging may occur.

Meissner's and pacinian corpuscles decrease by roughly two-thirds from age 30 to age 90,[9] causing a diminished sense of touch (Meissner's) and sense of pressure (pacinian). The older adult performing routine tasks is at risk for being burned and at increased risk for experiencing pressure necrosis as his or her perceived need to change position diminishes.

Fewer sweat glands coupled with decreased functional ability in the remaining glands cause older adults to have a decreased sweating response. There is also a tendency toward dry skin and altered thermoregulation. Fewer apocrine glands in the axillae and groin result in decreased body odor in older adults.

Sebaceous glands get larger as pore size increases with age. However, there is a 40 to 50 percent decrease in sebum production, resulting in dry skin.[10]

Normal integumentary system aging changes are summarized in Table 11–5.

TABLE 11–5 NORMAL INTEGUMENTARY SYSTEM AGING CHANGES

Normal Age-Related Changes	Clinical Implications
Renewal time for epidermal cells slowed	Easily torn and blistered skin
Decreased areas of contact between epidermis and dermis	Slow wound healing
Thinning of dermal layer	Poor wound closure and healing
Decreased vascularity	Reduced thermoregulation
	Decreased absorption of topical agents
Decreased number of Meissner's and pacinian corpuscles	Decreased sense of touch and pressure with increased risk of injury
Decline in number and functional ability of sweat glands	Decreased thermoregulation

Pathophysiology of Common Disorders

SKIN DAMAGE RELATED TO PHOTOAGING

Changes in the skin related to photoaging are most evident in regions of the skin exposed to the UV rays of the sun. Photoaging, or dermatoheliosis, is a condition of the skin resulting from UV damage. The face, neck, arms, and hands show these changes the most. These extrinsic changes in the skin are superimposed on the intrinsic changes, eventually masking the intrinsic changes completely.

Early changes are the result of chronic inflammation, known as elastosis.[1] Elastic fibers are gradually degraded, becoming thickened and tangled and rendering the skin lax and wrinkled. As the chronic inflammation continues and early changes give way to later changes, the skin is found to have absent inflammatory changes and quiescent fibroblasts. The overall amount of mature collagen decreases and small vessels begin to dilate, resulting in visible telangiectasia. In heavily sun-exposed body regions, especially the face, the sebaceous glands enlarge as pore size increases.[1]

Further late changes secondary to photoaging include a decreased protective response of the skin to the sun as melanin distribution lessens and becomes irregular. Thus, older adults are at increased risk for sun exposure skin damage.

Lesions typical of sun-exposed skin include seborrheic and actinic keratoses, solar lentigines, keratoacanthomas, basal cell epitheliomas, and squamous cell carcinomas.

SKIN DAMAGE RELATED TO PRESSURE

Older adults at high risk of pressure ulceration because of altered nutrition, altered protective pressure sensation, presence of chronic illness, self-care deficits, inadequate support at home, incontinence, mobility deficits, and altered levels of consciousness. In 1992, the first edition of *Pressure Ulcers in Adults: Prediction and Prevention* was published by the Agency for Health Care Policy and Research. This guideline is most beneficial in establishing a comprehensive program to identify at-risk individuals and early strategies for prevention and maintenance of skin integrity. Not all pressure ulcers can be prevented, but with consistent care and attention, many can be prevented or made less severe.

Pressure ulcers occur primarily over bony prominences but may occur in other areas where tissue is compressed. Tube sites, areas under restraints, and soft tissue areas under pressure from a splint or traction apparatus are a few examples of nonbony locations predisposed to pressure necrosis. Any tissue may ulcerate if exposed to external pressures greater than capillary closing pressures for a length of time. The degree of ulceration depends on many factors, both intrinsic and extrinsic. As pressure continues without interruption, the tissues become starved for oxygen and nutrients necessary for cell

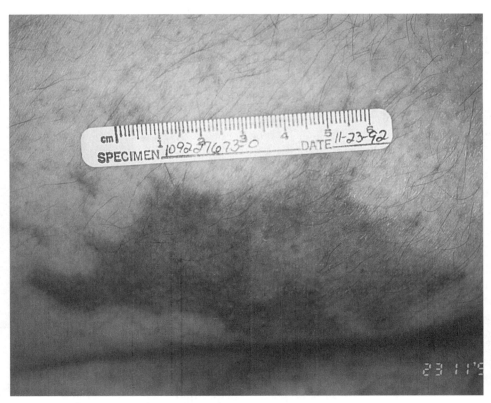

Figure 11–1 Stage 1 pressure ulcer.

metabolism and the cells become hypoxic and swollen. If pressure is relieved at this point, the tissue will become flooded with blood as the capillaries dilate and the area will redden, known clinically as regional hyperemia. The period of hyperemia will last approximately half as long as the period of hypoxia. At this point, the area under stress can completely reverse as risk factors are identified and eliminated and preventive measures are instituted. If the problem is not recognized at this point, however, pressure will not be relieved and the cellular edema will progress to small-vessel thrombosis, further compromising oxygen supply, and the tissues will begin to ulcerate.

A stage 1 lesion is seen as a red, firm area that does not blanch to light palpation, which indicates deeper tissue damage. However, with preventive strategies, a stage 1 lesion will not ulcerate or open to deeper tissue layers (Fig. 11–1). In a stage 2 lesion, the epidermis has sloughed, revealing the highly vascular dermis. When sensation is intact, the stage 2 lesion is quite painful (Fig. 11–2). As tissue layers necrose, the subcutis may become involved, leading to a stage 3 pressure ulcer. These ulcers may quickly undermine at the edges as the subcutaneous tissue layer necroses more rapidly than the highly vascular dermis (Fig. 11–3). Once the underlying muscle and bone become involved, the pressure ulcer is at stage 4. These stage 4 ulcers may result in local bone infection and are difficult and time-consuming to heal without surgical intervention (Fig. 11–4).

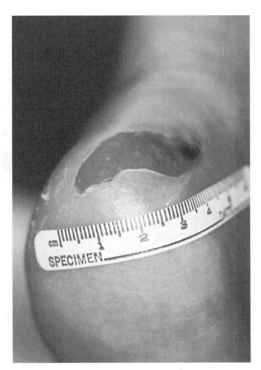

Figure 11–2 Stage 2 pressure ulcer.

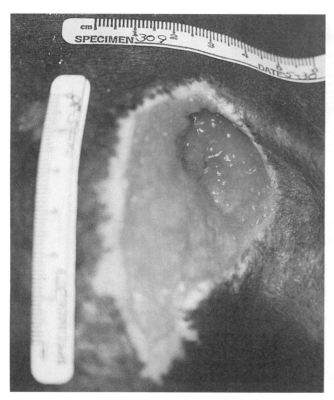

Figure 11–3 Stage 3 pressure ulcer.

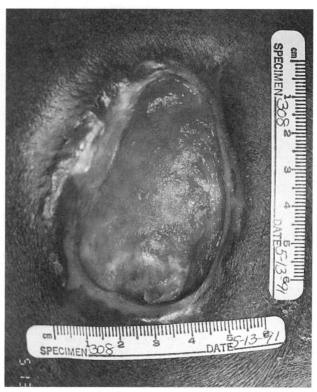

Figure 11–4 Stage 4 pressure ulcer.

Clinical Manifestations

ALTERED CELLULAR PROLIFERATION AND REPAIR

As the epidermal repacement time increases and cells are replaced more slowly, wound healing becomes prolonged and susceptibility to cutaneous trauma increases.[11] Delayed wound closure can lead to an increased risk of secondary infection because of the break in skin integrity. Secondary infection is often a result of staphylococcal or streptococcal growth from contamination of the wound with normal skin flora.

As the skin thins and loses elasticity, it becomes a target for trauma. A simple bump on the skin from the coffee table may become an ulcerated lesion taking weeks or months to heal. A small adhesive dressing covering a venipuncture site in the hospital may result in loss of an area of epidermis even greater than that of the original dressing if it sticks more strongly to the epidermis than the epidermis clings to the dermis. Clinically, the skin stretches easily under little pressure but then wrinkles and sags rather than rebounding from the stretch. This further predisposes the individual to trauma. Older adults are more susceptible to pressure-induced ulceration of the skin and deeper structures because of their diminished muscle and fat, as well as their lessened sensitivity to pressure and pain. Changes in tissue tolerance for distortion from stretch and pressure occur with increasing age as a result of diminished nutritional reserves, circulation, and sensory acuity.

Braden and Bergstrom[12] describe a conceptual schema for depicting interrelated factors of nutrition, moisture, sensory perception, activity, mobility, and friction-shear in the development of pressure sores. As nutritional reserves are depleted, less nutrition is available for times of stress. Fluid status declines, and skeletal muscle mass decreases. Tissue loses its structural integrity, and when trauma occurs, the damage is slow to repair. Peripheral circulation decreases, and the central pump may not have sufficient reserve to handle stress and an increased peripheral demand. The decrease in peripheral circulation and loss of subcutaneous fat reduce the individual's protection from heat and cold. Older adults have less insulation and a diminished capillary bed to facilitate cooling through vasodilation. The hyperemic response to local pressure may be delayed or nonexistent, resulting in prolonged tissue ischemia and consequent ulceration. A greater incidence of dependent edema is found in older people, causing the legs to feel heavy, ache, and ulcerate. The thin skin appears pale and fragile, bruising easily as a result of often unknown trauma.

The older person is less well protected from UV light as the presence and distribution of melanin pigmentation decrease. This predisposes the older person to both benign and malignant skin changes.[13,14]

The decline in cellular proliferation and longer turnover time results in a prolonged effect of local skin irritants such as liquid detergents and topical agents. The response to the irritant may be delayed, making it more difficult to isolate the offending agent. Therapy focuses on identifying the offending agent, removing it, and instituting treatment. However, absorption of topical agents for treatment is slowed, causing a sluggish response. Continuous monitoring is needed to accommodate the delay in absorption and response, as well as the delay in clearance, combining to prolong the topical effect. Transdermal delivery mechanisms for medication such as nitroglycerin must be monitored closely for dosage and intended systemic effect.

DIMINISHED IMMUNE COMPETENCE

Immune competence changes reflect changes in cellular immunity, as T and B cells diminish in function and number. Older adults show a reduced or muted inflammatory response. Fenske and Lober[15] reported that skin patch test sites should be monitored 3 weeks after application of a suspected irritant. The propensity for the older person to develop skin cancers is also a result of a compromised immune function. An increased susceptibility for cutaneous viral and fungal infections is another consequence of older adults' diminished immune competence. Fungal infections may spread rapidly, often caused by incontinence, and may be difficult to treat. Because of the rapid spread of cutaneous fungal infections, diagnosis and treatment must be rapid to avoid systemic consequences.

Management

1 Primary Prevention

Interpersonal Hazards

One of the more immediate, although not necessarily obvious, risks to the skin is dryness. As their skin becomes increasingly dry with a decrease in its normal lubricants, older adults experience more localized or generalized itching (pruritus). This may occur naturally or be exaggerated by frequent bathing or the use of strong detergents or deodorants. Should the pruritus become problematic and lead to skin ulceration from scratching, the ulcerations will be slow to heal and present an infection hazard. Conditions associated with pruritus in older adults include chronic renal failure, drug ingestion, extrahepatic biliary obstruction, hepatitis, polycythemia vera, Hodgkin's disease, other lymphomas and leukemias, multiple myeloma, iron-deficiency anemia, hyperthyroidism, diabetes mellitus, visceral malignancies, opiate ingestion, and psychosis.[16] Older adults must be encouraged to keep their fingernails trimmed and to avoid daily bathing. Use of mild soaps might reduce the drying effect. All people at risk for skin breakdown should have a systematic skin inspection at least daily.[17] Skin should be cleansed at the time of soiling and at routine intervals. Topical agents that act as barriers to moisture or those containing silicones and mucopolysaccharides to decrease friction may be beneficial.[18] Table 11–6 outlines the areas to emphasize with older adults to promote a healthy integument.

The client should be encouraged to remain as active as possible with the inclusion of rest periods to avoid

TABLE 11–6 TEACHING GUIDE: ESSENTIALS FOR PATIENT AND FAMILY EDUCATION

Avoid overexposure to the sun by applying sunscreen, wearing clothing with long sleeves, and wearing a wide-brimmed hat. Consider staying indoors during peak sun times of the day.
Avoid excessive bathing.
Avoid applying drying agents such as alcohol and deodorant soap to the skin.
Inspect the skin and its appendages every month.
Report any change in a mole or any change in size, shape, or color of an existing lesion.
Report any lesion that fails to heal.
Avoid use of over-the-counter preparations to treat corns, calluses, or ingrown toenails.
Cut nails straight across and even with the tops of the fingers and toes.

overtiring. When sitting, it is helpful for the client to elevate the legs at the level of the hip to promote the removal of edema from the legs. He or she should identify potential causes of trauma, such as sharp edges in the home. This potential hazard can be diminished if older adults wear protective long skirts or pants.

Decreased sensory perception places the older person at further risk for pressure sores and burns. Prevention may include encouraging the client to inspect the feet each day for 1 month after purchasing a new pair of shoes or establishing a habit of changing position slightly at each commercial break when watching television. Specialty mattresses, beds, and chair cushions may be used to decrease the external pressure load on the skin that comes in contact with a bed or chair.[19] Working around a hot stove presents special hazards that require teaching and may necessitate an occupational therapy consultation. Older adults must be taught to avoid reaching across a hot burner and to use hot pads and handle protectors. The use of an iron with an automatic shutoff feature is an excellent method of preventing injury. The home's water temperature should be adjusted at the water heater to prevent burning when showering or bathing. It takes only seconds to burn an older adult's skin when the temperature of the water heater is hot enough for running a dishwasher.

Environmental Hazards

As the skin becomes drier with age, low humidity predisposes older adults to the pruritus that results from dry skin. A humidity level of approximately 40 percent is considered the lowest humidity level well tolerated by the skin. The client's home can be humidified with a furnace attachment or a separate humidifier. Institutions usually have the capability to adjust humidity, although the typical institutional environment feels dry. The effects of low humidity can also be handled by maintaining an adequate fluid intake (which may be more effective than lotions), decreasing the frequency of bathing, and using topical lotions to prevent fluid loss.

An often undetected hazard to older adults is the change in environment that occurs with travel, hospitalization, or a residential move. The client should be encouraged to learn the furniture layout of a new environment, and once learned, the furniture should not be moved. It does little good to learn an obstacle course if the obstacles are constantly moving. The path to the bathroom and other vital areas of the dwelling should be identified and kept free of clutter and furniture to prevent or minimize trauma.

2 Secondary Prevention

Assessment

Important information from the health history includes history of trauma, history of skin allergies, any past problems with healing, and any current skin complaint such as wounds, ulcers, rashes, or abrasions. Older adults require a systematic skin inspection at least once a day, giving special emphasis to the bony prominences and, if incontinent, the perineum. A validated risk assessment tool should be used with anyone who presents with a mobility deficit.[19]

Skin is inspected for color, moisture, and turgor. Good lighting should be used when inspecting the color and pigment distribution of the skin. If open lesions are observed, clean disposable gloves will be needed. Skin lesions should be evaluated for size, depth, color, odor, and drainage consistency. The nurse should be aware of skin odors, usually noted in the skinfolds. Usually, skin color is uniform over the body. Hydration is reflected in the skin turgor and the moistness of the mucous membranes. Decreased perspiration and increased dryness are normal findings in older adults.[17]

Skin temperature reflects the amount of blood circulating through the dermis. There is a wide range of cool to warm skin temperatures. Any area of concentrated temperature change such as coldness of the fingers or toes from diminished blood flow or a reddened warm area over a bony prominence should be noted. Erythema and warmth should be expected over a bony prominence if pressure has recently been relieved. The absence of erythema over an area that has recently been subjected to pressure should be noted because this may provide a clue to the client who is unable to develop the hyperemic response to pressure and may therefore be at greater risk for skin breakdown. Skin temperature can be assessed using the dorsum of the nurse's hand, cutaneous temperature probes, or other research tools.

Skin texture should be assessed through palpation. Skin may feel rough and dry in exposed areas such as on the palms and soles of the feet. Skin may be flaking in areas and may appear leathery. Turgor may be assessed by lightly pinching and then releasing the skin on the client's forehead or sternum, although this method is unreliable.

During inspection and palpation, the skin may generally be free of odor; however, difficult-to-reach areas may have an odor if they are not cleaned. Lesions should be inspected, palpated, and measured. The lesion's two greatest perpendicular diameters and its depth should be measured, and the amount of undermining at the edge should be estimated. Erythema at the wound edge should also be assessed. It may also be useful to sketch the dimensions of the wound edge on a piece of paper to document its size and shape for reference over time.

Nursing Care

Nursing care is directed toward maintaining and restoring normal skin integrity (Table 11–7). The client's personal hygiene needs and his or her ability to meet these hygiene needs should be determined. If the client is at risk for skin breakdown, prevention strategies to maintain skin integrity should be planned. If skin breakdown exists, the nurse should plan to prevent further breakdown, prevent infection in the ulcerated area, control odor from necrotic lesions, and promote an environment supportive of wound healing.

Wound management must include consideration of systemic support for healing through adequate nutrition, hydration, and tissue perfusion, in addition to optimizing local care. An older adult who is losing weight, is unable to eat, or cannot buy food and prepare meals is at high risk for poor wound healing and wound infection. Homebound people should have a dietary consultation or find help through community resources. Wounds usually do not heal well in the absence of available protein, but even more at risk is the individual's available protein stores in the form of skeletal muscle, which will be catabolized in an effort to heal the wound.

A classic reason for poor wound healing is lack of blood flow to the site secondary to anemia, edema, or ischemia from vascular insufficiency or pressure. Anemia causes red blood cells to have a lower oxygen-carrying capacity. Edema further complicates the picture by increasing the distance for transport of oxygen and cellular wastes to and from the cells. A typical condition in which edema interferes with cellular activity is

TABLE 11–7 NURSING CARE PLAN

Nursing Diagnosis: High risk for impaired skin integrity related to immobility	
Expected Outcomes	*Nursing Actions*
Skin is intact, well-hydrated.	Bathe client every other day.
	Perform perineal care after each void.
	Use low-alcohol skin lotion to dry areas twice daily and as needed.
	Assess skin each shift for redness.
	Evaluate risk assessment every week.
	Establish turning and positioning schedule.
	Evaluate need for pressure-relief bed or mattress.
	Evaluate need for chair cushion.
	Evaluate need for additional consults (e.g., physical therapy, occupational therapy, dietary department).
	Offer fluids between meals.

chronic lower leg edema. Examination of the edematous lower legs will reveal shiny, thin, frail skin easily torn with trauma, and often blistering and ulcerating simply as a result of the edema. In this situation, adequacy of arterial blood flow must first be established, then efforts should be directed toward removal of the excess fluid. Impaired arterial flow causes hair loss on the lower anterior leg and shiny skin. Arterial impairment is distinguished from venous pathology by the pain and pallor associated with leg elevation.

Edema from venous insufficiency may be controlled by use of compression stockings (usually to the knee is adequate), Ace wraps, leg elevation, and compression pumps. Compression stockings may be difficult for the older adults to put on but are available with zippers and other adaptive devices. The client's fragile skin may be further at risk for trauma from the compression garment. A linear stocking may be used or a silicone-based lotion applied before donning the compression garment. Approximately every 2 to 3 hours the legs should be elevated above the level of the hip. Sitting or standing with the legs dependent should be avoided. Compression pumps may be useful; however, the client should be warned not to use the pump overnight to minimize the risk of congestive heart failure as fluid is forced into the vascular system. Compression pumps are typically ordered for intractable edema and should be used for 2 hours two or three times a day. It is sometimes necessary to supplement compression pump use with a diuretic; however, diuretics alone are not recommended for lower leg edema. Exercise (e.g., walking or biking) also is helpful in minimizing lower leg edema.

Ischemia, or lack of blood flow, is a critical factor in wound development and wound healing. Peripheral ischemia should be evaluated medically to determine correctable problems. With the pressure sore–prone client, it becomes the nurse's responsibility to explore alternatives for relieving pressure. Methods for pressure relief include proper positioning, frequent turning, and the use of pressure-relief beds or mattresses and chair cushions.[20]

Correct turning strategies involve proper body positioning and safe intervals. The sidelying position should be avoided because it puts pressure directly on the greater trochanter. A tilted position using a pillow under the shoulder and leg of the same side is preferable in order simply to rotate the body of midline.[20] Because the supine position is dangerous for the occiput, shoulders, spine, sacrum, and heels, it should be reserved for procedures and meals and limited to once per shift. When positioning a patient, the level of elevation of the head of the bed should be kept to no more than 30 degrees to avoid further increasing pressure over the sacrum and heels. Patients who are being tube fed or who are eating must be maintained at a higher degree of elevation for at least 1 hour after meals.[20]

Specialty beds and mattresses are useful adjuvants to relieving pressure in the bedbound or chairbound client. In general, low pressures can best be achieved through use of an air-supported mattress or bed. These types of surfaces should keep the person "floating" on the bed and should not allow the bony prominences to rest on the rigid mattress or bedframe. Any pressure-relieving mattress or bed should be used in compliance with the manufacturer's guidelines and not be viewed as a substitute for routine patient turning and positioning, but as an aid to routine nursing care.[21]

At regular intervals, wounds must be assessed, gently cleansed, and given a dressing that supports cellular repair. Most chronic wounds should be assessed and measured weekly; more frequent assessment may have little value because of the slow healing rate common in older adults. Wound cleansing is accomplished using gentle cleansers and minimal physical disruption of the wound bed.[22] Many cleansing agents contain harsh chemicals that destroy budding tissue; alternatively, the older adult may shower or use a whirlpool. The shower spray and the spray action of many wound cleansers provide gentle cleansing of the wound bed without disruption of its surface.

Dressings that do not leave debris in the wound should be chosen. The wound bed is cleansed before each new dressing is applied. Wound dressings are used to cover, protect, insulate, and provide an optimum moist environment for the body to make the repair necessary for healing. The dressing chosen should control drainage and odor and conform to the anatomical location of the lesion.[23] Table 11–8 describes wound dressing options based on the depth (partial or full thickness) and qualitative appearance of the wound.

Essential Documentation (See Also Chapter 5, "Legal Issues Affecting Older Adults")

The location, size, and appearance of any lesion noted during assessment should be documented. The use of a diagram allows consistent documentation for lesion location. Lesion size is measured when possible using the two greatest perpendicular diameters and lesion depth or elevation. If an appropriate measuring device is unavailable, the lesion can be described using fixed terms (i.e., the size of a dime rather than the size of a person's hand). The overall color and texture of the lesion are described. Is it red, yellow, black, or white? What portion of the lesion is what color? Sometimes drawing a diagram is helpful. Is the surface smooth or rough, shiny or dull? What does the edge look like: smooth, rounded, ridged, or irregular? Finally, it is often useful to document a skin lesion further with photography. If a photograph is taken, a metric ruler should be placed within the photographic frame to enable accurate comparison with future photographs (see Figs. 11–1 to 11–4).

3 *Tertiary Prevention*

The client who requires ongoing care for the skin usually needs much support and education. Slowly healing or nonhealing skin lesions may become malodorous and unsightly very quickly despite this slow improvement. Care may need to be directed toward symptom management rather than toward curing or healing the

TABLE 11–8   WOUND CARE GUIDE

Wound Stage	Appearance	Dressing Options
Partial thickness, stage 2	Clean, pink	Transparent film Transparent film over nonadherent gauze Composite dressings Hydrocolloid dressings Hydrogel dressings Polyurethane foam Nonadherent gauze
Full thickness	Pink base or <50% moist slough	Exudate absorbers Hydrogel dressings Hydrocolloid dressings Moistened gauze dressings
Full thickness	Moist slough, extends to muscle, fascia, and bone	Granular exudate absorbers Hydrogel dressings Calcium alginates Moistened gauze dressings
Full thickness	Dry, hard eschar	Surgical debridement by physician Conservative debridement: • Cross-hatch and apply transparent film, or transparent film over a hydrogel dressing • Enzymatic debriding agent • Dakin's solution, ¼- to ½-strength

lesion. For example, a debilitated older adult may have pressure sores over bony prominences. The ulcers may not be healing if caloric intake is inadequate. Methods available to treat such wounds are often expensive and, in the absence of adequate nutrition, are likely to be unsuccessful. The plan of care is then directed toward symptom management and includes controlling pain and odor, preventing additional breakdown when possible, and keeping the lesion free of infection and necrotic debris. Physical and occupational therapists may be consulted to provide appropriate activity and adaptive devices to optimize the patient's environment. Use of therapeutic devices, including speciality beds and mattresses and chair cushions, minimize the risk of developing pressure sores. Compression stockings or pumps might be used to decrease peripheral dependent edema, and whirlpool treatments may provide comfort as well as cleanse the wound. The goals are to optimize function whenever possible and to achieve the highest possible level of comfort and well-being.

Student Learning Activities

1 In your clinical agency, identify the various products available for prevention of skin breakdown. Compare the cost of the various products to the cost of an average length of stay for the diagnosis-related group related to decubitus ulcer, hospital-acquired.

2 Interview a local enterostomal therapist or skin care specialist regarding the specialized services needed by older adults.

3 Obtain a copy of the AHCPR *Guidelines for Prevention and Management of Decubitus Ulcers* by calling 202-521-1800. Identify specific strategies you will use from this guide in your clinical practice.

REFERENCES

1 Balin, AK, and Pratt, LA: Physiological consequences of human skin aging. Cutis 43:431, 1989.
2 Branchet, MC, et al: Skin thickness changes in normal aging skin. Gerontology 36:28, 1990.
3 Ortonne, JP: Pigmentary changes of the ageing skin. Br J Dermatol (suppl 35)122:21, 1990.
4 Gilchrest, BA, et al: Effect of chronological aging and ultraviolet irradiation on Langerhans' cells in human epidermis. J Invest Dermatol 79:85, 1982.
5 Thivolet, J, and Nicolas, JF: Skin ageing and immune competence. Br J Dermatol (suppl 35)122:77, 1990.
6 Cerimele, D, et al: Physiological changes in ageing skin. Br J Dermatol (suppl 35)122:13, 1990.
7 Cua, AB, et al: Elastic properties of human skin: Relation to age, sex, and anatomical region. Arch Dermatol Res 282(5): 283, 1990.
8 Montagna, W, and Carlisle, K: Structural changes in ageing skin. Br J Dermatol (suppl 35)122:61, 1990.
9 Kurban, RS, and Bhawan, J: Histologic changes in skin associated with aging. J Dermatol Surg Oncol 16(10):908, 1990.
10 Lapiere, CM: The ageing dermis: The main cause for the appearance of "old" skin. Br J Dermatol (suppl 35)122:5, 1990.
11 Young, EM, and Newcomer, VD: General aspects of aging. In Young, EM (ed): Geriatric Dermatology, Clinical Diagnosis and Practical Therapy. Igaku-Shoin, New York, 1989.
12 Braden, B, and Bergstrom, N: A conceptual schema for the study of the etiology of pressure sores. Rehab Nurs 12(1):9, 1987.
13 Kleinsmith, DM, and Perricone, NV: Common skin problems in the elderly. Clin Geriatr Med 5:189, 1989.
14 Glass, AG, and Hoover, RN: The emerging epidemic of melanoma and squamous cell skin cancer. JAMA 262:2097, 1989.
15 Fenske, NA, and Lober, CW: Skin changes of aging: Pathological implications. Geriatrics 45(3):27, 1990.
16 Gilchrest, BA: Skin diseases in the elderly. In Calkins, E, et al (eds): The Practice of Geriatrics. WB Saunders, Philadelphia, 1986.
17 DeWitt, S: Nursing assessment of the skin and dermatologic lesions. Nurs Clin North Am 25(1):235, 1990.
18 Panel for the Prediction and Prevention of Pressure Ulcers in Adults: Pressure Ulcers in Adults: Prediction and Preven-

tion. Clinical Practice Guideline no 3. AHCPR Publication no 92-0047. Agency for Health Care Policy and Research, Public Health Service, US Department of Health and Human Services, Rockville, Md, May 1992.

19 Seiler, WO, et al: Influence of the 30 laterally inclined positions and the super-soft 3-piece mattress on skin oxygen tension on areas of maximum pressure: Implications for pressure sore prevention. Gerontology 32:158, 1986.

20 Maklebust, J, and Sieggreen MY: Pressure ulcers. Nursing 26(12):34, 1996.

21 Skewes, SM: Skin care rituals that do more harm than good. AJN 96(10):33, 1996.

22 Litwack, K: Practical points on wound healing. J Post Anesthesia Nurs 10(1):29, 1995.

23 Panel for the Treatment of Pressure Ulcers: Pressure Ulcers in Adults: Treatment Guidelines. Clinical Practice Guideline no 15. AHCPR Publication no 95-0652. Agency for Health Care Policy and Research, Public Health Service, US Department of Health and Human Services, Rockville, Md, June 1995.

CHAPTER 12

The Aging Musculoskeletal System

Marilyn M. Pattillo / Mickey Stanley

OBJECTIVES

Upon completion of this chapter, the reader will be able to:

- Identify the normal changes in the musculoskeletal system that result from aging
- Differentiate among the following common musculoskeletal problems in older adults: osteoporosis, osteoarthritis, and rheumatoid arthritis
- State the common fractures that occur as a result of osteoporosis and the nursing interventions from the older adult and family
- Develop a plan for nursing intervention based on a systematic assessment of the older adult and family emphasizing safety, mobility, and continued function

Because activity and mobility are vital to the total health of the older adult, nurses must be knowledgeable in musculoskeletal assessment and intervention. Nurses play two important roles. First, practicing health promotion long before age 65 can delay and minimize the degenerative effects of aging. Musculoskeletal disease is not an inevitable consequence of aging and thus should be regarded as a specific disease process, not just the result of getting older. In teaching health promotion, nurses can help others cope with and delay the effects of the altered posture, decreased mobility, potential for injuries, and discomforts that normally accompany aging. The most credible nurses are those who promote their own health and incorporate into their own daily lives regular exercise, good posture, and correct diet. Second, when caring for older adults with musculoskeletal problems, nurses must have an understanding of the common musculoskeletal problems that affect older adults and an ability to distinguish between "rheumatic" complaints and those requiring more thorough evaluation and referral. Knowledge of osteoporosis, osteoarthritis, inflammatory articular disease, and fractures is necessary to help prevent complications and minimize their impact. Nursing care is grounded on the belief that maintenance of mobility is critical for health, well-being, and quality of life. Nurses also play an important role in recognizing and teaching others about the vulnerability of older adults because of the compounding factors of age-related changes and possible iatrogenic

impositions made on hospitalized older adults by their impaired mobility.

Normal Aging

Normal age-related musculoskeletal changes in older adults include decreased height, redistribution of lean body mass and subcutaneous fat, increased bone porosity, muscle atrophy, slowed movement, diminished strength, and stiffening of joints (Table 12–1). Changes in the bones, muscles, and joints are responsible for the altered appearance, weakness, and slowed movement that accompany aging.[1]

SKELETAL SYSTEM

Progressive decrease in height is universal among all races and in both genders and is attributed mainly to narrowing of the intervertebral discs and compression of the spinal column.[1] The shoulder becomes narrower and the pelvis wider, accentuated by the increase in anteroposterior diameter of the chest (see Fig. 12–1).

As people age, the amount of lean body mass decreases. Loss of peripheral subcutaneous fat tends to sharpen body contours and deepen the hollows around the orbits of the eyes, the axilla, the shoulders, and the ribs. Bony landmarks (vertebrae, iliac crests, ribs, scapula) become more prominent.

TABLE 12–1 NORMAL MUSCULOSKELETAL SYSTEM AGING CHANGES

Normal Age-Related Change	Clinical Implications
Progressive decrease in height caused by narrowing of intervertebral discs	Stooped posture with barrel-chest appearance
Stiffening of thoracic cage in expanded state	Increased risk of falls
Decreased production of cortical and trabecular bone	Increased risk of fracture
Decrease in lean body mass with loss of subcutaneous fat	Sharp body contours Assessment of hydration status difficult Decline in muscular strength
Prolonged time for muscular contraction and relaxation	Slowed reaction time Increased risk of injury
Stiffening of joints and ligaments	

Types of bone include cortical and trabecular bone, and each has a different structural role. Areas in which large-impact stresses are applied from many directions contain the trabecular bone pattern. Cortical bone's primary function is protection against torque and bending loads. The process by which calcium is absorbed from bone to maintain a steady blood calcium level and redeposited to form new bone is known as remodeling. This process of remodeling occurs throughout the life span. The rate of absorption does not change with age. The rate of new bone formation slows with age, resulting in the loss of total bone mass in older adults.

MUSCULAR SYSTEM

Muscular strength begins to decline around 40 years of age, with an accelerated decline after the age of 60. Changes in lifestyle and the decreased use of the neuromuscular system are the primary causes for the muscular strength loss. Muscle wasting occurs because of the decrease in the number of muscle fibers and general atrophy of organs and tissues. Regeneration of muscle tissue slows with age, and atrophied tissue is replaced with fibrous tissue.[1]

Slower, more sluggish movement is attributed to a prolongation of muscle contraction time, latency period, and relaxation period of the motor units in the muscle tissue. Joints such as the hips, knees, elbows, wrists, neck, and vertebrae become mildly flexed with older age. The increased flexion is caused by changes in the vertebral column, ankylosis (stiffening) of the ligaments and joints, shrinkage and sclerosis of tendons and muscles, and degenerative changes in the extrapyramidal system.[1]

JOINTS

Generally, there is deterioration of joint cartilage, most pronounced at the weight-bearing joints, and bone formation at the joint surface. Components of the joint capsule break down and the collagen content of connective tissues increases progressively, which, if disused, may cause inflammation, pain, decreased joint mobility, and deformity.[1]

1 *Primary Prevention*

The basis of preventive therapy lies in correcting known risk factors for bone loss and the problems asso-

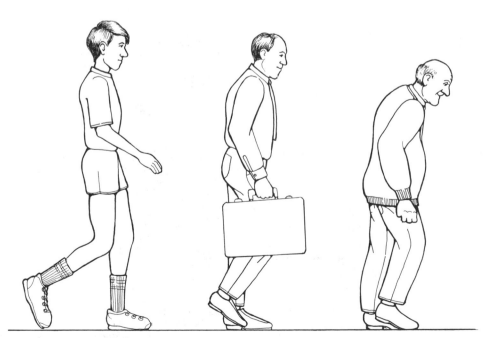

Figure 12–1 Comparison sketch of a man's loss of height caused by the aging process.

TABLE 12–2 RISK FACTORS FOR OSTEOPOROSIS

Female	High protein intake
Advanced age	High phosphate intake
White or Asian race	Certain medications, when taken
Thin, small-framed body	for a long time (high dosages
Positive family history	of glucocorticoid, phenytoin,
Low calcium intake	thyroid medication more than
Early menopause	2 grains)
(before age 45)	Endocrine diseases
Sedentary lifestyle	(hyperthyroidism, Cushing's
Nulliparity	disease, acromegaly,
Smoking	hypogonadism,
Excessive alcohol or	hyperparathyroidism)
caffeine	

TABLE 12–3 TRICKS TO HELP YOU GET ENOUGH CALCIUM (FOR NURSES AND THEIR CLIENTS)

- Add powdered nonfat dry milk to almost anything. Each teaspoon gives you 33 mg of calcium.
- Eat hot cereals for breakfast. This will increase your calcium intake and add bulk to your diet.
- Try tofu. You might like it.
- Remember that fish prepared with its bones (e.g., canned salmon and sardines) contains a high amount of calcium.
- If you take calcium supplements, spread them out over the day and take them with a little milk or yogurt. Also, take some calcium before going to bed, as more calcium is lost at night than during the day. Calcium supplements may cause gastric irritation and should be taken with food.

ciated with such disorders as osteoporosis (Table 12–2). Age-related factors that promote bone loss, including a decline in hormones and diet and lifestyle changes, are significant because the effects of bone loss encountered over a lifetime are cumulative.

ESTROGEN

Estrogen plays a major role in maintaining skeletal integrity in women. Bone loss occurs when estrogen levels fall. Estrogen-dependent bone loss is rapid during the 5 to 10 years after menopause.[2] Men are also at risk of bone loss because of the decline in hormonal function with advanced age. The rate of decline in these hormone levels is not as dramatic for men as that associated with menopause in women.[3]

A recent study identified that most older women do not take estrogen replacement therapy (ERT) because they believe that they do not need the therapy, they fear undesirable side effects from ERT, or they believe that the medication would harm them. Nurses have a key role to play in educating older women regarding the benefits of ERT and its role in the prevention of the painful and disabling effects of bone loss in old age.[4]

DIET

The dietary habits established throughout life influence bone mass at maturity. Balanced nutrition with adequate calcium and vitamin D intake is essential to maintaining bone structure and integrity at any age. The ability of the older adult's gastrointestinal tract to absorb and use dietary calcium shows a marked decline. Therefore, the recent recommendation for calcium intake for older adults is between 1000 and 1500 mg/day.[5] Suggestions to increase calcium in the diet must be creative and simple (Table 12–3). Nurses should pay special attention to the diet of homebound older adults living alone, for they are most at risk of dietary deficiencies and will need to seek family and community resources.

EXERCISE

Nurses can have a significant impact on the quality of life and disability associated with chronic diseases of the musculoskeletal system by encouraging and teaching a safe and effective exercise and fitness program (Table 12–4). Exercise has been demonstrated to delay the physiological changes that normally occur in musculoskeletal aging: decreased strength and flexibility, increased vulnerability to injury, increased body fat, decreased resilience of joint structures, and osteoporosis.[1] Lifelong exercise may protect older adults against falls and especially against the devastating effects of hip fractures. Starting late is far preferable to not starting at all. As epidemiologist Helmrich says, "Everything that gets worse as you age improves as you exercise."[6] A thorough discussion of the topic of activity and exercise for older adults is found in Chapter 20.

COUNTERING IMMOBILITY IN INSTITUTIONALIZED OLDER ADULTS

On the other side of the continuum, nurses can be instrumental in preventing further complications when caring for frail, ill older adults. Immobility, one of the

TABLE 12–4 TEACHING GUIDE: PROMOTING MUSCULOSKELETAL HEALTH

- Proper exercise promotes mobility, muscle strength, and endurance. The less active the person, the greater his or her chance of losing strength and flexibility.
- Encourage walking for enjoyment. However, any exercise, from passive range-of-motion exercises to swimming and aerobics, may be performed, depending on the level of fitness and functional abilities. Some weight-bearing exercises should be done daily.
- Instruct client to avoid fatigue and maintain a proper balance between rest and exercise.
- Encourage use of assist devices to conserve energy, decrease stress on joints and bones, and promote safety.
- Make home and other surroundings accident safe. Many self-help books and community services are available to the client and family for assistance.
- Assess client's diet to help him or her lose weight while maintaining proper nutrition. Emphasize the need to include calcium and other vitamins and minerals.
- Determine client's understanding of medications, their side effects, and interactions with certain foods.
- If advised by the physician, instruct client to take estrogen, progestin, or a combination of hormones as ordered.

most common problems among older adults, may lead to serious physiological and psychological consequences. Nurses should identify and incorporate into their health teaching the physical and architectural features that restrict mobility: waxed floors, lack of assistive devices, and physical and chemical restraints. From 10 to 15 percent of muscle strength can be lost each week that muscles are resting completely, and as much as 5.5 percent can be lost each day of rest and immobility. Although all joints can be affected by immobilization, the hips, knees, and ankles are especially susceptible because of the effects of gravity. To complicate the situation, contracture of the hip and knee make the client much less stable and therefore more prone to falls.[7]

2 *Secondary Prevention*

ASSESSMENT OF THE MUSCULOSKELETAL SYSTEM

History

Nursing assessment focuses on how age-related changes influence the functional status of older people and includes the following:

- Height, weight, posture, and gait provide baseline data that can indicate muscle wasting, obesity, or edema.
- Activity and rest patterns, past and present, should be noted. A person who has never exercised or participated in activities may have difficulty beginning an exercise program in later life, especially if the activity is painful or difficult.
- Dietary assessment includes nutritional intake of calcium and vitamin D. Obesity and malnutrition can affect mobility and muscle strength. Obesity predisposes older adults to instability in the ligaments, particularly in the lower back region and other weight-bearing joints.
- Medications, including over-the-counter drugs and home remedies, may make older adults susceptible to drug toxicities and side effects. Specific inquiries should be made about skeletal muscle relaxants, antirheumatoid agents, salicylates, nonsteroidal anti-inflammatory agents, and systemic steroids. Some drugs have been found to be detrimental to the musculoskeletal system: anticonvulsant (osteomalacia), phenothiazine (gait disturbances), steroids (abnormal fat distribution and muscle weakness), and potassium-depleting diuretics (cramps and muscle weakness). Amphetamines and caffeine can cause a generalized increase in motor activity.
- The combination of mobility, strength, and balance determines the functional capability of the client. A mobility assessment incorporates several aspects of mobility and functional capability.[8] For a thorough discussion of this concept, see Chapter 20.
- Past injuries (e.g., hip fracture) may indicate an osteoporotic condition. A history of joint pain and stiffness, weakness, or fatigue is often associated with the presence of osteoarthritis or rheumatoid arthritis (RA). Back pain and paresthesia or numbness of the lower extremities may be symptomatic of vertebral or intervertebral disc degeneration in the lumbar region. The list of minor or major injuries of the musculoskeletal system should include circumstances related to the injury, diagnostic evaluations, methods and duration of treatment, current status of the injury, need for assisting devices, and any interference with activities of daily living.
- Specific questions about the safety practices of the client as they relate to the job environment, living arrangements, safety hazards and safety aids in the home, recreation, and exercise should be asked to identify problems and direct client education.

Physical Assessment

Any kyphosis or scoliosis should be noted. Severe kyphosis can interfere with breathing and cardiovascular function. Tenderness over the spinous processes may portend a vertebral fracture. The joints are inspected next, particularly the joints of the hands. Osteoarthritis of the distal interphalangeal joints of the hands and knees is common. Bony overgrowths at the distal interphalangeal joint are called Heberden's nodes. Limitation of external rotation of the hip can be an early sign of osteoarthritic involvement. The range of motion of all joints should be assessed.

RA in the hands tends to affect the proximal interphalangeal joints. Swelling seen in rheumatoid joints is not bone but rather synovium and soft-tissue swelling. There may be ulnar deviation in the hands at the metacarpophalangeal joints, as well as a tendency for joints to sublux (partial dislocation due to instability). Morning pain and stiffness may last several hours for the client with RA, whereas the client with osteoarthritis is relieved from pain after a short period of limbering up the affected joints.[9]

Common Musculoskeletal Problems

OSTEOPOROSIS

Pathophysiology

Osteoporosis, a condition in which there is a decrease in total bone mass, is a crippling, often painful bone disease occurring in epidemic proportions. Although it is most commonly found in women, men are also at risk. The loss of bone substances causes the bone to become mechanically weakened and prone to either spontaneous fractures or fractures from minimal trauma.[10] When normal weight bearing is diminished or absent as a consequence of decreased or impaired mobility, disuse osteoporosis occurs. Osteoclastic activity, reabsorption of bone, and release of calcium and phosphorus are then accelerated.

Clinical Manifestations

The primary fractures most often seen in clients with osteoporosis are vertebral fractures, hip fractures, and forearm fractures. These fractures occur either from repetitive stress injuries or from acute trauma, which may be superimposed on these microfractures. As a consequence, it is uncertain what initiates hip fractures.[10]

Osteoporotic fractures tend to cluster in individuals, and the occurrence of one type of fracture usually indicates that a patient has an increased risk of subsequent fractures at other sites. Vertebral and lower arm fractures tend to occur earlier in life than hip fractures.[9] Fractures limit mobility and place patients at increased risk for subsequent decline of functional status and development of complications.

Incidence

The development of osteoporosis often begins at an early age and is influenced by endocrine and metabolic changes as well as by age- and gender-related effects on bone. Factors that affect attainment and maintenance of peak bone mass occurring after skeletal maturity (e.g., race, gender, and heredity) also determine who is at risk for developing osteoporosis. Postmenopausal, slender white women are the most susceptible group.[10]

Nevertheless, about 30 percent of women over 60 years of age have clinical osteoporosis. Bone mass declines by about 2 to 3 percent per year in women after menopause.[9] Bone loss progresses imperceptibly until a fracture develops.

Management

Nursing management of osteoporosis includes prevention through teaching with emphasis on reduction of risk factors, adequate calcium intake, adequate nutrition, physical activity, and ERT.[11]

Institutionalized older adults, whose mobility is impaired, are especially vulnerable because osteoporosis increases rapidly from the third day to the third week of immobilization and peaks during the fifth or sixth week. With ambulation, however, bone mineral is restored at a rate of only 1 percent per month, underscoring the importance of preventing the initial loss.[10]

OSTEOARTHRITIS

Pathophysiology

Osteoarthritis (also called degenerative joint disease, hypertrophic arthritis, senescent arthritis, and osteoarthrosis) is a slowly progressive, asymmetrical, noninflammatory disorder of mobile joints, particularly weight-bearing joints. It is characterized by degeneration of joint cartilage and by new bone forming at joint edges. The wear and tear on the joints with aging is thought to play a major role in the development of osteoarthritis. Degenerative changes cause the normally smooth, white, translucent cartilage to become yellow and opaque, with rough surfaces and areas of malacia (softening). As the layers of cartilage become thinner,

bony surfaces grow closer together. Secondary inflammation of the synovial membrane may follow. As the joint surface becomes denuded of cartilage, subchondral bone increases in density and becomes sclerotic.

Clinical Manifestations

Joint pain, stiffness, loss of motion, decreased function, and deformity are typically associated with inflammatory signs of tenderness, swelling, and warmth. Clients are likely to have a positive history of trauma, overuse, or previous joint disease.[12]

Initially, pain occurs with motion; later, it can also occur at rest. Examinations reveal tenderness, crepitus, diminished range of motion, often bony enlargement, and occasional inflammatory signs. Increasing pain is accompanied by progressive loss of function. Overall body coordination and posture may be affected as a result of the pain and loss of mobility.[12] Heberden's nodes, although not confined to older adults, are common manifestations of osteoarthritis. Reactive bony overgrowth located at the distal interphalangeal joints, Heberden's nodes are palpable protuberances that are often associated with flexion and lateral deviation of the distal phalanx. These nodes may become tender, red, and swollen, often beginning in one finger and spreading to others. Usually there is no significant loss of function, but clients are often distressed by the resulting disfigurement.[11]

Management

Management of this chronic disorder begins with discovering the activities of daily life that may be contributing to the stress on the affected joints, providing the client with assistive aids to alleviate weight bearing on affected joints, teaching the client to use these aids, and planning appropriate pain management. See Chapter 22 for a thorough discussion of pain management. If physical therapy and assistive devices do not lead to significant improvement and the pain is disabling, joint replacement surgery may be indicated.

Arthroplasty

Arthroplasty is the reconstruction or replacement of a joint. This surgical procedure is performed to relieve pain, improve or maintain range of motion, and correct deformity—conditions that could result from osteoarthritis, RA, or avascular necrosis. Arthroplasty can include replacement of part of a joint, surgical reshaping of the bones of the joints, or total joint replacement. Replacement arthroplasty is available for the elbow, shoulder, hip, knee, ankle, and phalangeal joints of the fingers. Hip reconstruction is often used in the treatment of clients with RA, osteoarthritis, and hip fractures.

Unremitting pain as a result of severe destructive deterioration of the knee joint is the main indication for knee arthroplasty. Part or all of the knee joint may be replaced with a metal and plastic prosthetic device. Within 2 to 5 days after surgery, the client is instructed to perform quadriceps-setting exercises and straight-leg raising. When the bulky dressing is removed, active flexion exercises are begun. Weight bearing is started as soon as the client can use a walker or crutches.[13]

INFLAMMATORY ARTICULAR DISEASE: RHEUMATOID ARTHRITIS

Pathophysiology

The most common inflammatory articular disease in older adults, RA, is a chronic, systemic disease, typically developing insidiously and characterized by recurrent inflammation of the diarthrodial joints and related structures. RA is often accompanied by rheumatoid nodules, arteritis, neuropathy, scleritis, pericarditis, lymphadenopathy, and splenomegaly.[14] RA is characterized by periods of remission and exacerbation.

Clinical Manifestations

In the older adults, RA can be categorized into three subsets.[11] Subset 1 is classic RA. The small joints of both hands and feet are predominantly involved. Rheumatoid factor is present, and rheumatoid nodules are common. Disease in this subset can lead to progressive joint damage.

Subset 2 includes clients who meet the American Rheumatologic Association criteria for RA because they have persistent, symmetrical inflammatory synovitis, often involving the wrist and finger joints.

Subset 3 synovitis affects primarily the proximal joints, shoulders, and hips. The onset is sudden, often with marked morning stiffness. The patient's wrist is often involved, with swelling, tenderness, impaired grip strength, and carpal tunnel syndrome. This subset represents a self-limiting illness that is well-controlled by low dosages of prednisone or anti-inflammatory agents and has a good prognosis.

If unarrested, RA progresses through four stages.[15]

1 There is joint inflammation with swelling of the synovial lining membrane and production of excess synovial fluid. No destructive changes are noted on radiograph. Evidence of osteoporosis may be present.

2 Radiologically, slight bone or cartilage destruction is seen. The client may have limitation of motion but no joint deformity.

3 Tough fibrous connective tissue replaces pannus, occluding the joint space. Fibrous ankylosis results in decreased joint motion, malalignment, and deformity. Radiologically, cartilage and bone destruction are evident.

4 As fibrous tissue calcifies, bony ankylosis may result in total joint immobilization. Extensive muscle atrophy and soft tissue lesions such as nodules may be present.

Management

Medical treatment depends on the stage of the disease when the diagnosis is made and the subset into which it fits. For pain relief using anti-inflammatory agents, the drug of choice is aspirin. However, aspirin's anti-inflammatory effect is not present in dosages of less than 12 tablets per day, which may cause gastrointestinal and central nervous system symptoms. Nonsteroidal anti-inflammatory agents are useful, but the manufacturer's recommended dosage is advised, and careful monitoring for side effects is necessary.[16] Corticosteroid therapy injected through the joints may be used for a flare-up in one or two joints. Rapid injections are associated with necrosis and collapse of bone. Generally, injection into any joint should not be repeated more than three times. Pain and swelling are usually relieved for 1 to 6 weeks.[15]

Nursing management emphasizes the client's understanding of the chronic nature of RA and the different subsets and stages to monitor disease progression. Clients must remember that although medications may reduce joint inflammation and pain, they must also maintain motion and strength to prevent deformities. A balanced program of activity and rest is important to prevent an increase in joint stress.

COMMON FRACTURES IN OLDER ADULTS

Fractures, especially those associated with osteoporosis, are considered the main causes of morbidity and disability in old age.[17]

Vertebral Compression Fractures

A common symptom of osteoporosis is back pain secondary to vertebral compression fractures. Acute pain in the middle to low thoracic vertebrae during routine daily activities may be the earliest symptom. These compression fractures may occur after minimal trauma such as stepping from a curb, opening a window, or even making a bed.

The focus of treatment for acute compression fractures is immediate symptomatic relief with bed rest in any position that affords maximum comfort. Muscle relaxants, as well as heat and analgesics, may be used when indicated. Short-term use of mild muscle relaxants diminishes the muscle spasms that often accompany these fractures.

As soon as pain permits, the client should attempt to move out of bed slowly and with support. Supervised exercises to correct postural deformities and increase tone are beneficial. Swimming, although not a weight-bearing exercise, maintains flexibility and may be most effective for clients with established disease. Clients should be taught how to prevent back strain by avoiding twisting and sudden forceful movements or bending. Safety measures regarding how to lift and carry heavy objects should be explained.[18]

Fracture of the Pelvis

Older clients usually sustain this injury from a fall. Although only 3 percent of all fractures are pelvic fractures, this type of injury accounts for 5 to 20 percent of the mortality among older adults from fractures. Pelvic fractures are ominous because they may also cause seri-

RESEARCH BRIEF

Bradley, CF, and Kozak, C: Nursing care and management of the elderly hip fractured patient. J Gerontol Nurs 21:15, 1995.

Bradley and Kozak used a posttest nonequivalent control group design to determine whether instruction regarding age-specific approaches for older patients with hip fracture would result in improved clinical outcomes. The content of the educational program included age-related changes, nutritional deficits, impaired physical mobility, voiding dysfunction, and acute confusion. The study results support that patients in the experimental group had a decreased length of time to first ambulation and a decreased length of stay on the orthopedic unit.

ous intra-abdominal injury such as colon laceration, paralytic ileum, intrapelvic hemorrhage, and rupture of the urethra or bladder.[19]

Fracture of the Hip

Although spinal fractures lead to deformity and pelvic fractures produce dysfunction, it is hip fractures that severely affect the quality of life and challenge survival in older adults. Holbrook[20] reports that 1 patient in 20 past the age of 65 currently occupying a hospital bed is recovering from a hip fracture. Even in the best hands, 40 percent of clients sustaining a hip fracture do not survive 2 years after this injury. Of the patients originating from a nursing home, 70 percent do not survive 1 year, only one-third of patients who survive a hip fracture return to a lifestyle and level of independence comparable to that enjoyed before the injury.

Between 75 and 80 percent of all hip fractures affect women, and almost 50 percent occur in persons age 80 or older. The clinical manifestations of hip fractures are external rotation, shortening of the affected extremity, and severe pain and tenderness at the fracture site. Displaced femoral neck fractures cause serious disruption of the blood supply to the femoral head, which can result in avascular necrosis.

Surgical repair is preferred when managing hip fractures. Surgical treatment allows the client to be out of bed sooner and prevents the major complications associated with immobility. Initially, the affected extremity may be temporarily immobilized by Buck or Russel traction until the client's physical condition is stabilized and surgery can be scheduled. Many believe that older adults are most healthy just after the accident and that surgery should be done as soon as possible.[19]

Management

Because many older clients tend to be in a compromised state before a fracture, nurses must be aware of certain preoperative and postoperative factors that, if not recognized, may tip the scales against the client. See "Research Brief."

Preoperative Factors

Chronic health problems such as diabetes, hypertension, cardiac decompensation, and arthritis may complicate the clinical picture. Severe muscle spasm can increase pain. These spasms are managed by appropriate medications, comfortable positioning (unless contraindicated), and properly adjusted traction, if it is being used. Massaging the affected limb is not recommended during the spasm.

Clients should be taught to exercise the unaffected leg and both arms. Preoperatively, clients should be instructed on how to use the trapeze bar and opposite side rail to assist in changing position. Because ambulation usually begins by the second postoperative day, the client should practice getting out of bed and transferring to a chair. Plans for discharge should be discussed and arrangements initiated with a social worker or the case manager for home care or skilled care.

Postoperative Factors

The initial care is similar to that of any geriatric surgical client: monitoring vital signs and intake and output, checking for changes in mental status (sensorium), supervising respiratory activities such as deep breathing and coughing, administering pain medications, and observing the dressing for signs of bleeding and infection. Before and after a reduction of a fracture, there is always potential for impairment of the circulation, sensation, and movement. Peripheral pulses distal to the affected limb must be assessed. The nurse assesses the client's toes for ability to move, warmth and pink color, numbness or tingling, and edema. The client's leg is kept elevated to prevent edema. An abductor splint is used between the client's knees when turning from side to side. Sandbags and pillows are helpful to keep the leg from rotating externally. The postoperative use of transcutaneous electrical nerve stimulator (TENS) units may significantly decrease the need for narcotics.

If the hip fracture has been treated by inserting a femoral-head prosthesis, the client and family must be fully aware of positions and activities that may cause dislocation (flexion, adduction with internal rotation). Many daily activities may reproduce these positions: putting on shoes and socks, crossing the legs while seated, lying on side incorrectly, standing up or sitting down while the body is flexed relative to the chair, and sitting on low seats. These activities must be strictly avoided for at least 6 weeks, until the soft tissue surrounding the hip has healed sufficiently to stabilize the prosthesis. Sudden severe pain and extreme external rotation indicate prosthesis displacement.

To prevent prosthesis dislocation, the nurse should always place three pillows between the client's legs when turning, keep leg abductor splints on the client except when bathing, avoid extreme hip flexion, and avoid turning the client onto the affected side. If the hip

TABLE 12–5 RESOURCES FOR MUSCULOSKELETAL INFORMATION

The National Osteoporosis Foundation
1625 I Street NW, Suite 1011
Washington, DC 20006
202-223-2226
 Voluntary foundation: publishes pamphlets and other client information.

National Arthritis and Musculoskeletal and Skin Disease
Information Clearing House
Box AMS
9000 Rockville Pike
Bethesda, MD 20892
301-495-4484
 Prepares bibliophiles, bibliographies, catalogs, guides, and reports on rheumatic, musculoskeletal, and skin diseases.

Office of Scientific and Health Communication
(NIAMS)
Building 31, Room 4C05
Bethesda, MD 20892
301-496-8188
 Supports in-depth research on rheumatoid arthritis, osteoarthritis, and osteoporosis.

fracture is treated by pinning, dislocation precautions are not necessary. Usually, the client is encouraged to be out of bed on the first postoperative day. Weight bearing on the involved extremity is not allowed until radiological examination indicates adequate healing, usually within 3 to 5 months.

3 Tertiary Prevention

The major nursing responsibility in rehabilitation is client and family teaching. In teaching the client, it is important to keep in mind that older adults are more likely to have multiple diagnoses that chronically affect several organ systems. Therefore, a comprehensive plan that focuses on the client's strengths and personal goals for a return to his or her previous level of independence as well as all health-care needs is essential. The geriatric case manager or discharge planner is an invaluable asset for the older adult who is recovering from a fracture. A list of organizations that provide resources for musculoskeletal information appears in Table 12–5.

Student Learning Activities

1 Keep a food diary for yourself for 3 days.
2 Calculate the amount of calcium you consumed during the 3 days.

3 Form small groups of three to four. Each group should select a cultural group that is represented in your area. Design a culturally sensitive menu for 1 week to ensure an adequate calcium intake for an older adult.

REFERENCES

1 Hamerman, D: Aging and the musculoskeletal system. In Hazzard, WR, et al (eds): Principles of Geriatric Medicine and Gerontology, ed 3. McGraw-Hill, New York, 1994.
2 Baylink, DJ, and Jennings, JC: Calcium and bone homeostasis and changes with aging. In Hazzard, WR, et al (eds): Principles of Geriatric Medicine and Gerontology, ed 3. McGraw-Hill, New York, 1994.
3 Gallo, J, et al: Handbook of Geriatric Assessment. Aspen, Rockville, Md, 1988.
4 Salamone, LM, et al: Estrogen replacement therapy: A survey of older women's attitudes. Arch Intern Med 156(1):1293, 1996.
5 Robb-Nicholson, C: Measuring our bones. Women's Health Watch 3(12):1, 1996.
6 US News and World Report 112(17):12, May 4, 1992.
7 Hogue, CC: Mobility. In Schneider, EL, et al (eds): The Teaching Nursing Home. Raven Press, New York, 1985, p 231.
8 Wagstaff, D, and Coakley, D: Physiotherapy and the Elderly Patient. Aspen, Rockville, Md, 1988.
9 Kaplan, F: Osteoporosis, pathophysiology and prevention. Clin Symp 15:39, 1987.
10 Chestnut, CH: Osteoporosis. In Hazzard, WR, et al (eds): Principles of Geriatric Medicine and Gerontology, ed 3. McGraw-Hill, New York, 1994.
11 Shah, S, and Tanner, E: Musculoskeletal disorders in the elderly. In Kaplan, P, and Tanner, E: Musculoskeletal Pain and Disability. Appleton & Lange, Norwalk, Conn, 1989.
12 Pompei, P: Osteoarthritis: New roles for drug therapy and surgery. Geriatrics 51:32, 1996.
13 Lewis, SM, and Collier, IC: Medical Surgical Nursing, Assessment and Management of Clinical Problems. McGraw-Hill, New York, 1987.
14 Calkins, E, et al: Rheumatoid arthritis in the older patient. In Hazzard, WR, et al (eds): Principles of Geriatric Medicine and Gerontology, ed 3. McGraw-Hill, New York, 1994.
15 Steinbrocker, O, et al: Therapeutic criteria in rheumatoid arthritis. JAMA 140:659, 1949.
16 Dunkin, MA, and O'Koon, M: The drug guide. Arthritis Today 9:27, 1995.
17 Bradley, CF, and Kozak, C: Nursing care and management of the elderly hip fractured patient. Gerontol Nurs 21:15, 1995.
18 Madson, S: How to reduce the risk of postmenopausal osteoporosis. Gerontol Nurs 15:9, 1989.
19 Lane, J, et al: Orthopedic consequences of osteoporosis. In Riggs, BL, and Melton, LJ (eds): Osteoporosis: Etiology, Diagnosis, and Management. Raven Press, New York, 1988, p 438.
20 Holbrook, TL: Specific musculoskeletal conditions. In Holbrook, TL, et al (eds): The Frequency of Occurrence, Impact and Cost of Selected Musculoskeletal Conditions in the United States. American Academy of Orthopedic Surgeons, Chicago, 1984.

CHAPTER 13

The Aging Neurological System

Linda A. Roussel

OBJECTIVES

Upon completion of this chapter, the reader will be able to:

- Identify the normal, age-related changes of the nervous system
- Discuss the clinical manifestations of the neurological deficits seen in older clients from a physical, functional, cognitive, sensory-perceptual, and psychosocial perspective
- Describe outcomes targeted toward primary prevention for neurological problems common among older adults
- Discuss outcomes associated with secondary prevention to address the needs of an older adult with a cerebrovascular accident
- Prepare a plan of care to address a unique need of an older adult with a cerebrovascular accident
- Outline the major outcomes of a stroke rehabilitation program for an older adult

People experience many psychological and physical changes through growth and maturity. Neurological changes depend on genetics, socioeconomics, self-esteem, and social factors. Although there are noted effects of aging on the nervous system, many changes can be slowed or decreased through a healthful lifestyle. Primary prevention, as a way of maintaining a healthful lifestyle, is a vital challenge to nurses and other health-care professionals.[1]

The Aging Neurological System

Envisioning the aging process from a broad perspective leads to more creative strategies for intervening with older adults. The intent is to develop partnerships to enhance quality of life. Cutillo-Schmitter[2] suggests viewing aging as a lifelong evolution as well as an ending stage, affording challenges and developmental opportunities for growth, change, and productivity. Health status, life experiences, nutrition, activity, and heredity influence the aging process. The neurological system, primarily the brain, is a major factor in adaptive aging. We know that neurons become increasingly complex and grow as we mature, but they do not regenerate. Current research on the brain indicates that although neurons die, the connections among the remaining cells increase and compensate for the void. This ability supports older adults' ability to continue to engage in cognitive tasks as in prior years, however slowly.[3]

The most notable structural changes occur in the brain itself, although the rest of the central nervous system (CNS) is affected as well. Brain size changes result from the atrophy of gyri and the dilation of sulci and ventricles. The cerebral cortex is the area of the brain most affected by neuronal loss. Decreases in cerebral blood flow and oxygen use are also noted to occur during the aging process. A decrease of cerebral blood flow and oxygen use may also occur with aging.[4]

Changes in the neurological system may include neuronal dropout and shrinkage, with a potential 10 percent loss noted by age 80. The uneven distribution of cholinergic neurons, norepinephrine, and dopamine are compensated by the loss of cells, resulting in little decline in intellect. However, mild parkinsonism may be experienced as the dopamine-blocking receptors are affected with aging. Increased levels of monoamine oxidase and serotonin and decreased levels of norepinephrine are noted, which may be associated with depression in older adults. These changes show wide variability among individuals.[5]

Depletion of dopamine and of some of the enzymes in the brain of older people contributes to functional neurological changes. A greater loss of dopamine has been noted in clients with Parkinson's disease.[5] Dopamine deficiency produces an overactive basal ganglia, causing bradykinesia, rigidity, and loss of postural mechanisms often seen in those with Parkinson's disease.[5]

Functionally, there may be a slowing in the deep tendon reflexes. There is a tendency toward tremor and short-stepped or broad-based gait with diminished associated movements. Increased muscle tone is noted, with the legs being involved more than arms, proximally more than distally. In addition, diminished muscle strength also occurs, with the legs demonstrating greater loss, proximally more than distally. A decrease in peripheral nerve conduction may be experienced. Reaction time is slower, with diminished or absent ankle jerk and reduction in knee, biceps, and triceps reflexes, primarily because of dendrite reduction and changes in synapses, which slow conduction.[4]

Functional changes may include decreased tactile discrimination and a raised pain threshold. This is particularly noticeable given the changes in the baroreceptors. However, alterations in the muscles and tendons may be a greater contributing factor to this than actual changes in the reflex arc.

The autonomic and sympathetic nervous system function may experience overall decline. Senile plaques and neurofibril tangles develop in older adults with and without dementia. The accumulation of the neuron pigment lipofuscin decreases the nervous system's control over circulation.[6] Congestion of the nervous system is thought to decrease cell activity, and the cell loses the ability to maintain itself.[7] The more active the cell, the less lipofuscin is deposited.

Drugs, oxygen depletion, lower vitamin E intake, and cirrhosis are external factors that affect lipofuscin deposits, predisposing the neurons to destruction. Along with this destruction is a decrease in protein synthesis and the ability of the hypothalamus to regulate heat production. This deregulation often results in heat loss.

Normal neurological system aging changes are summarized in Table 13–1.

TABLE 13–1 NORMAL NEUROLOGICAL SYSTEM AGING CHANGES

Normal Age-Related Changes	Clinical Implications
Slower peripheral nerve conduction	Slower deep tendon reflex and increased reaction time
Increased lipofuscin along neurons	Incomplete vasoconstriction and vasodilation
Less effective thermoregulation by hypothalamus	Danger of heat loss

Pathophysiology of Neurological Deficits

Clinical manifestations related to neurological deficits in the older client may be viewed from a number of perspectives: physical, functional, cognition-communication, sensory-perceptual, and psychosocial. Particular impairments appear when focal regions and neural systems in the brain are damaged by vascular compromise. Specific manifestations in each category are useful in assessing and developing a plan of care for the older client with neurological disorders.

PHYSICAL

The impact of aging on the CNS is difficult to determine, given the relationship of this system's function to other body systems. With altered perfusion and an interrupted cerebral blood flow, older adults are at greater risk for additional cerebral damage, renal failure, respiratory distress, and seizures. There is a known reduction in nerve cells, cerebral blood flow, and metabolism. With a lower nerve conduction velocity, slower reflexes and delayed responses to multiple stimuli are experienced; there is less kinesthetic sense. Because of the physiological changes in the nervous system occurring during the aging process, the sleep-wake cycle may be altered. Specifically, sleep disruptions affect 50 percent of people age 65 and older who live at home and 66 percent living in long-term care facilities. Sleep changes noted are increased sleep latency, early morning waking, and an increased number of daytime naps. A loss of effective circadian regulation of sleep is noted, with an associated increase in awakenings during sleep and in the composite of time spent awake during the night.[8]

FUNCTIONAL

Functional deficits in neurological disorders may relate to the older client's decrease in mobility, caused by declines in strength, range, and fluidity. With less freedom of movement, the older person may have difficulty in grooming, toileting, and eating. Decreased movement may be a result of kyphosis, enlarged joints, spasticity, and decreased muscle tone. Muscle fibers atrophy and decrease in number, with fibrous tissue gradually replacing muscle tissue. With the overall decline in muscle mass, strength, and movement, the older adult may exhibit generalized weakness. Muscle tremors may be associated with degeneration of the extrapyramidal system. Spasticity may result from an upper motor neuron injury within the CNS. Severe spasticity can result in a reduction of flexibility, posture, and functional mobility, as well as joint pain, contractures, and problems with positioning for comfort and hygiene. Tendons may undergo shrinkage and sclerosis, causing a decrease in tendon jerks. Reflexes are generally maintained in the knees, lessened in the arms, and nearly totally lost in the abdomen. Muscle cramping may be a common problem.

Functional mobility and movement deficits make the older adult vulnerable to alterations of skin integrity and falls.[9]

COGNITION-COMMUNICATION

Cognition and communication changes may be varied and severe. Premorbid communication style, intellectual ability, and learning styles are essential data used to prepare a realistic care plan for the older client. Our senses are essential to communication. A number of communication barriers may occur as a result of a cerebrovascular accident (CVA) or Parkinson's disease. Changes in sensation and perception can interfere with reception and expression of information and feeling.[10] Disruptions in taste, smell, pain, touch, temperature, and joint position sense may alter communication and our perceptual experience. With disorientation and confusion, our awareness of reality is markedly decreased. This decrease may be progressive, permanent, or transient, depending on the nature and extent of cerebral compromise.[11]

Memory may be altered in the aging process. Generally, memory for past occurrences is superior to the retention and recall of more recent information. Sensory deprivation may result from damage to the cerebral centers responsible for processing stimuli. Hallucinations, disorientation, and confusion may be results of sensory deprivation, not impaired mental ability. Sensations and perceptions may diminish further when CNS depressants are included in the pharmacological treatment.[10]

Sensory overload may result from the client's decreased ability to handle stimulation. The client may be unable to retain new information, which may cause more frustration and less tolerance for day-to-day activities. Aggression and agitation may occur as symptoms of sensory overload.

Agnosia, aphasia, and apraxia may be seen in clients with CVA or progressive dementia.[12] Agnosia is the inability to recognize common objects (comb, toothbrush, mirror) by using one of the senses, even though the sense is intact. Visual, auditory, and tactile agnosia occurs when there is damage to the parietal and occipital lobe, precentral gyrus, parieto-occipital region, and corpus callosum.[12]

Aphasia is an inability to use meaningful speech and the loss of verbal comprehension. There is a noted phonetic, semantic, or syntactic disintegration at the production or comprehension level of communication. Aphasia may be reflected in the client's vague, rambling, hesitant speech and difficulty finding the right words to express an idea.[12]

Apraxia is an inability to demonstrate a learned activity in the presence of the necessary motor function. It is the misuse of words in labeling things and the inability to recognize and name common objects and familiar people.[12] Disturbance of body image, space, distance, and movement perception often occurs with a CVA. The client may have a distorted view of self and may lack awareness of the use of certain body parts. Because of this distorted view and disuse, older adults may experience injury, weakness, inattention, and lack of care to the extremity.[12]

Memory deficits, aphasia, and confusion often found with strokes make communication a challenge. A multidisciplinary approach incorporates memory aids (watches, clocks, timers), oral-motor exercises, external modification of the setting, and a structured, consistent environment. Reality orientation that introduces familiar sights, sounds, smells, and experiences may keep the older clients in touch with the environment.

SENSORY-PERCEPTUAL

The five senses may become less efficient with the aging process, compromising safety, normal activities of daily living (ADLs), and overall self-esteem.[13] (Problems of the sensory system in older adults are covered in Chapter 10.)

PSYCHOSOCIAL

Neurological deficits causing withdrawal, isolation, and alienation may render the older client confused and disoriented. Loss of body function and altered self-image may contribute to loss of self-esteem. Concurrent physical and social changes cannot be isolated from psychological changes during the aging process. For example, sensory organ alterations (e.g., in vision or hearing) can impede interaction with the environment, influencing psychological well-being. General health status, genetic factors, and educational and vocational achievement are also influential in psychological functioning.

CEREBROVASCULAR ACCIDENT

CVA, or stroke, was the primary cause of death in 144,070 people in 1991, remaining the third leading cause of death in the United States; it is outnumbered only by cardiovascular disease and cancer.[12] Statistics from the Framington Heart Study indicate that the incidence of stroke in the United States is approximately 500,000 per year, resulting in significant morbidity, mortality, and disability in people over age 65. Hypertension, hyperlipidemia, gout, dehydration, severe atherosclerosis, mitral stenosis, silent myocardial infarction, anemia, and high serum triglyceride levels are risk factors associated with stroke.[12] In addition, cigarette smoking, physical inactivity, obesity, prior stroke, extracranial arterial disease, and left ventricular hypertrophy (LVH) were also found to be significant risk factors.[11] Aronow[14] reports that results of the Framington Study at 4-year follow-up revealed that echocardiographic LVH was predictive of new strokes in older men, independent of smoking, age, and other well-established factors.

A CVA may occur with or without the previous warning of a transient ischemic attack (TIA). Strokes can be distinguished between a syndrome and a disease. A syndrome has more than one cause, whereas a disease has but one. Stroke syndrome is caused by abnormalities of the cerebral blood vessels, collectively called cerebrovascular disease. Most strokes involve the carotid vascular distribution.[12]

Thrombotic strokes are often preceded by the appearance of one or more TIAs. A TIA is a syndrome manifested by the sudden or rapid nonconvulsive onset of neurological deficits that fit a known vascular territory, lasting for less than 24 hours. The patient returns to normal or back to baseline.[12] TIAs can be caused by any situation that decreases circulation. Such examples include hyperextension and flexion of the head when falling asleep in a chair, reduced blood pressure resulting from anemia, certain drugs (diuretics and antihypertensives), and cigarette smoking. Depending on the location of the ischemic area, hemiparesis, hemianesthesia, aphasia, vertigo, nausea, vomiting, and dysphagia may be signs manifested during a TIA. Medical treatment may include anticoagulant therapy or vascular reconstruction.

CVA symptoms persist more than 24 hours and are generally permanent. Specific neurological deficits result from damage to the brain tissue and depend on location and the extent of neuronal ischemia.[6] Dizziness, lightheadedness, headache, drop attack, and behavioral and memory changes may herald an impending CVA. A drop attack (a fall caused by a complete muscular flaccidity in the legs without alteration in consciousness) is a symptom requiring immediate attention.

As one ages, the risk of CVA increases. The vascular insufficiency CVA causes may lead to ischemia and sometimes necrosis of the brain tissue normally nourished by the affected vessels.

Major types of CVAs are thrombotic, embolic, and hemorrhagic. A thrombotic stroke begins with artheromas and ulcerative lesions within the large cerebral vessels. Thrombotic strokes are associated with atherosclerotic plaque formation, most often noted in the branching of the blood vessels. A blood vessel becomes narrow because of the plaque slowing or interrupting the flow. This process leads to the eventual progression of symptoms associated with CVA.

When a thrombus forms in a large vessel and breaks off, traveling to the brain, an embolic stroke may result. The thrombus usually lodges in a smaller vessel, obscuring blood flow. It may also break up and disperse, causing little or no damage. An embolic stroke may follow or may occur simultaneously. A common cause of the embolic stroke is a microembolus carried to the brain as a result of atrial fibrillation. The embolus is mobilized and enters the cerebral system, usually through the carotid arteries. On entering, it flows until the vessel is too narrow to allow further passage of the embolus, occluding the vessel and resulting in ischemia, which then leads to infarction. Rapid development is a hallmark sign of an embolus stroke, with maximal deficit present within seconds to a minute.

Hemorrhagic strokes are caused by the rupture of a blood vessel in the brain, usually a deep one. There are two categories of hemorrhagic strokes: intracerebral and subarachnoid. Bleeding into the brain tissue from rupture of a small vessel, most often a deep penetrating vessel, defines an intracerebral hemorrhagic stroke. A subarachnoid hemorrhage results from bleeding into the subarachnoid space, often in relation to a ruptured aneurysm or arteriovenous malformation. This prevents blood flow and the blood extravasates into the tissue. Neurological symptoms are often sudden and severe, resulting in immediate coma and respiratory distress. Common symptoms are headache (usually of sudden onset), nausea, syncope, tinnitus, and muscle weakness. In addition. sensory or motor loss and paralysis of the face or any extremity may occur. Aphasia (receptive or expressive), bowel or bladder incontinence, and seizures may also accompany a CVA.[6]

Christ and Hohloch[11] describe seven functions that may be affected by CVA: language, speech, sensation-perception, movement, behavioral style, memory, and holistic assessment.

Language

Language abilities are generally intact with left hemisphere involvement. Problems in language and perceptual abilities generally improve after stroke, but recovery is more variable than that seen in motor function. When testing language, an assessment of oral expression, verbal comprehension, naming, reading, writing, and repeating is essential in assessing the level of an individual's deficit. Aphasia (both receptive and expressive) may result from right-sided involvement.

Expressive (sometimes called nonfluent) aphasia results from damage to the region on the side of the frontal lobes, known as Broca's area. Destruction of Broca's area causes the client to have great difficulty speaking, often using faulty grammar. Some people with Broca's aphasia appear to have a disorder of omission of structural form and simplification of grammatical structure in speech.[10] With Broca's (expressive) fluency, expression, repetition, and naming are impaired, with a mild impairment in comprehension.

Receptive (sometimes called fluent or Wernicke's) aphasia results when there is injury to the cortex of the left hemisphere in the temporal lobes. Wernicke's area lies between the primary auditory cortex and a structure called the angular gyrus. A bundle of nerve fibers, the arcuate fasciculus, connects Broca's area to Wernicke's area. Wernicke's area is essential not only in speaking, but also in the comprehension of the spoken word in reading and writing.[12] With Wernicke's (receptive) aphasia, expression, comprehension, repetition, and naming are impaired; fluency is normal.

To better understand Broca's and Wernicke's aphasias, it is important to understand the normal process of receiving and expressing language. When a sound (word) is made, it cannot be heard until the signal is processed by Wernicke's area. Given a response (word), there is an indication that the spoken word is transmitted to Broca's area, which produces a program for articulation. This program is supplied to the motor cortex, which stimulates the muscles of the lips, tongue, larynx, and so forth. In reading words, the primary visual cortex registers the impression and then is thought to relay it to the angular gyrus. The angular gyrus relates the visual form (symbol) of the word with the equivalent auditory pattern in Wernicke's area. If injury is in both areas, the person experiences a global aphasia; that is, he or she experiences difficulty speaking and comprehending the spoken and written word. Fluency, expression, comprehension, repetition, and naming are all impaired.

Speech

Speech is altered in both left and right hemisphere involvement. Impaired nerve damage affecting the muscles of speech often results in aphasia (receptive, expressive, or global), dysarthria, and dysphagia. Dysarthria involves problems with articulation. The symbols (words) are used appropriately, but the speech may be slurred or distorted because of poor motor control. Assessment of subtle dysarthria may be detected by asking the client to say the following: "Me, me, me" (to test the lips), "La, la, la" (to test the tongue), and "Ga, ga, ga" (to test the pharynx).

Speech deficits are noted in left- and right-sided hemiplegia. Word-finding difficulties and dysarthria are particularly noted with right-sided involvement.[10]

Dysphagia is difficulty swallowing, related to poor motor control of the tongue and pharynx. The gag reflex may also be absent, creating a potential for aspiration when eating and swallowing. Clients with dysphagia may also have trouble handling excess secretions.

Sensation-Perception

Sensation is impaired in both right- and left-sided hemiplegia. Defective vision or visual field blindness on one side—the affected side—is known as hemianopsia and generally refers to bilateral visual defects. Right- or left-sided neglect may occur with or without a visual field defect. This distortion of perception makes it difficult for the client to judge depth and vertical and horizontal orientation in the environment. Sensation to pain, temperature, and proprioception may be diminished, although deep pain sensation is usually intact. Proprioception is a sense of feeling of joint position. If proprioception is altered, the client may not be aware of the position of the joint or limb, which may cause him or her to be at further risk for injury and skin breakdown. In addition, a hemispatial neglect may be manifested, which is a failure to report, respond, or orient to novel or meaningful stimuli presented to the side opposite a brain lesion.[12] Because of its negative impact on sitting balance, visual perception, wheelchair mobility, safety awareness, skin and joint protection, and fall risk, hemispatial neglect (neglect syndrome) contributes greatly to disability after stroke.

Movement

After a CVA, the affected side may initially be flaccid or limp because of paralysis. Spasticity and contractures may result if paralysis does not resolve.[12] Spasticity develops shortly after completed stroke, initially demonstrated as an increased phasic response to tendon tap and a slight catch with passive ranging. Ranging may become more problematic with evidence of tonic positioning in flexion or extension. Should voluntary motor activity return, a reduction in tone and reflex also is evident. If recovery is incomplete, spasticity generally remains, having implications for self-care skills and activities of daily living.[12]

As mentioned earlier, CVA can cause apraxia. The client's inability to continue doing learned, purposeful movements such as eating and dressing may lead to frustration and depression as he or she struggles to return to the premorbid state.

Behavioral Style

Altered behavioral style often takes the form of increased emotional lability, appearing as inappropriate laughing or crying. Typically, in left-sided hemiplegia, the client reacts quickly and impulsively, often overestimating abilities. The client may pace, often appearing to be searching for something, and, if not supervised, may wander. Compulsive ritualistic behaviors may also be manifested. Underestimation of abilities is often characteristic of right-sided hemiplegia. A thorough social and behavioral history (premorbid personality) is essential for appropriate and realistic care planning.[11] Depression is often a significant complication of stroke and may limit participation and positive psychosocial outcomes by inhibiting motivation and initiative. One-third to two-thirds of stroke survivors experience depression, manifesting loss of energy, sleep disorders, brooding, and hopelessness. Depression after stroke can be attributed to a combination of both organic and reactive causes.[12] Anxiety and fear after a stroke are common manifestations, often impeding future progress, quality of life, and functional gains.

Memory

Memory for new language formation is impaired in right-sided involvement. Remembering new information about the immediate environment, such as where the urinal is located, is often affected in left-sided hemiplegia.

Holistic Assessment

In summary, assessing the physical, functional, cognition-communication, sensory-perceptual, and psychosocial concerns affords the nurse a systematic method of evaluating the older client. Although the areas of assessment may overlap, this system better equips the nurse for a holistic approach to client care. In addition, the health promotion model provides a framework for assessing, planning, implementing, and evaluating the older client with neurological deficits related to CVA.

PARKINSON'S DISEASE

One of every 100 people over 50 years of age is diagnosed with Parkinson's disease. It is the most common neurological disease of the older adult. Of all people diagnosed with Parkinson's disease, 50 percent are over age 70. An estimated 50,000 new cases are diagnosed annually. Parkinson's disease is more common in men and is manifested most often in the fifth decade of life. Four prominent hypotheses regarding the cause of Parkinson's disease are accelerated aging, toxic exposure, genetic predisposition, and oxidative stress.[15]

Parkinson's disease affects the ability of the CNS to control body movements. Parkinson's disease is distinguished pathologically by degeneration of pigmented and other brain stem nuclei, particularly the substantia nigra, in association with the formation of eosinophilic neuronal inclusions called Lewy bodies.[12] The basal ganglia and the extrapyramidal motor system are involved in Parkinson's disease. Muscle tone control and smooth voluntary movements are governed by the basal ganglia. A balance of these two functions results from the excitatory effects of the reticular system and from the inhibitory action of dopamine. When the level of dopamine is decreased the basal ganglia become overactive, causing the classic symptoms of Parkinson's disease. Loss of cells in the substantia nigra correlates with the degree of dopamine shortage.[16] The depletion of dopamine in the corpus striatum contributes to the movement disorder found in those with Parkinson's disease. The corpus striatum has an essential influence on bodily movement. Muscle rigidity, tremors, involuntary movement, and bradykinesia (delay in starting movement) often are indicative of this degenerative neurological disease.

The first indication of Parkinson's may be a faint tremor that progresses over a long period. This tremor is reduced when the client is involved in purposeful movement. Drooling, difficulty swallowing, slow speech, and a monotone may be manifested and develop secondary to muscle rigidity and weakness. There may be an increase in appetite. Emotional instability and depression may be demonstrated. The client has a characteristic masklike appearance (masked facies). The classic pill-rolling gesture and shuffling gait, with the trunk leaning forward, are manifested as the disease progresses. The rate of gait increases as walking continues, and the client may be unable to stop voluntarily. Inability to ambulate may result as the disease progresses. Parkinson's disease continues to progress for an average of 10 years. Death is usually related to complications such as pneumonia and respiratory distress.

Diagnosing Parkinson's disease may be difficult. As noted, a masklike face characterized by a fixed facial expression is often seen in the disease. Tremors affecting the arms and hands are unique in that they are of a low frequency and almost rotary. These tremors generally increase when the limb is at rest and stop with purposeful movement. Cogwheel rigidity, often seen as jerking movements, with alternating periods of passive limb movement, is commonly observed. Initiation of movement is problematic. Absence of arm swing when walking and alterations in handwriting (micrographia) are early signs.[17] Being alert to signs and symptoms is essential because there are no definitive tests for diagnosing Parkinson's disease.[18]

Clients with Parkinson's disease are best treated using a multidisciplinary approach. Administration of dopamine is ineffective in the treatment of Parkinson's disease because it does not cross the blood-brain barrier.

However, levodopa, the metabolic precursor of dopamine, does cross the blood-brain barrier and presumably is converted to dopamine in the basal ganglia. If it is effective, the muscle rigidity, shuffling gait, drooling, and slowed body movements improve greatly. In addition, a mixture of levodopa and carbidopa, anticholinergics, antihistamines, antidepressants, and bromocriptine have also proved effective and may be included as part of the client's overall treatment plan. Physical therapy, assistive devices, and techniques for dressing, grooming, walking, and eating have also proved to be helpful in increasing the client's level of independence.[18] A multidisciplinary approach including the physician; physical, occupational, and speech therapists; a neuroeducator; and a nurse allows the older adult to be cared for holistically. This is discussed later in this chapter.

1 Primary Prevention

Using a health promotion model,[1] strategies and interventions can be identified from physical, functional, cognition-communication, sensory-perceptual, and psychological viewpoints.

EDUCATION

The most significant way to decrease stroke-related morbidity, mortality, and disability is to reduce the incidence of first-time and recurrent stroke. Increasing public awareness of modifiable risk factors, medical management of risk factors, and promotion of healthful lifestyles are essential.

Education is an essential component of primary prevention. As CVA continues to be a leading cause of morbidity and mortality among older adults in the United States, educational programs geared toward risk factors and prevention are crucial.[11] Smoking, diabetes mellitus, and hypertension are known risk factors that increase the client's likelihood of having a CVA, or more precisely, atherothrombotic brain infarction, its most common geriatric type.[14]

Hypercholesterolemia, type A personality behavior, obesity, lack of voluntary exercise, and family history not only influence the risk of stroke, but also affect the rate of disease progression. Older adults with coronary artery disease, especially women with prior myocardial infarction, are at higher risk for stroke.[14] LVH is a substantial independent risk factor.

Primary prevention is geared toward a healthful lifestyle, which includes a diet low in fat, salt, and sugar. Regular exercise, which becomes an important component of the older adult's schedule, can also contribute to prevention.

Although one cannot alter family history, teaching the older adult how to manage hypertension and diabetes can be an important primary preventive measure. Regularly monitoring blood pressure and properly administering antihypertensive medications are essential self-care measures for decreasing the risk of stroke. The older adult may be a candidate for antithrombotic (plasminogen activators) or antiplatelet (aspirin) therapy.[12,19] Routine use of such agents is discouraged and should be based on the client's risk for stroke or myocardial infarction as well as vulnerability to bleeding.[20,21] Management of diabetes requires regular blood glucose monitoring as well as adjustments of diet and insulin dosage.

A healthful lifestyle as primary prevention may include an educational program to decrease smoking, which carries a high risk of cardiovascular disease. In addition, knowing the target symptoms of TIAs and what can result if a TIA occurs may alert the older adult to seek attention promptly.

Educating clients about antihypertensive medication includes ensuring the correct dosage and time schedule, using memory aids to help the person follow the medication regimen, and teaching about special precautions to follow while taking antihypertensives and diuretics. Complications such as orthostatic hypotension must be addressed and prevented because of their potential to decrease the client's self-care capacity, increase disability, and cause eventual decline.

2 *Secondary Prevention*

Secondary prevention relates to assessment, diagnosis, goal setting, and intervention when neurological deficits exist. The overall goal is to prevent additional loss of health and to return clients to their maximum level of functioning.

ASSESSMENT

Assessment is the key component of accurate diagnosis, goal setting, and intervention. One component of physical assessment in neurological disorders is the testing of sensation, coordination, cerebellar functioning, reflexes, and cranial nerves. Past or present physical and functional problems such as defects in motor function, seizures, brain injury, cancer, abnormal reflexes, spasticity, and paralysis are triggers for further evaluation. In addition, cognitive-communicative deficits (in memory, thought-processing speech, abstractions, fluency), mental status and sensory-perceptual factors (orientation, level of alertness, unusual sensation), and psychological concerns (drug or alcohol use, employment history) guide the nurse in developing strategies to improve functional outcome. With a thorough assessment and understanding of the severity of the defects, the nurse is armed to work with the older client and family.

Stroke and Parkinson's disease often manifest similar neurological deficits. Keeping this in mind, the nurse should focus assessment, diagnosis, goal setting, and intervention on specific deficits rather than on the disease process. Teaching guides and discharge planning can also concentrate on specific deficits and problems with stroke and Parkinson's disease.

Once a client has had a stroke, arresting or retarding atherosclerosis is imperative to recovery. Stroke rehabilitation integrates an interdisciplinary approach incorporating medical stability, improved functional outcomes, and adjustment to residual long-term disability. Early rehabilitation measures instituted at the time of stroke are vital to the prevention of secondary complications.[12]

Acute stroke rehabilitation focuses on physical needs such as maintenance of a patient's airway and adequate nutrition. Body alignment, range of motion, and posture management are essential components of rehabilitation.[12] Preventing, recognizing, and managing comorbid illness and intercurrent complications, training for maximal functional independence, and fostering coping and adaptation should guide rehabilitation efforts. In addition, promoting community reintegration (return to home, family, and vocational activities) and improving quality of life are important outcomes in stroke rehabilitation.[22] The care plan in Table 13–2 outlines expected client outcomes and nursing interventions for the client at high risk for impaired airway clearance. Table 13–3 presents a teaching guide for chewing and swallowing problems.

POSITIONING AND EXERCISE

Positioning involves support of the paralyzed limb to prevent secondary problems such as contractures, pressure ulcers, and pain. Paralysis of the extremity prevents adequate venous return, thereby causing an accumulation of fluid in the tissue. This accumulation prevents adequate nutrition to cells, often leading to tissue breakdown. Positioning involves turning the client to facilitate good body alignment. During the acute phase, positioning involves placing the client on the unaffected side for 2 hours; the nurse should use a hand roll to keep the hand in functional position.[23]

Passive range-of-motion exercises decrease the client's risk of edema and contractures after a CVA. The exercise schedule set up by the physical therapist, which includes the frequency and repetitions, should be incorporated into the care plan. As the client's tolerance and endurance improve, exercises can be increased. The involved and uninvolved sides should both be exercised.

Exercises are carried out only to the point of resistance. The nurse continually evaluates the client's abil-

TABLE 13–2 NURSING CARE PLAN

Nursing Diagnosis: High risk for impaired airway clearance related to ineffective chewing or swallowing secondary to CVA	
Expected Outcomes	*Nursing Actions*
Patent airway Absence of evidence of aspiration	Assess for evidence of ineffective airway clearance (delayed swallowing, dyspnea, choking).
	Collaborate with speech therapist for muscle retraining.
	Assess gag reflex before administering anything by mouth.
	Supervise all meals once swallowing status has been determined.
	Keep patient in a fully upright position when administering anything by mouth.
	Observe every 8 hours for evidence of aspiration pneumonia (temperature elevation 1 degree above baseline, increased cough, adventitious breath sounds).

TABLE 13–3 TEACHING GUIDE FOR CHEWING AND SWALLOWING PROBLEMS

- Weigh the client once a week.
- Keep a log of the amount of food eaten for 3 days.
- Take the log to each follow-up appointment for evaluation.
- Obtain assistive devices as needed.
- Instruct client to cut up foods into small bites and chew well before swallowing.
- Encourage small, frequent meals in an unhurried environment.
- Keep a suction machine at hand until swallowing function returns.

ity to perform exercises alone. As the client stabilizes and activity tolerance increases, exercise should be incorporated into ADLs such as bathing, eating, bed positioning, transfers, and standing.

CVA AND NEUROLOGICAL DEFICITS

A thorough assessment includes the client's history of physical, functional, cognitive, communication, and psychosocial level and capabilities. With left-sided cerebral damage, the older client will generally exhibit right-sided hemiplegia, aphasia, dysphagia, memory deficits, and a slow, cautious behavioral style. An older adult with right-sided cerebral damage will probably demonstrate left-sided hemiplegia, spatial-perceptual deficits, memory deficits, unilateral neglect, and impulsivity. Emotional lability, ataxia, spasticity, paresthesia on the affected side, and bowel and bladder incontinence may also be characteristic of cerebral injury. A common emotional state manifested by the client is depression, usually as a response to loss of body image, function, role change, and changes in biochemistry. Depression is more commonly seen with left-hemisphere CVA. A CVA in the right hemisphere often produces emotional lability, which may take the form of mania.

NEUROLOGICAL DEFICITS IN OLDER ADULTS WITH PARKINSON'S DISEASE

The older client with Parkinson's disease may manifest bradykinesia, rigidity, loss of postural mechanisms, and tremors. There may also be loss of joint range of motion with flexion of the neck, hip, knees, and elbows, thus giving the older person a stooped body posture. Shuffling gait with or without propulsive or retropulsive movement, absent arm swing, masked facies, drooling, and bowel and bladder retention or incontinence are also characteristic of Parkinson's disease.

Cognitive disorders such as sleep disturbances and visual hallucinations progressing to paranoia and disorientation commonly occur in the later stages of the disease. Altered self-concept and altered social interaction often decrease the quality of life of the older adult with Parkinson's disease. Assisting the client to maintain optimal mobility and level of functioning and helping the family and client cope with self-care limitations and role changes are challenging goals. Such goals require continual evaluation and updating as the disorder progresses and functioning deteriorates. Neurological nurs-

ing assessment, which includes physical, motor, and sensory function and psychosocial evaluation, provides baseline data for care planning.

3 *Tertiary Prevention*

Tertiary prevention is aimed at decreasing the effects of illness and injury. This phase of health protection starts early in the period of recovery. Health supervision during rehabilitation to improve functioning, mobility, and psychosocial adjustment are expected outcomes of tertiary prevention. Living productively with limitations and deficits and minimizing residual disability are additional expectations. Tertiary prevention has much to add to the quality of life and overall meaning that life holds for the client.[1] Table 13–4 lists national support groups for neurological disorders.

STROKE REHABILITATION

Stroke rehabilitation encompasses the goals of geriatric rehabilitation. Prevention of complications and secondary limitations are major expected outcomes. Enhancing quality and meaning in life with the older client's limitations and deficits is also essential to the success of a stroke rehabilitation program.[24]

TABLE 13–4 COMMUNITY AND NATIONAL RESOURCES

American Deafness and Rehabilitation Association
Box 55369
Little Rock, AR 55369
501-663-4617

American Parkinson's Disease Association
116 John St, Suite 417
New York, NY 10038
212-732-9550

American Speech, Language, and Hearing Association
10801 Rockville Pike
Rockville, MD 20852
301-987-5700

Better Hearing Institute
Box 1840
Washington, DC 20013
703-642-0580

National Association for the Visually Handicapped
22 W 21st St
New York, NY 10010
212-889-3141

National Institute on Aging
National Institute of Health
Building 31, Room 5C35
Bethesda, MD 20105
301-496-1752

Parkinson's Disease Foundation
William Black Medical Research Bldg
Columbia University Medical Center
640–650 W 168th St
New York, NY 10032
212-923-4700

Stroke Club International
805 12th St
Galveston, TX 77550
409-762-1022

Activities of Daily Living

In addition to the positioning and range-of-motion exercises, a stroke rehabilitation program focuses on ADLs. Daily living activities include eating, grooming, hygiene, bathing, and the like. Incorporating physical and occupational therapies enhances the nurse's ability to plan care.

Evaluation of sensorimotor level, measurement of joint range of motion, and muscle strength are specific goals of the therapist and the nurse. Testing grip, triceps strength, and balance provides invaluable data for planning compensatory strategies for completion of self-care tasks.[25] Proprioception, sensation, and muscle tone are evaluated. A thorough assessment also includes the extent of neurological deficits the client may have experienced secondary to the stroke. Such data include the client's ability to bathe, dress, feed, toilet, and transfer. In addition, the status of the client's bowel and bladder function is essential information for care planning. Visual and hearing function are assessed and any deviation incorporated into the team approach.[24]

Once assessments are completed by members of the rehabilitation team, a plan identifying specific goals and assistance needed by the client is outlined to evaluate progress. Expectations should be realistic and measurable. New tasks should be introduced, using simple directions and giving one task at a time, as the client progresses through the program. Maintaining consistency with the therapy program helps the client learn new tasks and skills. A primary goal is to increase the client's independence by continuing to provide opportunities to do tasks that he or she is capable of doing. The nurse is the key care provider in the rehabilitation process, coordinating the nursing care and rehabilitative therapies. Keeping this goal in mind, the nurse can maximize the client's potential.

Cognition and Communication

Confusion, disorientation, and communication problems are common outcomes of stroke. Communication problems may result from aphasia, dysarthria, and dysphagia. With clients who have aphasia and dysarthria, the nurse should incorporate communication techniques that facilitate the client's ability to understand the world. Such techniques include speaking slowly, giving simple (one at a time) directions, limiting distractions, and listening actively. In addition, associating words with objects, using repetition and redundancy, and encouraging family to bring in small, familiar objects and to name them can improve communication patterns. Using alphabet boards, typewriters, and computer programs may also aid the client's understanding of the environment. Evaluating vision and hearing can also assist with ruling out problems that, once corrected, drastically improve communication.[10,24]

Psychological Support

The older client experiences many major losses with stroke, including body image, body functions, and role changes. Psychological support is aimed at dealing with these losses to encourage successful adaptation and adjustment. Realistic goals can be set only after the nurse has assessed the client's previous lifestyle, personality type, coping behaviors, and work activities. By providing situations for problem solving and decision making, the nurse gives the client a chance to gain control over his or her environment. Such situations can be as simple as allowing the client to choose between two activities, to decide on times for therapy, to select clothing, and to make meal choices. Focusing on strengths and abilities rather than on deficits encourages the client's hope.

Depression is common with loss of body function and changes in roles and body image. A mental health nurse may be consulted to help with this. The older client may experience a sense of isolation and alienation. The family may need emotional and psychological support when trying to understand what the loss means to the client. If this need for family support is not addressed, the client may consider suicide. Teaching family members about depression and alerting them to signs and symptoms are important in psychosocial support.[19] For a thorough discussion of depression in older adults, see Chapter 28.

Emotional lability and outbursts may occur after stroke. Family members who are taught communication strategies and how to role-play potential situations are more confident in caring for the client. Referring the client and family to support services such as home health, support groups, and respite care can lessen the burden of dependency that may follow stroke. The success of stroke rehabilitation involves managing the factors that ultimately make the difference in maintaining maximum independence and decreasing the secondary complications that can develop from disabling chronic diseases.

Student Learning Activities

1 Identify the nearest stroke rehabilitation unit in your area. Interview the stroke case manager or social worker to determine the range of services needed by an older adult who is to be discharged home following a CVA.

2 Compare the needed services with the results of your community assessment in Chapter 9.

3 What resources are available to cover the costs of these services?

REFERENCES

1 Pender, NJ (ed): Health Promotion in Nursing Practice, ed 2. Appleton & Lange, Norwalk, Conn, 1987, p 38.
2 Cutillo-Schmitter, TA: Aging: Broadening our view for improved nursing care. J Gerontol Nurs July:31–42, 1996.
3 Cavanaugh, JC: Adult Development and Aging. Brooks/Cole, Pacific Grove, Calif, 1993.
4 Ham, RJ: Assessment. In Ham, RJ, and Sloane, PD (eds): Primary Care Geriatrics: A Case-Based Approach. Mosby-Year Book, St Louis, 1992, p 87.
5 Routtenberg, A: The reward system of the brain. In Llinas, RR (ed): The Working of the Brain, Development, Memory, and Perception. WH Freeman, New York, 1987, p 78.

6 Calne, OB: Normal aging of the nervous system. In Anders, R, et al (eds): Principles of Geriatric Medicine. McGraw-Hill, New York, 1985, p 233.

7 Forbes, EJ, and Fitzsimmons, VM: The Older Adult. CV Mosby, St Louis, 1981, p 22.

8 Bohr, RT: Sleep Disturbances. In Stanley, M, and Beare, PG (eds): Gerontological Nursing. FA Davis, Philadelphia, 1995, pp 473–481.

9 Braddom, RL, et al: Physical Medicine and Rehabilitation. WB Saunders, Philadelphia, 1996.

10 Boss, BJ, and Abney, KL: Communication: Language and pragmatics. In Hoeman, S (ed): Rehabilitation Nursing, ed 2. Mosby, St Louis, 1996, pp 542–571.

11 Christ, MA, and Hohloch, FJ: Gerontological Nursing: A Study and Learning Tool. Springhouse Corp, Springhouse, Penn, 1988.

12 Roth, EJ, and Harvey, RL: Rehabilitation of stroke syndromes. In Braddom, RL, et al (eds): Physical Medicine and Rehabilitation. WB Saunders, Philadelphia, 1996, pp 1053–1087.

13 Gallman, RL: The sensory system and its problems in the elderly. In Stanley, M, and Beare, PG (eds): Gerontological Nursing. FA Davis, Philadelphia, 1996, pp 135–147.

14 Aronow, WS: Risk factors for geriatric stroke: Identification and follow-up. Geriatrics 9:37, 1990.

15 Jankovic, J: Theories on etiology and pathogenesis of Parkinson's disease. Neurology (suppl)43:S121–S123.

16 Nauta, WJ, and Feitag, M: The organization of the brain. In Llinas, RR (ed): The Workings of the Brain, Development, Memory, and Perception. WH Freeman, New York, 1987, p 24.

17 Dombovy, ML: Rehabilitation concerns in degenerative movement disorders of the central nervous system. In Braddom, RL, et al (eds): Physical Medicine and Rehabilitation. WB Saunders, Philadelphia, 1996, pp 1088–1099.

18 Booth, DE, and Morris, CL: Parkinson's disease. In Rogers-Seidl, FF (ed): Geriatric Nursing Care Plans. Mosby-Year Book, St Louis, 1991, p 217.

19 Waxman, SG: A treatment for stroke. Neuroscientist 2(3): 137.

20 Steering Committee of the Physical Health Study Research Group: Final report on the aspirin component of the ongoing physical health study. N Engl J Med 321:129–135, 1989.

21 Antiplatelet Trialists' Collaboration: Collaboration overview of randomized trials of antiplatelet therapy: Prevention of death, myocardial infarction, and stroke by prolonged antiplatelet therapy in various categories of patients. Br J Med 308:81–106, 1994.

22 Roth, EJ: Medical rehabilitation of the stroke patient. Be Stroke Smart 8:8, 1992.

23 Hickey, JV: Stroke. In Hickey, JV (ed): Neurological and Neurosurgical Nursing, ed 3. JB Lippincott, Philadelphia, 1992, pp 519–539.

24 Calvani, DL, and Douris, KB: Functional assessment: A holistic approach to rehabilitation of the geriatric client. Rehab Nurs 16(6):330, 1991.

25 Teuerkauf, A: Self-care and activities of daily living. In Hoeman, S (ed): Rehabilitation Nursing, ed 2. Mosby, St Louis, 1996, pp 156–187.

CHAPTER 14

The Aging Cardiovascular System

Mickey Stanley

OBJECTIVES

Upon completion of this chapter, the reader will be able to:

- Identify the normal age-related changes in the cardiovascular system of an older adult
- Discuss the common pathophysiological changes that accompany disease of the cardiovascular system in older adults
- Identify the components of a primary, secondary, and tertiary health protection plan for an older adult with cardiovascular disease
- Describe the alterations in care planning needed for older adults with cardiovascular disease
- List the recommended follow-up when total cholesterol level is elevated in an older adult

The heart and blood vessels provide every living cell with life-sustaining oxygen and nutrients. Without a functioning heart, life ceases. A decline in function of the cardiovascular (CV) system has an impact on all remaining systems. In the absence of severe disease, however, the older adult's heart is able to provide an adequate supply of oxygenated blood to meet the body's demands.

In the United States, CV disease is the leading cause of death and disability among older adults. Coronary artery disease (CAD) is responsible for 85 percent of the deaths attributed to heart disease.[1] Across the age span, the incidence of CV disease is higher among men than among women. By age 80, however, the prevalence rate is equal,[2] reflecting the increasing incidence of disease among older women. As the nation's population continues to age, the cost of care for older adults with all forms of CAD will increase dramatically, increasing the need for health promotion and health protection efforts among this population.[3]

The large number of older adults with CV disease makes it difficult to study normal aging of this system. A review of what is currently known of the normal aging process and the pathophysiology of common disorders affecting the CV system will provide a basis for discussion of health protection for the older adult with CV problems.

Normal Aging

With advancing age, the heart and blood vessels undergo both structural and functional changes. In general, changes caused by aging are slow and insidious in onset. This gradual state of decline is usually accompanied by a decreasing level of activity, which results in a decreased demand for oxygenated blood. The changes that accompany aging become apparent, however, when the system is stressed to increase its output to meet an increased demand.[1] Normal CV system aging changes are summarized in Table 14–1.

STRUCTURAL CHANGES

As a rule, the size of a person's heart remains proportional to body weight. Any significant hypertrophy or atrophy of the cardiac muscle is not normal, but rather a sign of cardiac disease.[2] The size of the chambers of the heart does not change with age. The thickness of the left-ventricular wall tends to increase slightly with age

TABLE 14–1   NORMAL CARDIOVASCULAR SYSTEM AGING CHANGES

Normal Age-Related Changes	Clinical Implications
Left ventricle thickens	Decreased contractile force
Valves thicken and form ridges	Impaired flow across valve
Number of pacemaker cells decreases	Dysrhythmias common
Arteries become stiff and tortuous in dilated state	Blunted baroreceptor response Blunted heat and cold response
Veins dilate, valves become incompetent	Edema to lower extremities with blood pooling

because of an increased density of collagen and loss of functioning elastic fibers.[3] Thus, the aging heart becomes less capable of distention, with a less effective contractile force.

Surface areas within the heart that have been subjected to high-pressure blood flow, such as the aortic and mitral valves, thicken and form ridges along the valve closure lines.[4] Stiffness at the base of the aortic cusps prevents complete opening, resulting in a partial obstruction to blood flow during systole. Incomplete ventricular emptying may occur during times of increased heart rate (e.g., fever, stress, and exercise) and compromise coronary artery and systemic circulation.

Structural changes affect the conduction system of the heart through an increase in the amount of fibrous and connective tissue. The total number of pacemaker cells decreases with age; therefore, only about 10 percent of the number found in young adults are present by age 75.[3] The bundle of His loses conduction fibers that carry impulses to the ventricles. In addition, a thickening of the elastic and reticular nets with an infiltration of fat occurs in the region of the sinoatrial (SA) node.[3]

With advanced age, the aorta and peripheral arterial system become stiff and tortuous. These changes result from an increase in collagen fibers and a loss of elastic fibers in the medial layer of the artery. The intimal layer of the artery thickens with increased calcium deposits.[1] This age-related process of increasing stiffness and thickness is called arteriosclerosis. As a compensatory mechanism, the aorta and other major arteries progressively dilate to receive a greater volume of blood.[2] The veins stretch and dilate in a similar fashion. The venous valves may become incompetent or fail to close completely.

FUNCTIONAL CHANGES

From a functional or performance point of view, the primary age-related change in the CV system is a reduced ability to increase output in response to an increased demand. The heart functions closer to its physiological limit under usual circumstances, leaving little physiological reserve. Cardiac output at rest remains stable or decreases slightly with advanced age,[3] and resting heart rates also decline. Because the myocardium is

thickened and less distensible, with stiffer valves, an increased diastolic filling time and increased diastolic filling pressures are required to maintain an adequate preload. The aged heart also depends more on an atrial kick, or the volume of blood delivered to the ventricles as a result of a coordinated atrial contraction. Two conditions that place older adults at risk for inadequate cardiac output are tachycardia, caused by a shortened ventricular filling time, and atrial fibrillation, caused by the loss of the atrial kick.[1]

The young heart meets an increased demand for oxygenated blood primarily by increasing heart rate in response to an increased level of circulating catecholamine. Although studies demonstrate that older adults do not have any reduction in catecholamine, their responsiveness to these chemical mediators is blunted.[1] In older adults, this phenomenon is revealed by a diminished heart rate response to exercise or stress. The principal mechanism used by the older heart to increase cardiac output is an increased end-diastolic volume, which increases stroke volume (known as Starling's law).[1,2] If the diastolic filling time is inadequate (as in tachycardia) or the ventricles become overdistended (as in heart failure), this mechanism may fail. The symptoms of dyspnea and fatigue occur when the heart cannot provide the body with an adequate supply of oxygenated blood to meet the demand or when it cannot effectively remove metabolic waste products.

The inherent rhythmic and coordinated electrical activity that controls the cardiac cycle becomes dysrhythmic and uncoordinated with advanced age. Loss of pacemaker cells and fatty infiltration into conductive tissue produce atrial and ventricular dysrhythmias. Sinus dysrhythmias, such as sick sinus syndrome and sinus bradycardia, are common and may produce dizziness, falls, palpitations, or a change in mental status.[2]

The principal functional age-related change associated with the blood vessels is a progressively increasing systolic pressure. The American Heart Association recommends that the value of 160 mm Hg systolic be considered the upper limit of normal for older adults.[5] No change in diastolic pressure is normal. Possibly resulting from the stiffened vessels or from years of high-pressure blood flow, the baroreceptors located in the aortic arch and carotid sinus become blunted or less sensitive.[4] This blunting produces the problems associated with orthostatic hypotension because it renders the vessels unable to vasoconstrict in response to a rapid change in position.

Pathophysiology

ATHEROSCLEROSIS

Atherosclerosis, by far the most common pathological process to affect the CV system, is a generalized disease process having an impact on virtually all of the arteries. However, individuals vary in the degree to which various areas of the body are affected. In many individuals, the obstruction occurs in a coronary artery, whereas in others it may occur in the cerebral or peripheral circulation.

The pathophysiology of atherosclerosis is no different in the young than in the old.[1] The disease process may be more pronounced in older adults because of a greater number of years of accumulation. Atherosclerotic disease affect primarily the intimal (innermost) layer of the arterial tree, which has a smooth endothelial lining that facilitates blood flow. Under normal circumstances, only the blood plasma comes in contact with the endothelial lining, with the cellular components (e.g., coagulation factors) remaining in the center of the bloodstream. When the smooth lining is roughened, however, the potential for thrombus formation exists as coagulation factors come in contact with the endothelium.[1]

Once initiated, atherosclerosis does not progress in a continuous fashion but involves a buildup-and-breakdown process.[1] The first stage may begin in childhood, progressing into the second decade of life. In this early stage, yellow streaks appear that consist mostly of lipids. These fatty lesions develop primarily in areas of turbulence such as a bifurcation.

In the second stage, fibrous plaques develop. These plaques are pearly white elevations that protrude into the lumen of the artery.[1] The principal change occurring in this stage is the growth of smooth muscle cells in the intima, an area that does not normally contain smooth muscle cells. The reasons for this proliferation are not well understood. Once the smooth muscle cells proliferate, they form a fibrous cap, which contains chiefly lipids in the form of low-density lipoproteins (LDLs), in addition to fibrin, fibrinogen, albumin, and white blood cells.[1]

As the lesion advances and enlarges, the core of this fibrous cap becomes necrotic and calcified, and the medial layer of the artery weakens. Areas of aneurysm that form on the wall of the plaque may rupture and hemorrhage into the core. The rupture may lead to thrombus formation, which further occludes the vessel lumen, with the potential for totally obstructing blood flow.

As previously stated, the process of atherosclerosis is not a continuous one. Rather, it is thought to be a process of building up and breaking down, with the concentration of LDLs contributing to the buildup phase and the concentration of high-density lipoproteins (HDLs) contributing to the breakdown phase. The role of hyperlipidemia is addressed more fully later in this chapter.

VALVULAR HEART DISEASE

The pathogenesis of valvular disease in the over-65 age group is primarily a combination of age-related stiffening and traumatic wear and tear from high-pressure blood flow.[6] However, rheumatic fever remains an important cause of valvular problems such as mitral stenosis and aortic and mitral regurgitation. An acute onset of valvular dysfunction may also be precipitated by papillary muscle rupture or endocarditis after an acute myocardial infarction (MI).

Clinical Manifestations

CORONARY ARTERY DISEASE

Although the pathophysiology of atherosclerosis is similar in the young and old, presenting signs and symptoms differ. Angina pectoris with physical exertion, commonly seen in the younger age groups, is often absent in older adults.[7] Many older adults respond to advancing age with diminished physical activity. Therefore, the supply-and-demand imbalance that typically produces angina pectoris may not emanate from increasing physical demands. When the demand for oxygenated blood does exceed supply, the most common symptoms are dyspnea, fatigue, and a change in mental status.[7]

As with angina pectoris, the symptoms of MI in older adults may be vague and difficult to recognize. Up to 42 percent of MIs may not present with chest pain.[8] The development of a Q wave on the electrocardiogram may also be absent. Difficulties involved in the history-taking process (i.e., recent memory loss, reluctance to admit sources of pain) and complications imposed by other, nonrelated chronic conditions (e.g., chronic obstructive pulmonary disease [COPD], arthritis, and hiatus hernia) make it difficult to obtain an accurate picture of CAD.

Gender differences have been noted in the relative importance of typical and atypical chest pain. Older women with atypical chest pain who have no history of MI are less likely than older men to have significant coronary artery stenosis or involvement of the left anterior descending (LAD) artery. Three-vessel, or LAD, artery disease (the more serious type of CAD) is almost nonextent in women with vague or nonspecific chest pain.[9] Classic or typical angina carries the same diagnostic significance for both genders.

Mortality rates after MI are higher among women than among men. Possible explanations for this finding include increased age at the time of infarction and the high prevalence of diabetes and hypertension in women who experience MIs.[9]

CONGESTIVE HEART FAILURE

Congestive heart failure (CHF) is the most common admitting diagnosis into acute-care agencies among older populations.[10] Approximately 50 percent of older adults admitted with a diagnosis of CHF are readmitted within 90 days for the same diagnosis. CHF may result from ischemic heart disease, hypertensive heart disease, or valvular disease. The clinical presentation of CHF in older adults is similar to that in younger persons, with the classic symptoms of dyspnea, orthopnea, paroxysmal nocturnal dyspnea, and dependent peripheral edema.[10] These same symptoms may also be found in other conditions often seen in older adults, such as COPD and nutritional anemia, thus complicating the diagnosis. A major emphasis for the future must be placed on proper management of this spiraling health-care problem through education and social support. The balancing act required for effective management is discussed in detail under "Tertiary Prevention" later in this chapter.

DYSRHYTHMIAS

The incidence of atrial and ventricular dysrhythmias is increased in older adults because of the previously described structural and functional changes of aging. The problems induced by an uncoordinated and dysrhythmic heart often manifest as behavioral changes, palpitations, dyspnea, fatigue, and falls.[11]

PERIPHERAL VASCULAR DISEASE

Arteriosclerosis is usually well advanced before symptoms of arteriosclerosis obliterans becomes obvious. The most common symptom is a burning, cramping, or aching pain that is brought on by exercise and relieved by rest. As the disease progresses, the pain is no longer relieved by rest. If the client maintains a sedentary lifestyle, the disease may be advanced when pain first occurs. Other accompanying signs and symptoms include cool extremities, trophic changes (i.e., uneven hair loss, deformed nails, and atrophied digits on the affected limb), diminished pulses, and numbness.[4]

VALVULAR HEART DISEASE

The clinical manifestations of valvular heart disease vary from the compensatory to the postcompensatory phase. During the compensatory phase, the body adjusts to the changes in the valve structure or function, producing few outward signs or symptoms. For example, as the aortic valve becomes stiff (i.e., aortic stenosis), the left ventricle hypertrophies to respond to the increased pressure gradient needed to propel the blood across the stiff valve.[4] In mitral stenosis, the left atrium may become enlarged to accommodate an increasing volume of blood.[4] The older adult may contribute to this compensatory phase through an increasingly sedentary lifestyle that places fewer demands on the heart for its cardiac output. Many older adults never progress past the compensatory phase of their valvular heart disease.

When the postcompensatory phase is reached, it usually indicates severe dysfunction of the affected valve. Symptoms vary depending on which valve is involved but generally consist of dyspnea on exertion, anginal-type chest pain, and symptoms of right or left (or both) heart failure.[4] A murmur is typically present on auscultation. Such diagnostic tests as Doppler studies, two-dimensional echocardiography, or right- and left-sided heart catheterization may be needed to diagnose the degree of valve dysfunction accurately.

Management

1 Primary Prevention

Efforts to reduce risk factors to prevent CV disease are viewed by most experts as the only reasonable answer to the spiraling health-care costs associated with the treatment of this number-one killer. Prevalence studies indicate a high incidence of risk factors for CV disease among older adults. An increasing body of research supports the effectiveness of an aggressive approach to risk factor reduction as a mechanism to reduce the morbidity and mortality associated with CV disease in this age group. In addition, improvement in quality of life have been shown through such efforts as increasing regular physical activity and reducing smoking.

Smoking

Tobacco smoking has a harmful effect on the heart by lowering HDL levels, increasing platelet adhesiveness and fibrinogen levels, displacing oxygen on the hemoglobin molecule with carbon dioxide, increasing myocardial oxygen consumption, and decreasing the ventricular fibrillation threshold during myocardial infarction. Today, cigarette smoking is the single most important preventable risk factor for CV disease. Increasingly, studies show the benefits for older adults who quit smoking. Therefore, all health-care providers must educate clients about the harmful aspects of smoking and the benefits to be gained by quitting smoking at any age.[12]

Hyperlipidemia

Total cholesterol levels gradually increase with age. The evidence is increasing that high levels of LDL cholesterol and low levels of HDL cholesterol are important predictors of CAD in both men and women over age 65.[13] For older adults with established coronary disease, elevated cholesterol substantially increases the risk of recurrent MI or death. Cholesterol lowering through low-saturated-fat diets has proven effective for older adults. For those who are unable to achieve the desired effects through dietary management, drug therapy is recommended.[12] The National Cholesterol Education Panel has provided guidelines for treatment of hyperlipidemia (Table 14–2).[14]

An area of concern regarding dietary restrictions with older adults is inadequate nutritional intake. Be-

TABLE 14–2 CLASSIFICATION AND FOLLOW-UP BASED ON TOTAL CHOLESTEROL LEVEL

Classification		Follow-Up
<200 mg/dL	Desirable	Repeat in 5 years
200–239 mg/dL	Borderline–high	Diet instruction
(without evidence of CHD or 2 risk factors)		Recheck annually
(with evidence of CHD or 2 risk factors)		Lipoprotein analysis
>249 mg/dL	High	Lipoprotein analysis

Adapted from Expert Panel: Report of the National Cholesterol Education expert panel on detection, evaluation, and treatment of high blood cholesterol in adults. Arch Intern Med 148(6):36, 1988.

cause many older adults have nutritional anemia or frank malnutrition, additional dietary recommendations that limit protein and fat intake must be made with caution. Older adults often need assistance to obtain a well-balanced diet that contains the appropriate distribution of calories and essential vitamins and minerals without the lipid-altering sources of animal fat.

Diabetes Mellitus and Obesity

Diabetes mellitus and obesity are independent risk factors for CV disease.[1] Weight reduction is beneficial not only to the diabetes but also to concomitant hypertension and hyperlipidemia. In addition to total body fat, the regional distribution of fat may also be of predictive value.[3] An increased abdominal-to-gluteal distribution ratio, known as an apple shape, indicates a higher risk category than the pear shape, or a decreased abdominal-to-gluteal distribution ratio. Unfortunately, ideal body weight and fat distribution charts have not been developed for older adults. Nevertheless, older diabetic or obese adults need support and encouragement to manage their diabetes effectively, to follow appropriate weight-reducing diets, or both to prevent the risks of CV disease. See Chapter 16 for a thorough discussion of diabetes in older adults.

Sedentary Lifestyle

"You're getting older now. It's time to slow down." This statement reveals a common attitude regarding physical activity and older adults. Rather than encouraging regular physical activity for all age groups, well-meaning friends, relatives, and even health-care professionals often promote decreasing levels of physical exertion for older adults. With a decline in physical exertion comes decreasing muscle tone; a loss of lean muscle mass, which is replaced by fatty tissue; and an increased risk of CV disease.[15] Primary prevention efforts aimed at combating this risk should focus on changing attitudes about the importance of regular physical activity for all age groups and promoting the belief that an appropriate activity program exists for everyone, regardless of the current level of fitness or presence of concomitant disease. Chapter 20 provides an in-depth discussion of physical activity for older adults.

Hypertension

Hypertension is a major risk factor for CV disease. When hypertension combined with diabetes or hyperlipidemia, the risk escalates dramatically.[16] Primary prevention of essential hypertension includes maintenance of ideal body weight, low-salt diet, stress reduction, and regular aerobic exercise. Early detection and effective management of hypertension are important to prevent any resulting hypertensive heart disease.[16]

Postmenopausal State

Before menopause, nondiabetic women enjoy a state of protection from atherosclerosis as a result of their natural hormones, principally estrogen. Although research in this area remains inconclusive, estrogen seems to increase the concentration of HDLs and to lower the concentration of LDLs.[17] Diabetic women lack this protection and develop atherosclerosis at a rate comparable with that of nondiabetic men. Prevention of CV disease in older women focuses on methods of estrogen replacement. Although estrogen replacement is effective in favorably altering lipids in postmenopausal women, this technique is not without risks, specifically the risk of endometrial cancer. The addition of progesterone to the estrogen regimen may prevent the malignant and nonmalignant consequences of unopposed estrogen.[17]

2 Secondary Prevention

History and Physical Assessment

The early detection and treatment of CV disease should begin with a thorough history and physical assessment. Table 14–3 provides questions used to elicit a history of CV problems. A physical assessment finding indicative of CV system problems is poor end-organ perfusion. For example, when cerebral perfusion is inadequate, behavioral changes can be observed such as restlessness, confusion, and falls. Older adults with poor renal perfusion in the absence of renal disease may have decreased urinary output over a 24-hour period. Signs and symptoms of inadequate peripheral perfusion may range from skin that is cool to the touch, with diminished capillary refill, to such chronic findings as faint or absent peripheral pulses, disproportionate hair loss on extremities, and nonhealing ulcers.

Edema, although a classic finding in CV dysfunction, also has noncardiac sources that require discrimination in older adults. Key differences include the distribution of the accumulated fluid and its diurnal variations. Edema of cardiac origin is soft and pitting, is symmetrical in distribution, and involves dependent body parts. This type of edema accumulates during the day (if the patient is ambulatory) and resolves or lessens at night or when the affected area is elevated. Edema associated with low levels of plasma albumin (from poor nutrition) or liver dysfunction involves all soft-tissue ar-

TABLE 14–3   QUESTIONS FOR CARDIOVASCULAR HISTORY

Do you ever have any of the following:
- Feelings of a pounding in your chest?
- Trouble catching your breath during normal daily activity?
- Clothes, shoes, or rings that become too tight?
- Swelling in your feet and legs?
- A feeling of extreme fullness after a small meal?
- The need to urinate frequently during the night (more than usual)?
- The need to prop up on pillows at night to sleep?
- A dry cough at night that goes away during the day?
- Dizziness or blackout spells after moving too quickly?

Data from Stanley M: Cardiovascular system. In Burggraf, V, and Stanley, M (eds): Nursing the Elderly: A Care Plan Approach. JB Lippincott, Philadelphia, 1989.

eas such as the face, eye orbits, and abdomen. This type of edema is usually worse in the morning and clears somewhat during the day if renal output is adequate. Edema that is isolated to one extremity more typically indicates venous occlusion from thrombus formation, a condition for which sedentary older adults are at risk. The various types of edema must be distinguished for appropriate care to be delivered.[18]

Auscultation of heart tones in older adults is often difficult because of senile emphysematous changes in the chest wall. If the heart tones are distant or difficult to hear, the client may be positioned on his or her left side with the left arm supporting the head. This position allows gravity to move the heart closer to the chest wall and thereby enhances the sound. With the stethoscope placed between the patient's chest wall and the bed at the fifth intercostal space and the midclavicular line, both normal and abnormal sounds are accentuated.[19]

In the cardiac assessment of older adults, "abnormalities" must be interpreted with caution. For example, shift of the point of maximal impulse (PMI) from its usual position may indicate left ventricular hypertrophy or may simply result from age-related changes in the anteroposterior diameter of the chest wall. In addition, a low-density systolic murmur or the presence of an S_3 or S_4 that would indicate pathology in younger adults may be a normal finding among older adults. Of greater significance than the presence or absence of these findings is their stability or instability over time. A new-onset systolic murmur, extra heart sound, or shift in the PMI requires careful medical evaluation and ongoing assessment.[19]

Although it is a routine assessment parameter, it is crucial to measure blood pressure accurately to avoid problems associated with unnecessary treatment of hypertension. Paying close attention to the details of cuff size and to activities preceding the measurement and maintaining a consistent technique are essential for accuracy.

Nursing Management

Nursing management for older adults during an acute or life-threatening situation can be conceptualized as a two-pronged approach: reducing the workload on the heart while improving its function.

Reducing Cardiac Workload

A variety of nursing efforts contribute to reducing the workload on the heart and CV system. Balancing rest with activity helps to maintain muscle tone and efficient oxygen extraction, which decreases the tissue demand for oxygenated blood. To accomplish this balance, activities should be spaced throughout the day. Major activities, such as meals, activities of daily living (ADLs), ambulation, or range-of-motion exercises, are followed by 20 to 30 minutes of rest. However, prolonged bed rest is to be avoided. Clients should be assisted out of bed, if necessary, once they are hemodynamically stable. Regular physical activity is the key to preventing any further decline in the CV system. See Chapter 20 for a discussion of nursing management of these problems.

The direct application of supplemental oxygen also decreases the workload on the heart by increasing the amount of oxygen carried on the hemoglobin molecule. Measures to relieve anxiety help stop the release of circulating catecholamines, which increase the demand on the heart. By reducing the client's circulating volume through fluid restriction or sodium restriction (if necessary), or both, or through administration of diuretics, the total blood volume that the heart has to handle is reduced. Dependent nursing measures to reduce the workload on the heart include the administration of β-adrenergic blocking agents to decrease the myocardial oxygen demand and drugs such as vasodilators to reduce the peripheral vascular resistance of the arterial system.

Improving Function

Effective functioning of the heart requires a delicate balance of contractility and a regular rate and rhythm. Nursing efforts to enhance contractility include monitoring electrolyte balance and administering the required supplements, insuring an adequate venous return through careful monitoring of blood pressure and fluid balance, and administering cardiotonic drugs such as digitalis preparations.

A critical nursing measure with this population is the careful assessment for side effects or untoward effects of digitalis preparations. Because older adults are especially sensitive to the toxic effects of these drugs, they require ongoing assessment.[20] Geriatricians often prescribe the pediatric strength of digoxin for older adults to allow once-a-day dosing without precipitating toxicity. Drugs that may be prescribed with digoxin (e.g., quinidine, verapamil, and to a lesser extent, nifedipine) increase the serum levels of digitalis. Thus, older adults receiving any of these combinations of drugs must be observed frequently for symptoms of overdose.[20]

A regular cardiac rate and rhythm are essential to effective function. Older adults often require antidysrhythmia agents to stabilize their heart rate and rhythm because of the loss of pacemaker cells in the sinoatrial and atrioventricular nodes. Although these drugs are commonly prescribed, the client's need for them must be reviewed regularly because of the side effects that occur with prolonged use. In addition, the use of pacemaker devices improves overall cardiac performance in older adults with sick sinus syndrome or symptomatic bradycardia and improves their activity tolerance.[20] As a rule, older adults adapt well to these devices with minimal support and encouragement.

Key elements for documentation include the development and resolution of signs and symptoms of the disorder and the client's response to therapy. Subtle changes in mentation or increasing shortness of breath upon exertion may indicate untoward drug effects or a worsening cardiac condition. Breath sounds must be auscultated and recorded regularly. The 24-hour fluid balance is a sensitive and early indicator of a changing cardiac status (in the absence of renal failure), and thus must be monitored regularly. Laboratory values should also be tracked frequently, because of their relationship to effective CV system functioning.

Documentation of the client's response to activity is critical. Heart rate and blood pressure are recorded before, during, and after exertion. The amount of activity must be quantified (i.e., in minutes or number of steps taken) to allow an evaluation of progress over time. In addition, the client's perception of the level of exertion, from "easy" to "very hard," is an important gauge of the workload on the heart.

NURSING DIAGNOSIS AND CARE PLANS

The principal nursing diagnosis associated with the CV system is decreased cardiac output. The defining characteristics and care plan for this nursing diagnosis can be found in Table 14–4.[21] The additional diagnosis of activity intolerance is covered in Chapter 20.

3 Tertiary Prevention

Balancing chronic CV problems with a health-promoting lifestyle requires a knowledge of how to balance the body's energy supply with the demand. Adjustments may be necessary in both lifestyle and environment to ensure that the older heart can meet the demand for oxygenated blood. See Chapter 20 on activity intolerance for a discussion of energy-conserving methods.

A program to assist with this balance begins with an assessment of the client's personal, modifiable risk factors. An understanding of the client's willingness and ability to follow the prescribed plan of care will direct nursing actions. Most older adults are willing to make adjustments to their lifestyles once they thoroughly understand the recommendations and their rationale. See

"Research Brief."[22] However, attempting to enforce radical or multiple lifestyle changes usually results in failure. Involving the client in establishing priorities for change and short-term goals fosters interdependence and enhances self-esteem. Each attempt to modify behavior, no matter how small, should be encouraged because it represents progress toward a long-term goal.

The nurse may need to accept the client's right to choose not to change certain lifelong habits such as smoking or a high-fat diet. The nurse has the responsibility to present or teach the content in a manner that the client can understand and accept. Once understanding has been reached, however, the principle of self-determination supports each individual's right to accept or reject the teaching.

The client's knowledge of his or her drugs, diet, and exercise plan must be assessed and supplemented as needed. The nurse should ask the client to describe a typical weekday and a typical weekend day. Each aspect of the plan of care should be discussed in terms of how it can be incorporated into the client's existing routines. Vague advice to take a medication three times a day with meals may be meaningless or confusing to an older adult who has only one meal a day. In addition, each client must understand the signs and symptoms of a worsening condition (Table 14–5) and have a plan for obtaining medical assistance when needed.

The nurse should assess the client's need for assistance with ADLs and instrumental ADLs. Is help available from family, friends, or community groups? Are these forms of assistance acceptable to the client? Previous studies have shown that a lack of appropriate discharge planning resulting in inadequate resources for mediation, food, and transportation, as well as a lack of

TABLE 14–4   NURSING CARE PLAN

Nursing Diagnosis: Alteration in cardiac output: decreased	
Expected Outcomes	*Nursing Actions*
Regular cardiac rate and rhythm	Assess regularly for evidence of expected outcomes.
Vital signs within normal limits	Balance rest with activity.
Clear lung sounds	Encourage client to perform ADLs to tolerance (assist as needed).
Palpable peripheral pulses	Monitor response to early and progressive exercise program.
Brisk capillary refill	Administer supplemental oxygen (as needed).
Alertness and orientation to surroundings	Reduce anxiety by:
Absence of edema	Using a calm and reassuring approach
Normal laboratory values	Providing information when client demonstrates readiness
Urinary output equal to fluid intake (minus insensible loss)	Relieving pain promptly
No chest pain or dyspnea with minimal exertion	Using touch and eye contact
	Providing comfort measures
	Maintain an adequate circulating blood volume by:
	Regulating fluid intake
	Restricting sodium intake (if needed)
	Elevating feet and legs while sitting
	Applying compression stockings during bed rest
	Ensure adequate nutrition intake.

RESEARCH BRIEF

Dellasega, C, et al: Cholesterol-related health behaviors in rural elderly persons. J Gerontol Nurs 21(5):6, 1995.

Using a survey design, this study determined that rural-living older adults had limited access to cholesterol screening. In addition, many older adults were uninformed regarding foods that are recommended for a low-cholesterol diet. Professional nurses in a rural setting have an opportunity to influence health promotion for older adults through teaching, providing routine cholesterol screening in such settings as Senior Centers and local churches or synagogues, and providing guidance to services that provide meals for older adults regarding appropriate food selection and preparation.

TABLE 14–5 TEACHING GUIDE: SIGNS AND SYMPTOMS OF A WORSENING CONDITION

Fatigue unexplained by daily activities
Shortness of breath caused by decreasing levels of exertion
Weight gain unrelated to intake
Shoes or rings that become too tight
Need to sleep using an increased number of pillows or to sleep sitting up
Nonproductive cough that develops at night and resolves during the day
Loss of appetite or sensation of fullness with minimal intake
Increasing forgetfulness or pattern of falls

understanding regarding medication regimen, resulted in an increased readmission rate for older adults with a diagnosis of congestive heart failure.[23] A referral to a social service or home health agency may be needed to ensure that the client has the support necessary to foster a health-promoting lifestyle.

Ongoing maintenance for CV problems can be viewed as a balancing act, depicted in Figure 14–1, in which the client is required to juggle medications, diet, and exercise to stay healthy. Many older adults benefit from a structured cardiac rehabilitation program, which offers professional assistance in attaining the balance needed after a cardiac event or when managing the long-term effects of CV disease.[15]

A structured cardiac rehabilitation program usually begins with early and progressive activity as soon as the CV system has stabilized. Educational elements are offered when the client demonstrates a readiness to learn. The program continues with a supervised exercise component. The synergistic effect of participating in a program with others in similar circumstances reduces the fear and isolation that often accompanies such an event. Motivation to make the necessary lifestyle changes is a

Balancing Act

Figure 14–1 Balancing act for cardiovascular problems.

key purpose of cardiac rehabilitation. Long-term compliance can be strengthened by the friendships that are formed during these programs.

Student Learning Activities

1 Collect recipes for low-cholesterol foods. Prepare a sample of the recipes and ask a group of clients to do a taste test.

2 Survey local establishments, such as enclosed malls, YMCA/YWCA, Senior Wellness Centers, retirement centers, and area parks and recreation facilities for information on walking or fitness programs for older adults. Are policies developed for the programs or are they informally operated?

REFERENCES

1 Fernandez-Ortiz, A, and Fuster, V: Pathophysiology of coronary artery disease. Clin Geriatr 12:1, 1996.
2 Gerber, RM: Coronary artery disease in the elderly. J Cardiovasc Nurs 4:23, 1990.
3 Morgan, S: Effects of age on cardiovascular functioning. Geriatr Nurs 14:249, 1993.
4 Blair, K: Aging: Physiological aspects and clinical implications. Nurs Pract: 15:14, 1990.
5 Kane, RL, et al: Essentials of Clinical Geriatrics, ed 2. McGraw-Hill, New York, 1989.
6 Lavie, CJ, et al: Prevention and reduction of left ventricular hypertrophy in the elderly. Clin Geriatr Med 12:57, 1996.
7 Fleg, JL: Angina pectoris in the elderly. Cardiol Clin 9:177, 1991.
8 Tresch, DD, and Aronow, WS: Clinical manifestations and diagnosis of coronary artery disease. Clin Geriatr Med 12:89, 1996.
9 Wingate, S: Women and coronary heart disease. Implications for the critical care setting. Focus 18:212, 1991.
10 Leibovitch, ER: Congestive heart failure: A current overview. Geriatrics 46:43, 1991.
11 Rodriguez, RD, and Schocken, DD: Update on sick sinus syndrome, a cardiac disorder of aging. Geriatrics 45:26, 1990.
12 Tresch, DD, and Aronow WS: Smoking and coronary artery disease. Clin Geriatr Med 12:23, 1996.
13 LaRosa, JC: Dyslipidemia and coronary artery disease in the elderly. Clin Geriatr Med 12:33, 1996.
14 Expert Panel: Report of the National Cholesterol Education Program expert panel on detection, evaluation, and treatment of high blood cholesterol in adults. Arch Intern Med 148(6):36, 1988.
15 Wenger, NK: Physical inactivity and coronary heart disease in elderly patients. Clin Geriatr Med 12:79, 1996.
16 Messerli, FH, and Grodzicki, T: Hypertension and coronary artery disease in the elderly. Clin Geriatr Med 12:41, 1996.
17 Nachtigall, LE, and Nachtigall, LB: Protecting older women from their growing risk of cardiac disease. Geriatrics 45:24, 1990.
18 Galindo-Ciocon, D: Nursing care of elders with leg edema. J Gerontol Nurs 21(7):7, 1995.
19 McGovern, M, and Kuhn, JK: Cardiac assessment of the elderly client. J Gerontol Nurs 18(8):40, 1992.
20 Karig, AW, and Hartshorn, EA: Counseling Patients on Their Medications. Drug Intelligence Publications, Hamilton, Ill, 1991.
21 Dougherty, CM: Decreased cardiac output. In Maas, M, et al (eds): Nursing Diagnoses and Interventions for the Elderly. Addison-Wesley Nursing, Redwood City, Calif, 1991.
22 Dellasega, C, et al: Cholesterol-related health behaviors in rural elderly persons. J Gerontol Nurs 21(5):6, 1995.
23 Vinson, JM, et al: Early readmission of elderly patients with congestive heart failure. J Am Geriatr Soc 38:1290, 1990.

CHAPTER 15

The Aging Pulmonary System

Kathryn A. Blair

OBJECTIVES

Upon completion of this chapter, the reader will be able to:

- Identify normal pulmonary changes associated with aging
- Understand the pathophysiological process of common pulmonary problems
- Recognize the clinical manifestations of common pulmonary problems
- Describe the pulmonary assessment of the older adult
- Discuss the nursing care of the older adult with pulmonary disease

Aging is a universal phenomenon that alters an individual's physiological reserve and ability to maintain homeostasis, particularly in time of stress (e.g., illness). Although the pulmonary system is bombarded daily with many insults (e.g., pollution, smoking) it has the capacity to sustain an individual throughout life. Most of the normal changes associated with aging are gradual, so the older person can adapt. The most profound change is related to the physiological reserve. The older adult can maintain homeostasis, but even minor insults can upset this precarious balance.

Normal Aging

The anatomic changes that occur with aging (Table 15–1)[1–7] contribute to changes in pulmonary function. Other changes such as loss of cilia and diminished cough and gag reflex alter the physiological reserve and protective ability of the pulmonary system (Table 15–2).[1–9]

Anatomic changes such as decreased lung and chest wall compliance contribute to an increase in the work of breathing by 20 percent at age 60 years.[3] Respiratory muscle atrophy and decreased respiratory muscle strength increase the older adult's risk of developing inspiratory muscle fatigue.[5] These changes can contribute to a decrease in maximum oxygen consumption. Alterations of parenchymal interstitium and a decrease in alveolar surface area can result in decreased diffusion of

oxygen.[3] These changes, when combined with an approximate 50 percent reduction in hypoxia and hypercapnia response at 65 years of age,[2] can result in decreased sleep efficiency and a diminished exertional capacity.

The clinical implications of changes in the respiratory system are many. The structural changes, alterations in pulmonary function, and an impaired immune system result in a susceptibility to respiratory failure caused by infections, lung cancer, pulmonary emboli, and chronic diseases such as asthma and chronic obstructive pulmonary disease (COPD). Normal pulmonary system aging changes and their clinical implications are summarized in Table 15–3.

Pathophysiology of Common Disorders

LOWER RESPIRATORY INFECTIONS

Lower respiratory infections are the second most common infection in older adults,[10] and pneumonia is the leading cause of death by an infectious process.[9] Ineffective airway clearance, increased colonization, and the impaired immune response of older adults can culminate in the development of pneumonia. Pneumonia can be classified by site of acquisition: community-acquired, nosocomial (hospital-acquired), aspiration, and nursing home-acquired.[10]

TABLE 15–1 ANATOMIC CHANGES AND ALTERATIONS OF PULMONARY FUNCTION

Change	Result	Alteration
Costal cartilage calcification	Increased anteroposterior diameter	Decreased Pao_2
	Increased abdominal and diaphragmatic breathing	
	Increased work of breathing	
Respiratory muscle atrophy	Increased risk for inspiratory muscle fatigue	Decreased maximum expiratory flow rates
Decrease in elastic recoil	Increased closing volume	Increased residual volume
	Increased air trapping	Decreased forced vital capacity
	Ventilation-perfusion mismatch	Decreased vital capacity
Enlargement of alveolar ducts	Decreased alveolar surface area	
Increased size and stiffness of trachea and central airways	Decreased diffusing capacity	
	Increased dead space	

Pneumonia affects the terminal airways. The invading organism multiplies and releases toxins that trigger inflammatory and immune responses. Subsequently, biochemical mediators are released that damage the bronchial mucous membranes and alveolocapillary membranes, causing edema. The acini (a respiratory bronchiole, alveolar duct, and alveolus) and terminal bronchioles fill with infectious debris and exudate.[11] Offending organisms are listed on Table 15–4.[10,12]

Institutionalized older people are prone to develop pneumonia because of altered consciousness (stroke and sedation) that may leave the airway unprotected. They may also experience impaired mobility, which may contribute to ineffective respiration. Older adults with recent viral infections (i.e., influenza) are at increased risk because the viral infection enhances mucosal adherence of bacterial and viral infections. Viral infections can also impair mucociliary transport.[13]

Tuberculosis is a growing epidemic among older adults who make up the fastest-growing segment of the U.S. population.[14] Whether these are new infections or reactivation of old infections is unclear. Older people are at an increased risk because of coexisting chronic conditions (e.g., diabetes), poor nutritional status, and immunosuppressive drugs or diseases.[14,15]

Tuberculosis (TB) is caused by *Mycobacterium tuberculosis,* and acid-fast bacillus. Typical transmission is via inhaled droplet. The microorganism usually lodges in the apices of the lung. It multiplies and causes a pneumonitis that triggers an immune response. Neutrophils and macrophages seal off and engulf the bacilli, preventing further spread. The sealing off results in the formation of a granulomatous tubercle. TB may remain dormant or be reactivated, or may never be contained because of an impaired immune response.[11] As is discussed later, the presentation of this disease in older adults is atypical.

LUNG CANCER

The leading cause of cancer-related death in men and women is bronchogenic cancer.[2] The incidence rate has been rising steadily, with the largest increase occurring in women. For a more detailed discussion of lung cancer in older adults, see Chapter 23.

CHRONIC OBSTRUCTIVE PULMONARY DISEASE

COPD is the fifth leading cause of death in older people. COPD encompasses three conditions that share one common feature, obstruction of expiratory flow. If the obstructive process is reversible, it is called asthma; if the obstruction is associated with mucous hypersecretion, it is called chronic bronchitis, and if there is destruction of alveolar tissue, it is known as emphysema.[2]

TABLE 15–2 CAUSES OF ALTERED PULMONARY PHYSIOLOGICAL RESERVE AND PROTECTIVE MECHANISMS

Change	Result	Consequence
Loss of cilia	Less effective mucociliary escalator	Increased risk of respiratory insult
Decreased gag and cough reflex	Unprotected airway	Increased risk of pulmonary injury
Blunted response to hypoxemia and hypercapnia	Decreased oxygen saturation	Decreased physiological reserve
Decreased T-lymphocyte function and humoral immunity	Decreased antibody response to specific antigens	Increased vulnerability to infections
		Diminished delay hypersensitivity response (false-negative response to purified protein derivative test)
		Decreased efficacy of vaccinations
Decreased β_2-receptor function	Decreased response to inhaled β_2-agonist	Increased difficulty in managing asthma
Decreased esophageal and gastric motility and loss of cardiac sphincter tone	Increased risk of esophageal reflux	Increased risk of aspiration

TABLE 15–3 NORMAL PULMONARY SYSTEM AGING CHANGES

Normal Age-Related Changes	Clinical Implications
Small and flabby lungs Loss of elastic recoil Enlarged alveoli	Decreased surface area for diffusion of gas
Decreased vital capacity and increased residual volume	Decreased O_2 saturation and decreased Pao_2
Hardened bronchi with increased resistance	Dyspnea on exertion
Costal cartilage calcification, stiffening of ribs in enlarged state	Senile emphysema Abdominal breathing
Loss of thoracic muscle tone, impaired inflation of lung bases	Diminished lung sounds at bases Atelectasis Fluid accumulation
Mucous glands less productive	Secretions thick, difficult to expectorate
Lower esophageal sphincter sensitivity	Loss of thirst sense Less active cilia Aspiration
Lower chemoreceptor sensitivity	No change in $Paco_2$ Less active lungs in acid-base disorders

Although these entities can occur separately, many times they occur together.

Asthma is reversible airflow obstruction triggered by hyper-responsiveness of the airways associated with inflammation.[1] The triggers for the inflammation can be viral, bacterial, or allergic. The release of inflammatory mediators produces bronchial smooth muscle spasms, vascular congestion, increased vascular permeability and leaking, and edema formation.[11]

Asthma is often unrecognized in older adults, although one-half of them develop the disease after age 65 years.[2,16] Typically, in older adults, allergens are less often involved, and esophageal reflux can be a common trigger for inflammation that causes bronchospasm.[3,8,17]

TABLE 15–4 OFFENDING ORGANISMS CAUSING PNEUMONIA

Community-acquired	*Streptococcus pneumoniae *Haemophilus influenza Branhamella catarrhalis *Staphylococcus aureus (postinfluenza)
Nosocomial	Klebsiella pneumoniae Escherichia coli Leionella species Other* (see above)
Nursing home-acquired	Two-thirds are K. pneumoniae and S. aureus
Aspiration	Aspiration of colonization of oropharynx Anaerobes
Vital/atypical pneumonia	Influenza A and B Respiratory syncytial virus Chlamydia pneumoniae Mycoplasma pneumoniae

Asthmatic older adults often experience a larger reduction in pulmonary function parameters and β-adrenergic receptor dysfunction.[1] Long-standing asthma can lead to irreversible airflow obstruction.[1,18]

Chronic bronchitis is a chronic cough of at least 3 months of a year for at least 2 years. The cough associated with chronic bronchitis is caused by bronchial hypersecretion.[17] The hyperplasia and hypertrophy of mucous glands and hypertrophied bronchial smooth muscle obstruct the airway, causing airway collapse during expiration.[11,17] Major contributors to the development of this condition are repeated infections or injury (inhalation of pollutants and smoking).

Emphysema can develop in response to these conditions or independently. Obstruction occurs as a result of changes in the lung tissue, specifically enlargement of the acini accompanied by the destruction of the alveolar wall. With the destruction of the alveoli, air trapping and loss of elastic recoil occur. The destruction of the alveoli occurs because of a loss of α_1-antitrypsin. This enzyme inhibits the actions of proteolytic enzymes, which can destroy the lung tissue. The loss of α_1-antitrypsin can be inherited or acquired (smoking).[11]

PULMONARY EMBOLI

Approximately 10 to 30 percent of older adults who were hospitalized or in nursing homes were found to have pulmonary emboli on autopsy.[2] Predisposing factors include hypercoagulability states, cardiac failure, dysrhythmias, cancer, immobility, and orthopedic procedure, all of which are common in older people.[17] The pathogenesis is venous stasis and thrombus formation with embolus development. Once the embolus enters the pulmonary circulation and occludes a vessel, hypoxic vasoconstriction results, causing pulmonary hypertension and systemic hypotension. Finally, decreased surfactant, pulmonary edema, and atelectasis develop.[11] Only 10 percent of pulmonary emboli produce infarction. If an infarction develops, it generally occurs with congestive heart failure, infection, or chronic lung disease.[19] If the emboli is large enough, death results.

Clinical Manifestations

Although there are specific manifestations for each disorder, the clinical manifestations of pulmonary dysfunction include dyspnea, abnormal breathing patterns, cough, hemoptysis, abnormal sputum, cyanosis, and chest pain.[2] These symptoms are consistent findings in older adults, but as each condition is discussed, it will become apparent that older people may manifest the disease differently than younger patients.

PNEUMONIA

The classic triad of cough, fever, and pleuritic pain may not be present in older adults.[10] Subtle changes such as increased respiratory rate (more than 25 breaths per minute), increased sputum production, confusion in frail older people, loss of appetite, and hypotension (less than 100 mm Hg systolic) may be clues to diagnosis of pneumonia.[9,10] Some of these signs and symptoms are a result of sepsis that commonly occurs with pneumonia.

Physical examination may reveal adventitious sounds (inspiratory crepitant rales),[12] dullness to percussion, and increased tactile fremitus. The definitive diagnosis is made by radiographic presentation. However, chest x-ray findings may lag behind clinical presentation[9] or may be masked by preexisting conditions such as congestive heart failure or COPD. Furthermore, in older adults, the classic presentation of certain pneumonias is absent. For example, the pattern for streptococcal pneumonia is lobar consolidation in younger adults, whereas in older adults, it may present with a bronchopneumonic pattern.[7] Laboratory data such as complete blood count should be examined for leukocytosis. Pulse oximetry is useful in evaluating oxygen saturation but depends on adequate blood volume and circulation. Sputum specimens (Gram's stain and culture) can be useful in identifying the organism, but these are often contaminated with oral flora. It should be recognized that many older adults have multiorganism pneumonias.[9] Blood cultures are still the standard for patients admitted to the hospital.

TUBERCULOSIS

The clinical presentation of TB in older adults is atypical and therefore may be missed or misdiagnosed.[14,20–22] Chronic cough, fatigue, and weight loss are attributed to aging or concomitant disease.[14] Radiographic patterns are interpreted as bronchogenic cancer or pneumonia.[14] Rather than the typical presentation of apical infiltrates, older people have midlobe and lower lobe involvement with less cavitation.[14,20–22] Because of an altered immune response, the purified protein derivative (PPD) skin test is not always reliable. Approximately 10 to 20 percent have a negative reaction because of a delayed hypersensitivity response or reactions may not peak until after 72 hours.[14] The definitive diagnosis is three fresh morning sputum specimens for smear and cultures for acid-fact bacilli, *M. tuberculosis*. If the older adult is unable to provide an adequate specimen, inhaled aerosol technique using hypertonic saline can be attempted.[14] Bronchoscopy with bronchial washing and alveolar lavage may be useful.

CHRONIC OBSTRUCTIVE PULMONARY DISEASE

Chronic obstructive disorders are characterized by cough, dyspnea, shortness of breath, and reduced exercise tolerance. Cough associated with chronic bronchitis is marked, with increased sputum, whereas emphysema has little sputum. Emphysema causes increased anteroposterior chest diameter, flattened diaphragm, and diminished breath sounds. In chronic bronchitis, there is no change in chest configuration, the diaphragm is normal, and breath sounds include rhonchi.[23] Wheezing is characteristic of asthma, but bronchospasm can be

found in both emphysema and chronic bronchitis. All may present with hypoxemia and reduced peak expiratory flow rates.

Of the three conditions, asthma is the most misdiagnosed. Asthma is a reversible airway obstruction, but in older adults there may be some fixed obstruction, and the methacholine challenge is less useful in older people regardless of the presence of asthma.[1] Asthma presentation includes chronic cough, wheezing, prolonged expiration, and decreased expiratory peak flow rates. Many times the older adult's condition is diagnosed as congestive heart failure, pneumonia, or bronchiogenic cancer.[1,18]

PULMONARY EMBOLI

The typical presentation of a pulmonary emboli is sudden onset of tachypnea, dyspnea, pleuritic pain, cough with hemoptysis, low-grade fever (37.7 to 38.3°C), and later the development of pleural friction rub. Sudden onset of atrial fibrillation may suggest pulmonary embolism. Diagnostic tests include arterial blood gases (hypoxemia), chest x-ray (typical wedge-shaped peripheral infiltrate), pulmonary ventilation-perfusion scan (decreased perfusion with ventilation-perfusion mismatch), and pulmonary arteriography.[19]

Management

1 Primary Prevention

Interpersonal Hazards

Although it has been established that pulmonary function declines with age, this decline is accelerated by smoking. Smoking contributes to pulmonary disease and has been linked to cancer and cardiovascular disease. Smoking is the one risk factor that can be eliminated, and smoking cessation can have beneficial effects even in older adults.[24]

The effects of smoking on the respiratory system are many. Carbon monoxide competes with oxygen on the hemoglobin molecule, thus reducing its oxygen-carrying capacity. Smoking promotes an inflammatory response that culminates in the reduction of α-antitrypsin activity. The inflammatory process contributes to a host of physiological alterations such as hyperplasia of mucosal glands, resulting in an increase in mucus production, bronchospasm, and diminished ciliary activity.

Other risk factors for pulmonary disease include impaired mobility, obesity, and surgery. All three contribute to impaired ventilation through inadequate lung expansion.

Environmental Hazards

Air pollution has a negative impact on the pulmonary system and, like smoking, has a cumulative effect, with an increase in risks with repeated exposure. Pollutants fall into four categories: fossil fuels, vehicle emissions, pesticides, and miscellaneous pollutants (those emitted from refineries and manufacturers using asbestos, lead, cadmium, and mercury).[25] Older adults are more likely to suffer the consequences of pollution because of a compromised pulmonary system and because hazardous substances in the workplace and environment were unregulated before the 1970s.[26]

Another well-known hazard is second-hand smoke. It contains about twice the tar and nicotine, three times the benzpyrene, five times the carbon monoxide, and fifty times the ammonia found in mainstream smoke.

2 Secondary Prevention

Assessment

Subjective information that addresses pulmonary problems includes information about cough, shortness of breath, chest pain with breathing, history of respiratory problems, cigarette smoking, and environmental exposure.[27] Each symptom should be explored in terms of onset, duration, frequency, character of symptoms, precipitating factors, ameliorating factors, past and current treatment, course of symptom (better, worse), and effect on activities of daily living. Questions about self-care behaviors such as last chest x-ray, screen for TB, and immunizations (influenza vaccine annually and pneumococcal vaccine once) should be included in the data collection.

Objective data are the same regardless of age, but the interpretation of these data may be different. Inspection includes skin and mucous membrane color, nail bed contour, thoracic shape, and configuration. Older adults may have kyphosis, which contributes to an increased anteroposterior diameter, resulting in a barrel chest appearance. Evaluation of the character and effort of breathing should include inspection for the use of

accessory muscles (sternocleidomastoid, trapezius, and intercostals). Although the chest wall becomes stiffer with age, expansion should be symmetrical. Palpation should demonstrate equal respiratory excursion and tactile fremitus. A resonant percussion note is the norm, but in some healthy older people, the note is hyperresonant. Before beginning the auscultatory examination, the patient should take a deep breath and cough to clear the airways and expand the alveoli in the bases. The patient should be sitting during the examination to allow full expansion of the lung bases. Vesicular breath sounds are heard over most of the posterior lung. The intensity of the breath sounds may be lessened as a result of changes in the chest wall and the decreased inspiratory effort of older adults.

Nursing Care

Nursing care of the older adult with pulmonary disease of potential for respiratory problems includes maintaining a patent airway, facilitating gas exchange, maximizing breath patterns, increasing or maintaining optimal activity, and providing education. See Table 15–5 for a care plan and Table 15–6 for a teaching guide.

Maintaining a patent airway in the neurologically impaired older adult can be accomplished by positioning and suctioning. For the alert older adult, simple coughing and deep breathing can promote an open airway and facilitate gas exchange.

Hydration is important to help thin and mobilize secretions. Water, fruit juices, and decaffeinated beverages should be encouraged. Milk should be avoided because it can thicken mucus. Adequate nutrition is necessary to provide energy and promote healing. Anorexia is common in older adults, especially in those with pulmonary disease. Frequent small feedings can provide an adequate caloric intake. High carbohydrate intake should be avoided because of the increased CO$_2$ load.

Another common problem for older adults with pulmonary disorders is sleep disturbances related to hypoxia, dyspnea, increased secretion, or a combination of these. For a more detailed discussion, refer to Chapter 34.

3 Tertiary Prevention

The goals of pulmonary rehabilitation are to maximize pulmonary function, avoid or minimize insults to the pulmonary system, and foster independence. Pulmonary rehabilitation requires a multidisciplinary approach that emphasizes patient education, exercise, and psychosocial support for the patient and family.

Educational content should address the specific pathophysiology and management of the pulmonary disease. The content can be delivered in a variety of ways but should be adapted to the patient's lifestyle and educational level.

Walking, indoors or outdoors, is an excellent form of exercise for older adults. It is simple and affordable and many malls offer walking programs that are climate

TABLE 15–5 NURSING CARE PLAN

Nursing Diagnosis: Impaired gas exchange	
Expected Outcome	*Nursing Actions*
Client will have adequate oxygen (O_2) and carbon dioxide (CO_2) exchange, as evidenced by Pao_2 >60 mm Hg, $Paco_2$ between 35 and 45 mm Hg, absence of cyanosis, and absence of confusion.	Administer low-flow O_2 per prescribed flow rate (usually 1–2 L/min). Assess and record respiratory status at least every 8 hours. Have the patient turn, cough, and deep-breath (every hour while awake). Monitor arterial blood gas values (consult with physician regarding need). Elevate head of bed (at least 30 degrees if possible). Assist client with self-care activities as needed. Provide breathing retraining (pursed-lip, abdominal). Encourage patient to pace daily activities and plan for rest periods. Many activities usually performed standing can be performed sitting (e.g., ironing, peeling vegetables). Refer client to pulmonary rehabilitation program.
Nursing Diagnosis: Ineffective airway clearance	
Expected Outcome	*Nursing Actions*
Client will maintain patent airway, as evidenced by absence of cyanosis and adventitious breath sounds and by respirations being even, unlabored, and within normal limits.	Increase fluid intake (water, fruit juices, decaffeinated beverages) to at least 2000 mL/24 hours (if not contraindicated by renal or cardiac impairment). Maintain humidity of room air at 30 to 50%. Assess and record characteristics of cough (moist or dry, frequency, duration, time of day). Assess and record characteristics of sputum expectorated (amount, color, consistency). Provide frequent mouth care with ½ saline and ½ peroxide (avoid use of lemon glycerine swabs). Perform postural drainage. Monitor effects of bronchodilators and expectorants. Encourage deep breathing and coughing; teach effective coughing by demonstration. Avoid giving very hot or cold fluids. Assess and record nature of breath sounds at least every 8 hours. Change client's position at least every 2 hours. Elevate head of bed.
Nursing Diagnosis: Ineffective breathing patterns	
Expected Outcome	*Nursing Actions*
Client will use effective breathing pattern, as evidenced by absence of nasal flaring and accessory muscle use, and by respirations being even, unlabored and within normal limits.	Verbally encourage use of abdominal and purse-lip breathing. Maintain low-flow oxygen at prescribed rate. Provide reassurance during periods of respiratory distress (stay with client; remain calm). Verbally encourage relaxation and meditation techniques (see Chapter 34). Elevate head of bed. Assess and record breathing pattern at least every 8 hours.

TABLE 15–6 TEACHING GUIDE FOR ELDERS WITH RESPIRATORY PROBLEMS

Signs of respiratory problems	Change in sputum. Increased shortness of breath. Fever. Change in activity tolerance.
Medications	Use as directed. Avoid over-the-counter medicines without consulting provider (e.g., aspirin interferes with coumadin: antacids can inhibit absorption of certain antibiotics). If adverse effects occur, notify provider. Pneumonoccocal vaccine.
Diet	Provide small frequent meals (avoid large meals because they may cause gastric distention and respiratory compromise). Provide a well-balanced diet (avoid high-carbohydrate diet because it will increase CO_2 content and increase ventilation). Maintain adequate hydration; approximately 1 L/day (avoid caffeine and milk products).
Exercise	Regular exercise to tolerance (enhances pulmonary reserve and improves venous return). Curtail activities when fatigued. Space activities with rest periods.
Environmental hazards	Avoid smoking/second-hand smoke. Avoid triggers for respiratory problems. Avoid outdoor activities when pollution levels are high.

and pollution controlled. Whatever activity the client chooses, it should be done regularly and gradually.

Pulmonary illnesses, whether acute or chronic, can cause anxiety and depression. Therapeutic communication is essential to identify client and family needs and feelings. Support groups are especially helpful for those with chronic pulmonary diseases. Ultimately, the client should be given the tools and support to successfully manage his or her pulmonary problem.

Student Learning Activities

1 Prepare an educational poster for older adults on the effects of smoking on the lungs and the advantages to be gained by stopping smoking. Place the poster in prominent areas that will be viewed by older adults in the community.

2 Provide additional information on smoking cessation programs available through the American Heart Association and the American Lung Association.

3 Investigate the number of options available for older adults to obtain flu shots in your community. Make plans to participate in community awareness programs to administer flu shots for older adults.

REFERENCES

1 Sherman, CB: Late-onset asthma: Making the diagnosis, choosing drug therapy. Geriatrics 50:21, 1995.
2 Addison, T: Pulmonary disease. In Lonergan, ET (ed): Geriatrics. Appleton & Lange, Stamford, Conn, 1996, p 139.
3 Morris, JF: Physiological changes due to age: Implications for respiratory drug therapy. Drugs Aging 4:207, 1994.
4 Grinton, SF: Respiratory limitations in the aging population. South Med J 87:S47, 1994.
5 Tolep, K, and Kelsen, SG: Effect of aging on respiratory skeletal muscles. Clin Chest Med 14:363, 1993.
6 Enright, PL, et al: Spirometry reference values for women and men 65 to 85 years of age. Am Rev Respir Dis 147:125, 1993.
7 Blair, KA: Aging: Physiological aspects and clinical implications. Nurse Practitioner 15:14, 1990.
8 Raiha, IJ, Ivaska, L, and Sourander, LB: Pulmonary function in gastro-oesphageal reflux disease of elderly people. Age Aging 21:368, 1992.
9 Moroney, C, and Fitzgerald, MA: Pharmacological update: Management of pneumonia in elderly people. J Am Acad Nurse Practitioners 8:237, 1996.
10 Fox, RA: Treatment recommendations for respiratory tract infections associated with aging. Drug Ther 3:40, 1993.
11 McCance KL, and Heuther, SE: Pathophysiology: The Biologic Basis for Disease in Adults and Children. CV Mosby, St Louis, 1994, p 1148.
12 Cunha, BA, Segreti, J, and Yamauchi, T: Community-acquired pneumonia: New bugs, new drugs. Patient Care 27:142, 1996.
13 Hecht, A, et al: Diagnosis and treatment of pneumonia in the nursing home. Nurse Practitioner 20:24, 1995.
14 Couser, JJ, and Glassroth, J: Tuberculosis: An epidemic in older adults. Clin Chest Med 14:491, 1993.
15 Liaw, YS, et al: Clinical spectrum of tuberculosis in older patients. J Am Geriatr Soc 43:256, 1995.
16 Bailey, WC, et al: Features of asthma in older adults. J Asthma 29:21, 1992.
17 Williams, JM, and Evans, TC: Acute pulmonary disease in the aged. Clin Geriatr Med 9:527, 1993.
18 Dow, L: The epidemiology and therapy of airflow limitation in the elderly. Drugs Aging 2:546, 1992.
19 Goldstone, J: Veins and lymphatics. In Way, W (ed): Current Surgical Diagnosis and Treatment. Appleton-Lange, Norwalk, Conn, 1994, p 738.
20 Chan, CH, et al: The effect of age on the presentation of patients with tuberculosis. Tubercle Lung Dis 76:290, 1995.
21 Davies, PD: Tuberculosis in the elderly. J Antimicrob Chemother 34: (suppl)A93, 1994.
22 Kosela, MK, et al: Tuberculosis in young adults and the elderly. Chest 106:28, 1994.
23 Stauffer, JL: Lung. In Tierney, LM, et al (eds): Current Medical Diagnosis and Treatment. Appleton-Lange, Norwalk, Conn, 1996, p 215.
24 Higgins, MW, et al: Smoking and lung function in elderly men and women. JAMA 269:21, 1993.
25 Stephenson, CA: Respiratory changes. In Esberg, KK, and Highes, ST (eds): Nursing Care of the Aged. Appleton & Lange, Norwalk, Conn, 1989, p 199.
26 Miller, CA: Nursing Care of Older Adults. Scott, Foresman/ Little, Brown, Glenview, Ill, 1990, p 330.
27 Jarvis, C: Physical Examination and Health Assessment. WB Saunders, Philadelphia, 1996, p 460.

CHAPTER 16

The Aging Endocrine System

Cheryl Dellasega / Mary Ellen Hill Yonushonis /
Arthur (Don) Johnson

OBJECTIVES

Upon completion of this chapter, the reader will be able to:

- Identify normal age-related changes in the endocrine system
- Discuss the pathophysiology of diabetes mellitus in the older adult
- Describe clinical manifestations of diabetes in the older client
- Apply principles of primary, secondary, and tertiary prevention to the management of diabetes mellitus in older clients
- Teach older clients needed information for complying with a diabetes self-care regimen
- Discuss findings from current research studies on diabetes in older adults
- Identify resources for support of the older client with diabetes
- Identify normal age-related changes in the thyroid gland
- Describe the pathophysiology of thyroid disorders
- Describe the clinical manifestations of thyroid disorders
- Explain the mechanisms responsible for the manifestations of thyroid disorders
- Identify differences between thyroid dysfunction in older patients and that in younger patients
- Discuss nursing care considerations for patients with thyroid dysfunction

Diabetes Mellitus in Older Adults

by Cheryl Dellasega / Mary Ellen Yonushonis

Diabetes, one of the top five chronic conditions affecting older adults, cannot be cured. Instead, the older adult with diabetes must learn to master a regimen of monitoring and treatment that involves a great deal of client participation. Many age-related changes may make it difficult for an older person to comply with the care plan. This does not mean that care should be delegated to others; instead, the nurse should work diligently with the client to compensate for age-related deficits to promote the client's ability to carry out as many self-care activities as possible.

Normal Aging

Although older people may experience diabetes more commonly than their younger counterparts, this condition is neither inevitable nor a normal consequence of the aging process. Several age-related changes increase the risk of diabetes, however, and may actually double the person's chances of developing the disease with each decade of life.[1] These include changes in nutritional status and endocrine function.

During the last decades of life, many older people tend to gain weight,[2] not because they consume more calories, but because of changes in the fat-to-muscle ratio and decreases in basal metabolism rates. As a result, a person who has been of normal weight throughout life may find that, with aging, their weight gradually increases. This nutritional imbalance can affect many body systems. In relation to the endocrine system, the added stress of unnecessary calories can predispose the person to diabetes.

Blood glucose values change as people get older. Adjustment of the normal range for the 2-hour postprandial blood sugar level to 140 to 200 mg/dL has been suggested.[3] An acceptable fasting glucose level for older adults is less than 140 mg/dL.[4] Kidney and bladder functions also change, making the testing of urine for glucose less reliable in the person over age 65.[5] These changes support the use of age-adjusted parameters in interpretation of laboratory values for the older client with diabetes.

Alterations in physical function that may occur in the later years may mask the signs and symptoms of diabetes and prevent the older person from seeking medical attention. Fatigue, needing to get up at night to urinate, and frequent infections are all possible indicators of diabetes that may be dismissed by the older person and family members because they are believed to be part of the aging process itself.

Pathophysiology

Diabetes mellitus is "a metabolic disorder involving a variety of physiological systems, the most critical of which involves glucose metabolism.[6] The vascular, renal, neurological, and visual function of people with diabetes are all jeopardized by the disease process, even though these changes occur in tissues that do not require insulin to function.[7]

Several conditions can predispose an individual to diabetes, although two types predominate. Insulin-dependent diabetes mellitus (IDDM), or type I diabetes, occurs when the person is unable to produce a sufficient supply of endogenous insulin to meet bodily needs. This type of diabetes afflicts primarily younger people. Non-insulin-dependent diabetes mellitus (NIDDM), or type II diabetes, is the more common form of the disease. Between 85 and 90 percent of people with diabetes have NIDDM, which is more closely associated with obesity than with the inability to produce insulin.[8]

NIDDM, the most common form of diabetes in older adults, is a serious threat to health for several reasons. First, the chronic complications experienced in relation to vision, circulation, and neurological and urinary function are superimposed on body systems already experiencing age-related declines. Second, hyperglycemic hyperosmolar nonketotic syndrome, a life-threatening complication of diabetes involving hyperglycemia, increased serum osmolality, and dehydration, occurs more often among older adults.[9]

Clinical Manifestations

Because many initial symptoms and signs of NIDDM may be vague and nonspecific, the older person may dismiss them as insignificant and fail to seek treatment. Therefore, in an older person, the actual diagnosis of diabetes is often made when the disease has reached an advanced state or has been precipitated by another medical problem. Retinopathy (pathological changes in the inner eye) may be detected during a routine eye examination, prompting further diagnostic studies. Elevated laboratory values discovered during hospitalization may also initiate a more detailed evaluation uncovering the presence of NIDDM.

Any persistent change in a client's usual health status should be investigated. Increased urination (polyuria), excessive thirst (polydipsia), marked hunger (polyphagia), and susceptibility to infections (especially yeast) are common indicators of the disease at any age and may be present to varying degrees in the older client as well. Blurring of vision, which results from the effects of hyperglycemia on the ocular lens,[10] may not be recognized as a symptom of diabetes in older adults.

Management

1 Primary Prevention

An estimated 65 to 80 percent of NIDDM cases could be prevented through a regimen of healthy nutrition.[11] Maintaining ideal body weight is an important consideration for all older people, not only to eliminate the stress on joints and enhance mobility but also to reduce the risk of developing diabetes. Unwanted pounds can be lost during the later years through a combination of optimal nutrition and exercise.

Financial problems may limit the older adult's ability to purchase nutritious food. Several excellent consumer guides on buying and preparing small quantities of inexpensive foods are available and may prove helpful (Table 16–1 provides resources to aid the client with diabetes). Assistance may be needed with transportation or special equipment to allow clients with disabilities to maintain independence.

Education on dietary requirements may be needed. A meal plan that consists of 10 percent fat, 15 percent protein, and 75 percent complex carbohydrates (percentages based on calories) is recommended to prevent diabetes. The low fat content in this diet not only deters atherosclerosis, but also increases the activity of insulin receptors.[11]

Exercise is also needed to help prevent diabetes. A pre-exercise screening examination should be performed to ensure that an older client is physically capable of beginning a fitness program. Assessment of the client's current activity level and lifestyle preferences can then help determine the type of exercise that might be most successful. Walking and swimming, two low-impact activities, are often excellent starters for new exercisers (see Chapter 20).

TABLE 16–1 RESOURCES FOR DIABETES INFORMATION

American Association of Diabetes Educators
500 North Michigan Avenue
Suite 1400
Chicago, IL 60611
312-661-1700

American Diabetes Association
PO Box 2055
Harlan, IA 51593-0238
1-800-ADA-DISC

Members receive 12 issues of the magazine *Diabetes Forecast* each year. Contact your local American Diabetes Association for information about diabetes support groups.

American Diabetes Association: Diabetes Information Service Center Hotline
1-800-ADA-DISC

American Diabetes Association National Service Center
1660 Duke Street
Alexandria, VA 22313
1-800-ADA-DISC

2 Secondary Prevention

Screening

Prompt detection and early intervention help limit the serious effects of NIDDM in the older adult. Careful history taking provides information on the client's usual state of health and indicates whether he or she has experienced any changes suggestive of NIDDM. In particular, obese people with a family history of the disease should be questioned carefully about the signs and symptoms previously discussed.

During a routine physical examination, several findings suggest that a more detailed workup is required. These include changes in vision, loss of skin integrity or frequent infections, change in body weight, altered circulatory patterns, evidence of cardiovascular disease, and symptoms of hyperglycemia such as increased thirst, appetite, and urination.

The fasting blood sugar level should be routinely checked as a component of any screening examination, but negative results in light of other symptoms should not be considered conclusive. The oral glucose tolerance test is generally considered to be a more sensitive and reliable indicator than the FBS level and should be performed for early diagnosis and treatment of NIDDM.

Once the client has been diagnosed as having NIDDM, treatment will focus on a regimen that involves everyday activities designed to control the disease. The more involved the client is in performing this care, the more easily adverse consequences of the disease can be limited. People with diabetes may still be able to enjoy optimal health by controlling nutritional intake, exercising regularly, taking medications as prescribed, monitoring blood glucose levels, and preventing well-known complications.

Nutrition

Nutritional therapy involves assessing current patterns. If the client is overweight, which is likely, planning must incorporate strategies for gradual, safe weight loss. Crash diets, use of food supplements or medications, and fasting are not only impractical approaches for older adults, but are life-threatening for those with NIDDM. In creating the client's meal plan, financial constraints must be considered. Loss of teeth and changes in taste perception can alter the client's food preferences. The client's input should guide all dietary modifications, and recommended changes must be realistic. Currently, meal planning for people with diabetes balances the diet using wise selections from each of the food groups.

The exchange system, which reflects a certain number of portions from each food group, is adjusted to meet caloric needs. A diabetic client will probably be placed on a meal plan consisting of 1800 to 2200 calories per day. If the client is also receiving insulin or an oral antidiabetic agent, he or she must make sure to divide these calories throughout the day to prevent hypoglycemia.[12] Although dietitians may be responsible for introducing the system to clients, nurses often help them apply this information to everyday life. Helping an older adult develop a few standard meal plans using the same types of food for each meal may be the best approach initially. Once the meal plan has been mastered, substitutions can be made with more confidence. Many older people tend to adhere to a fairly rigid meal plan for convenience as well as economic reasons.

The nurse who helps an older client plan meals can take this opportunity to educate him or her regarding general principles of sound nutrition. The nurse can teach the client about reading labels to avoid excessive sodium and fat intake, incorporating recommended food sources in the daily intake, choosing low-cholesterol food sources, and including adequate fiber in the diet.

The nurse's approach to teaching the diabetic client how to plan his or her nutritional intake is critical. If the nurse places the emphasis on the idea that healthier eating leads to an improved sense of well-being, the client may see the required changes in a more positive light. Also, it is important to teach the overweight client that losing a small amount of weight (10 to 15 lb) may result in major reductions in blood glucose levels.

Exercise

For the older adult with NIDDM, exercise can directly enhance physiological function by reducing blood glucose levels, improving physical stamina and emotional well-being, and promoting circulation.[13] In addition, regular exercise can help with weight reduction. However, it is important for the exercise program to be planned and not impulsive. The client who has poorly controlled diabetes (pre-exercise blood glucose levels greater than 250 mg/dL) may actually be harmed by a sudden increase in physical activity. Once blood sugar levels have stabilized and other medical conditions have been brought under control, the nurse and client can develop a plan for gradually increasing physical exercise. After constraints on the client's ability for exercise have been identified, short- and long-term goals should be set for implementing an exercise program.

Although swimming and brisk walking have been mentioned as excellent choices for the older person with NIDDM, other types of activity are equally beneficial. In particular, aerobic sports may offer the most benefit. A person with NIDDM should exercise at least once every 3 days.[14]

Medication

Oral Agents

Because the older person with NIDDM still has the ability to produce some insulin, dietary management may successfully control diabetes.[15] However, if the client has not or cannot follow the meal plan or if the disease is not detected early enough, an oral agent may be prescribed to stimulate secretion of insulin by the pancreas. The sulfonylureas are the drug group prescribed most often and are effective only in the treatment of NIDDM. Several different agents are available from within this drug class. However, chlorpropamide is contraindicated in older adults because of the increased risk of hypoglycemia associated with this drug.[10] In general, sulfonylureas that are excreted by the liver (e.g., Glucotrol) are advocated for use in older adults, whereas younger people may receive an agent cleared by the kidneys.[12] Gastrointestinal upset and adverse reactions to alcohol are the major untoward side effects of the sulfonylureas.

Second-generation sulfonylureas are now available. Glyburide (Micronase and DiaBeta) and glipizine (Glucotrol) are 100 to 200 times more potent than the first-generation agents, so they may be taken in smaller doses and only once a day instead of several times a day.[16] People receiving an oral agent for control of their NIDDM should be warned that they may still experience hypoglycemic side effects, particularly if their nutritional intake is not carefully monitored and controlled. Confusion, sweating, nervousness, pallor, and shallow respirations may indicate a hypoglycemic reaction in these people.

Glucophage (metformin hydrochloride) is an antihyperglycemic drug recently released by the Food and Drug Administration (FDA). It does not lower blood glucose levels but increases glucose use by peripheral tissues and the intestine. Glucophage should be taken with meals and is contraindicated in patients with renal impairments.[17]

Insulin

If the previous interventions are unsuccessful in modifying the blood sugar level and symptoms, insulin therapy will be needed to supplement the body's own supply. The goal of insulin therapy is to maintain blood glucose levels within prescribed parameters to limit the detrimental complications of the disease. A great deal of adjustment is often required to achieve a balance between optimal blood glucose readings and hypoglycemia. Many clinicians prefer a loose form of control in which blood sugar levels are occasionally allowed to rise slightly above normal to demonstrate that the client is not at risk for hypoglycemia. The time and frequency of insulin administration are adjusted to stabilize blood sugar levels. Insulin is occasionally administered concurrently with an oral agent, although the value of this practice has not been substantiated clinically. Although several different forms of insulin are available, the most common route of administration is subcutaneous injection. Refer to a basic pharmacology text for discussion of insulin types.

Teaching about insulin should involve storage of the insulin and syringes at home, the type of insulin to be used (human versus animal), the concentration (U-100), the expected mode of action (rapid, intermediate, long-acting, or a mixture), the prescribed dosage and conditions warranting adjustment of this dosage (exercise, illness), and possible side effects and their treatment. Older people in particular need to know the signs and symptoms of hypoglycemia because loss of adrenergic warning signals, a normal age-related change, renders them less sensitive to the condition.[17] Education on injection technique focuses on drawing up the correct dosage of medication, selecting and rotating injection sites, preparing the site, administering the medication itself, and reusing and disposing of syringes. For clients who need a combination of short-acting (regular insulin) and intermediate-acting (neutral protamine Hagedorn) insulin, premixed or 70%–30% insulins are now available.

Insulin pumps, infusers, and other devices intended to promote accurate delivery of the appropriate dosage of insulin may be prescribed for an older client. Magnifying sleeves and adaptive equipment for the client with arthritis can also facilitate insulin administration. In each case, the nurse must make sure that the client is able to see and read the printed parts of these devices and to understand the steps for their use.

Prevention of Complications: Hypoglycemia

Hypoglycemia in an older adult with NIDDM may be caused by not enough food, too much exercise, or too much medication. Older adults and family members should be taught the importance of preventing hypoglycemia, of having the client wear identification stating that he or she has diabetes, and of keeping a fast-acting sugar with the client at all times. Classic symptoms of hypoglycemia (e.g., tachycardia, perspiration, and anxiety) may be totally absent in older adults. Instead, symptoms in older adults usually consist of behavioral disorders, convulsions, confusion, disorientation, poor sleep patterns, nocturnal headaches, slurred speech, or unconsciousness.

Treatment for hypoglycemic reaction must be prompt. If the client is conscious, treatment should include a fast-acting sugar such as 4 oz of orange juice or regular (not diet) soda, followed by a carbohydrate and protein snack such as cheese and crackers or a peanut butter sandwich. The fast-acting sugar initially raises the blood glucose level, and the carbohydrate and protein prevent a sudden recurrence of hypoglycemia.

If the client is found unconscious, he or she should be treated with glucagon 0.5 to 1.0 mg intramuscularly or subcutaneously.[17] Family members may be taught these injection techniques as part of their basic diabetes teaching. If glucagon is unavailable, glucose gel or cake icing may be massaged into the inside of the person's cheek. After the unconscious person becomes fully awake, he or she should eat a carbohydrate and protein snack. The administration of glucose to an unconscious person may prevent tachycardia, dysrhythmias, myocardial infarction, or a cerebrovascular accident and will cause no harm if the person is unconscious because of hyperglycemia.

The older diabetic adult must prevent a variety of other complications as well. The first step in this process is self-monitoring of blood sugar levels. The currently accepted approach for self-monitoring is the use of a blood glucose meter, which directly measures the level of glucose in the blood. This method offers many advantages over urine testing but requires that the client have normal vision and the physical strength and coordination to perform the procedure. The client's age must not be a limiting factor when considering who can assume responsibility for daily monitoring of blood glucose because older adults in one study[18] who took charge of self-monitoring reported no change in the quality of their lives. Blood glucose monitoring times may be rotated among fasting, before meals, and 1 to 2 hours after meals to give the client and health-care team a range of blood glucose levels for planning treatment. Older clients need much hands-on practice with blood glucose meters because many of these devices may seem foreign to them. Hemoglobin A_{1C} is a laboratory test that measures an average blood glucose over 3 months. Clients should be encouraged to have this test done regularly.

Other steps for preventing adverse complications of NIDDM include yearly eye examination by an ophthalmologist (who will dilate the client's pupils to visualize the back of the eye, where retinopathy occurs), a foot care regimen that combines skin care and toenail maintenance, and regular visits to the primary care provider for screening and monitoring, including a yearly 24-hour urinalysis for protein to detect kidney changes.

Nurse's Role

The nurse plays the role of facilitator with older adults who have NIDDM. Although the initial stages of diagnosis and stabilization may require the nurse to play a more active role, the main nursing objective is to teach the needed skills for self-care. This process begins in the acute-care facility, with follow-through into the home. Encouraging the older client to assume responsibility for meal planning, medication administration, exercising, self-monitoring, and preventive care is the thrust of every nursing activity.

Nursing Management

Older adults with NIDDM have many safety needs. Accidents resulting from poor vision can be prevented by a careful assessment of the home environment and removal of potential hazards. Corrective lenses and adaptive devices are needed to compensate for visual deficits, as well as surgical procedures for some conditions.

Avoidance of burns and unintentional injury is also a consideration for the older diabetic client because diminished circulation and sensation in extremities render them prone to such incidents. Clients can be taught to check the temperature of bath water, wear proper clothing in cold weather, and use properly fitting shoes and stockings.

Nutritional needs may be complicated by age-related changes. Declines in perception of taste may lead older adults to compensate by using extra seasoning (e.g., salt). Loss of teeth can also pose special problems for an older person who must limit food choices to meet meal plan guidelines. The nurse can teach the client to use alternative measures for seasoning and preparing food to improve taste. A referral to the nutritionist may also supplement the nurse's efforts, particularly for clients with complex needs.

Clients should keep a written record of their medications and daily blood sugar levels and take responsibility for bringing these documents to their appointments with the primary care provider. These records can be reviewed by the nurse for stability and often serve as a useful teaching tool.

Because blood circulation to the extremities is compromised in people with diabetes, clients must learn the necessary methods for promoting healthy feet. Caring for toenails, preventing infections, using cotton socks and properly fitting shoes, and avoiding caustic agents on the feet are emphasized. Corns and bunions should be cared for by a podiatrist. (Table 16–2 provides a guide for foot care.)

The psychosocial aspects of coping with a chronic illness may present the most urgent needs from the client's perspective. The reality of needing daily medication (particularly injections), the perceived dietary deprivation, and the possible adverse consequences can be sources of anxiety, fear, and depression. Mental health problems can lead to a vicious cycle for the diabetic person. First, the client's need to adhere to a lifelong treatment plan precipitates feelings of anxiety, hopelessness, depression, or a combination of these. The client may then neglect his or her health and may even develop unhealthy habits that aggravate the diabetes (e.g., overeating or refusing to take medicine). Failure to comply with the treatment plan can cause a series of adverse physical responses that lead the client to feel even worse emotionally.[19]

Many older adults have experienced diabetes second-hand when a spouse, friend, or neighbor had the disease. This experience may foster misconceptions and fears that further impair coping. Nursing interventions to promote the use of lifelong coping skills and to teach new coping methods can help the older adult realize

TABLE 16–2 TEACHING GUIDE: FOOT CARE FOR THE OLDER CLIENT WITH DIABETES

- Wash feet daily; always dry carefully between the toes. Do not soak feet daily (this causes excessive drying).
- Keep feet warm and dry. Cotton socks are best because they do not hold moisture in. Do not apply hot-water bottles, heating pads, or battery-operated feet warmers.
- Use lotion on the dry areas of feet. Do not put lotion between toes, however, as this may contribute to the development of a fungal infection.
- A light dusting of nonperfumed powder between the toes can prevent excessive perspiration.
- Soak nails 10 to 15 minutes in warm water only on the days you trim your nails. Cut toenails straight across using a toenail clipper. If nails are too thick to cut yourself, have the podiatrist or physician do it.
- Inspect feet daily for cuts, blisters, reddened areas, and scratches. Use a magnifying glass or mirror to inspect feet, or have a family member or friend inspect them if you cannot see them well.
- Wear comfortable, well-fitting shoes. Good-quality athletic sneakers are stylish and comfortable and though they may seem expensive, will save money in the long run.
- Carefully break in new shoes, wearing them at first an hour each day, and then gradually increasing the time worn.
- Shake out shoes before putting them on to prevent injury from foreign objects or torn linings.
- Do not walk barefoot, even indoors. Sandals are recommended for beach wear so that hot sand, rough pavement, or sharp objects do not injure feet.
- Do not smoke. Smoking decreases circulation to feet and legs.
- Do not cut corns or calluses yourself; instead, have the podiatrist or physician treat tem.
- Do not use harsh commercial wart-removing products. These may remove not just the wart, but part of your foot as well.
- Call the physician for any problems such as tenderness, warmth, redness, drainage, ingrown toenail, athlete's foot, or pain in the feet or calves.
- Avoid wearing tight socks or garters and do not cross legs, as these may constrict blood flow to the legs.

that he or she can still enjoy a healthy lifestyle. Support from family, friends, and others with diabetes can be a helpful adjunct to the nurse's efforts. If severe or pronounced depression develops, the client should be referred for professional counseling (see Chapter 28 for more information on depression in older adults).

DISCHARGE PLANNING

If the older client is diagnosed with diabetes during an institutional stay and has been taught the details of a self-care regimen in that setting, the nurse must plan to transfer this information to the client's home setting. Purchase of syringes and medications, preparations of the meal plan, and transportation to the primary care provider for follow-up care are immediate needs to be anticipated before discharge. Emergency care, including telephone numbers and actions to be taken in a crisis, is reviewed and discussed with both the client and another

responsible adult before the client leaves the institution. Referrals to visiting nurse agencies should be in place before the client is scheduled to leave, with the nurse taking responsibility for conveying pertinent information to the home care counterparts.

3 *Tertiary Prevention*

To promote prompt rehabilitation and resumption of a normal lifestyle, the person diagnosed with diabetes should receive ongoing care that facilitates these goals. Sensory stimulation during acute care stays compensates for normal and disease-related deficits that can occur. For older clients, sensory stimulation in the form of appropriate verbal, auditory, and tactile cues not only fosters interaction with others, but also enhances performance of activities of daily living.[20]

Encouraging the older person to maintain or assume responsibility for as many aspects of care as possible signals to the client that a meaningful existence is possible, even in the face of chronic illness. The nurse who includes the client in decision making as well as physical tasks sends the message that the client is still a worthwhile human being able to contribute to his or her self-care. Foot, eye, and skin care, which are important components of the ongoing treatment plan, may be delegated to the client as soon as appropriate. The nurse should encourage the client to take the initiative in other health-promoting measures such as obtaining influenza and pneumonia vaccines as needed, working toward cardiovascular fitness, and modifying the home environment to foster safety.

Glycemic control, which involves maintaining blood sugar levels within a margin of safety usually established by the primary care provider, is especially important for older clients. One study[21] found that keeping blood sugar levels within a normal range prevented neurological deficits in some cases and regression of preexisting deficits in others. Results of the National Institutes of Health research study, conducted in 21 centers and called the Diabetes Control and Complications Trial, confirmed the widely held belief that maintaining the blood glucose levels within the normal range will prevent or slow the development of long-term diabetes complications.[16]

Special rehabilitative efforts may be needed if the client experiences profound circulatory deficits that eventually require surgery. Currently, most therapeutic amputations are performed on diabetic clients with peripheral vascular disease.[22] The type of amputation usually performed on an older person is the above-knee amputation. Once the acute postoperative period has passed, the nurse must help the client adjust not only to the physical demands of the amputation, but also to the emotional consequences of losing a limb.

A four-phase approach can be used to deal with the rehabilitative needs of older clients with diabetes who have undergone a lower-extremity amputation. First, the client must receive adequate nutrition and rest in a safe, quiet environment to recover properly from the trauma of surgery. The client must also be relieved of pain and discomfort, especially "phantom" pain in the missing limb, which is particularly distressing. Second, the residual limb itself must be monitored for signs of infection or other complications during the healing process. Third, a structured exercise program to prepare the client for walking with a prosthesis must be implemented, progressing appropriately as the client becomes increasingly mobile. Finally, the client must receive support and assistance as he or she grieves not only for the lost limb, but also for the person he or she was before the amputation. Exposure to others who have successfully dealt with this experience can be helpful and encouraging. Family members must be taught to support the client and understand the feelings of anger and despair. The client and significant others should be offered hope that a high-quality lifestyle is still possible despite physical disability.

TEACHING GUIDES

Any teaching endeavor undertaken to promote or maintain the health of an older individual must be tailored to individual needs. This is especially important because older clients with diabetes will be anxious about dealing with a life-threatening chronic disease, as well as perhaps having a visual impairment that limits the ability to read and to interact with others. A thorough evaluation of the client's vision, dexterity, memory, and mobility should precede any teaching intervention.[5]

The nurse who attempts to teach an older client every aspect of diabetes care in one session is destined to fail. Learning is far more likely to succeed if needs are put in order of priority and material is presented in small, manageable components. Learning about meal plans and medications should be the first priority, and these should involve the client and family from the beginning. Open-ended questions may be used to determine how much (or how little) the client has understood. Examples of these might be "Tell me what you will eat for breakfast now that your meal plan has changed" or "Describe how you will get your insulin ready in the morning."

The teaching plan for an older person with NIDDM should include nutritional instruction, medication awareness, exercise planning, glucose monitoring, foot care (see Table 16–2), and actions to prevent complications of diabetes. This content should be introduced over a span of time that makes teaching feasible for the nurse and learning possible for the client. One group of researchers[18] found that teaching older clients with diabetes over a 6-week period significantly increased their knowledge of the disease, enhanced their psychosocial function, and improved their metabolic control. Many hospitals across the United States offer 4- to 5-week outpatient diabetes classes. Further patient information may be obtained from state health departments or from the sources listed in Table 16–1.

Nurses who work with older clients should continue to evaluate their knowledge base and additional learning needs. This assessment can occur during a visit to the primary care provider or in the home setting by a visiting nurse.

Thyroid Disorders in Older Adults

by Arthur (Don) Johnson

Normally, the hypothalamus produces thyroid-releasing hormone (TRH) that stimulates the anterior pituitary to produce thyroid-stimulating hormone (TSH). The TSH then stimulates the thyroid to release triiodothyronine (T_3) and thyroxine (T_4). The T_3 and T_4 serve as a negative feedback to the hypothalamus to reduce the production of TRH and with subsequent reduction of TSH from the anterior pituitary. A larger proportion of T_4 is produced than T_3; however, about one-third of the T_4 is metabolized to T_3 in the peripheral tissues. T_3 is three to five times more potent than T_4. As people age, the thyroid gland becomes smaller and there is less conversion of T_4 to T_3. There is little change in the serum T_3 and T_4 concentrations in older adults, although there may be a slight decrease after the seventh decade of life. The half-life of T_4 increases in adults aged 80 to 90, and there is less thyroid production of T_4 with increasing age. Thyroid function seems to be well preserved until the eighth decade of life in normal individuals, but there is a decrease in TSH secretion contributing to a decline in serum T_3.[23] The half-life of serum T_4 increases with age from an approximate value of 4 days during youth to 7 days during young adulthood to 9.3 days during later life. Because less T_4 is produced by the thyroid gland with age, serum levels remain nearly constant.[24] Alterations occur in thyroid structure that include increased fibrosis, decreased follicular cellularity and size, and increased nodularity.[24] Baseline function and reserve capacity of the thyroid are usually sufficient to maintain a euthyroid condition in most healthy older adults.

Thyrotoxicosis

Hyperthyroidism is an excessive production and release of the thyroid hormones. A similar term, *thyrotoxicosis*, refers to the biochemical and physiological complex that results when the tissues have an excessive amount of thyroid hormones. The prevalence of thyrotoxicosis in older adults is approximately 2 percent.[23] About 15 percent of all thyrotoxic patients are over the age of 60. The pathophysiology of hyperthyroidism in older adults is not appreciably different, but some of the clinical manifestations may be more subtle or even dramatically different (Table 16–3).[25] Younger people who have thyrotoxicosis have elevated levels of both T_4 and T_3, whereas older people may have isolated elevations of either T_4 or T_3.

People age 60 or over may have apathetic hyperthyroidism, in which the older adult is not motivated to eat, move, or interact with others. Unfortunately, many people with apathetic thyrotoxicosis are mistaken to have a major depression.

Several variations of thyrotoxicosis exist, but Graves' disease is the most common form. Two major predisposing factors that influence the occurrence of Graves' disease are gender and heredity. Women are 3 to 10 times more likely to be affected than are men. The disease is believed to be an inherited defect of the immune system. Graves' disease is an autoimmune disorder in which the TSH receptor antibodies bind to and stimulate the thyroid gland, causing excessive secretion of T_3 and T_4. Like the course of many other autoimmune diseases, that of Graves' disease usually consists of periods of exacerbations and remissions. The serum of many patients with Graves' disease has long-acting thyroid stimulator that stimulates the thyroid function and is not inhibited by high levels of T_3.

Many effects of thyrotoxicosis resemble those induced by catecholamines, specifically epinephrine. These observations have been interpreted as an increased amount of catecholamines; however, studies have failed to provide this evidence. The apparent adrenergic hyperactivity appears to be a result of the direct effects of the excessive thyroid hormones or an additive effect of the catecholamines. Thyroid hormone increases the density of β-adrenergic receptors while it decreases the density of α-adrenergic receptors. The change in receptor density does not occur uniformly in all tissues but probably plays a role in increasing the sensitivity of some tissues to catecholamines.[26] Thyroid hormones also work at the postreceptor level to alter the responsiveness to catecholamines. For example, there is an increased response to norepinephrine in brown adipose tissue.[27]

TABLE 16–3 HYPERTHYROIDISM IN OLDER AND YOUNGER ADULTS[25]

Features	Older (%)	Young (%)
Tachycardia	50	100
Goiter	63	100
Nervousness	55	99
Heat intolerance	63	89
Palpitation	63	89
Fatigue or weakness	52	88
Weight loss	75	85
Thyroid bruit	27	77
Dyspnea	66	75
Eye signs	57	71
Diarrhea	12	23
Atrial fibrillation	39	10
Constipation	26	4

CLINICAL MANIFESTATIONS

Graves' disease is associated with various clinical manifestations that may involve almost any organ system. The mechanisms involved in producing the manifestations are not completely understood, but an increased sensitivity to the catecholamines may be involved.

Skin, Hair, and Appendages

Along with excessive amounts of thyroid hormones, there is an increase in metabolism and heat production. Peripheral vasodilation occurs to dissipate the excessive heat that results in warm, moist skin and increased perspiration. The hands are usually moist and red. The complexion is usually rosy, and the patient blushes easily. Excessive thyroid hormones cause an increased synthesis and degradation of protein and fat; however, the degradation exceeds the synthesis. Therefore, patients with thyrotoxicosis may have thin skin and hair and may state that the hair will not retain curl.

The fingernails are soft and friable. The distal margin of the nail may separate from the nailbed, with irregular recession of the junction, a characteristic finding known as Plummer's nails. Dirt accumulates under the nails and is difficult to dislodge, resulting in the appearance of dirty nails. The patient may have patchy vitiligo or areas of increased pigmentation. The pigmentation probably results from the excessive amount of thyroid hormones, which increases the metabolism of cortisol, a hormone from the adrenal cortex. The hypothalamus in the brain senses the low cortisol level and stimulates the anterior pituitary gland. This gland then releases adrenocorticotropic hormone (ACTH) to stimulate the release of cortisol from the adrenal cortex. When excessive ACTH is released, another pituitary hormone, melanocyte-stimulating hormone, is released in excessive amounts, resulting in pigmentation of the skin.[28]

Muscles

Because of the excessive amounts of thyroid hormones, synthesis and degradation of proteins increase. The degradation exceeds the synthesis, resulting in weakness and fatigability. The weakness is usually most prominent in the proximal muscles of the limbs, which causes the patient to have difficulty climbing stairs or to maintain the leg in an extended position. In some instances, there is muscle wasting, particularly in the proximal parts, that is out of proportion to the overall loss of weight.[29,30]

Cardiovascular System

Alterations in the cardiovascular system are among the most prominent features of thyrotoxicosis, particularly in older adults. Because of the hypermetabolism, there is an increased circulatory demand to dissipate the excess heat produced. Both stroke volume and heart rate are increased, resulting in an increase in cardiac output.

Because of the increased metabolic demands and because of the direct effects of the thyroid hormones, tachycardia is a common manifestation even at rest. Tachycardia caused by thyrotoxicosis can be distinguished from tachycardia caused by psychogenic stress by assessing the patient's pulse rate during sleep. If the tachycardia is caused by thyrotoxicosis, the resting pulse rate is usually 90 beats per minute or higher. The adrenergic-like effects of thyroid hormones on the heart cause an increased force of contraction, which results in increased blood pressure and complaints of palpitations. There is also an increase in heart sounds, and sometimes a systolic friction rub may be heard. Because of the altered protein metabolism, the papillary muscles may undergo changes that result in mitral valve prolapse.

Dysrhythmias are common. Paroxysmal supraventricular tachycardia and atrial fibrillation are the usual manifestations. Because of the increased metabolism and increased sensitivity of the heart to catecholamines, the older patient may not have enough reserve to support these dysrhythmias. Hence, congestive heart failure may occur. The response to digitalis preparations is decreased, possibly because the excessive thyroid hormones accelerate the metabolism of the drug.

Because degradation of protein exceeds the synthesis, the amount of protein within the blood vessels may be reduced, resulting in increased capillary fragility. Therefore, the patient may have petechiae and bruising.[29,30]

Respiratory System

Protein degradation in thyrotoxicosis results in degradation of muscles and subsequent weakness of the respiratory muscles, leading to a reduced vital capacity. Also, because metabolic demands are increased, there is a greater need for oxygen and a need to dissipate the increased amount of carbon dioxide. This results in a faster respiratory rate and feelings of dyspnea.[31]

Gastrointestinal System

The accelerated metabolism and protein and fat degradation result in increased appetite and food consumption in most older adults with thyrotoxicosis. The higher caloric intake may still be inadequate, however, and the client may lose weight. Another contributing factor is an increase in gastrointestinal motility, which decreases absorption of nutrients. Although an increase in appetite in thyrotoxic older adults is most common, anorexia occurs in about one-third of these people. Gastric emptying and hypermotility are common, causing an excessive number of poorly formed stools. In some instances, the hypermotility causes a slight malabsorption of fat. The mechanism causing this gastrointestinal hypermotility is unknown.

Autoantibodies may attack the parietal cells, causing a reduction in hydrochloric acid, which is necessary for proper absorption of vitamin B_{12}. Absorption of vitamin B_{12}, which is needed for maturation of red blood cells, is subsequently reduced, resulting in pernicious anemia. When the red blood cells in pernicious anemia, which are large and immature, enter the microcirculation, they burst, liberating bilirubin. The increased amount of bilirubin results in jaundice.[29,30]

Nervous System

The mechanisms responsible for changes in the nervous system have not been elucidated but may include an increased adrenergic activity. Consequently, it is common for patients to experience nervousness, emotional lability (which is usually prominent), hyperkinesia, and fatigue. The older adult may exhibit restlessness, manifested by a short attention span and a need to move about constantly.

Eyes

Older adults with thyrotoxicosis often appear to have a bright-eyed stare. Retraction of the upper eyelid occurs, as evidenced by the presence of a rim of sclera between the lid and limbus. There is also a lid lag, in which the upper eyelid lags behind the globe of the eye when the patient gazes downward. A globe lag also exists, in which the globe lags behind the upper eyelid when the patient gazes slowly upward. The movements of the lids are jerky, and there may be a fine tremor of the closed lids. These signs and symptoms are probably related to the increased adrenergic activity.

A major manifestation of Graves' disease is infiltrative ophthalmopathy, resulting in exophthalmos. The extraocular muscles swell and retro-orbital fat increases, causing the eyes to protrude. Early symptoms are irritation of the eyes and excessive tearing with injected conjunctivae. The patient may sleep with the eyes partly open, causing the conjunctivae to dry out, resulting in corneal ulceration or infection. Exophthalmos occurs bilaterally but is usually asymmetrical. Because of the infiltration of the extraocular muscles, the patient finds it difficult to achieve and maintain convergence, resulting in problems in focusing and diplopia.[32]

Calcium and Phosphorus

In thyrotoxicosis, increased amounts of calcium and phosphorus are excreted in the urine and stool. The body responds by releasing more parathyroid hormone, which extracts calcium from the bone to normalize the serum calcium level. There may be subsequent demineralization of bones and pathological fractures, particularly in older women.

Other Endocrine Effects

The thyroid hormones increase insulin metabolism. The client may have glucose intolerance or frank diabetes mellitus. It is important to note that clients with thyrotoxicosis along with diabetes have greater difficulty controlling the diabetes.

NURSING MANAGEMENT

The older adult with thyrotoxicosis should be given a quiet environment and encouraged to rest and enjoy quiet activities. Because the client may be hot, it is important to make the room cool. Because of increased perspiration, more frequent hygienic measures are usually needed. Cleansing of nails should be done cautiously. Separation of the nails may result in accumulation of dirt between the layers, so soaking may be necessary. Changes in the eye may require administration of artificial tears and application of cool, damp compresses to prevent drying of the cornea.

The pulse should be monitored frequently because tachycardia and atrial fibrillation are common. Because of the older adult's hypermetabolic state, a high-protein, high-calorie diet with supplemental feedings is to be encouraged. Nervousness is common, so caffeine should be restricted. The thyrotoxic patient may have neurological dysfunctions, weakness, and osteoporosis, which may cause an increased risk for injuries. A safe environment that prevents injuries from falls and from hot foods and drinks requires careful planning.

Propylthiouracil (PTU) and methylmercaptoimidazole (Methimazole, MMI) are the drugs most commonly used in the treatment of thyrotoxicosis. Both PTU and MMI act by inhibiting the iodination of thyroglobulin and iodotyronine coupling to reduce the amount of T_3 and T_4. PTU is preferred because it has the added benefit of inhibiting the peripheral conversion of T_3 and T_4. The usual initial dosage of PTU in the slightly thyrotoxic patient is 100 to 300 mg/day in divided doses; in the moderately thyrotoxic patient, 300 to 800 mg/day; and in the highly thyrotoxic patient, 800 to 1200 mg/day. In severe cases, it is recommended that PTU be administered with a loading dose of 600 to 1000 mg followed by 200 to 250 mg every 4 hours (1200 to 1500 mg total daily dose).

β-Blockers may be used along with PTU. Propranolol is a commonly used β-blocker that blocks the adrenergic effects and results in rapid improvement of many manifestations of thyrotoxicosis. The dosage range is 20 to 80 mg every 8 hours, depending on the severity of the symptoms. The therapeutic goal is restoration of the pulse to about 80 beats per minute and a subjective sense of improvement.[26]

Because older patients may not be good surgical candidates, radioactive iodine is usually the treatment of choice to destroy thyroid gland cells. The morbidity and mortality of this treatment are much less than those associated with thyroidectomy and with oral antithyroid drugs. [131]I is administered orally; the dosage is determined according to the laboratory test results and the severity of the thyrotoxicosis. Once accumulated within the thyroid, the iodine destroys the tissue through the emission of beta particles. Usually the desired effects occur within 12 weeks, with sufficient thyroid tissue destruction to render the patient euthyroid. The nurse should monitor for manifestations of hypothyroidism because excessive thyroid tissue destruction may occur. These symptoms may not appear until as long as 10 years after treatment. Because the destruction is permanent, these patients will require replacement thyroid hormones.[33]

Thyrotoxic Crisis

The nurse must be vigilant regarding the possibility of a thyrotoxic crisis or thyroid storm. This is an extreme exacerbation of severe hyperthyroidism. It usually occurs in patients who have not been diagnosed and in those with untreated thyrotoxicosis. Patients who cannot or will not routinely take antithyroid drugs are at high risk. Thyrotoxic crisis may result from increased amounts of thyroid hormones and catecholamines. Common physiological stressors that precipitate the condition include infections, diabetic ketoacidosis, and psychosocial problems such as family or occupational problems.[26] Thyrotoxic crisis may also occur as a complication of apathetic hyperthyroidism when an apathetic, anorexic older adult with tachycardia develops congestive heart failure, becomes somnolent, and lapses into a coma. The treatment includes the use of propranolol (1 to 3 mg intravenously in a slow drip every 4 hours), hydrocortisone (100 to 500 mg intravenously every 12 hours), PTU (100 to 200 mg orally every 4 hours), saturated solution of potassium iodine (5 drops orally three times a day), and supportive measures such as mild sedation, fluid replacement, oxygen, cooling, and an antibiotic as needed. Aspirin is contraindicated for the fever because aspirin displaces bound thyroid hormone from the serum protein and increases the amount of free, biologically active thyroid hormones.

Hypothyroidism

The clinical state called hypothyroidism results from a deficient production of thyroid hormones, T_3 and T_4, possibly caused by a loss or atrophy of the thyroid tissue. Hypothyroidism increases with aging and is more common in women. Up to 45 percent of thyroid glands from women over age 60 show evidence of thyroiditis.[25] Hypothyroidism may also be related to an insufficient stimulation of the thyroid as a result of hypothalamic disease. Less thyroid-releasing hormone is excreted from the hypothalamus, which reduces the amount of TSH. Pathology of the anterior pituitary also may cause a reduction in TSH. Because many signs and symptoms of hypothyroidism are nonspecific, early recognition occurs less often in older adults. Hypothyroidism is an age-prevalent disease that occurs most often in later life. Older adults may not be readily diagnosed because so many other problems that occur in later life may be confused with normal aging or other age-prevalent diseases. Therefore, it is recommended that all people over the age of 50 be screened for thyroid abnormalities.[24]

CLINICAL MANIFESTATIONS

Skin, Hair, Tissues, and Appendages

Decreased amounts of thyroid hormones cause a reduction in metabolism, producing hyaluronic acid and mucopolysaccharides. These materials bind water, causing edema, which is responsible for the thickened features and puffy appearance called myxedema. The edema is usually boggy and nonpitting, is most apparent around the eyes and the dorsa of the feet and hands, and causes an enlarged tongue and thickened pharyngeal and laryngeal mucous membranes, which results in a thick, slurred speech and hoarseness.

Because of the lowered metabolism, cutaneous vasoconstriction occurs to conserve heat, causing the skin to be pale and cool. These patients may also have anemia, which contributes to the pallor. The sluggish metabolism also causes less efficient metabolism of carotene; hypercarotenemia results, giving the skin a yellow tint. The skin tends to be dry and coarse because the secretions of the sweat glands and sebaceous glands are diminished.

A reduction in thyroid hormones, which normally maintain protein synthesis, causes decreased protein synthesis in the skin, hair, and vessels. The skin thus may be thin, and wounds may tend to heal slowly. The increased capillary fragility leads to a tendency to bruise. Because hair is made of protein, decreased protein synthesis causes the head and body hair to be dry and brittle and likely to fall out. Growth of hair slows, so haircuts and shaves may be required less often. The nails tend to be brittle and to grow more slowly.

Muscular System

Because of the infiltration of the muscles with fluid, the older adult may complain of stiffness and aching muscles. There is delayed muscle contraction and relaxation, causing a slowness of movement and delayed tendon reflex.

Cardiovascular System

With decreased thyroid hormones, the response to endogenous epinephrine is depressed with decreased adrenergic responsiveness. Heart rate may therefore decrease. There is loss of inotropic and chronotropic effects, resulting in a decrease in cardiac output and a lowered blood pressure. To retain heat, peripheral vascular constriction occurs, which causes a narrowing of pulse pressure. The decrease in cutaneous circulation leads to coolness and pallor of the skin and an increased sensitivity to cold. The effusion of proteins and mucopolysaccharides into the pericardial sac diminishes heart sounds. The effusion causes electrocardiographic changes including prolongation of the PR interval, low P-wave amplitude, and QRS complex.

Respiratory System

Because of the increase in mucopolysaccharides, pleural effusions are common. In severe cases, muscles of respiration may be involved, leading to hypoventilation.

Gastrointestinal System

Weight gain, common in patients with hypothyroidism, may be related to a decrease in metabolism but is usually caused by retention of fluid by the hydrophilic mucopolysaccharide deposits in the tissues. Peristaltic activity slows, often resulting in constipation. Achlorhydria, probably caused by an autoimmunity mechanism, leads to poor absorption of vitamin B_{12} and subsequent pernicious anemia.

Nervous System

Thyroid hormones are essential for the development and maintenance of the central nervous system. In hypothyroidism, there is general slowing of all intellectual functions of thinking, memory, and speech. Because of decreased cardiac output, cerebral blood flow may be diminished. Lethargy and somnolence are common sequelae. In the older patient, the mental aberrations may be mistaken for senile dementia. Because of the central nervous system edema, the median nerve may become depressed, resulting in carpal tunnel syndrome, and ataxia and tingling in the extremities may be present.[34]

Hematopoietic system

Because of reduced metabolism in the older adult, oxygen requirements diminish, so less erythropoietin is produced. In addition to the vitamin B_{12} deficiency, the reduction in erythropoietin causes a decrease in the red blood cell mass, further contributing to anemia.

Other Endocrine Effects

The decrease in thyroid hormones causes reduced metabolism of ADH and insulin. The amount of ADH therefore increases, which leads to more water reabsorption, a subsequent dilutional hyponatremia, and reduced urine output. The increased insulin level resulting from decreased insulin metabolism may cause hypoglycemia.[28,35]

MANAGEMENT

1 Primary Prevention

Because both hypothyroid and hyperthyroid conditions most often result from autoimmune disorders, they usually cannot be prevented. The exception is a goiter caused by inadequate iodine intake. A goiter is an enlargement of the thyroid gland caused by hyperplasia and hypertrophy of the thyroid gland cells. Iodine is necessary for the synthesis of T_3 and T_4. When the diet contains insufficient iodine, thyroid cells are produced in increased number and size to compensate for the low iodine level and to increase the avidity for the limited amount of iodine in the serum. This condition is rare in the United States because many foods contain iodine and most commercially available salt is iodized. Clinical findings include gradual enlargement of the thyroid gland, resulting in increased pressure in the neck that may cause difficulty in swallowing.

2 *Secondary Prevention*

Prompt detection and early intervention are important in limiting the serious effects of thyroid disease. The health history and physical examination should provide information about the potential diagnosis of hypothyroidism or thyrotoxicosis. T_3 and T_4 are the portions of the thyroid hormones in the serum that are not bound to proteins. Normal T_3 and T_4 levels by radioimmune assay are 75 to 195 ng/dL and 4 to 12 g/dL, respectively. These values are increased in thyrotoxicosis and decreased in hypothyroid conditions.

TSH may be measured to determine whether the pathology is caused by hypothalamic or anterior pituitary problems, as opposed to problems of the thyroid gland. The normal TSH value is 0.5 to 5 U/mL. A low TSH and low T_3 and T_4 indicate that the problem is hypothyroidism and the pathology is within the anterior pituitary. A high TSH and high T_3 and T_4 indicate thyrotoxicosis, with the pathology within the anterior pituitary. A high TSH and a low T_3 and T_4 indicate a hypothyroid condition, with the primary problem in the thyroid. The TSH is high because the anterior pituitary and hypothalamus attempt to stimulate the failing thyroid to produce normal levels of thyroid hormones. A low TSH and a high T_3 and T_4 indicate thyrotoxicosis, with the primary problem in the thyroid. The low TSH indicates that the hypothalamus and anterior pituitary are responding to the negative feedback of the increased serum levels of thyroid hormones.

With the thyrotropin-releasing hormone test, TRH is administered and the TSH and T_3 and T_4 levels are measured. If the anterior pituitary response is to increase the levels of TSH and subsequent T_4 levels, the pathology is probably within the hypothalamus. If there is little release of TSH and T_4, the failure is within the anterior pituitary.

Radioactive iodine uptake is a test that measures the amount of radioactive iodine that concentrates in the thyroid gland after administration of the substance. After 24 hours, a radioisotope detector determines the amount of radioactive iodine that has been absorbed by the thyroid gland. An elevated level of absorption indicates thyrotoxicosis and a depressed level indicates hypothyroidism.[36]

NURSING MANAGEMENT

The older adult with hypothyroidism requires enough rest to prevent fatigue and safety precautions to prevent falls. Because of the edema, reduced sweat, and sebaceous gland activity, skin breakdown is possible. Good skin care and frequent inspection of areas prone to decubitus formation are essential. Body heat can be conserved by providing extra layers of clothing or blankets. Roughage is encouraged to prevent the common prob-lem of constipation. The patient's bowel movements and bowel sounds should be assessed daily. The pulse rate and rhythm should be monitored carefully. Because drug metabolism depends on thyroid hormones, a hypothyroid patient receiving a digitalis preparation may require less than the usual dosage. As thyroid hormone replacement is initiated, a higher dosage may be needed to maintain the therapeutic effect. Likewise, if the hypothyroid patient is taking insulin, insulin metabolism may increase as replacement therapy is begun, with a need for a larger dosage. Therefore, it is important to monitor blood sugar levels frequently in these clients. Because of weakness of the respiratory muscles, respiration and indications of dyspnea must be evaluated. Drugs that depress respiration (e.g., narcotics, barbiturates, and tranquilizers) may be administered with caution. These drugs may have a prolonged and intensified effect because of a decreased metabolism.

Drugs

Several pharmaceutical preparations are available for the treatment of hypothyroidism. The usual thyroid hormone replacement agent is L-thyroxine, with a dosage for healthy patients under the age of 60 with no history of cardiac or respiratory disease of 1.6 to 1.8 μg/kg ideal body weight per day. Older patients require 20 to 30 percent less. Usually, the older adult is started out at no more than 50 μg/day, with the dosage increased by 25 μg at intervals of at least 6 weeks. This low dosage is recommended because an abrupt increase in metabolic rate and demand for increased cardiac output may precipitate angina, myocardial infarction, congestive heart failure, or dysrhythmias. If the patient exhibits no manifestations of cardiac decompensation after 6 weeks, the dosage may be increased by 0.025 mg/day.[37]

The nurse should monitor the client for myxedema coma, the life-threatening end-stage of untreated hypothyroidism. Myxedema coma initially presents as profound manifestations of hypothyroidism, including hypothermia, bradycardia, hypotension, and a depressed level of consciousness. Because of their decreased insulin metabolism, these patients may have increased levels of insulin, resulting in hypoglycemia. The coma may be precipitated by cold exposure, infection, trauma, surgery, or other stressors. It can also be brought on in older adults who stop their replacement therapy. Because hypothyroidism increases drug sensitivity, opiates, barbiturates, and anesthetics may cause the complication.

Patient Teaching

Patients with thyrotoxicosis should be taught the signs and symptoms of recurring hyperthyroidism. Also, because Graves' disease and its treatment may eventually lead to hypothyroidism, these patients must be taught the signs and symptoms of hypothyroidism. Patients with hypothyroidism should understand the manifestations of thyrotoxicosis because thyroid replacements may cause symptoms of that disorder; they also need to know the manifestations of hypothy-

TABLE 16–4 NORMAL ENDOCRINE SYSTEM AGING CHANGES

Normal Age-Related Changes	Clinical Implications
Blood glucose levels increase	Fasting blood glucose of 140 mg/dL considered normal
Renal threshold for glucose rises	2-hr postprandial blood sugar of 140–200 mg/dL considered normal
Residual urine in bladder increases	Urine glucose monitoring unreliable
Thyroid gland becomes smaller	Serum T_3 and T_4 remain stable
T_3 and T_4 production decreases slightly	
Half-life of T_3 and T_4 increases	

roidism because thyroid replacements may not be sufficient to maintain a euthyroid state. Other components that should be included in discharge planning are the importance of regular follow-up care to evaluate thyroid function for the remainder of the patient's life. The patient should also be taught the names, prescribed dosages, and potential side effects of the medications to maintain a euthyroid state.

3 Tertiary Prevention

To promote rehabilitation and resumption of a normal, healthful lifestyle, the patient with a thyroid disorder must receive ongoing medical care to facilitate maintenance of a euthyroid state. Because thyroid function fluctuates, regular follow-up care should be encouraged and the possibility of using visiting nurses considered. Programs of care are individualized according to the patient's manifestations and should be implemented to help the patient maintain an optimal level of wellness.

Summary of Normal Endocrine System Aging Changes

Normal aging changes to the endocrine system are summarized in Table 16–4.

Student Learning Activities

1 Identify the nearest community-based diabetes support group. What services does this group provide for community-living diabetic people?

2 For 1 week, consume only a 2000-calorie-per-day diet (10 percent fat, 15 percent protein, and 75 percent complex carbohydrates). In addition, limit the salt intake to 2 g/day. As a class, what difficulties did you have in accomplishing this task? What have you learned that will aid you in diabetic teaching in the future?

3 Survey the local emergency department personnel on their knowledge of the age-specific signs and symptoms of hyperthyroidism and hypothyroidism. Offer to present an inservice on the topic if needed.

REFERENCES

1 Marchesseault, L: Diabetes mellitus and the elderly. Nurs Clin North Am 18(4):791, 1983.
2 Havlik, RJ: Determinants of health: cardiovascular risk factors. In Havlik, RJ, et al (eds): Health Statistics, on Older Persons, United States, 1986. Vital and Health Statistics. Series 3, no 25, DHHS Pub no (PHS) 87-1409. Public Health Service, US Government Printing Office, Washington, DC, 1987.
3 Goldberg, A, et al: Diabetes mellitus in the elderly. In Andres, R, et al (eds): Principles of Geriatric Medicine. McGraw-Hill, New York, 1984, pp 750–764.
4 Kane, R, et al: Essentials of Clinical Geriatrics, ed 2. McGraw-Hill, New York, 1989.
5 Gray, D: Elderly diabetics and urine-testing. Geriatr Nurs 6(6):332, 1985.
6 Beare, P, and Myers, J: Principles and Practice of Adult Health Nursing. CV Mosby, St Louis, 1990, p 1475.
7 Porth, C: Pathophysiology: Concepts of Altered Health States. JB Lippincott, Philadelphia, 1986.
8 Matteson, M, and McConnell, E: Gerontological Nursing: Concepts and Practice. WB Saunders, Philadelphia, 1988, p 298.
9 Levine, S, and Sanson, T: Treatment of hyperglycemic hyperosmolar non-ketotic syndrome. Drugs 38(3):462, 1989.
10 Davidson, M: The Merck Manual of Geriatrics. Merck, Sharp, and Dohme Research Laboratories, Rahway, NJ, 1990.
11 Geriatrics Panel Discussion: Practical nutritional advice for the elderly. Part II: Modification and motivation. Geriatrics 45(11):45, 1990.
12 Kirchain, W: Treatment of diabetes mellitus. A continuing education program. Novo Nordisk Pharmaceuticals, Philadelphia, 1991.
13 Schwartz, R: Exercise training in the treatment of diabetes mellitus in elderly patients. Diabetes Care (suppl 2) 13(2):77, 1990.
14 Hollander, P, and Nordstrom, J: Exercise and diabetes: Great for type II, good for type I. Your Patient and Fitness 5(3):6, 11, 1991.
15 Grobin, W: A longitudinal study of impaired glucose tolerance and diabetes mellitus in the aged. J Am Geriatric Soc 37(12):1127, 1989.
16 The Diabetes Control and Complications Trial Research Group. The effect of intensive treatment of diabetes on the development and progression of long-term complications in insulin-dependent diabetes mellitus. N Engl J Med 329(14):977, 1993.
17 Bailey, EL: Biguanides and non-insulin-dependent diabetes mellitus. Diabetes Care 15(6):755, 1992.
18 Walter, R: Hypoglycemia: Still a risk in the elderly. Geriatrics 45(3):69, 74, 1990.
19 Gilden, J, et al: Effects of self-monitoring of blood glucose on quality of life in elderly diabetic patients. J Am Geriatr Soc 38:511, 1990.
20 Andron, V: Emotional health status can affect diabetes control. Diabetes 10(2):30, 1991.
21 Smith, C: Sensory stimulation and ADL performance: A single case study approach. Phys Occup Ther Geriat 6(1):43, 1987.
22 Riddle, M: Diabetic neuropathies in the elderly: Management update. Geriatrics 45(9):32, 1990.
23 Gambert, SR: Intrinsic and extrinsic variables: Age and physiologic variables. In Braverman, LE, and Utiger, RD (eds): Werner and Ingbar's The Thyroid: A Fundamental and Clinical Text. Lippincott-Raven, Philadelphia, 1996, pp 254–259.

24 Gambert, SR: Endocrinology and aging. In Reichel, W (ed): Care of the Elderly: Clinical Aspects of Aging. Williams & Wilkins, Baltimore, 1995, pp 365–379.

25 Byyny, RI, and Speroff, L: Thyroid and parathyroid disorders. In A Clinical Guide for the Care of Older Women: Primary and Preventive Care, ed 2. Williams & Wilkins, Baltimore, 1996, pp 397–412.

26 Tietgens, S, and Leinung, M: Thyroid storm endocrine emergencies. Med Clin North Am 79(1):169–184, 1995.

27 Silva, JE, and Landsberg, L: Catecholamines and the sympathoadrenal system in thyrotoxicosis. In Braverman, LE, and Utiger, RD (eds): Werner and Ingbar's The Thyroid. JB Lippincott, Philadelphia, 1991, pp 816–827.

28 Bernhard, JD, et al: The skin in thyrotoxicosis. In Braverman, LE, and Utiger, RD (eds): Werner and Ingbar's The Thyroid: A Fundamental and Clinical Text. Lippincott-Raven, Philadelphia, 1996, pp 595–597.

29 Larsen, P, and Ingbar, S: The thyroid gland. In Williams, R: Textbook of Endocrinology, ed 8. WB Saunders, Philadelphia, 1992.

30 Burman, K: Hyperthyroidism. In Becker, K, et al (eds): Principles and Practice of Endocrinology and Metabolism. JB Lippincott, New York, 1990.

31 Ingbar, DH: The respiratory system in thyrotoxicosis. In Braverman, LE, and Utiger, RD (eds): Werner and Ingbar's The Thyroid: A Fundamental and Clinical Text. Lippincott-Raven, Philadelphia, 1996, pp 616–627.

32 Alper, M: Endocrine ophthalmopathy. In Becker, K, et al (eds): Principles and Practice of Endocrinology and Metabolism. JB Lippincott, New York, 1990.

33 Cooper, DS: Treatment of Thyrotoxicosis. In Braverman, LE, and Utiger, RD (eds): Werner and Ingbar's The Thyroid: A Fundamental and Clinical Text. Lippincott-Raven, Philadelphia, 1996, pp 713–735.

34 DeLong, GR: The neuromuscular system and brain in hypothyroidism. In Braverman, LE, and Utiger, RD (eds): Werner and Ingbar's The Thyroid: A Fundamental and Clinical Text. Lippincott-Raven, Philadelphia, 1996, pp 816–820.

35 Jordan, RM: Myxedema Coma: Pathophysiology, therapy, and factors affecting progress. Med Clin North Am 79(1): 185–194, 1995.

36 Hancock, MR: Disorders of the thyroid gland. In Burrell, L (ed): Adult Nursing in Hospital and Community Setting. Appleton & Lange, Norwalk, Conn, 1992.

37 Brent, GA, and Larsen, PR: Treatment of hypothyroidism. In Braverman, LE, and Utiger, RD (eds): Werner and Ingbar's The Thyroid: A Fundamental and Clinical Text. Lippincott-Raven, Philadelphia, 1996, pp 792–795.

CHAPTER 17

The Aging Renal and Urinary System

Carolyn Kee

OBJECTIVES

Upon completion of this chapter, the reader will be able to:

- Describe age-related changes and associated clinical manifestations in the aging renal and urinary system
- Discuss parameters and measures for estimating creatinine clearance in older people
- Define the four types of urinary incontinence
- Discuss both nursing assessment and nursing management activities important to primary prevention
- Describe the three categories of iatrogenic complications and associated preventive nursing interventions
- Discuss renal diseases prevalent among older people
- Describe nursing management activities appropriate to each type of urinary incontinence
- Discuss issues important in tertiary prevention

Aging affects the renal and urinary system in a number of ways. In the healthy older person, age-related changes in the renal system are not overt because the kidney remains able to meet normal requirements. In times of stress, however, such as when physiological demand is abnormally high or when disease states exist, the aging renal system is vulnerable.

The urinary system is different, however. Although aging processes do not in themselves cause continence problems, conditions common in older people combined with age-related changes in the urinary system may precipitate incontinence.

Structure and Function of the Renal and Urinary System

The renal and urinary system is composed of the kidneys, ureters, bladder, and urethra. The ureters, bladder, and urethra are primarily a storage and transportation system for the removal of urine from the body once

it has been formed by the kidney. The kidney is more complex physiologically and is vitally involved in the performance of essential homeostatic functions. These functions include removing waste products from the body; regulating fluid and electrolytes; maintaining acid-base balance; producing renin, prostaglandins, and erythropoietin; metabolizing vitamin D into its active form; and degrading insulin. The urinary system serves two critical functions: passive storage and active removal of urine.

AGE-RELATED CHANGES IN THE RENAL SYSTEM

The functioning unit of the kidney is the nephron. In the young adult, there are approximately 2 million nephrons in the outer cortex and inner medulla of the kidney. By late adulthood, this number has been reduced by half. In addition, the remaining nephrons have more abnormalities than are found in the younger adult.[1] Although these changes seem dramatic, the fact that healthy individuals are able to donate a kidney without serious consequence provides a basis of comparison for the normal loss of nephrons in the older adult.

Age-related changes in the nephron and the vascular network of the kidney significantly affect kidney function (Table 17–1). Because the nephron is the mechanism through which blood is filtered, changes in vascular flow that accompany aging affect the ability of the nephron to accomplish its tasks. In turn, age-related changes occurring within the nephron itself affect the regulatory, excretory, and metabolic functions of the renal system.

Physiologically, blood is delivered for filtration through the renal artery to the afferent arteriole, from which blood enters the glomerulus (a capillary tuft). About 20 percent of the blood is filtered through the glomerulus at a rate of 125 mL/min. During the filtering process, all substances except proteins and red blood cells (RBCs) are removed, so the resulting liquid is essentially like plasma. The unfiltered blood, now with a higher proportion of protein and RBCs than before, proceeds to the efferent artery and into the vasa recta that surround the tubular system. The blood filtered through the glomerulus, now called the glomerular filtrate, passes through Bowman's capsule into a tubular system consisting of the proximal tubule, the loop of Henle, the distal tubule, and the collecting tubule. This tubular system is enmeshed in the vasa recta, a vascular bed. It is here, between the tubular system and the vasa recta, that fluid, electrolyte, and other exchanges occur. These exchanges are dictated by what is or what is not needed by the body. Fluids and substances that are required for homeostasis are returned to the circulation through the vascular bed and ultimately to the renal vein. Those that are not required eventually form urine and are delivered through the collecting tubules to the ureters. Most of the glomerular filtrate, both liquid and solutes, is reabsorbed so that only 1.5 L/day are finally excreted as urine.[2]

A number of changes have been noted in the aging nephron and circulatory system that affect exchange processes. In the nephron, changes occur in the glomerulus and the tubular system. In the glomerulus, the basement membrane thickens, focal areas of sclerosis are found, and the total glomerular surface decreases, resulting in less efficient filtration of blood. Both the length and volume of the proximal tubule decrease. Diverticula are seen in the distal convoluted tubule, causing the accumulation of debris. These tubular changes decrease the membrane surface area available for exchange processes. Vascular changes are caused by reduced cardiac output, the generalized vessel narrowing and sclerosing of aging, and the decreased size of the renovascular bed, which causes up to a 50 percent decrease in renal blood flow.[3] The compounded effect of these changes is that less blood is available for cleansing per minute and that exchange processes are less efficient and less effective.

Fluid balance is more precarious in an older person for several reasons. First, because older adults have reduced muscle mass and a corresponding increase in total

TABLE 17–1 STRUCTURAL AND FUNCTIONAL CHANGES IN THE AGING RENAL AND URINARY SYSTEM

Structural Changes	Functional Changes
Basement membrane of the glomerulus thickens.	GFR often decreases.
Total glomerular surface diminishes.	Concentration ability decreases.
Length and volume of proximal tubule decrease.	Nocturia is often present.
Distal tubule develops diverticula.	Serum creatinine may remain the same.
Renal circulation is altered or reduced.	Salt-losing tendency has been noted.
Bladder capacity decreases.	Calcium and vitamin D metabolism may be affected.
Residual volume increases.	Homeostatic mechanisms are altered and become more precarious.
Involuntary bladder (detrusor) contractions occur.	Frequency increases, interval decreases between urge and voiding.

body fat and because muscle contains more water than fat, there is an age-related net reduction in total body water. Second, a reduction in intracellular fluid occurs with normal aging.[4] Finally, compensatory mechanisms for water loss are altered in older people.

Fluid loss in a younger person results in a more concentrated urine, increased thirst sensation, and secretion of the antidiuretic hormone (ADH), so water is both retained and replaced in compensation for the loss. In contrast, in the aging adult the ability of the nephron to concentrate urine is compromised, response to ADH secretion is not as efficient, and thirst sensation may be diminished or even absent. Because of these factors, conditions that precipitate excess fluid loss and so disrupt homeostasis in an older person may quickly become serious because compensatory mechanisms are not as efficient or effective. These homeostatic deficiencies may not be important in healthy older people who maintain adequate fluid intake.[5]

The ability of the kidney to handle sodium is also affected by aging. Compared with younger people, older adults following salt-restricted diets demonstrated significantly less ability to conserve sodium because of nephron loss or impaired aldosterone secretion.[3,6] Reductions in sodium (hyponatremia) can cause increases in potassium retention (hyperkalemia). Hypernatremia is less common but can occur with dietary sodium excesses without sufficient water intake. Similarly, an excessive dietary intake of both sodium and water can cause hypervolemia. There is impaired excretion of acid and buffering systems are less efficacious.[3]

The secretion of the hormone 1,25-dihydroxyvitamin D by the kidney decreases in the aging adult. This hormone is important in calcium absorption in the gastrointestinal tract and in preventing mobilization of bone calcium for the purpose of maintaining serum calcium levels. Lack of this hormone may be one of the mechanisms implicated in the development of type II (senile) osteoporosis in the older adult.

AGE-RELATED CHANGES IN THE URINARY SYSTEM

The storage and discharge of urine at appropriate intervals is an intricately coordinated voluntary and involuntary process. The system must be physically and neurologically intact and there must be cognitive awareness of the urge to void and the appropriate place and circumstances in which to do so.

The bladder fills with urine discharged from the ureters at the rate of 2 mL/min. The bladder muscle (the detrusor) is relaxed to accommodate increasing volume while the internal sphincter at the bladder neck and the external sphincter at the pelvic muscle floor are constricted so that leakage does not occur. Normal bladder capacity ranges from 300 to 600 mL, with the urge to void sensed between 150 and 350 mL.[7] Voiding can be delayed for 1 to 2 hours once urge is recognized. When voiding or micturition occurs, the detrusor muscle contracts and the internal and external sphincters relax, opening the urethra. In young adults, virtually all urine is expelled in this process. In older adults, all urine may not be expelled, but a residual urine volume of 50 mL or less is considered adequate.[8] Amounts greater than 100 mL indicate significant urinary retention.[9]

Neurologically, pathways for relaxation and contraction are in the spinal cord at the sacral micturition center (S2-S4) and in T11 through L2. This localized control is superseded by the bladder control center in the cerebral cortex and by the brain stem. Disruption at any point in this system has consequences for continence.

TABLE 17–2   NORMAL RENAL AND URINARY SYSTEM AGING CHANGES

Normal Age-Related Changes	Clinical Implications
Thickening of basement membrane	Less efficient filtration of blood
Decreased glomerular surface area	
Decreased length and volume of proximal tubule	
Decreased vascular blood flow	
Decreased lean muscle mass	Decreased total body water
Increased total body fat	Risk of dehydration
Decreased intracellular fluid	
Decreased thirst sensation	
Decreased ability to concentrate urine	
Decreased hormone necessary for calcium absorption from gastrointestinal tract	Increased risk of osteoporosis
Decreased bladder capacity	Increased risk of incontinence
Increased residual volume	
Increased involuntary bladder contractions	
Generalized atrophy of bladder muscle	

For example, the demented patient with significant cognitive loss may no longer have a social inhibition against voiding in a hallway with other people present.

Changes commonly accompanying aging include a smaller bladder capacity, increased residual volume, and involuntary bladder contractions (see Table 17–1). In older women, decreased estrogen production results in atrophy of the urethral tissue and childbirth effects can be seen in weakened pelvic floor musculature. In older men, prostatic hypertrophy causes pressure on the bladder neck and urethra. Decreases in reaction time may affect neurological control of the bladder as well. The generalized muscle atrophy of aging affects the bladder musculature, so contractions are not as powerful as in younger years.

Normal renal and urinary system aging changes are summarized in Table 17–2.

CLINICAL MANIFESTATIONS

Most age changes in the renal system have no direct, observable clinical manifestations in the healthy older adult. Two parameters, glomerular filtration rate (GFR) and the concentration/dilution ability of the tubular system, can be assessed through indirect measures and indicate the effectiveness of kidney function in the older adult.

Age changes in the urinary system are of potentially greater significance. Nocturia is common and incontinence can be provoked to a greater or lesser degree. Incontinence is costly, in terms of both the psychosocial consequences to the patient and the enormous economic impact on society.[10] It is estimated that about 13 percent of the community-residing men and women aged 75 or over are incontinent, approximately 34 percent of men and 60 percent of women over 75 in acute-care institutions are incontinent, and about 50 percent of men and women in nursing homes are incontinent.[7] For older people, incontinence may be only an occasional annoyance or so significant that depression and social isolation ensue.

Glomerular Filtration Rate

Glomerular filtration occurs at the rate of 125 mL/min in young adults and can be measured clinically through serum creatinine or creatinine clearance. Longitudinal studies in healthy older subjects have demonstrated significant reductions in creatinine clearance rates over time, so by age 80, average GFR declined to 97 mL/min.[11] In this same group of subjects, however, about one-third showed no reductions in GFR and a few even showed improvement.[6] Recent evidence indicates that people with normal blood pressure and normal protein intake may retain functional renal reserve.[3]

GFR is estimated through determination of serum creatinine or creatinine clearance. The production of creatinine is directly related to muscle mass. Because muscle mass is normally less in the older adult and because creatinine is a by-product of muscle metabolism, less creatinine is produced as people age. If the kidney is accomplishing its cleansing task adequately, serum creatinine levels should be correspondingly lower to reflect reductions in muscle mass. Thus, a serum creatinine level that is within normal limits or slightly above normal might reflect a significant decrease in GFR in an older adult and is an indication for further evaluation.[12] A GFR of 60 mL/min or less was found in a significant number of healthy, ambulatory older subjects with normal serum creatinine and blood urea nitrogen (BUN) levels.[13] Therefore, measures of creatinine clearance are considered to be more accurate indicators of GFR than are measures of serum creatinine or BUN in the older adult. Creatinine clearance can be assessed through a 24-hour urine collection or estimated mathematically through application of the Cockcroft-Gault formula to serum creatinine level.[4] One study on older subjects[13] reported a correlation of 0.73 between 24-hour creatinine clearance and the Cockcroft-Gault formula. As shown in Figure 17–1, the Cockcroft-Gault formula incorporates the factors of age, muscle mass (as indicated through lean body weight), and gender differences. It has been suggested that the correction for women not be used for healthy older people.[13] Because error rate can be substantial in the process of collecting urine for a 24-hour period, no clear advantage for estimating GFR has been established for either of these two methods.[14]

Concentration and Dilution Mechanisms

Normal aging of the kidneys results in changes in the concentration and dilution mechanisms in the tubular system of the nephron. The inability of the older person to concentrate urine is related to the decreased number of total nephrons. Whether caused by increased solute load or increased blood flow to the remaining nephrons, the result is a more dilute, less concentrated, and therefore lighter-yellow urine.

Nocturia

The nocturia often observed in older adults is attributed to decreased ability to concentrate urine, to smaller bladder capacity (so that urine cannot be stored for long

$$\text{Creatinine Clearance ml/min} = \frac{(140 - \text{age}) \times \text{Weight (kg)}}{72 \times \text{Serum Creatinine (mg/dl)}}$$

$$\times\ 0.85\ \text{for Women}$$

Figure 17–1 The Cockcroft-Gault formula.[14,25]

periods), and to increased renal perfusion at night. It has been estimated that 75 percent of adults living in the community get up at least once during the night to void and that another 25 percent must get up twice.[15] This affects already altered sleeping patterns, contributes to daytime fatigue, and potentially causes falls with injury.

Incontinence

Although it is not considered a normal age-related change, aging processes and disease states may combine to result in incontinence. Long-standing incontinence is called established, persistent, or chronic incontinence. Incontinence of shorter duration is called transient or acute. Case-Gamble[10] comments that treatment of the cause usually resolves transient incontinence.

Four principal types of incontinence are recognized (Table 17–3). In older people, having more than one type, called mixed incontinence, is possible. Stress incontinence occurs with sudden increases in intra-abdominal pressure adding to pressure already present in the bladder. Thus, sneezing, coughing, laughing, exercising, or changing position by getting out of a chair or being turned can cause involuntary losses of small amounts of urine. It is more prevalent in women because of loss of pelvic floor tone attributed to childbirth, pelvic prolapse such as a cystocele, an anatomically shorter urethra, and sphincter weakness; in men, prostatectomy is a cause.[7,8]

Urge incontinence is associated with a strong, urgent desire to void with little ability to delay urination. In urge incontinence, the bladder is nearly full before the need to void is recognized and, as a result, small to moderate amounts of urine escape before a toilet can be reached. The sense of urgency is accompanied by frequency.[16] Cause is attributed to detrusor muscle in-

TABLE 17–3 TYPES OF INCONTINENCE

Type	Cause	Symptom
Stress	Loss of pelvic floor tone Pelvic prolapse Prostatectomy	Leaking of small amounts of urine when coughing, sitting up, etc.
Urge	Detrusor muscle instability	Very shortened interval between perceived need to void and occurrence of voiding
Overflow	Bladder overly distended but detrusor does not contract	Dribbling, reduced stream
Functional	Factors external to the urinary system itself such as a toilet too far away or cognitive impairment	Leakage or normal interval, amount, and flow

stability (overactivity) by itself or that associated with conditions such as cystitis, outflow obstruction, supra-sacral spinal cord injury, and stroke. Between 40 and 70 percent of incontinence in older people is urge incontinence.

Overflow incontinence is the loss of urine occurring with an overdistended bladder occurring in 7 to 11 percent of incontinent patients.[16] Capacity is exceeded, causing the bladder pressure to be greater than resisting urethral sphincter pressure. Because the detrusor muscle does not contract, dribbling and a reduced urinary stream result. Overflow incontinence is caused by a disruption in nerve transmission and by outlet obstruction such as that occurring with an enlarged prostate or fecal impaction.[8] It has also been called a hypotonic or atonic bladder. Postvoid residual urine is greater than 150 to 200 mL.

Functional incontinence is caused by factors other than a dysfunctional urinary system. Urinary system structures are intact and function normally but external factors impede continence. Dementia, other psychological impairments, physical weakness or immobility, and environmental barriers such as a distant bathroom are among these factors.[7]

1 *Primary Prevention*

The focus of primary preventive care for renal and urinary function in the healthy older adult incorporates assessment, monitoring, and educational nursing activities. As noted earlier, kidney function remains normal despite age-related changes. Renal reserve is diminished, however, so unusual physiological demands and minor illnesses are accommodated less easily. Factors potentially leading to continence problems may be present to one degree or another.

Primary nursing care is directed at minimizing the potential for exceeding renal reserve capacity (Table 17–4) and reducing the risks associated with developing incontinence. Assessment and monitoring of fluid balance and dietary habits are essential.

NURSING ASSESSMENT

Assessment for Fluid and Electrolyte Imbalance

The assessment of skin turgor as an indicator of fluid deficit can be inaccurate in the older adult because elasticity is normally reduced in this age group. Pinching the skin over the forehead or sternum has been recommended as a substitute because less elasticity is lost in these areas.[17] Testing the rapidity with which a vein on the dorsal aspect of the foot fills after occlusion and emptying at a distal point is an indicator of hydration in older adults.[17] Elevations of oral temperature often cannot be used as an indicator of dehydration in older people because thermal responses to fluid loss and even infectious processes are inhibited in many older adults. Signs of fluid excess are correspondingly easier to assess in the aging adult. The loss of skin elas-

TABLE 17–4 TEACHING GUIDE: HEALTH-PROMOTING ACTIVITIES FOR OLDER PEOPLE WITH AGE-RELATED DIMINISHED RENAL RESERVE

- Drink a minimum of 2½ quarts of water or other liquid each day.
- Spread the water intake evenly throughout the day.
- When engaging in physical exercise, drink more water more frequently than usual. Do not wait to feel thirsty.
- During hot weather, avoid exercising or engaging in other physical activity during the hottest periods of the day.
- If you have a mild illness with symptoms such as diarrhea, fever, or lack of appetite, be careful to continue to drink at least 1½ quarts of water or other liquid each day. Watch the color of your urine; if it becomes dark (rather than straw-colored), you need to drink more liquid.
- If a minor illness persists or if liquid and food cannot be retained, see a health practitioner.
- If voiding at night or incontinence is a problem, restrict liquids at night before bedtime but do not reduce the total amount for the day.
- If you are following a salt-restricted diet, do not have *less* salt than is prescribed.
- If you are not on a salt-restricted diet but food does not taste as good as it used to, do not add more salt. Try spices without salt or sodium, vinegar, or lemon juice instead.
- Ask a health practitioner to check all the medications you are taking, both prescription and over-the-counter, every 6 months. Make sure the labels are large enough for you to read and that the directions are clear.
- If you have arthritis or if you regularly take (or begin to take) medications such as aspirin, ibuprofen, indomethacin, or naproxen for any other reason, be sure to follow the prescribed amount and dosage intervals carefully. If your legs begin to swell or swell worse than usual, if the amount of urine voided is less than usual, the urine is foamy looking, or you just do not feel right, report this to your health practitioner.
- Ask your health-care practitioner about taking estrogen replacement therapy.

ticity and reduction in muscle mass make edema more readily apparent and neck or hand vein distention easier to assess.

Assessment for Nocturia

Assessing for the presence and frequency of nocturia is routine. Differentiating between age-related nocturia, medication-induced nocturia, or other causes provides the information necessary to determine whether intervention is required.

Assessment for Mental Status

Assessment for change in the mental status of an older adult provides an early warning sign for possible fluid and electrolyte imbalances and the delirium, depression, and dementia that contribute to the development of incontinence. The sudden onset of confusion or disorientation in the healthy older adult should immediately alert the nurse to assess hydration status and to anticipate functional incontinence.

Assessment of Diet

Assessing nutrition for adequacy of calcium intake is important in preventing osteoporosis. By the time clinical indicators such as kyphosis or multiple fractures are present, osteoporosis is well advanced. Although new drug therapies for osteoporosis have proven helpful, prevention remains the first line of defense.

Assessment of Incontinence Risk Factors

Assessment of risk factors for incontinence is aided by Ouslander's[7] DRIP mnemonic for recalling causes of transient incontinence. The DRIP system is also useful in identifying risk factors for incontinence. The *D* is for *delirium* (*depression* should be added for older people); the *R* stands for *restricted mobility* and *retention;* the *I* for *infection, inflammation,* and *impaction;* and the *P* for *polyuria* (such as that caused by diabetes or congestive heart failure) and pharmaceuticals or drugs. When one or more DRIP factors are present, continence is at risk and preventive action should be taken.

In addition, Donovan[18] advises early emphasis on prenatal and postnatal exercise to prevent weakened pelvic floor muscles later in life. Obesity adds further stress to these muscles. Donovan also suggests that lifelong attention to good bowel habits, high-fiber diets, general fitness, and estrogen replacement therapy all should promote continence in later life.

Asymptomatic bacteriuria is common and often transient in older people. Although infection is a potential risk factor for incontinence, most advise that if urinary tract infection (UTI) symptoms (frequency, urgency, and discomfort) are absent, bacteriuria should not be treated with antibiotic therapy.[19] Older people may not have the traditional symptoms of UTI but instead may have an altered mental status, decreased appetite, abdominal tenderness, or respiratory difficulty.[20]

NURSING MANAGEMENT

Monitoring of Physical Exercise

As a routine precaution, older adults can be taught to be aware of fluid deficits that may occur when engaging in physical exercise such as playing golf and gardening or when undertaking aerobic exercise such as rapid, sustained walking or jogging that may cause excessive sweating. Being alert for potential fluid deficits is particularly important in hot, humid weather. Fluid replacement must be a conscious, deliberate action. The older person should be taught to replace fluids frequently in small amounts rather than drinking boluses of liquid separated by long intervals.

Monitoring of Minor Illnesses

Episodes of diarrhea or vomiting, colds with accompanying fever, and viral illnesses or infections, normally regarded as minor illnesses to be managed at home, can quickly become critical if fluid deficits are severe. Older adults should be taught to monitor fluid balance carefully under these circumstances so that minimal daily fluid intake is sustained. Consultation with a health professional is necessary should these minor illnesses persist to prevent dehydration (hyperosmolar imbalance and hypernatremia) or hypovolemia.

Monitoring of Diet

An older person may independently restrict sodium in a misguided effort to prevent or manage hypertension. If hypertension is diagnosed and a moderately low-salt diet recommended, the person may severely restrict sodium in the belief that this would cause a greater reduction in blood pressure. Hyponatremia may be the result because of the aging kidney's normal tendency to lose salt. Sodium and fluid imbalance may also result from dietary excesses initiated in response to a reduced ability to taste salt. More dietary salt is added to compensate for decreased taste. Other spices or tart liquids such as lemon juice or vinegar can be used if this problem exists.

The older adult tends to have a lowered intake of dietary calcium.[21] Assessment of an older person's diet for adequate amounts of this mineral and vitamin D is important. Many physicians now recommend supplementary calcium for postmenopausal women because diets are so often inadequate.

Monitoring of Fluid Intake

In adults, minimal fluid intake is 1500 mL/day, with a more adequate range of intake between 2500 and 3500 mL/day,[22] assuming no contraindicating conditions. Replacement of water loss should proceed with caution in the older adult. Hypervolemia or a hypo-osmolar imbalance (hyponatremia) can be an untoward result of aggressive replacement therapy.

The older person who is continent may restrict fluid intake inappropriately in an attempt to prevent embarrassing episodes. Fluid intake reduction before bedtime can reduce nighttime incontinency, but more fluids should be taken during the day so that total daily intake remains the same.

Monitoring of Nocturia

Nocturia is an expected change with aging and is not problematic by itself. When present, however, fall prevention is a priority. Using a night-light and ensuring an unobstructed pathway to the bathroom are essential.

2 *Secondary Prevention*

The most common renal and urinary problems in older people are those caused by drugs, infections, hypertension, and incontinence.[23] Nursing management in terms of secondary prevention of these and other problems can be classified into three major areas. The first area is the prevention of iatrogenic complications that may occur either in the treatment of illnesses or other organ systems or during diagnostic procedures. The second area concerns diseases directly affecting the aging renal system that may ultimately cause renal failure. The third area is the nursing management of incontinence. Nursing interventions are summarized in Table 17–5.

NURSING MANAGEMENT OF IATROGENIC COMPLICATIONS

Pharmacotherapeutics

Prescribed medications can wreak havoc in older people. Absorption, metabolism, distribution, and excretion of drugs are altered. A number of drugs are excreted through the kidneys, and the altered physiology of the aging renal and urinary system requires adjustments in both dosage and dosage intervals. Older people consume more prescription and nonprescription drugs than do younger people. Visual difficulties, complicated instructions, and the sheer number of drugs taken further compound the propensity toward drug toxicities and adverse reactions including incontinence.

Declines in GFR affect the excretion of water-soluble drugs and result in higher-than-intended serum levels of certain drugs. The cardiac glycoside digoxin is cleared primarily through renal excretion, whereas digitoxin is deactivated in the liver. The antibiotic aminoglycosides such as gentamicin and kanamycin are affected by decreases in the GFR as well. This category of drugs has been identified as the most common cause of nephrotoxic acute tubular necrosis.[24] Other drugs that require lower dosages in older people if GFR is low include tetracycline, vancomycin, chlorpropamide, procainamide, cimetidine, and the cephalosporin antibiotics.[25,26]

Other medications contribute to hyperkalemia in older people by inhibiting the excretion of potassium in the kidney. Potassium-sparing diuretics such as spironolactone, the β-blockers, heparin, angiotensin-converting enzyme (ACE) inhibitors, and the nonsteroidal anti-inflammatory drugs (NSAIDs) all inhibit potassium excretion.[12] Potassium supplements and potassium-containing salt substitutes have also been identified as causes of hyperkalemia in older people. Hypokalemia has been found in older people with fecal impactions or who abuse laxatives and lose potassium in the stool.

Drugs that potentiate the secretion of ADH have also been identified as causing problems. The result of the syndrome of inappropriate ADH secretion is a hyponatremic, hypo-osmolar imbalance. Drugs implicated in this process include the psychotropics, chlorpropamide, carbamazepine, aspirin, acetaminophen, barbiturates, haloperidol, vincristine, and the thiazide diuretics.[25]

Diuretics increase urine volume and voiding frequency and cause or worsen incontinence. Sedatives inhibit awakening so that when need is perceived, urge is greater but time to reach the bathroom is too short and dangerous. Anticholinergic drugs cause urinary retention, contributing to overflow incontinence. Alcohol inhibits awareness of need to void and is a mild diuretic as well.[8]

Use of both prescription and over-the-counter (OTC) medications should be assessed and monitored by the nurse. Illnesses requiring pharmacological interventions are more common in older people. Commonly used drugs are often those that either alter kidney or urinary function or exacerbate age-related changes. Assessment for age-adjusted dosage drug interactions, untoward side effects, medication-induced incontinence, and inappropriate use should be done routinely. Observation for any changes in mental status is important because this may indicate problems with medications. Careful patient instruction, both verbal and written, with reinforcement and regular reassessment of prescription and OTC drug regimens is essential.

Parenteral Fluid Administration

A number of acute conditions occurring in older people required the administration of parenteral fluids. These solutions can be isotonic, hypotonic, or hypertonic and in themselves are a potential source of difficulty.

Correction for fluid and electrolyte imbalance from any cause can be challenging in older people. Because of the susceptibility of older people to changes in fluid status, the nurse needs to be particularly cautious in monitoring parenteral fluid administration in these patients. Replacement or corrective fluid therapy is usually done gradually, with frequent monitoring of laboratory values. If intravenous fluid administration is slower than that ordered for some reason, increasing the rate of flow

---

TABLE 17–5 SECONDARY PREVENTION: NURSING INTERVENTIONS

Pharmacological
  Monitor drug regimens frequently (prescription and over-the-counter).
  Evaluate any change in mental status.
  Validate that medication directions are clear, can be read, and are understood.
  Assess for untoward drug effects.
Parenteral fluids
  Monitor intake and output.
  Monitor vital signs.
  Keep intravenous fluids on schedule.
  Assess for signs and symptoms of volume and osmolar imbalances.
Diagnostic tests
  Monitor intake and output.
  Asses urine color and general fluid status.
  Evaluate potential ill effects of multiple testing procedures involving fluid restriction or fluid loss.
  Monitor response to tests that use radiographic contrast agents.
Kidney disease
  Consider the possibility of acute renal failure with all illnesses/surgery.
  Evaluate nonspecific symptoms for renal implications.
Incontinence
  Take history and perform physical examination.
  Identify type of incontinence and appropriate intervention.
  Suggest pelvic exercise for stress incontinence: Credé maneuver for overflow incontinence, bladder training for urge incontinence, scheduled/prompted toileting for cognitively impaired patients, and other interventions as indicated.
  Assess toileting facilities and general environment for safety, ease of access, and usability.

to remain on schedule is not an alternative for the older patient. Too rapid flow rates can lead to volume or osmolar imbalances because of delays in the excretion of excess water, and hyponatremia may develop.[27]

Diagnostic Tests

Diagnostic testing that includes fluid restriction, bowel-cleansing procedures, or radiographic contrast agents poses particular problems for the older person. People who undergo such tests range from those with minor illnesses to those with acute illnesses. Already homeostatically altered renal mechanisms are challenged further. Fluid restrictions combined with enemas in a mildly dehydrated patient can precipitate osmolar imbalances and hypovolemia. The contrast agents used in some radiographic procedures have a high osmolarity, which can create an obligate diuresis and potentially serious fluid loss.[28] Newer low-osmolarity contrast agents can also cause renal failure.[29] Extracellular fluid volume can increase and cause a circulatory overload. The use of renal ultrasound for diagnosis in place of intravenous pyelograms has reduced the renal risks associated with that procedure.

If possible, the nurse should ensure that the patient is adequately hydrated before being prepared for diagnostic procedures that involve fluid restriction or bowel-cleansing procedures. If this is not feasible, particular attention should be directed toward the assessment of fluid balance, including frequent assessment of mental status. Multiple tests over a short period, such as gastrointestinal series one day and a cholecystogram the next, should be avoided if possible. Monitoring fluid intake and urinary output (amount, frequency, and color) provide continuous data for assessing adequacy.

NURSING MANAGEMENT OF DISEASES OF THE RENAL SYSTEM

The older person with kidney problems may be asymptomatic or may report vague and nonspecific symptoms.[30] Other diseases further obscure the presence of kidney disease.[28] Proteinuria can be related to causes other than renal pathology; pyuria and hematuria usually indicate a problem of renal origin.[28]

Renal system disorders can be classified into four major categories: glomerular disease, tubulointerstitial disease, vascular disease, and obstructive disease. A study of 363 people over age 65 who had a renal biopsy performed showed that 75 percent had glomerular disease, followed by 11 percent with renovascular disease, 7 percent with tubulointerstitial disease, 5 percent with acute tubular necrosis, and 2 percent with other diseases.[31]

Glomerular Disease

Acute glomerulonephritis was once thought to be rare in older people. This may not now be the case, however.[32] Causes of acute glomerulonephritis in an older person include systemic diseases such as systemic lupus erythematosus; postinfectious disease such as may occur after a viral, pneumococcal, or even skin infection; or a primary glomerular disease of the kidney.

Although the symptoms are similar in all age groups (initially anorexia, nausea, vomiting, and muscle pain progressing to hematuria, proteinuria, azotemia, and hypertension), in older people, these are often attributed to the presence of an infectious disease or the exacerbation of a cardiovascular disease such as congestive heart failure. This results in late diagnosis or even none at all until after death has occurred. Prognosis in older people is poor.[29,32]

The nephrotic syndrome is evidenced by the symptoms listed earlier, all of which result from an increase in the permeability of the glomerular membrane. In older individuals, the nephrotic syndrome is often a result of diabetes mellitus, although it can be a consequence of other systemic diseases as well.[28]

Tubulointerstitial Disease

Tubulointerstitial disease (pyelonephritis) can be either acute or chronic in older people, affecting the renal tubules and interstitial kidney tissue. Pyelonephritis is considered the most common form of renal disease in older adults[30] and the most common cause of gram-negative bacteremia in patients admitted to acute-care institutions.[33] A weakened immune response and a lower resistance to infection contribute to the increased incidence in older adults.[30] Chronic pyelonephritis is often asymptomatic in older people, resulting in a late diagnosis of the disease when uremia is already present.

UTIs are another potential cause of pyelonephritis in older people. The most common cause of bacteremia in older people is a UTI.[20] Indwelling catheters, overflow incontinence from diabetes mellitus or a neurological disorder, prostate disease, and immobility have also been implicated in the development of pyelonephritis.[30]

Renal Vascular Disease

The generalized arteriosclerosis often found in older people extends to the renal arteries of the kidney. The concomitant presence of hypertension exacerbates an already compromised blood flow. Nephrosclerosis is the result, with eventual destruction of the glomeruli and renal ischemia.[28,30]

Renal artery emboli and thrombosis are other vascular complications disrupting blood flow to the kidneys. Hypertension, myocardial infarction, atrial fibrillation, and cardiac surgery are potential causes.[25]

Obstructive Disease

The most common cause of obstructive kidney disease in the older man is benign prostatic hypertrophy or prostatic malignancy. In older women, uterine prolapse, fibroid tumors, or malignancy have been identified as causes of obstruction.[24,30]

Kidney stones (nephrolithiasis) are more common among older men than among older women. The incidence of kidney stones in men has increased dramatically as the life span has lengthened.[34]

Acute Renal Failure

Iatrogenic complications, diseases of the kidney, other systemic diseases, surgery, urinary obstruction, and even mild illnesses with fluid losses can precipitate acute renal failure (ARF) in an older person. Those taking ACE inhibitors and NSAIDs are particularly at risk for ARF.[3] ARF is more common than chronic renal failure (CRF) in this age group because a mild to moderate degree of renal insufficiency may already be present and because of the increased presence of disease in general, the prevalence of obstructive urinary system disease, and the greater likelihood that a number of medications are taken.[3]

The older person can regain kidney function after ARF, although recovery may take longer and not be as complete.[28] Mortality from ARF is slightly higher in older people, but age did not reach statistical significance in one study, leading the authors to recommend that age not be considered in determining treatment decisions.[3] The pathophysiology of ARF and division of cause into prerenal, renal, and postrenal categories are essentially the same for adults in any age group.

As might be expected, however, the management of ARF is more complex in older people. Particularly close monitoring of fluid balance is warranted to avoid congestive heart failure. In older people with reduced muscle mass or those receiving dialysis, oral or parenteral nutritional supplementation is initiated earlier.[24,28] Infection, especially pneumonia, is common in older people with ARF.[24] Both hemodialysis and peritoneal dialysis should be used aggressively in older people because outcomes using these methods can be favorable.

As is evident, nursing measures must first be directed toward prevention through vigilant attention to the many potential causes of ARF and alertness toward apparently insignificant patient symptoms as well as to the more overt signs of kidney disease. Homeostasis is delicate in the aging kidney even when renal insufficiency does not exist. ARF can be precipitated easily. The monitoring of drug regimens, assessment of physical activity, attentiveness to the course of common illnesses such as colds, determining the ability of the older person to manage daily hygiene activities so that bacteria are not introduced through the urethra, and the monitoring of existing cardiac or other disease common to older people are essential. Overt signs of kidney failure do not occur until late in the process. The potential for renal failure should be considered at every assessment encounter in both community-residing and institutionalized older people, regardless of current health status or presenting illness.

NURSING MANAGEMENT OF INCONTINENCE

A problem of incontinence may go unrecognized because of an older person's reluctance to discuss so private and intimate a matter as urinary function. Questions must be direct and to the point. Observations of nonverbal behavior or hesitancy in answering may give clues to the need for further elaboration. A matter-of-fact attitude on the nurse's part, with a comment or two on the prevalence of this problem in older people, will do much to promote patient comfort.

A thorough history is the single most important initial step to be taken. This includes date of onset, prescribed and OTC medications being taken, other diagnoses present including surgeries, diet, parity if female, regularity of bowel function, and impact on lifestyle. The possibility of onset of a new illness such as diabetes mellitus must also be considered. A voiding pattern history includes when incontinence occurs, the frequency of occurrence, and whether hesitancy and prevoid or postvoid dribbling are present, voiding is painful, there is hematuria, large or small volumes of urine are released, flow is weak, and urgency is present. If answers to these questions seem vague, requesting that a voiding diary be kept for 1 week will supplement and clarify the initial data. Information to be recorded includes amount and time fluids are ingested and times, patterns, and circumstances of voiding.

Physical examination includes assessment for abdominal tenderness, costovertebral angle tenderness, bladder distention, fecal impaction, edema, genitourinary odor, rectal obstruction for men, and pelvic examination for women. Any observed difficulty in mobility of deficits in the neurological examination requires further, more detailed assessment. A urinalysis is done. Ouslander[7] recommends that catheterization or ultrasound to test for residual urine be included in the initial assessment. Further urodynamic testing is done pending the results of these assessments.

Assessment in the cognitively impaired patient is more difficult. A verbal history is usually supplemented by careful observation and record keeping. Mental status testing is added to the physical examination to indicate what can or cannot be expected from the patient. The environment also must be assessed. Location of the bathroom, toileting space especially if canes or walkers are used, height of the toilet seat, grip bars for lowering and standing, and privacy all are important in facilitating continence.

Interventions for incontinence include pelvic exercises, Credé maneuvers, bladder training, scheduled toileting, the use of external devices, intermittent catheterization, environmental modification, medication, and surgery. Choice depends on type of incontinence, but combinations are usually used.

Kegel pelvic exercise is recommended for those with stress incontinence (Table 17–6). The muscles involved can be identified by telling patients to stop voiding midstream. The muscles used to do this are those to be strengthened. The goal is to achieve 40 to 60 repetitions lasting 10 seconds every day.[8] Doing 15 repetitions at mealtimes and at bedtime is an easily recalled schedule. Improvement should be noticed in 4 to 6 weeks, with maximal improvement in 3 months. Using biofeedback equipment that records changes in pressure and electrical activity enhances exercise effectiveness. Cure rates using these exercises have been estimated to be as high

RESEARCH BRIEF

Flynn, L, et al: Effectiveness of pelvic muscle exercises in reducing urge incontinence among community residing elders. J Gerontol Nurs (20(5):23–27, 1994.

The effectiveness of pelvic muscle exercises in relieving urge and combined urge and stress incontinence was tested in 37 community-residing people whose ages ranged from 58 to 92. The number of incontinent episodes was reduced by 82 percent. The exercises were effective for both types of incontinence. Voiding intervals increased from a mean 2.13 to 3.44 hours.

as 77 percent.[16] Although pelvic exercise is usually suggested only for those with stress incontinence, it may be effective for those with urge incontinence as well. Findings form a recent study of 37 community-residing older people with urge or a combination of stress and urge incontinence showed significant success in using pelvic exercise as the only behavioral intervention.[35]

TABLE 17–6 TEACHING GUIDE FOR KEGEL EXERCISES AND BLADDER TRAINING

Kegel Pelvic Exercises

1 You will have to do these exercises for at least 6 weeks before you know whether they are helping. The muscles will take up to 3 months to be fully strengthened.

2 The muscles involved are those used to hold urine when you feel you have to go to the bathroom. Try going to the bathroom and then stop the flow of urine without tightening your stomach muscles. This is the way to do the exercises.

3 Contract and then relax these muscles 4 times a day and do 15 repetitions each time. Altogether, this is 60 times each day. An easy way to remember is to do them before meals and at bedtime.

Bladder Training

1 First, keep a 5-day diary to record the times you voided. Include all the times, whether you made it to the toilet or not.

2 Look at your diary and find the shortest interval that you had between these times.

3 Add 30 minutes to that interval. For example, if the shortest interval you had between one voiding and the next was 20 minutes, then you add 30 minutes and get 50 minutes.

4 For the next week, go to the bathroom every 50 minutes, whether you need to or not. If you have to go sooner, hold it and distract yourself by watching TV, talking on the telephone, or whatever else you can think of.

5 After the first week, add another 30 minutes (you would now be holding your urine for 1 hour and 20 minutes in the example).

6 Add 30 minutes every week until you are voiding 3 to 4 hours apart. This is what most people do, so you are back to normal. Make sure to check your interval every now and then to be sure that you are staying on this kind of schedule.

The Credé maneuver involves using pressure over the suprapubic region to manually compress the bladder during voiding; the Valsalva maneuver is done at the same time.[10] Case-Gamble[10] suggests a double voiding procedure. Here, the patient voids and then voids again minutes later using the Credé maneuver. These methods are used for overflow incontinence.

Bladder training is the traditional treatment for urge incontinence (see Table 17–6). Bladder training involves voiding on a predetermined schedule or by the clock every 30 to 60 minutes regardless of need.[8] If the urge to void comes sooner, the patient is advised to hold the urine until the scheduled time. Thirty minutes are added to the voiding interval each week until 3- to 4-hour intervals are achieved. As discussed earlier, pelvic exercise without bladder training was effective for a small group of patients with urge incontinence.

Scheduled or prompted toileting is used for cognitively impaired patients. Patients are either brought to the toilet or placed on a bedpan every 2 hours. Initial assessment of the frequency and time of incontinent episodes followed by toileting according to individual incontinence pattern promotes success. Patients able to respond can be asked on a regular basis whether they need to void.

External devices include external collection units such as a condom catheter connected to a leg bag, incontinence pants, pads, and commodes and urinals if toileting facilities are inaccessible to the patient.

Intermittent straight catheterization is preferred over indwelling catheters. This intervention may be necessary for those with overflow or functional incontinence. Clean technique is acceptable for those doing their own catheterizations. Clean technique may also be used in institutional settings. Here, however, scrupulous attention to cleanliness is required in handwashing as well as catheter cleansing and storage because of the danger of nosocomial infection.

Environmental modifications are indicated for those with impaired mobility or neurological deficit. Individual assessment indicates what is needed. A raised toilet at home might be sufficient or a bedside commode might be used in an institutional setting. Privacy is essential.

Medications are prescribed according to specific diagnosis. α-Adrenergic agonists and estrogen aid in stress incontinence. Bladder relaxants, tricyclic antidepressants, and anticholinergics increase bladder capacity and so help urge incontinence. A recent study shows that oxybutynin in combination with bladder training is more effective than bladder training alone in relieving incontinence in older patients.[36]

Surgical interventions include prostatectomy for men and pelvic floor, cystocele, or rectocele repair for women. Procedures vary for each of these categories. A new procedure using thigh muscle wrapped around the urethra is showing some success.[37]

3 Tertiary Prevention

CRF occurs less often in older people than in younger ones. The most common causes of CRF in older adults are vascular disease, chronic glomerulonephritis and pyelonephritis, diabetes mellitus, multiple myeloma, and progressive enlargement of the prostate.[23] CRF eventually progresses to end-stage renal disease (ESRD). As is the case with younger people, early symptoms are nonspecific and GFR can be as low as 8 to 10 mL/min before dialysis is initiated.[26] Serum creatinine values do not rise as much with CRF in older people because of reduced muscle mass and because of the nutritional deficits that accompany CRF. Dialysis and kidney transplantation are both options for the older person with ESRD. One study[29] reports that older patients prefer dialysis over transplantation.

Long-standing incontinence, particularly in the cognitively impaired or motor-impaired patient, is problematic for patients and caregivers. Aggressive intervention using appropriate treatment modalities and combined modalities (described earlier) should be initiated and assessed for effectiveness. Time and patience are necessary so that effectiveness can be evaluated critically. Skin problems are an outcome of long-term incontinence. Perhaps even more important are the psychosocial problems that result for the cognitively aware older person. Incontinence contributes to depression and social isolation. Such people may avoid embarrassment by staying at home and away from other people, but loneliness is a cause of depression.

Ouslander comments that urinary incontinence can be cured in many older people, or at least managed well enough for patient comfort and reduced caregiver burden. Quality of life can be significantly improved with conservative treatment alone.[38] Incontinence should not be accepted as normal by the patient or by the nurse.

Table 17–7 lists organizations through which further information is available.

TABLE 17–7 RESOURCES

American Kidney Fund 6110 Executive Boulevard No. 1010 Rockville, MD 20852 800-638-8299
American Nephrology Nurses' Association Easy Holly Avenue Sewell, NJ 08071-0056 609-256-2320
Continence Restored, Inc. 407 Strawberry Hill Stamford, CT 06905 914-285-1470
Help for Incontinent People (HIP) PO Box 8306 Spartansburg, SC 29305-8306 800-BLADDER
National Kidney Foundation, Inc. 2 Park Avenue New York, NY 10016 212-889-2210
The Simon Foundation PO Box 815 Wilmette, IL 60091 800-23-SIMON

Student Learning Activities

1 Obtain a copy of the AHCPR guidelines on urinary incontinence by calling 202-521-1800. Examine the information for specific information to be used in your clinical setting.

2 Do an assessment of a community-living older adult. Determine whether any of the medications he or she takes requires a normal GFR, or whether they have side effects that affect the renal-urinary system.

3 Do a self-assessment of intake and output for 3 days. Does your intake equal that recommended for normal kidney function? If not, how could you increase your recommended fluid intake? How can you apply this information to the care of older adults?

4 Look at media advertisements for products used for incontinence. What message does the advertiser give to the older adult?

REFERENCES

1 Lindeman, RD: The kidney. In Masoro, EJ (ed): CRC Handbook of Physiology in Aging. CRC Press, Boca Raton, FL, 1981, pp 175–191.

2 Price, SA, and Wilson, LM: Pathophysiology: Clinical Concepts of Disease Processes. McGraw-Hill, New York, 1986.

3 Pascual, J, et al: The elderly patient with acute renal failure. J Am Soc Nephrol 6:144–153, 1995.

4 Aaronson, L, and Seaman, LP: Managing hypernatremia in fluid deficient elderly. J Gerontol Nurs 15(7):29, 1989.

5 de Castro, JM: Age-related changes in natural spontaneous fluid ingestion and thirst in humans. J Gerontol 47(5):321, 1992.

6 Lindeman, RD, et al: Longitudinal studies on the rate of decline in renal function with age. J Am Geriatr Soc 33(4):278, 1985.

7 Ouslander, JG: Incontinence. In Kane, RL, et al (eds): Essentials of Clinical Geriatrics, ed 3. McGraw-Hill, New York, 1994, pp 145–196.

8 Palmer, M: Urinary Continence: Assessment and Promotion. Aspen, Gaithersburg, Md, 1996.

9 Gray, M: Assessment and investigation of urinary incontinence. In Jeter, K, et al (eds): Nursing for Continence. WB Saunders, Philadelphia, 1990, pp 25–63.

10 Case-Gamble, MK: Urinary incontinence in the elderly. In Stanley, M, and Beare, PG (eds): Gerontological Nursing. FA Davis, Philadelphia, 1995, pp 311–322.

11 Rowe, JW, et al: The effect of age on creatinine clearance in men: A cross-sectional and longitudinal study. J Gerontol 31(2):155, 1976.

12 Euans, DW: Renal function in the elderly. Am Fam Practice 38(3):147, 1988.

13 Friedman, JR, et al: Correlation of estimated renal function parameters versus 24-hour creatinine clearance in ambulatory elderly. J Am Geriatr Soc 37(2):145, 1989.

14 Weder, AB: The renally compromised older hypertensive: Therapeutic considerations. Geriatrics 46(2):36, 1991.

15 Ouslander, JG: Geriatric urinary incontinence. Dis Mon 38(2):71–149, 1992.

16 Chutka, DS, et al: Urinary incontinence in the elderly population. Mayo Clin Proc 71:93–101, 1996.

17 Metheny, NM: Fluid and Electrolyte Balance: Nursing Considerations. JB Lippincott, Philadelphia, 1989.

18 Donovan, B: Female incontinence. In Jeter, K, et al (eds): Nursing for Continence. WB Saunders, Philadelphia, 1990, pp 109–124.

19 Melillo, KD: Asymptomatic bacteriuria in older adults: When is it necessary to screen and treat. Nurse Pract 20(8): 50–66, 1995.

20 Nickel, JC, and Pidutti, R: A rational approach to urinary infections in older patients. Geriatrics 47(10):49, 1992.

21 Kochersberger, G, et al: The metabolic effects of calcium supplementation in the elderly. J Am Geriatr Soc 39(2):192, 1991.

22 Hoffman, NB: Dehydration in the elderly: Insidious and manageable. Geriatrics 46(6):35, 1991.

23 Timiras, ML: The kidney, the lower urinary tract, and body fluids. In Timiras, PS (ed): Physiological Basis of Geriatrics. Macmillan, New York, 1988, pp 315–333.

24 Seligson, GR: Acute renal failure in the elderly. In Michelis, MF, et al (eds): Geriatric Nephrology. Field, Rich and Associates, New York, 1986, p 103.

25 Rowe, JW: The renal system. In Rowe, JW, and Besdine, W (eds): Geriatric Medicine, ed 2. Little, Brown, Boston, 1988, pp 231–245.

26 Vitting, KE: Drug metabolism in the elderly nephrology patient. In Michelis, MF, et al (eds): Geriatric Nephrology. Field, Rich and Associates, New York, 1986, p 54.

27 Lonergan, ET: Aging and the kidney: Adjusting treatment to physiologic change. Geriatrics 43(3):27, 1988.

28 Golper, TA: Nephrology. In Cassel, CK, and Walsh, JR (eds): Geriatric Medicine, Vol 1: Medical, Psychiatric and Pharmacological Topics. Springer-Verlag, New York, 1984, pp 238–267.

29 Roy, AT, et al: Renal failure in older people: UCLA grand rounds. J Am Geriatr Soc 38(3):239, 1990.

30 Sourander, LB, and Rower, JW: The genitourinary system: The aging kidney. In Brocklehurst, JC (ed): Textbook of Geriatric Medicine and Gerontology, ed 3. Churchill-Livingstone, New York, 1985, p 608.

31 Preston, RA, et al: Renal biopsy in patient 65 years of age or older: An analysis of the results of 334 biopsies. J Am Geriatr Soc 38(6):6690, 1990.

32 Brown, WW: Glomerulonephritis in the elderly. In Michelis, MF, et al (eds): Geriatric Nephrology. Field, Rich and Associates, New York, 1986, p 90.

33 Gleckman, RA: Infectious problems in the geriatric nephrology patient. In Michelis, MF, et al (eds): Geriatric Nephrology. Field, Rich and Associates, New York, 1986, p 58.

34 Zebetakis, PM: Stone disease in the elderly. In Michelis, MF, et al (eds): Geriatric Nephrology. Field, Rich and Associates, New York, 1986, p 67.

35 Flynn, L et al: Effectiveness of pelvic muscle exercises in reducing urge incontinence. J Gerontol Nurs 20(5):23–27, 1994.

36 Szonyi, G, et al: Oxybutynin with bladder retraining for detrusor instability in elderly people: A randomized controlled trial. Age Ageing 24:287–291, 1995.

37 The good news. Time 148(5):22, July 22, 1996.

38 Fonda, D, et al: Sustained improvement of subjective quality of life in older community-dwelling people after treatment of urinary incontinence. Age Ageing 24:283–286, 1995.

CHAPTER 18

The Aging Gastrointestinal System, with Nutritional Considerations

Mickey Stanley

OBJECTIVES

Upon completion of this chapter, the reader will be able to:

- Identify normal age-related physiological changes in the gastrointestinal system
- Discuss commonly occurring pathophysiology within the gastrointestinal tract of the older adult
- Describe nursing measures aimed at primary, secondary, and tertiary prevention of these commonly occurring gastrointestinal disorders in older adults
- Explore teaching plans and methods that will enable older adults to maintain or regain maximal gastrointestinal health
- Discuss the nutritional needs of the older adult
- Outline the impact of nutrition on health and disease prevention in the older adult
- Conduct a nutrition screening on an older adult

Normal Aging of the Gastrointestinal Tract

The aging process affects nearly every part of the gastrointestinal (GI) tract to some degree (Table 18–1). However, because of the large physiological reserve of the GI system, few age-related problems are seen in healthy older adults. Many GI problems that older adults experience are more closely associated with their lifestyles. Common myths are associated with normal function of the GI tract and the changing nutritional needs of older adults. This chapter examines the common age-related problems seen in the GI system and the nutritional requirements of older adults.

ORAL CAVITY

Physical appearance, ability to communicate, and nutritional intake are enhanced by a healthy oral mucosa and retention of teeth.[1] Although tooth loss is not a natural consequence of aging, many older adults experience tooth loss as a result of the loss of supportive bone structures of the periosteal and peridontal surfaces. This bone loss also contributes to the difficulty associated with providing an adequate and stable support for dentures with advancing age. The teeth that are retained after age 70 often exhibit a flattening of the chewing surface. Shrinkage and fibrosis of the root pulp along with gingival retraction also contribute to tooth loss from periodontal disease.[1]

The oral mucosa appears red and shiny in older adults because of atrophy. The lips and gingivae appear thin because the epithelium has thinned and become more keratinized. The vascularity of the oral mucosa is decreased, with the gums appearing pale as a result of reduced capillary blood supply.[1]

Salivary flow remains normal in healthy older adults who do not receive medications that produce a dry mouth. Although there is some controversy over the loss of taste buds with aging, many older adults com-

TABLE 18–1 NORMAL GASTROINTESTINAL SYSTEM AGING CHANGES

Normal Age-Related Changes	Clinical Implications
Oral Cavity	
Loss of periosteal and peridontal bone	Tooth loss common
Retraction of gingival structures	Difficulty maintaining fit of dentures
Loss of taste buds	Altered taste sensations
	Increased use of table salt
Esophagus/Stomach/Intestines	
Dilation of esophagus	Increased risk of aspiration
Loss of cardiac sphincter tone	
Decreased gag reflex	
Atrophy of gastric mucosa	Slowed digestion of food
Slowed gastric motility	Decreased absorption of drugs, iron, calcium, and vitamin B_{12}
	Constipation common

plain of altered taste sensations and a decreased ability to perceive mild flavors.[1]

THE ESOPHAGUS, STOMACH, AND INTESTINE

Esophageal motility remains normal, although the esophagus does become slightly dilated with age. The lower esophageal (cardiac) sphincter loses tone. The gag reflex of older adults is weakened. These combined factors increase the risk of aspiration in older adults. Difficulty in digestion of foods results from atrophy of the gastric mucosa and decreased gastric motility. Atrophy of the gastric mucosa results in decreased secretion of hydrochloric acid (hypochlorhydria), with diminished absorption of iron, calcium, and vitamin B_{12}. Gastric motility is usually decreased, delaying the movement of partially digested food out of the stomach and through the small and large intestine.[2]

BILIARY TRACT, LIVER, GALLBLADDER, AND PANCREAS

The functional capacity of the liver and pancreas remains within normal range because of their large physiological reserve. After the age of 70, the size of the liver and pancreas decreases, reducing the storage capacity and the ability to synthesize protein and digestive enzymes. Insulin secretion is normal in the presence of high glucose levels (250 to 300 mg/dL), but insulin response is diminished with moderately elevated glucose levels (120 to 200 mg/dL).[2] See Chapter 16 for a thorough discussion of diabetes in older adults.

Aging modifies the proportion of biliary lipids without significantly changing the metabolism of bile acids.

This factor influences an increasing secretion of cholesterol. Many of the age-related changes occurring in the biliary tree are also noted in patients with extreme obesity.[2]

Nutritional Needs of Older Adults for Health Promotion

Adequate nutrition is an essential component of healthy aging. One's nutritional status affects every body system. Few guidelines have been published that speak directly to the nutritional needs of older adults. In part, this void exists because older adults are more heterogeneous than younger age cohorts and are less able to have their nutritional needs computed from a nomogram.[3] A lack of accurate and easy to understand information to guide older adults and practitioners has led to sobering statistics regarding the nutritional status of this nation's older adults.

Physiologically, energy needs are more closely related to physical activity levels than chronological age. The Recommended Daily Allowance (RDA) for calorie intake in an older adult between age 65 and age 75 is 2300 kcal. The RDA for those over age 75 is decreased to 2050 kcal; 55 to 65 percent of the calories should be consumed as complex carbohydrates, less than 30 percent as fat, and the remaining portion as protein.[4]

Other physiological factors related to the unique nutritional needs of older adults are decreased olfactory sensitivity, change in taste perception, and an increase in cholecystokinin, which may affect the desire to eat and increase satiety. Aging itself does not impair vitamin absorption to any great extent. However, recent reports indicate that older people are most likely to be deficient in vitamin B_{12} and D and folate.[5] Changes in mineral requirements include a lower need for iron in older women than in women during their reproductive years. Intake of calcium, another essential mineral for all older adults, is currently about 600 mg/day for women. This represents only 30 to 40 percent of the recommended levels. The new dietary guidelines suggest at least 1000 mg of calcium per day for all older adults and 1500 mg/day for older women who do not take estrogen.[6] Calcium supplements are not absorbed equally. Because of differences in the degree of acidity needed for proper absorption, calcium citrate malate may be the preferred form for an older adult with hypochlorhydria or achlorhydria.

With normal aging, an increase in adipose tissue normally accompanies a decline in lean body mass and total body water. Although studies show that Americans are consuming less fat, the prevalence of obesity has increased 133 percent in the last 10 years.[7] Excess body fat adversely affects older adults. The new dietary guidelines stress the importance of maintaining a stable weight and following a reasonable diet and exercise program throughout one's lifetime.[8]

RESEARCH BRIEF 1

Lindseth, G: Nutrition preparation and the geriatric nurse. West J Nurs Res 16:692, 1994.

A descriptive-correlational study design was used to evaluate registered nurses' knowledge of nutrition in older adults. A random sampling plan was used to select 13 long-term care facilities and swing-bed units in a midwestern state. Study findings reveal a knowledge deficit in such areas as digestion, absorption, and metabolism of nutrients, nutritional requirements throughout the life cycle, and diet and disease. The authors recommend the inclusion of nutritional needs of older adults in programs of nursing and continuing educational offerings for practicing nurses.

1 Primary Prevention

Aging affects nutritional needs and nutritional status of 30 million older adults, 6 million of whom are at high risk for malnutrition. Studies indicate that older adults who earn less than $6000 per year or who have less than $35 per week to spend on food, those who see friends or family less than twice a week, and those who are more than 50 lb overweight or more than 20 lb underweight are at high risk for malnutrition. An additional million are poorly nourished.[4]

Socioeconomic factors, as well as chronic disease and polypharmacy, contribute to the potential or actual problem of malnutrition in older adults. A screening tool, such as the one developed by the Nutrition Screening Initiative program, to determine nutritional status is recommended for use by all health-care providers.[9] Copies of this tool are available through the Nutrition Screening Initiative, 1010 Wisconsin Avenue NW, Washington, DC 20007. See Table 18–2. A consistent effort to identify older adults with nutritional disorders as well as those at risk for nutritional disorders must become a priority if the nation's goals for health promotion and disease prevention are to be realized.

Socioeconomic Factors

Socioeconomic factors that affect older adults include social isolation and low income. Mealtime is a social event in most cultures. When older adults live alone or spend most of their time alone, the motivation to prepare and consume nutritious meals may be lacking. Senior Centers across the nation often provide the social context that encourages older adults to consume a healthful diet on a regular basis. Because of budgetary constraints, many centers rely on processed foods that are high in saturated fats and salt. Methods of food preparation often include frying, which increases the consumption of saturated fats. Nurses have an opportunity to provide guidance in this area by serving in an advisory capacity to the facility as well as offering "lunch and learn" sessions on healthy eating.

Meals on Wheels is a federally funded program that provides one meal a day, Monday through Friday, for eligible older adults. Recent findings indicate only 7 percent of eligible older adults receive this service.[7] For homebound people, this service provides not only a nutritious meal, but also the opportunity for a responsible adult to look in on the older adult on a consistent basis. Nurses have the opportunity to educate those who coordinate these programs on the importance of not relying on processed foods or traditional cooking methods that include fried foods as a major component of the program.

Because they live on a reduced or fixed income, many older adults must choose between food, medicine, and rent. Poor protein, vitamin, and mineral intake may result from an inability to purchase appropriate foods. Advertisements that encourage older adults to use canned nutritional supplements to "put life back into their years" may mislead people into spending precious resources on these supplements rather than on more appropriate foods.

Many older adults are edentulous, have ill-fitting dentures, or have periodontal disease and cannot afford dental care.[1] High-quality meats, raw fruits, and vegetables are often avoided because they are too expensive or cannot be chewed and swallowed. Nurses may be able to collaborate with local dentists or dental schools to provide dental screenings at Senior Centers. Charitable community-sponsored events can be coordinated to

TABLE 18–2   NUTRITION SCREENING TOOL FOR OLDER ADULTS[9]

Read the statement. Circle the number in the Yes column for those that apply to you. Total your nutritional assessment score.

Nutritional Assessment Statements	Yes
I have an illness or condition that made me change the kind or amount of food I eat.	2
I eat fewer than two meals per day.	3
I eat few fruits, vegetables, or milk products.	2
I have three or more drinks of beer, liquor, or wine almost every day.	2
I have tooth or mouth problems that make it hard for me to eat.	2
I do not always have enough money to buy the food I need.	4
I eat alone most of the time.	1
I take three or more different prescribed or over-the counter drugs a day.	1
Without wanting to, I have lost or gained 10 pounds in the last 6 months.	2
I am not always physically able to shop, cook, or feed myself.	2
Total	____

If you scored 0–2: **Good!** Recheck your nutritional score in 6 months.

If you scored 3–5: **You are at moderate nutritional risk.** See what can be done to improve your eating habits and lifestyle. Recheck your score in 3 months.

If you scored 6 or more: **You are at high nutritional risk.** Take this checklist to your doctor, nurse practitioner, or home health nurse. Ask for help to improve your nutritional health.

provide the funding for needed follow-up for older adults in need of dental care who lack the available resources.

Chronic Diseases

Many chronic diseases, such as congestive heart failure and chronic renal failure, require therapeutic diets that severely restrict normal nutritional intake. These diets are often difficult to maintain and may contribute to nutritional deficiencies. Careful attention must be paid to those who require therapeutic diets to ensure adequate nutritional intake. In addition, chronic diseases, such as the malabsorptive disorders discussed later in this chapter, can contribute to nutritional problems in older adults.

Medications

Medications, such as diuretics, affect the fluid and electrolyte balance. Laxative abuse and a normal age-related decrease in the nephrons in the kidney may further compound this problem. Older adults may be more susceptible to adverse drug-nutrient interactions because of a decrease in metabolism and multiple drug use. Other side effects include increased or decreased appetite, constipation, nausea, and decreased absorption of nutrients. Alcohol also impairs absorption of the B vitamins and folate. Neuroleptics may depress the appetite, whereas other medications may increase it. Antihistamines may also contribute to a decreased appetite. Mineral oil, which is sometimes used as a laxative, may inhibit the absorption of A, D, and K fat-soluble vitamins.[3]

More older people are overweight now than ever before.[7] The condition of being overweight places the older adult at increased risk for such chronic conditions as hypertension, coronary artery disease, diabetes, and stroke.[7] In addition, it places additional strain on weakened joints and limits mobility and independence. Sound methods that include decreased caloric intake, moderate exercise, and increasing one's caloric intake from fruit and vegetable sources should be encouraged. Fishman[7] notes that although preventive measures to reduce one's risk of nutrition-related diseases are best started early in life, changes in diet and exercise patterns can improve health at any age. A thorough discussion of activity that is appropriate for older adults can be found in Chapter 20.

2 Secondary Prevention

Secondary prevention begins with a careful assessment of the client and efforts to identify the source of the nutritional disorder. Metabolic derangements must be corrected and medication regimens for chronic conditions may require adjustment to alleviate the side effects that are impairing normal nutrition. Undetected depression or early stages of dementia often result in poor dietary intake and malnutrition. In addition, a careful diet history and nutritional assessment are essential to establish appropriate and realistic goals for the older adult with a nutritional disorder.[10] The services of a registered dietitian can be beneficial.

Many older adults do not know how their nutritional needs have changed as a result of aging. Therefore, all health-care providers need to be prepared to provide current, accurate information about normal nutrition as well as the nutritional requirements that accompany disease processes. A recent study suggests that nurses are not adequately prepared to provide this type of instruction to their older clients.[11] See "Research Brief 1."

Nursing care is a key ingredient to boosting nutrient intake in the acute or long-term care institution. Dedication is needed to ensure that the client's nutritional needs are included in the total plan of care. Allowing cans of supplement to build up on the bedside table or to be returned to the dietary department does not facilitate adequate intake. Supplements are best used between meals and are often tolerated best when served cold. Alternatives to food, such as total parenteral nutrition and tube feedings, may be required if adequate intake cannot be maintained by the oral route.

Family involvement is essential to providing good nutrition in all settings. The ability to provide older adults with their favorite foods and provide the social atmosphere that encourages intake is what families do best. Families are often eager to participate in this way and respond well to the suggestions found in Table 18–3.[12]

Although supplements should not be used in place of a balanced diet, a recent report suggests the use of a multivitamin and calcium supplement if current dietary intake does not meet the recommended daily allowances. Excessive dosages above the RDA are not recommended at this time and may prove harmful if continued for a long period.[13] Additional recommendations include the use of dietary fiber to improve the intake of vitamins and minerals, aid glucose tolerance, prevent or treat some forms of cancer, and promote normal bowel elimination. Current recommendations for dietary fiber suggest 20 to 35 g of fiber per day.[14] For additional information on nutrition, see Table 18–4.

TABLE 18–3 TECHNIQUES FOR INCREASING INTAKE WHEN APPETITE IS POOR[12]

- Add nonfat dry milk powder to foods with a high liquid content (gravy, mashed potatoes, puddings, cooked cereal).
- Provide a variety of between-meal nourishments, varying the texture and sweetness.
- Offer the largest meal at the time of day when the older adult is hungriest (usually in the morning).
- Encourage finger foods that are easy to feed oneself.
- Add additional margarine to vegetables, sauces, and creamed foods.
- Serve nutritional supplements cold or prepared as a shake.
- Encourage the family to bring in the client's favorite foods.

TABLE 18–4 RESOURCES FOR NUTRITION INFORMATION

Center for Nutrition Policy and Promotion
USDA, 1120 20th Street NW
Suite 200, North Lobby
Washington, DC 20036

Food and Nutrition Information Center
USDA/National Agricultural Library, Room 304
10301 Baltimore Boulevard
Beltsville, MD 20705-2351

Disorders of the Upper Gastrointestinal System

PERIODONTAL DISEASE

Pathophysiology and Clinical Manifestations

Periodontal disease (gingivitis and periodontitis) is the inflammation of the structures that support the teeth, with resultant bone destruction. This destruction causes progressive loosening and ultimately loss of teeth. Gingivitis and periodontitis (pyorrhea) are caused by bacteria present in plaque.

Gingivitis is a superficial infection of the gums,[15] usually caused by poor dental hygiene. The first sign of gingivitis is reddened, swollen gums that bleed with brushing. If the infection progresses, bad breath (halitosis), a foul taste in the mouth, or presence of a purulent exudate around the gum line may be noted. Other conditions that can aggravate periodontal disease include oral infection, malocclusions, malnutrition, diabetes mellitus, and local irritation such as poorly fitting dentures.

1 Primary Prevention

Effective prevention involves regular toothbrushing and flossing and regular dental checkups for plaque and calculus removal two or three times yearly. Older adults should visit the dentist regularly even if they have partial dentures. Dentures should be checked periodically to ensure a snug fit and to prevent oral irritation.

2 Secondary Prevention

The client may complain of painful, swollen gums that make chewing difficult, or tooth loss, chipping, or a foul taste. The gums may bleed or a purulent exudate may be evident. The nurse should determine whether the patient visits a dentist and, if so, the date of his or her last dental checkup. If dental infection is present, inflammation may be observed.

Gingivitis can be cured with early dental intervention. Treatment involves a thorough cleaning by removing tartar and bacteria from under the gum line and from the surface of the root of the tooth.[15] This cleaning process is called root planing. If severe periodontal infection (pyorrhea) is present, treatment with an antibi-

otic may be necessary. Dental surgery may be needed to repair bones and tissues. With early intervention, periodontitis can usually be controlled. The nurse can help the patient to obtain treatment from an oral surgeon if tooth loss and gum disease are severe.

DYSPHAGIA

Although dysphagia was once thought to be a normal consequence of aging, structural, vascular, or neurogenic causes are now recognized as the underlying pathology. Dysphagia signals significant pathology in the older adult.[16] Regardless of the cause, the esophageal mucosa is usually irritated by food stasis. Heartburn or chest pain are noted. Generally, solids can be swallowed more easily than liquids, except when structural lesions are present. Regurgitation and pulmonary aspiration are common, as well as complaints of food sticking in the throat and coughing during swallowing.[16]

1 Primary Prevention

Dysphagia may result from paralysis, throat irritation, side effects of medications, structural lesions (tumors or strictures), motility disorders (achalasia or diffuse esophageal spasm), or vascular changes (dysphagia aortica). Strokes and neuromuscular disorders such as Parkinson's disease, polymyositis, myasthenia gravis, hyperthyroidism, and amyotrophic lateral sclerosis can cause dysphagia. Dysphagia resulting from vascular causes may result from dilation or an aneurysm of the aorta. All or part of the esophagus may be affected by structural or neurogenic abnormalities. The initiation of the swallowing mechanism or food propulsion into the stomach will be impaired.[2]

Dysphagia for any reason can be described in one of three ways: transfer dysphagia, transport dysphagia, or delivery dysphagia. A patient with transfer dysphagia has difficulty transferring food from the mouth to the esophagus. Transport dysphagia prevents the easy passage of ingested substances down the esophagus. This is usually caused by a neuromuscular (motility) defect or a structural lesion. Delivery dysphagia occurs when propulsion of a food bolus into the stomach is difficult because of a lesion or abnormally functioning sphincter.[17]

2 Secondary Prevention

A careful history is crucial to determine the client's response to dysphagia. Table 18–5 provides questions used to elicit a history of dysphagia. The nurse should observe the client at mealtime and note how he or she manages liquids and foods of different consistencies. The client's ability to produce saliva should be assessed. Adequate saliva assists with bolus formation of food. Thick, ropy saliva interferes with eating. Likewise, if xerostomia (dry mouth) is present, food may crumble in the mouth, causing the patient to choke.

While the nurse talks with the patient, speech pattern and tone abnormalities may be noticed. A paralyzed

TABLE 18–5   QUESTIONS FOR HISTORY OF DYSPHAGIA

- Do solid foods or liquids cause the presenting symptom?
- Is dysphagia consistently present or intermittent?
- Is heartburn associated with the dysphagia?
- When did the dysphagia begin?
- Are other symptoms present such as chest pain and nocturnal symptomatology?
- Has hoarseness, nasal regurgitation, or aspiration ever occurred?

palate and oropharynx can result in a hypernasal tone. Hoarseness may be caused by partial paralysis of the 10th cranial nerve.[17]

Prevention of regurgitation and aspiration is imperative, and assessing the patient's ability to swallow is the first step toward prevention. Hufler[18] recommends three tests with which to evaluate the client's swallowing reflex:

- Ask the patient to place his or her tongue against the palate. This movement is necessary to push food into the throat.
- Stroke the patient's tonsillar arch and soft palate with a moist cotton swab and ask whether this can be felt. Some feeling is necessary in these areas for swallowing to take place.
- Test normal pharyngeal contraction by stimulating the tonsillar arch with a cotton swab. The swab should be moistened with ice-cold lemon water to elicit contraction of the pharyngeal muscles.

The nurse can help the client position his or her tongue on the palate by practicing this maneuver with him or her in front of a mirror. Next, the tonsillar arch is massaged with a moistened cotton swab, which will help retrain the pharyngeal muscles. If the client regains the swallowing reflex, a soft diet such as pudding or strained baby food can be started. To prevent aspiration, the client should be positioned with the neck flexed slightly forward. This maneuver forces the trachea to close and the esophagus to open. Fluids should be avoided initially because dysphagic patients usually have difficulty swallowing liquids. Instead, liberal amounts of fluids should be mixed in with the introductory diet.

The nurse observes for weight loss or signs of dehydration. The client should be weighed at regular intervals. Fear of choking may cause the client to restrict food and fluid intake. If choking is a problem, have suction equipment readily available.[17] Table 18–6 provides a care plan for the dysphagic client.

Nursing care may involve the administration of nitrate drugs to relieve pain from esophageal spasm. The client must be informed of the side effects of these drugs.

GASTROESOPHAGEAL REFLUX AND HIATAL HERNIA

Gastroesophageal reflux is the backflow of gastric juices into the esophagus. The wall of the esophagus is thinner and more sensitive in older adults. In addition, dilation of the lower esophagus with relaxation of the lower esophageal sphincter (LES) makes esophageal reflux more likely. Hiatal hernias are often noted with LES pressure. However, many older adults have symptomatic reflux without hiatal hernia.[2]

A hiatal hernia is the protrusion of the stomach and other abdominal viscera into the thoracic cage through an enlarged esophageal hiatus in the diaphragm. Hiatal

TABLE 18–6   NURSING CARE PLAN

Nursing Diagnosis: Alterations in eating patterns: dysphagia	
Expected Outcome	*Nursing Interventions*
The client or caregiver demonstrates measures to reduce the likelihood of aspiration.	Assess ability to swallow.
	Position client comfortably in upright position. Have client flex his or her head forward.
	Obtain and set up suction equipment.
	Check client's mouth for presence of mucus and suction if necessary.
	Encourage taking only small bites of food at a time. Use teaspoon or syringe, if needed.
	Alternate liquids with solids, if the client can tolerate liquids.
	Put the food near the patient's back molars. Place food on the unaffected side if he or she is hemiplegic.
	Instruct the client to form a seal with the lips, assisting him or her if necessary.
	Check to see if the client is "pouching" food in the cheek. Check for residual food in the mouth at the end of the meal.
	If choking occurs, place the client's chin against the chest and flex his or her body at the waist. Suction food from the mouth.
	Leave client sitting upright for 30 minutes after the meal.

hernias occur in 40 to 60 percent of adults over age 60. There are two types of hiatal hernia. Type I, or sliding hernia, is a herniation of the stomach upward into the slightly enlarged diaphragmatic hiatus. The type I hernia is more common than the type II, or rolling, hernia, which is a herniation of a portion of the stomach alongside the esophagus, extending past the gastroesophageal junction.[2]

Clinical Manifestations

Symptoms of esophageal reflux may be absent or variable. Complaints usually include heartburn, regurgitation, "sour stomach," dysphagia, and odynophagia (painful swallowing). Heartburn is manifested as a retrosternal burning, usually after eating, that occurs when bending or reclining.[2]

Most hiatal hernias are asymptomatic. If symptoms do occur, the older adult may experience some degree of heartburn, flatulence, belching, dysphagia, or epigastric discomfort after eating certain types of foods. Symptoms of hiatal hernia are usually related to esophageal reflux, which results from regurgitation of gastric juices into the lower esophagus, causing irritation of the esophageal mucosa. If severe reflux esophagitis occurs, peptic ulceration and strictures may develop. Gastroesophageal reflux is more likely to occur with the type I, or sliding, hernia. Pain resulting from esophageal reflux must be differentiated from anginal pain. Reflux pain is usually associated with eating or lying supine, and is not associated with alterations in vital signs.[2]

2 *Secondary Prevention*

When obtaining a history, the nurse should ask about the presence of heartburn, dysphagia, belching, "sour stomach," or regurgitation. The nurse should determine what kinds of foods are associated with the onset of symptoms and whether certain activities (e.g., stooping, bending, or reclining) relieve or aggravate distress.

TABLE 18–7   TEACHING GUIDE: HIATAL HERNIA

Instruct the client or family member on the following:
- Avoid tight corsets, straining, or lifting. (This increases intra-abdominal pressure and, thus, esophageal reflux.)
- Elevate the head of the bed 4–6 in (for bedridden clients).
- Avoid eating or drinking 2–3 hr before bedtime.
- Lose weight, if obese.
- Eat smaller, more frequent meals.
- Eat slowly and chew food well.
- Sit upright during and for 1 hr after meals or walk slowly to promote gastric emptying.
- Take antacids as prescribed.
- Avoid foods (especially those high in fat, coffee, chocolate, mint, or alcoholic beverages) that may precipitate esophageal reflux.

TABLE 18–8   AGENTS THAT DIMINISH LES PRESSURE

Nicotine	Meperidine (Demerol)
Anticholinergic drugs	Estrogen
β-Adrenergic blocking drugs	Progesterone
Calcium channel blockers	Theophylline
	Diazepam (Valium)

Source: Adapted from Beare, PG, and Myers, JL: Adult Health Nursing, 3rd ed. Mosby, St Louis, 1998, p 1484.

Nursing Management

Nursing care of the older adult with esophageal reflux or hiatal hernia involves ongoing assessment, patient teaching, and monitoring of response to therapy. Because modification of lifestyle behaviors may help relieve symptoms, clients should be instructed about measures that decrease intra-abdominal pressure and aid digestion, as well as about prescribed medications and their side effects. The client should be encouraged to omit symptom-causing substances from the diet (Tables 18–7 and 18–8).

Disorders of the Small Intestine

MALABSORPTIVE DISEASE

The most common disorder of the small intestine associated with the older client is malabsorption, which is the impaired assimilation of nutrients from the small intestine. Reduced gastric acid secretion or chronic use of antacids fosters bacterial overgrowth, often causing malabsorption in older adults. Malabsorption may also be attributed to previous intestinal surgery or drugs, such as anticholinergics and narcotics that slow motility, thus increasing bacterial growth.[19] When intestinal immune mechanisms are compromised, as with chronic intestinal infections with *Giardia lamblia,* severe diarrhea and malabsorption result. Chronic pancreatitis may be responsible for a malabsorptive state because the flow of pancreatic juices is reduced, thus permitting ingested food to be only partially absorbed. Adult celiac disease or gluten enteropathy may also cause malabsorption because the gluten in the diet shrinks the intestinal villi and reduces the surface area available for nutrient absorption.[19]

Malabsorption in the older patient may also be secondary to mesenteric ischemia. When the blood flow to the bowel is compromised, the bowel's efficiency is reduced, thereby causing malabsorption. Small-bowel contamination by abdominal bacteria (the blind loop syndrome) may also cause malabsorption. The bacteria compete for vitamin B_{12} and also attack bile salts, impairing their detergent functions in fat absorption. This malabsorptive state is most often associated with small-bowel diverticulosis, stasis secondary to a constricted bowel, and stasis after partial gastrectomy.[19]

Clinical Manifestations

Malabsorption is not a normal result of aging, although malabsorptive problems can appear in older adults, often with subtle manifestations. Malabsorptive signs and symptoms are often seen in conjunction with inflammatory bowel disorders. Diarrhea, abdominal pain, and rectal bleeding are obvious symptoms. Those with celiac disease may have osteomalacia resulting from impaired absorption of vitamin D and an abnormal loss of calcium in the stool. The older adult appears thin and emaciated, with pale mucous membranes and dry, scaly skin. The blood pressure may be low and fever present if there is bacterial overgrowth in the bowel.

1 Primary Prevention

Primary prevention of malabsorption is aimed at modifying or eliminating contributing factors. Patients should be cautioned about excessive use of antacids that may cause harmful overgrowth of bacteria, leading to a malabsorptive state. Careful, ongoing monitoring of the client who is taking multiple prescription drugs is necessary to prevent a drug-induced decrease in intestinal motility.

The older patient should be taught to read labels and become aware of foods that produce signs of intolerance, such as milk and milk-containing products. Fermented dairy products, such as yogurt, are often tolerated better than other milk-containing products. Lactose intolerance may be counteracted with a lactose-hydrolyzed milk or an over-the-counter enzyme product, such as Lact-aid.

The client may have malabsorptive problems secondary to isolation and stressful life situations. Evaluation and modification of stressors in the older client's situation should be aimed at providing foods that are easily digested in a setting that is comfortable. Social contact and support are important factors that promote healthful eating habits for many older people.

2 Secondary Prevention

The patient should be asked about his or her normal pattern of elimination and dietary intake. If diarrhea is common, the character, consistency, color, and odor of stools should be noted. Assessment of the client includes watching for signs and symptoms of dehydration and electrolyte imbalance by checking daily weight, character of mucous membranes, and postural hypotension.

The dietary history provides a basis for making necessary modifications. The client can be taught to modify the diet by eliminating gluten and lactose. Because strict dietary restrictions are often a hardship for older adults, ongoing support may be needed to ensure compliance and to avoid further malabsorptive problems. As the patient improves, small amounts of gluten or lactose may be tolerated. Periodic consultation may help ensure adequate nutritional support. The client may show only vague signs of malabsorptive disease. Anemia, diarrhea, and weight loss may be the only signals that malabsorp-

tion is occurring. The nurse may be able to detect these signals, which may not seem significant to the client. Ongoing patient education is necessary to reinforce the importance of these subtle signs.

Disorders of the Large Intestine

The common disorders of the large intestine that affect the older adult are diverticulosis, cancer, constipation, and diarrhea.

DIVERTICULAR DISEASE

Diverticular disease is common among older adults. By age 80, at least 40 percent of people are affected. Our Western culture and diet that is typically low in fiber may be responsible for this high incidence of diverticulosis.[2] A colonic diverticulum is an outpouching or herniation through the colonic mucosa. There is usually a pronounced thickening of the colonic wall. The sigmoid colon is most often affected and may be the only part of the bowel affected in 50 to 65 percent of patients.[19]

Most people with diverticulosis are asymptomatic; however, some may experience constipation, bloating, and abdominal discomfort and distention. Complications from diverticulosis arise when there is acute inflammation (diverticulitis), rupture of one or more diverticula, hemorrhage, or obstruction. Diverticulitis results when there is microperforation and leakage of bowel content into the surrounding tissue, causing inflammation. The patient may experience pain, abdominal tenderness, fever, and often a palpable mass. Lower GI bleeding may occur in up to 15 percent of patients with diverticular disease. Often bleeding is present without significant abdominal pain.[19]

Disturbances in bowel motility are thought to predispose the older adult to the formation of diverticula. The occurrence of a ruptured diverticulum is life-threatening, resulting in major surgery and often a temporary colostomy. Intestinal obstruction and diverticular disease are the cause of most GI-related deaths in older adults.[19]

1 Primary Prevention

Older clients should be encouraged to have yearly fecal occult blood testing. A well-balanced diet with adequate fiber intake is advisable. Patients who have a sudden change in bowel habits or evidence of GI bleeding should seek medical attention. An active lifestyle should be encouraged because exercise and meaningful social contacts promote healthful patterns of eating and elimination.

2 Secondary Prevention

Careful questioning regarding bowel habits, particularly alternating constipation and diarrhea, is an essential part of assessment. Alternating diarrhea and constipation progressing to nausea and vomiting may signal a ruptured diverticulum or an obstruction. The patient's nutritional status, eating habits, and general knowledge regarding the disease process should be assessed.

Nursing care of older adults with diverticular disease includes pain management and dietary manipulation. Efforts to manage pain must avoid the use of opiates, which increase the sigmoid intraluminal pressure. See Chapter 22 for a thorough discussion of this problem. Dietary manipulation is an ongoing requirement that actively involves the client and caregiver. Thus, education begins during the acute phase of the disease process to teach the client the importance of fiber in the diet, avoidance of spicy foods, and control of constipation without the use of harsh laxatives.

INTESTINAL OBSTRUCTION

An intestinal obstruction is a partial or complete stoppage of the forward flow of intestinal contents, usually occurring as a result of an actual blockage of the lumen of the bowel. Obstruction can be caused by mechanical adhesions (from previous surgeries), volvulus, intussusception, tumors, neurogenic or paralytic ileus, or ischemic bowel disease.[2] Cancer of the colon is probably the most common cause of obstruction in the older adult.[20]

The bowel normally secretes and reabsorbs approximately 7 to 8 L of electrolyte-rich fluid each day. When an obstruction is present, large amounts of fluid, fermenting bacteria, and swallowed air build up in the bowel proximal to the obstruction. The patient experiences nausea, vomiting, and distention. Fluid shifts are common and capillary permeability decreases, causing bowel content seepage into the peritoneal cavity.

At first, the patient with an intestinal obstruction will have signs and symptoms that are related to the body's attempt to resolve the obstruction. Peristalsis will attempt to speed up to try to pass the bowel contents through the system. The patient will have high-pitched bowel sounds and cramping pain. As the obstruction progresses, bowel sounds become hypoactive, abdominal distention increases, and vomiting, often projectile, occurs if a nasogastric (NG) tube is not already in place. The patient will still have bowel movements even with an obstruction because the distal colon will continue to empty its contents. The older adult, who may be mildly dehydrated before the acute episode, will quickly advance to volume depletion. Signs of sepsis may develop secondary to bowel spillage into the abdominal cavity.

1 Primary Prevention

Prevention of intestinal obstruction in older clients may be accomplished by educating them about the warning signs of colon cancer. This involves the need to report changes in bowel habits to the primary care provider. Periodic stool testing for occult blood, along with education regarding other risk factors, such as family history and poor dietary habits, is also essential.

2 Secondary Prevention

Nursing assessment includes a careful history of the patient's pain. Abdominal assessment should include auscultation of bowel sounds and palpation. Orthostatic blood pressure assessment may reveal the fluid volume deficit. Laboratory data may suggest electrolyte imbalance and an elevated hemoglobin and hematocrit caused by hemoconcentration and fluid volume deficit. The patient may have a fever *or* a subnormal temperature if acute sepsis is present.

Nursing management will focus on careful replacement of fluid and electrolytes lost through vomiting or NG drainage. Fluids must be replaced slowly to prevent the complications of congestive heart failure. See Chapter 14 for a discussion of this problem. The client is usually maintained on bed rest during the acute phase. Care must be structured to avoid complications associated with immobility (see Chapter 20). Judicious pain management is essential to provide pain relief while avoiding the concomitant problems of confusion and disorientation. In addition, if the obstruction is not relieved within 48 hours, nutritional supplementation must be implemented.

CONSTIPATION

Peristalsis relies on a complex system of sympathetic, parasympathetic, gastric, and local neuronal effects and central nervous system integration. Certain foods, activity, medications, and emotions all affect peristalsis. Constipation is a common problem caused by decreased motility, lack of activity, and decreased strength and muscle tone. Dietary deficiencies in fluid and fiber intake also may lead to constipation. Many older adults experience constipation as a result of duller nerve sensations, incomplete emptying of the bowel, or failing to attend to signals to defecate.[21]

Constipation is a decrease in the frequency of bowel movement accompanied by a prolonged and difficult passage of stool.[22] Constipation may be further categorized as imagined, colonic, or rectal constipation.

1 Primary Prevention

Prevention of constipation in older adults begins with modifying beliefs about elimination. Educating the client about fluids, bulk, and fiber content in the diet and establishing a suitable exercise routine will aid in healthy elimination. Dietary fiber is helpful in preventing constipation because fiber holds water, making the stool bulkier, softer, and easier to pass. Because older adults have slowed GI motility, additional dietary fiber will decrease the time it takes for a substance to move through the bowel. From 20 to 35 g of dietary fiber is the recommended amount of daily dietary intake.[21] A mixture of bran, applesauce, and prune juice has been found to be an effective method of promoting normal bowel elimination.[23] See "Research Brief 2."[24]

RESEARCH BRIEF 2

Gibson, CJ, et al: Effectiveness of bran supplement on the bowel management of elderly rehabilitation patients. J Gerontol Nurs 21:21, 1995.

A quasi-experimental nonequivalent control group design was used to examine the effectiveness of a bran formula on laxative use among older clients in a geriatric rehabilitation unit of a large medical center. The bran formula consisted of Kellogg's All-Bran, applesauce, and prune juice. Results showed that the clients who received the bran formula had a significant decrease in the overall use of laxatives as compared with the baseline control group. Most subjects in the study found the formula to be palatable and easy to swallow.

Teaching includes providing information about cathartics, laxatives, and purgatives. Purgatives are not used because they cause such watery stools and violent cramping. Cathartics produce a soft stool but are associated with some abdominal cramping. Laxatives also act on the large intestine and are classified as bulk-forming, osmotic, surfactant (wetting agent), contact (stimulant, irritant), lubricant, or suppository and enemas. A bowel regimen consisting of a suppository as needed is preferable to a daily dose of Milk of Magnesia or Metamucil.[22] Liquids, especially water, are natural stool softeners. Encourage the client to drink several glasses of water daily. Coffee, tea, and juices act as diuretics, pulling water from the bowel, resulting in hard stool. Although coffee and tea, especially as a morning routine, may stimulate a daily bowel action, their intake should be minimal.

Exercise is an important factor in avoiding constipation. For the client whose immobility has slowed the gut motility, even turning in bed or shifting one's weight in a chair can have a positive effect on peristalsis. A program of increasing activity beginning with passive range-of-motion exercise is an essential component in preventing constipation.

2 Secondary Prevention

The nurse assessing the older adult for constipation must:

- Determine the type of constipation through a bowel history
- Identify factors that place the patient at high risk for constipation
- Isolate and modify elements that are contributing to the problem of constipation

Nursing management for older adults with imagined or perceived constipation focuses on education about normal bowel elimination. The nurse may help the client to examine the source of his or her attitudes and beliefs regarding elimination. The client is encouraged to establish a goal of every-other-day elimination

and to keep a calendar or diary as a reminder during the initial phase of behavior change. If long-term laxative abuse exists, colonic constipation may develop as these drugs are withdrawn. Therefore, the client will need to be taught preventive measures, as outlined earlier.

Additional measures for the older adult experiencing colonic constipation include establishing a toileting routine with adequate privacy. The most common time for toileting is 1 hour after breakfast. If the client's bowel history reveals a pattern of evening elimination, then 1 hour after the evening meal may be more productive. Providing warm fluids with the meal and helping the client into a comfortable upright position will aid the passage of stool.[23] Rectal constipation requires all the previously mentioned interventions. In addition, the older adult with rectal constipation may require retraining of the pelvic muscles. The exercises necessary to accomplish the retraining are described in Chapter 17.

DIARRHEA

Diarrhea is having bowel movements that are increased in frequency, more liquid, and difficult to control. Bacterial and viral infections, fecal impactions, tube feedings, and dietary excesses (particularly bananas) may cause acute diarrhea in the older adult. Diarrhea interferes with a normal lifestyle. For physically active older adults, it may limit social interaction. When the client is bedbound or less mobile, diarrhea may lead to serious problems, such as a urinary tract infection or decubitus ulcer.[25]

Chronic diarrhea may be caused by malabsorption, diverticular disease, inflammatory bowel disorder, or medications, especially antacids, antibiotics, antidysrhythmics, and antihypertensives. Systemic illnesses such as thyrotoxicosis, liver disease, diabetic neuropathy, and uremia may cause diarrhea. Ischemic disease among older adults, especially those with cardiac problems, may lead to ischemic colitis with diarrhea. Surgical procedures, such as a gastrectomy, and psychogenic disorders may also cause diarrhea.[2]

1 Primary Prevention

Prevention of diarrhea in older adults is aimed at educating the client about the causes of diarrhea and maintaining a balanced diet. Because diarrhea may be secondary to a more serious disorder such as intestinal obstruction or malignancy, all older adults should be encouraged to seek medical attention if diarrhea persists.[2]

2 Secondary Prevention

The older adult with acute-onset diarrhea is usually volume-depleted and may have fever, tachycardia, and postural hypotension. The skin turgor is poor. An elevated hemoglobin and hematocrit, as well as changes in the serum potassium and sodium levels, may exist. Initially, the nurse checks the patient for a fecal impaction. A stool count and an accurate intake and output measurement are recorded. Tube feedings administered too rapidly or those high in osmolarity may cause diarrhea. The patient's medications should be reviewed to observe for drugs with diarrhea as a potential side effect. The patient's abdomen is assessed for any pain or localized areas of tenderness.

The major focus of nursing management is to maintain adequate nutrition and electrolyte balance and to prevent skin breakdown, while finding and eliminating the cause of the diarrhea. Malnutrition may be both a cause and a result of diarrhea in older adults. A free amino acid formula administered slowly (20 to 30 mL/hr) via an enteric feeding tube may be needed to combat the malnutrition and promote absorption. In addition, the client should be adequately hydrated before any type of feeding program is instituted.

Preventing skin breakdown during episodes of diarrhea requires vigilance. The skin must be cleansed with a mild soap and warm water and dried thoroughly after each bowel movement. Protective emollient creams may provide a barrier to the acidity of the digestive enzymes.

Student Learning Activities

1 Visit a local supermarket or discount store and examine the number of products available over-the-counter for constipation and diarrhea. What are the principal ingredients of these products? What side effects do these products have in older adults? What impact would the use of these products have on an older adult who is taking medication for other common health problems?

2 Interview a community-living older adult regarding his or her dietary patterns for a period of 1 week. Does his or her intake equal that recommended in the chapter? What recommendations can you make to improve the dietary patterns for the individual?

3 Compare the recommendations for such products as Ensure or Sustacal with the current media advertisements. What messages do the advertisements contain?

REFERENCES

1 Martin, WE: Oral health in the elderly. In Chernoff, R (ed): Geriatric Nutrition: The Health Professional's Handbook. Aspen, Gaithersburg, Md, 1991, p 107.

2 Cashman, MD: The aging gut. In Chernoff, R (ed): Geriatric Nutrition: The Health Professional's Handbook. Aspen, Gaithersburg, Md, 1991, p 183.

3 Roe, DA: Nutritional needs of the elderly: Issues, guidelines, and responsibilities. Fam Community Health 12:59, 1989.

4 Nutrition Screening Initiative: American Academy of Family Physicians, American Dietetic Association, National Council on Aging, Washington, DC, 1991.

5 Russell, R: Vitamins B-12, A & Folate. Nutr Action Health Lett April:4, 1996.

6 Dawson-Hughes, B: Calcium and Vitamin D. Nutr Action Health Lett April:6, 1996.

7 Fishman, P: Healthy People 2000: What progress toward better nutrition? Geriatrics 51:38, 1996.

8 US Dept of Health and Human Services: Nutrition and Your Health: Dietary Guidelines for Americans, ed 4. US Government Printing Office no 1996-402-519, Washington, DC, 1996.

9 Determine Your Nutritional Health. National Screening Initiative. National Council on Aging, Washington, DC, 1991.

10 Mitchell, CO, and Chernoff, R: Nutritional assessment of the elderly. In Chernoff, R (ed): Geriatric Nutrition: The Health Professional's Handbook. Aspen, Gaithersburg, Md, 1991, p 363.

11 Lindseth, G: Nutrition preparation and the geriatric nurse. West J Nurs Res 16:692, 1994.

12 Yen, PK: Boosting intake when appetite is poor. Geriatr Nurs 15:284, 1994.

13 Crim, M: Protein. Nutr Action Health Lett April:8, 1996.

14 Yen, PK: Beyond the basic four. Geriatr Nurs 14:109, 1993.

15 Hardy, DL: Dental hygiene initiatives in gerontology. Dent Hyg News 6:11, 1993.

16 Castell, DO: Esophageal disorders in the elderly. Gastroenterol Clin North Am 19:235, 1990.

17 Maat, MT, and Tandy, L: Impaired swallowing. In Maas, M, et al (eds): Nursing Diagnosis and Intervention for the Elderly. Addison-Wesley, Redwood City, Calif, 1991, p 106.

18 Hufler, DH: Helping your dysphagic patient eat. RN 50:36, 1987.

19 Kerr, RM: Disorders of the stomach and duodenum. In Hazzard, WR, et al (eds): Principles of Geriatric Medicine and Gerontology, ed 3. McGraw-Hill, New York, 1994, p 693.

20 Carnevali, DL, and Reiner, AC: The Cancer Experience: Nursing Diagnosis and Management. JB Lippincott, Philadelphia, 1991.

21 McShane, RE, and McLane, AM: Constipation: Impact of etiological factors. J Gerontol Nurs 16:31, 1990.

22 Yakabowich, M: Prescribe with care: The role of laxatives in the treatment of constipation. J Gerontol Nurs 16:6, 1990.

23 Beverley, L, and Travis, I: Constipation: Proposed natural laxative mixtures. J Gerontol Nurs 18:5, 1992.

24 Gibson, CJ, et al: Effectiveness of bran supplement on the bowel management of elderly rehabilitation patients. J Gerontol Nurs 21:21, 1995.

25 Bennett, RG: Diarrhea among residents of long-term care facilities. Infect Control Hosp Epidemiol 14:397, 1993.

CHAPTER 19

The Aging Female Reproductive System

Jan Dodge Dougherty / Patricia Knutesen

OBJECTIVES

Upon completion of this chapter, the reader will be able to:

- Discuss normal gynecologic age-related changes
- Identify two common symptoms of vaginal disorders in older women
- Outline a routine for older women's health maintenance
- Describe a program of health promotion that includes primary, secondary, and tertiary prevention
- Discuss the importance of breast self-examination for older women

In 1995, 19.6 million women in the United States were over 65 years old. Today, a woman reaching age 65 can expect to live an additional 19.4 years, making this group the fastest-growing segment of our population.[1,2] These numbers highlight the importance of women's health needs, particularly in the postmenopausal years. Because menopause occurs at about age 50, the average woman can expect to live one-third of her life beyond menopause. During this same period, women may also be affected by metabolic, cardiovascular, and neoplastic disorders associated with or complicated by gynecologic signs and symptoms.[3]

Gynecologic care of younger women has received adequate medical and public attention; consequently, norms regarding function, screening, and treatment have been established. In older women, however, much less is known about the normal function of the reproductive system.[4] This is evidenced by the following facts:

- Only 25 percent of women over age 60 have ever had a mammogram.[5]
- There is a lack of regular Pap smear screening in the over-65 population.[5,6]
- Older women are less likely to use an obstetrician/gynecologist for routine care.
- Approximately 30 percent of community-dwelling older women have incontinence and routinely do not report this as a problem to a health-care provider.[7]

- Routine health screening of older adults is subject to controversy because of limited guidelines.[8]

These inconsistencies affect the attitudes of health-care providers and women alike regarding gynecologic care. Much of the literature to date regarding the postmenopausal years has been written in negative terms. Menopause, once considered a disease, was associated with depression, anxiety, obesity, and a decline of overall function. Such attitudes create barriers and must be overcome to achieve optimal health care for the older woman. Today, women and health-care providers are re-evaluating the postmenopausal years and studying this period in a woman's life as a normal part of aging.

This chapter focuses on common disorders of the genital tract and breast; however, other disorders associated with the gynecologic system such as urinary incontinence, osteoporosis, and sexuality are discussed in detail elsewhere in this text.

Normal Aging

Alterations in the production of sex hormones are the primary physiological event of natural menopause leading to age-related changes. A reduction in the amount of circulating estrogens and a relative increase in the amount of androgens in postmenopausal women are commonly associated with atrophy of the genital tract and breasts, a reduction in bone mass, and an increase in the rate of atherosclerosis (Table 19–1).[3]

CHANGES IN THE GENITAL TRACT

The vulva, consisting of the labia majora, labia minora, clitoris, and vestibule of the vagina, atrophies and the labia tend to blend into the surrounding skin. Loss of hair and subcutaneous fat creates an appearance of skin that is thin and flabby. The vagina undergoes a number of changes directly related to the reduction of estrogen. The vaginal epithelium becomes thin and loses vascularity and elasticity, thus appearing pale and dry. Vaginal secretions are diminished, resulting in decreased lubrication. The cervix shrinks and retracts, often becoming flush with the vaginal wall. The uterus likewise decreases in size and becomes much smaller than during the reproductive years. The ovaries atrophy and become nonpalpable on examination. Finally, the supporting connective tissue and muscles of the vagina and pelvic floor go through atrophic changes, which may lead to inadequate support for the pelvic organs.[3,9,10]

CHANGES IN THE BREAST

Age-related changes after menopause cause breast tissue, which during the reproductive years consists of fibrous connective tissue and mammary gland tissue, to atrophy and be replaced by fat. When excessive adipose tissue exists in the aging breast, palpable fatty lumps may exist, complicating the differential diagnosis of breast cancer. The nipples also atrophy and lose erectile ability. Thus, atrophy of breast tissue and decrease in elasticity of supporting ligaments may cause the breast to change in size and shape.[11]

Pathophysiology and Clinical Manifestations of Common Disorders

DISEASES OF THE VULVA

Pruritus Vulvae

Itching of the vulvar skin and mucous membrane is a common symptom of vulvar disease. This pruritus may be caused by infection, contact dermatitis, medications, or a systemic disorder such as diabetes. Because shrinkage, loss of elasticity, and dryness of the vaginal mucosa are often caused by estrogen withdrawal associated with menopause, estrogen cream applied directly to the vulva is the primary treatment.[3]

Vulvar Dystrophies

These involve hyperkeratosis with epithelial thinning, resulting in gross lesions of whitish-gray plaques, skin ulceration, or cracking of the skin. Symptoms in-

TABLE 19–1 NORMAL FEMALE REPRODUCTIVE SYSTEM AGING CHANGES

Normal Age-Related Changes	Clinical Implications
Reduction in circulating estrogen	Atrophy of breast and genital tissue
Increase in circulating androgens	Reduction in bone mass with risk of osteoporosis and fracture
	Increased rate of atherosclerosis

clude itching, dryness, and pain in the vulvar region. Biopsy generally is performed to determine whether the lesion is cancerous; however, the exact causes of vulvar dystrophies are unknown. Treatment consists of topical estrogen for symptomatic relief, treatment of specific infections, and perineal hygiene measures.[4]

Vulvar Carcinoma

Carcinoma of the vulva represents up to 5 percent of all genital malignancies and occurs most often in those over 65. More than 80 percent of vulvar cancers are squamous cell in type and are usually slow in growing and late to metastasize. Common presentations include long-standing pruritus and a lump, mass, ulceration, or wartlike growth. All lesions warrant biopsy. Radiation therapy may be used in some women; however, the primary treatment is surgical.[4]

DISEASES OF THE VAGINA

Atrophic Vaginitis

Atrophic vaginitis, inflammation of the vagina, is caused by a reduction in estrogen, which results in thinning and inelasticity of the vaginal epithelium. Vaginal secretions decline, but a thin, watery discharge may occur. The tissues become more susceptible to inflammation and ulceration from minor trauma or intercourse. Although estrogen deficiencies are associated with vaginitis, other contributing factors may include vitamin deficiencies (e.g., niacin), poor hygiene, allergies, and infections. Symptoms of vaginitis are vaginal itching and burning, urinary frequency and urgency, leukorrhea (a thin watery or bloody discharge), and dyspareunia. Estrogens are used to treat this condition when symptoms appear, which may reverse many of the atrophic changes.[12,13]

Vaginal Infections

Caused by *Candida* or *Trichomonas*, vaginal infections may be present in women with atrophic vaginitis. *Candida* infections, uncommon in most older women, usually are associated with diabetes mellitus or are a side effect of antibiotic therapy. Alterations in carbohydrate metabolism in diabetic patients and diminished vaginal flora after antibiotic therapy create a medium for this fungus to proliferate. Symptoms of *Candida* infection include vaginal and vulvar soreness; dyspareunia; thick, cheesy vaginal discharge; pruritus; and possible urinary tract infection. *Candida* infection is treated with a topical or oral antifungal agent, proper perineal hygiene, and antibiotic therapy for superimposed infections.[14]

Trichomonas infection is a sexually transmitted disease that may be present in 1 of 5 sexually active women.[9] This flagellated protozoan lives dormantly in the paraurethral glands until the pH of the vagina becomes more alkaline, thus enabling this infection to present. Symptomatic patients report profuse frothy yellow discharge. Marked pruritus may cause extreme discomfort and dyspareunia. A 7- to 10-day course of Flagyl (metronidazole) is the treatment of choice for the older woman and her sexual partner.[15]

Although sexually transmitted diseases are uncommon in older women, it must be remembered that sexually active older women with multiple partners are at risk for other infections such as *Chlamydia*, chancroid, gonorrhea, genital warts, *Mycoplasma* infection, pelvic inflammatory disease, pubic lice, scabies, and *Ureaplasma* infection. Proper hygiene should be emphasized, and the woman's sexual partner must also be treated.[16]

Disorders of the Pelvic Floor

Pelvic floor disorders can cause prolapse of the anterior vaginal wall, presenting as cystocele or urethrocele, whereas prolapse of the posterior vaginal wall results in rectocele. Varying degrees of uterine prolapse may accompany vaginal prolapse, resulting in a herniation of the uterus into the vaginal opening.[3,9] The pelvic organs, including the bladder, uterus, and rectum, are supported by various ligaments, the endopelvic fascia, and the levator muscles, forming a pelvic sling. Weakness or damage to the pelvic support may be attributed to parity, anatomic predisposition, or atrophy and weakening of the connective tissue.[3,17] Many older women may be asymptomatic. However, common symptoms of cystourethrocele include stress urinary incontinence, pressure, or discomfort in the pelvic or vaginal area. Those with rectoceles may experience constipation or problems emptying the rectum. Uterine prolapse may cause pressure or discomfort in the pelvis or vagina, particularly during walking.[3]

Mild uterine prolapse may be managed by teaching pelvic muscle exercises (Kegel) to strengthen pelvic support muscles, encouraging weight loss in obese women, and controlling a persistent cough to prevent further pelvic pressure. Pessaries may offer symptomatic relief in women experiencing symptoms such as urinary incontinence, pelvic fullness or pressure, and constipation. Moderate to severe prolapse generally requires surgical repair via vaginal or abdominal hysterectomy.

Symptomatic cystocele or rectocele is repaired along with the hysterectomy. Removal of the ovaries at the time of hysterectomy is controversial because intact ovaries continue to produce necessary hormones but may pose a future risk of ovarian cancer. Determination of oophorectomy may be based on physician opinion or preference and the woman's age and overall function.

DISEASES OF THE CERVIX

Cervical cancer is the primary disorder of the cervix found in older women. Because of increased use of the Pap smear and increased awareness in women, more cases of cervical cancer are being found in postmenopausal women. Human papillomavirus, considered the leading cause of cervical cancer, is thought to be sexually transmitted. Cervical cancer is a slow-growing cancer that progresses from minor dysplasia to carcinoma in situ and to invasive cancer if untreated. Vaginal spotting, staining, and discharge are the primary symptoms. Risk factors for cervical cancer include early menarche, young age at first intercourse and a large number of sexual partners, early and repetitive childbearing, history of sexually transmitted disease, smoking, and older age. Treatment involves surgery or radiation therapy.[18]

DISEASES OF THE UTERUS

Endometrial cancer is the fifth most common cause of cancer-related deaths in women over age 75. Risk factors for this disease are obesity, diabetes mellitus, hypertension, liver disease, and certain ovarian tumors. Endometrial cancer is believed to be related to excess estrogen stimulation. Exogenous estrogens have been found to increase the risk of endometrial cancer. Because abnormal postmenopausal bleeding is the primary symptom, endometrial cancer is often diagnosed in its early stages, thereby resulting in a high cure rate. Surgery, with or without radiation therapy, is the mode of treatment.[3,13,18]

DISEASES OF THE OVARY

Ovarian cancer has a low incidence but a very high mortality rate, with the peak incidence occurring around age 77.[9] The most common type of ovarian tumor is epithelial, arising from the mesothelial surface of the ovary. Ovarian cancer is usually asymptomatic in the early stages. By the time such symptoms as abdominal distention, vague abdominal discomfort, and pain occur, the ovarian cancer has progressed beyond its early stages. Treatment of ovarian cancer includes surgery, radiation, and chemotherapy.[3,9,18]

DISEASES OF THE BREAST

Breast cancer is the most prevalent cancer among older women, and the second most common cause of death in women. The incidence of breast cancer in women over age 65 is twice that in women between ages 45 and 64. In fact, the age-specific incidence of breast cancer continues to increase beyond age 80.[19] There are six histological types of breast cancer, with infiltrating duct cancer being the most common. Older women are less likely than younger women to have a biologically aggressive variant of breast cancer and often present with advanced stages of the disease.[20]

In about 80 percent of all women, a breast lump is usually the first sign of cancer. Other symptoms include nipple retraction, discharge, itching, a sensation of pulling in the breast, and localized breast tenderness.[20] Age is the most important risk factor but one that is often ignored. Risk factors also strongly associated with breast cancer are breast cancer in first-degree relatives (e.g., mother or sister) and a history of breast cancer. Additional risk factors include early menarche and late menopause, first pregnancy after age 35, obesity, and a high-fat diet.[21] Treatment strategies may include surgery, radiation, and chemotherapy.[22]

Management

1 Primary Prevention

In gynecologic care, primary prevention is associated with health education and health promotion. Because of the lack of information available to women regarding postmenopausal health, nurses have an opportunity and obligation to educate women about the normal aging process and routine care that is needed to promote optimal health. Health education about gynecologic issues should be incorporated into the overall health and function of older women. Similarly, primary prevention strategies for gynecologic health are pertinent in the prevention of numerous disorders (Table 19–2).

Primary prevention strategies that must be emphasized for many of the disorders discussed previously include health education regarding a healthful lifestyle, self-care, the normal aging process, and the importance of gynecologic care throughout life. Healthful lifestyle behaviors such as balanced diet and regular exercise are indicated in the prevention of many diseases and disorders. Maintaining an optimal weight and following a low-fat diet are considered preventive strategies for breast and endometrial cancers.[23] Exercise produces many positive physical and mental health effects. As part of a routine exercise program, women should be instructed on the benefit of Kegel (pelvic muscle) exercises throughout the life span to prevent further relaxation of the pelvic musculature. (This topic is thoroughly discussed in Chapter 17.)

Education about proper perineal hygiene should be included. Many women are unaware of the unhygienic practices that may lead to infections such as vaginitis, sexually transmitted disease, and urinary tract infections (Table 19–3). Breast self-examination (BSE) is an essential component of self-care for all women. Older women need to be educated about their risk of breast cancer and the need to perform monthly BSE. Strategies to promote BSE in older women are listed in Table 19–4.

Nurses need to stay current with information regarding normal age-related changes. The once-inevitable

TABLE 19–2   SUGGESTED PREVENTIVE HEALTH CARE FOR WOMEN 60 AND OVER WITHOUT SYMPTOMS

Examination or Test	Frequency
Physical examination	Every 1–3 yr until age 75, then annually
Pelvic examination	Annually
Pap smear	At least every 3 yr after 2 negative results 1 yr apart
Breast self-examination	Monthly
Breast examination by physician	Annually
Mammogram	Every 1–2 yr until at least age 85
Rectal examination	Annually
Stool for occult blood	Annually
Sigmoidoscopy	Every 3–5 yr after 2 negative results 1 yr apart
Blood pressure	Every 6 mo
Eye examination	Every 2 yr
Glaucoma testing	Every 2 yr
Medication review	Annually
Dental examination	Annually
Hearing test	Every 2–5 yr
Immunizations	
Flu vaccine	Annually
Pneumonia vaccine	Once after age 65
Tetanus booster	Every 10 yr
Comprehensive functional examination	Baseline data before age 80, then assessment every 1–2 yr or with any significant change in condition

TABLE 19–3   TEACHING GUIDE: PERINEAL HYGIENE FOR THE OLDER WOMAN

Teach the woman the anatomic relationship of the vagina, urethra, and rectum using drawings or a mirror to assist her in understanding her anatomy.

Instruct the woman to wipe and cleanse the perineum from front to back.

Instruct the woman to avoid use of harsh or scented soaps or deodorants in cleansing the perineum.

Teach the woman to towel dry the perineum gently or use a fan or hairdryer to dry an irritated perineum.

Obese women should give special attention to maintaining dryness in the genital folds, labia majora, and thighs, which may be moistened by perspiration and urine.

Instruct the woman with pruritus to apply a saline compress or ice bag to the perineum for relief from itching.

Discourage the use of douches.

Instruct the woman to wear cotton-lined underpants and avoid tight-fitting slacks and pantyhose. If a woman wears a pad for incontinence, it should be changed frequently.

Instruct the woman to avoid washing underpants by hand, as this may not destroy pathogens.

For the woman treated with vaginal creams, instruct her to use cream before bedtime to minimize leakage while maximizing absorption.

Instruct the woman to apply cream by lying on the back or standing with one leg elevated on a chair. The woman should use no more than half an applicator of cream, as more than this amount tends to mix with vaginal secretions, leak from the vagina, and cause irritation.

Instruct the woman to use a water-soluble lubricant (e.g., KY Jelly) before intercourse.

For the woman using a pessary for uterine prolapse, instruct her to report to her primary health-care provider immediately any vaginal bleeding or purulent drainage. Remind the woman that the pessary must be changed annually.

Instruct the woman to report any vaginal bleeding or malodorous discharge to her primary health-care provider.

TABLE 19–4   STRATEGIES TO ENHANCE BSE PERFORMANCE IN OLDER WOMEN

Areas Affecting BSE Performance	Strategies to Enhance BSE Performance
Cognition	Organize a small group discussion to review breast cancer issues. Use audiovisual materials designed to compensate for possible visual and hearing losses.
Memory	Provide a written guide that reviews BSE procedure. Encourage women to write down "Questions I Need to Ask" the physician or nurse.
Affect	Provide opportunity for small group or individual discussion time to review experiences, fears, or discomfort with self-breast inspection.
Tactile discrimination	Demonstrate BSE on breast models. Provide private supervision of BSE, addressing anatomic changes. For those with large, pendulous breasts, instruct the woman to support her breast against her hand to assist with thorough palpation.
Habit	Provide yearly calendar with agreed-upon dates for BSE (e.g., day of birthday); send reminder postcards biannually.
Reward	Distribute program attendance certificates; use lay volunteers to supplement professional instruction and provide additional positive feedback.
Professional contact	Provide memo pad and reminder calendar with names of nurses, physician, and clinic. Teach office nurses BSE technique. Consider community-based sites of instruction (e.g., churches, retirement centers, adult day-care centers, long-term care facilities, and mobile screening van programs).

Adapted from Welch-McCaffrey, D, and Dodge, J,[11] p 811, with permission.

decline associated with aging must be replaced with current information about how various health-promoting behaviors benefit the aging process. The "use it or lose it" theory is particularly important to maintain bone health, muscle mass, cardiovascular performance, memory, and sexual function. While teaching a woman about normal aging, the nurse may take the opportunity to discuss necessary health screenings such as Pap smear, mammography, and colorectal screening. In postmenopausal women, it is particularly important to emphasize ongoing care with a gynecologist, primary care physician, or nurse practitioner who routinely performs pelvic and clinical breast examinations and Pap smears and prescribes annual mammograms (see "Research Brief").

Hormone replacement therapy (HRT) may be considered a primary prevention strategy because its benefits have been demonstrated in the prevention of cardiovascular disease and osteoporosis in older women.[24] HRT may also play a role in the prevention of memory loss.[25] HRT decreases genital tract and breast atrophy and vasomotor symptoms such as hot flashes associated with menopause. Potential risks of HRT include increased risk of breast and endometrial cancers, hypertension, and thromboembolic disease. Women need to receive adequate information about HRT to make informed decisions.

2 *Secondary Prevention*

Secondary prevention is essential in providing optimal health care to the postmenopausal woman. Screenings for breast, cervical, and uterine cancer are necessary and yet rarely performed among most older women. This lack of screening relates to complex and multifaceted reasons involving the older woman herself, her health-care providers, and the entire health-care system.[5] Older women may have inaccurate perceptions about screening procedures such as fear of discomfort or embarrassment, denial of risk for cancer, concern regarding high costs, and cultural barriers.[26,27]

Because postmenopausal women tend to receive primary care from providers other than gynecologists (e.g., internists, family practitioners, nurse practitioners), these providers are responsible for performing necessary screening. It has been found that physicians perform fewer breast examinations on women over age 65 than on younger women. Only 37 percent of physicians surveyed by the American Cancer Society in 1989 followed the consensus guidelines for mammography.[19] This is further evidenced by the estimate that fewer than 50 percent of women over age 50 undergo yearly mammography.[28] In a study by nurse practitioners[29] of gynecologic health needs in older women, 77.4 percent of the women who participated stated that their physician had never recommended a Pap smear or mammogram. A recent study tracking compliance of older women's participation with the U.S. Preventive Services Task Force recommendations demonstrates that the proportion of women receiving Pap testing declined from 42 percent among the young-old to 16 percent in the old-old.[28]

The current health-care system also creates barriers to adequately screening older women. A tendency to focus on acute care has precluded consideration of sufficient outreach into rural, low-income, and various community-based and long-term care settings. Thus, inconvenient screening locations, difficulty in arranging appointments, and limited public transportation inhibit effective care.

Assessment

The nurse assessing the older woman for routine gynecologic care must be aware of certain special considerations. Providing a private and relaxed environment is necessary when taking a history, particularly when ask-

RESEARCH BRIEF

Denny, MS, et al: Gynecological health needs of elderly women. J Gerontol Nurs 15:33, 1989.

A project was developed to address gynecologic needs of older women through health assessment and education. Sixty-two women, aged 60 to 85, were recruited via lectures on women's health at six community sites. Appointments for screening tests were made at the lectures. Pelvic examinations and Pap smears were performed by a nurse, who also instructed the women on BSE with return demonstration, pubococcygeal (Kegel) exercises, personal hygiene, and sexual function. Of the women screened, 52 percent were found to have one or more abnormalities requiring physician follow-up. Abnormal findings included complaints of stress incontinence (33.9 percent), vaginal itching or discharge (21.0 percent), breast pain or discharge (6.4 percent), and abnormal Pap smear (38.6 percent). Of the 40 women receiving mammograms, 13.9 percent had abnormal results. These findings support the need for improved gynecologic screening in older women. Moreover, nurses can respond to older women's gynecologic health-care needs by providing education on self-care practices, by providing screening for gynecologic problems, and by referral for appropriate medical interventions.

TABLE 19–5   IMPORTANT ASPECTS OF THE GYNECOLOGIC HISTORY

Obstetric and gynecologic
 Obstetric
 Menstrual
 Postmenopausal
 Gynecologic surgery or procedures
 Estrogen replacement therapy
Genital tract
 Vaginal discharge
 Vaginal bleeding or spotting
 Vaginal dryness and itching
 Fullness or pressure in vagina or pelvis
 Painful intercourse
Breast
 Family history of breast cancer
 Breast lump
 Breast tenderness
 Nipple itching, discharge, retraction, or deviation
 Sensation of pulling in breast
Other factors
 Urinary incontinence
 Constipation
 Problems with evacuation of stool
Health maintenance
 Last pelvic examination
 Last Pap smear
 Last breast examination
 Last mammogram
 Performance of BSE

ing questions about the genital tract and breast. Table 19–5 outlines information that can help the nurse cover the important aspects of gynecologic health. The nurse should begin the history by questioning previous obstetric and gynecologic experience; however, some older women may be unable to supply accurate data about menopause. For example, a woman may not know whether her ovaries were removed at the time of her hysterectomy. Women should be questioned about a history or current use of hormone therapy including oral, intramuscular, and topics forms of estrogen. Inquiries about pelvic and clinical breast examinations, Pap smears, mammograms, and BSE will provide data about past screenings and create an opportunity for the nurse to reinforce the importance of each screening method.

Because the two most common genitourinary symptoms of older women are pruritus and dyspareunia, questions about vaginal health should include vaginal discharge, bleeding or spotting, dryness or itching, sensation of fullness or pressure in the pelvis or vagina, and painful intercourse. Questions about sexuality should reinforce that sexual activity is a normal part of later life. In assessing for possible pelvic relaxation, it is important to ask about any urine leakage, as well as about problems with constipation or evacuation of stool.

In taking a history of the breast, the nurse should ask about a family history of breast cancer, any breast tenderness or lumps, nipple itching or discharge, and the client's ability or willingness to perform monthly BSE. Functional assessment data will supplement the gynecologic history to provide information on any physical limitations that may require special adaptations in performing the gynecologic examination.

Because gynecologic examinations create anxiety in many women, nurses play a special role in helping older women prepare for the examination. Nurses provide older women with appropriate education and support to allay concerns about discomfort, embarrassment, and the procedure itself. Variations in positioning and examination techniques may be necessary to accommodate women with neurological, neuromuscular, or skeletal disorders. Two or three nurses or attendants may be needed to lift and position a woman for the gynecologic examination. Placing a pillow under the woman's head and supporting her legs, rather than using stirrups, may be more comfortable. The pelvic examination may be performed carefully using one finger and a small speculum. At times, it may be necessary to perform the pelvic examination with the client in the left lateral (Sims') position; however, a speculum should not be used with this type of examination.

Nursing Care

The nurse assesses, plans, intervenes, and evaluates the older woman for common vaginal symptoms and for lack of awareness about screening of the genital tract

TABLE 19–6 NURSING CARE PLANS

Nursing Diagnosis: Alteration in comfort: pain/pruritus related to atrophic vaginitis as evidenced by atrophy of the vaginal/vulvar tissue, vaginal erythema, vaginal bleeding, and complaints of vaginal itching, burning, discharge, and painful intercourse	
Expected Outcome	*Nursing Interventions*
Relief following treatment as evidenced by reduction or elimination of vaginal erythema and other vaginal symptoms	Instruct woman and caregiver to apply estrogen cream or suppository to affected vulva or vagina or both (see Table 19–3).
	Use Sitz bath or apply saline compresses, or both, to relieve irritation.
	Instruct woman and caregiver in optimal perineal care (see Table 19–3).
	Discourage use of douches, irritating or scented soaps, or deodorants on the perineum.
	Encourage the woman to wear cotton or cotton-lined underpants and discourage constant wearing of pantyhose, tight-fitting slacks, or multiple layers of clothing.
	For the woman experiencing dyspareunia, support and educate her regarding the cause, treatment, and need for a continued healthy sexual life.
	Instruct the woman to use a water-soluble lubricant (e.g., KY Jelly) before intercourse.
	For the woman with a secondary infection caused by a sexually transmitted disease, provide counseling and safe-sex education.
	In the confused or noncommunicative woman, be alert for restlessness, which may indicate irritation or pruritus. Assess for scratch marks in the perineal area.
Nursing Diagnosis: High risk for altered health maintenance related to insufficient knowledge of signs and symptoms of genital tract and breast cancers and of recommended screening guidelines	
Expected Outcome	*Nursing Interventions*
Verbalizes need for and participates in routine pelvic examination, Pap smear, mammography, and BSE	Educate the woman and family members regarding routine screening examinations via a primary health-care provider (see Table 19–2).
	Use patient education materials (e.g., *What you need to know: Cancer,* see Table 19–7) to reduce myths and fears regarding screening.
	Explore the woman's and family member's reaction to screening, to identify barriers and improve receptiveness to screening measures.
	In the outpatient setting, integrate screening and scheduled testing into routine visits to minimize the number of visits.
	Develop a reminder system to help the health professional track routine health maintenance examinations.
	Teach the older woman to perform BSEs (see Table 19–4).
	Provide a yearly calendar and mark dates to remind the woman to perform BSEs.
	Adapt and integrate screening principles into acute-care, long-term care, and community-based settings such as adult day care.

and breast. Nurses can integrate these concepts into routine care of all older women, thus educating them about gynecologic health-care needs (Table 19–6).

3 *Tertiary Prevention*

Tertiary prevention in gynecologic care serves to help older women maintain optimal function into late life. Women over 80 years of age may consider "female problems" such as urinary incontinence, vaginal dryness, and prolapse as an inevitable part of aging and not

report them to health-care providers. Older women may also think that they have outlived their risk of cancer and therefore may bypass secondary prevention measures. Consequently, these unreported and untreated problems may lead to social isolation and loss in overall function and well-being. By focusing on function and not on chronological age, nurses and other health-care providers should continue to assess and intervene in gynecologic health care. Table 19–7 provides a list of resources available to those seeking further information on this topic.

TABLE 19–7 RESOURCES

Self-Help Books Containing Gynecologic Health Information

Doress-Wolters, PB, and Siegal, DL: Ourselves, Growing Older: Women Aging with Knowledge and Power, ed 2. Simon & Schuster, New York, 1994.

For the woman approaching menopause. Mead Johnson Laboratories, Evansville, Ind, 1985.

Fries, JF: Aging Well. Addison-Wesley, Reading, Mass, 1989.

Hoffman, E: A Revolutionary Approach to Total Health Care for Women. Pocket Books, New York, 1995.

Nelson, EC, et al: Medical and Health Guide for People over Fifty. Scott Foresman, Glenview, Ill, 1986.

Porcino, J: Growing Older, Getting Better: A Handbook for Women in the Second Half of Life. Addison-Wesley, Reading, Mass, 1983.

National Resources

The National Cancer Institute provides various pamphlets containing cancer literature pertaining to women. Call 1-800-4-CANCER.
What You Need to Know About Cancer
What You Need to Know About Breast Cancer
Questions and Answers About Breast Lumps
Breast Biopsy: What You Should Know
Breast Exams: What You Should Know
Smart Advice for Women 40 and Over
What You Need to Know About Cancer of the Cervix

Local Resources

The American Cancer Society provides educational materials, equipment, and information on support groups.

Planned Parenthood provides a library of resources on women's health, Pap smears, pelvic and breast examinations, and counseling on women's issues.

Student Learning Activities

1 Prepare a poster on BSE and the importance of mammography for older women. Place the poster where it will be viewed by older women in your community.

2 Discuss the risks and benefits of HRT with the community-living older women in your neighborhood.

3 Survey the area physicians and nurse practitioners who provide primary care to older women about their current recommendations for HRT. Are there variations among the primary care providers? How do the current practice patterns differ from those recommended in this text?

REFERENCES

1 Blair, C, et al: Growing old in America. Information Plus, Wyle, Tex, 1996.

2 US Bureau of the Census: Statistical abstract of the United States: 1995, ed 115. Washington, DC, 1995.

3 Wingate, MB: Geriatric gynecology. Prim Care 9:53, 1982.

4 Ryan, KJ: Geriatric gynecology. In Andres, R, et al (eds): Principles of Geriatric Medicine. McGraw-Hill, New York, 1985, p 629.

5 Calle, EE, et al: Demographic predictors of mammography and Pap smear screening in US women. Public Health 83:53, 1993.

6 Blesch, KS, and Prohaska, TR: Cervical cancer screening in older women: Issues and interventions. Cancer Nurs 14:141, 1991.

7 National Institute of Health Consensus Development Conference Statement: Urinary Incontinence in Adults. National Library of Medicine, Bethesda, Md, 1988, p 1.

8 Wolf-Klein, G: Screening examinations in the elderly: Which are worthwhile: Geriatrics 44:36, 1989.

9 Barber, HR: Perimenopausal and Geriatric Gynecology. Macmillan, New York, 1988.

10 Masoro, EJ, et al (eds): Handbook of Physiology in Aging, CRC Press, Boca Raton, Fla, 1981.

11 Welch-McCaffrey, D, and Dodge, J: Planning breast self-examination programs for elderly women. Semin Oncol Nurs 15:811, 1988.

12 Staab, AS, and Lyles, MF: Genitourinary disorders. In Staab, AS, and Lyles, MF (eds): Manual of Geriatric Nursing. Scott, Foresman/Little, Brown Higher Education, Glenview, Ill, 1990, p 460.

13 Barber, HR: Geriatric gynecology. In Rossman, I (ed): Clinical Geriatrics, ed 3. JB Lippincott, Philadelphia, 1986, p 364.

14 Roberts, D, and Bancerwiez, D: Effective treatment for fungal skin infection. Geriatr Med 24:60, 1994.

15 Bergh, PA: Vaginal changes with aging. In Breen, JL (ed): The Gynecologist and the Older Patient. Aspen, Rockville, Md, 1988, p 299.

16 Talashek, ML, et al: Sexually transmitted diseases in the elderly: Issues and recommendations. J Gerontol Nurs 16:33, 1990.

17 McGuire, EJ, et al: Female genitourinary disorders. In Abrams, WB, and Berkow, R (eds): The Merck Manual of Geriatrics. Merck, Sharp and Dohme Research Laboratories, Rahway, NJ, 1990, p 624.

18 McGonigle, KF, et al: Ovarian, uterine and cervical cancer in the elderly woman. Clin Geriatr Med 9:115, 1993.

19 American Cancer Society: 1989 survey of physicians' attitudes and practices in early cancer detection. CA Cancer Clin 40:77, 1990.

20 Rybolt, AH, and Waterbury, L: Breast cancer in older women: Trends in diagnosis. Geriatrics 44:69, 1989.

21 Fiorica, JV: Breast cancer screening: Who, when and how. Am J Managed Care 2:839, 1996.

22 Singletary, SE, et al: Factors influencing management of breast cancer in the elderly woman. Clin Geriatr Med 9:107, 1993.

23 Fries, JF: Aging Well: A Guide for Successful Seniors. Addison-Wesley, Reading, Mass, 1989.

24 Speroff, L: Menopause and hormone replacement therapy. Clin Geriatr Med 9:33, 1993.

25 Robinson, D, et al: Estrogen replacement therapy and memory in older women. J Am Geriatr Soc 42:923, 1994.

26 Wheat, ME, et al: Pap smear screening in women 65 and older. J Am Geriatr Soc 36:827, 1988.

27 Weinberger, M, et al: Breast cancer screening in older women: Practices and barriers reported by primary care physicians. J Am Geriatr Soc 39:22, 1991.

28 Bergman-Evans, B, and Noble Walker, S: The prevalence of clinical preventive services utilization by older women. Nurse Pract 21:88, 1996.

29 Denny, MS, et al: Gynecological health needs of elderly women. J Gerontol Nurs 15:33, 1989.

Multisystem Alterations

CHAPTER 20

Immobility and Activity Intolerance in Older Adults

Kathryn A. Blair

OBJECTIVES

Upon completion of this chapter, the reader will be able to:

- Identify the importance of maintaining mobility in older adults
- Describe the physiological impact of immobility and inactivity
- Describe the appropriate nursing interventions that address primary, secondary, and tertiary prevention of immobility and activity intolerance
- List the physiological, psychological, and psychosocial benefits of exercise for older adults
- Describe the essential components of a regular physical exercise program for older adults
- Describe an appropriate exercise program for an older client with activity intolerance

Mobility is movement that affords a person freedom and independence. Although the types of activities change over one's lifetime, mobility is central to participating in and enjoying life. Maintaining optimal mobility is crucial for physical and mental health of all older adults.

Nature of the Problem

Mobility is not an absolute, static attribute determined by the ability to walk; rather, optimal mobility is an individualistic, relative, dynamic quality that depends on the interaction between environmental factors and social, cognitive, affective, and physical functioning. For one person, optimal mobility may be walking 5 miles every day; for another, it may involve limited movement with assistance.

Immobility is broadly defined as any activity level at less than optimal mobility. The nursing diagnoses of impaired physical mobility, potential for disuse syndrome, and activity intolerance offer a more restrictive definition of immobility and are subsumed under the broader definition of immobility. The definitions, defining characteristics, and related factors for these diagnoses are outlined in Tables 20–1, 20–2, and 20–3.[1,2]

Immobility, activity intolerance, and disuse syndrome are common in older adults. Studies on the incidence of nursing diagnoses used for institutionalized older adults reveal that impaired physical mobility was the first or second most common diagnosis.[3] The prevalence of this problem extends beyond institutional boundaries to include all older people.

Fatigue and weakness, defining characteristics of activity intolerance, have been cited as the second most common concern of older adults.[4] Approximately 43 percent of older adults have been identified as living sedentary lifestyles[5] that contribute to activity intolerance and disuse. Finally, about 50 percent of the functional decline in older adults is associated with disuse.[6]

The onset of immobility or activity intolerance for most people is not abrupt, going from full mobility to total physical dependence or inactivity, but rather develops slowly and progresses insidiously. Interventions directed at preventing untoward consequences of immobility and inactivity can decrease the slope of the decline. The likelihood for continued self-care and independence decreases if immobility decline is not interrupted or activity levels are not maintained.

The causes of immobility are numerous. In fact, there are as many unique causes for immobility as there are people who are immobilized. All disease and rehabil-

TABLE 20–1 IMPAIRED PHYSICAL MOBILITY

Definition
    A state in which one experiences a limitation of ability of
        independent physical movement
Defining characteristics
    Inability to move purposefully within the environment,
        including bed mobility, transferring, and ambulation
    Reluctance to attempt movement
    Limited range of motion
    Decreased muscle strength, control, or mass
    Imposed restrictions of movement, including mechanical
        and medical protocols
    Impaired coordination
Related factors
    Intolerance to activity
    Decreased strength and endurance
    Pain and discomfort
    Perceptual or cognitive impairment
    Neuromuscular impairment
    Depression
    Severe anxiety

Source: Carroll-Johnson RM (ed): Activity Intolerance, Definitions, Defining Characteristics, Related Factors. Proceedings of the Eighth Conference, North American Nursing Diagnosis Association, 1988, p 543.

itative states involve some degree of immobility. The multiple threats of physical immobility can be categorized as relating to the individual's internal and external environments or to his or her internal and external competence and resources.

INTERNAL FACTORS

Many internal factors result in immobility of the body or its parts (Table 20–4). Detailed discussions of the internal contributing factors to immobility may be found in related chapters in this text.

EXTERNAL FACTORS

Many external factors alter mobility in older adults. They include therapeutic regimens, resident and staff characteristics, the nursing care delivery system, barriers, and institutional policies.

TABLE 20–2 POTENTIAL FOR DISUSE SYNDROME

Definition
    A state in which one is at risk for deterioration of body
        systems as the result of prescribed or unavoidable
        musculoskeletal inactivity
Risk factors
    Paralysis
    Mechanical immobilization
    Prescribed immobilization
    Severe pain
    Altered level of consciousness

Source: Carroll-Johnson, RM (ed): Activity Intolerance, Definitions, Defining Characteristics, Related Factors. Proceedings of the Eighth Conference, North American Nursing Diagnosis Association, 1988, p 543.

TABLE 20–3 ACTIVITY INTOLERANCE

Definition
    A state in which one has insufficient physiological or
        psychological energy to endure or complete required or
        desired daily activities
Defining characteristics
    Verbal report of fatigue or weakness
    Abnormal heart rate or blood pressure to activity
    Exertional discomfort or dyspnea
    Electrocardiographic changes reflecting dysrhythmias or
        ischemia
Related factors
    Bed rest and immobility
    Generalized weakness
    Sedentary lifestyle
    Imbalance between oxygen supply and demand

Source: Carroll-Johnson, RM (ed): Activity Intolerance, Definitions, Defining Characteristics, Related Factors. Proceedings of the Eighth Conference, North American Nursing Diagnosis Association, 1988, p 543.

Therapeutic Regimens

Medical treatment regimens have a potent influence on the quality and quantity of the patient's movement. Examples of restrictive regimens include mechanical and pharmacological factors, bed rest, and restraints. Mechanical factors prevent or inhibit movement of the body or its parts by external appliances (e.g., casts and traction) or devices (e.g., those associated with intravenous fluid administration, gastric suctioning, urinary

TABLE 20–4 INTERNAL FACTORS CAUSING OR CONTRIBUTING TO IMMOBILITY

Decreased musculoskeletal function
    Muscles (atrophy, dystrophy, or injury), bones (infection,
        fracture, tumor, osteoporosis, or osteomalacia), joints
        (arthritis and tumors), or combination of structures
        (cancer and drugs)
Altered neurological function
    Infection (e.g., encephalitis), tumors, trauma, drugs,
        vascular disease (e.g., cerebrovascular accident),
        demyelinating disease (e.g., multiple sclerosis),
        degenerative disease (e.g., Parkinson's disease), exposure
        to toxic products (e.g., carbon monoxide), metabolic
        disorders (e.g., hypoglycemia), or nutritional disorders)
Pain
    Multiple and varied causes such as chronic illness and
        trauma
Perceptual deficits
    Sensory-perceptual input excess or deficit
Diminished cognitive ability
    Disruption of the cognitive processes, such as severe
        dementia
Falls
    Physical effects: injury or fractures
    Psychological effect: postfall syndrome
Altered social relationships
    Actual factors (e.g., loss of a spouse, moving away from
        family or friends)
    Perceived factors (e.g., altered thought pattern such as
        depression)
Psychological aspects
    Learned helplessness
    Depression

catheters, and oxygen administration). Pharmaceutical agents such as sedatives, analgesics, tranquilizers, and anesthetics used to alter a patient's level of awareness may reduce movement or eliminate it entirely.

Bed rest may be prescribed or may result from the treatment of disease or injury sequelae. As a prescriptive intervention, rest decreases metabolic needs, oxygen requirements, and workload of the heart. In addition, it allows the musculoskeletal system to relax, relieves pain, prevents excessive irritation of injured tissue, and minimizes the effects of gravity.[7] Bed rest may also be the result of other physiological or psychological factors such as hypoxia and depression. Physiologically, an inadequate supply of oxygen disrupts the maintenance of cellular function to promote activity. Psychologically, depression decreases available energy.

Physical restraints and bedrails are commonly used with institutionalized older adults. These devices contribute directly to immobility by restricting movement in bed and indirectly by increasing the risk of injury from falls as the person attempts to gain freedom and mobility.

Resident Characteristics

The level of mobility and behavior pattern of the client's peer group can influence his or her pattern of mobility and behavior. In a study on the mobility status of nursing home residents,[8] those who could walk were encouraged to ride in wheelchairs because of staff expectations for passive residents, modeling by other residents, understaffing, and an environment with slickly waxed floors and cluttered hallways. Conformity and excessive disability resulted.

Staff Characteristics

Three characteristics of the nursing staff that influence mobility patterns are knowledge, commitment, and number. Knowledge and understanding of the physiological consequences of immobility and of nursing measures to prevent or counteract their influence are essential to implementing care to maximize mobility. Adequate numbers of staff members with a commitment to help older adults maintain independence must be available to prevent immobility complications.

Nursing Care Delivery System

The type of nursing care delivery system used in the institution can influence the residents' mobility status. Functional or task allocation practice has been shown to increase dependency and complications from immobility.[9] When care is divided into tasks, the wholeness and interactiveness of the client are overlooked.

Barriers

Physical and architectural barriers may interfere with mobility. Physical barriers include lack of available aids for mobility, inadequate knowledge in the use of mobility aids, slippery floors, and inadequate foot support (i.e., house slippers instead of laced shoes). Often, the architectural design of the hospital or nursing home does not facilitate or motivate clients to be active and mobile. Hospital design is based on bed occupancy, with little space, if any, devoted to activity such as an exercise room or lounge. Hallways may be too narrow to handle the demands of the institution as well as its older residents. Hallways are often encumbered with obstacles and people. A person with decreased visual ability or one who requires an assistive device such as a walker or wheelchair may have difficulty moving in such an environment. The environmental stimuli to be active may also be lacking. Modeling from other residents, lack of a place to go, or inability to move independently may decrease mobility.

Institutional Policies

Another important environmental factor for older adults is institutional policies and procedures. These formal and informal governing practices control the balance between institutional order and individual freedom. The more restrictive the policy, the greater its effect on mobility.

Impact of the Problem on Older Adults

Older adults are highly susceptible to the physiological and psychological consequences of immobility. Age-related changes accompanied by chronic illness predispose older adults to these complications. Physiologically, the body reacts to immobility with changes similar to those of aging, thus compounding this effect.

An understanding of the impact of immobility can be derived from the interaction of physical competence, threat to mobility, and interpretation of the event. Immobility influences an already affected body. For example, after early adulthood there is a marked and steady decline in strength.[10] Between the ages of 20 and 60 years, muscle strength declines 10 to 30 percent; by age 80, about 50 percent of muscle is lost.[11] Whereas a 20-year-old person may use an estimated 50 to 60 percent of maximal voluntary contraction of the quadriceps muscles to rise from a low, armless chair, an 80-year-old person may use almost 100 percent of this muscle contraction force.[12] Thus, an older adult's physical competence may be at or near threshold level for certain mobility activities. Further change or loss from immobility may render the person dependent. The greater the number of causes for immobility, the greater the potential for untoward effects from immobility. Likewise, the person's perception of events influences the overall reaction to and potential for negating the physiological consequences of immobility.

The effect of immobility also depends on an assessment of resources and limitations within and external to the person and on the interactions between the internal and external environments. The internal environment, or the client's competence, is the most important determinant of mobility when lesser degrees of immobility are present. As the client's competence decreases, he or she relies more heavily on the external environment to maintain mobility. For example, if an older hemiplegic patient with severe muscle weakness is encouraged to use an electric wheelchair, the resources of the external environment help negate the limitations of the internal environment.

Clinical Manifestations

The physical impacts of immobility and inactivity are numerous and varied. Related problems can influence all systems of the body. The most common changes resulting from immobility are presented in Table 20–5.[13–15]

MANAGEMENT

1 Primary Prevention

For immobility and activity intolerance, primary prevention is both a lifelong and an episodic process. As a lifelong process, mobility and activity depend on functioning musculoskeletal, cardiovascular, and pulmonary systems. One of the biggest breakthroughs in health pro-

motion has been the recognition and acceptance of exercise as an integral component of daily life. As a primary preventive intervention, exercise is a lifelong investment. Exercise is beneficial both for older people who are healthy and for those who have a chronic physical or mental problem. Exercise and regular physical activity may retard the aging process and are associated with a sense of well-being, longevity, and improved cardiopulmonary function (Fig. 20–1).[15–17]

As an episodic process, primary prevention is directed at prevention of problems that can result from immobility or inactivity. Potential for disuse syndrome and activity intolerance are the nursing diagnoses associated with primary prevention. A prescription of activity and exercise will increase energy level, maintain mobility, and enhance cardiovascular and pulmonary reserves. Although exercise will not change the course of normal aging, it will prevent the deleterious effects of immobility and a sedentary lifestyle.

Older adults experience significant gains in health status with low to moderate leisure-time physical activity when these activities are practiced on a regular basis and are of sufficient duration and intensity.[18] As a

TABLE 20–5 PHYSIOLOGICAL IMPACT OF IMMOBILITY AND INACTIVITY

Effect	Result
Decreased maximum oxygen consumption	Orthostatic intolerance
Decreased left ventricular function	Increased heart rate, syncope
Decreased cardiac output	Decreased exercise tolerance
Decreased stroke volume	Decreased aerobic capacity
Increased protein catabolism	Decreased lean body mass Muscular atrophy Decreased muscle strength
Increased calcium wastage	Disuse osteoporosis
Slowed bowel function	Constipation
Decreased micturition	Decreased evacuation of bladder
Disordered glucose metabolism	Glucose intolerance
Decreased thoracic size	Decreased functional residual capacity
Decreased pulmonary blood flow	Atelectasis Decreased Po_2 Increased pH
Decreased total body water	Decreased plasma volume Decreased sodium balance Decreased total blood volume
Sensory disruption	Change in cognition Depression and anxiety Change in perception
Disordered sleep	Daydreaming Hallucinations

Figure 20–1 The benefits of regular exercise for older adults include slowing of the aging process, increased longevity, better cardiovascular function, and an enhanced sense of well-being.

result of exercise, the cardiopulmonary system gains in overall functioning,[19] the musculoskeletal system exhibits greater flexibility, nutritional habits are improved, and weight control efforts are enhanced.[20,21] Exercise training has also been associated with improvement in mood and levels of tension, anxiety, and depression. Several cognitive functioning scores have been improved in older adults participating in a program of regular exercise.[22] Various benefits result from exercise (Table 20–6),[15–22] but the major benefits of exercise are maintenance or improvement of physical, mental, emotional, and social functioning, which can result in greater self-sufficiency and independence.

Barriers to Exercise

A variety of barriers affect the participation of older adults in regular exercise. Interpersonal hazards include the social isolation that occurs when friends and relatives die, certain lifestyle behaviors (e.g., smoking and poor dietary habits), depression, sleep disorders, lack of transportation, and lack of support. Environmental barriers include the lack of a safe place to exercise and unfavorable climatic conditions. Cultural attitudes are another barrier to engaging in exercise. Our culture expects older adults to be inactive and dependent. Sedentary role models, distorted body image, and fear of failure or disapproval all contribute to the older adult's failure to participate in regular exercise. Gender can also be considered a barrier because physical activity is perceived as being more important for men than for women.

The nurse must assess all potential barriers before formulating an exercise program with the older adult. The program must be personalized for each client, consistent with his or her belief system, and feasible to accomplish, given individual abilities and lifestyles.

Developing an Exercise Program

A successful exercise program is individualized, balanced, and incremental. The program is structured to allow the client to develop a habit of regularly performing an active form of relaxing recreation, which affords a training effect.

The activity or exercise should conform to the client's capacity. Chair activities (Fig. 20–2) are suitable for the older adult who is afraid of falling or for one with limited balance; pool activities are appropriate when weight bearing is a problem, as in those with joint disease.

Before an older adult begins an exercise program, a pre-exercise assessment is recommended,[15] which should include at least a complete history and physical examination performed by a physician or nurse practitioner. Attention should be directed toward completing a thorough drug history (i.e., use of diuretics, β-blockers, tranquilizers, and hypoglycemic agents) and evaluating sensory neurological deficits, visual acuity, equilibrium, and gait. Exercise tolerance tests should be performed before an older adult engages in moderate to vigorous exercise, but this testing has little utility in most people over the age of 75 years.[15]

TABLE 20–6 BENEFITS OF EXERCISE

Cardiovascular
  Increased endurance capacity
  Decreased heart rate
  Increased oxygen transport
  Decreased cholesterol
  Decreased blood pressure in hypertensive clients
Respiratory
  Increased vital capacity
Musculoskeletal
  Increased muscle strength
  Increased range of motion
  Increased flexibility
  Increased remineralization of bone
  Increased balance
Endocrine
  Improved glucose metabolism
Psychological
  Increased sense of well-being
  Improved morale
Cognitive
  Improved logical glucose metabolism

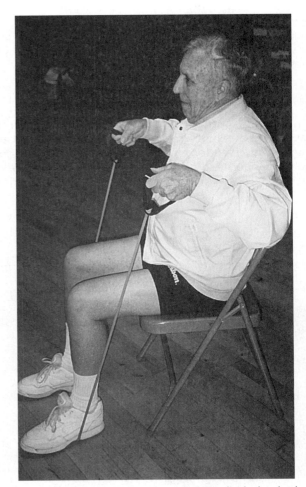

Figure 20–2 Chair exercises are safe for individuals who have limited balance and are at risk for falls.

Once the client has had a thorough physical evaluation, assessment of the following intervening factors will help to ensure adherence and enhance the experience:

- Current activity and physiological response (pulse before, during, and after a given activity)
- Natural propensity (predisposition or inclination toward a particular exercise)
- Perceived difficulty
- Goals and perceived importance of exercise
- Self-efficacy (degree of conviction that one will be successful)

On completion of the assessment, characteristics of an exercise program should be examined. The program must include exercises for flexibility, strength, and endurance.[23] Flexibility is attained by moving joints and their supporting structure through the normal range of motion. To maintain or increase muscle strength, muscle tension must occur, as with isotonic or isometric muscle contractions. Strength training increases muscle size and strength.[24] Endurance training requires aerobic exercise.

Safety

Once a specific exercise program has been formulated and accepted by the client, instructions regarding safe exercise are imperative. Teaching the client to recognize signs of intolerance or overexertion is as important as selecting the appropriate activity. Guidelines are addressed in Table 20–7.

2 Secondary Prevention

The downward spiral that results from acute exacerbation of immobility can be reduced or prevented by nursing interventions. Successful intervention stems from an understanding of the multiple factors that cause or contribute to immobility and of the physiological consequences of the interaction between immobility and aging. Secondary prevention focuses on maintenance of function and prevention of complications. The nursing diagnosis associated with secondary prevention is impaired physical mobility.

Assessment

An assessment of function provides evidence that immobility precipitates pathological changes in a body system. Assessment parameters are presented here by effects of immobility on body systems and by environmental factors.

Musculoskeletal Deterioration

Primary indicators of the severity of immobility on the musculoskeletal system are decreases in muscle tone, strength, size, and endurance; range of joint motion; and skeletal strength. Periodic assessment of function can be used to monitor change and effectiveness of interventions.

To evaluate muscle tone, the client's muscle is observed in a relaxed, comfortable position. Tautness indicates tone. Strength is evaluated either subjectively by the degree of resistance of muscle groups or objectively by the use of an ergometer. Circumferential measurements of appendages provide evidence of muscle size.

Indicators of endurance are evident from usual activities. Reduced muscle endurance results in the reduction of time that general activities can be sustained or in complaints of weakness or tiredness. Also, decreased endurance results in increased heart and respiratory rate during and after the activity.

Joint mobility can be evaluated by measurement of functional ability, by observation of normal activities such as the manipulation of a fork to eat, or by measurement of the degrees of movement with a goniometer. Both functional ability and range of joint motion provide evidence of overall ability and do not duplicate information. Functional mobility may be derived from the observation of the essential components of ambulation. The assessment begins with the client seated in a hard, straight-backed, armless chair.

Functional mobility may be derived from the observation of the essential components of ambulation. The assessment begins with the client seated in a hard, straight-backed, armless chair. The client is asked to stand, turn, walk with the usual aids, and sit.[25,26] Assistance must be available to prevent injury. The ability to perform these maneuvers with or especially without assistance indicates degree of mobility.

Cardiovascular Deterioration

Cardiovascular signs or symptoms do not provide direct or conclusive evidence of the development of complications of immobility. Few reliable diagnostic clues are present with thrombosis formation. Signs of thrombophlebitis include erythema, edema, tenderness, and positive Homans' sign. Orthostatic intolerance may manifest itself after assumption of an upright position as

TABLE 20–7 TEACHING GUIDE: EXERCISE PROGRAM

- Warm up and cool down for 3–5 min before and after each session.
- Perform muscle stretching exercises before and after each session.
- Do not overdo it. If you experience shortness of breath or rapid pulse or both for more than 10 min after exertion, then you have overdone it.
- Gradually increase exercise.
- If you experience chest pain, chest pressure, fainting, or pallor, *stop* the exercise and notify your physician.
- Avoid jerking, bouncing, or twisting movement.
- If you experience pain other than chest pain (e.g., leg, shoulder), this may be a sign that you need to slow down, rest, and continue the activity only if it no longer causes pain.
- Morning and evening are usually the best times to exercise.
- Exercise should be performed regularly and the exercise program should be simple.
- If possible, exercise with friends.
- Always monitor your pulse and *listen to your body.*

symptoms of increased pulse rate, decreased blood pressure, pallor, tremor of the hands, sweating, difficulty in following commands, and syncope.

Respiratory Deterioration

Indications of respiratory deterioration are evidenced from signs and symptoms of atelectasis and pneumonia. Early signs include elevation in temperature and heart rate. Changes in chest movement, percussion, breath sounds, and arterial blood gases indicate extent and severity of involvement.

Integumentary Changes

The first indicator of ischemic injury to tissue is the inflammatory reaction. The earliest changes are noted on the skin surface as irregular, poorly defined areas of erythema over a bony prominence that do not fade within 3 min after the pressure has been relieved.[27]

Urinary Function Changes

Evidence of changes in urinary function include physical signs of small, frequent voiding, distended lower abdomen, and palpable bladder margin. Symptoms of micturition difficulty include statements of inability to void and pressure or pain in the lower abdomen.

Gastrointestinal Changes

Subjective sensations of constipation include lower abdominal discomfort, sense of fullness, pressure, incomplete emptying of the rectum, anorexia, nausea, restlessness, malaise, mental depression, irritability, weakness, and headache. In addition, the stools are small, hard, and dry and deviate from the client's normal pattern and character.

Environmental Factors

The environment in which the client lives provides evidence for intervention. In the home, bathrooms without hand supports, loose rugs, inadequate illumination, high steps, slippery floors, and low toilet seats decrease the client's mobility. Institutional barriers to mobility include obstructed hallways, beds in high position, and liquid on floors. Identification and removal of potential barriers enhance mobility.

Therapeutic Management

Medical therapeutics are directed toward treating the disease or illness that is producing or contributing to the immobility problem and treating the actual or potential consequences of immobility. Examples of approaches to treatment of immobility include physical therapy to maintain joint mobility and muscle strength, intermittent pneumatic compression or gradient compression stockings to promote venous return and prevent thromboembolism, incentive spirometry for hyperinflation of the alveoli, and bed rest except for elimination.

Interventions

Five goals direct nursing interventions to prevent or negate the physiological sequelae of immobility. The first goal involves maintenance of strength and endurance of the musculoskeletal system, which includes a daily conditioning exercise program of both isometric and isotonic muscle contraction, strengthening and aerobic activities, nutrition to promote protein anabolism and bone formation, and an attitude of commitment to exercise. Second, maintenance of flexibility of joints involves range-of-motion exercises, proper positioning, and activities of daily living. Third, maintenance of normal ventilation involves hyperinflation and mobilization and removal of secretions. Fourth, maintenance of adequate circulation involves supportive measures to maintain vascular tone (including changing of body position in relation to gravity), compression stockings to provide external pressure to the legs, and adequate fluid intake to prevent dehydration effects on blood volume. Active movement influences orthostatic tolerance. Last, maintenance of normal urinary and bowel function depends on nutritional support and structuring of the environment and routines to facilitate elimination. A discussion of the interventions is presented here.

ISOMETRIC MUSCLE CONTRACTIONS

Isometric muscle contractions increase muscle tension without changing the length of the muscle moving the joint. These contractions are used to maintain the strength of the muscles of upright mobility (i.e., the quadriceps, abdominal, and gluteal muscles) and to provide stress to bone in people with and without cardiovascular disease. Isometric contractions are performed by alternately tightening and relaxing the muscle group.

ISOTONIC MUSCLE CONTRACTIONS

Resistive or isotonic muscle contractions are useful for maintaining the strength of muscles and bone. These contractions change the length of a muscle without changing the tension. As muscles shorten and lengthen, work is accomplished. Isotonic contractions can be accomplished while in bed, with legs dangling over the side of the bed, or while sitting in a chair by pushing or pulling against a stationary object. As the arm or leg is exercised both the flexor and extensor muscles should be involved.

STRENGTH TRAINING

Strengthening activity is progressive resistance training. The force the muscle must generate increases over time.[24] Weight training with increasing repetitions and weight is a strength-conditioning activity. This training increases muscle strength and mass and prevents the loss of bone density and total body mineral content (Fig. 20–3).[24]

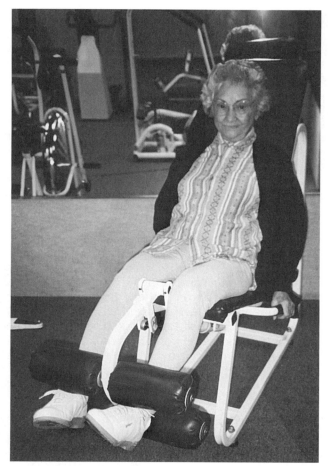

Figure 20–3 Strength training using progressive resistance can increase muscle strength and mass and prevent loss of bone density and total body mineral content.

AEROBIC EXERCISE

Aerobic exercise is activity that results in an increase in heart rate to 60 to 90 percent of one's maximal heart rate for 15 to 60 minutes and should be done three or more times per week.[28] Maximal heart rate is calculated as (220 − person's age) × 0.7.[28] The aerobic activity chosen should use large muscle groups and should be continuous, rhythmic, and enjoyable. Examples include walking, swimming, bicycling, and dancing (Fig. 20–4).

ATTITUDE

A major intervening variable to successful intervention for the immobilized individual is the attitude of the nurse and the client regarding the importance of exercise and activity in the daily routine. The nurse's attitude affects not only a commitment to incorporate exercise as an ongoing component of daily life but also the active integration of exercise as an intervention for older adults in all settings: the community, hospital, and long-term facility. Likewise, the client's attitude affects the quality and quantity of exercise.

Often, a person does not value the benefits of early and repeated exercise during a period of decreased activity. General beliefs are that the need for exercise decreases with age, that people must rest when they are ill, and that exercise will not change anything. Approaches to negate such beliefs include increasing cognitive knowledge about the importance of exercise and benchmarking by directing attention to abilities that have been retained or improved.[29]

RANGE-OF-MOTION EXERCISE

Active and passive range-of-motion exercises provide different benefits. Active exercise helps maintain joint flexibility and muscle strength and improve cognitive performance.[29] In contrast, passive motion, in which one's joints are moved through their range of motion by another person, helps maintain only flexibility. To maintain range of motion, joints should be exercised twice daily for three repetitions.[30] If pain or inflammation of the joint is present, gentle motion or a referral to physical therapy is indicated.

POSITIONING

Alignment of the body, regardless of position, affects mobility. All positions (sitting, side-lying, and lying

Figure 20–4 Walking is an excellent aerobic exercise for older adults.

RESEARCH BRIEF

Dawe, D, and Moore-Orr, R: Low intensity, range-of-motion exercise: Invaluable nursing care for elderly patients. J Advocate Nurs 21:675, 1995.

This study examined the effects of range-of-motion and stretching activities on cognitive performance of nursing home residents. Recall (immediate and delayed) was improved in the exercise group. The authors concluded that range-of-motion and other nonstrenuous activities are beneficial to older adults and can be incorporated in routine nursing care.

prone or supine) should be evaluated using the normal upright position as a reference. In the supine position, the body should be kept straight, the neck without lateral or anterior flexion, and the extremities in extension. Special care must be taken to prevent flexion contracture of the hips, knees, and ankles.

Positioning is also used to promote venous return. If a person is positioned with legs dependent, pooling and decreased venous return occur. A normal chair-sitting position with legs dependent is potentially dangerous for a person who is at risk for the development of venous thrombosis. Positioning the legs with minimal dependency (e.g., elevating the legs on a footstool) prevents blood pooling in the lower extremities.

Care Plan

The nursing care plan for immobility aims at maintaining abilities and functions and preventing impairment. The plan encompasses the nursing diagnoses of impaired physical mobility, potential for disuse syndrome, and limited components of activity intolerance (Table 20–8).

ESSENTIAL DOCUMENTATION

Specific documentation for immobility and activity intolerance involves recording baseline information, the response to interventions, and any changes in mobility patterns. Baseline information should document resources and limitations for each potential deterioration or change. Documentation for each system includes the following:

- For musculoskeletal: muscle strength, size, tone, and endurance; joint mobility, including both range of motion of joints and functional assessment of ability; use and abuse of assistive devices; problems of mobility; and presence of pain
- For cardiovascular: orthostatic changes in blood pressure and pulse
- For respiratory: lung assessment
- For integumentary: characteristics of the skin over bony prominences
- For urinary: frequency and amount of urination
- For gastrointestinal: character and pattern of stools and usual aids to facilitate elimination

TABLE 20–8   CARE PLAN FOR OLDER ADULTS WITH IMMOBILITY PROBLEMS AND ACTIVITY INTOLERANCE

Nursing Diagnosis: Impaired physical mobility related to activity intolerance; high risk for disuse syndrome	
Expected Outcome	*Nursing Interventions*
The client maintains strength and endurance of musculoskeletal system and flexibility of joints.	Observe for signs and symptoms of decreased muscle strength, decreased joint mobility, and loss of endurance.
	Observe patient's respiratory status and cardiac function.
	Observe environment for potential safety hazards.
	Encourage isometric muscle contraction (quadriceps, abdominal, and gluteal muscles).
	Encourage isotonic muscle contraction (flexor and extensor muscle groups).
	Provide range-of-motion exercise (active or passive).
	Provide a diet with adequate protein, calories, and calcium.
	Maintain proper body alignment.
	Encourage activities of daily living.
	Encourage adequate rest periods.
	Use supportive devices (e.g., walker, cane).
	Refer client to physical therapy, if medically indicated.
	Encourage attitude restructuring (benchmarking).
	Alter environment to decrease safety hazards.
	Teach importance and purpose of exercise.
	Teach appropriate use of assistive devices.
	Teach the signs and symptoms of overexertion.

Ongoing documentation should include type, tolerance, and effect of intervention. For example, for moving from supine to dangling the legs over the side of the bed, documentation should include whether movement was active or passive, baseline and upright heart rate and blood pressure, statements of tolerance, and length of activity. Changes in mobility pattern and activity tolerance should be documented and observed over time.

3 Tertiary Prevention

Rehabilitative efforts to maximize mobility for older adults involve a multidisciplinary effort composed of nurses, a physician, physical and occupational therapists, a nutritionist, a social director, and family and friends. For a thorough discussion of this topic, see Chapter 9.

Student Learning Activities

1 Visit a senior aerobics class at an area retirement center, YMCA/YWCA, or Senior Center. Observe for the types of activities that are included. How does this class differ from aerobics classes for younger adults?

2 As a class, identify the major components of an exercise or activity program for older adults with degenerative joint disease. How can these people maintain mobility?

3 In your clinical setting, observe for the amount and kinds of activities that are encouraged for older adults. Is the emphasis on prevention of the hazards of immobility appropriate? What recommendations could you make based on your assessment?

REFERENCES

1 Carroll-Johnson, RM (ed): Classification of Nursing Diagnoses: Proceedings of the Eighth Conference. JB Lippincott, Philadelphia, 1989.

2 Esposito, MC, et al: Nursing diagnosis: Potential for disuse syndrome. In Carroll-Johnson, RM (ed): Classification of Nursing Diagnoses: Proceedings of the Eighth Conference. JB Lippincott, Philadelphia, 1989, p 464.

3 Hardy, MA, et al: The prevalence of nursing diagnosis among elderly and long-term residents: A descriptive comparison. Recent Adv Nurs Sci 21:144, 1988.

4 Brody, EM, and Kleban, MH: Day-to-day mental and physical health symptoms of older people: A report on health logs. Gerontologist 23:75, 1983.

5 Woolf, SH, et al: The periodic health examinations of older adults: The recommendations of the US preventive services task force. J Am Geriatr Soc 38:817, 1990.

6 Smith, E, and Gilligan, C: Physical activity prescription for the older adult. Physician Sports Med 11:91, 1983.

7 Milde, FK: Physiological immobilization. In Hart, LK, et al (eds): Concepts Common to Acute Illness. CV Mosby, St Louis, 1981, p 67.

8 MacDonald, M, and Butler, A: Reversal of helplessness: Producing walking behavior in nursing home wheelchair residents using behavior modification procedures. J Gerontol 29:97, 1974.

9 Miller, A: A study of the dependency of elderly patients in wards using different methods of nursing care. Age Ageing 14:132, 1985.

10 Bosco, C, and Komi, PV: Influence of aging on the mechanical behavior of leg extensor muscles. Eur J Appl Physiol 45:209, 1980.

11 Lexell, J, et al: What is the cause of the aging atrophy? J Neurol Sci 84:275, 1988.

12 Young, A: Exercise physiology in geriatric practice. Acta Med Scand (suppl)711:227, 1986.

13 Bortz, WM: Disuse and aging. JAMA 248:1203, 1982.

14 Harper, CM, and Lyles, YM: Physiology and complications of bed rest. J Am Geriatr Soc 36:1047, 1988.

15 Barry, HC, and Eathrone SW: Exercise and aging: Issues for the practitioner. Med Clin North Am 78:356, 1994.

16 Paffenbarger, RS, et al: The association of changes in physical activity level and other lifestyle characteristics with mortality among men. N Engl J Med 328:538, 1993.

17 Healthy People: National Health Promotion and Disease Prevention Objectives. US DHHS Publication 91-505212, 1990.

18 La Porte, RE: The health benefits of exercise. Physician Sports Med 15:115, 1987.

19 Hopkins, DR, et al: Effect of low impact aerobic dance on the functional fitness of elderly women. J Gerontol Soc Am 30:189, 1990.

20 de Coverly Veale, DMW: Exercise and mental health. Acta Psychiatr Scand 76:113, 1987.

21 Rogers, RL, et al: After reaching retirement age physical activity sustains cerebral perfusion and cognition. J Am Geriatr Soc 38:123, 1990.

22 Elward, K, and Larson, EB: Benefits of exercise for older adults. Clin Geriatr Med 8:35, 1992.

23 Teague, ML, and Hinnicutt, BK: An analysis of the 1990 public health service physical fitness and exercise objectives for older Americans. Health Values 13:15, 1990.

24 Evans, WJ: Effects of exercise on body composition and functional capacity of the elderly. J Gerontol 50A:147, 1995.

25 Tinitti, ME, and Ginter, SF: Identifying mobility dysfunctions in elderly patients. JAMA 259:1190, 1988.

26 Tinitti, ME: Performance-oriented assessment of mobility problems in elderly patients. J Am Geriatr Soc 34:119, 1986.

27 Frantz, RA: Impaired skin integrity: Decubitus ulcer. In Maas, M, et al (eds): Nursing Diagnoses and Interventions for the Elderly. Addison-Wesley Nursing, New York, 1991.

28 Caldwell, JD: Exercise in the elderly: An overview. Activities, Adaptation and Aging 20:3, 1996.

29 Daeve, D, and Moore-Orr, R: Low intensity, range-of-motion exercise: Invaluable nursing care for elderly patients. J Advocate Nurs 21:675, 1995.

30 Kottke, FJ: Therapeutic exercise to maintain mobility. In Kottke, FJ, et al (eds): Krusen's Handbook of Physical Medicine and Rehabilitation, ed 4. WB Saunders, Philadelphia, 1990, p 389.

CHAPTER 21

Assessment and Prevention of Falls

Joanne M. Miller

OBJECTIVES

Upon completion of this chapter, the reader will be able to:

- Identify why it is important to prevent falls
- Perform an assessment for gait and balance
- List 10 factors that increase the risk of falling in older adults
- Identify what needs to be assessed in developing a fall prevention program
- List at least six interventions to prevent falls
- Recognize the necessity of fitting interventions to need and maintaining a safe but satisfying quality of life
- Identify essential elements of patient and family teaching

Falling used to be considered a natural consequence of growing old. We now understand that falls are not part of the normal aging process, but annually about 30 percent of older adults in the community fall. The annual fall incidence among older adults in the community increases from 25 percent at 70 years of age to 35 percent after age 75.[1] Institutionalized older adults fall more often than older adults in the community because they are typically more frail and have more disabilities. Annually, about 50 percent of institutionalized older adults fall and many of these people fall several times.[1]

These percentages are probably an underestimation of the problem because the statistics are based on reported falls. Falls in the community may go unnoticed or may be forgotten. Institutional policies and norms vary as to what type of fall is reported and even whether a fall is reported. Institutions may report a fall only if there was a risk of injury or liability.

Older adults have a very realistic fear of falling. Only about 5 to 6 percent of falls result in a serious injury,[1] but the consequences of a fall may be more than just a serious injury. Falls can also be embarrassing and painful and can lead to a restriction of activities and independence or to a loss of confidence. Older adults who have fallen and need to be treated in a hospital have a 17

to 50 percent chance of dying within the following year.[2,3] These deaths do not result directly from the fall itself but rather from fall-related consequences such as immobility, infections, or embolism.

Internationally, sustaining a fall without a fracture is the most common cause of an older person being admitted to a geriatric hospital, nursing home, or retirement home.[4] Even if no serious injury results from the fall, families, caregivers, and staff members may feel guilty that they did not prevent the fall and further restrict the person's activities and independence. Once activity, mobility, and independence are restricted, a downward trajectory is begun. These consequences and the risk of another fall must be weighed against maintaining normal functioning.

An international work group[4] has defined falls as "an event which leads to the conscious subject coming to rest inadvertently on the ground" and excludes falls from violent blows, loss of consciousness, seizures, or the sudden onset of paralysis. These latter falls are from specific causes that differ in type and consequence from those of a conscious fall. This definition still covers a wide range of possible causes for a fall. The causes and interventions to prevent falls vary greatly depending on a person's age, level of mobility, physical health, and cognitive ability.

Clinical Manifestations

Falls can result in many types of physical and psychological injuries and damage. The most feared consequence of a fall is a broken hip. Other common types of fractures from a fall are wrist, upper arm, and pelvis. Osteoporosis, which is more common in women, may be an important factor contributing to the higher incidence of fractures among women under 75 years of age.[5]

Other consequences of falling include soft-tissue damage and the results of a long lie, which is lying on the ground for at least 5 minutes after a fall. The inability to get up without help after falling, even with no injury, occurs in up to 50 percent of falls in the community.[3,6] A long lie is a marker for weakness, illness, and social isolation. Both hip fractures and a long lie are associated with a high mortality rate. The fear of a fall and not being found or able to call for help are two reasons older adults may be institutionalized. These factors also provide a market for electronic devices designed to assist in calling for help.

The psychosocial manifestations of a fall can have as much impact on an older adult as a physical injury, if not more. Even if a physical injury did not occur, the shock of the fall and the fear of falling again can have many consequences, including anxiety, loss of confidence, social withdrawal, restrictions in daily activities, postfall syndrome ("clutch and grab"), "fallaphobia," loss of independence and control, depression, feelings of vulnerability and fragility, and concerns regarding death and dying, becoming a burden to family and friends, or requiring institutionalization.[4,7,8]

The psychosocial consequences of a fall can range from minor to severe. A healthy balance should be maintained between realistic limitations and disproportional restrictions. A study of older adults in the community[9] reported that 48 percent of the participants were afraid of falling. Twenty-six percent had curtailed activities such as shopping and housecleaning because of this fear. The fear of falling can affect even those who have not fallen. Anxiety, loss of confidence, social withdrawal, and restriction of activities that are related to falling can occur because a person is afraid he or she will fall.

It is important to distinguish between a fear of falling and a concern about falling. Some modifications in activities are adaptive and appropriate to age-related physical changes. A concern about falling may signal to an older person the need to adapt to a loss of ability, to make corrections in the environment, or to follow up on a physical problem.

The other consequences of falling (i.e., loss of independence and control, sense of loss, feelings of fragility, concerns regarding death, and fear of becoming a burden to family and friends) are issues related to aging. Falling and the fear of falling may intensify these issues and force an older adult and his or her family to deal with them. Institutionalization is often considered after a fall. A fall can trigger a whole set of forces that will affect the older adult's quality of life. This intervention should be in proportion to the older adult's real need and ability and should not be a response to the older adult's fear or fears of family and caregivers.

Management

Falling is not a random event but rather one that is influenced by other factors.[6] This is an important point because if falls were random events, they would be very difficult to predict and prevent. Because people usually fall wherever they spend the most time, environmental (external) factors must be considered. Falls may also be caused by intrinsic (internal) factors. Internal factors are variables that determine why one person might fall at a particular time and another person in similar circumstances might not fall. Both types of factors must be considered in preventing a fall.

1 Primary Prevention

The goal of primary prevention is to minimize the risk of falling among older adults and, it is hoped, to prevent a fall. Interventions for primary prevention include a thorough physical and psychosocial assessment, review of the use of drugs, an environmental assessment (Table 21–1), and correction or management of any potential problems.

Physical Assessment and Interventions

Regular thorough physical examinations can identify potential problems and changes that may affect an older person's risk of falling. Vision, proprioception, and vestibular function interact with adequate central processing and appropriate muscle, joint, and reflex responses to maintain postural control and efficient gait. Age-related changes occur in all these systems and result in an increased risk of falling for all older adults. The physical examination should target sensory changes, as well as the cardiovascular, musculoskeletal, neurological, and urological systems. Other areas to be examined are feet and nutritional status (see Table 21–1). Early correction of, or assistance in adapting to, age-related changes and abnormalities could prevent a fall.

Sensory

The use of proper eyeglasses when needed and the appropriate treatment of cataracts, glaucoma, or macular degeneration help prevent falls. Hearing aids and periodic removal of impacted cerumen improve hearing acuity and therefore the ability to use auditory cues.

Cardiovascular and Blood Pressure

Proper treatment of cardiac dysrhythmias and regulation of blood pressure and orthostatic changes decrease the older adult's risk of falling. Orthostatic changes in some people do not cause any symptoms. Therefore, a drop of 20 mm Hg or more should warrant

TABLE 21–1 ASSESSMENT FOR FALL RISK

Physical	*Sensory changes:* Glasses, hearing, proprioception, visual contrast sensitivity
	Cardiovascular: Dysrhythmias, orthostatic blood pressure, dizziness
	Musculoskeletal: Mobility, strength, gait and balance (getting up from a chair, turning while walking, step height, sitting down) (see Table 21–2), ankle dorsiflexion strength, cerebrovascular disease
	Neurological: Tremors, gait and balance, reaction time
	Urological: Incontinence, urgency, micturition hypotension, diuretic use
	Nutrition: Anemia, fluid or electrolyte imbalance, malnutrition
	Acute illness: Infection, mental status changes
Psychosocial	*Emotional health:* Stress
	Behavior and cognitive ability: Confusion, depression, anxiety, dependency, agitation, denial, fear of falling, concern about falling
	Living situation
	Caregivers
	Pattern of activity: How far from home does the person venture and how often?
	Type of activity
Drug use and effects	*Number of drugs* (include over-the-counter)
	Alcohol use
	Interactions and side effects: orthostatic hypotension, dizziness, change in mental status
Environmental	*Inspection or discussion of home hazards* inside and outside the home and wherever the person spends a significant amount of time (stairs, handrails, bathroom, rugs, cabinets, clutter)
Fall history (secondary prevention)	*Events leading up to a fall:* What was the person doing? Any warning? Where? How? When?
	What happened after the fall?
	Has the person fallen before (including falls without injuries)?

an investigation into the cause (e.g., hypovolemia, neurological disease, reaction to medications, or postprandial reductions).[8]

Musculoskeletal, Neurological, and Gait and Balance

Exercise programs improve muscle tone, strength, endurance, flexibility, general fitness, confidence, and general social well-being. Small improvements in balance may prove effective in reducing falls.[4,10] See Chapter 20 for a thorough discussion of this topic.

A person's gait and balance provide valuable information for preventing future falls. Impaired gait or balance has been implicated as a significant fall risk factor in almost every recent study.[4,6,11] A simple assessment of routine daily mobility maneuvers can provide better clinical information about a fall risk than a standard neuromuscular examination.[12] The ability to walk or move about safely involves both gait and balance. The assessment focuses on four activities: getting up from a chair, turning while walking, raising the foot completely off the floor (step height), and sitting down (Table 21–2). This assessment includes many higher-level functions such as vision, muscle strength, position sense, reflexes, hip and knee flexion, coordination, and integration of input from various sources into the complicated actions of changing positions and walking. A person need only have difficulty with one of the maneuvers to be at risk of falling. The more difficulties a person has, the greater his or her risk. The advantage of clinically assessing gait and balance is that it does not focus on finding a specific diagnosis or cause because falls result from many interrelated factors, both intrinsic and extrinsic.

The use of assistive devices for stabilization requires another caution. If necessary, these devices should be sized correctly and the person instructed in their proper use. Assistive devices do not correct for poor sensory input and can even cause a fall themselves or can hamper the person's attempt to restore his or her balance.[4]

Urological

Urological problems and incontinence are not normal aging changes and should be investigated seriously. Toileting schedules, incontinence pads, pelvic floor exercises, and fluid management are possible interventions. The need for elimination has been identified in some studies[13,14] as being related to falls. The person experiences a sense of urgency to use the bathroom and rushes to avoid an accident. Rushing and possibly slipping in urine can result in a fall. The use of diuretics and laxatives, combined with impaired mobility, make for a dangerous situation. See Chapter 17 for a thorough discussion of incontinence.

Foot Disorders

Good podiatric care and use of proper footwear can help the older adult avoid falls. Treating any foot deformities (e.g., painful bunions), keeping nails cut, and shaving calluses will help. Shoes should fit properly and be low-heeled, with nonskid soles. Walking in stocking feet should be avoided. However, for those who have worn high-heeled shoes all their life, switching to one with a low heel may cause instability rather than reduce it. Thus, even this intervention must be individually evaluated for appropriateness and effectiveness.

TABLE 21–2 POSITION CHANGES, BALANCE MANEUVERS, AND GAIT COMPONENTS INCLUDED IN FUNCTIONAL MOBILITY ASSESSMENT

Mobility Maneuvers	Conditions Defining Maneuvers: Done with Difficulty
Position Change or Balance Maneuver	
Getting up from chair*†	Does not get up with single movement, but pushes up with arms or moves forward in chair first, is unsteady on first standing
Sitting down in chair*†	Plops in chair, does not land in center
Withstanding nudge on sternum (examiner pushes lightly on sternum three times)	Moves feet, grabs object for support, feet not touching side by side
Eyes closed	Same as above (tests patient's reliance on visual input for balance)
Neck turning	Moves feet; grabs object for support; feet not touching side by side; complains of vertigo, dizziness, or unsteadiness
Reaching up	Unable to reach up to full shoulder flexion while standing on tiptoes, unsteady, grabs object for support
Bending over	Unable to bend over to pick up small object (e.g., pen) from floor, grabs object to pull up on, requires multiple attempts to arise
Gait Component or Maneuver‡	
Invitation	Hesitates, stumbles, grabs object for support
Step height (raising feet while stepping)‡§	Does not clear floor consistently (scrapes or shuffles), raises foot too high (>2 in)
Step continuity§	After first few steps, does not consistently begin raising one foot as other foot touches floor
Step symmetry§	Unequal step length (pathological side usually has longer step length; problem may be in hip, knee, ankle, or surrounding muscles)
Path deviation¶	Does not walk in straight line, weaves from side to side
Turning†	Stops before initiating turn, staggers; sways; grabs object for support

From Tinetti, ME, and Ginter, SF,[12] p 1191, with permission, copyright 1988, American Medical Association.

*Hard, armless chair.

†Included in analysis.

‡Patient walks down hallway at usual pace and comes back, using usual walking aid. Examiner observes single component of gait at a time (analogous to heart examination).

§Best observed from side of patient.

¶Best observed from behind patient.

Nutrition

Proper nutrition and fluids also improve the older person's chances of avoiding a fall. Dehydration and electrolyte imbalances often can increase the risk of falling.

Psychosocial Assessment and Interventions

Good emotional health and the management of stress and tension may help the older adult maintain awareness of possible risks and dangerous situations. These psychosocial aspects enable older adults to make appropriate lifestyle changes. Isaacs[15] noted that there is a time in life between 60 and 75 years of age when falls result from imprudence. Older adults need to recognize the change in their abilities and endurance as they age; they can prevent falls by either slowing down or limiting what they do in accordance with their abilities. The person's living situation, social network, and pattern of activity also should be assessed.

Behavior and cognitive ability affect a person's risk of falling and the probable cause of a fall. For an alert and functional older adult, environmental or external factors play more of a role in a fall. Mental and emotional status affect awareness, judgment, gait, balance, the processing of information needed for safe transfers or mobilization, agitation, and the motivation to be active. Confusion and impaired cognitive ability have been cited in many studies[4,6,12,16] as contributing to the risk to fall.

Drug Use and Effects and Interventions

Medications have been well-documented as contributing to falls.[4,8] Many older adults take several medications on a regular basis. A clear association among specific medications, alcohol use, and falls has not been established.[4,17] Medications have been studied extensively, but no one medication has consistently been implicated in falls. Because of the changes in the older person's metabolism, excretions, and absorption, a safe medication for a 50-year-old person may be toxic for a 75-year-old person. Medications may be a marker for or may represent the illness they are being used for rather than contributing to falls themselves. The more medications a person uses, the greater are his or her chances of experiencing drug interactions, drug side effects, and a fall.[4,6] The number of drugs being used (usually three or more) is itself a fall risk factor.[11]

Several types of medication (e.g., those that reduce mental alertness, affect balance, lower blood pressure, and increase frequency of urination) seem to increase the risk of falling.[8] Many types of drugs may affect blood pressure or may cause dizziness. Antihypertensives, vasodilators, diuretics, antipsychotics, antidepressants or tricyclics, some β-blockers, sedatives and hypnotics, and hypoglycemics may lower blood pressure. Older adults may take many of these drugs at the same time. Orthostatic blood pressure measurements should be included in all assessments on admission to a facility. Blood pressure must be rechecked periodically because the older adult's blood pressure can vary with factors such as adding or deleting medications, a change in physical condition, or prolonged immobility (even a few hours). Providing the person with understandable information about his or her medications, side effects, and interactions will prevent complications that may lead to a fall. These people should have a physician periodically review all of the prescription and over-the-counter drugs they use to avoid overmedication and drug interactions.

A change in mental status is another drug side effect capable of increasing the risk of falling. Narcotics, hypnotics, antidepressants, sedatives, antipsychotics, and alcohol alter a person's ability to mobilize safely and their judgment. The assessment of an older adult's use of alcohol can signal an area of concern. The exact influence of alcohol on the risk of falling is unknown, but alcohol does impair judgment and coordination.

Environmental Assessment and Interventions

External or environmental factors almost always contribute to some degree to a fall. Reducing home hazards is an important primary prevention measure. Both the outside and the inside of a home should be assessed for safety (Table 21–3). Many safety-promoting suggestions are simply common sense. In the home, stairs are probably the most serious area of risk. The bathroom is

TABLE 21–3 ENVIRONMENTAL SAFETY

Area	Assess For
Outside the home	Level, unbroken sidewalks
	Handrails (both sides if possible)
	Lighting
	Objects to trip over
	Slippery surfaces (wet leaves, water, ice)
Inside the home	Stairs (bottom stair marked, in good repair)
	Handrails
	Adequate, nonglare lighting
	Floors free of spills and dust
	Nonskid rugs (rugs tacked down)
	Cords covered or out of way
	Traffic areas free of clutter
Bathroom	Grab bars for tub and toilet
	Raised toilet seat
	Shower chair
	Nonskid mats or decals in tub
Kitchen	Sturdy stepstool
	Objects arranged to minimize reaching and bending
Furniture and bed	At proper height to aid transfers
	Not easily movable

TABLE 21–4 TEACHING GUIDE: TEACHING OLDER ADULTS ABOUT FALL PREVENTION

- Discuss the concept that the risk of falling can be minimized and that falling is not a normal part of aging.
- Teach the client that falls can be an early sign of an illness that may require treatment.
- Review the list of possible home hazards and explain the need to correct any existing hazards.
- Discuss the need to stay as active as possible, both before and after a fall.
- Instruct the client in proper exercises and activities for his or her level of ability.
- Instruct the client to report any changes in his or her balance, gait, or muscle strength to the clinician for follow-up.
- Explain the need for regular blood pressure testing, physical examinations, and proper diet.
- Instruct the client in the proper use and fitting of assistive devices and equipment (walkers, wheelchairs, and canes).
- Instruct the client to minimize sudden movements, rushing, or quickly changing positions.
- Inform the client of the need to be seated while eating, drinking, or taking medication.
- Explain the need for sensible, nonskid footwear.
- Educate the client on the need for regular foot care.
- Discuss the client's fear of falling and the impact this fear can have on his or her quality of life.
- Explain that the fear of falling is a realistic and common fear.
- Discuss the possible responses to a fall emergency, including how to get up from a fall.
- Reinforce the value of social activities and involvement with others.
- Discuss the need to be alert for sensory changes and to correct them as soon as possible.
- Reinforce the need to use prescribed eyeglasses and hearing aids.
- Demonstrate the proper method of lifting or transferring people or heavy objects.
- Review the proper method of calling for assistance.

another site of frequent falls. Clients can be taught the proper way to bend and reach for objects. Furniture and beds should be at the proper heights to aid transfers. (See Table 21–4.)

Older adults may require extra time and care when in a new situation or environment. The older person knows his or her own home the best, and unfamiliar surroundings can be hazardous. Extra precautions are needed when older adults visit friends' and children's homes, when hospitalized, or when in any less familiar environment. With careful assessment, minor modifications, and forethought, some falls can be prevented.

2 Secondary Prevention

The goal of secondary prevention is to prevent the older adult from having another fall. Everyone falls sometimes, but a fall may not be considered significant to an older adult unless it results in an injury. Defining a fall in these terms influences the falls a person reports and how the person perceives his or her fall risk.

Assessment

Assessment is the foundation for the development of nursing diagnosis and interventions. Fall assessment includes gathering and organizing information about the fall, the person, and the environment (see Table 21–1).

Fall History

A prior fall is usually a reliable predictor of another fall, so it is important to collect a detailed history of any previous falls. The nurse must ask the person directly about any previous falls and ask specifically about falls that did not result in an injury. People do not generally offer this information unless they are asked. The more recent the fall, the more significant the information.

Data about events leading up to the fall, what happened afterward, and any previous falls are needed (see Table 21–1). The activity a person was engaged in can suggest appropriate interventions. For example, a fall caused by tripping over a loose rug would be managed differently from a fall occurring while getting up from a chair.

Falling can be a signal or symptom of psychological distress as well as physical distress. Depression can limit socialization and mobility and impair judgment. Catchen[16] noticed that people who fell more than once were unable to accept their physical or mental impairment. They were described as strong-willed or determined people. Anxiety, fear of falling, and agitation influence judgment.[6,8,13]

Interventions

The objective for all nursing interventions related to falls is to minimize the risk of falling and to prevent another fall. Prevention of all falls would involve an unrealistic amount of nursing time and impose severe restrictions on the older adult's activities. The key to fall prevention is to be knowledgeable about the possible causes for falls, the person, the environment, and the person's fall history. The first step in nursing intervention is a complete assessment (see Table 21–1). Direct observation of the person's ability to change positions and walk is essential (see Table 21–2). This assessment can help identify people at risk as well as situations in which falls are most likely to occur. By combining the data gathered from each area, the nurse can target potential problems or risk factors for intervention.

Once the information is collected, the nurse must decide how much the person is still at risk. No single fall prevention plan will fit everyone. Interventions should aim at maintaining physical and psychosocial health, educating older adults about home safety, and keeping activities appropriate to their ability. The discovery and correction of possible fall risks is the best intervention.

Correctable Causes

People do not usually seek help for a problem until they see a need; the first fall may be the event that triggers action. By referring older adults to a physician or other specialist to correct possible disease- or medication-related causes of falls, nurses can reduce their risk of falling. A referral for proper eyeglasses, podiatry treatment, review of medications, and treatment of anemia, depression, or any other fall-related disorder will help.

Even though the nurse refers a client for correction of a problem, unless the client sees the problem as a threat to his or her immediate safety, he or she may not comply. The client also needs the resources to comply. For example, if a home assessment is done and it is determined that handrails are needed in the bathroom, the client may be unable to afford them or to install them or may not even agree with the need to change. The nurse needs to consider all of these factors when making suggestions.

Education

Older adults need to know about all appropriate interventions. Nursing interventions can target physical activity, knowledge deficits, and nonadherence. Encouraging and assisting older adults to be as active as possible is important, especially if they have fallen. This will help them regain confidence. Older adults need to know about medication side effects, how to take their own blood pressure or to have it taken regularly, and home safety. The National Safety Council, American Association of Retired Persons, and the Department of Aging offer programs and literature on home safety and fall prevention. Some Senior Centers have their own programs or literature.

Nurses can teach about fall risks and fall prevention to individuals, groups of older adults, or families. Caregivers and the older adults can be involved in learning safe techniques for transferring, reaching, timing activities, and medication taking. Older adults should be instructed to take time to regain their balance when changing positions. Learning to bend and reach properly and avoiding rushed or sudden movements can help. The nurse may suggest that the person tell friends to let the telephone ring 10 times or more to allow them time to get to the telephone without rushing.

The older adult can be taught to get up after a fall or to crawl to the telephone to get help. Squires and Bayliss[18] report that some older adults have forgotten how to get up after a fall. They suggest several methods of getting up. One method is to roll onto the stomach, get up on all fours, and crawl to a nearby piece of furniture. Another method is to shuffle on the bottom or side to a telephone or piece of furniture. The client can also scoot up the lower stairs until able to stand. If an injury makes it impossible to get up, the person should be instructed to use anything available to keep warm, such as a coat, rug, or blanket. It is helpful to discuss an emergency plan with the older person and his or her caregivers that determines who and when to call for help.

These interventions do not guarantee a person will not fall. Discussing the possibility of a fall with the client can help reduce some fears and anxiety about falling. Helping the person prepare for a fall can renew some lost confidence. Devising a system for calling for help or using a security alarm system can prevent a long lie and the feeling of helplessness. Putting a loud bell under a chair or the telephone on a low stool, with emergency numbers handy, are simple safeguards.[4] Services are available that call a person daily on the telephone for extra reassurance.

High-Risk Times

Older adults and their caregivers should be made aware of high-risk times for falling: during an acute illness, when in a new environment, while wearing new eyeglasses, during any change in medication, at times of stress or anxiety, and right after a previous fall. The older adult can be sensitized to watch for small changes that can result in a fall. Complaints of dizziness, leg weakness, or "not feeling right" should be taken seriously. As mentioned earlier, any fall, even with no associated injuries, can be a sign of an underlying illness.

Acute illnesses may precipitate a fall. In the older adults, a change in mental status may be the first noticeable sign of a developing problem (e.g., infection, hypoxia, fluid or electrolyte imbalance). This change in mental status may be manifested as a fall. When an older adult falls, this is a well-recognized nonspecific indicator for many illnesses.[17] A clustering of falls may occur also before death.[19] The more frail an older person is, the greater is his or her risk of falling.

Fall Prevention in Acute-Care and Long-Term Care Settings

In institutions, falls among older adults are a serious problem. In the institutional setting, nurses have more control over and responsibility for the environment, and the nursing staff is held more liable for providing a safe environment. An older adult's first fall is usually unexpected and therefore the most unpredictable.

Because a previous fall is one of the best predictors of a fall, a crucial nursing intervention is to ask about prior falls on admission and to learn the circumstances of the fall. This information can then be used along with the assessment of the person to identify the degree of risk and what specific interventions are needed to prevent a fall.

Fall prevention is a 24-hour responsibility. In developing a care plan, intervention must be tailored to the person's needs. In addition, these needs can vary on different shifts. A person with Alzheimer's disease, a mild balance problem, and some urinary urgency may be a serious fall risk at night or in the late evening, when he or she is more confused. During the day the person may be able to be up independently. This middle ground of moderate fall risk and its set of interventions is called modified fall prevention.[13] Older adults with moderate fall risk are usually cooperative but may have periods of increased risk after a procedure, during an acute illness, when toileting at night if sedated, or in the early morning because of muscle rigidity. At these times of higher fall risk, nursing supervision or assistance should be provided for toileting, activities of daily living, or other needs. Once the higher risk period is over, the person should be considered independent again. Nurses must evaluate the specific interventions for need and effectiveness. It is important that the specific interventions be written on a care plan and relayed through reports.

Identifying older adults who are likely to fall has been the subject of several articles.[13,20,21] Whether by orange dots, labels, or a special set of letters, people at a moderate or serious risk of falling must be identified (see "Research Brief"). This identification needs to be communicated to any personnel who might come in contact with the at-risk person.

Fall prevention cannot be one nurse's responsibility; rather, it should be a way of thinking and a priority for everyone working with the older adults. The major problem with any identification system is that it can be overused: If too many older adults are identified as fallers, the labels will lose their impact. A unit that used dots found that almost everyone ended up with one and the system failed because the dots lost their intended meaning. Any system must include clear boundaries and periodic evaluation.

Some specific interventions help decrease the risk of falling. It is helpful to assist the older adult in toileting and to anticipate their other needs in the early morning as well as before and after meals, staff breaks, meetings, or any other time the nurse will be away from the client for long. The nurse should communicate explicitly to those caring for the person exactly what he or she needs to ensure safety. The older adult should be made aware of their risk of falling. The nurse should involve the person in planning interventions as much as possible.

The environment must be checked constantly for safety. Handrails in the halls, bathrooms, and rooms help. Keeping clutter and movable furniture out of the way prevents some falls. The older adult should be discouraged from using rolling tables and intravenous infusion setup poles as supports. Wheelchairs and beds should be locked in place. The use of nonskid slippers and properly fitting shoes is a simple but effective measure. Keeping the call signal, telephone, water, and urinal or bedpan within easy reach will avoid falls from over-reaching. Leaving a dim light on at night may enable the person to find the bathroom safely. Furniture should be impossible to tip over and at the proper

RESEARCH BRIEF

Hendrick, A, et al: Hospital falls: Development of a predictive model for clinical practice. **Appl Nurs Res** 8(3):129, 1995.

The purpose of the study was to develop a practical risk model using logistic regression that would identify various levels of risk for falling in acute-care patients. Seven risk factors were identified: recent history of falls, depression, altered elimination patterns, dizziness, primary diagnosis of cancer, confusion, and altered mobility.

height for easy standing and sitting. Spills or liquids should be wiped up quickly. Carpets, lights, beds, and any other equipment should be repaired as soon as possible when damaged.

Restraints

The use of restraints raises ethical and legal issues. It cannot be assumed that restraint vests, sheets, belts, side rails, gerichairs, or other devices will prevent falls. They have even been known to increase the incidence of falls or the chance of injury from a fall.[16,22] Someone climbing over a side rail to get to the bathroom is more likely to get tangled in the rails and fall, fall over the rails, or slip in urine because of the delay in reaching the bathroom. The use of half-rails and bedside commodes may help more than restraints and full side rails. However, there is still no substitute for direct supervision of the client and prompt answering of call signals. The older adult's fear of wetting the bed has led to many falls. Listening for side rails rattling or beds squeaking can alert a night nurse to check on a person.

Restraints can also contribute to falls by decreasing muscle strength from prolonged sitting or lying or by increasing agitation. Restraints can be used only when they are part of the medical treatment, other interventions have been tried and other disciplines consulted, and there is proper documentation. The older adult can see restraints as punishment or may experience anger and depression over being "tied down." This can have a major impact on a person's psychological well-being.

All institutions have policies on the use and proper application of restraints. Even with policies, nursing judgment is the factor that determines when a restraint is used.[23] Creative measures to free older adults from restraints can be successful.[24] Changing the time of giving laxatives or diuretics and the use of special chairs, frequent walking or toileting, diversional activities, commodes, half-rails, bed alarms, or other ideas can be tried. By understanding and addressing the cause of the person's behavior, physical restraints can often be avoided and used only when appropriate, thereby limiting the risk for a fall.

Serious Fall Risk

The older adult who is a serious risk of falling can be a special challenge to nursing. These people are often confused, are impulsive, or have poor judgment. They may have unreliable or unpredictable behavior and have gait or balance difficulties. The intensity or time needed to supervise and assist the person at serious fall risk is much greater than that needed when precautions are considered "modified." Hernandez and Miller[13] have labeled this set of precautions "strict." Unlike the moderate-risk faller, the serious-risk faller cannot reliably follow instructions or restrictions. This difficulty can come from memory or cognitive impairment, difficulty accepting the need for activity restrictions, depression, or other factors.

The unpredictable behavior necessitates a different set of interventions. Older adults at serious fall risk need to be supervised constantly on an individual basis when walking or transferring. They must never be left alone in the bathroom. Supervision at the level needed for strict precaution is draining and almost impossible for one nurse to do if he or she has to care for other people. Monitoring people this closely becomes a unit responsibility: Everyone in the unit must know who is at serious risk of falling and what care they need. Grouping several people together for a limited time will allow the assigned nurse time to attend to his or her other patients. People at a high risk of falling also can be located closer to the nurse's station or in any area that allows close ob-

TABLE 21–5   CARE PLANS

Nursing Diagnosis: Potential for injury: fall related to (specify risk)	
Expected Outcome	*Nursing Actions (Moderate Risk)*
The person will be free from injury.	Assess fall history, intrinsic factors, and environmental factors.
	Assess medication effects and side effects.
	Anticipate need for increased supervision at high-risk times.
	Provide a safe environment.
	Consult physical therapist for gait training, transfer techniques, and activity program.
	Teach client and family the need for proper foot care and shoes, personal fall risks, ways to respond in the event of a fall.
	Nursing Actions (Serious Risk)
	Locate client near supervision.
	Supervise all activity.
	Provide for regular activity.
	Assess for cause of agitation or restlessness, and correct.
	Encourage family, volunteer, or other caregiver to participate in supervision.
	Use mechanical bed alarms or other warning systems.

servation. Family members or sitters can be used to watch a person if a nurse is not available for close supervision.

Care Plans

Care plans for fall prevention should be individualized to provide the most safety with the fewest restrictions. The nursing actions are appropriate for older adults living both in the community and in institutions. Nursing actions for the person in the community at a serious risk of falling would have to be implemented by a family member with some type of assistance. This level of care can be difficult and draining on the primary caregiver (Table 21–5). See also Chapter 5, "Legal Issues."

3 *Tertiary Prevention*

Tertiary prevention is important in restoring older adults to their optimum level of functioning after a fall. This level of prevention addresses older adults who have become seriously injured by a fall, have become seriously psychologically impaired by a fear of falling, or are subject to repeated falls.

For older adults seriously injured by a fall, the need is to try to recover mobility as quickly as possible. Good nursing and medical care (Table 21–6), appropriate stimulation, and a focus on speeding the recovery will improve the chance of regaining some measure of previous functioning.

The psychological impairment from a fall or even from the fear of a fall can lead the older adult on a downward trajectory and can severely limit mobility. If psychiatric care can be started, this process may be reversed or at least minimized. Having patience, going slowly, and taking things in small, concrete steps may help some older adults regain their confidence and mobility.

For the older adult who experiences repeated or recurrent falls, restrictions on activities and an aggressive investigation into the cause of the falls may be needed. Institutionalization is one possible solution. Older adults with multiple chronic problems are at risk of falling, but addressing and controlling the chronic problems will reduce that risk (Table 21–7). Chronic problems can be improved only to a point, after which measures must be taken to keep the person safe while still maximizing his or her mobility.

Older adults who have recurrent falls can also be cognitively impaired, uncooperative, or unable to accept or adapt to their need for increased assistance. Older adults who want to be independent but cannot safely do so commonly have repeat falls.[6,11] Keeping activity restrictions to a minimum and searching for creative ways to allow independence help to maintain a person's sense of well-being. People need to perceive that they have control over some part of their lives, and having to wait for a nurse or depending on others lessens this sense of control. The use of restraints and the suggestion of institutionalization should be avoided unless other measures (e.g., home care, visiting nurses, and adult day care) have been tried. However, it is important to remember that restraints do not prevent falls or replace nursing supervision or nursing assistance. Restrictions should be specific and limited, and they should be evaluated frequently. The goal is to keep a person as mobile and independent as possible, considering his or her limitations. If restrictions are specific and tailored to a particular fall risk factor, then this goal can be attained.

Closely observing and assisting a person with Parkinson's disease in the early morning or when symptoms are worst, and then decreasing restrictions at other times, is an example of specific limitations. Safety is maintained at high-risk times and more independence

TABLE 21–6 THERAPEUTIC MANAGEMENT

Medical
- Be aware that falls are not a random event or a normal part of aging.
- Perform complete physical examination.
- Diagnose and treat specific illnesses.
- Evaluate gait, balance, muscle strength, and endurance.
- Obtain a fall history (ask when was the last time client fell).
- Treat injuries resulting from a fall.
- Manage medication (focus on keeping medications to the lowest possible number).
- Provide appropriate referrals for follow-up and home assessment.

Physical Therapy
- Assess gait, balance, muscle strength, and endurance during activities of normal living.
- Evaluate need for assistive devices for ambulation or transfer.
- Provide and instruct in the proper use of assistive devices.
- Provide gait training and exercises to strengthen muscles and improve balance.

Occupational Therapy
- Assess ability to function in living situation.
- Evaluate need for adaptive devices.
- Provide adaptive devices if needed and instruct in their proper use.

Visiting Nurse, Social Worker, Physician
- Visit home to assess for safety hazards.
- Educate client about need to correct any existing safety hazards.
- Provide resources, if available, to correct hazards.

Dietitian
- Educate and assist in providing adequate nutrition.

TABLE 21–7 RESOURCES

National Safety Council
444 North Michigan Avenue
Chicago, IL 60611
800-621-7619, ext. 6900

Pamphlets: *Preventing Falls—A Safety Program for Older Adults*
Falling—The Unexpected Trip
Your Home Safety Checklist
Ladder Safety

American Association of Retired Persons
1909 K Street, NW
Washington, DC 20049

Booklet: *Dangerous Products, Dangerous Places*

encouraged at lower-risk times. The risk of a fall will always be present, but the importance of independence to a satisfying quality of life also must be recognized.

Student Learning Activities

1 Work in pairs observing older adults walking, sitting, and standing up, using the mobility assessment tool from this chapter. Possibly sites for observation are physical therapy, waiting rooms, Senior Centers, or churches. Compare your observations about older adults' risk of falling.

2 Develop a patient education booklet to inform older adults in your community about the risk factors for falling, ways to reduce these risks, how to do a home assessment, and how to question health-care providers on their medications.

3 Review an older adult's medication list (both prescribed and over-the-counter) and identify factors that could increase the risk of falling.

REFERENCES

1 Commodore, DIB: Falls in the elderly population: A look of incidence, risks, healthcare costs and preventative strategies. Rehab Nurs 20(2):84, 1995.
2 Rubinstein, LZ: Falls in the elderly: A clinical approach. West J Med 38:273, 1983.
3 Wild D, et al: How dangerous are falls in old people at home? BMJ 282:266, 1981.
4 Kellogg International Work Group in the Prevention of Falls in the Elderly: The prevention of falls in later life. Danish Med Bull (suppl 4)34:1, 1987.
5 Cummings, SR, et al: Epidemiology of osteoporosis and osteoporotic fractures. Epidemiol Rev 7:178, 1985.
6 King, MG, and Tinetti, ME: Falls in community-dwelling older adults. J Am Geriatr Soc 43:1146, 1995.
7 Murphy, J, and Isaacs, B: The post-fall syndrome: A study of thirty-six elderly patients. Gerontology 28:265, 1982.
8 Tideiksaar, R: Falling in Old Age: Its Prevention and Treatment. Springer, New York, 1989.
9 Tinetti, ME, et al: Risk factors for falls among elderly persons living in the community. N Engl J Med 319:1701, 1988.
10 Tinetti, ME, et al: A multifactorial intervention to reduce the risk of falling among elderly people living in the community. N Engl J Med 331:821, 1994.
11 Tinetti, ME, et al: Risk index for elderly patients based on the number of chronic disabilities. Am J Med 80:429, 1986.
12 Tinetti, ME, and Ginter, SF: Identifying mobility dysfunctions in elderly patients. JAMA 259:1190, 1988.
13 Hernandez, M, and Miller, J: How to reduce falls. Geriatri Nurs 7:97, 1986.
14 Rainville, NG: Effect of an implemented fall prevention program on the frequency of patient falls. QRB 10:287, 1984.
15 Isaacs, B: Clinical and laboratory studies of falls in old people. Clin Geriatr Med 1:513, 1985.
16 Catchen, H: Repeaters: Inpatient accidents among the hospitalized elderly. Gerontologist 23:273, 1983.
17 Tinetti, ME, and Speechley, M: Prevention of falls among the elderly. N Engl J Med 320:1055, 1989.
18 Squires, A, and Bayliss, DE: Rehabilitation of fallers. In Kataria, MS (ed): Fits, Faints and Falls in Old Age. MTP Press, Lancaster, UK, 1985.
19 Gryfe, CI, et al: A longitudinal study of falls in an elderly population. I: Incidence and morbidity. Age Ageing 6:201, 1977.
20 Fife, DA, et al: A risk/falls program: Code orange for success. Nurs Manage 15:50, 1984.
21 Spellbring, AM: Assessing elderly patients at high risk for falls: A reliability study. J Nurs Care Qual 6(3):30, 1992.
22 Evans, L, and Strumpf, N: Tying down the elderly: A review of the literature on physical restraint. J Am Geriatr Soc 37:65, 1989.
23 Matthiesen, V, et al: Hospital nurses' views about physical restraint use with older patients. J Gerontol Nurs 22(6):8, 1996.
24 Coberg, A, et al: Harnessing ideas to release restraints. Geriatr Nurs 12:133, 1991.

CHAPTER 22

Pain Management
in Older Adults

Lora McGuire

OBJECTIVES

Upon completion of this chapter, the reader will be able to:

- Examine the reasons for undertreatment of pain in older adults
- Differentiate between acute and chronic pain
- Discuss three ways pain in older adults can be controlled
- Describe six factors to be considered in assessing pain in older patients
- Discuss two principles of pain assessment in the nonverbal patient
- Describe the role of nonopioid analgesics in the management of pain in older adults
- Discuss and compare opioid analgesics and routes of administration for the older patient in pain
- Discuss the importance of adjuvant analgesics in the management of chronic pain in older adults
- List four common types of pain in the older patient
- Describe the role of the nurse in pain management in the older patient

Pain is a problem for patients in all age groups. Studies consistently show undertreatment of pain. The classic study by Marks and Sachar[1] reported that 73 percent of hospitalized medical patients experienced moderate to severe pain despite receiving parenteral narcotic analgesics. Donovan, Dillon, and McGuire found that 353 medical inpatients had pain, and 58 percent said it was excruciating.[2] This study found that pain was asked about or recorded in fewer than half of the patients.

Fewer than 1 percent of 4000 papers published on pain each year focus on older adults.[3] The studies that do exist consistently show undertreatment of pain as a problem (see "Research Brief 1"). Analgesic use decreases with age, and the older adults make up a smaller number of pain clinic admissions.[4] A study of older nursing home residents reported that 83 percent had pain, many in the severe range.[5]

There are several reasons why pain and its lack of treatment may be a problem for older adults. First, the prevalence of painful conditions and illness is common in old age. More than 50 percent of the cancer in the United States occurs in people over the age of 65 years, and 60 to 80 percent of patients with cancer have moderate to severe pain. Arthritis pain occurs in more than

half of all older adults with osteoarthritis being responsible for more chronic pain than any other condition.[4] Other common types of pain in older adults are headaches, low back pain, and lancinating, burning neuropathic pain (e.g., phantom limb, diabetic neuropathy, postherpetic neuralgia, trigeminal neuralgia, and causalgia).

Although nurses are taught McCaffery's definition, "Pain is whatever the person says it is, and exists whenever (s)he says it does,"[6] some patients are not always believed. Because pain is subjective, it may be difficult for some patients to communicate their pain. Older adults may be reluctant to say they have pain, and if they do, their report is often discounted by health-care providers who mistakenly believe that older adults either do not feel pain or are unreliable judges. Therefore, their pain may be undertreated or untreated.

Older people may not tell their physicians about their pain for several reasons: They like their physicians and do not want to disappoint them, they are not used to complaining, and they may believe that pain is a normal part of growing old.

Older adults may be coping with several stressors, such as financial insecurity, absence of support persons,

RESEARCH BRIEF 1

Brockopp, DY, et al: Nursing knowledge: Acute postoperative pain management in the elderly. J Gerontol Nur pp 31–37, November 1993.

This study compared the level of knowledge of practicing nurses with that of senior nursing students regarding pain management in older patients. Although practicing nurses scored higher than student nurses, the study found that both groups appeared to lack an understanding of pain management. This lack was apparent in the nurses' attitudes, misconceptions, and poor knowledge of narcotics and the components of pain assessment in older adults.

rejection, chronic illness, limited mobility, and diminished visual and auditory acuity. They may also fear pain medications and potential side effects and have an exaggerated fear of addiction. These additional stressors may produce increased anxiety.

Pain itself can have a major impact on a patient's quality of life. The effects of pain may cause decreased activity, social isolation, sleep disturbances, and depression. Depression is more common in older adults than in younger adults, yet it is diagnosed and treated less among this age group.[7] This topic is discussed more fully in Chapter 28.

Lack of education contributes to the inadequate management of pain in older adults. Of 11 leading geriatric medical textbooks, only 2 devoted chapters to pain. In 8 geriatric nursing textbooks, fewer than 18 pages out of 5000 addressed pain relief.[8]

The Nature of the Pain Experience

ACUTE AND CHRONIC PAIN

Pain may be acute or chronic. Acute pain results from injury to the tissues (e.g., surgery, inflammation, trauma) and notifies the person that help is needed. Acute pain is pain that lasts from a second to usually less than 3 months. Acute pain has an identifiable cause, is of short duration and sudden onset, is limited, and decreases with healing. It is usually accompanied by anxiety. The management of acute pain in older adults is similar to that in younger patients. Acute pain usually subsides after the cause has been treated by medications, rest, surgery, heat or cold, or immobilization.

Chronic pain is common in older adults. An estimated 80 percent of older adults have at least one chronic condition associated with pain.[9] Chronic pain is any pain lasting longer than 3 months. The cause may be known to be persistent or progressive (e.g., rheumatoid arthritis or cancer) or unknown or difficult to find. When no organic basis is evident, the nurse must remember McCaffery's[6] definition of pain and believe the patient's report of pain even if objective signs and symptoms are absent. The person feels pain and, indeed, may be disabled by it. These patients are likely to be untreated or undertreated because their report of pain is not believed, either by health professionals or by family and friends. Rejection of their report of pain as not being "legitimate" only increases their suffering.

The nurse has a valuable role in helping manage the patient's pain. One of the simplest ways to do this is to believe the patient and acknowledge that the pain is real. Support should be given to show that the nurse is trying to understand the pain.

Older adults are more likely to have chronic pain, but the nurse must be aware that both types may exist in the same person, and each type requires specific treatment. For example, in a person with osteoarthritis who needs abdominal surgery, the reduced activity resulting from the surgery may aggravate painful joints. The patient may need opioid analgesics for the acute pain and nonopioid or adjuvant analgesics to relieve the chronic pain, along with careful positioning and range of motion.

PAIN TRANSMISSION

The three types of neurons (nerve cells) involved in pain reception and transmission are afferent or sensory neurons, efferent or motor neurons, and interneurons or connector neurons. All of these nerve cells consist of cell body, axon, and dendrite. Neurons have receptors on their endings that cause the pain impulse to be conducted to the spinal cord or the brain. These receptors (nociceptors) have highly specialized endings that initiate the impulse in response to physical or chemical changes. Injury to cells or tissue stimulates the nociceptors to release a variety of chemical substances that initiate pain impulses and mediate pain responses. These substances occur naturally and include histamine, substance P, cholinesterase, bradykinin, and prostaglandins. Once released, these substances sensitize nerve endings and transmit pain impulses to higher levels in the brain.

Peripheral nerve fibers conduct the pain impulse to the central nervous system (CNS). The pain response activates the peripheral A-delta fibers. The impulse travels quickly to the substantia gelatinosa in the dorsal horn of the spinal cord, where the gating mechanism operates. The afferent (sensory) impulse enters the dorsal horn of the spinal cord. The impulse exits the spinal cord via the efferent (motor) impulses from the anterior horn. The pain impulse is transmitted over the nerve synapse with the help of neurotransmitters such as acetylcholine, norepinephrine, epinephrine, serotonin, and dopamine.

Next, the pain impulse crosses over to the opposite side of the spinal cord and ascends to higher centers in the brain via the spinothalamic tract. The spinothalamic tract enters the brain and travels to the thalamus. The thalamus plays a role in memory, recall, and emotional responses. From the thalamus, the impulse goes to the cortex and other areas. All higher levels in the brain play a part in processing the painful stimuli (thalamus, hypothalamus, brain stem, and cortex). When the pain transmission is relayed to the brain, pain is then perceived subjectively. The descending paths of the efferent fibers extend from the cortex down to the spinal cord and can also influence impulses at the level of the spinal cord.

The Gate Control Theory

The gate control theory of pain was proposed in 1965 by Melzack and Wall.[10] This theory states that pain impulses from the periphery travel to the gray matter in the dorsal horn of the spinal cord, where a gating mechanism exists, called the substantia gelatinosa, which can either open or close the transmission of pain impulses to the brain. The gating activity depends on the amount of stimulation large and small nerve fibers receive. In general, these nerve fibers compete with each other; if more large fibers are stimulated than small, pain transmission is inhibited. In essence, the gate is closed, and pain impulses are not transmitted to the brain; therefore, no pain is felt. If more small nerve fibers are stimulated than large, pain transmission is facilitated, or the gate is open.[11]

In addition to the gating mechanism in the spinal cord, there are other places in the CNS where pain impulses can be inhibited. Impulses from the brain stem, caused by sensory input such as distraction or imagery, or those from the cerebral cortex and thalamus, caused by relaxation techniques and anxiety reduction, may close the gate to painful stimuli.

The cerebral cortex contains motor, sensory, and associational centers and memory. It functions in awareness, thought, problem solving, imagery, and communication. The cortex in the brain plays a large role in pain perception and response. There is no consensus in the literature regarding changes in perception caused by aging. The brain perceives tissue injury or pain. Then it analyzes the pain's characteristics, including location, intensity, and quality, comparing this event with previous pain experiences. The brain interprets the meaning and significance of this pain event, records a memory of it, and decides on the response. The response may be biochemical, releasing endogenous opiates (enkephalins), which are produced in the pituitary gland and periaqueductal gray matter, circulate in the cerebrospinal fluid and blood, and attach to receptors in the spinal cord and viscera. The deficiency of these natural analgesics increases pain and suffering, as those endogenous opiates are decreased in chronic pain.[12]

PSYCHOSOCIAL ASPECTS OF PAIN

Part of the response to pain generated by the brain is an emotional component. Because of the uniquely personal nature of the pain experience, older adults may feel alone and anxious. They may fear the pain will never go away or, if it does, that it will return. Their anxiety may be combined with depression, thus further interfering with pain control. In addition, older adults often have sustained many losses for which they may be grieving: economic security, friends and relatives who can be supportive, independence, health, vigor, and bodily comfort. They may feel powerless to control the pain and its impact on their lives. Additional problems that may compound pain management are chronic dis-

RESEARCH BRIEF 2

Ferrell, B, et al: Pain in the nursing home. J Am Geriatr Soc 38:409, 1990.

These researchers interviewed 97 nursing home residents for pain information. Results showed that 71 percent had at least one pain complaint. Of those with pain, 34 percent had continuous pain and 66 percent had intermittent pain. Only 15 percent of residents with pain had received any pain medications within the previous 24 hours.

ease, multiple drug regimens, and age-related effects on the brain's chemistry, including reduced levels of the endogenous opiates.

The older adult may be confused because of diminished cerebral blood flow, drug effects, and pain. There may be memory deficits, which may interfere with self-medication and accurate descriptions of pain. Previous pain events may also have an effect on the current pain experience. Older adults have accumulated many memories of painful events. Depending on how well or poorly past events were handled, these memories may influence the patient's perception of the current pain state.

Older adults with chronic pain may become hostile or abusive. These many stressors often affect interpersonal relationship adversely. Relatives and friends may withdraw, as may the patient. Family members need to be helped to understand what the pain experience is like, to help the patient talk about these feelings and find ways of gaining control.

Nurses can assist these patients in pain simply using good interpersonal skills. Listening to older patients can strengthen their coping ability. Encourage the patient to stay as active as possible. Information is paramount to helping these patients achieve some control over their pain. Most patients want to know about their health and condition, even if the news is not pleasant. The nurse's role should be to help the older patient in pain maintain as much comfort as possible and a good quality of life.

Nursing Management

Several aspects of pain management are discussed here, including prevention, assessment, interventions, evaluation of relief, and teaching to restore optimal health.

1 Primary Prevention

Older adults are subject to acute pain from infections, surgery, and trauma. Problems with balance, vertigo, joint instability, muscle weakness, and reduced visual acuity predispose older adults to accidents. To prevent and cope with pain, it is important to maintain optimal health. Nutrition, hydration, sleep, and activity may need improvement. Pain is best prevented and treated by recognizing the holistic nature of a person. Pain is a stressor that affects all aspects of a person's life.

2 *Secondary Prevention*

Assessment

Most health professionals have little knowledge of the prevalence of pain in older adults because of a lack of assessment and documentation. To be treated, pain must first be identified and documented. Many people believe that pain is inevitable with aging. Older adults may deny pain because of fears of cancer, medical treatments, cost, being a burden to family, or possible institutionalization.

Several helpful tools are available for assessing pain. One of the most convenient is the 0-to-10 scale of pain intensity (Fig. 22–1). Using this scale, the nurse asks the patient: "On a sale of 0 to 10, with 0 representing no pain and 10 the worse pain imaginable, how severe is your pain? What is the best or lowest number achieved in a 24-hour period? What is the worse or highest number achieved?"

Scales provide a more objective understanding of the person's pain. They are easily used in any setting. The "faces of pain" chart and a picture of a body chart are other useful tools. The older person should be asked to describe qualities of the pain, using his or her own words. The nurse may ask the patient to determine what makes the pain better and what makes it worse. It is important to know which pain is being described. It may be the one for which the person is being treated or it may be a chronic pain or a complication of the acute condition. Encourage the patient to point to the area of pain or to mark the location on a body chart.

If the older person is experiencing acute pain, only the most essential questions should be asked. Often positioning or immobility may aggravate the pain. Appropriate questions are as follows: When did the pain start? What are its qualities, including intensity? What has been done to relieve it? When was that? Do you have chronic pain? Where is it? What are its qualities? What measures provide relief? What help do you want? The

questions related to chronic pain may be delayed for a brief time until the person is more comfortable. However, if acute pain will be treated by surgery, the nurse needs to know preoperatively about chronic pain, which may confound pain management in the postoperative period. Being positioned on the operating table and being lifted while unconscious may exacerbate chronic pain.

To perform a complete pain assessment, the nurse should ask the patient about his or her medical history. Often, when a patient is in pain, he or she may go to several physicians and receive many different prescriptions. The nurse should find out about medications the patient takes, both prescribed and over-the-counter. If concomitant disease is present, there is risk of toxicity and sensitivity reactions because of an intake of incompatible drugs. Does the patient use any home remedies for the pain? How does the pain affect the client's quality of life? activities? social functioning? Is the patient depressed because of the pain?

The nurse should establish trust by initially letting the patient know that he or she is believed. The nurse must appear to be unhurried in the assessment, giving the patient time to respond. The nurse should face the person, talking slowly and distinctly. The patient may have mild or severe cognitive problems, and perhaps visual or hearing problems as well. The nurse should be prepared to read or show the questions or describe the number scale to the patient.

A bedside record of the pain experience should be established, using a flow sheet. This simple sheet should include on a 0-to-10 scale, a description of the pain, interventions used, and evaluation of their effectiveness. Entries can be made at half-hour intervals for an hour or so. Shared with the physician, this record provides data about the quality of relief being obtained and any needed changes in analgesic orders. A log or daily diary of the pain and any medications or activities taken to help control it can be used in the outpatient setting.

Evaluation of relief obtained is essential to prevent pain peaking beyond tolerable levels. The nurse cannot depend on the patient to report inadequate relief because he or she may believe that the relief obtained is the best that can be achieved or that another request for help may be denied. The patient should be encouraged to verbalize pain and to let the caregiver, family member, nurse, or physician know if pain is not controlled. The nurse should never promise the patient that the pain can be taken away completely, however. The goal is to get the pain down to a tolerable, functional level.

Difficulties in pain assessment may occur in older adults who are nonverbal, comatose, or confused. These patients often have pain but cannot express it. Certain behaviors may express pain such as moaning, restlessness, or withdrawal. Also, nurses should be aware that any conditions or treatments that a verbal patient says cause pain probably cause pain also in a nonverbal patient in a similar situation. Whether a person can verbalize pain or not, the reaction to treatment may be the same. Examples of these conditions are positioning patients with fractures or contractures, dressing changes,

Pain Intensity Scale

```
No                                              Worst
Pain   :   :   :   :   :   :   :   :   :   :    Pain
       0   1   2   3   4   5   6   7   8   9  10 Imaginable
```

Pain Relief Scale

```
No                                              Complete
Relief :   :   :   :   :   :   :   :   :   :    Relief
       0   1   2   3   4   5   6   7   8   9  10
```

Figure 22–1 Pain assessment scale.

and tube feeding. These patients should be medicated for pain even though they cannot verbalize reports of pain.

Pharmacological Nursing Interventions

Analgesics continue to be the mainstay of therapy in pain management. Unfortunately, one of the biggest reasons for undertreatment of pain in the United States is lack of knowledge of the pharmacology of analgesics. To achieve optimal pain control through the use of analgesics, one must understand basic principles of analgesic administration. Although these principles apply to all patients in pain, several specific points will be addressed regarding the use of analgesics for older adults.

Three types of medications are used for pain control: nonopioid and opioid analgesics and adjuvants. Adjuvants are not true analgesics, but they can help certain types of pain, mainly chronic pain.

NONOPIOIDS

Acetaminophen (Tylenol) and aspirin are the two most common types of nonopioid (non-narcotic) analgesics. These drugs work primarily at the peripheral level to relieve pain. They are equal in analgesic effect (1000 mg/dose is optimal) but vary in their anti-inflammatory effects. Because acetaminophen has very little anti-inflammatory effect, it is not usually helpful for managing inflammatory pain such as rheumatoid arthritis or osteoarthritis. Although acetaminophen is generally safe, inexpensive, and easy to purchase, it has a major side effect of hepatotoxicity. This is crucial for the nurse to explain to the patient and family. Many analgesics contain acetaminophen that the patient may be unaware of (Darvocet N 100, Vicoden, Lortab, Tylox). Patients may also take over-the-counter acetaminophen mistakenly thinking it is not harmful. The nurse should monitor daily doses of acetaminophen to make sure it is less than 4000 mg/day.

Aspirin is one of the nonsteroidal anti-inflammatory drugs (NSAIDs). Valuable pain relievers for many types of pain, the NSAIDs work by inhibiting the synthesis of prostaglandins, important mediators in pain and inflammation. In the United States, the number of prescriptions for NSAIDs in older adults is 356 percent higher than for younger patients.[13] This figure is not surprising because the NSAIDs are effective in decreasing pain and inflammation in so many conditions common in older adults: rheumatoid arthritis, osteoarthritis, back and neck pain, postoperative pain, dental pain, and bone metastasis pain.

The NSAIDs are not without side effects, the most common being gastrointestinal (GI) upset. In fact, 30 percent of patients who take NSAIDs have this side effect.[13] Other possible side effects include GI bleeding (two-thirds are asymptomatic before bleeding), fluid retention, and renal complications. The nurse should especially be aware of possible renal effects from the NSAIDs, which are most likely to occur in patients with congestive heart failure or liver disease or those taking

RESEARCH BRIEF 3

Ferrell, BA, et al: Pain in cognitively impaired nursing home patients. J Pain Symptom Manage 10(8):591–598, 1995.

These researchers found that pain is common in older people requiring skilled nursing home care. Of 217 cognitively impaired residents from 10 nursing homes, more than 60 percent had pain, mainly from musculoskeletal or neuropathic causes. Pain management techniques (both pharmacological and nonpharmacological) in skilled nursing homes were found to be limited. Although patients with cognitive impairment are sometimes difficult to assess, it can be accomplished through time and frequent assessment of pain at the moment.

diuretics. It is important to monitor renal function closely in all patients taking NSAIDs routinely. Monitor patients taking long-term NSAIDs for adverse effects. Do they have any GI pain or edema? Encourage routine tests to assess stool for occult blood, renal, and hepatic functions.

Many different types and classes of NSAIDs are available. The reader is referred to the American Pain Society.[14] Several NSAIDs are suggested for older adults because they cause less GI irrigation: salsalate (Disalcid), choline magnesium trisalicylate (Trilisate), diflunisal (Dolobid), and nabumetone (Relafen). In addition, salsalate, choline magnesium trisalicylate, and sulindac seem to have a lesser effect on the kidneys.[14] If GI problems persist, misoprostol (Cytotec) may be ordered to counteract the NSAID-induced GI side effects.

Piroxicam (Feldene) is an NSAID with a long half-life that can lead to accumulation problems, especially in anyone with hepatic or renal dysfunction. Indomethacin (Indocin) is another NSAID that seems to have an increased effect on the kidneys. These two NSAIDs should not be recommended for older adults.

When starting an older adult on an NSAID, physicians often prescribe one-half to two-thirds the recommended dosage. The dosage is then increased slowly (weekly) until the recommended dosage is reached. All nonopioid drugs have a ceiling effect. Once the optimal dosage is reached the patient will have no more pain relief, only side effects. If the NSAID has been given an adequate trial (2 to 3 weeks) and pain relief has not been achieved, the physician should be informed. The patient may then be given an NSAID in a different class until the optimal combination has been determined that provides pain relief without distressing side effects.

The NSAIDs are valuable pain relievers for many types of pain common in older patients. The nurse has a major responsibility to teach the patient and family the important points regarding these medications (Table 22–1).

TABLE 22–1 TEACHING GUIDE: INSTRUCTION FOR OLDER ADULTS TAKING NSAIDS

- Be sure to give an NSAID an adequate trial (2–3 weeks) before deciding whether it is effective.
- Never take more than one NSAID at a time. (This includes aspirin.)
- Comply with routine stool tests for occult blood and renal and hepatic function tests.
- Do not take NSAIDs with steroids.
- Take the NSAID with meals or milk to prevent GI upset.
- Inform the physician of any adverse effect.

OPIOIDS

The opioid (narcotic) analgesics work by attaching to specific pain receptors in the CNS. The opioids are recommended for moderate to severe pain. There are two types of opioids: the pure agonist (morphinelike) analgesics and the mixed agonist-antagonists pentazocine (Talwin), nalbuphine (Nubain), and Butorphanol (Stadol).

The mixed agonist-antagonists are discussed first because they have no real advantage over the pure agonists (particularly in the management of cancer pain) and they do have several disadvantages not found in the pure agonists. First, because they are partial agonist-antagonists, they will precipitate withdrawal in patients receiving pure agonists. Second, they have a very high incidence of psychotomimetic side effects (confusion, seizures, agitation). Last, the only agonist-antagonist available orally is pentazocine (Talwin), which has the highest incidence of psychotomimetic effects.

The pure agonists have an important place in pain relief. These drugs differ mainly in their potencies, duration of action, and side effects in older adults. The pure agonists have the advantage of being available in many different routes and varieties, and their analgesic effect has no ceiling.

Morphine is the standard opioid analgesic against which all others are compared. Morphine, oxycodone (oxycontin), and hydromorphone (Dilaudid) are recommended orally for older adults in severe pain. Fentanyl (Duragesic patch) is useful for severely or chronically ill inpatients who cannot swallow. Codeine and oxycodone (Percodan, Tylox) are recommended for mild to moderate pain. Dolophine (Methadone) and levorphanol (Levodromoran) should be avoided in older adults because these drugs have long half-lives and may accumulate and cause oversedation and other CNS problems.

Another common opioid, but one that should be avoided for chronic pain is meperidine (Demerol). This drugs has a very poor oral-to-intramuscular (IM) ratio: 300 mg orally equals 75 mg IM.[14] It is painful and irritating to administer IM, and there can be problems with absorption. It also is short-acting. One of the most serious concerns with meperidine is in its active metabolite, normeperidine. This metabolite may accumulate with repetitive dosing, causing CNS toxicities (e.g., twitching, numbness, confusion, hallucinations, and seizures). This accumulation is most likely to occur in older adults because of the decreased elimination of drugs in the kidneys.[15]

The opioids are effective for almost all types of pain. Most pain literature recommends "starting low and going slow" when choosing initial opioid doses for older adults.

Fear of Addiction

Health professionals, patients, and the public still seem to have many fears and misconceptions about opioids. Several reasons may contribute to these fears: lack of education in medical, pharmacy, and nursing schools; misuse of terminology; and the social, government, and media pressure to "say no to drugs." It is unfortunate that in some parts of this country, patients in severe pain are being denied opioids because of exaggerated fears of addiction.

Drug addiction is a voluntary behavioral pattern in which a person is obsessed with obtaining drugs for their psychic effects, for reasons other than pain relief. This phenomenon is rarely seen when a patient takes the narcotics for pain relief. Studies show that regardless of dosages or length of time receiving narcotics, the incidence of addiction is less than 1 percent. Porter and Jick[16] found that out of almost 12,000 medical inpatients receiving narcotics, only 4 patients had possible problems with addiction.

Physical dependence is an involuntary physiological response to narcotics, such that if the drug is abruptly discontinued, unpleasant withdrawal symptoms will occur. Prolonged use of narcotics may result in physical dependence. Tolerance may also occur, which means that increasing dosages are needed to get the same result. Both conditions can be treated and do not constitute a reason for withholding narcotics from patients in pain.

The word *addiction* has negative connotations and should be avoided. People too often confuse physical dependence with addiction. Drug addicts take drugs to get high; patients take drugs for pain relief. These definitions of drug addiction and physical dependence are used by the World Health Organization, the American Pain Society, and other organizations. Nurses, physicians, and other health professionals are becoming increasingly aware of the differences and are speaking out on behalf of adequate pain management for older adults.

Side Effects

Because of the physiological changes associated with aging and the problem of multiple conditions possibly being treated, observing for interactions and signs of toxicity is crucial. Signs of adverse reactions may not be recognized because they mimic the signs of impaired old age such as confusion, tremor, depression, weakness, constipation, and loss of appetite.

Constipation and nausea or vomiting are two common side effects of opioids. GI motility may be diminished, resulting in constipation. Nausea is a common side effect of opioids that is mistaken for an allergic reac-

McCaffery M, and Ferrell, BR. Patients age: Does it affect your pain control decisions? Nursing 91, pp. 44–48, September 1991.

These authors surveyed 359 nurses regarding the effect of patient age on their decisions regarding pain control. The survey found that respondents were more willing to believe an older patient's rating of pain but less likely to increase opioid analgesic dosing.

tion. For regularly scheduled opioids given around the clock, especially with cancer pain or any chronic pain, antiemetics should be given until the nausea subsides. Sedation is another possible side effect. However, sedation does not equal pain relief. The patient may need to be awakened to take the opioid on schedule. If sedation is a problem, determine whether the patient is receiving any other medication that could be contributing to the sedation.

Respiratory depression is a commonly feared side effect of opioids. However, respiratory depression is rarely seen in patients taking opioids over the long term because pain or stress (or both) is a stimulus to breathe. Patients do not succumb to respiratory depression while awake.[14]

Older adults are more sensitive to the actions and side effects of drugs, especially hypnotics and opioids.[17,18] Body size and total body volume are reduced.[17] As a result of reduced hepatic and renal clearance, the duration of drug action is longer, allowing toxic levels to accumulate in the body.[17] Dehydration and consequent hemoconcentration, common in older adults, compound this problem. In addition, serum albumin levels fall, affecting the protein binding of many drugs, including the narcotics.[17] Generally, the dosage of protein-bound drugs should be reduced initially and titrated upward until relief is safely obtained.[19]

PRINCIPLES OF ANALGESIC ADMINISTRATION

The best way to manage pain is to prevent it before it becomes severe. The patient should be taught to take pain medication on a regular schedule to achieve adequate blood levels of the drug. Unfortunately, most analgesics are ordered as needed, or PRN. Often, patients know neither that they have to request a pain medication nor how often they can receive it. Again, teaching is a vital component of adequate pain management.

Oral Route

The oral route is the preferred route for analgesics. Most analgesics are available and effective when given orally, in adequate dosages, and before pain peaks in intensity. The oral route in less expensive and easier to use

than other routes. If a client is unable to swallow but has a nasogastric or gastrostomy feeding tube, the oral analgesics should be given through the tube.

Intramuscular and Subcutaneous Injections

Injections are the worse way to manage pain, especially chronic, long-term pain. Injections are painful to administer, may have problems with absorption, are short-acting, could possibly cause muscle or nerve damage, and must be administered by someone else. Aging affects the way the body processes drugs. Muscle mass and subcutaneous tissue decrease, as does circulating blood volume.[17] The rate of absorption may be unpredictable when medications are administered intramuscularly or subcutaneously. Opioids deposited in either site may not be absorbed fully until after a second dose has been given, possibly resulting in respiratory depression or oversedation. This absorption problem is seen more in those with acute pain than in those with chronic pain.

Most people believe that injections are best for relieving pain because they have a quick onset of action, but that action does not last long. Patients in pain should be encouraged to take oral medications regularly around the clock instead of receiving painful injections.

Rectal Route

The rectal route is still an underused route of analgesic administration. The rectal route should be recommended when a patient cannot take oral analgesics. Morphine, hydromorphone, and oxymorphone are currently available as suppositories. These drugs generally last about 4 to 5 hours, and most patients can easily administer them themselves. If a patient has leftover oral analgesics, they can simply be put in a gelatin capsule and given rectally. The patient should check with his or local pharmacist and physician before doing so. This route should not be used for patients who are thrombocytopenic, however.

Patient-Controlled Analgesia

If a patient is alert and able, patient-controlled analgesia (PCA) is an effective way to maintain a therapeutic blood level while at the same time providing the patient with a sense of control. PCA pumps allow for analgesics to be administered intravenously or subcutaneously. A 10- to 20-minute lockout system prevents the person from getting doses too often. This method avoids fluctuating concentrations of the opioid in the bloodstream and can maintain a more adequate level of analgesia. Patient teaching is an important factor in determining whether PCA will be an effective way to manage pain.

Fentanyl Patch

Another useful noninvasive route is the transdermal patch containing the opioid fentanyl (Duragesic). Problems relating to dosing have been seen with this route of administration, and there is a 12-hour delay in onset.

The patch is a 72-hour analgesic, but most patients require something for breakthrough pain. Patients need to be monitored 24 to 36 hours after removal. Because Duragesic is costly and there are few studies of its use in older adults, it is not recommended as a first line of treatment for a patient able to take analgesics orally.

ADJUVANTS

As mentioned earlier, adjuvants are medications that are not analgesics but still have a valuable role in pain relief. These medications can be used alone or in combination with other analgesics. They are recommended primarily for chronic pain.

Not surprisingly, many patients with chronic pain are depressed and may benefit from the use of a tricyclic antidepressant. The patient must be informed that these medications may take 2 to 3 weeks to build up an adequate blood level before any antidepressant effect is felt. Fortunately, pain-relieving effects are felt must sooner, sometimes after 3 or 4 days. Tricyclic antidepressants have been found to be effective for neuropathic pain, which is caused by a destruction of nerves in the CNS. Examples of neuropathic pain are phantom limb pain, diabetic neuropathies, trigeminal neuralgia, causalgia, and post–cerebrovascular accident pain. Another common type of neuropathic pain in older adults is postherpetic neuralgia (shingles) or herpes zoster. Neuropathic pain can be one of the most difficult types of pain to treat. Patients describe this pain as very intense and burning. The anticonvulsant medication carbamazepine (Tegretol) has been found to be effective in treating neuropathic pain.

The tricyclic antidepressants should be administered once a day at the hour of sleep because sedation is a common side effect. The initial dosage should be very low (10 mg). Dosages to relieve pain are much lower than those needed to relieve depression. Other anticholinergic side effects may be seen, including blurred vision, dry mouth, urinary retention, and hypotension. Extreme caution should be used when these drugs are given to patients who have narrow-angle glaucoma or urinary retention. Nortriptyline (Pamelor) causes less sedation and doxepin (Sinequan) has fewer anticholinergic effects than tricyclics, so these are two of the antidepressant drugs recommended for older adults.

Steroids can be used as adjuvants for pain control. Prednisone or dexamethasone (Decadron) can be effective for tumors with nerve root involvement or headache pain caused by brain metastasis. Steroids can elevate mood and increase appetite. However, because steroids can cause GI ulcers or bleeding or both, they should never be given to a patient who is also taking an NSAID.

The older adult in pain should avoid taking sedative-hypnotic medications because they do not help relieve pain. They are CNS depressants, which could affect the client's safety, especially if he or she is also taking an opioid analgesic.

Phenothiazines such as promethazine (Phenergan) are not narcotic potentiators.[14,20] In fact, these drugs may counteract the effect of the narcotic and cause increased pain.[20] They also depress the CNS and lower the seizure threshold. Phenothiazines have no place in pain management, especially in older adults. Table 22–2 provides suggestions for the pharmacological management of common types of pain in older adults.

NONINVASIVE INTERVENTIONS

Although pain is primarily managed through the use of medications, several noninvasive techniques may also help control pain: massage, relaxation and imagery, transcutaneous electrical nerve stimulation (TENS), heat or cold application, therapeutic touch, meditation, hypnosis, and acupressure. These techniques are generally safe, are easily available, and can be done at home or in an acute-care setting.

There are a few important points to keep in mind when using heat or cold therapy or TENS for an older adults's pain. Caution should be used when using heat or cold therapy on a patient with a history of vascular disease or diabetes. Thermal or ice burns can easily occur in someone with decreased sensation or level of consciousness. TENS is contraindicated in older adults with cardiac pacemakers because the electrical stimulation may interfere with certain types of pacemakers.

Relaxation Strategies

These exercises are designed to enable an anxious, stressed person to relax. They effectively reduce pain by combating the stress component. Relaxation strategies include guided imagery, progressive muscle relaxation, and medication. Nurses can easily teach patients to do simple forms of relaxation such as deep breathing and focusing on an object. This short form of relaxation can be effective for controlling short-term, procedural-type pain.

For a more in-depth relaxation technique, the nurse should interview the person to determine what strategy would be preferable and appropriate. The nurse needs to pay attention to the person's reality orientation, mood, and motivation, which are crucial to success. For those who will use imagery, after determining their favorite place to relax, the nurse incorporates this site into the script. The person is talked through the exercise, or the nurse may write a script, which can be read into a tape recorder by a nurse or family member for repeated use. Commercial tapes are available but should be evaluated for content and quality before being used by a patient. For detailed instructions for relaxation techniques, the reader is referred to Benson[21] and McCaffery and Beebe.[6]

The patient and family must be taught the importance of keeping active. Performing isometric exercises and active and passive range-of-motion exercises, along with the use of splints and braces to increase activity, will add to the client's physical and mental health.

Because the older adult has a wealth of life experiences, simple distraction techniques may be encouraged by asking the patient to reminisce about happy times in the past, by looking at photo albums, and by telling stories into a tape recorder. Any technique that is safe and

TABLE 22–2 SUGGESTIONS FOR THE PHARMACOLOGICAL MANAGEMENT OF COMMON TYPES OF PAIN IN THE OLDER PATIENT

Type of Pain	Nonopioid	Opioid	Adjuvant
Inflammatory pain (rheumatoid arthritis, osteoarthritis)	Any one of the following NSAIDs: Clinoril, Trilisate, Disalcid, Dolobid, Ecotrin, Rimadyl (For all types of pain listed, avoid Feldene and Indocin.)		Tricyclic antidepressant such as Pamelor or Sinequan (For all types of pain listed, use Endep and Elavil cautiously, as more anticholinergic effects are seen.)
Cancer pain	Any one of the above NSAIDs, especially if bone metastasis present	Oral morphine or oral dilaudid (For all types of pain listed, avoid Demerol, methadone, Talwin, Nubain, Stadol.)	Tricyclic antidepressant such as Pamelor or Sinequan
Low-back pain	Any one of the above NSAIDs	Oral oxycodone, oral codeine	Tricyclic antidepressant such as Pamelor or Sinequan
Neuropathic pain (post-CVA, diabetic neuropathy, postherpetic neuralgia, phantom limb pain, causalgia, trigeminal neuralgia)		Oral codeine, oral oxycodone, oral morphine, oral Dilaudid	Anticonvulsant such as Tegretol and tricyclic antidepressant such as Pamelor or Sinequan Topical anesthetics (EMLA cream, capsaicin, Lidocaine) Clonidine Baclofen

easy for the patient to do on his or her own is beneficial to pain management (Table 22–3). Tables 22–4 and 22–5 may assist the nurse in care of the older patient with pain.

Essential Documentation

Acute Pain

Acute pain should be assessed and described at regular intervals and when there is a change in its location or qualities. The following should be recorded:

- Location and movement
- Appearance of site
- Intensity on 0-to-10 scale, where 0 = no pain and 10 = worst pain
- Relief or comfort on 0-to-10 scale, where 0 = complete relief and 10 = no relief
- Adjectives patient uses
- Relief measures used
- Effectiveness of interventions on 0-to-10 scale

Chronic Pain

Chronic pain should be assessed and described once a day and when there is a change in its occurrence or qualities.

- Location and movement
- Intensity on 0-to-10 sale, where 0 = no pain and 10 = worst pain
- Relief or comfort on 0-to-10 scale, where 0 = complete relief and 10 = no relief

- Adjectives patient uses
- What aggravates the pain?
- What makes the pain better?
- Effect on sleep, appetite, and mobility
- Relief measures used
- Effectiveness of interventions on 0-to-10 scale

TABLE 22–3 TEACHING GUIDE: PHARMACOLOGICAL MANAGEMENT OF PAIN IN OLDER ADULTS

- Keep a diary or log about your pain and what makes it feel better or worse.
- Take the prescribed pain medications around the clock on a set schedule.
- Take aspirin or other nonnarcotic anti-inflammatory medication with meals or milk to decrease the changes of an upset stomach.
- Inform the nurse or physician of all medications you are taking (both prescription and over-the-counter).
- Prevent the common side effect of constipation, if taking narcotics, by increasing liquids and bulk in your diet.
- Do not worry about addiction if you are taking narcotics for pain relief.
- Report any adverse effects of medications to the nurse or physician.
- Let the nurse or physician know if pain occurs between your regularly scheduled doses of pain medication.
- Keep as active as possible.
- Remember, you are the authority on your pain; only *you* know how it feels.

TABLE 22–4 NURSING CARE PLAN

Nursing Diagnosis: Acute pain related to fractured femur with an intratrochanteric pin	
Expected Outcomes	*Nursing Actions*
Patient verbalizes a marked reduction in pain.	Assess patient's report of pain, noting location, intensity using 0–10 pain scale, every 2 hours.
	Teach patient to request PRN pain medication *before* pain becomes severe.
	Administer analgesic medication every 3–4 hours around the clock for 48 hours.
	Monitor effectiveness of analgesics and state of alertness. Notify physician if analgesics not effective.
	Support the operated leg in proper alignment with a trochanter roll and pillow.
	Avoid flexion of the body.
	Monitor for evidence of complications.
Patient uses alternative ways of reducing associated stress.	Assist patient to use relaxation strategies, including guided imagery and progressive muscle relaxation.
	Maintain adequate fluid-electrolyte balance.
	Help the person to rest by closing curtains and door. Put note on patient's door saying, "Patient resting until _____."

3 Tertiary Prevention

Nurse as Patient Advocate and Patient Educator

The nurse's position in caring for an older adult with pain includes being a role model to others to examine attitudes and biases toward the patient with pain. The nurse advocate teaches older adults and their families to expect adequate pain relief. The government has developed clinical practice guidelines for acute pain, low back pain, and cancer pain through the agency of Health Care Policy and Research. These standards, when consistently applied, should have a significant impact on the problem of pain. Nurses must become aware of the resources available on pain and its management to assist older adults in pain (Tables 22–6).

Pain is not and should not be a normal part of aging. Through advocacy and teaching, nurses' efforts and the efforts of many others committed to pain relief are the first step in combating the problem of pain in older adults.

Student Leaning Activities

1 Identify older clients in your clinical area with a range of pain experience from chronic to acute forms. Using the pain scale from the chapter, assess the client's perception of pain and his or her expectation for relief.

TABLE 22–5 NURSING CARE PLAN

Nursing Diagnosis: Chronic pain related to rheumatoid arthritis	
Expected Outcomes	*Nursing Actions*
Patient states that pain is tolerable on 0–10 scale.	Assess pain on 0–10 scale every 3–4 hours.
	Have patient or family or both keep a log or flow sheet on the pain intensity.
	Encourage patient to take medication *before* pain becomes severe.
	Help patient or family or both to apply splints and observe for or prevent pressure areas.
	Help with warm bath or shower.
	Review lifestyle in relation to avoidable sources of stress and pain aggravators.
	Ensure adequate rest, nutrition, and hydration.
	Support the person's use of positive coping measures such as prayer, meditation, relaxation, or distraction.
Patient maintains as much joint function as possible.	Help the patient take NSAIDs with food in the dosage and at the time interval ordered.
	Assess nausea and other side effects.
	Ensure that the prescribed exercises are performed correctly.
	Ask the patient or family or both to demonstrate any exercises that are to be performed after discharge.

TABLE 22–6 RESOURCES

Agency for Health Care Policy and Research
PO Box 8547
Silver Spring, MD 20907
900-358-9295

American Chronic Pain Association
PO Box 850
Rocklin, CA 95677
Support groups, manuals, tapes: 916-632-0922

American Pain Society
4700 W Lake Ave
Glenview, IL 60025-1485
847-375-4715

American Society of Pain Management Nurses
2755 Bristol Street, Suite 110
Costa Mesa, CA 92626
714-545-1305

Resource Center for State Cancer Pain Institutes
1300 University Ave, Room 3671
Madison, WI 53706
608-265-4013

2 Discuss the types of home methods the client uses for pain relief. Are these culturally based?

3 Develop a culturally sensitive pain assessment scale for the dominant ethnic groups in your area.

REFERENCES

1 Marks, RM, and Sachar, EJ: Undertreatment of medical patients with narcotic analgesics. Ann Intern Med 78:173, 1973.
2 Donovan, M, et al: Incidence and characteristics of pain in a sample of medical-surgical inpatients. Pain 30(1):69, 1987.
3 Melding, P: Is there such a thing as geriatric pain? Pain 46:119, 1991.
4 Portenoy, RK, and Farkash, A: Practical management of nonmalignant pain in the elderly. Geriatrics 43(5):29, 1988.
5 Wall, RT: Use of analgesics in the elderly. Clin Geriatr Med 6(2):345, 1990.
6 McCaffery, M, and Beebe, A: Pain: Clinical Manual for Nursing Practice. CV Mosby, St Louis, 1989, p 37.
7 Tollison, JW, and Longe, RL: Special considerations in pharmacologic pain management. II. The elderly. Pain Manage 41:29, 1991.
8 Ferrell, BA: Pain management in elderly people. J Am Geriatr Soc 39(1):64, 1991.
9 Butler, R, and Gastel, B: Care of the aged: Perspectives on pain and discomfort. In Ng, L, and Bonica, J (eds): Pain Discomfort and Humanitarian Care. Elsevier/North Holland, New York, 1980, pp 297–311.
10 Melzack, R, and Wall, PD: The Challenge of Pain. Basic Books, New York, 1983, p 1.
11 Bonica, JJ: The Management of Pain, vol 1, ed 2. Lea & Febiger, Philadelphia, 1990, p 28.
12 Aronoff, GM: Evaluation and Treatment of Chronic Pain. Urban & Schwarzenberg, Baltimore, 1985, p 408.
13 Murray, MD, and Brater, DC: Non-steroidal anti-inflammatory drugs. Clin Geriatr Med 6(2):365, 1990.
14 American Pain Society: Principles of Analgesic Use in the Treatment of Acute Pain and Chronic Cancer Pain, ed 3. American Pain Society, Skokie, Ill, 1992.
15 Kaiko, RF, et al: Central nervous system excitatory effects of meperidine in cancer patients. Ann Neurol 13:180, 1983.
16 Porter, J, and Jick, H: Addiction rate in patients with narcotics. N Engl J Med 302:123, 1980.
17 Hughey, JR: Pain medications and the elderly. Top Emerg Med 11(3):62, 1989.
18 Harkins, SW, et al: Pain and suffering in the elderly. In Bonica, JJ (ed): The Management of Pain, vol 1, ed 2. Lea & Febiger, Philadelphia, 1990, p 558.
19 Thienhaus, OJ: Pain in the elderly. In Foley, KM, and Payne, RM (ed): Current Therapy of Pain. BC Decker, Philadelphia, 1989, p 88.
20 McGee, JL, and Alexander, MR: Phenothiazine analgesia: Fact or fantasy. Am J Hosp Pharmacol 36:633, 1979.
21 Benson, H: The Relaxation Response. William Morrow, New York, 1975, p 23.

CHAPTER 23

Cancer in Older Adults

Linda Sarna

OBJECTIVES

Upon completion of this chapter, the reader will be able to:

- Identify common cancers and cancer-related deaths in older adults
- Identify measures for early detection of cancer in older adults
- Describe the role of the nurse in primary and secondary cancer prevention for older adults
- Describe the impact of aging on treatment of major cancers
- Discuss significant nursing assessment and intervention strategies for cancer-related problems in older adults

Most cancers in the United States are diagnosed in people 65 years of age and older.[1,2] Cancer is the second leading cause of death for older adults in the United States, affecting more than 200,000 adults 75 years of age and older.[2] More than 50 percent of all cancers and cancer deaths occur in those age 65 and older, despite the fact that this group makes up only 13 percent of the population.[1] One in 4 adults aged 60 to 79 will develop cancer during his or her lifetime.[1] The most common cancers in women over 65 years of age are breast, lung, colorectal, pancreatic, urinary, bladder, stomach, and ovarian.[3] Cancer is more common in older men. The most common cancers include prostate, colon, lung, urinary bladder, stomach, and pancreatic.[3] Over the past 20 years, there has been a 32 percent increase in cancer incidence among adults aged 65 and older and a 16 percent increase in cancer mortality.[1] However, adults who survive to very old age (near 90 to 100 years) rarely die of cancer.[4]

Carcinogenesis and Old Age

There are many different types of cancer with different attributable causes, presenting signs and symptoms, treatments, and prognoses. The causation of cancer (carcinogenesis) is a complex multistage phenomenon with initial exposure to carcinogens or growth-altering events (initiation) causing irreversible deoxyribonucleic acid (DNA) and cellular damage.[5] Genes are directly implicated in cancer. These genes are categorized as oncogenes, which cause activation of growth mechanisms, and tumor suppressor genes, which can alter cell proliferation and division by deletion or mutation of certain genes.[5] Continued exposure to cancer-promoting factors may increase the potential development of preneoplastic lesions. Finally, additional genetic damage results in development of a malignant tumor capable of invading adjacent tissues and spreading to distant sites. The link between exposure to a specific carcinogen and the subsequent development of cancer is not clear for many malignancies, but increasing age does appear to be a risk factor.[6] Spontaneous mutations may lead to cancers that are not related to an environmental factor.

The reasons for the increasing risk of cancer with age, especially after age 50, are under scrutiny. This increased risk is thought to be caused primarily by accumulated exposure to carcinogens (e.g., tobacco) over time and the long latency period before cancer is detectable.[6] An example of latency can be seen in the development of skin cancer from sun tanning, which may not be diagnosed as cancer until 40 years after skin damage has occurred.[7]

Age-related alterations in the immune system have been linked to increased malignancies, but the data are inconclusive.[6,8] This theory involves the decreased ability of the aging immune system to detect cancer cells as foreign bodies. Aging also is associated with an increased susceptibility to DNA damage by carcinogens and the reduced ability to repair damaged DNA. Because both cancer and aging relate to cellular growth and mortality, further discoveries about cancer may lead to new knowledge about aging and vice versa.

1 *Primary Prevention*

Although the risk of cancer may be caused in large part by cumulative exposure to carcinogens over time, primary preventive behavior can decrease the risk even for older adults. For example, the damage done by exposure to some carcinogenic substances may be reversible with the natural healing process (e.g., lung changes after smoking cessation).[9] However, most prevention activities focused on older adults are secondary prevention or focused on early detection of cancer to decrease mortality and morbidity.

ASSESSMENT OF RISK FACTORS FOR CANCER

Assessment of risk factors for cancer in older adults can provide a basis for intervention programs directed at risk reduction.[9] Examples of these behavioral changes include smoking cessation, diet modification, weight reduction, increased exercise, alcohol reduction, and sun exposure prevention. Even in older adults, assessment of other risk factors such as family history of cancer, personal history of cancer, hormonal influences, comorbid diseases related to increased cancer risk, and iatrogenic cancer effects of medications and treatments can help focus screening and early detection efforts. Interventions are now being investigated for reversal of the effects of exposure to known carcinogens.[5]

Family History

Adults with strong family histories of cancer should be monitored carefully through screening programs. Recent discoveries of genes linked to breast cancer (BRCA1 and BRCA2) and other cancers may have important implications for cancer screening and treatment.[3] However, tumor types with a genetic predisposition, such as breast and colon cancer, occur more often in younger adults. Most breast and colon cancers occur in people without any known genetic link.[8]

Smoking and Tobacco Use

Smoking is related to one-third of all cancer deaths, specifically cancers of the lung, head and neck, bladder, kidney, esophagus, pancreas, and cervix.[10] Currently, smoking is related to 45 percent of all cancer deaths in men and 21.5 percent of cancer deaths in women.[11] Most lung cancers are attributed to smoking (85 percent).[12] More than 20 percent of the U.S. population still smokes.[13] The cumulative exposure to cigarette smoking places the current cohort of male smokers in their 70s in the highest risk group for lung cancer.[3] Lack of knowledge about the smoking–lung cancer link, the heavy promotion of smoking by the tobacco industry, the increase in smoking during World Wars I and II, the lag time in carcinogenesis, and the delayed manifestations of lung cancer (20 to 40 years) have contributed to the high incidence of lung cancer among older adults.[11,12] Chewing tobacco (also called spit of smokeless tobacco) is related to a higher risk of oral cancers.

Older adult smokers are more likely to continue to use the more carcinogenic high-tar (nonfilter) cigarettes.[14] Even those who smoke filter cigarettes may compensate by increased inhaling. Older adults can still benefit from smoking cessation, but it take 15 to 20 years to lower a former smoker's risk of cancer to that of a nonsmoker.[12,14] Health-care personnel must also educate older adults about the risks of exposure to environmental tobacco smoke.[15]

Diet, Weight, and Exercise

Diet is linked with one-third of all cancer deaths.[16] A lifetime diet of foods high in animal fat and low in fiber is associated with an increased risk of colon, breast, and prostate cancers.[16] Dietary interventions to reduce the risk of cancer include a decrease in dietary animal fat and an increase in fruits, vegetables, and dietary fiber. Foods high in nitrates (e.g., smoked fish) have been linked to increased risk of colon and stomach cancers. Obesity and a high-fat diet are associated with an increased risk of breast and colon cancers.[16] Lack of exercise also is linked to increased risk of colon cancer. Heavy alcohol use is related to cancers of the head and neck area and to cancer of the liver.[16]

Sun Exposure

Skin cancers (basal cell, squamous cell, and melanoma) are a common problem among older adults; their incidence increases with age because of sun exposure over time.[7] The most lethal skin cancer, malignant melanoma, is increasing at the greatest rate of all cancers. Primary prevention includes minimizing exposure to ultraviolet rays in sunlight by using sunscreens, wearing protective clothing, and limiting outdoor activities to nonpeak sun hours (before 10 AM and after 3 PM). Sunscreens may still be useful in older adults, especially for those who have a history of skin cancer or evidence of premalignant lesions.

Environmental Hazards

Previous exposure to workplace carcinogens such as asbestos is very important to assess in older adults.[9] Chemicals and other substances in the workplace that have been linked to an increased incidence of cancer include chromium (ore miners), Benzene, (varnish and glue factory workers), and asbestos (shipyard workers). For many of these carcinogens, exposure combined with smoking significantly increases the risk.

Hormonal Influences

The risk of breast cancer increases dramatically with age.[17] Menopause after 55 years of age is associated with twice the risk of breast cancer as menopause before 45 years (including surgically induced menopause). The use of oral contraceptives has been inconclusively linked to an increased risk of breast cancer, but their use appears to reduce the risk of endometrial cancer (e.g., with estrogen opposed by progesterone).[9]

History of Cancer

A personal history of cancer places a person at higher risk for development of other types of primary cancers. Preventive behaviors are important for the millions of Americans currently living with a history of cancer.[9]

Other Medical Problems and Treatments

Cancer can be related to the presence of, or sometimes the treatment of, other medical conditions. Risk of stomach cancer, for example, is increased in the presence of other gastric diseases such as gastritis, achlorhydria, and stomach ulcers.[18] Diabetes and hypertension have been linked to an increased risk of endometrial cancer. A history of exposure to radiation can be a risk factor for a variety of cancers. Use of immunosuppressive drugs has been linked to cancers of the immune system such as lymphoma. Chemotherapy agents used to treat cancer can themselves be carcinogenic (e.g., chemotherapy for Hodgkin's disease can lead to leukemia).

2 *Secondary Prevention*

The early detection of cancer through screening (before signs or symptoms of cancer are present) is critical to minimize the disability of cancer treatment by detecting tumors when they are small, as well as by increasing the opportunities for cure and long-term survival. Even though older adults are the group at highest risk for cancer, they may be the age group least likely to participate in an early detection program.[19] Therefore, the revised public health goals listed in Healthy People 2000 specifically focus on increased cancer screening in those 70 and older.[20]

OLDER ADULTS AS A TARGET GROUP FOR EARLY DETECTION

Older adults may delay seeking medical attention because of depression, diminished mental status, limited financial resources and access to medical care, misperception of the importance of symptoms, and fear of cancer.[6,21] Social support can be an important factor in encouraging the older adult to seek medical attention. Older adults have been noted to have significantly more negative attitudes about cancer and many older people do not consider themselves at increased risk for cancer.[22]

Current American Cancer Society (ACS) guidelines for early detection of cancer are listed in Table 23–1. Guidelines for cancer screening are controversial, especially regarding age limits for testing, and not all agencies agree with the recommendations set forward by the ACS.[23] Cancer screening methods may have to be modified for older adults in nursing homes, for those with compromised mental status, and for the physically frail. However, most older adults can benefit substantially from cancer screening programs.[1,23] Strategies for decreasing the physical discomfort associated with some screening tests (e.g., sigmoidoscopy) in older adults with

TABLE 23–1 AMERICAN CANCER SOCIETY GUIDELINES FOR THE EARLY DETECTION OF CANCER IN ADULTS 65 YEARS AND OLDER

Test	Sex	Frequency
Health counseling and cancer checkup*	M and F	Every year
Breast self-examination	F	Every month
Mammogram	F	Every year
Breast clinical examination	F	Every year
Pelvic examination	F	Every year or at advice of physician
Pap test	F	Every year or at advice of physician
Digital rectal examination	M and F	Every year
Stool guaiac slide test	M and F	Every year
Sigmoidoscopy	M and F	Every 3–5 years at advice of physician
Prostate-specific antigen blood test	M	Annual

*Including examination of thyroid, prostate, ovaries, lymph nodes, oral cavity, and skin.
Source: Adapted from Cancer Facts & Figures, 1994. American Cancer Society, Atlanta, 1994.

decreased functional mobility or with other comorbid conditions (e.g., arthritis) must be evaluated. The emotional distress associated with fears of cancer and misconceptions about cancer must be considered when promoting the benefits of screening. Transportation to screening locations may be essential for programs targeted at older adults.

SCREENING AND EARLY DETECTION

Physical Examination

Annual cancer-related checkups may facilitate the early detection of malignancies and afford an opportunity to assess risk factors and to counsel and refer the patient for risk reduction (e.g., smoking cessation, reduction of sun exposure, diet and nutritional alterations). During the examination, the nurse can evaluate the older adult's knowledge about cancer screening and secondary prevention practices.

Cancer may present with multiple signs and symptoms, some that are specific to the site involved and others that may be nonspecific (e.g., malaise and weight loss). The nonspecific signs and symptoms might be incorrectly attributed to the aging process in older adults.[16]

Colorectal Cancer

Colorectal cancers are common among older adults (two-thirds of patients are older than age 60).[2,3] It is the second most common cause of cancer death in women 75 years and older and in men 55 to 74 years.[2]

Screening for the early detection of colon cancer includes an annual stool examination (i.e., guaiac) to detect occult blood, which is recommended for adults age

50 and over.[23] Collection of the specimen may be awkward for older adults limited in mobility and dexterity. Only 20 percent of women and 16 percent of men age 70 and older were recently tested.[19] A digital rectal examination to detect lesions in the anus should be performed yearly for those 40 years of age and older, but only one-third of older adults were recently examined.[19]

Examination of the colon using a flexible proctosigmoidoscope is recommended for adults age 50 and over every 3 to 5 years. This test can be the most effective in eliminating polyps, potential precursors of colon cancer, but only 15 percent of older women and 8 percent of older men were recently evaluated.[19] All three screening techniques should be used because of their lack of sensitivity and the risk of possible false negatives if only one or two of these techniques is used.

Signs and symptoms of colon cancer in the older adult may include rectal bleeding, red or black blood in the stool, and a change in bowel habits (constipation or diarrhea, narrowing of stool). Tumors in the right colon can become large and cause vague, dull pain and abdominal discomfort. Those in the left colon are likely to be smaller and more infiltrating, with bleeding and bowel obstruction possible. Older adults may ignore or minimize these symptoms.[22] Rectal bleeding may be incorrectly attributed to other causes such as hemorrhoids or constipation. Anemia may result from the chronic blood loss associated with colon cancer, a sign that also may be misinterpreted as a result of aging. Fatigue, dyspnea, and generalized weakness may result from substantial blood loss. Weight loss is usually a symptom of advanced disease.

Lung Cancer

Lung cancer is the leading cause of cancer death for both men and women aged 55 and older, and its incidence is increasing among older adults.[2,3,12] More than 60 percent of all lung cancers occur in men and women over 65 years of age.[3] The impact of the later uptake of smoking among women is not affecting the increased incidence of lung cancer; the incidence rates for women 65 years and older increased almost 200 percent in the past 20 years, but lung cancers among men increased only 20 percent.[12] The risk of lung cancer is 10 times higher for smokers than for nonsmokers. It is particularly high for those with a 20 or more pack-year history of smoking and for those with exposure to asbestos. Unfortunately, almost 90 percent of older adults diagnosed with lung cancer will eventually die of that disease.[2,12] The high mortality rate of lung cancer is caused in part by delayed diagnosis, the aggressive biology of the tumor, its frequent metastasis to the brain and other vital organs, and the ineffectiveness of conventional treatments. Even patients with lung cancers that are discovered early (about 20 percent) have only a 37 percent 5-year survival.[3]

No mass screening methods have been proven effective for the early detection of lung cancer.[23] Chest radiographs and sputum cytology may be useful in confirming the diagnosis but are not recommended for screening because early detection has not been found effective in prolonging survival. Most lung cancers have already spread by the time of diagnosis and are thus incurable. Older adults may present with less advanced disease at diagnosis[24] and a higher percentage of squamous cell cancers, which are associated with a better prognosis. Chest radiographs may be used to evaluate high-risk asymptomatic people but are not warranted for nonsmokers.[23]

Unlike breast cancer, early detection of lung cancer does not necessarily ensure a good chance for cure. Symptoms of a persistent cough, coughing up bloody sputum, or difficulty breathing may indicate lung cancer. Fatigue and sudden weight loss often are symptoms of advanced disease.

Lung cancers are categorized as small cell and non–small cell. Older adults with small-cell lung cancers may benefit from chemotherapy.[24] Even patients older than 70 can be successfully treated with surgery. Despite clinical response to chemotherapy or radiation therapy, these may not prolong survival but can be used for palliation. Many current studies consider the impact of treatment on the older person's quality of life along with the expected length of survival.

Breast Cancer

The incidence of breast cancer escalates with age, with the highest rates in women aged 80 to 84.[4] Women over age 65 represent 13 percent of the population in the United States but account for 50 percent of all cases of invasive breast cancer.[1] Breast cancer is the most common cause of cancer-related death in women 65 to 69, and the third most common cause of death for women aged 75 and older.[2] Risk of breast cancer increases for older women with a history of breast cancer and those who have never had children (or had their first child after age 30). Because the incidence of breast cancer does not routinely increase with age in other parts of the world, environmental factors (e.g., diet) are being investigated in the United States.

Screening for the early detection of breast cancer is critical for older women. Women over age 50 should have an annual mammogram to detect breast cancer before it can be palpated.[23] Early detection of small lesions can lead to curative treatment. Some studies suggest that older women may have more advanced disease at diagnosis because of lack of screening.[25] The importance of physician referral for mammogram has been indicated as an essential factor in compliance with the screening recommendations. Medicare currently provides coverage for mammograms every other year. Only 39 percent of women aged 60 to 69 and 28 percent of women 70 and older have had a recent mammogram, and the frequency of clinical breast exam among older women is not much greater.[19]

Normal age-related changes in the breast include the decrease in dense fibrous and glandular tissue and its replacement with increasing amounts of fat. These changes actually facilitate screening for breast cancer in older women because of the greater contrast in density between malignancy and fatty tissue. Although not universally recommended for cancer screening, monthly breast self-examination is still an important health-care practice for breast cancer detection.[23] Development of the benign breast lesions associated with fibrocystic disease decreases in older women. Therefore, any new mass or thickness in the breast should be regarded with suspicion. Strategies for modification of breast self-examination instructions for older women are presented in Chapter 19.

In addition to mass, other signs of breast cancer are skin retraction or dimpling and a change in the usual contour of the breast. Serosanguinous nipple discharge (rare) in women over 50 is often associated with breast cancer.[9] Adjunctive tests if a lump is found or if the mammogram is suspicious, or both, may include aspiration of fluid from the cyst, ultrasound of the area, and biopsy of the lesion.

The risk of metastasis in breast cancer generally increases with tumor size and the presence of positive lymph node involvement, negative estrogen receptor status, and increased DNA index. Postmenopausal women have a higher percentage of estrogen receptor–positive tumors (a more favorable predictor) than premenopausal women.[26]

Curative treatment options for breast cancer in older women include surgery (mastectomy, lumpectomy) and radiation (used as an adjunct to surgery). An axillary lymph node dissection may be performed to determine lymph node involvement for prognostic assessment and to help reduce the risk of metastasis; however, this is done less often in older women.[1,17,26] Surgery is a good option for curative treatment for older women in good health. Adjuvant therapy is offered to reduce the risk of disease recurrence.[27] Tamoxifen, an antiestrogen agent, is offered to postmenopausal women with positive lymph node involvement and estrogen receptor–positive tumors and for those too frail to undergo standard surgical treatment. Because breast cancer will recur in 25 percent of women who do not have positive lymph node involvement in diagnosis, adjuvant chemotherapy (e.g., a regimen of Cytoxan, methotrexate, and fluorouracil) may be given for 6 months. Older women may be less likely to be offered adjuvant treatment, even though they might benefit from it.[27] Stage of disease as well as clinical parameters (e.g., indicators of aggressiveness of the tumor) are more important prognostic indicators than advancing age.

Gynecologic Cancers

The most common gynecologic cancer, ovarian cancer, increases with age, with 50 percent occurring in women age 65 and older, and the highest incidence rate among 75 to 79-year-old women.[2,3] It is the fifth most common cause of cancer death for women aged 75 and older. Unfortunately, there are no recommended screening procedures for this lethal tumor, although transvaginal ultrasound and biochemical assessment with CA125 are under investigation.[23] Associated risk factors include a family history of ovarian cancer and infertility. Enlarging girth and abdominal discomfort are possible symptoms of ovarian cancer. The pelvic examination is gener-

ally not sensitive enough to detect early stage disease, and 76 percent of tumors have spread at the time of diagnosis.[3] Surgery is used for diagnosis, staging, and curative treatment. Palliative treatment includes chemotherapy regimens with paclitael and platinum for advanced stage disease.[28]

The incidence of endometrial cancer increases with age, and the highest incidence in women aged 70 to 74. It is a leading cause of cancer death among women 75 years of age and older.[2,3] A history of infertility, obesity, estrogen therapy (unopposed by progesterone), menopause after age 50, diabetes, and high blood pressure are associated risk factors. An endometrial biopsy at menopause is recommended for early detection of this common female malignancy. Important symptoms include painless bleeding or spotting a year or more after menopause.

Cervical cancer is still an important cancer in older women, accounting for 25 percent of new cases, but cases have been decreased 44 percent in the past 20 years.[3] Mortality rates are highest for women aged 65 to 69. The most important screening examination is the Pap smear, which should be performed annually (or less frequently at the discretion of the physician if there is a history of previously normal examination results).[23] Only 43 percent of women age 70 or older have had a Pap smear in the last 3 years.[19] Unusual vaginal discharge and pain during intercourse should be assessed carefully as possible symptoms of cervical cancer. Undertreatment of older women with cervical cancer, especially those with low income, increases with age.[29]

Prostate Cancer

Prostate cancer is the second leading cause of cancer in older men and is the third leading cause of cancer death in men age 65 and over, and its incidence has increased more than 100 percent in the past 20 years.[2,3] In fact, 84 percent of all prostate cancer occurs in men over age 65.[1] African-American men in the United States have the highest rate of prostate cancer of any group in the world. Unfortunately, more than 50 percent of men with prostate cancer are diagnosed with advanced disease. Symptoms do not occur until the cancer has locally invaded or spread, and generally include difficulty urinating, hematuria, and back or bone pain. Digital examination of the prostate can be performed at the same time as the digital rectal examination.

Early prostate cancer can be cured with surgery or radiation therapy, but impotence may result, depending on the extent of treatment.[30] For frail older men with many comorbid diseases, supportive care alone may be used. Because testosterone production stimulates tumor growth, blocking the production of this hormone may shrink the tumor and provide palliation of symptoms. Methods of reduction of testosterone production include surgical removal of the testicles, estrogen therapy, and luteinizing hormone–releasing hormone (LH-RH) therapy with or without the use of an antiandrogen (e.g., flutamide).[31] Sexual dysfunction may result from this treatment as well.

Skin Cancer

Self-examination of one's skin can be useful for the early detection of suspicious skin lesions that may be cancerous or premalignant.[7,9] A history of degree of sun exposure is essential in determining risk of skin cancer, particularly in those at higher than average risk (fair haired with blue eyes). Common premalignant skin lesions include actinic keratoses and leukoplakia. Any changes in wart or moles should be assessed. The most serious skin cancer, malignant melanoma, is more lethal in older adults, and has increased dramatically in those 65 years of age and older in the past 20 years.[7]

Gastrointestinal Cancers

A variety of gastrointestinal (GI) tumors are important causes of morbidity and mortality in the older population.[3,18]

Stomach Cancer

Stomach (gastric) cancer is a significant cause of death in older men and women.[2] Symptoms usually occur after the disease has advanced and include epigastric pain, weight loss, a sense of fullness after eating small amounts of food, and hematemesis.[9] No recommended screening methods exist for early detection.[23] Surgical intervention is generally the only possibility for cure.

Pancreatic Cancer

Pancreatic cancer is most prevalent in older adults, with highest risk for those 75 years and older.[3] It is the fourth most common cause of cancer death for women 75 and older and for men 55 and older.[2] Tobacco use and chronic pancreatitis are important risk factors.[9] Routine screening is not recommended and symptoms may be nonspecific. Because of advanced stage at diagnosis, the prognosis is generally grim, with only 2.3 percent of those diagnosed surviving longer than 5 years. Surgery may be curative, but chemotherapy and radiation are more commonly used for palliation.[18]

Esophageal Cancer

Difficulty swallowing and epigastric pain are potential symptoms of esophageal cancer. This tobacco-related cancer is most prevalent in those in their 60s and 70s and is often diagnosed with advanced disease.[3] Surgical intervention may be curative, but most patients receive chemotherapy or radiation therapy for palliation.[18]

Bladder Cancer

The likelihood of being diagnosed with advanced bladder cancer increases with age, especially over 70 years.[3] No routine screening recommendations exist for bladder cancer. Hematuria, urinary frequency, and difficulty urinating, which are common symptoms of bladder infection, also can be symptoms of bladder cancer.[9] Symptomatic patients require a workup including cystoscopic examinations of the bladder, including biopsy. Tobacco also is a risk factor for this cancer.

Head and Neck Cancers

Cancers in the head and neck are common in older adults, particularly in older men.[3] Alcohol consumption and tobacco use are important risk factors. Assessment of the oral cavity is critical. Many of these cancers are proceeded by preneoplastic lesions and can be visualized easily.[32] Difficulty swallowing, hoarseness, neck mass, or the occurrence of new lesions in the oral area should be assessed further. Surgery and radiation therapy may be curative but can result in significant morbidity and psychological distress.

Hematologic Malignancies

Hematologic malignancies, such as leukemias and lymphomas, increase with age.[33-35] Older adults, as a group, have poorer outcomes. Treatment options may be modified or limited by age as well as comorbid conditions. Treatment should not be limited by age alone, especially as data are very limited.[36] Other hematologic disorders, such as myelodysplastic syndromes, are more common in older adults and can transform into acute myelogenous leukemias.[37] Anemia and fatigue, common symptoms of hematologic malignancies, can be confused with less serious comorbidities of aging.

Cancer Treatment in Older Adults

Cancer is treated with four major modalities: surgery, radiation, chemotherapy, and biological response modifiers. There are still limited data to define the risks and benefits of modifications or alterations of traditional cancer treatment in older adults, particularly those 70 and older.[1,6,38-41] Such issues as quality of life, symptom distress, functional impairment resulting from cancer treatment, and concerns about the caregiver are being investigated.[42-45] In some cases, a wish to spare the patient the side effects of cancer treatment may actually result in more suffering from the cancer.[1,6] Other barriers to effective cancer treatments include economic, physical, social, and cultural barriers.[39] With decreasing hospital stays, the majority of the nursing care for older people with cancer occurs in private offices, outpatient clinic settings, and the home. For many adults, the need for transportation to cancer treatment facilities can seem like an insurmountable problem. Many local ACS units in the community provide a volunteer-supported transportation program to enable patients to receive treatment when transportation is a problem.

CHEMOTHERAPY

In general, healthy older adults who have received cancer treatment do not have significantly greater toxicity from systemic antineoplastic chemotherapy.[6] However, older adults may be a higher risk for some of the side effects resulting from chemotherapy because of age- and disease-related physiological changes in cardiac, pulmonary, hepatic, and renal function that may adversely affect drug metabolism.[6] In addition, decreased total body water, increased adipose tissue, reduced lean body mass, and presence of comorbid disease make drug absorption distribution and excretion less predictable in the aging body (see Chapter 8).

Data to support universal drug reduction based on chronological age are unavailable, but less effective treatment regimens have been prescribed for older adults predicated on this assumption.[1,6,26] All drugs used in the treatment of older adults must be reassessed before the initiation of chemotherapy to prevent untoward drug interactions and risks. For example, aspirin, which many older patients take for arthritis, can cause a greatly increased risk of bleeding if taken by patients receiving bone marrow suppressive chemotherapy.

Bone Marrow Suppression

Recent reviews of chemotherapy toxicity have failed to support an increase in problems of older adults with solid tumors (e.g., breast, colon, lung) based on chronological age alone.[36] However, the older adults in these studies are otherwise healthy and may not be representative of older adults with chronic illness. Chemotherapy has the greatest impact on rapidly dividing cells, especially precursor cells in the bone marrow (red blood cells, white blood cells, and platelets). Leukopenia (decreased white blood cell count) and thrombocytopenia (decreased platelet count) are common and potentially life-threatening side effects of chemotherapy. In older adults, the bone marrow is less cellular (has fewer functional elements) and has a smaller reserve capacity; thus, it is more vulnerable to the impact of chemotherapy. Older adults with hematological malignancies may experience more toxicity.[36] The nadir (time of lowest blood count) requires careful assessment for evidence of infection and bleeding and can be anticipated for different drug protocols. The advent of hematopoietic growth factors such as granulocyte colony stimulating factors can allow for the safe administration of higher dosages of chemotherapy. The prophylactic use of growth factors can be used to support the most effective treatment and prevent unnecessary morbidity and mortality.[46]

Renal Toxicity

Preexisting kidney disease and age-related declining renal function (decreased glomerular filtration rate) may prevent the use of chemotherapeutic drugs that are excreted by the kidney.[6] The decrease in renal function may compromise its capability, so certain chemotherapy drugs (e.g., methotrexate at high dosages) cannot be used safely for treatment. Other drug dosages may need to be decreased if there is diminished creatinine clearance (less than 60 mL/min).

Cardiovascular Toxicity

Comorbid cardiac problems may make it inappropriate to use drugs with associated cardiotoxicity, particularly the anthracyclines. Cardiac function can be monitored during treatment. Diethylstilbestrol at high dosages (used for the treatment of prostate cancer) has been as-

sociated with irreversible cardiac complications in older adults with a history of heart disease.[46] Additional risk factors for cardiac toxicity include radiation to the chest. Preoperative cardiac and pulmonary status may preclude more extensive surgical interventions.[38,47,48]

Central Nervous System Toxicity

Central nervous system (CNS) toxicity is of particular concern in older adults. Biochemical abnormalities resulting from cancer and cancer treatment (e.g., hypercalemia) may indirectly lead to confusion and disorientation.[49] Advanced age is a risk factor for drug-related peripheral neuropathy. Assessment of muscle weakness is critical. Cisplatin has been associated with hearing loss.[1,3] Combination radiation therapy to the brain and systemic chemotherapy may substantially increase neurotoxicity in older adults.[1,3]

Other Toxicities

Chemotherapy is associated with a wide range of toxicities that affect rapidly growing cells. Because of the sensitivity of hair follicles, alopecia (hair loss) is a side effect of many chemotherapy drugs. Although a certain degree of hair thinning and loss may be a preexisting problem for older men and, to some extent, also for older women, it should not be presumed to be less traumatic among this age group. The severity of alopecia and the quality of hair regrowth after treatment have not been specifically described according to age. Changes in aging skin, especially the decrease of subcutaneous tissue and elasticity, may make venous access for the delivery of intravenous chemotherapy agents more difficult. Increased risk of extravasation (leaking of vesicant chemotherapy drugs into the tissue) has not been reported in older adults. Increased risk of mucositis in older patients has been reported.[50]

Patient Teaching

Most older patient receive chemotherapy on an outpatient basis. Patient education for self-care of common side effects for early recognition of serious toxicities is an essential role for the nurse. Many patients are unaware of simple strategies to prevent or decrease the severity of side effects of chemotherapy. Older adults have more difficulty complying with complex medication treatment regimens. However, compared with younger adults, older patients deal more effectively with the physical side effects of chemotherapy.[44,45] The caregiver at home should be included in educational efforts. A telephone call to assess side effects at the critical time may be important in preventing serious toxicities.

RADIATION THERAPY

External beam radiation therapy is a noninvasive treatment and may be suggested more often for older frail adults unable to withstand surgery. However, it still is associated with threatening site-specific side effects, which require careful monitoring and self-care. Like chemotherapy, radiation more often affects rapidly dividing cells, but the effects are seen primarily in the areas treated with radiation. Severity of radiation side effects depends on the dosage, site, and volume irradiated. Systemic side effects may occur as well. Myelosuppression, skin, and GI side effects may be more pronounced in older adults.[6] Recovery from skin lesions might be compromised and require special nursing care to prevent secondary infection.

Older adults with concurrent diseases (e.g., emphysema) will be at greater risk for side effects in the areas affected (e.g., lung), and dosage reduction may be necessary. Radiation may be used for curative, adjuvant, or palliative treatment for advanced disease. Treatment with this modality also may be limited if significant comorbid disease exists. Most courses are 5 days a week for 4 to 6 weeks. This might cause transportation problems and may increase the risk of debilitation. Shorter courses of treatment with rest periods have been suggested but may be less effective. Fatigue is commonly experienced during radiation, generally increasing during the course of treatment. This difficult-to-control symptom may complicate involvement in household tasks and meal preparation. See Chapter 20 for a thorough discussion for the management of fatigue.

SURGERY

Surgery may be curative or used to improve quality of life (e.g., breast reconstruction). Surgery can be less debilitating than chemotherapy or radiation therapy for patients well enough to undergo anesthesia and is the only therapy for many older patients with cancer.[1,38] Surgery also may be used to palliate the effects of incurable cancers by removing obstruction and stopping bleeding. Risk of mortality increases with age, particularly in conjunction with diminished cardiac, pulmonary, and renal function.[1,3,4,7] In addition to comorbid diseases, obesity, nutritional deficits, and compromised immune function increase the surgical risk. Nursing of older adults undergoing cancer surgery must involve careful operative assessment, including a comprehensive plan for recovery and rehabilitation. Postoperative complications are similar to those for other procedures but may be more prevalent because of the radical nature of some cancer surgeries. Older patients with cancer have reported less intense postoperative pain.[44]

BIOLOGICAL RESPONSE MODIFIERS

Biological response modifiers are drugs that affect the biological responses of the body (including the immune system) to tumor cells or drugs that fight cancer biologically in a direct fashion. Examples of this new classification of antineoplastic therapy include monoclonal antibodies directed against antigens of tumor cells; interferons, which have multiple effects including modulating the immune system; and interleukins, which enhance aspects of the immune system. A recent advance in cancer treatment is the use of colony-stimulating factors (hematopoietic growth factors) to decrease the toxicity of bone marrow–suppressive chemotherapy agents by enhancing granulocyte recovery.[46] This may be particularly useful in older adults, who are more vulnerable to the side effect of bone marrow suppression. Differences by chronological age alone in side effects and toxicities of these experimental agents are not well documented.

BONE MARROW TRANSPLANTATION

The transplantation of a patient's bone marrow with that of a donor (preferably an identical twin) has not been successful in treating leukemia in older adults.[33,36] Use of bone marrow transplantation in autologous transfusions (in which a patient has stored his or her own marrow before undergoing bone marrow–suppressive chemotherapy) is currently under study for those with breast cancer and other solid tumors, but morbidity increases substantially with age.[51]

Peripheral stem cell transfusion, a form of bone marrow transplantation, is increasingly being used to support patients during the period of bone marrow suppression associated with chemotherapy. Peripheral stem cell transfusions are used for a variety of malignancies and provide support after high-dose ablative chemotherapy. Nursing care problems are complex and require sophisticated assessment and interventions.[52]

Gerontology-Oncology Nursing Problems

Cancer nursing care may have to be modified to suit the special needs of older adults.[41] Vigorous assessment of symptoms related to cancer or cancer treatment is essential in older adults. For example, the manifestations of infection in older adults may be different from those in younger patients. Cancers and cancer treatments also can suppress the immune system, increasing the risk of infection. Increased risk of bleeding in older adults may be magnified by normal age-related skin changes, which make it less elastic, thinner, and more vulnerable to breakdown (Table 23–2).

Pulmonary side effects can result from cancer or its treatment. Preexisting pulmonary disease and a history of smoking may make the older person more vulnerable to the symptoms of dyspnea. Radiation to the chest may substantially compound this problem. Symptoms of this toxicity include progressive difficulty with dyspnea, dry cough, and tachypnea (see Chapter 15).

Altered mobility is an important concern for older adults with cancer. The impact of the disease and its treatment may result in longer in bed times, which may promote physical inactivity. Older patients with cancer have reported greater need for help with household maintenance.[51] Poorer physical function can decrease social contacts and support. Hypercalcemia, a serious problem in those with breast and lung cancer, is aggravated by prolonged bed rest. The nurse must be aware of the risk of falls in older adults with cancer, especially those with impaired mobility.

TABLE 23–2 NURSING CARE PLAN

Nursing Diagnosis: High risk of injury: alteration in oral mucous membranes	
Expected Outcome	*Nursing Interventions*
Oral mucous membranes remain intact.	Assess dental status before cancer treatment; refer to dentist for treatment as needed.
	Assess oral mucous membranes every 4 hours.
	Provide soft toothbrush for oral hygiene and ½ hydrogen peroxide and ½ sterile water to rinse mouth before and after meals.
	Apply local anesthetic for pain relief before meals.
	Offer soft, cool foods and popsicles frequently.
	Eliminate hot, spicy, or acidic foods from diet.

Older adults may be at greater risk for the nutritional problems related to cancer and cancer treatment. These include nausea and vomiting, dehydration, taste alterations, anorexia, cachexia, and bowel alterations.[50] In addition, problems related to the purchase of food and meal preparation for patients with cancer may contribute to the risk of inadequate dietary intake. Changes with aging (e.g., taste alterations) and concurrent illnesses may contribute to compromised nutritional status. Alterations in metabolism can be caused by the tumor alone, especially that associated with advanced lung and colon cancers, and may contribute to a profound malnourished state, despite adequate intake.[50]

Nausea and vomiting are common side effects of chemotherapy and a possible side effect of radiation therapy. In general, older adults experience less chemotherapy-related nausea and vomiting than do young adults.[4,5] However, older adults may be at higher risk of dehydration if nausea and vomiting, mucositis, anorexia, or diarrhea results from the cancer or its treatment. Uncontrolled vomiting or diarrhea can result in electrolyte disturbances, dehydration, and weight loss. The dosage of chemotherapy may need to be limited if these side effects cannot be controlled. Nausea and vomiting caused by chemotherapy can now be effectively and safely controlled in most cases with drug therapy.[7] However, delayed-onset nausea and vomiting are still difficult to control (Table 23–3).

Disruptions in sexual function have been noted by adults of all ages undergoing cancer treatment. Nursing assessment of sexual functioning in older adults with cancer must be sensitive to the changes that occur with aging. Interventions that include exercise, nutrition, and psychosocial support can be effective in facilitating return of function (see Chapter 30).

The emotional impact of cancer varies in older adults.[44,45] Aging and cancer are both isolating phenomena. The fear of dependency brought on by the diagnosis of a potentially disabling and terminal illness may be an older adult's primary concern. Several investigators have reported that the emotional stress related to the impact of cancer and cancer treatment may be less severe in older adults.[45] Preexisting psychiatric disorders and substance abuse are predictors for problems in coping with cancer. In addition, the older adult may be more resistant to seeking psychiatric therapy for serious problems in coping with the disease. Shielding the diagnosis of cancer from the older adult, by the family or physician, is less common today but still occurs. Family members are particularly afraid that the older person will be unable to cope with the impact of the diagnosis and the sometimes accompanying risk of death. It is important to include the older adult in the treatment plan and to consider his or her needs, fears, concerns, and desires.

Cognitive and mental status changes may occur with cancer and its treatment. Changes in mental status may be the first symptoms of malignancy, and these may be mistaken as dementia in the older adult.[50] The older adult with cancer may be more susceptible to episodes of confusion and mental status changes caused by infection, chemotherapy side effects, radiation to the brain, tumors (primary and metastatic), bleeding, and trauma to the CNS. Metabolic abnormalities (e.g., hypercalcemia or hypoxia) caused by specific cancers and cancer treatment can cause mental status changes. Older patients with cancer are twice as likely as young patients to experience an organic mental disorder.[50] However, multiple-drug therapy, especially with tranquilizers and analgesics, may contribute to an appearance of altered mental status. Irritability, mood swings, confusion, dis-

TABLE 23–3 NURSING CARE PLAN

Nursing Diagnosis: Potential for alteration in nutrition: less than body requirements	
Expected Outcome	*Nursing Interventions*
Patient maintains normal body weight.	Assess nutritional status before treatment.
	Weigh patient daily during active treatment; otherwise, weigh weekly.
	Assess pattern of nausea and vomiting.
	Provide antiemetic drugs before treatment (also after treatment if delayed nausea is noted).
	Provide small, frequent meals whenever patient is free of nausea. Keep odors and sight of food out of patient area during periods of nausea.
	Maintain adequate calorie count if patient is unable to consume diet.
	Supplement diet with high-calorie foods.
	Maintain intake and output record.
	Assess need for assistance with meal preparation before discharge if community living.

orientation, recent memory loss, and altered thinking processes may be early symptoms of delirium caused by the effects of cancer and cancer treatment.

3 *Tertiary Prevention*

An essential aspect of cancer diagnosis is a focus on recovery and rehabilitation. Quality of life is a major goal, especially for older adults, for whom attention on maximum preservation of health and physical function is as important as length of survival. The impact of functional changes associated with aging and response to cancer treatment has been an important area for research.[51,52] Even in older adults, temporary as well as permanent side effects of cancer and cancer treatment must be considered at the time of diagnosis to initiate a proactive plan of care. Consideration of premorbid conditions may require modification of exercise programs and adjustment for appropriate goal setting. Evaluation of the longer-term effects of cancer treatment for adults in their 80s who received treatment in their 60s has yet to be examined.

The use of at-home and in-hospital hospice care for older adults dying from cancer may be important to minimize pain and suffering and enhance functional capabilities as long as possible.[41-43] High-quality nursing care can ensure that symptoms are not discounted and that relief is a priority.

Student Learning Activities

1 From your university or community college library, assess the most common forms of cancer in your state. What are the known causes of these forms of cancer? What risk factors exist in the population for these diseases?

2 Develop a poster or pamphlet about prevention and early detection for these known cancers, to be distributed to local churches and Senior Centers.

3 Visit a local cancer support group. What services does this group provide for older adults with cancer?

REFERENCES

1 Yancik, R, and Ries, LA: Cancer in older persons: Magnitude of the problem: How do we apply what we know? Cancer 74:1995, 1994.

2 Parker, SL, et al: Cancer statistics, 1996, CA 4:5, 1996.

3 Ries, LAG, et al (eds): SEER Cancer Statistics Review, 1973–1991: Tables and Graphs. NIH Pub no 94-2789. National Cancer Institute, Bethesda, Md, 1994.

4 Smith, DWE: Cancer mortality at very old ages. Cancer 77:1367, 1996.

5 Mastrangelo, MJ, et al: Gene therapy for human cancer: An essay for clinicians. Semin Oncol 23:1, 1996.

6 Cohen, HJ: Oncology and aging: General principles of cancer in the elderly. In Hazzard, WR (ed): The Elderly in Principles of Geriatric Medicine and Gerontology. McGraw-Hill, New York, 1994, pp 77–89.

7 Marks, R: Prevention and control of melanoma: The public health approach. CA 46:4, 1996.

8 Miller, RA. The aging immune system: Primer and prospectus. Science 273, 1996.

9 Frank-Stromborg, M, et al: Evaluating cancer risks and preventive oncology. In McCorkle, R, et al (eds): Cancer Nursing: A Comprehensive Textbook, ed 2. WB Saunders, Philadelphia, 1996, pp 213–264.

10 Fiore, MC, et al: Smoking cessation: Information for specialists. Clinical Practice Guideline. Quick Reference Guide for Smoking Cessation Specialists, no 18. AHCPR Pub no 96-0694. US Department of Health and Human Services, Rockville, Md, April 1996.

11 Garfinkel L, and Silverberg, E: Lung cancer and smoking trends in the United States over the past 25 years. CA 41:137, 1991.

12 Peto, et al: Mortality from smoking in developed countries: 1950–2000. Indirect estimates for vital statistics. Oxford University Press, New York, 1994.

13 US Department of Health and Human Services. State-specific prevalence of cigarette smoking: United States, 1995. MMWR 45:4, 1996.

14 Rimer, BK, and Orleans, CK: Tailoring smoking cessation for older adults. Cancer (suppl)74:2055, 1994.

15 US Environmental Protection Agency. Respiratory health effects of passive smoking: Lung cancer and other disorders. Office of Health and Environmental Assessment, Office of Research and Development, Washington, DC, 1992.

16 American Cancer Society 1996 Advisory Committee on Diet, Nutrition, and Cancer Prevention: American Cancer Society guidelines on diet, nutrition, and cancer prevention: Reducing the risk of cancer with healthy food choices and physical activity. CA 46:325–342, 1996.

17 Muss, HB: Breast cancer in older women. Semin Oncol 23:1, 1996.

18 Wallach, CB, and Kurtz, RC: Gastrointestinal cancer in the elderly. Gastroenterol Clin North Am 19:419, 1990.

19 US Department of Health and Human Services. Trends in cancer screening: United States, 1987 and 1992. MMWR 45:3, 1995.

20 US Department of Health and Human Services: Healthy People 2000. Appendix B: History of the objective development and the midcourse revision processes. Jones & Bartlett Publishers, Sudbury, Mass, 1995, pp 271–274.

21 Weinrich, SP, et al: Teaching older adults by adapting for aging changes. Cancer Nurs 17:494–500, 1994.

22 Weinrich, SP, et al: Knowledge of colorectal cancer among older persons with cancer. Cancer Nurs 16:322–330, 1992.

23 US Preventive Services Task Force: Guide to Clinical Preventative Services, ed 2. US Government Printing Office, Washington, DC, 1996.

24 Lindsey, A, and Sarna, L: Lung cancer. In McCorkel, R, et al (eds): Cancer Nursing: A Comprehensive Textbook, ed 2. WB Saunders, Philadelphia, 1996, pp 611–633.

25 Constanza, ME: The extent of breast cancer screening in older women. Cancer 74:2046, 1994.

26 Lyman, GH, et al: Age and the risk of breast cancer recurrence. Cancer Control 3:5, 1996.

27 Muss, HB: Chemotherapy of breast cancer in the older patient. Semin Oncol 22:1, 1995.

28 Teneriello, MG, and Park RC: Early detection of ovarian cancer. CA 45:71–87, 1995.

29 Hoffman, MS, and Cavanagh, D: Cervical cancer: screening and prevention of invasive disease. Cancer Control 2:503–509, 1995.

30 Middleton, RG: The management of clinically localized prostate cancer: Guidelines from the American Urological Association. CA 46:6, 1996.

31 Kantoff, PW: New agents in the therapy of hormone-refractory patients with prostate cancer. Semin Oncol 22:1, 1995.

32 Shah, JP, and Lydiatt, W: Treatment of cancer of the head and neck. CA 45:6, 1995.

33 Feldman, EJ: Acute myelogenous leukemia in the older patient. Semin Oncol 22:1, 1995.

34 Lichtman, SM: Lymphoma in the older patient. Semin Oncol 22:1, 1995.

35 Balducci, L, and Ballester, OF: Non-Hodgkin's lymphoma in the elderly. Cancer Control 3:5, 1996.

36 Lipschitz, DA: Age-related declines in hematopoietic reserve capacity. Semin Oncol 22:1, 1995.

37 Utely, S: Myeolodysplastic syndrome. Semin Oncol Nurs 12:51–58, 1996.

38 Farrow, D, et al: Tempora and regional variability in the surgical treatment of cancer among older people. J Am Geriatr Soc 44:559–564, 1996.

39 Trimble, EL, et al: Representations of older patients in cancer treatment trials. Cancer 74:2208, 1994.

40 Taplin, SH, et al: Stage, age, comorbidity, and direct costs of colon, prostate, and breast cancer care. J Natl Cancer Inst 87:6, 1995.

41 Boyle, DM, et al: Oncology Nursing Society position paper on cancer and aging: The mandate for oncology nursing. Oncol Nurs Forum 19:914, 1992.

42 Ferrel, BR, et al: Pain management for the elderly patients with cancer at home. Cancer 74:2139, 1992.

43 Ferrel, BR, et al: The impact of cancer pain education on family caregivers of elderly patients. Oncol Nurs Forum 22:1211, 1995.

44 Mor, V, et al: The psychosocial impact of cancer on older versus younger patients and their families. Cancer 74:2118, 1994.

45 Given, CW, et al: The influence of cancer patients' symptoms and functional states on patients' depression and family caregivers' reaction and depression. Health Psychol 12:277–285, 1997.

46 Vose, JM: Cytokine use in the older patient. Semin Oncol 22:1, 1995.

47 Wei, JY: Cardiovascular comorbidity in the older cancer patient. Semin Oncol 22:1, 1995.

48 Ginsberg, SJ, and Comis, RL: The pulmonary toxicity of antineoplastic drugs. Semin Oncol 9:34, 1982.

49 Weinrich, S, and Sarna, L: Delirium in the older person with cancer. Cancer 74:7, 1994.

50 Mitchell, EP, and Schein, PS: Gastrointestinal toxicity of chemotherapeutic agents. Semin Oncol Nurs 9:52, 1982.

51 Sarariano, WA: Comorbidity and functional status in older women with breast cancer: Implications for screening, treatment, and prognosis. J Gerontol 47:24–31, 1992.

52 Sarariano, WA: Aging, comorbidity, and breast cancer survival: An epidemiologic view. Adv Exp Med Biol 330:1–11, 1993.

CHAPTER 24

HIV Disease in Older Adults

Demetrius Porche

OBJECTIVES

Upon completion of this chapter, the reader will be able to:

- Define HIV disease and AIDS
- Identify the modes of HIV transmission
- Discuss the phases of HIV disease
- Identify risk factors for HIV transmission in older adults
- Describe the nursing management for an older adult with HIV disease

Human immunodeficiency virus (HIV) disease is a pathological process that consists of an illness spectrum from asymptomatic HIV infection to the last stage, known as acquired immunodeficiency syndrome (AIDS). HIV disease is caused by the HIV virus, which is spread through behaviors or products that expose older adults to an infected person's blood or other body fluids. HIV infection and AIDS are often associated with gay men or injecting drug users (IDUs) who are young or middle-aged. However, HIV infection and AIDS are not limited to any specific risk group or age category. Any behavior by a person of any age group that exposes the individual to an infected person's blood or body fluids increases the risk of HIV transmission.

Since the first cases of AIDS were reported in 1981, the biological and epidemiological knowledge of the syndrome has rapidly increased. The identification of HIV in 1984 and the development of a specific HIV antibody test in 1985 permitted further investigation of HIV transmission modes and patterns. Epidemiological data and clinical studies have discovered the natural history of HIV disease. However, there remains a paucity of literature on HIV disease in older adults.

Epidemiology in Older Adults

As of 1996, an estimated 21.8 million adults and children were living with HIV/AIDS throughout the world. Of the adults, 12.2 million (58 percent) were male and 8.8 million (42 percent) were female. The increase in the number of HIV-infected adults is evident: 10 million infections were reported in 1990, but 25.5 million infections were reported by mid-1996.[1] In 1995, 513,486 adult cases of AIDS were reported to the Centers for Disease Control and Prevention (CDC). Of these adult AIDS cases, 52,097 (10.1 percent) were in people 50 years of age or older. Of the 52,097 AIDS cases in older adults, the risk categories were as follows: men who have sex with men, 26,416 (50.7 percent); IDUs, 8426 (16.2 percent); heterosexuals, 5486 (10.5 percent); transfusion recipients, 3687 (7.1 percent); men who have sex with men and inject drugs, 1296 (2.5 percent); and people with hemophilia/coagulation disorder, 477 (0.9 percent). The remaining 6309 (12.1 percent) did not report or identify risk factors. Of those infected through transfusions, almost half (3687, or 47.3 percent) of the total number of AIDS cases were 50 years of age or older, which is a disproportionately large percentage.[2] However, of those 50 years of age or older who are HIV infected, most report high-risk behaviors.

Pathophysiology of HIV

HIV is the virus that causes HIV disease.[3] HIV belongs to a family of viruses called retroviruses, which convert genetic ribonucleic acid (RNA) to deoxyribonucleic acid (DNA) once they enter the host cell. They infect the host target cell by binding and fusing to a receptor site. Once the virus is bound and fused, its genetic material is injected into the host cell. The virus uses an enzyme, reverse transcriptase, to transcribe its RNA into a single strand of viral DNA using the host cell's DNA. The strand then replicates itself into a double-stranded viral DNA. The viral DNA can enter the host cell's nucleus and become a permanent component of the host cell's genetic material. Therefore, any future replication of the host cell directs the cell to reproduce HIV.

The human immune system consists of various mechanisms and immunological processes that work together to protect the body against foreign substances such as bacteria, fungi, and viruses. In immunodeficiency disorders, there may be malfunction in the immune cells, antibody formation, or other alterations in the immune response. HIV infects several cells of the immune system, including monocytes, macrophages, and lymphocytes, causing an acquired immunodeficiency. The cells that the virus infects and destroys are critical to the regulation of the immune system and immune response. HIV destroys CD4+ lymphocytes through several mechanisms: continual viral replication and budding that destroys the lymphocytes cell membrane, fusion of infected cells into syncytium (forms a clump of cells that may be nonfunctional), and destruction of HIV-infected cells by antibodies. The destruction of CD4+ lymphocytes results in a depletion of CD4+ lymphocytes. The depletion in CD4+ cells is also accompanied by an impairment in virtually every component of the immune system, including monocyte and macrophage function and B-cell or humoral immunity.[4] Clinically, CD4+ cell abnormalities are manifested as lymphopenia, an altered CD4+-to-T8 cell ratio. This process leaves the person at risk for opportunistic infections by infectious organisms that would not harm a healthy person. These people are also at risk for various cancers.

Diagnosis of HIV Infection and AIDS

HIV infection can be detected as early as 2 weeks after infection, but most people have detectable HIV antibodies between 3 weeks and 6 months after initial infection. Therefore, a window of 3 weeks to 6 months can exist during which an infected person may not test positive for HIV antibodies.[5] Testing for HIV infection involves diagnostic tests that screen the blood for antibodies to HIV or for HIV antigens. HIV testing is initially done with a highly sensitive enzyme-linked immunosorbent assay (ELISA) to detect HIV antibodies in the patient's blood. If the test is positive, it is repeated. A positive test on the second ELISA is confirmed with a more specific test known as the Western blot (WB). If the WB test is positive, the patient is diagnosed as HIV-infected.[5] HIV infection can also be diagnosed through polymerase chain reaction test and viral cultures. These tests are more specific and attempt to identify the HIV antigen.

Late-stage HIV disease is diagnosed as AIDS, the last phase of HIV disease. The AIDS diagnosis is based on CDC criteria. These criteria were established to ensure uniformity in the diagnosis and reporting of AIDS cases. However, it must be realized that these criteria were based on male symptomatology, specifically those of gay men and IDUs, and do not include several of the presenting symptoms and illnesses specific to HIV-infected women. The diagnosis of AIDS is based on HIV infection and at least one of the following conditions: CD4+ lymphocyte count less than 200 cells/μL; specific opportunistic diseases specified by the CDC such as cytomegalovirus; candidiasis of the esophagus, bronchi, trachea, or lungs; *Pneumocystis carinii* pneumonia; chronic herpes simplex ulcers or herpetic bronchitis, pneumonitis, or esophagitis; toxoplasmosis; *Mycobacterium avium intracellulare;* opportunistic cancers such as Kaposi's sarcoma, Burkitt's lymphoma, and primary lymphoma of the brain; HIV dementia; and wasting syndrome (defined as a loss of 10 percent or more of ideal body weight).[6]

Modes of Transmission

Although HIV infection is a communicable disease, it is not easily transmitted from one person to another. An infected person can transmit the virus to others through childbirth, contact with infected blood, and unprotected sexual contact. The virus cannot penetrate unbroken skin.

The virus is thus transmitted from person to person through the exchange of infected body fluids. The risk of infection is greatest if the infected body fluid reaches the uninfected person's bloodstream. HIV has been found in blood, semen, female genital secretions, saliva, spinal fluid, tears, urine, and breast milk. Some of these fluids (e.g., blood and semen) contain high concentrations of the virus, whereas others (e.g., saliva, tears, and urine) contain little. Knowing which fluids contain the virus helps determine what behaviors are more likely to transmit the virus from one person to another. HIV is not transmitted through tears, saliva, or sweat.[3,4]

BLOOD

Transfusing blood from an infected person to another seems to be the most effective way of transmitting HIV. Before 1985, before blood was tested for HIV antibodies, people with hemophilia and patients undergoing surgery may have contracted an HIV infection from HIV-contaminated blood or blood products. The time that elapses between transfusion with HIV infected blood and the diagnosis of AIDS in older adults is shorter than in younger people.[7]

IDUs represent 128,696 (25 percent) of U.S. AIDS cases as of December 1995.[2] IDUs often draw blood back into the syringe to be sure the needle is in a vein. Sharing a needle with a second person poses risk of HIV infection for the second person because some of the first person's blood may remain in the needle and syringe. This shared use of contaminated equipment is the mode of transmission for most IDUs.

Any break in an uninfected person's skin is a potential mode of HIV transmission into the bloodstream. Blood from an infected person that has direct contact with a break in the skin could provide an entry for the virus. This may occur through direct contact with blood or through an accidental needle-stick. Contamination may also be caused by using needles or surgical or dental instruments on more than one person without sterilization.[8]

SEXUAL TRANSMISSION

HIV can be transmitted sexually through the exchange of body fluids, especially semen, vaginal secretions, and blood. An uninfected person must come in direct contact with body fluids of the infected person for transmission to succeed. It is not the risk group that a person belongs to, but rather the high-risk behaviors engaged in that make an older adult at risk for HIV infection. High-risk behaviors are unprotected sexual activities that increase the risk of transmitting HIV, such as anal or vaginal intercourse without a condom, oral-anal contact, semen in the mouth, manual-anal penetration, contact with blood, and the sharing of sex toys that have come in contact with semen or blood.[9]

In homosexual and bisexual men, the greatest risk of exposure to HIV is from unprotected anal intercourse, unprotected sex with multiple sexual partners, and other sexual practices that may cause trauma, such as fisting. Heterosexuals are at greatest risk of exposure to HIV through unprotected vaginal or anal intercourse.

There is an increase in the number of women diagnosed with HIV disease. Scura and Whipple[7] reported that 25 percent of their sample of older adults (60 years and older) who were HIV-positive were women. Although the percentage of women with AIDS in the United States in 1995 was 19 percent according to the CDC, this number may be underestimated because of under-reporting of AIDS in women, especially older women, who are not recognized as being at risk for HIV.[2,7]

MYTHS OF TRANSMISSION

HIV is not transmitted by casual contact between people. This means that it is not spread by shaking hands, sneezing, coughing, being near people who are HIV-infected, closed-mouth kissing, sitting on toilet seats, using telephones, or swimming in a pool. HIV is not spread by mosquito bites. Some body fluids in which HIV has been found but that have not been known to transmit the virus are tears, urine, saliva, and sweat.[3,4]

Spectrum of HIV Disease

INITIAL INFECTION PHASE

The initial infection phase is also known as the acute retroviral syndrome.[4] After a person is infected with HIV, seroconversion is often manifested as flulike or mononucleosis-like symptoms such as fatigue, headaches, fever, nausea, pharyngitis, or a diffuse rash. These symptoms are called the acute retroviral syndrome. This syndrome typically occurs 1 to 3 weeks after initial infection and last for 1 to 2 weeks.[4] During this time, these symptoms are not usually associated with HIV infection. During this phase, the immune system is responding to the presence of HIV. Usually in 3 weeks to 6 months (although in some people it may be many years), an infected person's blood will develop antibodies to the virus. At this time, an HIV antibody test using the blood is the only way to determine whether a person has been infected. Once a person is infected with HIV, with or without symptoms of infection, the person is considered infectious for life and can transmit HIV to others through unprotected sexual activities or injecting drugs.

EARLY INFECTION PHASE

The early infection phase may also be called the asymptomatic phase. Most people then enter a period of many years during which they feel healthy. However, the immune system still contains the virus, and CD4+ lymphocyte counts remain normal or slightly decreased. During this phase, the virus is not latent; it is continually replicating and destroying the immune system by producing HIV.

In the early infection phase, the symptoms may be as vague as fatigue, diarrhea, headache, low-grade fevers, swollen lymph nodes, and night sweats. Other symptoms may be more serious, such as neurological changes manifested as visual deficits or confusion. During this phase which may last from weeks to many years, not all infected people develop symptoms. Many people may not know about their HIV infection during this asymptomatic phase.

SYMPTOMATIC PHASE

During this phase the number of CD4+ cells continues to decline while the immune response becomes weaker. This early phase was initially called AIDS-related complex, a term that is no longer used. Although these people will have greater immune suppression, they may not meet the CDC definition of AIDS. The constitutional symptoms during this phase are persistent fevers, recurring night sweats, chronic diarrhea, headaches, fatigue, and fungal infections. Other complications during this phase include local infections, lymphadenopathy, and neurological problems. Common neurological manifestations are headaches, aseptic meningitis, cranial nerve palsies, myopathies, and peripheral neuropathy.[4]

AIDS PHASE

The AIDS phase begins when a person is diagnosed as having AIDS. An AIDS diagnosis is based on the presence of a CD4+ lymphocyte count less than 200 cells/μL, opportunistic infection, opportunistic cancer, HIV dementia, or wasting syndrome.[6] Most people have more than one infection during this phase. A variety of factors influence the specific infections that occur in a person with AIDS. Some of these factors are related to the person's occupation or lifestyle, some are related to the area in which they live or travel, and others depend on their age or gender.

A person can die from the infection or other causes during any of these phases. However, just because a person reaches the AIDS phase does not automatically mean that death is imminent. Pharmacological interventions have transformed HIV disease into a chronic illness. The same principles that guide nursing care for people with a chronic illness should be applied when caring for a client who has HIV or AIDS.

The phases described here were developed to help nurses recognize a variety of symptoms in a developmental timeline. This description should not be confused with the CDC classification system for HIV infection.

Female-Specific Symptoms

Women are the fastest-growing population that is at risk for HIV infection and AIDS in the United States and around the world.[2] Symptoms of HIV disease in women differ from those of HIV disease in men. Little is known about the unique aspects of HIV disease in women. Gynecologic symptoms are often the first signs of HIV disease in women.[10] The most common clinical manifestations of HIV disease in women are vulvovaginal candidiasis, pelvic inflammatory disease, and cervical dysplasia.[10] Women with HIV disease may not be diagnosed or considered at risk for HIV disease because health-care professionals may lack knowledge of the clinical manifestations of HIV disease in women.[11] HIV-infected women may progress to AIDS and death faster than men. This faster progression is associated with several factors such as failure to diagnose and later entry into health-care delivery system; also, women may put the health-care needs of others ahead of their own.[10]

Sexually transmitted diseases (STDs) that create genital ulcers such as chancroid, syphilis, and herpes act as cofactors in the HIV epidemic. Genital ulcerative STDs characterized by ulceration have been shown to increase the risk of HIV infection. There is a strong association between HIV infection and abnormal Pap smears; therefore, it is important for older women to have routine Pap smears and gynecologic examinations.

Health-care providers, along with certain feminist and activist groups, are encouraging the CDC to include more of the female-specific symptoms in the CDC definition of and criteria for AIDS. If these symptoms are included, women who do not manifest the male-specific symptoms would still be eligible for clinical drug trials, disability benefits, and services.[12]

Older Adults: Are They at Risk for HIV Infection?

The issues of HIV disease in older adults have not been adequately addressed in the literature. Older adults have largely been ignored and not considered at risk for HIV infection. The older adult is often considered by society to be asexual and not an IDU.[13-16] Older adults are usually excluded from donating blood because of age limits imposed by blood banks, and they are therefore not identified as being HIV-positive during routine screening of blood. In fact, older adults themselves do not believe that their present or past behaviors may put them at risk for HIV infection. Few older adults consider using latex condoms because they are not concerned with birth control and believe this to be the only reason for latex condom use.

Older adults are sexually active. Sex is a healthy and fulfilling part of an older adult's life. If older adults are healthy and have an interesting and interested partner, they should be able to enjoy sexual relationships into very old age. However, society thinks otherwise.[8] The myths, stigmas, and negative societal beliefs about older adults, such as being incapable of sexual activity or interest, are often accepted by older adults. Older adults may incorporate the judgment of society and think of themselves as "dirty old men" or "dirty old women" when they have sexual desires or relationships.[8]

Sexual expression and intercourse are not limited to older adults who are heterosexual. Older gay men may not be as open about their sexual orientation because of years of concern about disclosure.[17] Older adults who are 60 years or older have lived half of their lives before the 1969 Stonewall Rebellion in New York City. The Stonewall Rebellion was the beginning of the modern gay liberation movement in the United States.[15] Many of these people are reluctant to disclose their homosexuality to health-care professionals. Instead, these people often live a lifetime of secrecy, which is the result of internalized homophobia as a result of society's beliefs about homosexuality. Internalized homophobia is a risk factor for HIV infection. People with internalized homophobia often do not express their sexual orientation overtly. These people do not reach out to the HIV/AIDS education and services provided to the gay community. Nor do these people participate in gay dating because of failure to identify with or reveal their sexual orientation; therefore, these people may seek anonymous sexual encounters such as sex in parks, gay theaters, or private club rooms or with prostitutes. Many older gay adults who grew up during a period of antigay discrimination become alcoholics or substance users as young men as a means of coping with society's marginalization, stigmatization, and oppression of homosexuals.[15] Because of the poor judgment that may occur when engaging in sexual activities under the influence of alcohol or other substances, alcohol or substance use is a risk factor for HIV infection. Some older gay adults may have formed long-term relationships. However, after the death of a long-term partner, an older gay man may turn to more available younger partners who may have a greater chance of being HIV infected.[8]

Along with expressing themselves sexually, older adults may be IDUs. Older adults may also have received HIV-infected blood via transfusion before 1985. Therefore, because of previous and present sexual behavior, older adults may be at risk for HIV infection and AIDS.

1 Primary Prevention

Nursing care of older adults affected or infected by HIV infection is challenging. Nurses are expected to be knowledgeable about a disease that has several emotional challenges and stigmas for clients and families. Nurses are key health-care professionals who have the ability to provide care for individuals and families affected or infected by HIV. Nursing care must encompass the entire spectrum of HIV disease, from an individual with no symptoms of AIDS to the dying patient and grieving family. Nurses also need help coping with their own concerns and fears and the concerns and fears of their family members and significant others. Obtaining knowledge about the disease, physiology of the immune system, and HIV prevention is an essential first step for nurses to cope with this disease. Nurses can then direct their care toward prevention and early treatment, focusing on the older adult and his or her family.

EDUCATION

In all environments, nurses must educate older adults about the modes of transmission of HIV infection and the ways to prevent the spread of the infection. Despite a willingness of the older adult to learn about HIV disease, there is a considerable knowledge deficit regarding risk factors for HIV transmission among older adults.[18] A sexual history provides an excellent opportunity for the nurse to discuss sexual activity and risk factors of HIV with the older adult. See Chapter 30 for a discussion of this topic.

Educational programs that incorporate information about HIV transmission and the current testing and treatment modalities available to older adults are appropriate forums for nurses not only to educate older adults, but also to give the message that nurses are knowledgeable and available to discuss issues of HIV disease. Older adults who are relatives of HIV-infected people need information about the modes of transmission, the disease itself, and community resources so that they can assist with or provide care and emotional support. The older adult relative is often the only caregiver for the person living with HIV disease (PLWHIV) at a time of life when his or her own resources may be severely limited. Older adults often assume the care and responsibility of their grandchildren if the child has HIV disease. To provide care, older adults may have to move to the PLWHIV's geographic location or move the PLWHIV to their geographic location. Any change in geographic location creates stress for the person who moves because of the loss of close contact with his or her usual sources of social support.

2 *Secondary Prevention*

ASSESSMENT OF THE OLDER ADULT FOR HIV AND AIDS

In the aging process, the immune system undergoes changes that are complex and individually variable. The body's psychological and immunologic responses to HIV infection are similar to normal aging changes. In older adults, the reduction in the types and amounts of antibody response that accompanies aging is attributed to the increased incidence of cancer and infectious and autoimmune diseases that occur in this age group. The dramatic decline in cell-mediated immunity, especially the CD4+ cell component, is an important contribution to the immune deficiency that occurs with aging. This decline in cellular immunity is characteristic of HIV infection, which presents as opportunistic infections, cancers, and autoimmune disorders. Depression and bereavement, often experienced by older adults, are also often associated with immunosuppression.

CARE OF THE OLDER ADULT WITH HIV DISEASE

If the history or physical assessment leads the nurse to suspect HIV infection, HIV testing should be recommended. The purpose of the test needs to be explained to the older adult, and permission for testing must be obtained. Confidentiality is to be strictly maintained. If the older adult is not cognitively compromised, no family member or friend may be informed about the test without the older adult's full consent. The person tested is to be informed of the test results. Counseling should always accompany HIV testing.[9] If the test result is negative, the older adult needs information about the possibility of HIV infection and the appropriate preventive procedures, as well as the availability of further testing. If the test result is positive, the older adult needs counseling about treatment modalities and methods to prevent the spread of infection to others. HIV-infected older adults need follow-up counseling, including information about resources available to them and their significant others. Nurses need to encourage older adults to seek eduction about and treatment of HIV disease. Nurses an contact the CDC in Atlanta, Georgia, or their state's Department of Health for the location of counseling, testing, and treatment centers. In addition, HIV-infected older adults should be referred to a support group.[19]

The same principles that the nurse uses in any counseling situation apply to counseling people about HIV infection. That is, the nurse develops a rapport with the client, makes the client feel comfortable, and explains that anything discussed in the counseling session is strictly confidential. Counseling should be done in a nonjudgmental manner.

When counseling an older adult about HIV infection, the nurse first assesses the client's knowledge of the various phases of HIV disease, the modes of transmission, and methods to prevent infection and clarifies any misconceptions. It is important for clients to know that they can contact the nurse if they have any questions or need to talk, regardless of whether they are HIV-infected themselves or they are the caregiver for an HIV-infected family member. In addition to counseling, the nurse provides appropriate referrals when needed.

In caring for older HIV-infected adults, nurses need to educate these clients about prevention of opportunistic infections by avoiding contact with people who have infectious diseases as well as to how to prevent the spread of infection to family members and significant others. Teaching older adults to strive toward an optimal nutritional status and emphasizing the important of routine exercise and rest promotes the infected person's physical and emotional well-being. Table 24–1 lists suggestions for secondary prevention for the HIV-infected older adult.

HIV Dementia

HIV may infect the central nervous system and present as a neuropsychiatric disorder. This neuropsychiatric disorder is known as AIDS dementia complex, HIV dementia, or HIV encephalopathy. It is believed that HIV

TABLE 24–1 SECONDARY PREVENTION STRATEGIES FOR THE HIV-INFECTED OLDER ADULT

- Eat a balanced, low-microbial diet that is high in calories and proteins.
- Plan regular exercise and rest periods.
- Practice safer sex with all sexual partners.
- Use sterile needles and syringes.
- Avoid crowds.
- Avoid contact with people who have communicable illnesses, especially children.
- Receive yearly influenza vaccinations and receive pneumococcal vaccine.
- Wash hands before preparing meals and eating.
- Cook all meats thoroughly.
- Avoid foods that include uncooked animal products, such as Caesar salads.
- Peel or wash all fruit and vegetables before eating.
- Use gloves for gardening. Wash hands after removing gloves.

TABLE 24–3 HIV DEMENTIA MANIFESTATIONS

Early Manifestations

Forgetfulness and loss of concentration
Blunted or flat affect
Trouble with activities of daily living
Loss of balance or leg weakness, clumsiness
Falls or history of tripping
Alterations in fine motor movements, such as handwriting changes
Anxious, hyperactive, or inappropriate behavior
Social withdrawal
Verbal and motor slowing
Gait ataxia
Hyperreflexia, especially in lower limbs

Late Manifestations

Spontaneous tremors
Paralysis
Urinary or fecal incontinence
Inappropriate behavior
Severe cognitive dysfunction
Mutism
Coma

enters the brain via infected macrophages. HIV is harbored in the microglial cells or neurons.[20] There are no definitive diagnostic tests to differentially diagnose Alzheimer's disease, except brain biopsy; therefore, HIV dementia may present as an imitator of Alzheimer's disease. A thorough evaluation of a patient who has dementia symptoms should attempt to identify the cause of the dementia so that disease management can be initiated. Table 24–2 identifies the tests commonly used in an evaluation of HIV dementia.

HIV dementia presents as an impairment in cognitive, motor, and behavioral functions. The presentation of HIV dementia is often described in terms of early and late manifestations. HIV dementia is different from that of Alzheimer's disease in that it is a subcortical dementia whose extrapyramidal symptoms resemble parkinsonism, without the resting tremor.[20] In addition, HIV dementia has a sudden onset without aphasia, whereas Alzheimer's disease typically presents with word-finding difficulties and aphasia and has a gradual onset.[20] Despite these differences, older adults with HIV dementia are often misdiagnosed as having Alzheimer's disease.[21] See Table 24–3 for the characteristics of early and late HIV dementia.

TABLE 24–2 HIV DEMENTIA ASSESSMENT

The following laboratory and diagnostic tests may be prescribed for a routine dementia evaluation.

Complete blood count
Complete chemistry profile
B_{12} and folate level
Drug levels
Veneral disease research laboratory test
Computed axial tomography scan of the head
Magnetic resonance imaging
Electroencephalogram
Lumbar puncture
Mental status exam and other neuropsychiatric testing

The older adult with HIV infection or AIDS also needs comprehensive nursing care that incorporates age-related changes. Nursing care for clients with HIV dementia should promote the older adult's optimal functional ability. Emphasis should be placed on good nutrition, rest, and exercise, and encourage mental activity. Nursing interventions for HIV-demented older adults include monitoring disease progression; establishing a safe environment; maintaining a stable environment; providing a routine schedule of daily events; providing written directions; posing simple questions; providing memory aid such as pill boxes, notes, alarms; and providing assistive devices.[14]

3 Tertiary Prevention

As more middle-aged people with HIV disease live longer, they become part of the older adult population who need long-term care. More structured residential housing is needed, and long-term care becomes necessary for older as well as younger people with HIV disease. This puts older adults in competition with younger adults for health care and creates an even greater stress on a system that is already undersupported. Older adults with HIV disease have expressed concerns that they are taking services from younger people who may be more deserving.

Fortunately, nurses who work in residential housing and long-term care facilities have many of the skills needed to provide care not only for older adults but also for younger HIV-infected people. Housing young HIV-infected adults in a residential facility for older adults may create concerns among the older adult residents. Older adults often equate the HIV epidemic with previous infectious disease outbreaks such as typhoid and tuberculosis, which creates distress amongst these residents.[22] Therefore, nurses must address the issues of misinformation or lack of information and educate older adults who are neighbors to HIV-infected residents.

Most of the resources provided in response to the AIDS epidemic are directed toward children and young adults. Older adults are an overlooked and forgotten population. The fear of being stigmatized prevents older adults from discussing HIV infection and AIDS with their peers and family. Older adults may fear disclosure of their HIV infection status to their children, grandchildren, and friends. Support groups can help older adults cope with these issues and concerns. Nurses as counselors can organize peer support groups for older adults with goals specific for this age group.

Nurses who care for older adults need to be aware of and practice standard precautions (formerly known as universal precautions) to prevent occupational exposure to HIV. Because the nurse often teaches intimate personal care to families and ancillary health-care workers, the proper use of standard precautions must be emphasized in all health-care settings.

There is a growing demand for home care of PLWHIV. Care of HIV-infected older adults may be provided by community-based organizations that typically do not provide health-care services but do provide early intervention or basic HIV care, such as AIDS service organizations.

Nurses also care for PLWHIV in acute-care settings. Despite the awareness of HIV infection and AIDS and the use of standard precautions, not all HIV-infected people who are hospitalized, especially those who are older, receive adequate health teaching about their infection and disease process.[7]

The largest group of people with AIDS consists of people between 30 and 40 years of age.[2] This means that their parents are part of the older adult population. If people 30 to 40 years old contract HIV infection, their parents become caregivers at a time in their life when grandparenting is the usual developmental expectation. The issues that these older adult caregivers are confronted with are secrecy, fear of rejection, stigma, homophobia, shame, and embarrassment. These feelings often lead to family conflicts and isolation. Collaboration between nurses in the acute-care setting and nurses in the community can help facilitate appropriate nursing interventions for PLWHIV, their families, and their older adult caregivers.

Future Research

Nurses in various settings have the opportunity to identify researchable questions and to implement nursing research studies. Nursing research studies should explore the lived experience of HIV infection in the older adult. Nursing research studies should compare and contrast the presentation and progression of HIV disease in the older adult, especially HIV dementia. Research studies should be designed to evaluate the outcomes of nursing interventions that are implemented to improve immune status and prevent the development of opportunistic infections.

Information in itself is not enough to promote behavior change. Nurses can investigate the motivation

and knowledge of older adults to determine what factors help them change behavior to prevent the spread of HIV. Coping strategies of HIV-infected older adults and older adults who are caregivers of HIV-infected people should be described and explored.

Student Learning Activities

1 As a class, develop a knowledge assessment tool about the risk factors for HIV in the older adult. Visit your local Senior Center and ask the members to complete the questionnaire. Summarize the results.

2 Prepare an education program to address any misconceptions held by the seniors.

REFERENCES

1 Porche, D: One world. One hope. Eleventh International Conference on AIDS. J Assoc Nurses AIDS Care 7(5):94–100, 1996.
2 Centers for Disease Control and Prevention: HIV/AIDS surveillance report. Department of Health and Human Services, Atlanta, 7(2):15, 16–17, 29, 1996.
3 Barre-Sinoussi, F: HIV as the cause of AIDS. Lancet 348:31–35, 1996.
4 Feinberg, M: Changing the natural history of HIV disease. Lancet 348:239–246, 1995.
5 Gurtler, L: Difficulties and strategies of HIV diagnosis. Lancet 348:176–179, 1995.
6 Centers for Disease Control and Prevention: 1993 revised classification system for HIV infection and expanded surveillance case definition for AIDS among adolescents and adults. MMWR 41(RR-17):1, 1992.
7 Scura, KW, and Whipple, B: Older adults as an HIV-positive risk group. J Gerontol Nurs 16:6, 1990.
8 Whipple, B, and Scura, K: HIV and the older adult: Taking the necessary precautions. J Gerontol Nurs 15(9):15–19, 1989.
9 Porche, D, et al: HIV counseling and testing: A primer for health care professionals. AIDS Patient Care 6(3):130–133, 1992.
10 DeHovitz, J: Natural history of HIV infection in women. In Minkoff, H, et al (eds): HIV Infection in Women. Raven Press, New York, 1995.
11 Smeltzer, SO, and Whipple, B: Women and HIV infection. Image Nurs Sch 23:249, 1991.
12 Smith, J: AIDS and Society. Prentice-Hall, Englewood Cliffs, NJ, 1996.
13 Butler, R: AIDS: Older patients aren't immune. Geriatrics 48(3):9–10, 1993.
14 Whipple, B, and Scura, K: HIV in older adults. Am J Nurs 96(2):23–28, 1996.
15 Grossman, A: At risk, infected, and invisible: Older gay men and HIV/AIDS. J Assoc Nurses AIDS Care 6(6):13–19, 1995.
16 Wallace, J, et al: HIV infection in older patients: When to suspect the unexpected. Geriatrics 48(6):61–70, 1993.
17 Kelly, J: The aging male homosexual: Myth and reality. Gerontologist 17:328, 1977.
18 Hinkle, KL: A literature review: HIV seropositivity in the elderly. J Gerontol Nurs 17:12, 1991.
19 Lavick, J: Psychosocial considerations of HIV infection in the older adult. AIDS Patient Care 8(3):127–129, 1994.
20 Scharnhorts, S: AIDS dementia complex in the elderly: Diagnosis and management. Nurse Pract 17(8):37–43, 1992.
21 Weiler, PG, et al: AIDS as a cause of dementia in the elderly. J Am Geriatr Soc 36:139, 1988.
22 Allers, C: AIDS and the older adult. Gerontologist 30(3):405–407, 1990.

Individual and Family Psychodynamics

CHAPTER 25

Developmental Tasks and Development in the Later Years of Life

Cathy S. Heriot

OBJECTIVES

Upon completion of this chapter, the reader will be able to:

- Compare four theories of developmental tasks as they relate to the later years
- Describe the concept of interiority
- Apply the nursing process to older adults experiencing developmental difficulties
- Conduct life reviews with older clients
- Discuss areas of research needed regarding the developmental tasks of older adults

To older people should be told, Never Quit
Please don't call me old
And don't ever tell me to quit
For as long as I live
I expect to do a little bit
There may be something
That I can do or say
To help somebody just a little
I'll keep on trying anyway
Some words in the Bible
To older people should be told
It tells we can bear fruit
Even though we are old
You can read it in Psalms
In the 14 verse of Chapter 92
These words are in the Bible
And I know they are true.[1]

Mayme Carpenter, age 98*

---

*Mrs. Carpenter was led through a life review by an undergraduate nursing student. She was so grateful when the author provided her with a copy of the student's paper that resulted from the life review that she sent the author a copy of her book of poems, Don't Call Me Old, which she published when she was in the eighth decade of her life. This is one of the poems from that book, reprinted with her permission.

They shall bring forth fruit in old age; they shall be fat and flourishing.

Psalms 92:14[2]

Human development is the continuous evolvement of the person toward increasing complexity and diversity.[3] It is viewed as an inherently dynamic process that carries the person to higher, more satisfying levels of existence. Human development has been studied in terms of the intertwining of biological endowments, personal life experiences, the interdependence of person and environment, and processes of social interaction that transform the person. It has been most commonly studied through an analysis of developmental tasks that people must achieve at various times in their lives.

Older adults have the potential to continue the growth they started early in life. Reed[4] supported this premise, noting that "aging has for too long been associated primarily with decline rather than with development . . . There has, however, been an upsurge of theoretic and empiric information that development is a lifelong process and can occur in the presence of obvious physical changes and deterioration commonly associated with aging." Henri Matisse provided us with an excellent example of this ability to transcend the physical changes of aging. At the age of 84, although bedridden, he produced some of his most daring and beautiful pictures.[5]

Developmental Tasks

HAVIGHURST

Developmental tasks are tasks that arise "out of or about a certain period in the life of the individual, successful achievement of which leads to happiness and to success with later tasks, while failure leads to unhappiness in the individual, disapproval by the society, and difficulty with later tasks."[6] This definition suggests that developmental tasks are jobs to be done to facilitate one's development and further implies that people assume responsibility for their own development.

There are many sources of developmental tasks. They arise from physical maturation, cultural pressure of society, and personal values and aspirations. Old age is a period in which there is unique developmental work to be accomplished. "The major developmental task in old age is to clarify, deepen and find use for what one has already obtained in a lifetime of learning and adapting."[4] Developmental theorists believe it is crucial for older adults to continue to grow, develop, and transform themselves if health is to be maintained and promoted.[7,8]

ERICKSON

Erickson's theory of psychosocial development "broadens the understanding of factors involved in personality development to include social forces."[9] The theory describes the challenge or need facing each of eight age groupings and suggests that ego strength is achieved when each stage is successfully attained. Erickson was one of the first to address human development throughout the life span. According to Erickson, a feeling of satisfaction is experienced when ego integrity is achieved by successful progression through all the stages. Satisfaction is manifested through both a positive self-concept and a positive attitude toward life. Although the theory associates needs with specific age groupings, it is not meant to denote a linear progression. When a stage has been achieved, it is not necessarily mastered for life. Likewise, issues of one stage may appear earlier or later than the age of life Erickson noted it is the most likely to occur. For example, the older adult may experience issues related to identity versus role confusion, whereas the adolescent may face questions related to integrity versus despair.

The primary developmental task of all age groups is ego integrity versus despair, with the concomitant virtue of wisdom. Integrity is "the acceptance of one's one and only life cycle as something that had to be and that, by necessity, permitted no substitutions."[7] Despair results when there is disappointment over one's life. People who fail to accept their lives while simultaneously realizing that there is no time to start in a new direction may feel despair. Failure to achieve ego integration may manifest itself in disgust and fear of death. Disgust may

present itself as disdain, for one's self or for a particular or generalized other.[10]

The reader who is interested in further understanding Erickson's theory is referred to the following videos, available from Davidson Films, Inc. (231 E Street, Davis, CA 95616, 916-753-9604).

On Old Age I: A Conversation with Joan Erickson at 90
On Old Age II: A Conversation with Joan Erickson at 92
Erik H. Erickson: A Life's Work

PECK

Erickson's single task is all-encompassing; it incorporates tasks that other theorists have outlined more specifically. Peck[8] is one of the theorists who refined Erickson's single task of old age. He conceptualized three tasks that he purported influenced the outcome of the conflict between integrity and despair.

- *Ego differentiation versus work role preoccupation.* This task requires a shift in one's value system, which allows older adults to re-evaluate and redefine their work. This reappraisal leads the older adult to substitute new roles and activities for those that have been lost. Older adults are then able to find new ways of seeing themselves as worthwhile other than the parental and occupational roles.

- *Body transcendence versus body preoccupation.* Most older adults experience some physical decline. For some people, pleasure and comfort mean physical well-being. Those people may experience the greatest difficulty transcending their physical state. Others have the ability to engage in pleasurable psychological and social activities despite physical changes and discomforts. Peck proposed that in their value systems, "social and mental sources of pleasure and self-respect may transcend physical comfort, alone."[8]

CASE 1   Mrs. M, an 84-year-old woman, has lost her sight and is unhappy because her children are insisting that she find a live-in companion. She states that she is unable to engage in pleasurable psychological and social activities because of her illness. Mrs. M told her granddaughter, who conducted a life review with her, that the Lord promises that being with Him means a better life than the one you have had on Earth, and she is ready for that. She clarified this thought by adding, "Not that I'm planning to make it happen or anything; I'm just ready for it to happen because I want to be happy again."[11] This case illustrates the despair and hopelessness that may accompany failure to achieve body transcendence.

- *Ego transcendence versus ego preoccupation.* Peck proposed that the most constructive way of living the final years of life might be defined in the following way: "To live so generously and unselfishly that the prospect of personal death—the night of the ego, it might be called—looks and feels less important than the secure knowledge that one has built for a broader, longer future than any one ego ever could encompass."[8] People accomplish this through their legacies, their children, their contributions to society, and their friendships. They want "to make life more secure, more meaningful, or happier for the people who will go on after they die."[8] To clarify, "long-lived individuals seem to be more concerned with what they do than who they are. They live outside themselves rather than dwelling egocentrically on their own personalities."[5]

To achieve integrity, then, one must develop the ability to redefine self, to let go of occupational identity, to rise above physical discomforts, and to establish personal meaning that goes beyond the scope of self-centeredness.[12] These goals, however commendable, may be difficult for some older adults. Not all older adults have the fortitude or energy to laugh in the face of adversity or overcome the assaults of old age. Stenback asserts:

> Particularly in old age, active interest taken in personal preventive health care and tenacious care of a chronic disease are adequate and necessary "preoccupations" with the body. When body stamina decreases and the body becomes ailing, foreboding disability and death, depressive preoccupation with the body has to be deemed normal rather than neurotic.[13]

HAVIGHURST AND DUVALL

Havighurst believed that "living is learning and growing is learning."[6] Old age demonstrates this, according to Havighurst, because older adults "still have new experiences ahead of them, and new situations to meet."[14] Retiring, moving to a retirement community, adjusting to the effects of chronic illnesses, and losing a spouse and cohorts are some of these new experiences and situations.

The Committee on the Dynamics of Family Interaction[15] extended the concept of developmental tasks to the family as a whole. The family life cycle proposed by Duvall consists of eight stages, the last of which is the aging family. The last stage of the family cycle begins with retirement, proceeds through the death of the first spouse, and ends with the death of the second spouse.

The developmental tasks presented by Havighurst[14] and Duvall's committee[15] are almost comparable, as shown in Table 25–1. Both address life changes required in relation to living arrangements, retirement, income, interpersonal relationships, social activities and obligations, and death. The primary difference is that Havighurst addresses the individual, whereas Duvall uses a family framework.

Applying the Nursing Process to Development in the Later Years

ASSESSMENT

To determine the extent to which older clients have achieved the developmental tasks of old age, the nurse

TABLE 25–1   DEVELOPMENTAL TASKS IDENTIFIED BY HAVIGHURST AND DUVALL

Havighurst	Duvall
Adjusting to decreasing physical strength and health	Finding a satisfying home for later years
Adjusting to retirement and reduced income	Adjusting to retirement income
Adjusting to death of spouse and significant other	Establishing comfortable household routines
Establishing an explicit affiliation with one's age group	Nurturing each other as husband and wife
Meeting social and civic obligations	Facing bereavement and widowhood
Establishing satisfactory physical living arrangements	Maintaining contact with children and grandchildren
	Caring for older relatives
	Keeping an interest in people outside the family
	Finding meanings in life

Source: Developed from Havighurst[6] and Duvall.[15]

will conduct a careful interview. Beaton recommends the use of life stories as a routine part of clinical assessment, "not only because the content of stories is valuable, but also because the process of telling and listening enhances the relationship with the client."[16] Aside from eliciting clients' life stories, suggestions for specific questions include the following:

- As you look back over your life, do you see that it occurred as it had to?
- Do you have any unresolved regrets or griefs?
- Is there anything you failed to achieve or gain out of life that you feel was needed or deserved?

Information should also be elicited regarding the client's work or retirement status, finances, living arrangements, spirituality, and social support systems. It is also important that the nurse remember that older adults may express their psychosocial problems through physical symptoms (e.g., fatigue, depression, anxiety, and vague aches and pains).

NURSING DIAGNOSES

Analysis of the data gathered during the assessment phase usually leads to the following nursing diagnoses:

- Altered growth and development related to unfulfilled life dreams
- Ineffective individual coping related to depression
- Alteration in family processes related to developmental crisis

Related diagnoses that may also be discovered include the following:

- Disturbance in self-concept related to loss of work role
- Dysfunctional grieving related to unfinished business with the deceased
- Hopelessness related to unsuccessful reintegration of life events
- Spiritual distress related to lack of meaning and purpose in life

INTERVENTIONS

Clayton[17] raised some doubt that integrity is the ultimate task of old age, or at least that it is ever attained. She concluded that most people "either seek foreclosure or enter prolonged moratoriums after adolescence." In other words, they do not choose to proceed with their maturation, electing not to encounter and resolve future developmental conflicts. Clayton's thesis points to the need for interventions to help adults, particularly older adults, attain the last stage of development.

Most interventions to help older adults achieve the final developmental task involve them in reflection on their lives. The most well-researched intervention is the life review, developed by Butler,[18] who saw the process as a way to achieve reintegration of the ego. Stimulation of life memories helps older adults to work through their losses and maintain self-esteem. Life review provides older adults with an opportunity to come to grips with guilt and regrets and to emerge feeling good about themselves.

Haight[19] developed a comprehensive list of questions designed to prompt memories related to childhood, adolescence, family and home, and adulthood. Haight's Life Review and Experiencing Form also includes summary questions aimed at eliciting the older person's perceptions of his or her life (Table 25–2). At the completion of the interview, the nurse is able to determine the degree to which the client has achieved ego integrity. Life review has been shown to have a significant effect on both life satisfaction and psychological well-being.[20]

Wysocki[21] provides the nurse with a detailed guide to performing the life review with older adults. She offers specific suggestions for initiating the process, handling each visit, managing specific difficulties such as the apathetic and withdrawn client, ending the interview, and terminating the sessions.

Older adults may benefit from writing about their own life experiences.[22] Autobiography is a helpful way of giving meaning to one's present life. Birren stated that "writing an autobiography puts the contradictions, paradoxes and ambivalence of life into perspective."[22] Something happens when people go beyond merely recollecting and writing about their experiences to sharing those life experiences with others. The interaction that occurs when people divulge their deeply personal selves with those in their social environment reveals new dimensions of the self. Nurses need to encourage older adults to write phenomenological accounts of their experiences with the aging process.[23] The autobiographical technique can be used with both institutionalized and noninstitutionalized older adults. Birren[22] notes that guided autobiographies are the most useful. Nurses might assign topics such as the roles of money, health, exercise, food, and humor in the older adults' lives. After a week of remembering and writing or tape-recording their life experiences, the older adults are asked to share those experiences with others in the group.

Ebersole and Hess[12] have offered another, more direct intervention to assist older adults in achieving full developmental maturity. They suggest that nurses ask older adults how they have defined the tasks of aging for themselves.

In the earliest presentation of his developmental theory, Erickson[7] noted that only those who have taken care of things and other people will eventually mature through the stage of integrity. Erickson and his wife,[24] along with Kivnick, have continued Erickson's earlier work and believe that caring, especially for one's children and grandchildren, is the quality that provides the greatest sense of continuity. Through caring, older adults experience the human need for connectedness. They further challenge older adults "to accept from others that caring which is required, and to do so in a way that is itself caring."[24] This suggests that it may be useful for nurses to help their older clients continue to express their caring and demonstrate grace in their acceptance of caring from others.

Most older adults have been brought up with the dichotomous concepts of independence and dependence. The recent trend is to view such concepts as existing on a continuum so that most people live lives of varying degrees of interdependence. O'Bryant claims that "a society that over-values independence may unwittingly create pressure on its elderly to be too independent . . . In an ideal society, older persons and their support systems would work toward a viable exchange of services, so that interdependence would become the most valued lifestyle."[25] Nurses can help their older clients recognize that they have been interdependent and can continue to be so.

EVALUATION OF NURSING CARE: PROCESS AND OUTCOME

To evaluate the process, nurses must look at what transpired between them and thier clients. Did the nurse participate by sharing his or her life as the client was asked to do? Did the nurse experience a feeling of connectedness with the client? Did the client express awareness of this connectedness? More specifically, did the client express pleasure with the interventions used?

The best-researched outcome of developmental interventions with older adults thus far is life satisfaction. Other indicators of whether older clients have achieved ego integrity are expressions of disgust with self or others and their views of death. Do they express fear of death that extends beyond a normal fear of a painful dying process? How are they spending their days? Although social activity may not be an indicator of integrity, older people should have things to do that bring them pleasure.

Perhaps the most significant measure of the effectiveness of nurses' efforts to support the continued development of older adults will be significant decreases in their rates of suicide. Currently, older Americans, who make up just 12.6 percent of the population, represent 20.3 percent of suicides (1991 data).[26] The U.S. Department of Health and Human Services included in its Healthy People 2000 National Health Promotion and Disease Prevention Objectives a goal to reduce the rate of suicides to "no more than 39.2 per 100,000" by the

TABLE 25–2 HAIGHT'S LIFE REVIEW AND EXPERIENCING FORM

Childhood

1 What is the very first thing you can remember in your life? Go as far back as you can.
2 What other things can you remember about when you were very young?
3 What was life like for you as a child?
4 What were your parents like? What were their weaknesses and their strengths?
5 Did you have any brothers or sisters? If so, tell me what each was like.
6 Did someone close to you die when you were growing up?
7 Did someone important to you go away?
8 Do you ever remember being very sick?
9 Do you remember having an accident?
10 Do you remember being in a very dangerous situation?
11 Was something that was important to you lost or destroyed?
12 Was religion a large part of your life?
13 Did you enjoy being a boy or girl?

Adolescence

1 When you think about yourself and your life as a teenager, what is the first thing you can remember about that time?
2 What other things stand out in your memory about being a teenager?
3 Who were the important people for you (parents, brothers, sisters, friends, teachers, those you were especially close to, those you admired, those you wanted to be like)? Tell me about them.
4 Did you attend church or synagogue and youth groups?
5 Did you go to school? What was its meaning for you?
6 Did you work during these years?
7 Tell me of any hardships you experienced at this time.
8 Do you remember feeling that there was not enough food or necessities of life as a child or adolescent?
9 Do you remember feeling left alone, abandoned, or that you did not have enough love or care as a child or adolescent?
10 What were the pleasant things about your adolescence?
11 What was the most unpleasant thing about your adolescence?
12 All things considered, would you say you were happy or unhappy as a teenager?
13 Do you remember your first attraction to another person?
14 How did you feel about sexual activities and your own sexual identity?

Family and Home

1 How did your parents get along?
2 How did other people in your home get along?
3 What was the atmosphere in your home?
4 Were you punished as a child? For what? Who did the punishing? Who was "boss"?
5 When you wanted something from your parents, how did you go about getting it?
6 What kind of person did your parents like the most? the least?
7 Who were you closest to in your family?
8 Who in your family were you most like? In what way?

Adulthood

1 Now I'd like to talk to you about your life as an adult, from when you were in your 20s up to today. Tell me of the most important events that happened in your adulthood.
2 What place did religion play in your life?
3 What was life like for you in your 20s and 30s?
4 What kind of person were you? What did you enjoy?
5 Tell me about your work. Did you enjoy your work? Did you earn an adequate living? Did you work hard during those years? Were you appreciated?
6 Did you form significant relationships with other people?
7 Did you marry?
　(Yes)　What kind of person was your spouse?
　(No)　Why not?
8 Do you think marriages get better or worse over time? Were you married more than once?
9 On the whole, would you say you had a happy or an unhappy marriage?
10 Was sexual intimacy important to you?
11 What were some of the main difficulties you encountered during your adult years?
　a Did someone close to you die? go away?
　b Were you ever sick? Have an accident?
　c Did you move often? change jobs?
　d Did you ever feel alone? abandoned?
　e Did you ever feel needy?

TABLE 25-2   HAIGHT'S LIFE REVIEW AND EXPERIENCING FORM *(Continued)*

Summary

1   On the whole, what kind of life do you think you have had?
2   If everything were to be the same, would you like to live your life over again?
3   If you were going to live your life over again, what would you change? leave unchanged?
4   We have been talking about your life for quite some time now. Let's discuss your overall feelings and ideas about your life. What would you say have been the three main satisfactions in your life? Why were they satisfying?
5   Everyone has had disappointments. What have been the main disappointments in your life?
6   What was the hardest thing you had to face in your life? Please describe it.
7   What was the happiest period of your life? What about it made it the happiest period? Why is your life less happy now?
8   What was the unhappiest period of your life? Why is your life more happy now?
9   What was the proudest moment in your life?
10 If you could stay the same age all your life, what age would you choose? Why?
11 How do you think you have made out in life—better or worse than what you hoped for?
12 Let's talk a little about you as you are now. What are the best things about the age you are now?
13 What are the worst things about being the age you are now?
14 What are the most important things to you in your life today?
15 What do you hope will happen to you as you grow older?
16 What do you fear will happen to you as you grow older?
17 Have you enjoyed participating in this review of your life?

Source: Barbara K. Haight, RNC, Dr. PH, Professor of Nursing, College of Nursing, Medical University of South Carolina, Charleston, SC 29425-2404, 1982, with permission.

year 2000. If this objective is to be achieved, life satisfaction among older adults must be immediately and earnestly targeted for special intervention measures.

Research Highlights

A resurgence of interest in the development of older adults has begun. The renewed interest has provoked the initiation of more research efforts into the development of both healthy and ill older adults.

Finding that theories of human development were, for the most part, limited to their impact on healthy people and failed to sufficiently address the impact of illness or disability on developmental processes, Wright et al.[27] sought explanations through an exploration and analysis of the current literature. The chronic illnesses of Alzheimer's disease and cerebral vascular accidents were investigated to illustrate emerging changes in human development over the course of illness. They concluded that, among ill older adults and their family members, interaction with and attachment to another person, whether family member or professional caregiver, assumed increasing importance. As this attachment links ailing older adults to their environments, it becomes crucial to continued development.

Leidy and Darling-Fisher[28] studied the usefulness of the Modified Erickson Psychosocial Stage Inventory (MEPSI) as a tool for operationalizing and testing Ericksonian developmental theory in adults. The MEPSI is a simple survey measure designed to assess the strength of psychosocial attributes that arise from progression through Erickson's eight stages of development. The researchers studied four diverse samples: healthy young adults, hemophiliac men, healthy older adults, and older adults with chronic obstructive pulmonary disease.

As noted earlier, suicide rates among older adults are appallingly high. It is apparent that detecting older peo-

ple at risk for developing serious mental disorders is vital. Depression is the most common mental disorder among older adults. They may experience depression as they confront developmental tasks. Zauszniewski[29] contends that the first step in helping older adults to appraise their situations more positively and cope with their losses more effectively is assessment of the cognitive processes that may predispose or contribute to development of depressive illnesses. Zausniewski is currently developing a tool to accomplish this task, the Depressive Cognitions Scale (DCS) for older adults. The scale is derived from Erickson's psychosocial theory. "Each item reflects a depressive cognition that may arise from less than successful resolution of one of Erickson's developmental phases."[29] Preliminary psychometric testing of the DCS in a convenience sample of 60 healthy older adults has provided promising evidence of reliability and validity of the scale.

Implications for Research

With the fastest-growing age group being those over 85 years of age, the nation is seeing rapidly increasing numbers of people who become centenarians. There are 35 years of potential growth between the ages of 65 and 100. Yet developmental tasks of old age address this vast period as if it represented a single stage. Are there different developmental tasks for the young-old, middle-old, and old-old age groups? Is chronological age the best way to divide these tasks, or do better criteria exist?

Are there other interventions that will help older adults achieve the developmental tasks of old age? How does the guided autobiography compare with life review as an intervention technique used with older adults? Nurses need to research only a few of the many areas to enlarge the body of knowledge about development and developmental tasks during the later years of life.

Wright et al.[27] suggested the following areas of study for future research: "How can we structure environments, both home and institutional, to facilitate dependent elder persons' help-seeking behavior?" "Assuming that fear of abandonment leads to agitation, clinging and demanding behavior, depression, and overall, less cooperation from the ill person, how can we empower care givers to minimize this fear in their afflicted family members?" "Assuming that an alternate, but consistently available significant other or professional care giver can reduce detachment, are there ways to substitute an attachment figure if the primary care giver dies or is emotionally or physically unable to provide positive interactions?"

The work of Leidy and Darling-Fisher and Zauszniewski suggests that nurses must continue to develop tools for exploring questions pertaining to human development among older adults.

Summary

All the work that has been conducted in the area of development and aging points to the need to prepare for old age throughout one's life. When adequate preparation has not been made, however, the nurse can still help older adults reflect on their lives and accept that those lives transpired as they had to. A sense of peaceful satisfaction may then be experienced that allows the older adult to face death with equanimity.

Student Learning Activities

1 View the film *The Whales of August.* How does the film depict such issues as the need for independence, self-maintenance, and an individual's unique coping patterns?

2 The continuity theory of aging suggests that the quest for continuity is the central task of old age. How does this film present the need for continuity as a dominant theme?

3 How will you use the insights you gained from the film in your professional nursing practice?

4 Select a community-living older adult and conduct a life review using Haight's Life Review and Experiencing Form. Summarize your findings and present them to the class.

REFERENCES

1 Carpenter, M: Don't Call Me Old: A Book of Poems, revised ed. 314 W 5th North St, Summerville, SC 29483, 1985, p 71.
2 The Holy Bible, King James Version. World Publishing, Cleveland, p 501.
3 Rogers, ME: Nursing: A science of unitary man. In Riehl, JP, and Roy, C (eds): Conceptual Models for Nursing Practice, ed 2. Appleton-Century-Crofts, New York, 1980, pp 329–337.
4 Reed, P: Implications of the life-span developmental framework for well-being in adulthood and aging. Adv Nurs Sci 6:19, 1983.
5 Morris, D: The Book of Ages. Viking, New York, 1983.
6 Havighurst, R: Developmental Tasks and Education. David McKay, New York, 1952, p 92.
7 Erickson, E: Childhood and Society, ed 2. WW Norton, New York, 1963.
8 Peck, RC: Psychological developments in the second half of life. In Neugarten, BL (ed): Middle Age and Aging. University of Chicago Press, Chicago, 1968, p 88.
9 Leddy, S, and Pepper, JM: Theories as a basis for practice. In Leddy, S, and Pepper, JM (eds): Conceptual Basis of Professional Nursing, ed 2. JB Lippincott, Philadelphia, 1989, p 166.
10 Fiske, M: Tasks and crises of the second half of life: The interrelationship of commitment, coping, and adaptation. In Birren, J, and Sloane, R (eds): Handbook of Mental Health and Aging. Prentice-Hall, Englewood Cliffs, NJ, 1980, p 337.
11 Cooper, A: Life review. Paper submitted to Medical University of South Carolina, College of Nursing, 1990.
12 Ebersole, P, and Hess, P: Toward Healthy Aging: Human Needs and Nursing Response. CV Mosby, St Louis, 1990.
13 Stenback, A: Depression and suicidal behavior in old age. In Birren, J, and Sloane, B (eds): Handbook of Mental Health and Aging. Prentice-Hall, Englewood Cliffs, NJ, 1980, p 616.
14 Havighurst, RJ: Developmental tasks of later maturity. In Developmental Tasks and Education. David McKay, New York, 1952, p 92.
15 Duvall, E: Family Development, ed 3. JB Lippincott, Philadelphia, 1967.
16 Beaton, SR: Styles of reminiscence and ego development of older women residing in long-term care settings. Int J Aging Hum Dev 32:53, 1991.
17 Clayton, V: Erickson's theory of human development as it applies to the aged: Wisdom as contradictive cognition. Hum Dev 18:119, 1975.
18 Butler, R: Successful aging and the role of the life review. J Am Geriatr Soc 22:529, 1974.
19 Haight, BK: Life review: Part I, A method for pastoral counseling. J Religion Aging 5:17, 1989.
20 Haight, BK: The therapeutic role of a structured life review process in homebound elderly subjects. J Gerontol 43:40, 1988.
21 Wysocki, MR: Life review for the elderly patient. Nursing 13:46, 1983.
22 Birren, J: The best of all stories. Psychol Today 21:91, 1987.
23 Burnside, I: Nursing and the Aged: A Self-Care Approach, ed 3. McGraw-Hill, New York, 1988, p 77.
24 Erickson, EH, et al: Vital Involvement in Old Age: The Experience of Old Age in Our Time. Norton, New York, 1986, pp 33, 74.
25 O'Bryant, SL: Older widows and independent lifestyles. Int J Aging Hum Dev 32:41, 1991.
26 McIntosh, JL: Suicide facts and myths: A study of prevalence. Death Studies 9(3/4):267–281, 1985.
27 Wright, LK, et al: Human development in the context of aging and chronic illness: The role of attachment in Alzheimer's disease and stroke. Int J Aging Hum Dev 41(2):133–150, 1995.
28 Leidy, NK, and Darling-Fisher, CS: Reliability and validity of the Modified Erickson Psychosocial Stage Inventory in diverse samples. West J Nurs Res 17(2):168–187, 1995.
29 Zauszniewski, JA: Development and testing of a measure of depressive cognitions in older adults. J Nurs Meas 3(1):31–41, 1995.

CHAPTER 26

Family Dynamics

Barbara K. Haight / Kelly H. Leech / Joelle A. Graham*

OBJECTIVES

Upon completion of this chapter, the reader will be able to:

- Describe how power structure and role structure influence the functioning of the family
- Discuss the varying family processes that affect the psychodynamics of family interactions
- Identify the clinical manifestations of problems occurring within the family as a result of the age-related impact on structures, functions, and processes
- Describe the primary and secondary prevention strategies a nurse would use with an older adult facing retirement, reduced income, relocation, isolation, or powerlessness

Today's aging family differs greatly from aging families as we knew them in the past. As families change, so do the dynamics within the family. Thus, the dissensions, problems, and practices of today's aging families are unique to the 1990s.

The nuclear family is no longer the traditional family; neither is the extended family. Increasing divorces, single parenthood, and nontraditional unions have all led to a new image of family. Single parents manage more than one-third of today's families. Because of the lengthening life span, these single parents may be responsible for the care of an aging family member as well. Nursing management cannot happen in isolation but must be couched in the family system to be successful.

History

The best way to understand family functioning in old age is to gain knowledge of past family functioning through a family review. Just as a life review gives clues to people's coping skills and responses to crisis,[1] a family review provides information on family functioning.[2] A family review or history provides an understanding of the way families assign meaning to certain events. The review provides a historical perspective on family interactions, cultural influences, social class information,

feelings of filial obligation, and religious preferences. A family history also can provide information regarding health status and the family's view of health.

Many family researchers report that family history repeats itself. A genogram also may provide background for interventions to interrupt the family history and change the course of events. For example, Great Uncle Henry was an alcoholic and a loner. At age 18, his father kicked him out of the house. He has not interacted with the family for 20 years. Information about Uncle Henry provides knowledge for the present generation; there is a history of alcoholism, and there is little tolerance within the family for deviant behavior. Great-Grandfather's act of kicking Henry out showed a quick temper, lack of tolerance, and a sense of finality and disengagement in his approach to family problems. Uncle Henry's response shows a lack of forgiveness and a wish to function away from the family. These past actions may provide an understanding for Grandson Ben's affinity to alcohol and for how the present client, Grandma Ellen, is coping with the problem.

Unit of Study

Fink advises that one must study the family using a unit approach and looking at the influence of resources and demands on the entire family unit.[3] It is also essential to determine the unit of study when dealing with the aging family. Over time, the unit changes, as do affil-

---

*Special thanks to Kathy Brungard and Matthew Leech for their assistance in the preparation of this chapter.

iations and needs. Now, the most common unit is the nuclear family; however, the nuclear family unit will change with age. Troll[4] provided excellent insight into the changing family structure over time. Using her own family to exemplify the tier concept, Troll described her original first-tier family as her parents and herself, with the extended family subsumed in the second tier. After marriage, the first tier changed to become husband and children, with parents and siblings joining the second tier of the extended family. As time passed, Troll's children grew and left home. Then Troll and her husband separated, resulting in an isolated existence for her with no first tier, and her children becoming part of the second tier. Later, when Troll's mother moved in, a new first tier formed, composed of Troll and her mother. However, the roles had reversed, so Troll was now the primary caregiver.

Troll's description of tiers is similar to a description of primary and secondary relationships. For a period, such as the time Troll lived separated from all family tiers, the primary relationships of an older person may not even be with family members. The significant other may be someone with whom the older person can discuss problems and share confidences. Research shows that life satisfaction increases for older people in the presence of a significant other, who often substitutes for first-tier family relationships.[5]

Structure

To gain a better understanding of the aging family unit, one must be aware of different configurations and the impact of the configuration on the unit. The configurations include married, divorced, widowed, childless, and remarried people. Each of these configurations affects the status of the aging person within the family system. Therefore, the approach to care in each configuration is different. Table 26–1 describes the concerns unique to each family configuration.[2] The story of Mrs. J illustrates the problem of remarrying in old age.

CASE 1 Mrs. J was withdrawn, uncommunicative, and apparently depressed. She spent most of her day drawn into herself or crying. During the interview with Mrs. J, the nurse found that Mrs. J had remarried 10 years ago against the wishes of her children and her new husband's children. Despite the lack of support for their union, Mr. and Mrs. J were blissfully happy and the marriage was a success. However, like most older people, Mr. and Mrs. J became more frail with each passing year. Both Mr. and Mrs. J had chronic illnesses, were failing in eyesight and hearing, and found they had to call on their children for help. For a while, the children were responsive but eventually decided it was too much trouble to travel to another town to help their parents. Finally, the children decided that each family would be responsible for its own parent. Mr. J's family took him 50 miles away to live with his daughter, and Mrs. J's family placed her in a nursing home. The children did not consider the effect of the separa-

tion on Mr. and Mrs. J. The children considered the problem solved, and the parents had to comply because they were dependent on their children. As Mrs. J talked, she said, "The hardest thing is not knowing how he is or where he is. I won't even know when he dies!" That is the plight of one reconfigured family as independence is lost and control is taken away.

POWER STRUCTURE

In a normally configured family, a variety of structures exist. One is the power structure, which the nurse should assess in working with the family. In Case 1, the power moved from the parents to the children as the parents began to lose their physical ability to maintain the power. Every family has a power structure that is a reflection of the family's unwritten rules and underlying value system.[6] Knowledge of the power structure helps the nurse understand the family dynamics. Those with the power make the decisions that influence all family members.

In most traditional North American families, the power often lies with the father or chief male, but as the family ages and the father retires, much of the power reverts to the mother. The mother is usually in charge of the home and has a set management routine and certain ways of doing things. If a decision must be made re-

TABLE 26–1 RECONFIGURED FAMILIES AND RESULTING CONCERNS

Configuration	Concerns
Married couple	Change in roles More time together Task sharing Retirement and income Mutual support
Divorce	Decreased income Decreased social interaction Lost family interaction Need for new identity New daily routines Discrimination and alienation
Widowhood	Bereavement Loneliness Decreased income Possible relocation Decreased intimacy and support Decline in health Decreased social network
Remarriage	Alienated children Need to establish new patterns and relationships Issues of adjustment New family
Childlessness	Decreased sense of legacy Decreased primary relationships Isolation Fewer family contacts Fewer social contacts Increased institutionalization

garding the home, the mother often makes it. As the family continues to age and the parents become more frail, the power is passed on to the children, who assume the decision-making powers of the parent, sometimes regardless of the parent's wishes.

Understanding the power structure in the family is essential in formulating nursing interventions. For example:

> CASE 2   Mrs. L needed to visit the physician weekly to get a vitamin B$_{12}$ shot. She did not drive and had no one to take her to the doctor, so she had to rely on taxis, which were expensive. As Mrs. L talked about the expense, she laughingly called her husband "Mr. Budget" and said, "He'll never let me take a taxi every week." Thus, "Mr. Budget" could have affected Mrs. L's compliance with treatment if he exerted his power and decided the treatment and travel were too expensive. The nurse had to work through the husband's value system and power base to ensure that Mrs. L would continue with her treatment.

The abuse of power exists in many families. Violence is a learned way of life, and the powerful father may use force in his disciplinarian role. Often, one child becomes the victim of this discipline and endures much distress throughout a lifetime. As the family ages, the balance of power shifts. This same victimized child, as an adult, may then hold power over the abusive parent. Battering or other mistreatment of the parent is often the result. If the child uses power as learned from the father, the father may become the victim. The adult child may not even realize that he or she is "getting even" for past abuses.

The nurse can assess the power in the family by observing family interactions and communications. Another way the nurse may assess this power is by asking questions such as the following: "Who pays the bills?" "Who decides where to work and live?" "Who decides how to spend an evening, whether to buy a car, and when to visit relatives?" and "Who's really in charge?" Many people think they are in charge when they really are not. One partner allows the other to make most of the decisions, but they are nonpowerful decisions such as what movie to see or what color to paint the kitchen. The truly powerful partner retains the right to make the life decisions but is skillful enough to keep that knowledge private.

ROLE STRUCTURE

Each family member plays a role according to position and status in the family system. Roles are based on the expectations of others and self. In a young family, the mother plays the role of nurturer, the father that of provider. The mother often also assumes the role of peacemaker, the person who translates actions and thoughts for other family members. However, Figure 26–1 shows that removing the peacemaker improves communication between the remaining family members. An analysis of the peacemaker role shows that some assumed roles create pitfalls rather than enhance the family relationship.

As the family ages, the roles change. The father-provider becomes more nurturing,[7] resulting from the self-examination that occurs with aging. During this self-examination, the father-provider finds he was so busy working that he never got a chance to establish close relationships with his children. In young-old age, he may have his last chance to do so. The father may become the family communicator, the one who keeps in touch with the children. This newly nurturing father often has a chance to enjoy his grandchildren more than he did his own children. There may actually be more role-sharing in the aging family.

For the aging woman, the empty nest syndrome may be met with joy instead of sadness because the change provides an opportunity for the mother to explore her own potential. Of course, there is the other type of aging woman who is so imbedded in the role of parent and wife that the empty nest brings unhappiness. The ability of the family to respond to change via role flexibility is of utmost importance in successful family functioning. This may be particularly true for the aging family.

Processes and Functions

Various family processes and functions affect the psychodynamics of family interactions at all ages. These are the communication process, the family's value orientation, and the affective and socialization functions of the family.

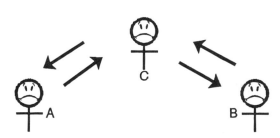

Communication with Peacemaker

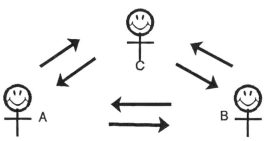

Communication without Peacemaker

Figure 26–1   Family peacemaker role.

COMMUNICATION PROCESS

Processes, within a family, are the results of family functioning. Each family communicates in its own way, some more effectively than others. Unclear communication is a major contributor to poor family functioning. Nonverbal behavior is as important to the communication process as verbal behavior. All behavior is a form of communication, of one person sending a message to another. An observant nurse can assess family functioning by observing communication without hearing a word.

Functional families openly express emotions and feelings to one another. They show a mutual respect for one another's feelings and listen to and respond to one another. A certain level of trust and self-esteem permeates the communication patterns of functional families. Because of this trust, family members freely use self-disclosure. People who feel safe with one another can manage conflict and disagreement. Through conflict, family members get to know and understand each other better. If openness exists, conflict can be a positive thing that leads to increased family functioning.

The nurse should assess certain aspects of family communication. First, the nurse should examine the pattern of communication in the family. Is it direct and are communication lines open among subsystems? Is the method of communication open or closed? What is the content of the communication? Are there affective messages? How are feelings expressed and received? Do family members demonstrate respect for one another, at any age?[8]

VALUE ORIENTATION

Family values often have a cultural focus that may influence the family's health-care practices. The value systems of the nurse and of the family may differ also. The nurse needs to recognize any disparity between his or her value system and that of the client's family. These differences must be recognized, accepted, and overcome for the nurse to function effectively with a particular family member. The following example illustrates disparity of values between nurse and client.

CASE 3 Mr. F was an 85-year-old Lutheran minister who was dying and lived alone at home. The hospice nurse visited Mr. F twice weekly to bathe him and to provide comfort. Mr. F looked forward to these visits and often fell to talking about the past and reminiscing with the nurse. The nurse had read about reminiscing and life review and knew that it would be therapeutic for Mr. F to reminisce. Thus, the nurse encouraged Mr. F to talk about his past. One day he said, "I have a little story you will enjoy," and he proceeded to describe his ministry to his congregation during World War II. The church was in the Midwest, and its members were farmers, many able to speak only in German. As a result, the church members experienced prejudice from other "all-American" farmers. The American farmers viewed the Germans with suspicion, sometimes even as Nazis. It was Mr. F's job to build morale among his parishioners. To do so, he initiated a church fair, with the proceeds to be donated to the Red Cross. When the fair was over and donations counted, Mr. F and the church's board of directors decided to play a trick on the prejudiced American farmers, so they donated the proceeds to the German war effort. Mr. F chuckled and laughed as he relived his cleverness during that time.

The nurse was appalled. Should the nurse tell Mr. F he had committed an act of treason? Should the nurse impose patriotic values on Mr. F? The answer is no: The nurse in the role of caregiver is there to support Mr. F's dying, to encourage his recall, and to help him be at peace with himself. The nurse needed to disregard part of her own value system while caring for Mr. F and accept Mr. F for himself. Values, whether cultural or inherited, must be understood fully to understand family behavior. Nursing interventions must be couched in the family's own value system to be effective.[9]

AFFECTIVE FUNCTION

The affective function is the internal function of the family, the meeting of the psychosocial needs of family members by other family members. In aging families, a significant other often fulfills the affective function, particularly when the aging family member lives alone. Part of social support is love and affection.[10] Love and affection must be examined separately as a part of care and concern in affective family functioning.

As families age, they tend to lose some of the affective function that binds them together. When spouses die and children move away, siblings again assume a greater level of importance in the affective relationship, as the following example illustrates:

CASE 4 Mrs. K grew up with nine siblings and enjoyed their company. When she married, Mrs. K moved away to her husband's home town and assumed closer relationships with her husband's family than with her own family of origin. She kept in touch with her siblings by attending family reunions and holiday gatherings throughout her marriage. Fifty-five years later, Mr. K died. Mrs. K's daughters lived in other cities. As Mrs. K grieved, her sisters became a strong source of support. They took turns calling her and seeing to her needs. One weekend, the sisters all returned to the original homestead and enjoyed a pajama party, at which they reminisced about the past. The sisters made plans to travel and enjoy future events together. After 55 years, siblings again supported Mrs. K, demonstrated love and affection, and became important to Mrs. K's affective functioning.

Siblings provide a unique social resource in old age. Although they may have little contact throughout certain parts of a lifetime, they have bonded early and shared a past. Even though frequency of contact decreases, affectional closeness may increase. Siblings may not help each other often, but they are there in the background, performing a "watchdog" function and becoming available when needed.[11] Female siblings nurture this sibling attachment more than male siblings. Women often persist in being the keepers of the affective family function throughout a lifetime.[12]

SOCIALIZATION FUNCTION

Socialization is a group of learning experiences provided within the family that teaches family members how to function and assume roles in adult society. If the family uses self-care in time of illness, the family member socialized by this process will probably use self-care in later life.

Much of the current family socialization process falls to the school or other institutions. Current learned behavior may teach adult children to put their parents in nursing homes, just as their parents put them in child care in their youth. The notion of not interrupting a career to care for a family member may persist throughout a generation.

Grandparents often fulfill the socialization functions in families. In a study of expectations of grandparents, Kennedy[13] found that young people thought grandparents were important role models. They were loving, helping, and comforting and provided some of the socialization neglected by parents.

Aging parents are also family resources. Aging family members often provide parenting to help adult children cope with life stresses. The movement of reserve troops in the war in the Persian Gulf highlighted older adults as resources, many of whom interrupted their "golden years" to care for young children left behind by military parents. Thus, aging parents may become significant resources for their children.[14]

A new issue of the socialization process may be the continued socialization of grown children who never leave home. In difficult economic times, grown children often live at home and maintain the role of child. Thus, new problems emerge as aging parents and grown children renegotiate their roles. Aquilino and Supple[15] found that coresidence is possible when the people living together engage in mutually pleasurable activities. Coresidence can enhance intergenerational solidarity in old age.

Clinical Manifestations

Clinical manifestations of problems occur within the family as age affects each of the structures, functions, and processes. Transitions are normal passages that present themselves as families age. There is a trajectory in which one transition instigates another, resulting in still another, and manifesting problems for the family as a unit. Because the family is a unit composed of differing parts, a change in one part will cause change in another part. Aging has a cause-and-effect relationship in families. For example, during the first transition of aging—retirement—there is not only role loss for the person who retires, but also a shift in the power system within the family and changes in the communicative and affective functions of the family.

Money also may become a problem in retirement. Age reduces income for most people, and reduced income means that certain choices that may influence family well-being and interfere with family functioning must be made. People may have to change location, adjust their diets, and change their expectations. Reduced income can cause major lifestyle changes.

Relocation is another transition. Many families relocate as they age. Sometimes relocation is by choice; sometimes reduced income and inability to manage a home force relocation. Whatever the cause, relocation requires a period of adjustment. The family may encounter unforeseen problems that require adjustment and change.

As age progresses and transitions occur, death may cause bereavement for significant others. Older people often experience bereavement. As people age, their cohorts and family members die. These deaths first produce bereavement, then loneliness and isolation. Bereavement alone can cause confusion, malnutrition, depression, and sickness in the surviving spouse, other family member, or significant other.

Isolation and loneliness are particularly problematic for people in reconfigured families who have experienced divorce or who are childless. Aging people may lack the energy to keep up former social contacts. Retreating to home can cause an isolation resulting in loneliness, particularly if no first-tier family members are present to combat that loneliness. An isolated older person may no longer benefit from the affective and socialization processes of the family and may lack the energy to reach out to others.

Finally, increased frailty occurs, which raises caregiving issues. For the older person, the result of frailty is a loss of control and a growing dependence on others. Frailty may cause the older person to change living arrangements and search for support systems. Frailty begins the downward spiral ending in powerlessness. Often, with this decline, one spouse must become caregiver for another, resulting in caregiver stress in the well spouse, leading to even more difficulties for aging families.

Management

RETIREMENT AND ROLE LOSS

For some, retirement is a joyous event; for others, a source of unhappiness. Many losses may occur with retirement: loss of role, identity, collegial relationships, significant others, and direction in life.[16] Retirement is particularly stressful for the person devoted to work who has not developed other interests and hobbies. Johnston[17] studied the effect of retirement on marriages and found that men were happier than women in retirement. She added that during retirement, spouses become increasingly aware of their partners' faults. Although children served as an important source of conversation, retired couples did not increase time spent with them, nor did they increase time spent together. Those less satisfied in retirement have unfinished agendas at work and perceive retirement as unfeasible. These people deny the existence of retirement and make no plans to adjust. Their impact on family functioning may be crucial as they manifest signs of boredom, apathy, and lack of meaning in life. An example is given in the case of Mr. S, age 56, who is exhibiting physical signs of stress:

> CASE 5   Mr. S came into the clinic complaining of increasing abdominal pain over the past several weeks, with weight loss, decreased appetite, fatigue, and inability to sleep. He related, "My wife said if I didn't come in to get checked, she would kill me. I guess I'm driving her crazy."
>
> A thorough physical examination and medical tests revealed no physiological cause for Mr. S's complaints. The nurse practitioner reviewed Mr. S's family health assessment and found that he had just retired. The nurse learned that Mr. S was a successful law enforcement officer with 25 years' experience who had been forced to retire because of personnel cuts. He had devoted most of his adult life to his job, working long hours and successfully progressing from an entry-level position as a uniformed officer to a senior detective in the homicide division.
>
> Meanwhile, Mrs. S had been a homemaker except for limited part-time jobs to supplement the family's income. She had managed all household and financial decisions for the family and raised three children to adulthood with little assistance from her husband. Since then, Mrs. S has been an active volunteer with a close circle of friends, spending four or five evenings a week with them.
>
> Mr. S stated, "I guess I'm just getting under her feet; she doesn't need me; the force dumped me. I guess I'm no good to anyone, and now, on top of that, I'm sick!"
>
> The nurse practitioner suspected that Mr. S's unexpected retirement and consequential role loss had caused tension in the family unit and a decrease in Mr. S's self-esteem, resulting in his physical complaints.

1 Primary Prevention

Retirement is a significant life event that requires planning and realistic expectations of life changes. Primary prevention of problems associated with retirement deal mainly with increasing the family unit's awareness of these changes before they occur. Table 26–2 outlines anticipatory actions the retiring person can take.

An assertive primary prevention tool suggested by Johnston[17] is a marital enhancement program at retirement (MEPR). The MEPR addresses the demands and adjustments made on the family unit before and during the retirement transition. It includes counseling time for couples to identify and appreciate their partners outside

TABLE 26–2 ANTICIPATORY ACTIONS FOR THE RETIRING PERSON

- Planning ahead to ensure adequate income.
- Developing friends not associated with work.
- Decreasing time at work in the last years before retirement by taking longer vacations, working shorter days, or working part-time.
- Developing routines to replace the structure of the work day.
- Relying on people and groups other than spouse to fill leisure time.
- Developing leisure time activities before retirement that are realistic in energy and monetary cost.
- Preparing for exhilaration followed by ambivalence before satisfaction with one's lifestyle develops.
- Assessing living arrangements, and if relocation is necessary, expending time in developing new social networks.
- Expecting role loss to have a short-term impact on self-esteem and one's marital relationship.[16]

the roles they had played during the career portions of their marriage, helps them identify what the new roles should be, and helps them organize and define these new aspects of their lifestyles.

2 Secondary Prevention

If the family unit heads into retirement without considering these factors, or does so with unrealistic expectations and goals, perhaps not even discussed with the rest of the family unit, difficulties will arise that the health-care professional may need to address and treat. Nursing diagnoses applying to problems associated with retirement are anxiety, decisional conflict, altered family processes, fear, knowledge deficit, personal identity disturbance, self-esteem disturbance, and social isolation.

Of these, the most common problem for the retired person is self-esteem disturbance. Self-esteem is one's assessment of self-worth, a positive or negative interpretation of the extent that the person views himself or herself as being capable, worthy, and significant. Feelings of self-worth are often closely associated with a person's career. Thus, retirement may reduce self-esteem. Table 26–3 plans care for decreased self-esteem.

Research Findings

In the literature, certain similarities have been found among retirees who had anticipated and planned for this life event. These retirees enjoyed the retired phase of life, particularly the freedom and the time to travel, and were very family focused.[14] Other research[16] found that those who had enjoyed their work were more healthy after retiring, and Fletcher and Hansson[18] reported retirement anxiety in people who usually had difficulty with major life transitions.

TABLE 26–3 NURSING CARE PLAN FOR THE CLIENT EXPERIENCING DECREASED SELF-ESTEEM RELATED TO RETIREMENT

Nursing Diagnosis: Self-esteem disturbance related to major life event, role disturbance	
Expected Outcomes	*Nursing Interventions*
Client and spouse will identify and express feelings and concerns related to retirement.	Encourage role playing by having the partners assume one another's roles.
Client and spouse will relate these concerns to present situation, identifying areas of dissatisfaction.	Help them identify feelings and concerns.
Client and spouse will identify new interests and role expectations and adapt to changing lifestyle in a positive manner.	Have the couple identify specific qualities about each other unrelated to the work experience that will help them begin to view each other positively in retirement.
	Encourage the client to explore areas of interest not yet experienced by listing activities he or she had enjoyed or would like to enjoy that are unrelated to work.
	Assist the couple in exploring these new activities.
	Discuss ways to incorporate them into each other's changing lifestyles.

Moneyham and Scott suggest that there is an emerging view of older adults as capable of developing meaningful lifestyles.[19] The newest research recommends that one look at families as a whole unit to determine the time of retirement. Smith reported that family world view and communication style significantly influenced both family and individual adaptation to retirement.[20] Physical health greatly affects retirement. Men reported pulmonary disease and heart attack as decreasing quality of life in retirement, whereas women were more affected by arthritis.[21]

REDUCED INCOME

Retirement means reduced income for many older adults. After struggling financially throughout a lifetime to buy a home and raise a family, many people fail to plan financially for retirement. Problems associated with reduced income vary, depending on the extent of the income reduction and on the actual and perceived adjustments a family must make to meet new financial realities. If the lifestyle changes result in loss of activities and friends, the client could experience fear, anxiety, self-esteem disturbances, social isolation, and perhaps even a personal identity disturbance.

1 *Primary Prevention*

Primary prevention of problems associated with a reduction in income include education and awareness about the meaning of the reduction to the family. Proper financial planning and investments made while the client is still working may offset the expected reduction of income enough to maintain a similar standard of living into the retirement years. Thus, primary prevention should begin early in the family's life span. If that is impossible, the identification of the problem at an early stage of old age will enable the client to plan for future lifestyle changes. Planning will allow more control in decision making and add an increased sense of autonomy.

Research Findings

Once the initial financial effects on retirement income take place, retirees adjust to the reduced resources. Krause, Liang, and Jay[22] studied financial strain in both American and Japanese populations, discovering that financial strain eroded feelings of self-worth and control in both cultures. In a study of older widow lifestyles, O'Bryant[23] reported that widows with adequate income were more independent because they could hire someone to help with traditionally male tasks such as minor household repairs and car care. Because of this impact of income on independence and psychological well-being, responsible financial planning should be encouraged during the middle years.[24]

RELOCATION

Relocation may occur through both necessity and choice. Some older people neither plan nor think through relocation. The "snowbird" couple is the most common example of those who relocate in an unplanned manner, settling in a new place with no established ties, no place of worship, no family, no friends, no history. Then these couples must begin again. Often, one spouse adjusts well to the relocation and the other does not. This lack of adjustment affects the family socialization process and may mean the loss of significant others, family, network, and support systems.

Connidis and Davies[5] researched the place of family and friends as companions and confidants in later life. They describe a companion as a person who shares activities and may or may not be a confidant. Geographic proximity affects companion status. Thus, relocation affects the confidant and companion network among older adults.

Nurses often see older people before, during, and after a transfer from one environment to another, such as relocation to a nursing home far from familiar surroundings. Relocation may be less stressful and life more satisfying when the degree of change in physical and psychosocial environments is not great.[25] The change should be slow and gradual. The older people involved should be at the center of the decision-making process.

It is important for nurses who work with the elderly in institutions and in the community to be aware of translocation stress. Nurses should develop the environmental and procedural changes necessary to help minimize the harmful effects of relocation. Once sensitized to the psychological and physical impact of translocation, nurses can strive for ways to minimize inherent risks. Nurses who have a basic understanding about the effect of the environment on an individual's mental and physical well-being have much to contribute toward alleviating the patient's translocation stress.[25]

1 Primary Prevention

Primary prevention of problems related to relocation focuses mainly on relocation of older people from one health-care facility to another, but these interventions can be adapted to relate to older people experiencing any type of relocation. Preparatory programs for relocation are helpful. In these programs, older adults visit the new site and are informed of various aspects of the new location. Support systems and counseling should be available before, during, and after the relocation to facilitate adjustment, particularly in institutions.

2 Secondary Prevention

Clinical manifestations vary according to the type of relocation. An older person who is moved to a nursing home without his or her consent or knowledge might experience increased confusion, memory deficits, bizarre behavior, decreased trust, and increased dependency. Older adults who find themselves without usual activities and support mechanisms may experience insecurity about new living arrangements, increased stress and anxiety, decreased life satisfaction, and decreased levels of social activity.[25]

Research Findings

Most of the relocation literature addresses institutional relocation. Wives of institutionalized men are passing through the first stage of the transition to widowhood. These women, though experiencing a decrease in burden, also experience low morale, poor health, and increased depression. Matzo and Bernsee[26] describe a different type of relocation, that of the chronically mentally ill older adult from the institution to the community. They describe a model project known as Heritage House as a way to meet these older people's needs. Nurses must remember that relocation, even from bed to bed in a hospital setting, can create new problems that must be attended. Currently, many believe that older people prefer to age in place and remain connected to home and environment.[27] However, this belief may be refuted by the growing number of retirees who choose to move to the south or live in retirement communities.[28] Children seem to pick the relocation site regardless of parental needs, but when the parents require care, distance becomes a factor and the nearest child often becomes the caregiver.[29]

ISOLATION AND LONELINESS

There seems to be a natural trajectory in the life span as each of these transitions creates another transition. The widow may need to move back home to be supported by children; the childless person may choose to live near siblings. People need close ties with family toward the end of life. Although their confidants may not be family members, there is some need to be near family as age progresses and death nears. Considering the shifts in family function that occur over time, the family maintains an even more important role in old age.[30]

Although isolation is an environmentally created situation and loneliness an inner sense, the two are closely related. One can feel lonely in the midst of a large group, particularly with the loss of a spouse, whereas isolation occurs situationally. Those who are most isolated are those who have moved away from family or whose children have moved away. The 1970s and 1980s produced many transplanted families as a result of occupational relocation. These families, as they grow older, may be among the most socially isolated. The trend toward small families also may contribute to isolation among older adults. People retain a need for interpersonal intimacy and human contact until they die.[31]

1 Primary Prevention

Primary prevention of problems associated with isolation and loneliness involves the education of people providing care to older adults. Being aware of the potential for isolation and knowing the signs of loneliness may help prevent these in older adults.

Older people become isolated or experience loneliness for a variety of reasons. Factors identified by Elsen and Belgen[32] include decline or lack of physical abilities, loss of social roles and relationships, anxieties about or deficiencies in social skills, lack of a shared language, or decreased desire to communicate. These factors need not be mutually exclusive. One person may avoid interactions because of anxieties caused by illness. Isolation in others may be caused by multiple factors such as illness concurrent with a decrease in relationships. One older person may be uncommunicative because of difficulty hearing, another because of a lack of shared language.

Characteristics of isolation can be as subtle as a tendency to avoid social gatherings or to be preoccupied with one's own thoughts and memories, or as obvious as withdrawal, with lack of eye contact and flat affect. Isolated older people may be uncommunicative, avoid eye contact, appear to be sad, or have few significant others with whom to interact. They may express feelings of aloneness, rejection, and insecurity in their ability to interact successfully.

2 *Secondary Prevention*

A thorough assessment is necessary to identify causes for isolation and plan goals and interventions to overcome it. A highly effective method of assessment is that of direct observation in older people's everyday surroundings. A self-reporting questionnaire may provide an insight into the older person's perceptions of his or her social skills and reasons for avoiding interactions not readily obtained through observation. Table 26–4 presents a helpful tool for assessing social skills.

Several nursing diagnoses may be used to identify problems of loneliness, the most pertinent of which is social isolation. The nursing diagnosis of social isolation or impaired social interaction may be based on other causes (e.g., social isolation related to decreased desire to communicate, secondary to impaired physical mobility).

Research Findings

Uhlenberg and Cooney[30] found that women with more children communicated more with family members and that large families were more likely to help aging parents. The communication patterns developed early in life can follow a family as they age and if the patterns are poor, they can interfere with family interactions and important decisions throughout a lifetime.[9] There was also a significantly positive relationship between mothers and children in large families. Mullins and Dugan[33] examined the impact of various social rela-

TABLE 26–4   SOCIAL SKILL CHECKLIST

Please rate aspects of the resident's social behavior on the following scale.
  1 equals Serious difficulty in this area, disturbing to others
  2 equals General difficulty in this area, interferes with social interaction
  3 equals Difficulty in some situations or with some people
  4 equals Generally appropriate, does not interfere with social interaction
  5 equals Very appropriate, definite asset
  N.O. equals Not observed
Your assessment should be based on observations of the resident's behavior in a number of different settings over a period of 2 weeks.
  Remember to add comments as necessary and to summarize the information at the end.

Nonverbal Behavior	Rating	Comments
1 Facial expression		
2 Eye contact		
3 Body posture		
4 Body movements		
5 Social distance		
6 Tone of voice		
7 Loudness of speech		
8 Speed of speech		
9 Spontaneity of speech		
10 Hesitations in speech		
11 General appearance		
12 Holding casual conversations		
13 Showing interest in what other people say		
14 Expressing feelings appropriately		
15 Disagreeing with people without getting upset		
16 Keeping symptoms from being intrusive		
17 Asking for help when needed		
18 Accepting compliments		
19 Cooperating with others		
20 Responding to criticism		
21 Other problems (please specify)		

Please also comment on the following:

22 Social supports in the community		
23 Friendships in the hospital		
24 Degree of social anxiety		
25 Response to organized social activities		
26 Interest in social activities		

Summarize key areas in need of some intervention.

tionships on levels of loneliness and found that those who were dissatisfied with their relationships were more lonely. It did not matter whether the relationships were with siblings, neighbors, children, or grandchildren. In a clinical report, Palmer[34] saw failure to thrive as an outcome of social isolation and warned against the development of failure-to-thrive syndrome. Two nurse researchers suggest that we interview older people who are alone but not lonely and teach their strategies of coping to other old people who suffer from loneliness.[35]

FRAILTY AND DEPENDENCE

Increased frailty is a condition of advancing age that leads to increasing dependence. A role exchange occurs at this time, particularly between mothers and daughters, possibly resulting in role strain for those mothers and daughters with previously unsatisfactory relationships. The role strain results from role demand overload and perceived role inadequacy, particularly when the daughters become the primary caregivers.

In other research on mother-child relationships,[8] mothers were found to be unhappy with their adult children. Many mothers reported providing children with substantial goods and services at great personal cost to themselves. Still other older people report a feeling of subordination to their adult children, which leads to dependence. Many older people fear becoming dependent more than they fear death. Having been in charge of themselves for an entire lifetime, they find it hard to give up that control even when they can no longer manage for themselves.

Frailty and dependence, then, cause a complete change in the family system. The frail older person no longer retains power. Roles change, with the frail older person assuming a dependent role. The communication process may become one of imparting information and giving commands, instead of the give-and-take that normally occurs in families. Although frailty brings dependence, it may not necessarily bring loss of control, particularly if the family's affective function and communication processes have been good. An illustration of exemplary family functioning in the face of an older person's frailty follows.

> CASE 6   Mrs. D weighed 85 lb. She was never hungry and often forgot to feed herself. Because of increasing weakness, it was impossible for her to shop in the grocery store and carry the groceries home. She began to rely on the milk her milkman left for her only nutrients. As she became weaker and weaker, she could no longer clean or manage her house. Finally, she fell, broke her hip, and was hospitalized. Mrs. D knew she could no longer continue by herself, but she loved her independence. Mrs. D's family talked with her and said they felt she could no longer manage alone. The family said they understood Mrs. D's need for independence and wanted to foster her independence while caring for her. They offered Mrs. D several options and gave her time to deliberate. Mrs. D chose to move in with a daughter, into the maid's apartment, to which she could bring her own furniture. She put her things in

her own sitting room and arranged her bedroom and bath as it had been in her old house. As was her habit, she stayed up late at night and was a late riser. Each morning she had coffee on a tray by her bed. At noon, she went to the kitchen, where brunch was waiting to be heated up. Dinner was a social event with the entire family. As she began to eat, she became stronger and more interested in her surroundings. She began to enjoy television and telephone calls with old friends.

Frailty and dependence cause a myriad of problems for aging families, such as altered family processes, ineffective coping by the individual or the family, powerlessness, self-esteem disturbances, and financial difficulties. Without kin, Mrs. D would not have had such a variety of choices or the independence to try to make it alone within a more sheltered environment.

Research Findings

Soldo, Wolf, and Agree,[36] discussing family and household arrangements of frail older women, concluded that the simple availability of kin is an important constraint on living and care arrangements. Without children, older people have few resources for assistance and thus must resort to institutions for help their families would ordinarily provide. Maddox, Clark, and Steinhauser found that income is an independent predictor of status and health.[37] Clark and Standard suggested that total family systems (or the family unit) must be considered in developing clinical interventions.[38]

LOSS OF CONTROL

A different outcome may have resulted for Mrs. D if her daughter had not been able to take her in. The outcome of a different arrangement, such as nursing home placement, may have been one of loss of control. Often, for the isolated older person institutionalization in a nursing home is the only choice. For some reason, when institutionalization occurs, the frail older person may be viewed as a nonthinking person incapable of making decisions. Consider the outcome for Mrs. D had she been institutionalized:

> CASE 7   Mrs. D entered the nursing home at her family's insistence. It was a strange environment for her and one in which the required routine was very different from her own routine. Mrs. D often slept late in the morning so that she could watch David Letterman at night. Not only were her sleep habits different, but her eating habits were different as well. In the past, she enjoyed morning coffee, a brunch at noon, and a late dinner after cocktails. During her late-night television viewing, she enjoyed snacks.
>
> The first day in the nursing home, the nurse woke Mrs. D at 5 AM for a shower, and breakfast was bacon, eggs, and grits at 7 AM. Mrs. D could not eat; she was confused. At night, she was wide awake looking for the television room. The staff described her as confused

and wandering. They asked for a restraint and sleeping pill order at night, so she wouldn't disturb the other residents. The next night she became violent, aggressive, and disoriented as she fought the restraints. She began to exhibit anxiety at the thought of being restrained again.

Mrs. D did not like the nursing home. When her family visited, she always pleaded with them to take her out. Her daughter was overwhelmed with guilt and her son-in-law very angry about the situation. When the family left the nursing home, they fought about the situation. The son began to drink, and the daughter became depressed. Mrs. D didn't eat or drink well, and in time, she became dehydrated. Others began to make all her decisions as she became too weak and confused to make her own. The entire family was unable to cope.

1 Primary Prevention

A consequence of loss of control, perceived or actual, is anxiety for the entire family, often resulting in ineffective coping. Anxiety is characterized by feelings of powerlessness and helplessness that may overcome coping skills and paralyze the person. Anxiety is different from fear, in which the threat is a specific thing or person. Anxiety results from a variety of sources, such as loss of objects or support systems, loss of social control, declining mental or physical abilities, and the fear of losses caused by aging.[37] Prompt primary prevention minimizes anxiety and stops ineffective family coping from becoming an even more serious problem or from exacerbating preexisting physical problems. One can achieve primary prevention by explaining details to older people and alleviating fears before they start. Family coping may be improved with support groups. One national nursing home chain sponsors a group for families in which the families explore their feelings of guilt about the nursing home placement. These families and

their significant others adjust effectively to the changes caused by the placement.

2 Secondary Prevention

How do nurses assess ineffective coping in families? Ineffective family coping can happen on many levels; it may be compromised or disabling, or on a more positive level, it may show potential for growth. The family described in Case 7 demonstrates disabling coping. The son and daughter express despair through drinking and depression, Mrs. D by withdrawing into herself. Their behavior suggests abandonment, rejection, and desertion, in addition to neglectful relationships within the family. Family members cannot restructure their lives and make meaningful changes for themselves because they are overwhelmed by the problems caused by nursing home placement.

In Mrs. D's case, hopelessness related to the recent loss of control in many areas of her life caused anxiety, confusion, and memory loss. Loss of physical control resulted in a loss of social control, as family members made most of the decisions about home, finances, and medical care. Family members then became dysfunctional as they were overwhelmed. Table 26–5 addresses ineffective family coping.

Research Findings

Rodin[39] described good health as being important to an older person's sense of control. Studies show that loss of control has a detrimental effect on health, and the nurse should be aware of mechanisms mediating the control-health relationship. Pagel, Becker, and Coppel[40] studied loss of control in spouses caring for patients with Alzheimer's disease. They found that loss of control increasingly correlated with depression. Thus, control is important to both ill older people and their caregivers.

TABLE 26–5   NURSING CARE PLAN FOR THE FAMILY EXPERIENCING INEFFECTIVE FAMILY COPING

Nursing Diagnosis: Ineffective family coping, disabling	
Expected Outcomes	*Nursing Interventions*
Family/significant other(s) are expressing more realistic understanding and expectations of patient.	Provide supportive environment and encourage Mrs. D to express feelings and concerns surrounding her recent life change and loss of autonomy.
Family is visiting regularly.	Through counseling, increase awareness of Mrs. D's recent life changes and the family's subsequent actions.
Significant other(s) are expressing feelings openly and honestly, as appropriate.	Establish rapport with family members.
Mrs. D will regain control of areas of her life through means both feasible and acceptable to herself and her family unit.	Acknowledge difficulty of situation for family.
	Allow free expression of feelings, including frustration, anger, hostility, and hopelessness.
	Include significant other(s) in plan of care and help them to learn necessary skills to help patient.
	Help family identify coping skills.

POWERLESSNESS

Powerlessness is the end of the trajectory. The powerless person who has lost all control is at the mercy of caregivers, family, and others.

The transition has gone full circle. The powerless person becomes the child, and because of the resulting helplessness, family members and caregivers must be careful not to take advantage of the powerlessness. The epitome of a powerless family member is a nursing home resident with mid- or end-stage Alzheimer's disease.

CASE 8 Mrs. J was the wife of an Army colonel. When she was in her 50s, she began to have difficulties with her memory and her condition was diagnosed as Alzheimer's disease. She entered a nursing home against her will. In the beginning, she felt powerless to cause change. As her disease progressed, she no longer recognized family members. By age 75, she lay in bed all day in a fetal position. She was incontinent of feces and urine. She could not feed herself, often forgetting to swallow. Mrs. J had no power over her own existence. She was at the end of the trajectory.

1 Primary Prevention

The concept of powerlessness is the perception by the individual that one's own actions will not significantly alter an outcome. According to O'Heath,[41] powerlessness is a potential problem when a power resource is compromised. These resources include physical strength, psychological stamina, self-concept, energy, knowledge, motivation, and belief system. Factors contributing to powerlessness include the health-care environment, previous experience, lack of knowledge (including perceived or actual lack of provision of information), a lifestyle of helplessness, and a perceived or actual loss of control or influence over a situation, self, environment, or outcome.[41] Nurses can prevent powerlessness by being aware of the older person's need to participate in decision making and by encouraging and ensuring his or her participation.

2 Secondary Prevention

Assessment of powerlessness involves obtaining both subjective and objective data. Defining characteristics may be seen as a lack of information-seeking behavior, a refusal or reluctance to participate in decision making, actual verbalization of loss of control, or behavioral responses such as anger and hostility, apathy, resignation, aggression, and withdrawal.[41]

Research Findings

Marchione and Stearns[12] discuss ethnic tradition as sources of family power and encourage all nurses to be aware of them. Horowitz, Silverstone, and Reinhardt[42] suggest an expanded definition of autonomy, emphasizing the importance of goal-directed behavior and the need for personal control when possible. However, when there is a need to relegate decision making to other family members, older people expect them to make the right decisions.[43]

CAREGIVER STRESS

As families age, they become once again a dyad, a husband and a wife. When one of them cannot respond to the stresses of aging, the other often assumes the role of caregiver. Because they both are older, the caregiving role produces a burden, resulting in caregiver stress.

Most caregivers are women, either adult daughters or wives. Husbands account for 13 percent of the caregiver group and experience increased difficulty in this unusual role.[44] Consider the following case study:

CASE 9 If Colonel J could not afford to place Mrs. J in a nursing home, he would have been a caregiver for 25 years. Colonel J is unskilled in homemaking, and he always depended on Mrs. J for most of his own personal needs. Twenty-five years of assuming the homemaker role and providing total care for Mrs. J would undoubtedly prove a burden and provide multiple stressors.

1 Primary Prevention

Primary prevention of caregiver stress must begin as soon as the diagnosis is made. One important source of primary prevention for caregivers of patients with Alzheimer's disease is the Alzheimer's support group, in which involved families learn about the disease and benefit from other families' experiences. Thus, they are able to anticipate the progression of the disease while learning about services in the community and benefiting from others' experiences. Even though some caregivers find these sessions depressing, they serve the important function of letting the older person know what to expect as a caregiver. The sessions are very educational about the disease itself. Although these support groups are universal, they are not currently reported in the literature.[45]

2 Secondary Prevention

Respite care is a major help in secondary prevention of stress for the caregiver. Often, convincing the caregiver to take advantage of respite care is difficult. Caregivers must learn to look for and recognize stress in themselves before the stress becomes a problem. Adler[46] reports on a respite care program at a Veterans' Administration hospital. Although family caregivers spoke favorably of the experience, they often noted functional deterioration in the impaired person as a result of the respite. Berry, Zarit, and Rabatin[47] examined two different respite care programs and found very high ratings of program satisfaction. In a survey of caregivers' needs,[48] caregivers reported the need for high-quality educational material, improved training for health professionals about Alzheimer's disease, and communication with other caregivers. All such services would be helpful in the secondary prevention of caregiver stress.

3 Tertiary Prevention

As the disease progresses, every caregiver begins to feel stress, much of it caused by a commitment to see the ill person through to the end. Although men may be involved in the caregiving at the beginning of the disease, they often must seek help as the disease progresses.[49] Reed, Stone, and Neale[50] found that caregivers felt more stress in their marriages as the patient's disease progressed but that they did not experience more disruption of social events and recreational activities at this time. However, when the care is as intense as that required for Mrs. J, often the only treatment of the stress is institutionalization of the patient. Brody, Dempsey, and Pruchno[51] studied the mental health of sons and daughters whose parents were institutionalized and found that those with poor physical health were much more depressed than others. Adult children who felt that they were still useful to the parent were less depressed, however. Spouse caregivers have an even bigger problem with institutionalizing their loved one. They may recall the marriage vow phrase "until death do us part" and may therefore believe they are not fulfilling their part of the marriage contract. Spouse caregivers must be made to feel comfortable with their nursing home decision and begin to care for themselves.

Research Findings

Studies on caregiver stress have been abundant in the past 10 years. Kosberg, Cairl, and Keller[52] wrote of the components of burden and talked about the implications for interventions. Albert[53] scaled caregiver tasks and found them to be multidimensional. After examining caregiving among multigenerational families, Baum[54] found that regardless of family size, one caregiver shouldered most of the burden of caregiving. The research agrees that caregiving is a burden and that ways to alleviate that burden must be found.

Summary

The family is a major component of geriatric care. Previous textbooks in gerontological nursing have not included family as an entity in aging. However, those who have read this chapter can readily appreciate the need to consider the family. The family is key in implementing interventions and pursuing them to fruition. In pediatrics, the family is always an essential component of care. Nurses and their clients need to recognize that the family once again becomes primary in successful nursing care for older adults.

Student Learning Activities

1 View the film *Driving Miss Daisy*. How is the concept of first-tier relationships depicted in this film? Discuss the concept of support as a reciprocal process in light of the film.

2 How will you use the insights you gained from the film in your nursing practice?

REFERENCES

1 Haight, BK, and Burnside, I: Reminiscence and life review: Conducting the process. J Gerontol Nurs 18(2):39–42.

2 Brubaker, TH: Families in later life: A burgeoning research area. J Marriage Fam 52:959, 1990.

3 Fink, SV: The influence of family resources and family demands on the strains and well-being of caregiving families. Nurs Res 44(3):139, 1995.

4 Troll, LE: New thoughts on old families. Gerontologist 28(5):586, 1988.

5 Connidis, IA, and Davies, L: Confidants and companions in later life: The place of family and friends. J Gerontol Soc Sci 45(4):S141, 1990.

6 Friedman, MM: Family Nursing: Elements and Style, ed 3. Appleton-Century-Crofts, Norwalk, Conn, 1992.

7 Ebersole, P, and Hess, P: Toward Healthy Aging: Human Needs and Nursing Response, ed 4. CV Mosby, St Louis, 1993.

8 Talbott, MM: The negative side of the relationship between older widows and their adult children: The mothers' perspective. Gerontologist 30(5):595, 1990.

9 Bata, EJ, and Power, PW: Facilitating health care decisions within aging families. In Smith, GC, et al (eds): Strengthening Aging Families: Diversity in Practice and Policy. Stanford University Press, Newbury Park, Calif, 1995, p 143.

10 Rosenthal, CJ, and Dawson, P: Wives of institutionalized elderly men. J Aging Health 3(3):315, 1991.

11 Bedford, VH: A comparison of thematic apperceptions of sibling affiliation, conflict, and separation at two periods of adulthood. Int J Aging Hum Dev 28(1):53, 1989.

12 Marchione, J, and Stearns, SJ: Ethnic power perspectives for nursing. Nurs Health Care 11(6):296, 1990.

13 Kennedy, GE: College students' expectations of grandparent and grandchild role behaviors. Gerontologist 30(1):43, 1990.

14 Kelly, JR, and Westcott, G: Ordinary retirement: Commonalities and continuity. Int J Aging Hum Dev 32(2):81, 1991.

15 Aquilino, WS, and Supple, KR: Parent-child relations and parent's satisfaction with living arrangements when adult children live at home. J Marriage Fam 53:13, 1991.

16 Herzog, AR, et al: Relation of work and retirement to health and well-being in older age. Psychol Aging 6(2):202, 1991.

17 Johnston, T: Retirement: What happens to the marriage? Ment Health Nurs 11:347, 1990.

18 Fletcher, WL, and Hansson, RO: Assessing the social components of retirement anxiety. Psychol Aging 6(1):76, 1991.

19 Moneyham, L, and Scott, CB: Anticipatory coping in the elderly. J Gerontol Nurs 21(7):23, 1995.

20 Smith, C: Family worldview: Problem-solving communication style and adaptation during retirement. Unpublished doctoral dissertation. University of South Carolina, College of Nursing, Columbia, SC, 1996.

21 Loveys, B: Transitions in chronic illness: The at-risk role. Holistic Nurse Pract 4(3):56, 1990.

22 Krause, N, et al: Financial strain and psychological well-being among the American and Japanese elderly. Psychol Aging 6(2):170, 1991.

23 O'Bryant, S: Older widows and independent lifestyles. Int J Aging Hum Dev 32:41, 1991.

24 Cutler, NE, and Gregg, DW: The human "wealth span" and financial well-being in older age. Generations 15:45, 1991.

25 Remer, D, et al: Translocation syndrome. In Maas, M, et al (eds): Nursing Diagnoses and Interventions for the Elderly. Addison-Wesley Nursing, Redwood City, Calif, 1991, p 495.

26 Matzo, M, and Bernsee, ML: Independent after all these years! Geriatr Nurs 11:268, 1990.

27 Mulschler: Where elders live. Generations 16(2):7–14, 1992.

28 Dobbin: If you build it, they may not come. Generations 16(2):31, 1992.

29 Stern, S: Measuring child work and residence adjustments to parents' long-term care needs. Gerontologist 36(1):76, 1996.

30 Uhlenberg, P, and Cooney, TM: Family size and mother-child relations in later life. Gerontologist 30(5):618, 1990.

31 Davidhizar, R, and Shearer, R: It can never be the way it was: Helping elderly women adjust to change and loss. Home Healthcare Nurse 12(1):43, 1994.

32 Elsen, J, and Belgen, M: Social isolation. In Maas, M, et al (eds): Nursing Diagnoses and Interventions for the Elderly. Addison-Wesley Nursing, Redwood City, Calif, 1991.

33 Mullins, LC, and Dugan, E: The influence of depression, and family and friendship relations, on residents' loneliness in congregate housing. Gerontologist 30(3):377, 1990.

34 Palmer, RM: "Failure to thrive" in the elderly: Diagnosis and management. Geriatrics 45(9):47, 1990.

35 Rane-Szostak, D, and Herth, KA: A new perspective on loneliness in later life. Iss Ment Health Nurs 16:583, 1995.

36 Soldo, BJ, et al: Family, households, and care arrangements of frail older women: A structural analysis. J Gerontol Soc Sci 45(6):S238, 1990.

37 Maddox, GL, et al: Dynamics of functional impairment in late adulthood. Soc Sci Med 38(7):925, 1994.

38 Clark, M, and Standard, PL: Caregiver burden and the structural family model. Fam Community Health 18(4):58, 1996.

39 Rodin, J: Aging and health: Effects of the sense of control. Science 233:1271, 1986.

40 Pagel, MD, et al: Loss of control, self-blame, and depression: An investigation of spouse caregivers of Alzheimer's disease patients. J Abnorm Psychol 94(2):169, 1985.

41 O'Heath, K: Powerlessness. In Maas, M, et al (eds): Nursing Diagnoses and Interventions for the Elderly. Addison-Wesley Nursing, Redwood City, Calif, 1991, p 449.

42 Horowitz, A, et al: A conceptual and empirical exploration of personal autonomy issues within family caregiving relationships. Gerontologist 31(1):23, 1991.

43 High, DM: All in the family: Extended autonomy and expectations in surrogate health care decision-making. Gerontologist (suppl)28:46, 1988.

44 Brackley, MB: Caregiver stress (doctoral dissertation). The University of Texas Health Science Center at San Antonio School of Nursing, 1990.

45 Barer, BM, and Johnson, CL: A critique of the caregiving literature. Gerontologist 30(1):26, 1990.

46 Adler, G: Dementia caregivers: Expectations of respite care. Am J Alzheimer Dis Related Disord Res 7(2):8, 1992.

47 Berry, GL, et al: Caregiver activity on respite and nonrespite days: A comparison of two service approaches. Gerontologist 31(6):830, 1991.

48 Fortinsky, RH, and Hathaway, TJ: Information and service needs among active and former family caregivers of persons with Alzheimer's disease. Gerontologist 30(5):604, 1990.

49 Stoller, EP: Males as helpers: The role of sons, relatives, and friends. Gerontologist 30(2):228, 1990.

50 Reed, BR, et al: Effects of caring for a demented relative on elders' life events and appraisals. Gerontologist 30(2):200, 1990.

51 Brody, EM, et al: Mental health of sons and daughters of the institutionalized aged. Gerontologist 30(2):212, 1990.

52 Kosberg, JI, et al: Components of burden: Interventive implications Gerontologist 30(2):236, 1990.

53 Albert, SM: Cognition of caregiving tasks: Multidimensional scaling of the caregiver task domain. Gerontologist 31(6):726, 1991.

54 Baum, M: Caregiving and multigenerational families. Gerontologist 31(6):762, 1991.

CHAPTER 27

Elder Mistreatment

Terry Fulmer

OBJECTIVES

Upon completion of this chapter, the reader will be able to:

- Describe the nature and clinical manifestations of elder abuse
- Discuss the theories of causation of elder abuse
- Identify secondary and tertiary prevention strategies for elder abuse

Nature of the Problem

Elder mistreatment (EM) is a serious, underreported, underdetected phenomenon that afflicts thousands of older adults annually. Estimates suggest that nearly 700,000 to 1.2 million older adults are victims of EM each year. This translates into 32 per 1000 individuals.[1]

A roundtable discussion before the Special Committee on Aging of the U.S. Senate[2] further defined the problem as one especially salient among women. In 1993, more than 1 million women were victims of violence in this country, with 700,000 midlife women between the ages of 45 and 65 physically abused by a spouse and 400,000 older women living in institutions victimized physically or sexually; women over 65 were twice as likely as younger women to be mugged at or near their homes. That same report noted that 1 in every 100 women age 50 to 64 years is likely to be a victim of violent crime, and 2 of every 100 women age 65 or older is likely to be a victim of theft. The issue is serious for both genders, and the frailty and vulnerability that come with advancing age create a state of fear and even hopelessness for those with the least resources to cope.

There is much debate over why EM occurs and the underlying theoretical thinking for the same. Definitions of EM, as well as the categories of activities that lead to EM, are also contentious. Mandatory reporting laws vary from state to state, with certain amounts of overlap in these definitions.[3–5]

Although the issue of varying definitions limit the ability of practitioners and policy makers to compare ideas or research, most state reporting laws reflect one or more of the following categories: physical abuse, neglect, exploitation, abandonment, and psychological abuse.[6] See Chapter 5 for more on the legal aspects of EM.

The American Medical Association has published diagnostic and treatment guidelines for the appropriate detection and intervention in EM cases, which provide screening and intervention decision trees (Figures 27–1 and 27–2). These same guidelines provide commonly accepted definitions to frame the problem.[5]

Physical abuse is generally regarded as an act of assault or battery, whereas neglect is an unreasonable withholding of some goods or services necessary for physical or mental health. Exploitation usually means taking advantage of an older adult for personal or financial benefits, and abandonment is desertion of an older person or withdrawal of care with no provision for alternative care.

Clinical Manifestations

Signs and symptoms of physical abuse reflect the result of direct beatings, infliction of physical pain, or physical coercion and might include abrasions, lacerations, contusions, burns, sprains, and dislocations. Neglectful actions such as the withholding of food or fluid, inadequate medical attention, and inappropriate clothing or shelter might result in poor nutrition, poor hygiene, frostbite, hypothermia, or hyperthermia. Exploitation may occur in the form of taking and cashing Social Security checks, or taking their possessions either against their will or on the threat of withholding care. This may result in poverty, depression, and ultimately, a loss of ability to sustain oneself financially. Abandonment may occur when a caregiver drops off the older adult at an emergency room, for example, with no intention of coming back. This may cause the older adult to be unable to continue living with current arrangements or to try and fail at great personal risk. Psychological abuse

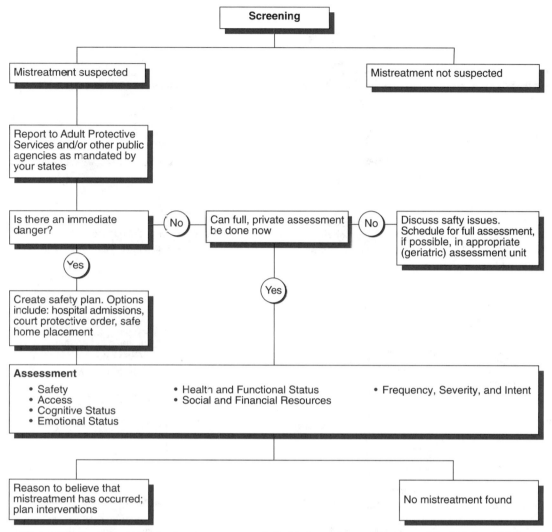

Figure 27–1 Intervention and case management: Part I. Screening and assessment for EM should follow a routine pattern. Assessment of each case should include the steps shown. (Reprinted from Diagnostic and Treatment Guidelines on Elder Abuse and Neglect, American Medical Association, copyright 1992.)

(also called mental anguish) is more difficult to define but usually refers to unreasonable verbal abuse or hostile behavior toward an older adult, with resultant deleterious effects.

Psychological abuse such as continuous denigrating comments, threats, withdrawal of all acts of affection, or scare tactics may lead to physical illness, sleep deprivation, depression, withdrawal, and an inability to care for self (Table 27–1).

Management

1 Primary Prevention

THEORIES OF CAUSATION OF ELDER ABUSE

Dependency in old age may increase the risk of abuse and neglect. Abuse might result when the degree of dependency overwhelms the caregiver to the extent

that hostile and aggressive behavior that may harm the older adult ensues. Neglect is highly likely to occur when an older person becomes increasingly dependent because he or she cannot or will not keep up with care needs. Neglect by people other than the older adult (self-neglect) implies the presence of dependency. Neglect accounts for a large percentage of EM referrals, with Massachusetts reporting more than 70 percent of its protective service referrals in the category of neglect and Illinois reporting 33 percent.[7] Neglect cases exemplify the role of dependency in EM. Some researchers believe that it is dependency of the caregiver on the older adult that creates a high-risk situation.[8]

Psychopathology of the abuser is another theory of causation for EM. This theory holds that people who are mentally ill, substance dependent (e.g., drugs or alcohol), or mentally retarded are "non-normal" and do not have the same ability to control their behavior as healthy people would. Although this attractive theory would explain abhorrent behavior, Straus[9] attributes

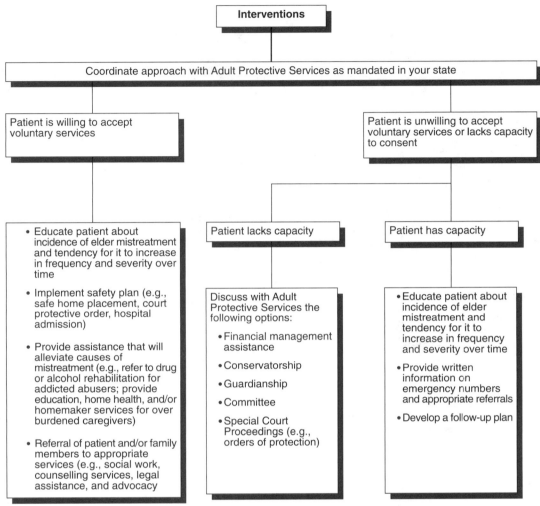

Figure 27–2 Intervention and case management: Part II. Case management should be guided by choosing the alternatives that least restrict the client's independence and decision-making responsibilities and fulfill state-mandated reporting requirements. Intervention depends on the client's cognitive status and decision-making capability and whether the mistreatment is intentional or unintentional. (Reprinted from *Diagnostic and Treatment Guidelines on Elder Abuse and Neglect*, American Medical Association, copyright 1992.)

fewer than 10 percent of all instances of family violence to mental illness or psychiatric disorders, and no one has conducted a cohort analysis to study this specifically in older adults. Gelles and Cornell[10] describe the causative factors of alcohol and drug abuse as myths and claim that although there is considerable association between drinking and violence, it has never been proved that drugs and alcohol cause violence or are proven disinhibitors. He reminds us that common sense leads us to one conclusion, whereas research points in another direction. Still, any emergency room record will support the theory that substance abuse plays a prominent role in violent behavior.

Transgenerational violence is another popular theory that has not been firmly established. This theory focuses on violence as a learned behavior that is passed down from generation to generation in some families because violence has been modeled as an acceptable

coping behavior, with no substantial penalties for the behavior. This model suggests that a child who grows up in a violent family will also become violent. Some believe that EM may be related to retribution on the part of an adult offspring who was abused as a child.

The stressed caregiver theory is one that researchers are all too ready to give up, whereas clinicians stand by it faithfully. Stress is believed to be responsible for the ultimate outcome of violent behavior. Examples might include single parents, "women in the middle,"[11] or any person who is pressed beyond his or her tolerance level. This is also called the social situational model,[12] which includes structural stress and cultural norms.

The exchange theory,[13] probably the most respected theoretical model for explaining EM, refers to the human drive to obtain rewards and avoid punishment. This model looks at the relationship between the older adult and the abusive caregiver and postulates that as

TABLE 27–1 PHYSICAL INDICATORS OF ABUSE AND NEGLECT

Type of Abuse or Neglect	Possible Physical Indicators

Physical abuse	Unexplained bruises and welts:
	  On face, lips, or mouth
	  On torso, back, buttocks, or thighs
	  In various stages of healing
	  Clustered, forming regular patterns
	  Reflecting shape of article used to inflict (electric cord, belt buckle)
	  On several different surface areas
	  Regularly appearing after absence such as weekend or vacation
	Unexplained burns:
	  Cigar or cigarette burns, especially on soles, palms, back, or buttocks
	  Immersion burns (socklike or glovelike doughnut-shaped burns on buttocks
	    or genitalia)
	  Patterned like electric burner, iron, and so on
	  Rope burns on arms, legs, neck, or torso
	Unexplained fractures:
	  To skull or nose or other facial structure
	  In various stages of healing
	  Multiple or spiral fractures
	Unexplained lacerations or abrasions:
	  To mouth, lips, gums, or eyes
	  To external genitalia

Physical neglect	Consistent hunger, poor hygiene, inappropriate dress Consistent lack of supervision, especially in dangerous activities or long periods Consistent fatigue or listlessness Unattended physical problems or medical needs Abandonment
Sexual abuse	Difficulty in walking or sitting Torn, stained, or bloody underclothing Pain or itching in genital area Bruises or bleeding in external genitalia, vaginal, or anal areas
Emotional maltreatment	Habit disorder (e.g., sucking, biting, rocking) Conduct disorders (e.g., antisocial, destructive) Neurotic traits (sleep disorders, speech disorders, inhibition of play) Psychoneurotic reaction (hysteria, obsession, compulsion, phobias, hypochondria)

Source: Indicators of Abuse and Neglect. United States Department of Health and Human Services, US Government Printing Office, Washington DC, 1980.

long as abusers gain from the interaction, they will continue to be abusive. If the exchange becomes negative, as in the case of the threat of sanctions, lack of monetary gain, guilt, and so on, the behavior stops. Sanctions can be imposed through the introduction of an observer such as a home health aide.

ENVIRONMENTAL HAZARDS

EM occurs in an environmental context, and it is important to recognize what aspects of the situation or setting make it unsafe.

Keeping active helps maintain an older adult's visibility. An older adult who is engaged in activity is more likely to be missed if anything happens to prevent the activity, such as illness or assault. Families are encouraged to maintain close ties with aging relatives and talk to them about sensitive issues such as living wills and financial concerns. Communities are urged to provide public awareness programs on the problem of EM and support for older adults and family members who are overwhelmed or troubled.[14] Table 27–2 lists activities that can help older adults avoid abuse.[14]

2 Secondary Prevention

ASSESSMENT

Once an older adult has been mistreated, the abuse must be detected as soon as possible. Social service agencies, emergency departments, and police departments are the most likely agencies to be contacted in EM. EM should be assessed in the routine history in the emergency unit. Questions should be tactfully yet clearly stated in order to determine whether any EM has occurred. It may help to provide a statement followed by a question (e.g., "Some older adults are treated poorly by other people and may even be slapped or screamed at. Has this ever happened to you?" or "I see that you live with your son. Is he good to you?"). This format provides a clear message to the client regarding the information the nurse is seeking. These questions should be asked privately, and any unusual dynamics between the client and any accompanying caregivers should be observed (see "Research Brief").

Physical findings that should be noted include any unusual physical signs or symptoms, especially those that conflict with or contradict the history. Possible

TABLE 27–2   TOWARD PREVENTION: SOME DOS AND DON'TS

For Individuals

Do

- Stay sociable as you age; maintain and increase your network of friends and acquaintances.
- Keep in contact with old friends and neighbors if you move in with a relative or to a new address.
- Develop a buddy system with a friend outside the home. Plan for at least once-a-week contact and share openly with this person.
- Ask friends to visit you at home. Even a brief visit can allow observations of your well-being.
- Accept new opportunities for activities. They can bring new friends.
- Participate in community activities as long as you can.
- Volunteer for or become a member or officer of an organization. Participate regularly.
- Have your own telephone; send and open your own mail. If your mail is being intercepted, discuss the problem with postal authorities.
- Stay organized. Keep your belongings neat and orderly. Make sure others are aware that you know where everything is kept.
- Take care of your personal needs. Keep regular medical, dental, barber, hairdresser, and other personal appointments.
- Arrange to have your Social Security or pension check deposited directly to a bank account.
- Get legal advice about arrangements you can make now for possible future disability, including powers of attorney, guardianships, or conservatorship.
- Keep records, accounts, and property available for examination by someone you trust, as well as by the person you or the court has designated to manage your affairs. Review your will periodically.
- Give up control of your property or assets only when you decide you can no longer manage them. Ask for help when you need it. Discuss your plans with your attorney, physician, or family members.

Don't

- Don't live with a person who has a background of violent behavior or alcohol or drug abuse.
- Don't leave your home unattended. Notify police if you are going to be away for a long period. Don't leave messages on the door while you are away.
- Don't accept personal care in return for transfer or assignments of your property or assets unless a lawyer, advocate, or another trusted person acts as a witness to the transaction.
- Don't sign a document unless someone you trust has reviewed it.
- Don't allow anyone else to keep details of your finances or property management from you.

For Families

Do

- Maintain close ties with aging relatives and friends. Keep abreast of changes in their health and ability to live independently.
- Discuss an older relative's wishes regarding health care, terminal medical care alternatives, home care in the case of incapacitation, and disposition of his or her personal assets.
- Find sources of help and use them. Chore services, housekeeping, home-delivered meals, senior recreation, day care, respite care, and transportation assistance are available in many communities.
- With the older person's consent, become familiar with his or her financial records, bank accounts, will, safe deposit boxes, insurance debts, and sources of income before he or she becomes incapacitated. Talk and plan together now about how these affairs should be handled.
- Anticipate potential incapacitation by planning as a family who will take responsibility, such as power of attorney or in-home caregiving, if an aging relative becomes incapacitated.
- Closely examine your family's ability to provide long-term, in-home care for a frail and increasingly dependent relative. Consider the family's physical limits.
- Plan how your own needs will be met when your responsibility for the dependent older relative increases.
- Explore alternative sources of care, including nursing homes or other relatives' homes, in case your situation changes.
- Discuss your plans with friends, neighbors, and other sources of support before your responsibilities become a burden. Ask for their understanding and emotional support because you may need them.
- Familiarize family members with emergency response agencies and services available in case of sudden need.

Don't

- Don't offer personal home care unless you thoroughly understand and can meet the responsibilities and costs involved.
- Don't wait until a frail older person has moved in with you to examine his or her needs. You should consider access, safety, containment, and special needs. (Do you need a first floor bathroom, bedroom, or entry ramp? Will carpets or stairs become barriers? Do you need a fenced yard to prevent the loved one from wandering away? Does your kitchen allow you to prepare special diets or store medications properly? Can you move the person safely in case of fire?)
- Don't assume that poor interpersonal relationships between you or other members of the household and the older person involved will disappear.
- Don't expect irritating habits or problems (e.g., alcohol abuse) to stop or be controlled once the dependent person moves into your home.
- Don't ignore your limitations and overextend yourself. Passive neglect could result.
- Don't hamper the older person's independence or intrude unnecessarily on his or her privacy. Provide a private telephone if you can and make other changes if possible.
- Don't label your efforts a failure if home care is not possible and you must seek an alternative.

TABLE 27–2 TOWARD PREVENTION: SOME DOS AND DON'TS (*Continued*)

For Communities

Do

- Develop new ways to provide direct assistance to caregiving families. Improve crisis response to help families that face the difficult decision to discontinue home care.
- Through public awareness programs, advocate the cause of caregiving families and the needs of victims of mistreatment.
- Ask other community groups to become more involved in aging service programs, including those at nursing homes or senior citizen housing projects. Their involvement can lead to improved facilities and services. Encourage both public and private employers to help caregiving families, especially those with caregivers nearing or beyond retirement age, with fixed incomes and increasing health problems.
- Publicize available support services and professionals available to caregivers such as senior day-care centers, chore services, companions, and housekeeping services. Caregivers may not know about them.
- Give public agency employees basic training in responses and case management. They can be trained to recognize some of the causes of neglect or abuse of older people and can help in support roles.
- Provide training for community gatekeepers and service workers (primary care physicians, public health and social workers, law enforcement officers, transportation and utility workers, postal employees, and others) to help them recognize at-risk situations and take appropriate action.
- Expand Neighborhood Watch programs and similar community groups to include training on home care of frail older adults, identification of the signs of mistreatment, and preventive actions to reduce such victimization.
- Open your eyes and ears to the possibility that mistreatment is occurring. Became aware of people who are at risk. Develop procedures for investigation, public education, and public support of assistance to troubled families.
- Recognize that many forms of mistreatment or abuse are crimes. Volunteers can help victims file formal complaints, seek compensation for losses, seek prosecution of guilty parties, and give the victim assistance subsequent to prosecution. Prosecution can result in sentencing, diversion, training, counseling, or other types of family assistance services as alternatives to criminal sanction. Urge public support of agencies to provide the necessary services.

Don't

- Don't ignore family caregivers of dependent older adults. They are significant parts of the community. Community services can try to involve isolated people in appropriate services or self-help programs. Those at risk, or living in isolation, simply may lack knowledge or information and may welcome community outreach.
- Don't assume that gerontology is a study confined to universities and hospitals. Begin to educate the entire community about aging. (This should be as common in public education as information about child care.)
- Don't sensationalize stories of abuse of older people. Instead, try to arouse public interest in techniques and strategies to prevent abuse.
- Don't start a major intervention just because an older person is alone or is considered eccentric. The goal is to seek the least intrusive alternative.

Source: Reprinted with permission from American Association of Retired Persons: Domestic Mistreatment of the Elderly: Toward Prevention—Some Do's and Dont's. AARP, Washington, DC, 1990.

RESEARCH BRIEF

Phillips, LR, and Rempusheski, VF: A decision-making model for diagnosing and intervening in elder abuse and neglect. Nurs Res 34:134, 1989.

This study examined decision making related to diagnosis and intervention in abuse and neglect of older adults. Characteristics of both the abuser and the older adult were found to have an effect on the way the professional interpreted the situation and intervened.

The study of EM is in its seminal stages and much research is needed before any consensus will be reached regarding the nature of this problem, its causes, and, most importantly, the key aspects of its prevention. For a detailed analysis of EM research, see Hudson and Johnson.[15]

abuse indicators include bruises, lacerations, fractures, or any of the aforementioned in various stages of healing. This would indicate that the client has sustained repeated injury over time. Any statement by the client regarding abuse should also be documented and prompt the nurse to ask questions.

Neglect indicators include contracture, decubiti, dehydration, malnutrition, urine burns, poor hygiene, repetitive falls, or any statement by the client regarding neglect. It is important to note that any of these neglect indicators could also result from a disease state and thus may not be related in any way to neglect.

Exploitation indicators include any evidence of misuse of the client's money, reports of demands for goods in exchange for services, an inability of the client to account for money or property, or any statement regarding exploitation.

THERAPEUTIC MANAGEMENT

EM management depends on the severity of the situation. Life-threatening problems should be triaged accordingly and a protective service report called in. Once the older person is medically stable, an investigation can be conducted by appropriate state agencies. Health-care professionals are responsible for reporting any suspicions of EM. The investigatory work is then conducted by regulatory agencies, which can determine whether the case is corroborated. No health-care professional who acts in good faith can be sued for libel because most states provide for anonymity of the reporter and protection against such suits.

Cases can be evaluated while the client is hospitalized, but often he or she is not admitted to the hospital and therefore may be sent back to an unsafe situation. When this happens, it is especially important to have a good working relationship with the adult protective service agencies in the area, who will then follow up once the client is back at home. Cases may repeat themselves. Some individuals and families are well-known to the protective service agencies.

In these cases, it is useful to have a primary nursing care delivery system in the emergency department so that the same nurse can work with the client each time. Such continuity of care helps ensure consistency in care planning, as well as early and rapid detection.

NURSING INTERVENTIONS

Once a nurse determines that a client may have been mistreated, a formal call should be made to alert either the EM resource team at that institution or the appropriate state agency. Every effort must be made to ensure the client's safety, which may entail getting permission to "socially admit" the client to the hospital until a safe discharge plan can be developed. Close collaboration between medicine and social work is very important in such cases. A particularly difficult situation arises when the client is clearly mistreated, but is mentally competent and chooses to go back to the setting in question. The nurse should explain the possible consequences of such a choice (e.g., further beatings, malnutrition), document the discussion, and then provide a follow-up telephone number for the client to call for assistance in case there is a change of mind. Nurses often feel angry and powerless in such a situation, but if not cognitively impaired, clients have the right to self-determination and their choice must be respected.

In summary, key nursing interventions involve educating the staff and community to be aware of the existence of EM and using nursing systems that lead to the prevention, detection, and resolution of EM cases. Community awareness programs, educational material development and distribution, and a clear protocol that ensures thorough detection and follow-up of EM are all within the purview of professional nursing.

3 Tertiary Prevention

Rehabilitation can be difficult after EM has occurred. Trust is often shattered, and choices related to new living arrangements can cause serious strain on any older adult, whether it is the victim or another who is forced to move. Nursing home placement may be war-

TABLE 27–3   RESOURCES

American Association of Retired Persons
601 E Street NW
Washington, DC 20049

National Committee in the Prevention of Elder Abuse
c/o Rosalie Wolf
University Center on Aging
University of Massachusetts Medical Center
55 Lake Avenue
North Worcester, MA 01655

ranted, in which case the client is likely to have intense personal reactions. Being aware of these potential reactions, the nurse should do everything possible to prepare the client and significant others for such reactions. For those who choose to remain in the setting in which EM occurred, every effort should be made to improve the setting. Assistance through daily home health care or Meals on Wheels can reduce stress and develop a safer environment.

Ongoing surveillance is essential and this can take place through regular telephone communication with the client or with the community agency that oversees support programs.

Summary

EM is a serious and prevalent problem that can be eradicated by aggressive public awareness campaigns and careful screening programs. Nursing professionals are in an optimal position to lead programs dedicated to EM prevention because of the variety of nurses' work settings and the obvious mechanisms available to nurses for following clients across settings. As the population ages, more older adults will become victims of EM in the absence of such effort. Table 27–3 lists some resources that may be useful to those dealing with this problem.

Student Learning Activities

1 Invite a representative from the Area Agency on Aging to visit the class and discuss the issue of EM. Identify services available to assist abused older adults in your area.

2 Identify the factors that contribute to the invisible nature of this problem.

3 Plan a primary prevention measure that can be implemented in your community to combat this growing problem.

REFERENCES

1 Pillemer, K, and Finkelhor, DH: The prevalence of elder abuse: A random sample survey. Gerontologist 28(1):51–55, 1988.
2 US Senate Special Committee on Aging. Elder Abuse and Violence Against Midlife and Older Women. May 4, 1994 ser-

ial no. 103-19. US Government Printing Office, Washington, DC, 1994.

3 Totara, T: An Analysis of State Laws Addressing Elder Abuse, Neglect, and Exploitation. The National Center on Elder Abuse, 1995.

4 Baumhover, LA, and Beall, SC: Abuse, Neglect and Exploitations of Older Persons: Strategies for Assessment and Intervention. Health Professions Press, Baltimore, Md, 1996, pp 9–27.

5 American Medical Association: Diagnostic and Treatment Guidelines on Elder Abuse and Neglect. AMA, Chicago, Ill, 1992.

6 Johnson, TF: Elder Mistreatment: Decide What Is at Risk. Greenwood Press, New York, 1991, pp 21–45.

7 Neale, AV, et al: The Illinois Elder Abuse System: Program description and administrative findings. Gerontologist 36(4):502–511, 1996.

8 Pillemer, KA: Risk factors in elder abuse. Results from a case-control study. In Pillemer, KA, and Wolf, RS (eds): Elder Abuse Conflict in the Family. Auburn House, Dover, Mass, 1986, pp 239–263.

9 Straus, M: A sociological perspective on the causes of family violence. In Gillen, MR (ed): Violence and the Family. Westview, Boulder, Colo, 1989, pp 7–31.

10 Gelles, RJ, and Cornell, CP: Intimate Violence in Families, ed 2. Family Studies Text Series no 2. Sage, Newbury Park, Calif, 1990, pp 11–24.

11 Brody, SJ, et al: The family care unit. A major consideration in the long-term care support system. Gerontologist 8(6):556, 1978.

12 Gelles, RJ, and Cornell, CP: Intimate violence in families, ed 2. Family Studies Text Series no 2. Sage, Newbury Park, Calif, 1990, pp 112–113.

13 Gelles, RJ, and Cornell, CP: Intimate violence in families, ed 2. Family Studies Text Series no 2. Sage, Newbury Park, Calif, 1990, pp 118–119.

14 American Association of Retired Persons: Domestic mistreatment of the elderly: Towards prevention—some do's and don'ts. AARP, Washington, DC, 1990.

15 Hudson MF, and Johnson, TF: Elder neglect and abuse: A review of the literature. Annu Rev Gerontol Geriatr 6:81, 1986.

CHAPTER 28

Depression and Suicide

Kathleen C. Buckwalter

OBJECTIVES

Upon completion of this chapter, the reader will be able to:

- Discuss the prevalence of depression in older adults as a significant public health problem
- Identify the risk factors, signs, and symptoms of depression in an older adult and provide reasons why this common problem is often misdiganosed or overlooked in older adults
- List two atypical presentations of affective disorder that are more common among older adults
- Outline theoretical perspectives and nursing management concerns for older adults with depression and those who are at risk for suicide in terms of primary, secondary, and tertiary prevention
- List assessment and documentation strategies, nursing diagnoses, interventions, and expected outcomes for each level of prevention
- Analyze the problem of suicide among older adults in terms of prevalence, clinical manifestations, assessment, nursing diagnoses, and management issues
- Plan nursing care for a suicidal older adult, highlighting nursing interventions, psychotherapeutic approaches, expected outcomes, and documentation

This chapter presents an overview of depression, a psychiatric syndrome often encountered in older adults, and then discusses suicide, one of the most devastating consequences of depression in this population. Although these conditions are clearly related, to guide nursing actions, primary, secondary, and tertiary prevention are considered separately in this text. The research brief and tables containing teaching guides and resources are combined because they apply to both depression and suicide.

Depression

Depression affects nearly 10 million Americans of all ages, socioeconomic classes, races, and cultures. Among older adults, depression continues to be a serious mental health problem despite recent advances in our understanding of its causes and the development of many effective pharmacological and psychotherapeutic treatments. Epidemiological studies of depression among community-dwelling older adults report widely varying rates, ranging from 2 to 44 percent, depending on the criteria used to define depression (e.g., strict DSM-IV criteria versus feelings of despair and a low mood) and the method used to evaluate it (e.g., self-report or brief rating scales versus in-depth clinical psychiatric evaluation). Most rigorous studies suggest that important symptoms of depression affect approximately 10 to 15 percent of all noninstitutionalized people over age 65. These depressive symptoms are often associated with adjustment to late life losses and stressors (e.g., enforced retirement, death of a spouse) and physical illnesses.[1] Rates of depression increase dramatically among institutionalized older adults, with as many as 50 to 75 percent of long-term care residents having mild to moderate depressive symptoms. Of these, a significant number of noncognitively impaired adults (10 to 20 percent) experience symptoms severe enough to meet diagnostic criteria for clinical depression.[1] Thus, depression is a significant public health problem; it is the most common and, happily, the most treatable psychiatric disorder among older adults. Almost 80 percent of all people with serious depression are successfully treated and return to health.

Although depression is common among older adults, it is often misdiagnosed or overlooked. A number of factors account for this circumstance, including the fact that in older adults, depression may mask or be masked by other physical disorders. In addition, social isolation, ageist attitudes, denial, and ignorance of the normal aging process contribute to underdetection and undertreatment of this disorder.[2] Unfortunately, some health-care professionals and many older people still mistakenly view depression as a natural part of growing older and thus fail to distinguish between expected behaviors and a treatable illness.[3]

This is particularly unfortunate for a variety of reasons. Depression may shorten life expectancy by precipitating or aggravating physical deterioration. Its greatest impact is often in the area of diminished satisfaction and quality of life, inhibiting fulfillment of late-life developmental tasks. Moreover, depression can be both emotionally and financially draining for the affected person as well as his or her family and informal and formal social support systems.[2] Finally, a high rate of suicide is perhaps the most serious consequence of untreated depression, as discussed in detail later in this chapter.

CLINICAL MANIFESTATIONS

The symptoms of depression, which remain the same throughout the life span, may be divided into three main groups, often called the depressive triad, listed in Table 28–1. Although the symptoms of depression in older adults are the same as those exhibited by a younger person with a depressive disorder, older adults, more than any other cohort, do not fit neatly into psychiatric categories. In many cases, the differential diagnosis of depression in later life is complex and difficult. For example, psychiatric health-care providers must distinguish between major depressive episodes (single, recurrent, or bipolar) and other diagnoses that manifest depressive features commonly found in older adults. Bereavement, adjustment disorders with depressed mood, and other conditions often associated with depression (e.g., dementia, hypochondriasis, sleep disorders) are common.

To complicate matters further, atypical presentations of depression are more common in older adults than in any other age group. These include a milder form of depression that seems to come and go with no clear-cut environmental precipitant and unremitting or intractable forms of depression that are seemingly resistant to treatment. Another type of bipolar illness known as rapid cycling exists, during which the mood of the older person changes rapidly (often over the course of several days) from a euphoric, manic state to profound depression.

MANAGEMENT

1 *Primary Prevention*

A number of interpersonal and environmental hazards common in later life may combine to put older adults at greater risk for depression. Some, such as adverse medication reactions, may be preventable; others,

such as the onset of dementia or death of a spouse, are not. Nevertheless, nurses should be aware of these factors and intervene to prevent the onset of depression when possible.

With increasing age, people continue to confront normal developmental tasks, which require the ability to adjust to a variety of changes, as discussed in more detail in Chapter 25. Nurses are ideally suited to help older clients to work through these changes, using interactive strategies such as reminiscence and life review that emphasize pleasant life events and positive contributions and accomplishments (see Chapter 25). Referrals to local bereavement support groups or widow-to-widow programs may also be indicated. Nurses can ensure appropriate and least-restrictive levels of care for the client by making referrals for home care and home-delivered meals and by recommending environmental modifications (e.g., ramps, adequate lighting) to maintain an optimal level of independence. Educating the client and family about normal and pathological aging processes is also an essential nursing task.

A number of theoretical perspectives are valuable in understanding the multiple causes of depression in older adults and guiding preventive nursing actions in this area. According to Erikson's[4] theory of psychosocial de-

TABLE 28–1 SIGNS AND SYMPTOMS OF DEPRESSION

Pervasive Disturbance of Mood

Sadness, discouragement
Crying
Anxiety, panic attacks
Brooding
Irritability
Statements of feeling sad, "blue," depressed, "low," or "down in the dumps" and feeling that nothing is fun
Paranoia

Disturbances in Perception of Self, Environment, Future

Withdrawal from usual activities
Decreased sex drive
Inability to express pleasure
Feelings of worthlessness
Unreasonable fears
Self-reproach for minor failings
Delusions
Hallucinations (of short duration)
Criticism aimed at self and others
Passivity

Vegetative

Increased or decreased body movements
Pacing; wringing hands; pulling or rubbing hair, body, or clothing
Difficulty getting to sleep, staying awake, waking early
Decreased or (sometimes) increased appetite
Weight loss or (sometimes) gain
Fatigue
Preoccupation with physical health, especially fear of cancer
Inability to concentrate, think clearly, or make decisions
Slowed speech, pauses before answering, decreased amount of speech, low or monotonous speech
Thoughts of death
Suicide or suicide attempts
Constipation
Tachycardia

velopment, the older adult who has not successfully worked through the necessary developmental tasks and arrived at a sense of cohesion, inner peace, and satisfaction with his or her life (a state he called ego integrity) risks despair.

Furthermore, many older adults face a variety of stressors, often cumulative, that may predispose them to depression. These stressors include economic, social, physical, and emotional stressors and activity losses. Sociological theory suggests that these stressors and losses may combine to produce a loss of role status and social support systems, a view reinforced by the prejudicial, ageist attitudes often held by society. From an existential perspective, these changes can result in a loss of meaning and purpose in life, thus leading to depression. Nurses who encounter older adults who have experienced major, and often cumulative, losses may help them avoid depression by redirecting their interests, encouraging meaningful new activities and relationships, and bolstering their social support network. These interventions may take the form of very concrete tasks, such as making sure the older adult has access to a telephone or knows how to use public transportation, as well as facilitative strategies, such as encouraging the family to visit on a more regular basis, helping the client enroll in a folk dancing class at the local Senior Center, or recommending a preretirement counseling course.

Psychoanalytical theorists propose object loss, aggression turned inward, and loss of self-esteem as critical factors in the onset of depressive symptoms, whereas cognitive theories suggest that the older person's negative cognitive sets and distorted interpretations of self and environment lead to and reinforce depression. Behavioral theorists postulate that learned helplessness secondary to aversive stimuli and resulting in rewards is a basis for depression, and theorists in the biological camp set forth neurotransmitter and neuroendocrine dysregulation and malfunctions as the cause of depression. If psychodynamic, cognitive, behavioral, or biological mechanisms are suspected of putting the older adult at risk for depression, the nurse should refer him or her to psychiatric specialists for comprehensive evaluation and, if needed, for talking or pharmacological therapies.

In addition, a broad range of physical illnesses common in older people may create symptoms of depression. These include metabolic disturbances, endocrine disorders, neurological diseases, cancer, viral and bacterial infections, cardiovascular disorders, pulmonary problems, musculoskeletal disorders, gastrointestinal disorders, genitourinary problems, collagen vascular diseases, and anemias. Moreover, many of the medications commonly used to treat these disorders may produce a secondary depression. Examples include antihypertensives, psychotropics, antiparkinsonians, narcotic and non-narcotic analgesics, cardiovascular preparations, oral hypoglycemics, antimicrobials, steroids, cancer chemotherapeutic agents, and cimetidine.[5] Alcohol also can cause secondary depression.[5] When an older client has one of the physical illnesses listed here, the nurse should first make sure he or she is receiving adequate medical care and then discuss the relationship between the illness and its treatment with the person's primary care physician. Sometimes medications can be changed or dosing patterns altered to eliminate or diminish depressive side effects. In some cases, neither the disease nor its treatment is amenable to intervention. In this situation, it is often helpful for nurses simply to explain to the client that the disease or the medicine essential to treatment is causing the depression. This stops the person from assuming (falsely) that the depression is something he or she has caused and allows the person to feel less stigmatized. Physical illnesses can also trigger depression because they may cause chronic pain, disability, and loss of function; diminish self-esteem; increase dependence; or cause fear of pain or death. The nurse should openly discuss these issues with the older adult and work with the primary care physician to ensure that no unnecessary suffering occurs. Referrals to occupational, speech, and physical therapists may prevent unnecessary disability and loss of function and self-esteem. Factors associated with physical illnesses such as isolation, sensory deprivation, and enforced dependency may also contribute to the development of depression and are often amenable to selected social and environmental interventions.[6]

Many factors may be responsible for the onset of depression in later life. All of the theories highlighted here have merit with regard to depression in this population, which is probably multifactorial in nature. Thus, the nurse who is assessing an older person for depression must consider a variety of issues—environmental, spiritual, interpersonal, social, biological, behavioral, physical, cognitive, psychodynamic, existential, and treatment-related—if the assessment is to be comprehensive and valid.

2 *Secondary Prevention*

Assessment

Because of the stigma often associated with any form of mental illness in this age group, many depressed older adults have somatic or physical complaints, stating that they must have cancer, heart trouble, or some other malady that is making them feel bad, rather than attributing their symptoms to an emotional cause. A critical part of interviewing depressed older adults is using their terminology. For example, if the older adult states, "Oh, I'm not depressed, I've just been down in the dumps for the past 6 weeks," then it is best to continue the interview by inquiring how he or she feels when "down in the dumps" rather than using medical or psychiatric labels and jargon. This will provide richer, more valid interview data on which to base further assessment, diagnostic, and therapeutic activities.

Given all the factors that can cause or contribute to depression in older adults and the varied signs and symptoms associated with depression in this age group, how can the nurse best go about identifying a depressed older adult? It is best to begin by reviewing the signs and symptoms of the depressive triad (see Table 28–1) and ascertaining via face-to-face interview with the client what his or her symptoms are or have been, how long they have lasted, and whether these symptoms occurred before. It is also essential to note whether a clear-cut environmental precipitant or loss (e.g., forced retirement) may have triggered the depressive symptoms.

If depression is suspected, the nurse should administer a standardized assessment tool that is reliable and valid and has been designed for and tested on older adults. Several such tools are available,[7] but one of the easiest to use and interpret in a variety of settings is the Geriatric Depression Rating Scale (GDRS).[8] The 30-item GDRS was developed as a screening tool for depression in older adults. It uses a simple yes-or-no self-report format or can be read to a vision-impaired person, and takes about 10 minutes to complete. The GDRS is psychometrically sound and excludes somatic items that do not correlate well with other measures of mood. Scores greater than 10 suggest the need for referral for a more detailed psychiatric evaluation of depression; the GDRS is only a screening tool.

Because depression is often associated with or may even mimic dementia in older adults, it is also advisable for the nurse or another member of the health-care team to administer a mental status screening examination such as the mini-mental status exam (MMSE)[9] to assess for cognitive status.

Nursing Interventions

Every interaction with a depressed client has therapeutic potential. Nurses can offer safety and comfort by supporting and encouraging the client to try new things, by providing structure in daily activities, by encouraging interaction and involvement that adds meaning and purpose to life, and by validating the client's worth as a person by the way he or she is treated.[6] Four main first-line interventions can be performed by nurses with any level of professional preparation: letting the client know that he or she is cared about, helping the client see that he or she is unusually sad or blue, providing accurate information about depression, and creating a healthful physical and social environment.

Communicate Caring. Nurses must be sensitive to the feelings of depressed older adults and recognize the stigma attached to any form of mental illness in this cohort. Clients should be told directly that the nurse cares about and values them, even if they do not seem to care about themselves. The nurse should ask them how they feel and think and should encourage them to talk about what has happened in their life, and about their hurts and fears. Then the nurse should try to understand the situation from the client's point of view. It is also essential to recognize and accept that these clients are feeling great sadness. There are many easy ways to communicate acceptance of depressed older adults and their problems, such as being nonjudgmental and nonpunitive, conveying interest, talking and listening to them, and permitting them to express strong emotions (e.g., anger, sadness).[6]

Help Clients Realize That They Are Unusually Sad or Blue. Nurses can help depressed clients realize that they are unusually sad or blue by asking questions that help them identify the things that they feel sad about, such as any losses they have suffered and are grieving over. Reminiscence and guided life review focusing on past positive events (e.g., family visits, hobbies and leisure activities, contributions to others) also help the depressed person see that things have not always been this bad. It is often necessary for nurses to point out the positive things they see in their depressed clients, thus reinforcing the notion that they still have worth.[6]

Provide Information About Depression. Clients deserve accurate information about depression, including the fact that it is a common illness in all age groups, and like many physical illnesses, it probably is treatable. Depressed older clients need to understand that their symptoms are part of this illness and that the symptoms will go away when the depression lifts. The nurse should emphasize that taking their prescribed medications and talking about their feelings help reduce or eliminate the symptoms of depression (Table 28–2). Finally, nurses may need to remind older adults that they have lived a long life, have had many valuable experiences, and have survived many difficulties that can help them cope with this problem.

Modify the Physical and Social Environment. A number of environmental strategies are appropriate with depressed older adults. Examples include increasing sensory input by turning on lights, increasing touch and massage, making sure that the client is using assistive devices such as eyeglasses and hearing aids, and using plants or animals (pet therapy) to increase the client's bond with growing things to add to his or her sense of being loved, accepted, and needed. Providing structure, security, and consistency by explaining institutional routine clearly increases the client's sense of safety. Setting limits on clients' behavior only when really necessary and doing things for them only when they really cannot do them for themselves helps prevent dependency and learned helplessness.

The nurse should encourage the depressed client's participation in self-care and other activities and enhance his or her self-concept by introducing opportunities to do something (no matter how small) and to do it

TABLE 28–2 TEACHING GUIDE: DEPRESSION

Instruct the older client in assertiveness, problem solving, and stress management techniques.

Make sure the client understands the nature of depression and also how factors such as social isolation and alcohol abuse may contribute to suicidal thoughts or actions.

Teach clients about their medications (their purpose, possible side effects, and how to deal with them).

Include family members when possible.

Use a group format. Older adults seem to benefit greatly from sharing these very stigmatizing experiences, and the group encounter diminishes their sense of social isolation.

Provide ongoing educational sessions. Content of these sessions should include a focus on the aging process, signs of depression, and characteristics of suicidal intent, emphasizing the fact that suicide is preventable and depression highly treatable.

right. Older clients need to be taught how to be assertive and encouraged to tell the staff whatever is on their minds. Finally, opportunities should be created for interaction with others, including staff, other patients or residents, family, and friends.

Medication Management

Although antidepressant medications are the most common form of treatment for depression,[10] a number of potential problems are associated with their administration. Nurses are in the best position to recognize early adverse side effects (Table 28–3) and to report them to the prescribing physician. Nurses should also encourage older clients to take their medications as prescribed, remind them that these drugs do not work overnight (often taking 2 to 3 weeks to become effective), and continue to monitor their symptoms for improvement.

Table 28–4 provides suggested interventions for the nurse caring for a depressed older adult. Nurses interested in a more in-depth discussion of the use of somatic therapies (e.g., medication selection and management and electroconvulsant therapy) in the treatment of depression, as well as a review of cognitive and interpersonal psychotherapies, are encouraged to read Buckwalter and Babich's[5] review of the psychological and physiological aspects of depression, the report of the National Institutes of Health [NIH] Consensus Development Panel on Depression in Late Life,[11] the guidelines for treatment of depression published by the Agency for Health Care Policy and Research,[10] and Schneider's review of the efficacy of clinical treatment for mental disorders in older people.[12]

Documentation

Documentation of depression covers a variety of verbal, nonverbal, physiological, and emotional parameters. As noted in Table 28–4, the nurse must regularly monitor and record items such as weight, intake, and hours of sleep. Patient reports of symptoms (e.g., agitation, self-reproach) are also essential aspects of documentation in addition to the nurse's own observations of activity levels and social interaction. Depression tends to be a recurrent illness that often has a genetic or hereditary component (i.e., runs in families), and the nurse must therefore obtain and document information about previous episodes of affective illness and family history.[13] Because depression is often related to physical illness and medications in this population, it is critical to document medical history as well. Present symptoms, scores on self-rating scales such as the GDRS, and precipitating factors (e.g., psychosocial stressors such as loss of a loved one) should be charted and communicated with other members of the health-care team. The family is an excellent resource to provide information or to corroborate data obtained from the older client. Social support information, including both informal and formal support mechanisms, is an area of documentation that is key to the discharge planning process.[14]

TABLE 28–3 COMMON ANTIDEPRESSANT SIDE EFFECTS AND INTERVENTIONS

Blurred vision: Reassure the older client that this is a medication side effect and that it is temporary (often resolving after taking the medication for several months and disappearing when medication is stopped); provide support and assistance as necessary; check for environmental hazards if needed.

Constipation: Increase client's water and fluid intake; suggest natural dietary laxative (e.g., prunes, fiber); request prescription stool softeners; monitor bowel habits to avoid impactions; use laxatives only as last resort.

Dry mouth: Encourage fluids to reduce discomfort; check dentures for proper fit; monitor for sores or lesions that may cause discomfort and interfere with eating.

Urinary retention: Monitor voiding patterns (scantiness, difficulty starting, frequency) and assess for subjective distress (feeling of fullness or incomplete emptying, pain); monitor color and odor of urine (urinary stasis leads to infection); report findings to physician for possible catheterization and medication change.

Excessive perspiration: Offer comfort measures (e.g., dry clothes, handkerchiefs, tissues); inform client that sweating is a side effect of medication.

Orthostatic hypotension: Check the client's lying and standing blood pressures for 2 to 3 weeks when the medication is started; monitor for dizziness and light-headedness; inform client that this is a side effect of the medication and that falls may occur if he or she gets up too quickly; instruct client to dangle feet over bedside when getting up from a reclining position; instruct client to rise slowly and stand supported for a few minutes before walking.

Fatigue, weakness, drowsiness: Administer medications in the evening to facilitate sleep and reduce daytime drowsiness; monitor level of sedation and fatigue over time (getting worse versus getting better) to differentiate between medication side effects and symptoms of depression (fatigue caused by the depression should decrease with medication); assess activities of daily living (ADLs) and activity level for declines; monitor sleeping patterns for increased daytime sleeping; notify physician if symptoms seem to get worse as medication is increased.

Tremors, twitches, jitteriness: Monitor severity of symptoms and their interference with ADLs and other activity; assess subjective distress; provide information and encouragement that this is a medication side effect rather than a permanent impairment and that it will subside when the medication is discontinued; notify the physician if these symptoms are prolonged and severe.

Hallucinations, delusions: Establish onset to differentiate between psychotic depression and medication side effect; if associated with medication, hold additional doses and notify the physician; monitor client for safety and reassure him or her if hallucinations or delusions are frightening or upsetting; provide reality orientation; acknowledge that the hallucination *seems* real but assure client that it is an adverse side effect of the medication, that it will soon go away, and that you will keep client safe until then.

Source: Smith, M, and Buckwalter, KC,[6] with permission.

3 Tertiary Prevention

Group Modalities

Because being with other people is important in the process of ongoing care and rehabilitation of depression, group therapies are often successful among depressed

TABLE 28–4 CARE PLAN

Nursing Diagnosis: Depression	
Expected Outcome	*Nursing Actions*
Client demonstrates fewer vegetative signs and symptoms.	*Diagnostic/Monitoring* Monitor appetite, weight loss, sleep and elimination patterns, levels of fatigue and activity, body movements. Observe patterns of speech, concentration and decision-making abilities, and preoccupation with physical health. *Therapeutic* Encourage participation in self-care activities. Provide support, structure, and consistency. Modify the physical and social environments to increase sensory input and create opportunities for successful task completion. Encourage involvement with plants and pets. Set limits only as necessary.
Client demonstrates more positive mood and perceptions of self, environment, and future.	*Diagnostic/Monitoring* Assess mood, using GDRS. Monitor medication compliance and adverse side effects. Intervene as necessary (see Table 28–3). Monitor improvement. Observe social interactions with staff, other patients, family, and friends. Assess for delusions, hallucinations, or paranoid ideations. Monitor activity levels, feelings of worthlessness, and unreasonable fears. Observe symptoms of crying, irritability, and anxiety. *Therapeutic* Communicate caring directly. Validate and accept client's sad mood through nonpunitive, nonjudgmental behaviors. Convey interest and ask questions that help client identify losses and hurts. Listen and permit expression of strong emotions. Help client discover that he or she is unusually sad or blue. Facilitate recall of past positive events and reinforce self-worth. Provide accurate information about depression and its treatment. Encourage verbalization of problems and feelings. Teach client how to be assertive. Increase sense of mastery, belonging, and shared experiences. Encourage decision making to increase sense of control. Facilitate psychosocial rehabilitative therapies, either by leading groups or referring clients to mental health professionals. Administer prescribed medications.

older adults.[15] Many types of psychosocial rehabilitative therapies are possible: those that focus on activities and promote a sense of relatedness to others (e.g., movement, music), those that encourage reminiscing or life review and thus help resolve old problems and increase identification with past accomplishments (see Chapter 25), those that teach about health and stress management, those that stimulate the senses and improve responsiveness to the environment, those that help fulfill the need to love and be loved (e.g., pet therapy), and those that encourage renewed interest in surroundings and stimulate thought and discussion of topics related to the real world, such as remotivation therapy.

Any of these modalities can help depressed older adults by promoting social interaction and relationships, increasing self-worth by providing an opportunity to master an activity and thus feel a sense of accomplishment, and increasing the sense of shared experience.[6] The essential ingredient to psychosocial interventions, whether on a one-to-one basis or in a group, should be the desire to improve patient care. This desire stimulates interest in the patient, better communication among staff members, and improved interpersonal relationships overall. The therapeutic method used is much less important than the interaction between the nurse and the older patient.

Table 28–10 at the end of this chapter lists several sources of information related to the topic of depression among older adults.

Suicide

Suicide is perhaps the most devastating consequence of depression. It is a universal phenomenon that affects both the old and the young. In the United States, the suicide rate of older adults has been increasing since 1981.[16] However, most gerontological nurses know little about the magnitude of the problem, its assessment and prevention, and management of suicidal behavior in older adults. As Osgood[17] has noted, although suicide in older adults is a major social problem, it has been virtually ignored in the United States. Attention has consistently focused on adolescent suicide, demonstrating our culture's emphasis on youth and devaluation of older adults.

Older white men have a higher suicide rate than any other age, gender, or race category.[18] Analysis of suicides by age indicates that they are accounted for largely by people over the age of 75. In fact, the suicide rate for white men over age 75 increased from about 46 to 60 percent between 1981 and 1986, whereas that for white men in the 65- to 74-year-old category grew from 30 to 38 percent.[16] These statistics have implications for the environmental and interpersonal factors related to suicide in older adults.

Unlike many young people, most older adults who attempt suicide really do want to kill themselves. Seldom is suicide merely a cry for help or an attention-getting mechanism among older adults.[19] Two reasons the attempts-to-completion ratio is so much lower in older adults are that they tend to use more violent and lethal means (e.g., gunshot to the head) and that they tend to communicate their suicidal intentions less often than do people in other age groups.[17] Interestingly, the frequency of suicidal thoughts such as "I'm sick and tired of living this way" remains constant across the life cycle, whereas suicidal attempts (deliberate acts of suicide in which the person cannot be sure of survival) are actually lower among older adults. However, the critical statistic is the attempts-to-completion ratio which is about 20:1 for people under age 40 and only 4:1 for those over age 60. These ratios mean that suicide must be considered serious in older adults, who are five times more likely to actually kill themselves than are younger people.

Furthermore, even as dramatic as the suicide statistics are for older adults, they probably grossly underestimate the true magnitude of the problem for two reasons. First, even if suicide is suspected, it is often not listed as the actual cause of death on most death certificates. Second, these data do not reflect the number of older adults who indirectly or passively commit suicide by starving themselves, abusing alcohol, mixing or overdosing on medications, purposely discontinuing life-sustaining medications, or simply giving up the will to live.

TABLE 28–5   RISK FACTORS ASSOCIATED WITH SUICIDE

Widowed or divorced
Retired or unemployed
Living alone
Poor physical health
Drug abuse (including therapeutic drugs)
Access to lethal means
Depression
Alcohol abuse
Sense of hopelessness
Previous suicide attempt
Bereavement
Family history of depression or suicide

CLINICAL MANIFESTATIONS

Although the major risk factors for suicide (Table 28–5) remain virtually the same throughout the life span, many of these factors become more common as one ages. As with younger people, the single best predictor of suicide attempts in late life is a previous attempt.

Given the difficulty inherent in identifying an older person with suicidal potential, what signs and symptoms, or "defining characteristics" in North American Nursing Diagnosis Association (NANDA) parlance, should the nurse look for in older clients?[20] The most immediate response to this question is that the defining characteristics can be extremely varied and often relate to factors associated with depression. Some of the more prominent signs and symptoms are listed in Table 28–6.

MANAGEMENT

1   Primary Prevention

Although there is no single cause of suicide, what interpersonal and environmental hazards, in addition to the risk factors noted in Table 28–1, may account for the increasing suicide rate, especially among white men over age 75? Social scientists, psychiatrists, and epidemiologists have set forth a number of explanatory environmental hypotheses, including technological and medical advances that extend the number of years lived but di-

TABLE 28–6   DEFINING CHARACTERISTICS OF SUICIDE POTENTIAL

Hopelessness or helplessness
Psychomotor agitation or retardation
Verbalization of suicidal ideation
Ruminations about death
Hostile behavior
Impulsive behavior (e.g., giving away valued possessions)
Social isolation; withdrawn behavior
Depressed, flat affect
Changes in appetite and sleep patterns
Indecisiveness
Cognitive disturbances including impaired concentration and "tunnel vision"

minish the quality of life, the cost of treatments that impoverish older adults and their families,[21] a sense of perceived failure and retirement from the workforce, and declining health.[22] The latter factors represent a loss of both economic and social status, especially among white men. At present, it is impossible to assess the full impact of the advent of prospective payment systems such as diagnosis-related groups (DRGs) on the health and well-being of older adults and the relationship among diminished medical coverage, shorter hospital stays, and quicker discharge on suicide rates in this population.[16]

Nurses can initiate primary prevention efforts by knowing which clients are at greatest risk for suicide. Often, the profile is of an older person, especially an older white man, who is in poor health and may be economically stressed, is socially isolated, and is bereaved or depressed because of the death of a spouse or enforced retirement. When such a profile of cumulative interpersonal and environmental hazards is detected, the nurse should act immediately to prevent suicide by making referrals for psychiatric evaluation and possible treatment of depression, making referrals to appropriate social service agencies for economic assistance, and implementing strategies to increase social interaction by encouraging the client to attend functions such as congregate meals or bingo at local Senior Centers. These Senior Center activities are available for no or minimal cost in most communities under the auspices of local Area Agencies on Aging and funded through the Older Americans Act. In addition, initial assessment efforts should always target the risk factors noted in Table 28–5, especially drug and alcohol abuse (often overlooked among older adults), availability of a means to commit suicide, family history of depression or suicide, and previous suicide attempt.

2 Secondary Prevention

Assessment

It is essential that nurses who work with older adults in a variety of settings (acute-care and long-term care as well as community-based practice) become attuned to the demoralized statements that may indicate suicidal ideation in their clients, such as "Things only get worse the older I get," "I'm of no use to anyone," or "Life just doesn't bring me any satisfaction." When the nurse hears statements of this nature or when the older client is at risk for depression or suicide (see Table 28–5), the nurse should assess for suicidal potential. This is most easily accomplished through the series of hierarchical questions presented in Table 28–7.

TABLE 28–7 SUICIDE ASSESSMENT QUESTIONS

"Have you thought life is not worth living?"
"Have you considered harming yourself?"
"Do you have a plan for hurting yourself?"
"Have you ever acted on that plan?"
"Have you ever attempted suicide?"

Many older adults respond affirmatively to the first question; a few admit to having considered harming themselves but often qualify this remark with statements such as "But I could never go against my religion that way" or "I would never do that to my wife. Who would look after her when I'm gone?" Older adults who admit to planning to harm themselves and who have access to the means to do so must be considered potentially suicidal and should be referred immediately for further psychiatric assessment and treatment. Because of the extremely high risk in this population, nurses must document their assessment findings and share them with other members of the health-care team. Nurses should also re-evaluate potential for suicide in any depressed older adult every 3 months, noting any changes in responses to assessment questions.

Nursing Interventions

Although suicide cannot always be prevented, when the risk is recognized, some preventive measures can be instituted. The nurse can play a vital role in instructing family members to prevent access to or remove medications that may be harmful if consumed in large quantities (e.g., sleeping pills, tranquilizers), as well as knives, guns, or ropes, which could become instruments of suicide. If the suicidal risk is great, the older person should be hospitalized under the care of psychiatric specialists. Thus, nurses must decide the appropriate level of observation for the older client.

Crisis Intervention. Nurses, especially those working in outpatient settings, can also use principles of crisis intervention in dealing with older adults who are suicidal. The crisis intervention approach consists of five basic steps:

1 Focusing on the current hazard or crisis to which the client is responding (e.g., loss of a loved one)
2 Decreasing any immediate danger (removing implements, providing hospital supervision)
3 Comparing the costs and benefits of continuing to provide medications to the client (which he or she may use in an overdose attempt) on an outpatient basis
4 Discussing the situation openly with the client's family
5 Negotiating a suicide contract with the client[23]

Therapeutic Alliance. Another key element in the prevention of suicide is therapeutic alliance building. This process entails forming a bond of trust and a rapport with older clients and always keeping promises made to them (e.g., "I will call you at home over the weekend to see how you are feeling"). The nurse should set clear limits and make firm therapeutic recommendations, while encouraging older clients to verbalize any concerns they have. Another critical element in therapeutic alliance building among this age group is the need to set short-term goals, which focus on daily, weekly, or at most, monthly objectives.[23]

Skills Training. The nurse may facilitate referrals (e.g., to family therapy sessions) or may play a more direct therapeutic role by teaching older clients communication skills, assertiveness skills, and stress management techniques and by providing information about depression and the medications prescribed to treat it. At all times, the nurse should encourage and facilitate the client's independence, assisting with activities of daily living only as needed.

Psychotherapeutic Approaches. The nurse may also teach the older client how to cope with dysfunctional and self-destructive thoughts and behaviors related to suicide. For example, the client should be taught how to identify and then curb dysfunctional thoughts that generate inappropriate guilt, depression, and a sense of hopelessness (e.g., overgeneralizations, black-and-white thinking patterns). An example of this is the older person who says, "If I had only insisted my wife see the doctor last month, she never would have died. It's my fault that she's dead." Behavioral techniques are similarly designed to help the older client link certain events with negative or depressed feelings, and then to identify ways these events can be changed or eliminated. For example, "Every time I visit with my sister-in-law, I feel rotten afterward."

When these interventions are used, the older person often develops a safe and trusting relationship with the nurse, one in which the client discusses his or her suici-dal feelings rather than acting on them. These clients should also exhibit fewer of the defining characteristics of suicidal potential, becoming less withdrawn, feeling less depressed, and taking a more active part in their own care and the rehabilitation process. They should have developed the ability to identify, and when possible to avoid, factors that may trigger depression and a sense of hopelessness; they should also have developed some skills with which to better cope with their immediate and recurrent problems. Among the most important evaluative elements to be documented are that the older client no longer verbalizes suicidal intent and agrees to continue treatment.

Care Plans

The principles of prevention, acute management, and ongoing care and rehabilitation of the suicidal older person are highlighted in Table 28–8. Many related diagnoses, listed in Table 28–9, have been approved by NANDA, and their risk factors and defining characteristics are important to understanding and preventing suicide in older adults.

The defining characteristics of suicide potential were set forth in Table 28–6. This nursing diagnosis is most clinically useful if related factors are explicated (as

TABLE 28–8 CARE PLAN

Nursing Diagnosis: Suicide potential	
Expected Outcomes	*Nursing Actions*
Client feels safe. Client reports any suicidal ideation to nurse. Client negotiates written contract not to harm self. Client does not harm self.	*Diagnostic/Monitoring* Assess potential for suicide. Decide on appropriate level of observation (e.g., outpatient, hospital). *Therapeutic* Reduce environmental hazards; instruct family to do so. Use crisis intervention techniques. Use therapeutic alliance building. Provide structure and diminish social isolation.
Client takes more active role and interest in self-care activities and in the rehabilitation process. Client increases interactions with staff, family, and friends. Client discusses issues related to suicide with staff and participates in setting therapeutic goals, renegotiating contracts, and planning for continued care after discharge. Client demonstrates enhanced ability to cope with problems that may precipitate suicidal behavior. Client verbalizes no suicidal ideation and feels diminished sense of hopelessness. Client keeps aftercare appointments, complies with prescribed medication regimen, and understands its purpose. Client demonstrates skills (e.g., problem-solving, assertiveness) in role-play situations. Client identifies stress management techniques and other alternative strategies to deal with feelings of despair.	Promote social interaction. Include client in goal-setting and discharge-planning activities and, if appropriate, in family therapy. Promote independence in self-care activities (e.g., grooming) and enhance decision-making opportunities. *Diagnostic/Monitoring* Ensure adequate mental health follow-up and monitoring for suicide in the aftercare period. *Therapeutic* Teach client assertiveness, communication, stress management, and problem-solving skills. Inform client of aftercare and community resources available. Use cognitive, behavioral, or family therapy strategies, or make referrals to psychiatric specialists for same. Teach client (and family if available) about the nature of depressive illness and medication side effects and management.

TABLE 28–9   NANDA-APPROVED NURSING DIAGNOSES RELATED TO SUICIDE POTENTIAL

Hopelessness
Violence
High risk, self-directed
Grieving, dysfunctional
Coping, ineffective individual
Self-esteem, low: situational
Social isolation
Spiritual distress

in "Suicide potential related to depression and loss of functional ability secondary to CVA").

Documentation

As always, nurses must document their assessment findings and communicate them to other members of the health-care team. More specifically, the nurse should note whether a previous suicide attempt has been made and, if so, the circumstances surrounding that attempt. The precise nature of the suicide plan must be detailed as well. The nurse should report any significant recent events (e.g., death of a favorite grandchild) that may have precipitated suicidal ideations or actions and note any other pertinent features of the crisis experience (e.g., chronic or acute stressors). The older client's social support network and available resources should be documented, as well as lifestyle factors and previous strategies used to cope with stress. Any thorough evaluation includes detailed demographic data and documentation of the client's psychiatric history, family history, and medical history, paying particular attention to current or life-threatening illnesses.

Another form of documentation, the suicide contract, was mentioned earlier and deserves further elaboration. In the written contract, older clients help develop and then sign a contract in which they state that they will not harm themselves and in which they agree to inform the health-care professional if they are feeling suicidal, rather than acting on the destructive feelings. Contracts vary in terms of the specific behaviors they cover, but all share the common elements of clearly defined problems and objectives to be met by specified dates. The responsibilities of both the client (e.g., "I will not harm myself before the Monday morning session, and if I am suicidal over the weekend I will call the nurse at home") and the health-care professional are laid out clearly. Written contracts are useful in both inpatient and outpatient settings and should be revised periodically in keeping with the client's mental health status and short-term goals.

3   Tertiary Prevention

As previously mentioned, the single best predictor of suicide is a previous suicide attempt. This risk factor must always be considered in the care and rehabilitation process, particularly if the precipitating factor (e.g., a diagnosis of cancer, death of a spouse) is unresolved. After the client is discharged to the community from an acute-care psychiatric setting and has granted consent, other members of the health-care network (e.g., homemaker or home health aide, visiting nurses) who have frequent contact with the client must be apprised of the suicidal risk and encouraged to report to mental health professionals any observed changes in mood or behavior that may indicate suicidal ideation. To this end, nurses who are active members of case management networks for older adults can inform other caregivers of the risk and can educate them regarding signs and symptoms of suicidal behavior and what to do if the behavior occurs. This educational function must extend to any family members or people in the informal social support network, such as friends and neighbors, who have close and ongoing contact with the client in the aftercare period.

Posthospitalization follow-up is essential to combat the high rate of recidivism in this population. Initially after discharge, psychiatric follow-up should be scheduled on a weekly basis for about 3 months. Thereafter, if the client is stable and no longer manifests symptoms of suicidal potential, the primary clinician may choose to see the client less often (e.g., monthly) or as needed.

Ideally, psychotherapeutic strategies such as cognitive and behavioral approaches used during inpatient

RESEARCH BRIEF

Mellick, E, et al: Suicide among elderly white men: Development of a profile. J Psychosoc Nurs 30(2):29–34, 1992.

A pilot study sought to determine the social, psychological, physical, economic, and demographic variables associated with suicide among older white men. A small sample of white male suicide victims age 60 and over who had been residents of Scott County, Iowa, were retrospectively compared with a control group of white male older residents of the same area who had died of natural causes during the 5-year period of 1983 to 1988. Data were obtained through interviews with surviving spouses. Both groups shared many characteristics, but statistically significant differences were found in four main areas of interest to nurses. The older men who had committed suicide were more likely than those of the control group to have left a suicide note, experienced chronic sleeping problems during the year before death, had some sort of degenerative illness, and experienced considerable pain or discomfort in the year before death. Interestingly, 25 percent of the suicide notes were found by nurses and 60 percent of the subjects who committed suicide had been seen by a physician in the month before death. This study was an initial step toward the refinement of a profile of the older white male suicide victim.

TABLE 28–10   RESOURCES

Helpful Facts about Depressive Disorders. U.S. Department of Health and Human Services, No ADM 87-1536, 1987. One copy free, minimal charge for more; excellent patient education brochure.

What Everyone Should Know About Depression. A Scriptographic Booklet. Channing L. Bete Co, South Deerfield, MA 413-665-7611 for order information.

Depression/Awareness, Recognition, Treatment (D/ART) Pamphlet on the National Education Program on Depressive Disorders. U.S. Department of Health and Human Services, 1987.

For further information about depression and suicide, write to: National Institute of Mental Health Public Inquiries

Room 15C-05
5600 Fisher's Lane
Rockville, MD 20857
301-443-4513

D/ART Fact Sheet
For further information on the D/ART program write to:
Director, D/ART Program
National Institute of Mental Health
5600 Fisher's Lane
Rockville, MD 20857
301-443-4140

treatment as well as skills training are reinforced during the rehabilitation phase by practitioners knowledgeable in these areas. Even clients who appear symptom-free in the aftercare period often benefit greatly from periodic booster or refresher sessions that remind them of the relationship between dysfunctional thoughts and actions and depression, particularly on the anniversary of their suicide attempt. Similarly, written suicide contracts (discussed earlier) can be effective in the rehabilitation period. Nurses providing ongoing care after a suicide attempt should regularly inquire about feelings of hopelessness, isolation, and depression (see Tables 28–5 and 28–7) and are encouraged to readminister the GDRS every 6 months to monitor changes in mood from baseline (discharge) levels. A final, critical element of ongoing care and rehabilitation involves careful monitoring and adjustment of any psychotropic medications the older client has been prescribed on discharge, as well as periodic review and evaluation of the potential for adverse interactions of these medications and others that may have been prescribed for the treatment of unrelated physical disorders. The Research Brief describes one effort to characterize older adults who attempt suicide. Table 28–10 lists resources to be consulted for further information.

Student Learning Activities

1 Form two teams. Discuss whether depression should be considered a normal part of the aging process. One team will argue for and one against the issue.

2 Review the diagnoses and medication records of three older nursing home residents. Identify the medications and illnesses that might lead to a secondary depression.

3 Discuss how current changes in the health-care system (managed care/HMOs, decreased funding for the Older Americans Act) might affect suicide rates among older adults.

REFERENCES

1 Blazer, DG: Current concepts: Depression in the elderly. N Engl J Med 320:164, 1989.

2 Love, CC, and Buckwalter, KC: Reactive depression. In Maas, M, et al (eds): Nursing Diagnoses and Interventions for the Elderly. Addison-Wesley, Menlo Park, Calif, 1991, p 419.

3 Billig, N: To Be Old and Sad: Understanding Depression in the Elderly. Lexington Books, Lexington, Mass, 1987.

4 Erikson, EH: Childhood and Society. Norton, New York, 1950.

5 Buckwalter, KC, and Babich, KS: Psychologic and physiologic aspects of depression. In Gift, A, and Jacox, A (eds): Nursing Clinics of North America. WB Saunders, Philadelphia, 1990.

6 Smith, M, and Buckwalter, KC: Training manual: Geriatric mental health training in long term care. Abbe Center for Community Mental Health Aging Education, Cedar Rapids, Ia, 1994.

7 Kane, RA, and Kane, RL: Assessing the elderly: A practical guide to measurement. DC Heath and Co, Lexington, Mass, 1981.

8 Yesavage, J, et al: Development and validation of a geriatric depression screening scale: A preliminary report. J Psychiatr Res 17:215, 1983.

9 Folstein, M, et al: Mini-mental state: A practical method for grading the cognitive state of patients for the clinician. J Psychiatr Res 12:189, 198, 1975.

10 Agency for Health Care Policy and Research: Depression Guideline Panel: Depression in primary care, vol 2. Treatment of major depression. AHCPR Pub no 93-0551, Silver Spring, Md, 1993.

11 NIH Consensus Development Panel on Depression Late Life (1992). Diagnosis and treatment of depression in late life. JAMA 268(8):1018–1024, 1992.

12 Schneider, LS: Efficacy of clinical treatment for mental disorders among older persons. In Gatz, M (ed): Emerging Issues in Mental Health the Aging. American Psychological Association, Washington, DC, 1995.

13 Zauszniewski, JA: Potential sequelae of family history of depression: Identifying family members at risk. J Psychosoc Nurs 32(9):15–21, 1994.

14 Kurlowicz, LH: Social factors and depression in late life. Arch Psychiatr Nurs 7(1):30–36, 1994.

15 Clark, WG, and Vorst, VR: Group therapy with chronically depressed geriatric clients. J Psychosoc Nurs 32(5):9–13, 1994.

16 McCall, PL: Adolescent and elderly white male suicide trends: Evidence of changing well-being? J Gerontol 46(1): S43, 1991.

17 Osgood, NJ: Suicide in the Elderly. Aspen, Rockville, Md, 1985.

18 Osgood, NJ, and McIntosh, JL: Suicide and the Elderly: An Annotated Bibliography and Review. Greenwood Press, New York, 1986.

19 Miller, M: Suicide after Sixty: The Final Alternative. Springer, New York, 1979.

20 McLane, A: North American Nursing Diagnosis Association: Nursing Diagnoses: Definitions and Classification, Mosby, St Louis, 1995–1996.

21 Tolchin, M: When long life is too much: Suicide rises among elderly. New York Times, July 19, 1989, p 1.

22 Woodbury, M, et al: Trends in US suicide mortality rates 1968 to 1982: Race and sex differences in age, period and cohort components. Int J Epidemiol 17:356, 1988.

23 Blazer, DG: Depression in the elderly. Presentation at the American Society on Aging Conference, Mental Health of the Elderly, San Francisco, November, 16, 1988.

CHAPTER 29

Spirituality in Older Adults

Helen L. Halstead

OBJECTIVES

Upon completion of this chapter, the reader will be able to:

- Differentiate religiosity, spirituality, and spiritual well-being
- Describe the spiritual aspects of an integrated older adult
- Explain the impact of developmental stages and tasks on spirituality in the older person
- Justify continuity theory as a basis for spirituality and religiosity in older adults
- Contrast the deleterious spiritual effects of loss and the beneficial effects of hope on the older adult
- Discuss the influence of spirituality on the older person's view of death and preparation for it
- Define nursing roles and characteristics that facilitate spirituality for the older person
- Evaluate the status of his or her own current level of religiosity and spirituality
- Discuss the influence of spirituality, or the lack of it, on older adults that the reader knows

Impervious to race, color, national origin, gender, age, or disability, spirituality is a basic human quality, experienced by older adults of all faiths and those of no faith at all. Spirituality surmounts lifelong losses with hope. Nursing care for spiritual needs flows from the nurse's spiritual reservoir. Nurses cannot nourish spiritual needs without having their own spiritual nourishment.

Spirituality

Definitions of spirituality and descriptions of its characteristics in older adults abound in the literature.[1] Spirituality is a two-dimensional concept with both vertical and horizontal dimensions.[2] The vertical represents a relationship with God, and the horizontal, relationships with others. "Spiritual refers to the transcendent relationship between the person and a Higher Being, a quality that goes beyond a specific religious affiliation, that strives for reverence, awe, and inspiration, and that gives answers about the infinite."[3] It has been described as a source of strength and hope.[4] Banks[5] calls it a unifying force, providing meaning in life and consisting of individual values, perceptions, and faith as well as being a common bond among individuals. The 1971 White House Conference on Aging affirmed that all people are spiritual, even if they have no use for religious institutions and practice no personal pieties.[6] Spiritual needs were identified as a basic need of any age. Fish and Shelley[7] identify spiritual needs as the requirements for meaning and purpose, for love and relatedness, and for forgiveness.

Spirituality is often used synonymously with *religion* or *religiosity* but is actually distinct from it. Spirituality has to do with one's internal beliefs and personal experiences with God, whereas religion is only one way of expressing the inner aspects of one's personal beliefs. Religion or religiosity has more to do with creeds, communal practices, and external behaviors. Spiritual needs may be met by religious acts such as prayers or confession, but many such needs are met through caring human relationships.[8] Spirituality includes religiosity, but religiosity does not necessarily include spirituality.

Religiosity

Religiosity is "the degree and type of religious expression and participation of the aging."[9] A number of indicators of religiosity have been determined from research: church attendance, participation in church-related activities, knowledge of creeds and theology, prayer, Bible reading, and devotional time.[10]

The religious and spiritual needs of older adults in one study were the "need for opportunity for liturgical worship in my own denomination, especially on Sunday" and the "need for resources to maintain and nurture my inner life—the Bible, books, records, tapes, and TV programs."[11,12] Palmore[13] emphasizes that the church or synagogue is the "single most pervasive community institution to which the elderly belong."

In a society that includes more than 1200 different religious groups and innumerable subgroups and sects, nurses must obtain basic information about the common religious groups in their region. Although the various religions differ, some commonalities among religions are notable. Six common characteristics include a basis of authority or power, sacred scriptures, an ethical code defining right and wrong, a group identity, aspirations or expectations, and a view of what happens after death.[14] Most religions also have a respect for older adults.

Responsiveness of the church or synagogue to the needs of older adults is growing. Fifty-two different services that are provided by various churches have been identified. The four major roles of the church are providing religious programs, pastoral care, and social services and passive hosting of service agencies.

Finally, the church or synagogue provides a caring community when the older person most needs it. Steinitz[15] indicates that for many, it becomes the surrogate family, made up of "mothers," "fathers," "sisters," and "brothers" of all ages. The church or synagogue provides a support group unparalleled by others in the community. The report of the National Interfaith Coalition on Aging (NICA) further emphasizes that older people's affirmations of life are deeply rooted in their participation in a community of faith.[16] Fellowship in the community promotes acceptance of the past, enjoyment of the present, and hope for future fulfillment.

Spiritual Well-Being

Spiritual well-being permeates and binds the component parts of the person into a fulfilled being. It encompasses both the aspects of religious activity and spiritual meanings to describe a state of spiritual contentment.[17] Growing out of the 1971 White House Conference on Aging, NICA, in 1972, defined spiritual well-being as "the affirmation of life in a relationship with God, self, community, and environment that nurtures and celebrates wholeness."

Kahn[18] explores the relationship with God as a caring one that supports growth not only in the young but throughout the life span. He points out that the root meaning of *nurture* in the ancient Hebrew is "nursing father" and refers to the spiritual connotations of fathering in Psalm 91: "He who dwells in the shelter of the Most High will rest in the shadow of the Almighty." This nurturing of growth contributes to ongoing develop-ment as a person with value and meaning regardless of chronological age. Kahn advocates a rite of passage to help older adults recognize that they are still achieving, that maturity is affirmed, and that ultimate peace is ensured.[19]

Nursing Diagnosis

The interrelated human dimensions—physical, psychological, social, and spiritual—are inseparable, integral components of the whole person.[20] Spiritual concerns are not well developed in nursing practice and content. In 1973, the National Conference on Classification of Nursing Diagnosis of the North American Nursing Diagnosis Association (NANDA) identified the classification "Faith, alteration in."[21] As the taxonomy evolved, the current designation, "spiritual distress," was accepted and developed with definitions, descriptors, and defining characteristics.[22]

An alternative view of nursing diagnoses that emphasizes the health viewpoint has been developed by Houldin and colleagues.[4] Their materials parallel the NANDA format but present a wellness approach. Their designation for the area of spirituality is "spiritual support," which is characterized by spiritual strength. Contributing factors and defining characteristics are presented from a spiritual health perspective. Several contributing factors include firm spiritual identity, maintenance of a belief system despite adversity, empathy for others' values and beliefs, sense of spiritual fulfillment, ability to cope with barriers to the practice of religious rituals, an adaptable belief system, and the meaning of life, suffering, and death.

Integration

The need to view a person from a holistic perspective rather than focusing on a particular disease is increasingly crucial as the older person loses various aspects of his or her health, possessions, abilities, and roles. The losses in body function and mental capacity are often not counterbalanced by social and spiritual gains. The body, mind, and spirit of the person can be taken over by chronic disease. Demographics show that most older people have at least one chronic condition and that many have more than one. Exact rates of concomitant depression, anxiety, alcoholism, and suicide have not been documented, but they are common among older adults with multiple physical disabilities. Grief, pain, and loss of control affect the older adult's personal integrity. This impact may be neutralized or diminished by a strong spiritual life. Just as Frankl[23] found inner strength that enabled him to find purpose and survive imprisonment in a Nazi concentration camp, many older adults gain strength from their faith as they find meaning in suffering.

Maslow[24] called the highest two levels of hierarchical achievement self-esteem and self-actualization, which encompass enrichment, adaptive flexibility, creativity, and acceptable life patterns. Gould[25] described transformation in later life that arise from changes in the inner life. The development conceptualization implies that successful achievement of earlier stages and tasks contributes to the success of the final stages. It is assumed that each person has evolved through the stages in his or her own manner, thus achieving an integrity unique to that person.

In regard to religious practices and spiritual interests, a person who is active in the church or synagogue as a younger person is more likely to be religiously involved in later life. Despite a departure from it in young or middle adulthood, the value is embedded and is more likely to resurface in later years. Those who never experienced or who actively rejected religious experiences are less likely to find religion a solace and support in later life. Brennan and Missine[26] found that religion was one of the three most important things to the older adults they surveyed. Their study seems to support the view that religiosity or the lack of it evolves over the life span.

Loss versus Hope

The concept of loss infiltrates the aging process, with its cumulative decrements in mental, physical, and social realms. *Loss* is the one word that best sums up the problems of old age, which include loss of work, loss of time, loss of self-esteem, loss of personal dignity, loss of physical health, loss of social contacts, loss of roles, loss of income, loss of material possessions, loss of mental acuity, loss of energy, and the inevitable loss of life itself.

Loss is registered by present deprivation in relation to past status, although the intensity of the loss depends on the person's value system. When the frequency and intensity of the losses accelerate, the person is less able to adapt and reintegrate, thus jeopardizing his or her mental and physical health. Garret[27] identifies influences on the griever's ability to cope as advanced age, past negative experiences with loss, lack of preventive methods of coping, limited use of a support system, inability to maintain control, decreased mental and physical health status, and lack of belief in a power greater than oneself. One's attitude toward all these losses, more than the number or kind of losses, affects the quality of one's old age.

The cumulative effects of lifetime losses, particularly after age 75, are experienced as valuelessness and abandonment.[28] Vulnerability escalates when the older adult lacks interpersonal skills, motivation, spiritual strength, meaningful social contacts, adequate finances, or a positive perception of health. Burnside[29] encourages the use of "loss-facing" strategies and support to promote well-being. The negative concept of loss is illustrated in the upper portion of Figure 29–1.

Balancing the concept of loss is another concept: hope. To some extent, hope negates the potentially catastrophic effects of cumulative loss for the older adult. Hope, as an expectation of fulfillment, counteracts the inevitable losses that accumulate from childhood onward. Hope is an anticipation of an improved status or relief from perceived entrapment.[30] It is based on belief in the possible, support from meaningful others, a sense

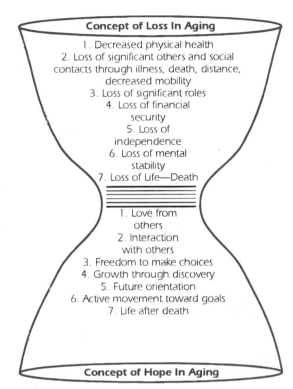

Figure 29–1 Schematic of loss and hope in aging.

of well-being, overall coping ability, and purpose in life. It is a motivating, energizing force that can move the older adult out of the morass of losses to a higher level of function. Hickey[31] uses the term *enabling hope* to describe the nurse's role in caring for patients with cancer. Faith in God provides a reason for older adults to live and hope, as long as they are willing to make the effort to achieve it.

Hope is an essential characteristic of Erikson's last stage of integrity. Hope, as an integral thread woven into the warp and woof of a lifetime, serves as a functional stabilizer in old age. In the older adult, the concept of loss is most destructive when it produces a loss of meaning in life. Loss of meaning and purpose, and therefore of hope, is the ultimate loss in life—a living death. Long ago, Gibbon[32] wrote, "The failure of hope darkens old age." Loss without hope puts out the very light of life. The positive aspects of hope are depicted in the lower portion of Figure 29–1.

Nursing Roles in Spirituality

Nursing roles in promoting the spirituality of older adults must be highly individualized, yet several categories are common to older adults in general.

- *Assessor:* Perhaps the most important function of the nurse, or of anyone working with older adults is that of assessment. Spiritual assessment includes both collecting information about spiritual history and current status and analyzing the significance of these findings. Assessment data collected from the older client and family and environmental influences provide extensive information regarding spiritual health. Data obtained become the basis for subsequent nursing intervention. The requisites for making skillful assessments include attentive listening, skillful questioning, thoughtful observing, and critical thinking.

- *Friend:* As older adults' social contacts diminish, their mental stimulation and self-esteem are undermined. They need someone who understands the normal aging processes and the disease processes of later life. The most important need of older adults is for someone to care about them as individuals. The caring nurse makes time available for older adults, allows them to be themselves, and recognizes their value as individuals. Perhaps the greatest gift one can give an older person is time. That time may be spent in sharing life interests, praying over problems, reading devotional material, laughing over a cartoon, or sitting together quietly listening to music or watching a sunset. The quantity of time is less important than the quality. The inherent skills required are demonstrating the caring presence of God, listening attentively, opening up conversational leads into spiritual topics, and being available regularly.

- *Advocate:* The nurse's advocacy role for the older person includes obtaining spiritual resources based on the client's unique background. It may be necessary to support the client's desire for participation in religious services by obtaining suitable transportation or arranging for the local clergy to visit. It may involve promoting friendships with other older adults at the church or synagogue. In some cases, the nurse may mediate between the client and estranged friends or family members. At times, the nurse may help the client and family deal with such ethical issues as euthanasia, continuation of life support systems, or prolongation of nutritional support. It may involve intervening on the client's behalf with his or her physician regarding prolongation of medical care. The nurse's advocacy role may include writing letters, making telephone calls, or lobbying for a cause affecting the client's welfare. Some special nursing skills include the ability to remain calm when others are upset, a belief that God is at work in difficult situations, a desire to promote reconciliation, a concern for justice for older adults, and the ability to express ideas clearly.

- *Caregiver:* The nurse as caregiver is an astute assessor who not only performs thorough basic assessments of spiritual status, but also continues to assess the client throughout the relationship. The nurse translates assessments of spiritual deficits into spiritual care interventions or fosters spiritual wellness by strengthening spiritual support. The nurse recognizes that spiritual status has a powerful effect on health maintenance as well as on disease prevention or resolution. Older adults may need specific assistance to attend religious services, listen to radio or television services, have

undisturbed quiet time to meditate or receive the sacraments, or vent anger about their suffering. Nursing skills include being sensitive to unspoken needs, promoting a hopeful attitude, listening for clues of spiritual distress, and giving physical and spiritual care simultaneously. It is often difficult for the caregiver because an older adult's physical needs can be so extensive that little time or energy is left for spiritual care.

- *Case manager:* The nurse who is serving as a case manager in the area of spirituality must be knowledgeable about the older adult and the community. A case manager working with older adults is most likely to be coordinating care for frail clients who need assistance because of advanced age, low income, multiple disease problems, or a limited support system. Often, the nurse may need to negotiate among family members, various caregivers, or agencies providing assistance. Particular nursing skills include managing limited resources for maximal benefit, organizing care for the client to minimize fatigue and anxiety, encouraging acceptance of assistance without undue dependency, and promoting fellowship with one's religious community of origin.

- *Researcher:* The nurse researching spiritual aspects of older adults must guard the human rights of older adults who are sought as research subjects. The relevant ethical considerations involved in the proposal must be carefully evaluated and explained. It is apparent from a review of the research literature and available test instruments that religiosity is an easier concept to study than is spirituality. Investigations have principally involved organizational religious behavior, personal religious behaviors, and the correlation of religious activities with health, personal adjustment, and other practices. Spirituality research has been hampered by several factors. Spirituality is ephemeral and difficult to define. Conceptual frameworks are encumbered by the multidisciplinary components, and valid instruments must be developed or refined to assist in quantification. Furthermore, research efforts in spirituality have not been widely supported by government or private funding sources.

Nursing Interventions

Nursing interventions are as diverse as the people giving and receiving them. Nursing interventions must be individualized to the unique spiritual needs determined by baseline and ongoing assessments. Many systems have been developed by a number of disciplines, exemplified by Fitchett's[33] seven-by-seven model, which includes seven dimensions of assessment and seven aspects of the spiritual dimension. Although this particular format was developed by an interdisciplinary team headed by a chaplain in a hospital setting, it has relevance in many circumstances. A structured interview developed in a nursing context by Carpenito[22] is easy to incorporate into many institutional and community situations. The questions are as follows:

1 Is religion or God important to you? If yes, to what religion do you belong, or in what do you believe? If no, do you find a source of strength or meaning in another area?

2 What effect do you expect your illness (hospitalization) to have on your spiritual practices or beliefs?

3 Are there any religious books (statues, medals, services, or places) that are especially important to you?

4 Do you have a special religious leader (priest, pastor, rabbi)?

5 How can I help you maintain your spiritual strength during this illness (hospitalization).

In addition to the answers to these questions, the interviewer has the added opportunity to evaluate the client's affect during the interview. Overall assessment is enhanced by observation and contact over an extended period.

One of the most demanding (but highly effective) interactions is spending time with the older person. Time is a valuable commodity that even in small increments reinforces the self-esteem of older adults. It represents the pervasive, loving presence of God. Even time spent in silence conveys the impression of worth and value. For example, Anna Lou, a poststroke resident, was unresponsive to anyone or anything for weeks. After the nurse sat and held her hand for 10-minute intervals every day for 3 weeks, she wept when the nurse was transferred. Supportive silence accompanied by touch conveys a depth of acceptance and compassion. Time could be spent with a background of religious music, observing a sunset over the lake, walking along the river, or simply hugging or holding hands. When the older person is ready to talk about matters of personal importance, he or she will initiate conversation.

Appropriate touch enhances a relationship because many older people have decreased opportunities to touch and be touched, along with a decreased sensory sensitivity. Touch powerfully communicates worth and value to the older person. Holding hands in prayer or giving a gentle backrub is another expression of compassion and mutual agreement. Touch can be especially reassuring and comforting in the many instances of loss and discouragement characteristic of aging.

Prayer is communication with God that can occur anytime, any way, anywhere: aloud or silent, alone or with others, at noon or midnight. The comfort of knowing the presence of an almighty power in the face of great losses and readjustments in life sustains older adults. There is assurance in repetition of childhood prayers, in agonized groans of the inner spirit, in the gut-wrenching "Help me," that an Unseen Person cares and reaches to help.

The nurse can give a silent prayer for the nursing process and for patients but can offer to pray aloud with or for older adults as well. It is more beneficial for older clients to actively participate in a prayerful confession, request, or thanksgiving, but it is also helpful for the client to know that he or she is uplifted in prayer by others. A prayer book or devotional guide may serve as the stimulus to initiate this activity.[34]

Conversation about spiritual concerns, spiritual benefits of sickness and hardship, and preparation for death are some of the many topics most older people welcome an opportunity to reflect upon. Often, reminiscing about life events and spiritual journeys enables older adults to reaffirm themselves as people with a purpose. This reminiscence may be initiated and enhanced by looking through a photograph album, reviewing a personal journal of life events, or examining mementoes collected over a lifetime. Asking the older person's opinion and evaluation of his or her experience provides affirmation for both the speaker and the listener. The amount of time spent is less significant than regularity. Consistency of contact in a nonjudgmental atmosphere provides comfort and security to the older adult. Considerable gain in morale, sociability, and memory has been achieved through individual or group reminiscence therapy. Reflecting on the landmarks in one's spiritual life has a therapeutic effect.[35]

An uplifting aspect of one's spirituality is music. By humming a hymn while working with an older person, soothing a sleepless older adult at night, or joining in a group hymn sing, nurses can optimize the positive effects of music. Often, demented persons participate in singing when they are unable to converse. Depressed adults may respond to upbeat music. The burdens of life are eased by the joy of music.[36]

Many older adults enjoy the fellowship of one-on-one group scripture study. A single verse or scriptural thought may be focused on in even a brief contact, giving the older person a positive thought to ponder. One older woman found solace in a plaque on her wall at eye level that said, "I will never leave thee nor forsake thee." Sometimes reading or repeating familiar scriptures together is useful.

Opportunity to attend organized services may be limited by disability or lack of transportation, but weekly services that are wheelchair-accessible or include hearing aids may be available. Some churches provide bus transportation with a lift to provide door-to-door assistance. Most areas have radio or television programs that air religious services or programs. The nurse can obtain lists of available services and assist in tuning radios or televisions to the correct frequencies. Audiotapes and videotapes are often available, if time schedules conflict with direct listenings. Personal visitation by clergy is another avenue of support and encouragement. When the older person is limited in capacity, it may be desirable to provide the rituals of the church at the client's bedside.

Another spiritual care approach that is helpful for some older adults is journaling, which could be done in relation to travel, study of the scriptures, a reading program, or simple recording and response to daily events. Meditation, prayer, guided imagery, and study may accompany reflective writing. When re-examined over an extended period, the reminders of progress, positive coping, and divine intervention are a source of encouragement. It may also be helpful to engage the older person in a written life review to explore and affirm his or her past and present. This may involve family members, resulting in solidified relationships and an ongoing sense of their legacy.[37]

Another aspect of spiritual care involves the family and friends who are caregivers. They often have spiritual distress as a result of their caregiving role. As spiritual care and support is given to the caregiver, the benefits seep through to the client through a strengthened, encouraged caregiver. The burden of caregivers tends to increase with the long-term, cumulative illnesses of older adults, depleting physical, emotional, and spiritual reserves, thus reducing their ability to provide a positive milieu for the client. Respite (time away, religious services or retreats, attendance at a support group, or conversing about problems of caring for an older person) may sustain the caregiver through the difficulties.[38]

Interview Pearls

In conducting structured interviews about spirituality, religiosity, and life satisfaction in older adults over the past 6 years, the author has been enriched by many adults nearing the end of their spiritual journey. Some older adults have left indelible words of wisdom, spoken from the depths of their spirits:

It's been a long way, but I've never been alone. I gave myself to the Lord when I was ill. . . . He's brought me this far, without any hitches . . . reckon I'll go the rest of the way home with him.
84-year-old former mechanic

My idea of Heaven is that we won't be old anymore, or have all these aches and pains, or have to take all these old pills. . . . No more diets, and no more doctors—just lolling around soaking up God's love, and strumming on my harp.
87-year-old retired teacher

So I got off the track a couple of times . . . the important thing is I'm back on it now to stay. God doesn't hold grudges. Even when I was in that foxhole in Normandy, I just knew He was looking after me. He said He would, and I believed Him then, and I believe Him now.
79-year-old retired accountant

Getting old is the pits—everything's broken down, except my mind and my soul, and I'm not sure about my mind! My soul? Oh, it's in good hands . . . better than ever . . . the future is the best part of my life.
82-year-old homemaker

I see the Lord in the Mass—these problems just shrink away—I couldn't miss my appointment with the good Lord unless my body gave out, 'cause it sets me straight on things.
92-year-old former sales clerk

Heck, I've been everywhere. . . . I done about everything I ever wanted. . . . It's hard to think about the end of it all, but I sure don't want to go back! I don't just know what's ahead, but God's at the wheel, and He knows what He's doing.
80-year-old former truck driver

These pearls of spiritual insight are more impressive than all the studies, publications, and speeches because they are real, poured out of distorted bodies with wrinkled faces and callused hands. These pearls are the products of the hardships and triumphs of older adults' spiritual journeys.

Literature Pearls

There is much to learn from those who have previously walked the aging path. Their observations from the trail ahead provide pointers for those who follow.

Life is a journey. . . . [God] is leading me along the new paths of old age. It is He who has made the unity of my life.
Paul Tournier, MD[39]

One ought to enter old age the way one enters the senior year at the university, in exciting anticipation of the summing up and consummation.
Abraham Hershell, rabbi[40]

Don't think about the end. . . . God has lovingly planned that, and you will be as unaware of your passing out as you were of your coming in.
F. B. Meyer, DD[41]

I do not want to miss my old age any more than I would choose to have skipped childhood or adolescence. . . . For growing old is an ongoing project of self actualization throughout the life-span.
Robert Kastenbaum, PhD[42]

If we have longed for solitude and learned to have it because we find God there, it should be that the last years of a long life will be the happiest of all, so close to Him that His love and life can shine through us to countless souls.
Mary Evening, author[43]

God is not exclusively youth oriented. . . . Age is immaterial to a God who knows no time as we measure it. His personal interest in our welfare does not wane in the passing years.
J. Oswald Sanders, author[44]

We are to be like God, to have in us the mind that was in Christ Jesus. We are called to be someone as well as to do something. . . . We are called to become old.
Paul Maves, consultant and author[45]

Summary

Spirituality in the older adult is a universal, intrinsic, and individual process, progressing through the life span. Because of the drain of cyclic losses punctuating the older adult's life, equilibrium is maintained partially by the positive effects of hope offsetting those losses. Older adults who have learned to cope with the vicissitudes of life through mechanisms of faith are eventually confronted with the final challenge of death. Hope enables those with spiritual or religious faith to tran-

TABLE 29–1   SOURCES OF INFORMATION REGARDING MAJOR WORLD RELIGIONS

General

Bach, M: Major Religions of the World. DeVorss, Marina Del Rey, Calif, 1984.

Carson, VB: Spiritual Dimensions of Nursing Practice. WB Saunders, Philadelphia, 1989.

Mead, FS: Handbook of Denominations. Abingdon, Nashville, 1990.

Melton, JG: Encyclopedia of American Religions. Gale, Detroit, 1993.

Watson, W: Concise Dictionary of Cults and Religions. Moody, Chicago, 1991.

Williamson, WB: Encyclopedia of Religions in the United States: Religious Groups in America Speak for Themselves. Crossroad, New York, 1991.

Specific

Christianity

 Barros, C: Catholicism, lifestyles, and the well being of the elderly. J Religion Aging 4(3/4):109, 1988.

 Kromkowski, JA: Elderly urban Catholic ethnics: Their churches and neighborhoods. J Religion Aging 3(3/4):61, 1987.

 Missine, LE: Christian perspective on spiritual needs of a human being. J Religious Gerontol 7:90, 1991.

Confucianism

 Odada, T: The teaching of Confucianism on health and old age. J Religion Aging 4(3/4):101, 1988

Buddhism

 Chit, DKM: Add life to years the Buddhist way. J Religion Aging 4(3/4):39, 1988.

 Lesco, PA: Aging through Buddhist eyes. J Religion Aging 5(3):59, 1989.

Shintoism

 Mitsuhashi, T: A study of the health of the elderly from the standpoint of Shinto. J Religion Aging 4(3/4):127, 1988.

Taoism

 Fukui, F: On perennial youth and longevity: A Taoist view on health of the elderly. J Religion Aging 4(3/4):119, 1988.

Judaism

 Berkowitz, P, and Berkowitz, N: The Jewish patient in the hospital. AJN 67:2335, 1967.

 Davies, AM: Judaism: Lifestyles leading to physical, mental, and social well being in old age. J Religion Aging 4(3/4):97, 1988.

 Katz, RL: Jewish values and sociopsychological perspectives on aging. In Hiltner, S: Toward a Theology of Aging. Human Sciences, New York, 1979.

 Meier, L: Filial responsibility to the suicide patient. In Thorson, JA, and Cook, TC: Spiritual Well Being of the Elderly. Charles C. Thomas, Springfield, Ill, 1980, p 161.

Islam

 Said, HM: Islam and the health of the elderly. J Religion Aging 4(3/4):27, 1988.

scend the crises of loss of life to death. Nursing roles in meeting the spiritual needs of the older adult are assessor, friend, advocate, caregiver, case manager, and researcher. Numerous nursing approaches are used to provide spiritual care. Nursing roles must support those in spiritual distress and promote spiritual health and strength in those with spiritual well-being. Table 29–1 provides a list of resources on various faiths that may be helpful in nursing specific patients with spiritual needs.

Perhaps the best conclusion has already been written by Nouwen and Gaffney,[46] who wrote a thought-provoking volume on aging as life fulfillment from a spiritual perspective:

> We believe that aging is not a reason for despair, but a basis for hope, not a slow decaying, but a gradual maturing, not a fate to be undergone, but a chance to be embraced. We therefore hope that those who are old, as well as those who care, will find each other in the common experience of aging, out of which healing and new life can come forth.

Student Learning Activities

1 Compare the spiritual needs of ambulatory well older adults with those of hospitalized older adults.

2 Form debate teams to address whether nurses should provide the spiritual support for clients manifesting spiritual needs.

3 How would you manage a clinical situation in which you enter to find your older client moaning and crying, "I don't see why God keeps me here when I am so useless!"?

REFERENCES

1 Johnson, BC: Spirituality in the later years. J Religion Aging 6(3/4):125, 1989.
2 Stoll, R: The essence of spirituality. In Carson, VB (ed): Spiritual Dimensions of Nursing Practice. WB Saunders, Philadelphia, 1989, p 7.
3 Murray, RB, et al: The Nursing Process in Later Maturity. Prentice Hall, Englewood Cliffs, NJ, 1990, p 361.
4 Houldin, AD, et al: Nursing Diagnosis for Wellness. JB Lippincott, Philadelphia, 1987, p 141.
5 Banks, R: Health and the spiritual dimension: Relationships and implications for professional preparation programs. J School Health 50:196, 1980.
6 Moberg, DO: Religiosity in old age. Gerontologist 5:80, 1965.
7 Fish, S, and Shelley, JA: Spiritual Care: The Nurse's Role. Inter Varsity, Downers Grove, Ill, 1978, p 37.
8 Agostino, JN: Religiosity and religious participation in the later years: Reflection of spiritual needs of the elderly. J Religion Aging 4(2):85, 1988.
9 Bardon, AJ: Toward new directions in aging: Overview of issues and concepts. J Religion Aging 2(2):143, 1986.
10 Young, C, and Dowling, W: Dimensions of religiosity and old age. J Gerontol 42:379, 1980.
11 Thibault, J, et al: A conceptual framework for assessing the spiritual function and fulfillment of older adults in long term care settings. J Religious Gerontol 7:38, 1991.
12 Tobin, SS, et al: Enabling the Elderly. State University of New York Press, Albany, 1986, p 15.
13 Palmore, E: The social factors in aging. In Busse, E, and Blazer, D (eds): Handbook of Geriatric Psychiatry. Van Nostrand Reinhold, New York, 1980, p 192.
14 Murray, RB, and Zentner, JP: Nursing Concepts for Health Promotion. Prentice-Hall, Englewood Cliffs, NJ, 1985, p 475.
15 Steinitz, LY: The local church as support for the elderly. J Gerontol Social Work 4:46, 1981.
16 Thorson, JA, and Cook, TC (eds): Spiritual Well Being of the Elderly. Charles C. Thomas, Springfield, Ill, 1980, p xvi.
17 Moberg, DO: The development of social indicators of spiritual well being for quality of life research. In Moberg, DO (ed): Spiritual Well Being: Sociological Perspectives. University Press of America, Washington, DC, 1979.
18 Kahn, RI: Spiritual well being: A relationship that nurtures. In Thorson, JA, and Cook, TC (eds): Spiritual Well Being of the Elderly. Charles C. Thomas, Springfield, Ill, 1980, p 41.

19 New International Version of the Holy Bible: Psalm 91:4. Zondervan, Grand Rapids, Mich, 1988, p 900.

20 Gress, LD, and Bahr, RT: The Aging Person: A Holistic Perspective. CV Mosby, St Louis, 1984, p 4.

21 Gebbie, KM, and Lavin, MA: Classification of Nursing Diagnosis. CV Mosby, St Louis, 1975.

22 Carpenito, LJ: Handbook of Nursing Diagnosis. JB Lippincott, Philadelphia, 1985, p 87.

23 Frankl, V: Man's Search for Meaning. Beacon, Boston, 1963.

24 Maslow, AH: Toward a Psychology of Being. Van Nostrand Reinhold, New York, 1962.

25 Gould, R: Transformations. Simon & Schuster, New York, 1978.

26 Brennan, CL, and Missine, LE: Personal and institutional integrity of the elderly. In Thorson, JA, and Cook, TC (eds): Spiritual Well Being of the Elderly. Charles C. Thomas, Springfield, Ill, 1980, p 94.

27 Garrett, JE: Multiple losses with older adults. J Gerontol Nurs 13(8):10, 1987.

28 Pruyser, PW: Aging: Downward, upward, or forward? In Hiltner, S (ed): Toward a Theology of Aging. Human Sciences Press, New York, 1979, p 111.

29 Burnside, I: Working with the Elderly. Wadsworth, Monterey, Calif, 1986.

30 Miller, JF: Inspiring hope. AJN 85:23, 1985.

31 Hickey, SS: Enabling hope. Cancer Nurs 9(3):133, 1986.

32 Gibbon, E: The Autobiography of Edward Gibbon. Dent, London, 1939, p 93.

33 Fitchett, G: Assessing Spiritual Needs: A Guide for Caregivers. Augsburg, Minneapolis, Minn, 1993.

34 Shelley, J, and Fish, S: Praying with patients. J Christian Nurs 12(1):18, 1994.

35 Lashley, M: Reminiscence: A biblical basis for telling our stories. J Christian Nurs 9(3):4, 1992.

36 Lescheid, HG: Singing in the face of death. J Christian Nurs 11(1):18, 1994.

37 Bianchi, EC: Life review through meditative journaling. J Religious Gerontol 8(4):73, 1992.

38 Fischer, KR: Spirituality and the aging family. J Religious Gerontol 8(4):1, 1992.

39 Tournier, P: Learn to Grow Old. Harper & Row, New York, 1972, p 214.

40 Davies, AM: Judaism: Lifestyles leading to physical, mental, and social well being in old age. J Religion Aging 4(3/4):97, 1987.

41 Meyer, FB: Tried by Fire. Zondervan, Grand Rapids, Mich, 1967, p 60.

42 Kastenbaum, R: Growing Old. Nelson, Melbourne, 1979, p 121.

43 Evening, M: Who Walk Alone. Hodder & Stoughton, London, 1974, p 182.

44 Sanders, JO: Your Best Years: Staying Young While Growing Old. Moody, Chicago, 1982, p 123.

45 Maves, PB: Faith for the Older Years. Augsburg, Minneapolis, 1986, p 185.

46 Nouwen, HJ, and Gaffney, WJ: Aging: The Fulfillment of Life. Image, Garden City, NY, 1974, p 20.

CHAPTER 30

Sexuality and Aging

Beverly K. Johnson

OBJECTIVES

Upon completion of this chapter, the reader will be able to:

- Define sexuality and sexual health for older adults
- Describe the knowledge and attitudes of society, older adults, nurses and nursing students, and the reader toward sexuality and aging
- Describe a tool for sexual assessment: the sexual interview; describe areas of sexual assessment (normal changes of aging, medications, menopause, and erectile dysfunction)
- Discuss the effect of significant health issues for older adults (heart attack, stroke, chronic obstructive pulmonary disease, diabetes, arthritis, cancer, and institutionalization) on sexuality in older adults
- Identify nursing diagnoses related to alterations in sexual health and sexuality patterns
- Describe selected nursing roles related to sexuality and aging
- Apply levels of prevention (primary, secondary, and tertiary) to selected health conditions related to sexuality and aging

We must learn not to ignore the disquieting sexual aspects of a patient's humanity: nor should we overtly or covertly stigmatize him or her. We are health care providers, not theologians, law enforcement officers, or moralists. We cannot be committed to total patient care without considering the patient as a sexual being.

Marianne Zalar, RN[1]

Sexuality has often been described from a holistic perspective as "the integration of the somatic, emotional, intellectual, and social aspects of sexual being in ways that are positively enriching and that enhance personality, communication, and love."[2] Johnson's study of sexuality and aging supports this biopsychosocial view of aging and sexuality.[3] Late life changes can directly or indirectly affect the patterns of sexuality and sexual health of older adults.

The loss of sexuality is not an inevitable aspect of aging, and most healthy people remain sexually active on a regular basis until advanced old age. However, the aging process does bring with it certain changes in the physiology of the male and female sexual response, and these along with a number of medical problems that become more prevalent in the mature years play a significant role in the pathogenesis of the sexual disorders of older adults. The typical patient over 50 has only a partial degree of biological impairment, which has been escalated into a total sexual disability by a variety of cultural, intrapsychic, and relationship stressors. Fortunately, these problems are often amenable to an integrated, psychodynamically oriented sex therapy approach that emphasizes the improvement of the couple's intimacy and the expansion of their sexual flexibility.[4]

Myths, Taboos, and Stereotypes

Myths, taboos, and stereotypes about sexuality and aging exist in our society. Kuhn[5] and Murray[6] list the following:

- Sexual activity does not matter in old age.
- Interest in sexuality is abnormal for old people.
- Remarriage after the loss of a spouse should be discouraged.
- It is acceptable for old men to seek younger women as sex partners, but the reverse is unacceptable.
- Semen emission begins to weaken in old age, which causes coital inability.

- Menopause and hysterectomy mean the end of a woman's sex life.
- It is sick for older people to masturbate.
- Older people are too fragile to make love.

These sexual myths imply that older people are not sexually attractive, interested, or capable.

Older adults' self-perceptions of their sexuality are related to beliefs held by society and their family and friends. Among nursing home residents, White[7] found that sexual knowledge showed little relationship to sexual attitudes but that both knowledge and attitudes were closely associated with the frequency of sexual activity. Recent studies show that older men and women are knowledgeable about sexuality and aging and have liberal attitudes in this area.[3,8]

In a survey of health-care professionals, Woods[9] found the following phrases used to describe sexual activity in older people: *difficult to imagine, nonexistent, discouraged by society, normal, impossible, slower, healthy,* and *infrequent.* A study of home staff found that staff identified certain sex talk and behaviors of the residents as sexual and problematic but that hugging and kissing on the cheek were okay.[10]

Sexual Assessment: The Sexual Interview

Because sexual health involves a complex interaction of social, psychological, physiological, and biochemical factors, the nurse's sexual assessment should include both areas of normal changes associated with aging and possible effects of changes in the older adult's life caused by changes in physical and psychoemotional health (role changes, loss of partner, lowered self-esteem). Initially, the nurse should examine her own knowledge and attitudes about sexuality and aging and be aware of the current societal attitudes in this area. Myths about aging and sexuality can affect both health-care providers' approaches to sexual concerns of older adults and older adults' self-esteem, sexual interest, and activity. Table 30–1 provides resources for learning more about aging and sexuality.

Areas to include in the sexual interview and history are described in Table 30–2.[11] This general framework provides a guide for the nurse to initiate a sexual interview, an activity crucial to identification of the client's sexual concerns, questions, and needs. Before the sexual interview, the nurse should be thoroughly knowledgeable about the client's overall health status, including past and present health problems (disease, surgery, medications). Elder[12] suggests the following points to remember in taking a sexual history:

- Feel comfortable discussing sexuality and be aware of your own values and beliefs about the topic.
- Be respectful of attitudes and behaviors that differ from yours.
- Help the client explore his or her own answers and describe what is normal for himself or herself.
- Ensure privacy and confidentiality.
- Allow enough time to explore feelings, values, expectations, concerns, and fears.
- Be open, honest, reassuring, and empathetic.
- See the client and partner as a unit.
- Clarify words and help the client describe the issue or question accurately in his or her own words.
- Observe nonverbal communication such as lack of eye contact or not sitting next to one's partner.
- Be aware of signs of anxiety such as jokes, silence, or vague complaints.

Key nursing roles during the assessment can include validating the normalcy of questions and concerns and giving permission to discuss sexual concerns.[13] Older adults themselves suggest that health-care providers should be frank, well-informed, and accepting and should listen when helping older adults with their sexual concerns.[14]

Initially, the sexual history progresses from least sensitive to more sensitive topics. For example, an initial question can be "How is your relationship with your spouse (partner)?" or "Are you having any concerns about your intimate or personal relationship with your partner?"; a more directive question may be "Are any specific areas of your sexual relationship causing you

TABLE 30–1 RESOURCES

American Association of Sex Educators, Counselors, and Therapists
435 North Michigan Boulevard
Suite 717
Chicago, IL 60611
312-644-0828

Senior Action in a Gay Environment (SAGE)
208 West 13th Street
New York, NY 10011
212-741-2247

Sex Information and Education Council of the United States (SIECUS)
130 West 42nd Street
Suite 250
New York, NY 10036
212-819-9770

TABLE 30–2 AREAS OF SEXUAL CONCERN TO BE ASSESSED

Availability of a partner if appropriate to the person's situation
General mental health, including depression
Evaluation of gynecological and urological status, perhaps including hormonal levels
Presence of chronic illness or symptoms such as chronic pain or decreased mobility for possible effect on self-image as sexually undesirable
Use or abuse of prescribed medications and alcohol for effect on the sexual response cycle
Unhealthful ideas, attitudes, and behaviors that interfere with healthful sexual expression
Factors of living arrangements (congregate or institutional) that may encourage older adults to think of themselves as nonsexual beings

Source: Kaplan, HS,[11] with permission.

concern?" Questions may be prefaced by a statement to validate the normalcy of sexual concerns: "Often older men find they do not have erections as often or that their erections are not as firm as when they were younger. Are you having any concerns about this?" and "Often older women find that they have vaginal dryness and find sexual intercourse uncomfortable. Do you have any concerns in this area?"

Physiological Changes of Aging

Masters and Johnson's classic research on the normal physiological changes of aging and their effect on the sexual response cycle has been summarized by Woods.[15] The concept of "slowing down" can apply to these changes in the sexual response cycle of older men and women. Normal sexual effects of aging may be exaggerated by events such as acute or chronic illness or the death of a life partner.

Numerous health variables (disease, surgery, medications) have been included in studies of human sexuality; the impact on the sexual response cycle and sexual relationship varies among individuals. In her study of 161 men and women age 55 and older, Johnson found that older adults who were healthy had positive self-images and intimate relationships and were sexually active, sexually satisfied, and liberal in their attitudes toward sexuality and aging.[3]

Different categories of drugs are associated with varied interruptions in the sexual response cycle. Because older adults often take a number of different drugs and drug metabolism is affected by the aging process, nurses should be aware of possible drug effects on the sexual response cycle and that a change in dosage or drug type may reverse the sexual symptom. The nursing assessment should include an evaluation of the older adult's sexual functioning before the onset of the illness and use of the drug and evaluation of other factors possibly related to the sexual symptom such as other psychological problems or relationship concerns.[16]

MENOPAUSE

Sarrel[17] described five basic menopause-related changes in sexual function in the literature: decreased sexual responsiveness, pain with intercourse, decreased sexual activity, decreased sexual desire, and the presence of a partner with sexual problems. He reported that sexual arousal, including sensory perception, central and peripheral nerve discharge, peripheral blood flow, and the capacity to develop muscle tension, sexual interest, and activity can all be influenced by ovarian hormone levels. The age-related physiological changes affecting sexual function in the older woman can be explained in the context of changes in sensory stimulation and blood flow secondary to declining estrogen levels. Estrogen-sensitive cells have been identified throughout the central and peripheral nervous systems; the sequence of activities involved in sexual response within the nervous system involves a chain of estrogen-sensitive cells. A decrease in levels of estradiol appears to affect cells throughout the system and thus affects nerve transmission. Because the cardiovascular system is replete with cells sensitive to ovarian hormones, cardiac output, rate of blood flow, and vasomotor stability are affected by these hormones. A decrease in estradiol influences the response of peripheral blood flow to sensory stimulation and, as a result, affects the timing and degree of vasocongestive response during sexual activity.[17] Biopsychosocial and cultural factors are related to the sexual response of the older woman.[17,18] Assessment factors of the woman's sexual health should include the following[8]:

- Evaluation of subjective symptoms related to the physiological changes of aging related to decreased ovarian function (vaginal dryness, vaginal itching and burning, pain with intercourse, decreased lubrication, leg cramps, palpitations)
- Hormonal assessment for possible hormonal therapy
- Physical assessment for vaginal atrophy, vaginismus, and infection
- Evaluation for presence of other conditions such as diabetes, congestive heart failure, angina, arthritis, changes in mentation, cancer, gynecological surgery, and ostomies
- Evaluation of psychosocial factors such as anxiety or depression, availability of a sexual partner, attitudes toward sexuality (personal and societal), religious or spiritual level, and living situation allowance for privacy

The use of hormone replace therapy and its associated risks and benefits should be discussed by the older woman and her health-care provider. The nurse can be an important source of information for the older woman in this area.[19]

ERECTILE DYSFUNCTION

Erectile dysfunction is "the inability to attain and/or maintain penile erection sufficient for satisfactory sexual performance; the likelihood of erectile dysfunction increases progressively with age but is not an inevitable consequence of aging. Other age-related conditions increase the likelihood of its occurrence." Any condition that impairs arterial blood flow to the penis may be the cause of erectile dysfunction.[20] Men's lack of information about causes, both physical and psychological, may worsen this sexual symptom and keep them from seeking help.

Psychological factors affecting erectile dysfunction include anxiety, guilt, and anger.[21] Life events (retirement, illness, injury, or loss of a significant other) may cause the older man to feel less attractive, lose his self-esteem, and feel inadequate and sexually inhibited. He may not communicate his concern to his partner. Fear of repeated failure of erection may lead to less sexual activity or a repeated cycle of inability to achieve or maintain an erection.

Organic impotence occurs most commonly in older men and often the onset is slow and erectile dysfunction is ongoing.[22] The initial symptom of difficulty maintaining an erection may then progress to difficulty in achieving an erection. The older man may have erectile problems both with masturbation and with a partner. He may find that morning erections are either absent or are not firm for long.[22]

Organic causes include neurogenic, systemic, vascular, endocrine, and pharmological.[21] Neurogenic factors may interrupt or reduce the conduction of nerve impulses to the penis. Surgical procedures (radical prostatectomy, abdominal-perineal resection, retroperitoneal lymphadenectomy, sympathectomy, renal transplant, aortoiliac bypass, abdominal aortic aneurysm resection, cystectomy, proctocolectomy, and peritoneal irradiation) and spinal cord injury or peripheral neuropathies may interrupt or reduce the conduction of nerve impulses to the penis. Diabetes, the leading cause of impotence, reflects a combination of factors related to erectile dysfunction (hormonal, vascular, and neurologic).[23]

Systemic diseases such as alcoholic cirrhosis, with abnormal testosterone and estrogen metabolism, and chronic renal failure and systemic sclerosis, affecting both the vascular and neurogenic systems, cause erectile dysfunction. Erectile dysfunction can result from varying degrees of occlusion of the blood vessels. In the older man, atherosclerotic plaques in the large blood vessel supplying the penis and pelvis can reduce blood flow to those areas. Vascular changes in blood vessels can impair erection.

The National Institutes of Health (NIH) Consensus Conference on Impotence suggested the following assessment for men with erectile dysfunction: medical and detailed sexual history, physical and psychosocial evaluation, and basic laboratory studies.[20] The nurse must give the older man permission to discuss his sexual concerns, provide information about possible causes of the sexual symptom, and then refer him for a thorough medical assessment.

SIGNIFICANT HEALTH ISSUES FOR OLDER ADULTS

Illness can affect sexual behavior because the body uses its energy to meet the demands of the body's symptoms and little energy may remain for sexual activity, especially if the illness is lengthy or becomes chronic. The physical impact of the illness may be enhanced by psychological, emotional, and relationship concerns.

Stroke

The sexual activities that decrease for people who have had a stroke include mutual verbal and nonverbal responsiveness, caressing and touching without sexual intent, and intimate foreplay and caressing in established relationships.[24] Psychosocial issues may involve decreased self-esteem, performance anxiety, and increased dependency on the partner for assistance with activities of daily living. Sexual information and counseling before hospital discharge to both poststroke clients and their partners have been lacking. When provided, such information or counseling was positively received by both clients and partners.[24]

Chronic Obstructive Pulmonary Disease

Mooradian and Grieff[18] have suggested that chronic obstructive pulmonary disease (COPD), which has been found to reduce serum testosterone levels in men, may have a similar effect on serum estrogen levels in women. The high stress and use of high-dose glucocorticosteroids associated with this disease may affect these serum levels for women. Physical changes such as dyspnea, coughing, sense of suffocation during increased activity, reduced nutritional intake, and sleep disorders may alter the sexual health of older adults with COPD.[25] Symptoms in men with COPD may include a decrease in libido and erectile dysfunction. Men who have achieved an erection may find themselves too dyspneic before ejaculation and thus unable to complete intercourse.[26] The person with COPD may try to avoid the physical effects associated with intimate activity and forgo emotional intimacy. Dependency on others, drug effects, and possibly respiratory equipment may decrease the person's self-esteem and increase depression, thus reducing sexual interest and activity.

Diabetes

Sexual symptoms related to diabetes include problematic erections during intercourse, normal or increased libido, lack of morning erection, and partial or total lack of erections during masturbation.[27] Women have reported one or more of the following symptoms: decreased libido, slow arousal, inadequate lubrication, lack of orgasm, and pain with sexual intercourse. Recurring vaginal infections and poor vaginal lubrication in the older woman can lead to painful intercourse.[28]

Cancer

Cancer can affect one or more body systems, the individual's body image and self-esteem, and relationships. "Cancer and its therapies can affect all systems necessary for normal sexual function, impairing hormonal, vascular, or neurological function or damage genital structure."[29] Cancer-related surgeries (prostatectomy, mastectomy, hysterectomy, or ostomy) may change the older adult's body image and may cause anxiety or embarrassment in an intimate relationship.

For women, the hormonal impact on sexuality most commonly results from removal of the ovaries in radical pelvic surgery, damage to ovarian function caused by pelvic radiotherapy or high dosages of chemotherapy, or use of antiestrogen drugs to treat metastatic breast or uterine cancer. Chemotherapy may also cause temporary vaginal irritation and discharge.[29]

For men, testicular cancer may be treated by removal of only one testicle; if the other is healthy, testosterone remains sufficient. Treatment of metastatic cancer of the prostate involving removal of the testicles or use of estrogens or progesterones can lead to decreased sexual interest, impotence, and orgasmic difficulty.

In a recent review of the literature on cancer and aging, Shell and Smith concluded that exercise, nutrition, and self-esteem intervention programs together with strategies to promote sexual activity that account for normal changes of aging can help the older adult improve sexual functioning.[30] This information is important for the nurse to know during a sexual assessment of an older adult with cancer.

Institutionalization

Expressions of sexual interest or behavior may be an important issue for older adults who reside in a long-term care facility, as well as for staff and family members.[31] Staff members and administration should examine and discuss their own values about sexuality and aging in a safe and open atmosphere. Table 30–3 suggests questions for staff and administration to discuss and consider in adopting sexual health-care plans for their facility. Nurses can promote sexual health in residents by providing options for privacy, educating staff about sexuality and aging, allowing spousal visits or allowing residents to have home visits, assessing decision-making capacity of residents with cognitive changes, evaluating residents' concerns about sexual functioning, encouraging assessment of medications that can affect sexual function, and providing information about sexuality to interested residents.[32]

Prevention as a Framework for Intervention

Nurses need to initiate discussion and respond to sexual concerns more often with their patients. Within all levels of prevention the nurse can validate the normalcy of sexual concerns, give permission to discuss sexual issues, provide limited information directly related to their sexual concerns to dispel myths and stereotypes, and provide specific suggestions as needed.

1 Primary Prevention

Primary prevention involves health promotion through health education, with emphasis on development of a healthful lifestyle to promote an optimal level of functioning (nutrition, exercise, sleep, recreation, relaxation, and no use of alcohol, tobacco, and other drugs), development of a healthy personality, marriage counseling, and development of a healthful social environment.[33] An example of primary intervention is a community education program for healthy older adults about sexuality.

The nurse's role during the group session includes facilitating an atmosphere open to discussion of sexual health: normal physical changes in sexual response related to aging; possible effects of disease, surgery, and medications on sexual response; possible effects of changes in roles, body image, and communication with sexual partner on sexual response, societal and personal attitudes about sexual interest and activity in older adults, and any questions about sexuality and aging. At the group session, nurses validate the normalcy of the

TABLE 30–3 STAFF-ADMINISTRATION DISCUSSION QUESTIONS TO ENHANCE THE SEXUALITY OF INSTITUTIONALIZED OLDER ADULTS

- If there is a problem related to sex, with whom is the problem? Patient? Staff? Family? What can I do about it?
- Are physical problems related to sexuality, such as senile vaginitis, catheters, and the like, well taken care of in your institution?
- Are you helping the staff examine the stereotypes of "the dirty old man" and "the shameless old woman"?
- Are you aware of the isolation and sensory deprivation of the immobile patient?

Can you:

- Provide more touch, hugging, kissing, handholding, and intimacy such as back rubs and body massages?
- Build sexuality into (rather than separate it from) the spiritual and emotional well-being of your patients?
- Accept and allow masturbation and help your staff deal with it?
- Provide more touching and feeling things to handle, fondle, and hold, such as yarn balls, prayer beads, and stuffed animals?
- Bring live pets into your setting and allow patients to feel and cuddle them?
- Provide more music: romantic, sentimental, sensuous?
- Encourage opportunities for sexes to meet, mingle, and spend time together, such as in small television rooms, without structuring a "trusting time or place" too rigidly?
- Provide double beds for married couples?
- Counsel families, particularly adult children of patients, about sexual needs of older people?
- Manipulate the environment to make your facility a therapeutic milieu?

Finally:

- Do staff and patients laugh (and maybe cry) together?
- Do you have a Bill of Rights for sexual freedom in your facility?

Source: Adapted from Steiffl, B: Sexuality and aging: Implications for nurses and other helping professionals. In Solnick, RL (ed): Sexuality and Aging. Ethel Percy Andrews Gerontology Center, University of Southern California Press, Los Angeles, 1978, p 132, with permission.

elders' questions or concerns and provide anticipatory guidance, limited information, and specific suggestions (Table 30–4).

Sexuality is affected by the health of body and mind. Physical fitness helps provide an overall sense of well-being; a daily program of walking and stretching in addition to exercises specific to toning and strengthening the muscles of the stomach, thighs, breasts, back, and pelvis can promote sexual health. Maintaining well-balanced nutrition, as well as eating smaller meals and avoiding overindulgence of food and drink before sexual activity, can assist older adults. Getting adequate rest can enhance sexual interest and activity. Stress management activities suited to the individual or couple can increase well-being. Warm baths or a massage from one's partner can encourage sexual desire in older adults. Self-care of one's body and physical appearance (e.g., good hygiene, proper hair care, and attractive clothing) can help older men and women feel sexually attractive. Engaging in sexual activity in the morning after a night's rest or in sexual activities other than intercourse for sex-

TABLE 30–4   HEALTHY ADAPTATIONS: MAINTAINING SEXUAL FUNCTIONS

Age-Related Changes	Adaptations and Management
Vaginal dryness and dyspareunia	Use of lubricant before coitus Estrogen replacement Intercourse on a regular basis Dilaters
Diminished sexual desire (male and female)	Testosterone replacement Fantasy and erotica Treatment of depression Treatment of substance abuse
Lengthened male refractory period Softer penile erections	Less frequent intercourse; emphasize quality rather than quantity Use coital methods that facilitate intromission (e.g., stuffing) No condoms More reliance on manual and oral stimulation More emphasis on clitoral orgasm
High penile threshold for mental and physical stimulation	More partner-provided physical stimulation More rapid lovemaking Erotica and fantasy Morning sexual intercourse

Source: Kaplan, HS,[4] p 192, with permission.

ual pleasure can enhance sexual health. These basic components of a healthful lifestyle can be emphasized by the nurse engaging in primary prevention to promote sexual health in older adults.

GENERAL GUIDELINES FOR TEACHING DURING SECONDARY AND TERTIARY PREVENTION

The following general guidelines for teaching about sexuality can be discussed with the older adult who is recovering from an acute illness episode (heart attack) or undergoing the phase of rehabilitation (arthritis).

- Seek as much information as possible about the usual effects of your health problem on sexuality. Ask any member of the health team in whom you have confidence or trust. The information can help you plan how to deal with the sexual issues relevant to you and your partner.
- Remember that the ability to feel pleasure from touching does not change because of your health concern. Pleasure and satisfaction are possible for both men and women in a variety of ways.
- As much as possible, have an open mind about different ways to feel sexual pleasure. Explore mutual caressing and stimulation, masturbation, or just cuddling. Many sexual activities besides sexual intercourse can lead to pleasure and satisfaction for both you and your partner.
- Try to have good communication with your partner. Share your concerns, fears, anxieties, and questions with your partner; your partner needs to hear what you are thinking and feeling about your sexual relationship.

A final important area of information for teaching is as follows:

- Generally, a person who has a change in health status (heart attack, arthritis) that affects sexual

interest, activity, or satisfaction can benefit from understanding family, friends, a loving and sensitive partner who is open to changes and adaptations as needed, skilled and caring health-care professionals, and even a support group for discussing common concerns.

Secondary Prevention

Heart Attack

Cardiovascular disease is the main cause of death and disability in older Americans. After a heart attack, the older adult may be fearful of resuming sexual ac-

RESEARCH BRIEF

Johnson, BK: Older adults and sexuality: A multidimensional perspective. J Gerontol Nurs 22(2):6, 1996.

To investigate sexuality and aging in older adults residing in the community, 92 women and 69 men, age 55 and older, completed a survey on self-esteem, intimacy, health, sexual knowledge, attitudes, interest, participation, and satisfaction. Health was significantly positively correlated with intimacy, self-esteem, sexual attitudes, sexual participation, and sexual satisfaction. Age was significantly negatively correlated with intimacy and sexual attitudes, sexual interest, and sexual participation. Study results can increase our understanding of the aspects of sexuality in older adults and assist clinicians in their assessment of sexual concerns and design of appropriate interventions.

tivity, although recent research suggests the risk of myocardial infarction after sexual activity is low and regular exercise is important in the reduction of this risk.[34] Men have reported reduced frequency of orgasms and sexual intercourse after a heart attack for reasons such as less sexual desire, fears, anxiety, partner's decision not to have sex, and depression.[35]

The nurse's role initially is to reassure the man that it is common for men who have had a heart attack to be anxious about resuming sexual activity and give him permission to express sexual concerns and ask questions. The nurse's introductory statement could be as follows: "Many older men who have had a heart attack have questions about their sexuality, especially about when and how to resume sexual activity. Do you have questions in this area?" Providing education (limited information, specific suggestions) and referring the older man to other health-care professionals for further in-depth assessment or counseling can also be part of the nurse's role. The nurse should intervene as soon as possible to try to alleviate some of his (and his partner's) questions and concerns about resuming sexual activity after a heart attack. Table 30–5 provides a teaching guide to be used by the nurse in the educator role.

3 Tertiary Prevention

Arthritis

Arthritis affects 37 million Americans, two-thirds of whom are women. Arthritis, causing pain, stiffness, limited movement, and occasionally deformity, can affect the older woman's sexual interest, sexual activity, and self-image, and thus her sexual relationship.

The older woman with arthritis may find that physical sexual activity can precipitate or aggravate joint pain; she may lose her interest in sexual activity. "People who have chronic diseases and those with whom they are intimate often have inaccurate or incomplete information about the impact of their illness on sexual expression and they may know little about what treatment options are available. Accurate information is key in dispelling the myths and misconceptions."[35]

To allow and encourage her to express sexual concerns and questions, the nurse can give the older woman permission to talk about the subject by stating, "Many older women with arthritis who experience pain, joint stiffness, limited movement, or fatigue have found it somewhat difficult to engage in some types of sexual activity. Has this been an area of concern for you and your partner?" More specific questions can follow: "How is the pain affecting your sexual activity at present? Have you found anything that helps decrease the pain? How do you and your partner feel about any changes in sexual activity to alleviate your discomfort? Do you have specific questions about arthritis and sexuality?"

The nurse should also assess the older woman's overall health history (other health problems, use of medications, experience with menopause, and normal sexual changes with aging). The primary nursing role for intervention is educator: to dispel myths and misinformation about aging and sexual changes and to provide limited information and specific suggestions regarding sexuality and arthritis. (See Table 30–6 for a teaching guide on arthritis.)

TABLE: 30–5 TEACHING GUIDE: BETTER SEX FOR OLDER ADULTS WITH HEART DISEASE

- Having a heart attack can affect how you feel about yourself as a man and thus can affect your sexual relationship.
- Many men, after having a heart attack, are fearful and anxious about when and how to resume sexual activity.
- The following guidelines may be helpful to you and your partner. It is important to remember to ask your health-care provider regarding when to resume sexual activity. Also, remember to report any symptoms you experience during or after sexual activity possibly related to your heart.
- Select a familiar, quiet setting; a strange environment often adds to heart stress.
- Choose a time for sex when you are rested, relaxed, and free of stress. The best time may be early in the morning after a good night's sleep or during the day after taking a nap.
- Postpone intercourse for 1 to 3 hours after eating a full meal so that adequate digestion can take place.
- Use whatever sexual position is most comfortable and familiar. It is not generally necessary to change sexual positions after a heart attack to decrease possible strain on the heart.
- Take medications, such as nitroglycerin, as prescribed before intercourse to prevent chest pain.
- Foreplay is helpful: it gradually prepares the heart for the increased activity of intercourse.
- Be aware that your heart rate during intercourse is roughly similar to your heart rate during other normal daily activities. Most patients with angina can have a normal sex life.
- If you experience prolonged angina, severe difficulties, or a very rapid heart rate, be sure to report these symptoms to your physician for appropriate treatment and relief.

Source: Data from Cohen, JA: Sexual counseling of the patient following myocardial infarction. Crit Care Nurse 6(6):156, 1986; Wohl, AJ: Sudden anginal pain. Medical Aspects of Human Sexuality 24(2):57, 1990; and Woods.[9]

Student Learning Activities

1 Give the list of myths about sexuality and aging in this chapter to your peers, a group of older adults, and a group of nurses who work with older adults. Compare the findings of the three groups. Do the myths continue? What can you do to dispel these myths?

2 View the film *Grumpy Old Men*. What issues of sexuality among older adults are portrayed in this film?

3 Interview a local nursing home administrator regarding the facility's policies on married couples sharing rooms.

TABLE 30–6 TEACHING GUIDE: ARTHRITIS

- Pain, joint stiffness, limited movement, and fatigue are symptoms of arthritis. These symptoms of discomfort may affect your sexual interest, participation, and satisfaction.
- Arthritis may affect how you feel about your body and your sexual attractiveness, and your sexual relationship may also be affected.
- Specific suggestions to help with your sexual relationship include the following:
  - Try to be sexual when you feel most rested and after taking pain medications.
  - Pace your usual activities before a sexual episode.
  - Taking a warm bath or shower may relax you and relieve joint pain and stiffness.
  - A side-by-side position with your partner may be more comfortable if you have hip pain, pain in the upper part of your body, or lack of strength.
  - Range-of-motion exercises before sexual activity may be helpful as long as you do not engage in the exercises to the point of fatigue.
  - Use a water-soluble lubricant such as KY Jelly if you have decreased lubrication.
  - Obtain a copy of the pamphlet titled "Arthritis, Living, and Loving: Information about Sex" from the Arthritis Foundation in Atlanta.
- There are four important ideas to keep in mind as you think about your sexual life:
  - Seek as much information as possible about the usual effects on sexuality of having arthritis. Ask any member of the health team in whom you have confidence and trust. The information can help you plan how to deal with the sexual issues relevant to you and your partner.
  - Remember that the ability to feel pleasure from touching usually remains the same even though you have arthritis. Pleasure and satisfaction are possible for both men and women.
  - As much as possible, have an open mind about different ways to feel sexual pleasure. Explore mutual caressing and stimulation, masturbation, or just cuddling. Many sexual activities besides sexual intercourse can lead to pleasure and satisfaction for both you and your partner.
  - Try to have good communication with your partner. Share your concerns, fears, anxieties, and questions with your partner; your partner needs to hear what you are thinking and feeling about your sexual relationship.
- Generally, a person with arthritis can benefit from understanding family and friends, a loving and sensitive partner who is open to changes and adaptations as needed, skilled and caring health-care professionals, and even a support group for discussing common concerns.

Source: Data from Woods[9] and Katzin.[35]

REFERENCES

1 Downey, GW: Sexuality in a health care setting. Modern Healthcare 6(5):20, 1976.
2 Shope, DT: Interpersonal Sexuality. WB Saunders, Philadelphia, 1975.
3 Johnson, BK: Sexuality and aging: A multidimensional perspective. J Gerontol Nurs 22(2):6, 1996.
4 Kaplan, HS: Sex, intimacy, and the aging process. J Am Acad Psychoanal 18(2):187, 1990.
5 Kuhn, ME: Sexual myths surrounding aging. In Oaks, WW, et al (eds): Sex and the Life Cycle. Grune & Stratton, New York, 1976, p 177.
6 Murray, R: The Nursing Process in Later Maturity. Prentice-Hall, Englewood Cliffs, NJ, 1980.
7 White, CB: Sexual interest, attitudes, knowledge and sexual history in relation to sexual behavior in the institutional aged. Arch Sex Behav 11(1):11, 1982.
8 Steinke, EE: Knowledge and attitudes of older adults about sexuality in aging: A comparison of two studies. J Adv Nurs 19:477, 1994.
9 Woods, NF: Sexuality and aging. In Reinhardt, AM, and Quinn, MD (eds): Current Practice in Gerontological Nursing. CV Mosby, St Louis, 1979, pp 151, 156–159.
10 Szasz, G: Sexual incidents in an extended care unit. J Am Geriatr Soc 31(7):407, 1983.
11 Kaplan, HS: The Evaluation of Sexual Disorder. Bruner & Mazel, New York, 1983.
12 Elder, MS: The unmet challenge: Nurse counseling on sexuality. Nurs Outlook 18(11):38, 1970.
13 Smedley, G: Addressing sexuality in the elderly. Rehab Nurs 16(1):9, 1991.
14 Johnson, BK: Frankness about sexuality endorsed by elderly clients. Aging Digest (Texas Dept Aging) 1(5):2, 1990.
15 Woods, NF: Human Sexuality in Health and Illness, ed 3. CV Mosby, St Louis, 1984.
16 Buffum, J: Prescription drugs and sexual function. Psychol Med 110:181.
17 Sarrel, PM: Sexuality and menopause. Obstet Gynecol 75(4):265, 1990.
18 Mooradian, AD, and Grieff, V: Sexuality and the older woman. Arch Intern Med 150:1033, 1990.
19 Hofland, SL, and Powers, J. Sexual dysfunction in the menopausal woman: Hormonal causes and management issues. Geriatr Nurs 17:161, 1996.
20 NIH Consensus Development Panel on Impotence: Impotence. JAMA 270:83, 1993.
21 Marshall, S: Evaluation and management of simple erectile dysfunctions in office practice. Medical Aspects of Human Sexuality 23(4):4, 1989.
22 Mulligan, T: Impotence in the older man. Medical Aspects of Human Sexuality 23(4):32, 1989.
23 Bernstein, G: Counseling the male diabetic patient with erectile dysfunction. Medical Aspects of Human Sexuality 23(4):20, 1989.
24 Sjogren, K: Sexuality after stroke with hemiplegia (II) with special regard to partnership adjustment to fulfillment. Scand J Rehabil Med 15(2):63, 1983.
25 Campbell, ML: Sexual dysfunction in the COPD patient. Dimensions of Critical Care Nursing 6(2):70, 1987.
26 Fletcher, EC: Sexual dysfunction in men with chronic obstructive pulmonary disease. Medical Aspects of Human Sexuality 18(5):151, 1984.
27 Cooper, AJ: Diagnosis and management of endocrine impotence. BMJ 2:34, 1972.
28 Campbell, LV, et al: Factors in sexual dysfunction in diabetic female volunteer subjects. Med J Aust 151:550, 1989.
29 Schover, LR, and Jensen, JB: Sexuality and Chronic Illness: A Comprehensive Approach. Guilford Press, New York, 1988.
30 Shell, JA, and Smith CK. Sexuality and the older person with cancer. Oncol Nurs Forum 21:553, 1994.
31 McCartney, JR, et al: Sexuality and the institutionalized elderly. J Am Geriatr Soc 35:331, 1987.
32 Richardson, JP, and Lazur, A: Sexuality in the nursing home patient. Am Fam Physician 151:121, 1995.
33 Archer, SE, and Fleshman, RP: Community Health Nursing: Practice and Patterns, ed 2. Duxbury Press, North Scituate, Mass, 1979.
34 Muller, JE, et al: Triggering myocardial infarction by sexual activity. JAMA 275:1405, 1996.
35 Katzin, L: Chronic illness and sexuality. AJN 90(1):55, 1990.

CHAPTER 31

Alcohol Problems in Older Adults

Beverley E. Holland

OBJECTIVES

Upon completion of this chapter, the reader will be able to:

- Differentiate between alcohol abuse and alcohol dependence
- Compare early and late onset of alcohol problems in older people
- Recognize the effects of alcohol use and consequences of alcohol dependence
- Describe interactions between alcohol and aging processes
- Delineate issues in the identification of alcohol problems in older adults
- Discuss attitudes of health-care providers toward older adults with alcohol problems
- Describe nursing interventions in alcohol withdrawal and postwithdrawal periods
- List nursing diagnoses common to older adults with alcohol problems
- Identify an overall goal in tertiary prevention in the management of alcohol problems in older people

Most older people do not experience difficulties associated with alcohol use, but for some, the use of alcohol adversely affects many aspects of later life. Concern about the incidence and prevalence of alcohol use and abuse by older adults has increased dramatically over the last 20 years.[1] Still, problems related to alcohol use are often given a low priority when addressing the needs of older people. A challenge to health-care providers is to identify and treat older adults experiencing alcohol-related problems.[2]

Health professionals are in a good position to identify alcohol-related problems in older adults. In all areas of service, they encounter people who may have alcohol problems that require assessment, diagnosis, and treatment. Helping an older person deal with an alcohol-related problem requires that the health-care provider possess a critical knowledge base and a heightened sensitivity to the reactions associated with alcohol problems in later life.

Problematic drinking by older people can be arrested and treated successfully. After the diagnosis is established and accepted, the overall goal of treatment is to make life worth living again and to make the later years rewarding.

Nature of the Problem

When does the use of alcohol become a problem in later life? Alcohol use patterns in older adults vary, and problematic use can be different for each individual. The older person who began excessive alcohol use in early adulthood and shows alcohol dependence and problematic drinking throughout life is easily recognized. In contrast, the older adult may escalate alcohol use in late life in response to life events such as unresolved grief, poor health, or loneliness. These older adults may be hidden from public view and not easily detected, especially if they live alone. Furthermore, identification of alcohol-related problems in older adults is complicated by symptoms of chronic alcohol abuse that often mimic clinical features of aging and some chronic health conditions. Alcohol use may mask symptoms of an illness and result in treatment delay of an emerging health condition.

A problem with alcohol may be described as "whenever drinking interferes with a person's daily life and relationships" and "whenever alcohol is more important to the older person than the problems it's causing."[3] Common adverse consequences of alcohol abuse by older adults include resulting or aggravated physical health problems, disturbed relationships, impaired memory, shortened life expectancy, and reduced quality of life.

DEFINITION AND DESCRIPTION

It is important to be familiar with the definition of alcohol abuse and dependence and the effects alcohol can have. Many definitions and descriptions are used by health-care providers.[4,5] Two of the most acceptable are the definition issued by the National Council on Alcoholism and Drug Dependence (NCADD) and the American Society of Addiction Medicine (ASAM)[6] and the criteria contained in the *Diagnostic and Statistical Manual of Mental Disorders,* Fourth Edition (DSM-IV).[7] According to the NCADD-ASAM,[6] alcoholism is defined as follows:

> [Alcoholism is] a primary, chronic disease with genetic, psychosocial and environmental factors influencing its development and manifestations. The disease is often progressive and fatal. It is characterized by impaired control over drinking, preoccupation with the drug alcohol, use of alcohol despite adverse consequences and distortions in thinking, most notably denial.

DSM-IV, which has no alcoholism category, does have other alcohol-related criteria in its section on substance use disorders. Some of the criteria make reference to older adults, but critics believe there should be more age-specific descriptions and explanations. Gomberg[8] has called for the following:

> Relevant criteria for a definition of elderly problem drinking or alcoholism. Such criteria should include falls or accidents, nutritional inadequacy, family problems, including social isolation, and—most of all—medical problems associated with heavy alcohol intake.

Ingestion/Intoxication

Evidence of alcohol ingestion is seen in the classic neurological and behavioral effects as a result of dose-dependent depression of the central nervous system (CNS) function. Basic CNS effects are seen as a symptom sequence of euphoria, decreased inhibitions, impaired vision, muscular incoordination, lengthened reaction time, and impairment of judgment and reasoning.[9]

Intoxication (0.1 percent blood alcohol concentration [BAC] is the legal level for intoxication in many states) is evident in the drinker when he or she slurs words and is unable to walk, turn, or stand with precision. These effects can be measured in most people when the BAC is between 0.1 and 0.2 percent. These effects become more pronounced as the BAC is elevated to 0.2 percent (e.g., inability to remain in an upright position without support). When the BAC approaches 0.3 or 0.4 percent, there is impending or actual coma in the average person. At this level, the depressant effect on the respiratory center is critical; a diagnosis of death

due to the primary action of alcohol can be made at a BAC of 0.5 percent in an otherwise healthy naive drinker.[9,10]

Tolerance

Chronic exposure to alcohol results in apparent tolerance. Tolerance is said to develop when a person's response to the same amount of alcohol is decreased with repeated use and a greater amount is needed to produce the same effect.[9]

Dependence and Withdrawal

The term *dependence* signifies both psychological dependence and physical dependence. Psychological dependence refers to repetitive and excessive self-administration of alcohol for its reinforcing properties. Alcohol becomes central to the person's thought, emotions, and activities, so it is virtually impossible to stop using it. Physical dependence is a physiological state of adaptation to a drug, normally following the development of tolerance, which results in a characteristic set of withdrawal symptoms (often called abstinence syndrome) when administration of the drug is stopped.

Withdrawal signs and symptoms for any drug are generally opposite to the effects induced by the drug itself. Withdrawal from alcohol can be viewed as a state of hyperexcitability representing a rebound phenomenon in the previously chronically depressed nervous system. Early common features of alcohol withdrawal include anxiety, anorexia, insomnia, tremor, irritability, internal shaking, and tachycardia. The symptoms begin within a few hours of cessation of alcohol intake and tend to peak after 24 to 36 hours and then rapidly disappear. Significant tachycardia reflects continuing toxicity, and the pulse may reach 120 to 140 beats per minute. Elevation of pulse rate may warn of impending delirium tremens and the need for additional sedation.[11]

Delirium tremens is the most severe withdrawal state. *Delirium* refers to hallucinations, confusion, and disorientation. *Tremens* refers to the heightened autonomic nervous activity, producing tremulousness, agitation, tachycardia, and fever. The state of delirium tremens may occur as early as 1 or 2 days after the last drink and as late as 14 days; it is usually seen in the daily drinker who consumes a large quantity over a long time. Significant mortality can attend this state and is usually associated with secondary complications related to illness, infection, or injury. Convulsive grand mal seizures may occur, usually during the first 48 hours of abstinence but possibly days later. Anticonvulsant therapy should be used during withdrawal of any person with a history of seizures, and hospitalization is required for detoxification.[11]

Differentiation of Abuse and Dependence

Alcohol abuse and alcohol dependence are two distinct forms of problematic drinking. A person abusing alcohol may have problems that arise from impaired

RESEARCH BRIEF

Mudd, SA, et al: Alcohol withdrawal and related nursing care in older adults. J Gerontol Nurs 20(10):17–26, 1994.

The purpose of this study was to describe how alcohol withdrawal differs in older adults compared with their younger counterparts. The groups differed in that the older adults were found to have more liver and cardiac disease and longer duration of problematic drinking than the younger clients, but no significant differences were found in current quantity and recentness of drinking or in the number of previous hospitalizations. The study found that older clients had significantly more occurrences and types of alcohol withdrawal symptoms, for a longer duration, and they required a greater number of nursing assessments and interventions than younger clients. The nurse should be aware that the older adults in treatment for alcohol problems have more symptoms of alcohol withdrawal and withdrawal occurs for a longer duration and can more individualized care.

judgment, diminished concern for the consequences of behavior, and physical effects of alcohol consumption. They may find that alcohol causes interpersonal, occupational, or legal problems. A person who is alcohol-dependent has the problems seen with alcohol abuse and also manifestations of tolerance and the craving for alcohol, which becomes the center of his or her life. The person who is alcohol-dependent also shows evidence of withdrawal when he or she ceases drinking.[7,12]

ETIOLOGICAL FACTORS

How do people become alcoholic? There is no simple answer to this question. Research suggests that alcoholism develops from an interplay of genetic and environmental factors.

Genetic, Psychosocial, and Cultural Factors

Evidence for genetic transmission of vulnerability for alcoholism has been provided by studies of twins and adopted children. Studies[12] have shown that sons of alcoholics were more likely to be alcoholic themselves, whether raised by their alcoholic parent or by a nonalcoholic foster parent. Cloninger[13] has described two types of alcoholism related to inheritance factors. Type 1 is characterized by onset after age 25 and loss of control or binge drinking; it occurs in male relatives of alcoholic women. Type 2 is characterized by onset before age 25 and an inability to abstain from alcohol; it occurs in male relatives of alcoholic men.

There is supporting evidence that ethanol metabolism is genetically determined. Early studies[14] showed that 85 percent of Asian subjects had a variant of alcohol

dehydrogenase, which could be responsible for the flush reaction when alcohol is ingested.

Patterns of alcohol use may vary according to acceptability of use in different ethnic or societal groups. For example, certain religions prohibit the use of alcohol, whereas others offer alcohol as part of religious ceremonies. Other cultural groups view drinking alcohol as a part of masculine behavior. Psychosocial factors such as peer influences, expectancies about alcohol's effects, subjective experiences of alcohol's pharmacological effects, and social context of alcohol use have been found to influence drinking behavior.[12]

Impact on Older Adults

PREVALENCE

The actual prevalence of alcohol problems among older adults is unknown. Most markers of alcohol abuse are not appropriate for older adults who live alone, are widowed, are unemployed, and do not drive a car. One survey[15] showed that at least 10 percent of older adults have alcohol-related problems, and higher rates of alcohol abuse have been found in nursing homes and acute medical wards.[16] Many of the homeless are older persons with substance abuse problems.[4]

Age differences may be attributed to the prevailing historical and cultural influences for each generation. Longitudinal studies that track people over several years show that consumption patterns do not change substantially over time but tend to remain stable as the person ages.[17,18]

Although overall prevalence of drinking problems in later years has decreased, alcohol use with onset in late life has escalated. A review by Atkinson[19] suggested that late-onset heavy drinking may begin in response to stressful life experiences such as bereavement, poor health, economic changes, or retirement and appears to be more common among people of higher socioeconomic status. Furthermore, many alcohol problems of older people may not be properly identified because of lack of adequate screening methods and diagnostic criteria appropriate for older adults.

Alcohol problems will probably increase among older adults. Studies[20] show a lower percentage of abstainers, an increase in the level of drinking among the younger age groups, and a tendency for people to carry drinking patterns of younger years into old age as long as circumstances and health permit. It appears that future generations of older people will present a larger proportion of drinkers and more people who continue to drink at higher levels into old age.[12,21]

USE OF ALCOHOL BY OLDER ADULTS

Not all older adults use alcohol, but among those that do, various patterns of use can be seen. In predicting problems in use of alcohol, volume and frequency of alcohol consumption are less significant in older people than in younger ones. Studies[18,21] have shown that although the frequency of drinking does not decrease with age, the average number of drinks per occasion does. This is related partly to age-related changes in alcohol metabolism and body water.[2,22]

Manifestations of alcohol-related problems in older adults are associated with both length of time and pattern of alcohol use. Some older adults develop alcohol problems only in later life, whereas others have experienced these problems since youth or early adulthood.[19]

Early Onset

Older adults who have had alcohol problems since their early years, referred to as the early-onset group, are estimated to represent two-thirds of older adults manifesting alcohol dependence. Characteristics of the early-onset group include tolerance, physical dependence, psychosocial and behavioral disturbances (e.g., social isolation, intellectual deterioration), and alcohol-related physical health problems. The physical problems often include pathophysiological symptoms of prolonged alcohol abuse such as gastrointestinal disturbances, cardiovascular problems, coagulation disorders, increased susceptibility to infection, and cirrhosis of the liver.[2,23] They typically manifest a long-established drinking behavior pattern that has affected significant portions of their lives and relationships. If these people continue to drink, severe life-threatening withdrawal is a critical health consideration.

Late Onset

The late-onset group includes the other third of older adults with alcohol problems, those who begin excessive alcohol consumption after age 40. Those with late onset do not manifest the severity of cognitive, affective, behavioral, and somatic problems common to those with early onset. Their alcohol problems are more often related to coping problems associated with life events such as depression, bereavement, loneliness, retirement, marital stress, and other health problems. Signs and symptoms of physical dependence on alcohol may be absent in this group. Rather, nonspecific factors such as falls, accidents, and injuries associated with excessive alcohol intake may lead to a diagnosis of alcohol problems in the late-onset group.[2,23]

Intermittent or Variant

Several other patterns of life history use of alcohol have been observed. For example, Gomberg[24] described an intermittent pattern of alcohol consumption that involved periods of heavy drinking on weekends with abstention or moderate drinking on other days. Maintenance drinking or periodic binges interspersed with periods of abstinence have adverse consequences for health because of their effect on lifestyle behaviors. These people may fail to keep medical or other appointments, neglect tasks such as grocery shopping and doing laundry, and experience financial hardships incurred by the cost of alcohol. It is important for nurses to recognize these patterns and assess for life history alcohol use patterns.

ETIOLOGICAL CONSIDERATIONS

Each older person who has alcohol problems has a set of circumstances leading to the occurrence, continuation, or cessation of alcohol use. Etiological factors unique to the older adult are important in the development of alcohol problems.

Psychosocial Factors

Use of alcohol to decrease tension and to fulfill unmet needs may be a predisposing factor to the development of alcohol problems. Increasing alcohol use and excessive use of alcohol in later life is often triggered by trying to cope with major life changes and their accompanying stressors. Examples of these are retirement (e.g., lack of interests to replace activity structure, reduced social controls and purpose of work roles), loss of relationships (e.g., loneliness, death of a significant other), poor health (e.g., negative self-image, illness, impaired mobility, pain, fatigue), relocation from a familiar neighborhood and home, and other psychological states (e.g., depression, alienation).

Myths, Stereotypes, and Stigma

Myths, stereotypes, and stigma can be barriers to identifying and intervening with an older person who has alcohol problems. Our culture conveys mixed messages about the desirability of alcohol use. This is particularly true for older adults. The belief that an older person should not be deprived of one of his or her "few remaining joys" is, unfortunately, still widely held.[21] On the other hand, older adults with a drinking problem are negatively viewed and offend the social sensibilities of those with whom they come in contact.[25] Many health professionals are exposed only to early-onset, late-stage older alcoholics and may see few who are recovering, thus reinforcing a stereotype of the older "skid row" alcoholic.[21] The stigma of drinking by older adults is greater for women than for men. This results in women hiding their alcohol use and experiencing shame, guilt, and social isolation.

PHARMACODYNAMICS OF ALCOHOL

The active ingredient in beer, wine, and distilled spirits is ethyl alcohol, or ethanol.[26] One drink equals about 1.2 oz of distilled spirits, 4 oz of wine, or 12 oz of beer. In people who are not alcohol-dependent, alcohol is metabolized at the rate of about one drink (15 to 20 mL of ethanol) per hour.[26] Pharmacologically, alcohol belongs to the class of sedative-hypnotics similar in their action of CNS depression. The initial effect of sedative-hypnotics is to depress inhibitory synapses of the brain, which results in excitation. This is why alcohol is sometimes categorized as a stimulant rather than a depressant. The disinhibition may initially manifest itself in high spirits or euphoria, but the depressive effects of alcohol soon catch up.[26]

Absorption and Distribution

Alcohol is absorbed from both the stomach and duodenum, with approximately 20 percent of the absorption taking place in the stomach and 80 percent in the intestinal tract. It rapidly enters the bloodstream from the stomach and intestine unless food delays exist. Once alcohol enters the bloodstream it is distributed to and affects every cell in the body. The resulting complete body distribution is the reason that alcohol abuse can harm so many different organs, although its action on the nervous system is by far the most critical.[26]

Metabolism

Three different enzyme systems are capable of oxidizing ethanol: liver alcohol dehydrogenase (LAD), catalase, and the microsomal ethanol-oxidizing system (MEOS). LAD is the primary enzyme system capable of oxidizing ethanol. LAD uses a three-stage process for metabolism of alcohol. The first stage converts alcohol into acetaldehyde. In the second stage, acetaldehyde is converted to acetate, and finally acetate undergoes a complex series of metabolic reactions that break down ultimately into carbon dioxide and water, which are eliminated.[26] The two alternate pathways, MEOS and catalase, assume a more significant role with prolonged, heavy alcohol consumption.[26]

The drug disulfiram (Antabuse) blocks the conversion of acetaldehyde to acetate, leading to accumulation of acetaldehyde, which is highly toxic, in the body. This property has led to its use in the treatment of alcohol dependence by providing a deterrent to alcohol consumption. The person who has consumed Antabuse cannot drink alcohol without becoming acutely and severely ill. The intensity of the effects is related to quantity of alcohol taken and the dosage of disulfiram, but the general effects are flushed skin, decreased blood pressure, increased heart rate, and particularly, dizziness with nausea and vomiting.[9]

Elimination

Metabolic breakdown is the primary route of elimination, with 95 percent of alcohol leaving the body by this route. The remaining 5 percent of alcohol is eliminated in expired air, urine, feces, sweat, and breast milk.[9]

PHYSIOLOGICAL AND PATHOPHYSIOLOGICAL CONSEQUENCES OF ALCOHOL USE IN OLDER ADULTS

Age-related changes in the older body, from the cellular level to the gross anatomic level, may influence responsiveness to and disposition of alcohol. Alcohol changes organs involved in the processing and elimination of drugs. Many ethanol-related disorders are associated with alcohol dependence. Physiological changes that occur with advancing age are particularly important for older adults who use alcohol. Certain specific changes in body composition and kidney, nervous, gastrointestinal, and cardiovascular systems may heighten the older adult's risk for adverse effects from alcohol and other drugs.[23,27]

Body Composition

The ratio of lean body weight-to-fatty tissue changes along with a reduction in the intracellular and extracellular fluids. These changes result in the reduction of fluid volume available for the distribution of water-soluble agents such as alcohol.

Kidneys

With age, the ability to concentrate and dilute urine decreases, as does the ability to conserve sodium. Thus, the excretory functions of the kidney to preserve the volume of body fluids and to maintain the proper composition of these fluids are affected.

Nervous System

With age, cellular brain mass and blood flow decrease, sensory conduction time increases, and the permeability of the blood-brain barrier probably increases. These changes may result in decreased physical coordination, prolonged reaction time, and an increased number of falls. Also, the brains of older people appear to be more sensitive to the side effects of alcohol and drugs in general. Several conditions occurring in the nervous system are closely associated with long-term alcohol dependence.

The most prevalent condition is Wernicke's encephalopathy. This condition is related primarily to thiamine deficiency. It is characterized by mental confusion, disorientation, ataxia, and ocular abnormalities. Treatment with thiamine replacement can have very positive results.[22] Korsakoff's psychosis is another CNS problem seen with chronic alcohol ingestion. Korsakoff's is characterized by severe memory impairment with confabulation, disorientation, and overall intellectual deterioration. It is believed to be caused by the direct neurotoxic effects of ethanol on the brain tissue and there is no effective treatment.[28]

Gastrointestinal System

Both structural and functional changes associated with aging are responsible for the stomach's reduced secretion of protective mucus. These changes, added to the irritating effect of alcohol on mucosal tissues, heighten the risk of gastric injury. Prolonged alcohol consumption affects the absorption, use, and storage of ingested nutrients, leading to nutritional deficiencies. Alcohol interferes with normal peristaltic movements. People with alcohol dependence often have symptoms of erratic bowel function and gastrointestinal hemorrhage or peptic ulcer.

Age-related changes cause decreased blood flow in the liver and may slow down the liver's microsomal metabolism. Because of these changes, alcohol is metabolized and eliminated more slowly, resulting in exposure of body tissues to higher levels of alcohol for longer periods. Under these conditions, tissue damage increases. Reduced ethanol metabolism can result in states of hypoglycemia, hyperlipemia, ketosis, acidosis, and hyperuricemia.[29]

The liver and pancreas are seriously affected by chronic alcohol abuse. Fatty liver may occur in anyone ingesting moderate amounts of alcohol but occurs more often in those drinking heavily over long periods. Alcoholic cirrhosis, which is generally irreversible, occurs in about 10 percent of people with alcoholism. Acute or chronic pancreatitis is characterized by severe abdominal pain.

The association between drinking and cancer of the mouth, pharynx, esophagus, and liver, which has been observed clinically for many years, may result from the prolonged effects of alcohol on body tissues and the possible presence of carcinogenic substances in some alcoholic beverages.[30]

Cardiovascular System

Aging is associated with structural changes in the heart and blood vessels, which include major negative changes in electrical, mechanical, and biochemical properties. Alcoholic cardiomyopathy and heart disease may occur in people with a history of alcohol abuse. Hypertension may also be adversely affected by alcohol use. The adverse effects of ethanol on hematopoiesis result in abnormalities of red blood cells, white blood cells, and platelets. These, in turn, may give rise to anemias and interference with clotting mechanisms. Blood abnormalities are reversible with alcohol abstinence and proper nutrition.[28]

PSYCHOSOCIAL CONSEQUENCES OF ALCOHOL USE IN OLDER ADULTS

Denial of alcohol abuse or alcohol-related problems may be more intense among older people because of strict moral codes acquired in early life. Grief issues are often present in the older heavy drinker. Although grief is a universal human experience, heavy drinking interferes with one's ability to process and integrate the grief (i.e., grief work stops when heavy drinking begins). If alcohol dependence is present, an older person may grieve over lost opportunities, relationships, health, and so on. These issues may make it more difficult to confront the situation because of anticipated pain and self-doubt about a successful outcome.

Chronic pain and other disability may offer a ready excuse for drinking. Furthermore, the client may believe that nothing else can help relieve the problem. This attitude can alienate potential helpers and increase isolation of the drinker. Older people may complain of falling and trauma, but alcohol dependence can present as almost any medical illness.[21] One consequence of alcoholism in the community-residing older adult may be the so-called senior squalor syndrome (i.e., squalor and self-neglect without dementia or other chronic illness).[30] This syndrome was originally described in people age 60 to 92, most commonly women living alone.

The constellation of drinking problems in older adults includes hangovers and blackouts, psychological dependence, health problems, accidents, and financial problems related to alcohol use, problems with spouse or relatives, and problems with friends or neighbors.[31] The older problem drinker is less likely than the younger problem drinker to be involved in alcohol-related traffic accidents, have much contact with the police or criminal justice system, or be implicated in job or marital and other family problems indicative of alcohol abuse. To a large extent, these people are hidden from public view because they reside outside the mainstream of activity.[20]

Management

1 Primary Prevention

Primary prevention is directed at lowering the incidence of alcohol problems in older adults and reducing the risk for vulnerable people to develop late-onset problems of alcohol abuse. Intervention strategies target preretirement and retirement planning groups,[32] education regarding alcohol and how to cope with stressors associated with aging,[33] and self-help groups.[22]

Preretirement Planning

Preretirement and retirement planning groups are often a part of personnel services in industry and business and in labor and professional groups and organizations. The focus of these planning groups may include role transition issues, increased leisure and management of time, structuring daily activities, and determining the nature of and access to resources in the neighborhood and community. Health-promotion factors may be addressed as substance use in general, exercise, nutrition, and so forth.

Education Programs

Education programs at Senior Centers that target stressors of aging can help prevent ineffective coping responses such as escalating alcohol use. Topics may include issues around stress management, grieving, loneliness, living alone, declining physical health with age, and death and dying issues. The recognition that alcohol or drugs or both might offer temporary control and relief of stressors experienced must be countered with the adverse consequences that can result from excessive use of alcohol such as incoordination, falls, and fractures. In some instances, a comprehensive course teaching the nature and effects of alcohol use may be desirable and can result in vigorous and informative discussions. See Table 31–1 for resources for information and education programs.

TABLE 31–1   RESOURCES

Addiction Research Foundation
33 Russell Street
Toronto, Ontario, Canada M5S 2S1

Al-Anon Family Group Headquarters
PO Box 182
Madison Square Station
New York, NY 10010

Alcohol and Drug Abuse Nursing Program
Department of Psychosocial Nursing SC-76
University of Washington
Seattle, WA 98195

Alcoholics Anonymous
General Service Office
PO Box 459
Grand Central Station
New York, NY 10164-0371

Hazelden
Pleasant Valley Road, Box 176
Center City, MN 55012-0176

National Clearinghouse for Alcohol and Drug Information
PO Box 2345
6000 Executive Boulevard
Suite 402
Rockville, MD 20857

National Council on Alcoholism
12 West 21st Street
New York, NY 10010

National Institute on Alcohol Abuse and Alcoholism
US Department of Health and Human Services
5600 Fisher's Lane
Rockville, MD 20857

National Nurses Society on Addiction
2506 Gross Point Road
Evanston, IL 60201

Rutgers Center of Alcohol Studies
Rutgers University
Smithers Hall, Busch Campus
Piscataway, NJ 08855-0969

Vista Hill Foundation
Drug Abuse and Alcoholism Newsletter
Suite 100
3420 Camino del Rio North
San Diego, CA 92108

Women for Sobriety, Inc
Box 618
Quakertown, PA 18951

Self-Help Groups

Self-help groups can be developed in the community under the sponsorship of Senior Centers, community mental health centers, voluntary organizations, church groups, and so forth. Special topics could be derived from selected memberships, as well as from literature, music, and other humanities. Literature such as novels, short stories, and poems written by their peers have special relevance and meaning for older adults.

2   Secondary Prevention

Secondary prevention involves reducing the prevalence of alcohol abuse or dependence through early case finding and prompt, effective treatment.

Identification Issues

One difficulty involved with identification of alcohol problems in older adults is that some people are isolated from the social groups that might draw attention to compulsive alcohol use. Some tend to drink alone or in family groups. Older people are often protected by relatives who fear stigma of having a parent labeled "alcoholic." When older adults do come to the attention of the health-care system, they are often misdiagnosed or treated ineffectively.

A second difficulty that may cause the older drinker to be overlooked is that many of the instruments used to investigate potential alcohol or drug abuse problems are based on younger populations, relying on indicators that may not be relevant for older people (e.g., employment problems, marital problems, and occurrence of driving while intoxicated and other legal problems).[34] In one age-integrated substance abuse treatment program, most older adults admitted for treatment drank at home alone and in response to depressive states. Few were employed, few were active drivers, and many were widowed, divorced, or socially isolated.[35]

Older people with alcohol problems are more likely to be found among those seeking medical or psychiatric attention; thus, case finding might be conducted through the health-care system. However, Solomon[36] notes that the diagnosis of alcohol dependence in older people is often missed by clinicians because of a low index of suspicion, concealment by patients and families, and attribution of symptoms to advancing age. Older adults with alcoholism rarely seek treatment for alcohol problems because of their denial, and clinicians either fail to recognize the problem or ignore it. Furthermore, people tend to under-report alcohol consumption when questioned directly.

Attitudes of Health-Care Providers

The health-care provider also must be aware of and be able to confront his or her own feelings and attitudes toward older people, alcohol use and abuse, and dependence. Education about alcohol problems, diagnosis, and treatment in older adults is inadequate for most health-care professionals.[21,37] When skills are perceived as lacking, competency to deal with alcohol problems is also lacking. Feelings of hopelessness and incompetence can be a potent combination leading to avoidance of the problem. Hopelessness about alcoholism in general may be magnified under the mistaken belief that the prognosis for change is poorer in the older population.[21]

Denial is often present in the older person and his or her family members. The denial associated with alcohol dependence is often poorly understood by health-care professionals. Although affected people tend to deny they have a condition that is beyond their control, these same people usually share specific experiences, behavior, and events in their lives that relate to drinking (e.g., troubled relationships, physical side effects). The DSM-IV criteria serve as a valid and reliable source of such experiences that are specific for diagnostic purposes.[7]

Assessment

Assessment of alcohol abuse and dependence requires both psychosocial and biochemical indices.[38] Screening questions for alcohol use must be incorporated into everyday practice as opposed to reliance on cues to trigger an evaluation of alcohol use. Questions about history of falls or accidents, acute-onset dementia, symptoms of neglect including nutritional deficiencies and weight loss, or a recent loss or change in living situations such as from death of a significant other can be asked along with questions regarding other health-related behaviors such as tobacco use and exercise. The overall assessment goal is to determine the nature of alcohol use in order to identify health risks or alcohol dependence.

Psychosocial Indices

Various screening tools are available to aid in assessment. These include the Michigan Alcoholism Screening Test (MAST)[39] or short version (SMAST),[40] the CAGE (which consists of four questions from the MAST),[41] and HEAT[42] (Table 31–2). SMAST, CAGE, and HEAT are brief, routine, standardized alcohol problem screening tools to use with older people. If any positive response is elicited, a full substance use history is indicated and a diagnosis established according to the DSM-IV criteria. Any answer that raises suspicion is considered a positive response (e.g., defensiveness, anger, embarrassment, discomfort). If the older person drinks alcohol but not compulsively, or in a way that causes problems, it is necessary to assess whether the alcohol use may cause or worsen other health problems or their therapeutic management.

A brief depression assessment is helpful in suspected abusers. An association has been found between alcohol consumption and depression.[22] In some instances, alcohol may be used to self-medicate a primary disorder of depression; in other instances, the use of alcohol has caused the depression. Somatic complaints may indicate depression as well. The Geriatric Depression Scale[43] was developed specifically for use with older adults and serves as an adjunct to case finding.

Cognitive effects of alcohol may mimic changes normally associated with aging or organic brain syndrome. Bienefeld[22] reported that 25 to 65 percent of older alcoholics have a dementia syndrome and further noted that at least 10 percent of clients with dementia have alcohol-related brain disease, with only a small proportion having the classic Wernicke's encephalopathy.

Zimberg[44] has outlined key problem areas that can be queried to facilitate diagnosis in situations in which alcohol problems in an older person are more difficult to discern. In each problem area, it is necessary to determine whether its occurrence is associated with drinking behavior. They include recent changes in behavior or personality, recurring episodes of memory loss and confusion, increased social isolation and staying home most of the time, increased argumentativeness and resistance to help offered, neglect of personal hygiene, irregular eating habits, failure to keep appointments, neglect of medical regimen, inability to manage income, legal troubles, and problems with neighbors. The information should be obtained from the client as well as from relatives and friends. If the information obtained from the client or other source indicates that any of the problem areas seem to be associated with use of alcohol, the client probably has an alcohol problem requiring attention.

Biochemical Markers

Biochemical markers are laboratory tests that provide information about a person's alcohol use independent from self-report. Blood and urine screens show recent ingestion but must be performed before the alcohol is metabolized and eliminated. The most commonly used markers for alcohol include γ-glutamyl transpeptidase, mean corpuscular volume, liver enzymes, and high density lipoproteins. Abnormalities in these tests are not highly sensitive or specific to alcohol. The tests do tend to show abnormality in cases of chronic liver pathology associated with alcohol dependence and long-term use. Elevated findings must be evaluated in conjunction with other physical findings, medication usage, and psychosocial reports.

Therapeutic Management and Nursing Interventions

Detoxification: Alcohol Withdrawal Syndrome

Nurses working with older clients in alcohol withdrawal note that older adults present greater complexity and diversity in alcohol withdrawal symptoms and these symptoms continue for longer periods and are often more severe than those seen with younger adult abusers[45] (see "Research Brief"). Because of autonomic and cardiovascular instability of older adults, detoxification is often safer if carried out in a controlled inpatient setting.[22]

Management of withdrawal includes appropriate nutrition with attention to vitamin and mineral deficiencies (especially thiamine and magnesium), hydration (avoiding excessive glucose solutions to prevent hyperglycemia), and a safe environment.[46] Medications commonly used for detoxification such as the benzodiazepines must be used cautiously because of their potential to produce confusion and delirium. Benzodiazepines

TABLE 31–2 SCREENING TOOL FOR ALCOHOL USE: HEAT

A brief screening tool for alcohol use that can be remembered by the mnemonic *HEAT*. A positive answer indicates the need for further assessment. The first question is a subjective, open-ended question designed to elicit subtle defensiveness on the part of the respondent. The following three questions were found to identify 95 percent of alcoholics in a hospital setting.

H **H**ow do you use alcohol?
E Have you ever thought you used to **E**xcess?
A Has **A**nyone else ever thought you used too much?
T Have you ever had any **T**rouble resulting from your use?

with a short half-life, such as lorazepam (Ativan) or oxazepam (Serax), are recommended and often given in dosages one-half to one-third normal adult dosages.[46] Disulfiram (Antabuse) is seldom used because of the potential toxic risks caused by the compromised cardiovascular status of the older abuser.[46]

The focus of nursing interventions during the alcohol withdrawal and detoxification period is to provide a safe, quiet environment. Ensuring adequate rest, reducing sensory stimuli and interpersonal contacts, and providing reassurance and reality orientation help reduce anxiety, disorientation, and confusion.[47] Monitoring vital signs and other symptoms is important because tachycardia and elevated temperature indicate the severity of withdrawal.[11] The prevention of seizures, especially if they were experienced during prior detoxification episodes, may necessitate anticonvulsant therapy during the withdrawal period. The nurse is responsible for ensuring that the client receives adequate nutrition, hydration replacement therapy, and sedatives to promote stabilization and as smooth a withdrawal period as is possible. Also important is physical health-care and assistance with activities of daily living.

Postwithdrawal Period

The postwithdrawal period follows stabilization of body and behavioral functioning accomplished during detoxification and withdrawal. Recovery from alcohol dependence is a long and difficult course in which physical and behavioral symptoms and the effects on cognition, memory, and mood may resolve slowly.[45,46,48] For many, recovery from alcohol dependence is complicated by lapses or a return to alcohol use. Restoration of body and behavioral functioning after long periods of using the depressant alcohol requires total alcohol abstinence and establishment of health-promoting lifestyle behaviors. This restoration of function may also require treatment of emergent or coexisting health problems previously masked by alcohol use.

During the postwithdrawal period, the nurse assesses the seriousness of the client's alcohol use pattern. The decision to discontinue, reduce, or continue current alcohol use belongs to the client. It is important to establish a working relationship with the person. It may be easier to deal initially with health issues such as nutrition and concurrent health problems and then to move into the more sensitive issues associated with the alcohol abuse.

Before engaging the person in management strategies for alcohol use, the nurse may need to work through the client's denial that his or her current alcohol use is a problem. In some cases, the person may refuse assistance offered, despite a working relationship with the health-care provider. Readiness is an important factor in altering a long-standing alcohol use pattern that may have met and still does meet various needs of the client. However, it is still important for health-care providers to share their concerns about the person's existing alcohol use and to discuss resources to help the client attain health goals.

Treatment Options

Continued alcohol abuse treatment after the withdrawal phase depends on comprehensive discharge planning (see Table 31–3 for nursing care plan). Referral often requires coordinating with an alcohol treatment program (inpatient facility, outpatient mental health program, intensive programs, or halfway house), close and ongoing alliance with a health-care provider for associated medical problems, guidance directed toward avocational/leisure pursuits, and peer group interaction.[46] Older alcohol abusers require the same range of services as younger abusers, but the focus of treatment may differ.[21,46] Health-care providers disagree about whether age-specific or mixed-age group programs are most successful for treatment of older abusers.[23] It is important that the older patient choose the type of program most suitable to their needs and one that is available, affordable, and accessible.

When the client completes treatment, he or she must be connected with an aftercare program. Aftercare programs, such as Alcoholics Anonymous, Women for Sobriety, peer counseling, and self-help groups have demonstrated positive results in helping many older adults remain in recovery and helping their families provide support. Some older adults also benefit from con-

TABLE 31–3 CARE PLAN

Nursing Diagnoses: Knowledge deficit related to the effects of alcohol abuse and consequences of alcohol dependence
Knowledge deficit related to physiological changes of aging and their interaction with alcohol intake
Perceptual alterations related to alcohol use pattern, alteration in self-concept related to alcohol use
Alteration in family process related to alcohol abuse
Perceptual and cognitive alterations related to alcohol withdrawal syndrome

Expected Outcomes	*Nursing Interventions*
Client participates in treatment and abstains from alcohol.	Refer to Alcoholics Anonymous or other agency.
Client lists signs and symptoms of alcohol dependence.	Identify support people who can be available if help is needed.
Client discusses impact of aging on alcohol use.	Discuss the treatment plan with family or significant other. Encourage their support.
Client reports improved family relationships	
Client engages in leisure activities that provide an opportunity to experience a more positive self-concept; reports intent to abstain from alcohol use following detoxification.	Identify health-positive leisure activities or healthful alternatives to alcohol-related activities.

tinuing care groups and individual counseling. In most cases, medical and social services and a supportive social network are essential to continued recovery. All these programs emphasize recovery as a lifelong process.

Several alcohol treatment programs targeted for older adults provide a sampling of varied intervention approaches in different settings.[49] Recently, Dupree and West[50] outlined their program for older adults, which targets alcohol self-management in high-risk situations. Other programs emphasize health-promoting lifestyles, intensive day care, and a variety of intervention strategies such as reminiscence groups in a continued care program.[51] Still other approaches have targeted homeless people and those in low-income housing for older adults in metropolitan areas in which multiple health issues and alcohol-related problems are addressed.[52]

During treatment, group therapy for older abusers may deal with age-related losses, depression, boredom, loneliness, negative self-esteem, decreased socialization and rebuilding social support networks, general problem solving, and involvement in community networks.[21] There is evidence that organically impaired older abusers do better in less structured programs, using stress reduction techniques and one-to-one counseling, whereas those who are unimpaired seem to benefit from more traditional treatment approaches.[45] It is important when planning treatment for older abusers to know community agencies that have programs individualized to older adults, including payment plans, discounts, and acceptance of Medicare.

3 Tertiary Prevention

Tertiary prevention is aimed at reducing the severity of consequences of alcohol dependence and the disability associated with alcohol abuse. Rehabilitation involves sustaining gains made in treatment and changing activities associated with previous pretreatment alcohol use patterns.

Continuing care after discharge is essential to support the client in his or her recovery maintenance program. The risk and prevalence for lapses and a return to alcohol use must be recognized and dealt with. An overall goal of rehabilitation is to help the person assume a lifestyle of alcohol abstinence, use appropriate coping and recovery methods, and participate in aftercare programs, with the intention of improving quality of life.

Student Learning Activities

1 What factors contribute to the invisible nature of alcoholism in older adults?

2 Discuss the impact of alcoholism on the management of such chronic diseases as diabetes and heart disease.

REFERENCES

1 Maddox, GL (ed): The Encyclopedia of Aging. Springer, New York, 1995, pp 53–54.
2 Council Report. Alcoholism in the elderly. JAMA 275(10): 797–801, 1996.
3 Schmall, VL, et al: Alcohol Problems in Later Life. Oregon State University, Eugene, 1989, p 5.
4 National Institute on Alcohol Abuse and Alcoholism: Seventh Special Report to the US Congress on Alcohol and Health. US Dept of Health and Human Services, Washington, DC, 1990, pp 1–12.
5 Institute of Medicine: Causes and Consequences of Alcohol Problems. National Academy Press, Washington, DC, 1987, p 17.
6 Morse, RM, and Flavin, DK: The definition of alcoholism. JAMA 268(8):1010–1014, 1992.
7 American Psychiatric Association: Diagnostic and Statistical Manual of Mental Disorders, ed 4. APA, Washington, DC, 1994.
8 Gomberg, ESL: Drugs, alcohol and aging. In Koglowski, LT, et al (eds): Research Advances in Alcohol and Drug Problems, vol 10. Plenum, New York, 1990.
9 Loomis, T: The pharmacology of alcohol. In Estes, NJ, and Heinemann, ME (eds): Alcoholism, ed 3. CV Mosby, St Louis, 1986.
10 Antai-Otong, D. Helping the alcoholic patient recover. AJN 8:22–30, 1995.
11 Butz, RH: Intoxication and withdrawal. In Estes, NJ, and Heinemann, ME (eds): Alcoholism, ed 3. CV Mosby, St Louis, 1986.
12 Seventh Special Report to the US Congress on Alcohol and Health. US Department of Health and Human Services, Rockville, Md, 1990.
13 Cloninger, CR: Neurogenic adaptive mechanism in alcoholism. Science 236:410, 1987.
14 Stamatoyanopoulos, G, et al: Liver alcohol dehydrogenase in Japanese: High population frequency of atypical form and its possible role in alcohol sensitivity. Am J Hum Genet 27:789, 1975.
15 Bienenfeld, D: Alcoholism in the elderly. Am Fam Physician 36(2):163, 1987.
16 Atkinson, RM: Aging and alcohol use disorders: Diagnostic issues in the elderly. Int Psychogeriatr 2(1):55, 1990.
17 National Institute on Alcohol Abuse and Alcoholism: Alcohol and aging. Alcohol Alert 2:1, 1988.
18 Stinson, FS, et al: Alcohol-related morbidity in the aging population. Alcohol Health Res World 13(1):80, 1989.
19 Atkinson, RM: Alcohol and substance use disorders in the elderly. In Birren, J, et al (eds): Handbook of Mental Health and Aging. Academic Press, New York, 1992.
20 Williams, M: Alcohol and the elderly: An overview. Alcohol Health Res World 8:3, 52, 1984.
21 Willenbring, M, and Spring, WD: Evaluating alcohol use in elders. Generations 12(4):27, 1988.
22 Bienefeld, D. Substance abuse. In Bienefeld, D (ed): Verwoerdt's clinical geropsychiatry. Williams & Wilkins, Baltimore, 1990, pp 164–177.
23 McMahon, AL: Substance abuse among the elderly. Nurse Pract Forum 4(4):231–238, 1993.
24 Gomberg, EL: Patterns of alcohol use and abuse among the elderly. In National Institute on Alcohol Abuse and Alcoholism: Special Population Issues. Alcohol and Health Monograph no 4, Rockville, Md, 1982.
25 Maddox, GL: Aging, drinking, and alcohol abuse. Generations 12(4):14, 1988.
26 Levin, JD: Alcoholism: A Biopsychosocial Approach. Hemisphere, New York, 1990.
27 Lamy, PP: Actions of alcohol and drugs in older people. Generations 12(4):9, 1988.
28 Ciraulo, DA, and Renner, JA: Alcoholism, In Ciraulo, DA, and Shader, RI (eds): Clinical Manual of Chemical Dependence. American Psychiatric Press, Washington, DC, 1991, pp 1–93.
29 Heinemann, ME, and Hoffman, AL: Alcoholism. In Carnevali, D, and Patrick, M (eds): Nursing Management for the Elderly. JB Lippincott, Philadelphia, 1986, pp 301–317.
30 Kafetz, K, and Cox, M: Alcohol excess and the senile squalor syndrome. J Am Geriatr Soc 30:706, 1982.
31 Mishara, BL: Perspectives on alcohol and old age. In Bergener, M, and Finkel, S (eds): Clinical and Scientific Psy-

chogeriatrics: The Holistic Approach, vol 1. Oxford University Press, New York, 1990, pp 277–286.

32 Gomberg, ESL: Alcohol use and alcohol problems among elderly. In Special Population Issue, Alcohol and Health Monogram no 4. National Institute of Alcohol Abuse and Alcoholism, Washington, DC, 1984, pp 263–290.

33 Brody, JA: Aging and alcohol abuse. J Am Geriatr Soc 30(2):123, 1982.

34 Graham, K: Identifying and measuring alcohol abuse among the elderly: Serious problems with existing instrumentation. Stud Alcoholism 47(4):322, 1986.

35 Schonfeld, L, and Dupree, L: Older problem drinkers: Long long-term and late-life onset abusers. In Aging (no 361). US Department of Health and Human Services, Washington, DC, 1990, pp 5–8.

36 Solomon, DH: Alcoholism and aging. In West, LJ (moderator): Alcoholism. Ann Intern Med 100:411–412, 1984.

37 Hoffman, AL, and Heinemann, ME: Substance abuse education in schools of nursing: A national survey, J Nurs Educ 27(7):282, 1987.

38 Barry, PP: Chemical dependency in the elderly. In Hazzard, WR, et al (eds): Principles of Geriatric Medicine and Gerontology, ed 2. McGraw-Hill, New York, 1990.

39 Selzer, ML: The Michigan Alcohol Screening Test: The quest for a new diagnostic instrument. Am J Psychiatr 127(12):89–94, 1971.

40 Pokorny, AD, et al: The brief MAST: A shortened version of the Michigan Alcohol Screening Test. Am J Psychiatr 129(3):342–345, 1972.

41 Mayfield, D, et al: The CAGE questionnaire: Validation of a new alcoholism screening instrument. Am J Psychiatr 131(10):1121–1123, 1974.

42 Woodruff, RA, et al: A brief method of screening for alcoholism. Dis Nervous System 37:434, 1976.

43 Sheikh, JJ, and Yesavage, JA: Geriatric Depression Scale (GDS): Recent evidence and development of a shorter version. Clin Gerontol 5(1/2):165–172, 1986.

44 Zimberg, S: Alcohol abuse among the elderly. In Carstensen, LL, and Edelstein, BA (eds): Handbook of Clinical Gerontology. Pergamon, New York, 1987.

45 Mudd, SA, et al: Alcohol withdrawal and related nursing care in older adults. J Geriatr Nurs 20(10):17–26, 1994.

46 Mackel, CL, et al: The challenge of detection and management of alcohol abuse among elders. Clin Nurse Specialist 8(3):128–135, 1994.

47 Estes, NJ, and Hoffman, AH: Postacute withdrawal syndrome: A nursing challenge in maintaining recovery. Perspect Addiction Nurs 3:7, 1992.

48 Estes, NJ, and Hoffman, AL: Post acute withdrawal syndrome: A nursing challenge in maintaining recovery. Perspect Addiction Nurs 3:7, 1992.

49 Program profiles. Alcohol Health Res World 8(3):40, 1984.

50 Dupree, LW, and West, H: Alcohol self-management in high risk situations: A group training manual for older adults (FMHI Pub Series 1922). Florida Mental Health Institute, Tampa, 1990.

51 Starr, J: Outpatient speciality clinic. Strategies for promoting health in the later years: Alcohol and the Older Adult. Northwest Geriatric Education Center, September Conference, Seattle, September 21, 1991.

52 Haynes, M: Community clinic. Strategies for promoting health in the later years: Alcohol and the older adult. Northwest Geriatric Education Center, September Conference, Seattle, September 21, 1991.

CHAPTER 32

Homeless Older Adults

Shirley Damrosch / Judith A. Strasser

OBJECTIVES

Upon completion of this chapter, the reader will be able to:

- Describe the phenomenon of homelessness in America
- Discuss the impact of homelessness on older adults
- Identify the barriers to health promotion and health protection for a homeless older adult
- Discuss the primary and secondary strategies for homeless older adults

Poverty in America

Americans who have grown up in comfortable circumstances may find it difficult to understand how hard life is for those who are poor. Being poor is like trying to run life's race with both legs tied together. Pesznecker[1] has summarized what is known about poverty into an explanatory model, which she calls the adaptational model of poverty. Figure 32–1 illustrates how the factors in this model each interact with one another.

Personal factors in the model include individual variables such as a person's early childhood experiences, the quality of available role models, and the other advantages or disadvantages in his or her life. Examples of environmental factors are the amount of stressful life events and the presence or absence of discrimination and stigmatization. Mediating factors include public policy concerning adequate or inadequate funding of social and health programs designed to aid the poor, or variables such as social support from friends, family, and community.

As seen in Figure 32–1, the model emphasizes the interactive nature of these factors: People living in poverty must each day confront the disadvantages of being poor in the total context of all these factors.

THE HOMELESS IN AMERICA

Homeless Americans are the poorest of our country's poor. There are many unsettled issues involving the homeless, including how to define a homeless person and how many people are homeless in America. The National Governor's Association defined a homeless person as "an undomiciled person who is unable to secure permanent and stable housing without special assistance (p. 7)."[2] A definition that focuses on the socioemotional aspects of homelessness comes from Ellen Bassuk, a psychiatrist who specializes in research on the homeless. She characterizes homelessness as "extreme disaffiliation and disconnection from supportive relationships and traditional systems that are designed to help (p. 1550)."[3] Bassuk adds that homelessness is often "the final stage in a lifelong series of crises and missed opportunities (p. 43)."[4]

Because of the difficulty of counting the homeless, experts disagree on how many Americans are homeless, with estimates ranging from 200,000 to 3 million. The Urban Institutes survey of 178 cities yielded an estimate of 500,000 to 600,000, a count that has become the gold standard.[5] There is consensus that the number is growing.

Contrary to any stereotype Americans have of the homeless, the population of homeless people is extremely diverse. Some major classifications of the homeless include the chronically mentally ill, chronic alcoholics and other drug abusers, street people, and the situationally distressed.[6,7] Naturally, a particular homeless person may be found in any one or several categories. Also, no classification system can do justice to the unique identity of any homeless person. In fact, there is growing recognition of the multiplicity of mental and physical disorders in many homeless people. For example, the widespread coexistence of mental disorders and substance abuse problems has led to the term *dually diagnosed*. Moreover, the overlap of alcohol and drug abuse and mental disorders is further complicated by their association with physical comorbidities.[8]

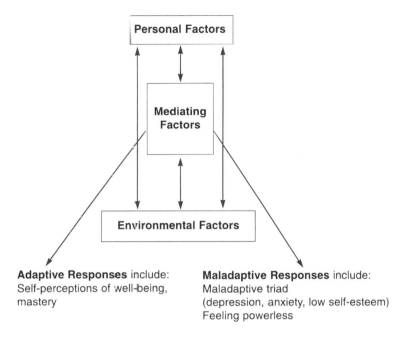

Personal Factors

Mediating Factors

Environmental Factors

Adaptive Responses include: Self-perceptions of well-being, mastery

Maladaptive Responses include: Maladaptive triad (depression, anxiety, low self-esteem) Feeling powerless

Figure 32–1 Pesznecker's adaptational model of poverty. (Adapted from Pesznecker.[1])

The Chronically Mentally Ill

Zuk reported estimates that 20 to 30 percent of the homeless have major mental problems.[9] Deinstitutionalization policies beginning in the 1960s resulted in releasing mentally ill patients from institutions to the community. Many communities failed to provide proper outpatient treatment and housing for the discharged patients, some of whom became homeless.

Current legal restrictions in most jurisdictions make it almost impossible to involuntarily commit any mentally ill person, no matter how severe the condition, unless clear evidence exists that the person is a danger to self or others.[10] For example, a homeless woman, whom we will call Dora, came to the court's attention when social workers become concerned about her well-being. Dora refused any food offered to her, preferring to hunt for meals among the garbage in dumpsters and trash cans. After a psychiatric evaluation of Dora, it was decided that eating garbage was insufficient grounds for involuntary commitment, and Dora was discharged, free to continue this practice.[11]

Despite the high percentages (0 to 30 percent) of homeless people with major mental diagnoses, it is estimated that fewer than 5 percent receive Supplemental Security Income (SSI) benefits.[9] Nurses, nursing students, and social workers can be useful in helping the homeless negotiate the complexities of SSI and other entitlements.

Chronic Alcoholics and Other Drug Abusers

Although alcohol abuse exists in all categories of homelessness, chronic alcoholics are hard-core, down-and-out homeless people whose lives are driven by alcohol. Chronic alcoholics tend to be predominantly men 40 and older. Alcoholism magnifies the distress of the homeless by complicating the provision of health care and other services to them, intensifying their financial problems, endangering their health, and straining their social support networks of family and friends.

Nationwide, alcohol is the most commonly abused drug among the homeless. However, other kinds of drug abuse are prevalent and may differ depending on geographic region. For example, a 1989 study concluded that among men in New York City shelters, cocaine (or crack) abuse was a greater problem than alcohol abuse.[6] Although experts cite substance abuse as one important cause of homelessness,[12] the degree of such abuse among the homeless may also reflect the stresses of their harsh lifestyle.

Street People

Street people come closest to many people's stereotype of the homeless. These "bag ladies" and "grate men" stand out in public because of their especially shabby clothing and appearance; many tote all their possessions in a grocery cart or shopping bag, which they take wherever they go. Their daily struggle to survive probably takes all their time and energy.[13,14] Although few in number, street people may represent the most severely disturbed category of homelessness.

The Situationally Distressed

The situationally distressed are people who, because of factors such as economic recession and shortage of low-cost housing, are occasionally homeless. For example, in 1996 federal legislation set a lifetime limit of 5 years on welfare payments for most families. Moreover, states may set stricter limits: South Carolina has imposed a 2-year limit. Such restrictions are likely to increase the number of homeless people of all ages. In many cities, the waiting list for subsidized housing is so long that many older applicants die before being assigned an apartment.

Some experts consider the situationally distressed to be victims primarily of economic and other outside forces. However, other experts cite factors such as educational or intellectual handicaps, personality disorders, and substance abuse as significant in contributing to the person's current homelessness.[15] This issue is important because experts disagree on whether the situationally distressed need access merely to low-cost housing and other economic support or to remedial services as well.

Which Is Cause and Which Is Effect?

Many factors listed as potential causes of homelessness may also be potential consequences. Wright[12] summarizes relevant data from care providers working in clinics for the homeless. These providers assessed a list of 22 factors that could be implicated in causing someone to become homeless. Alcohol and drug abuse, chronic mental illness, and chronic physical illness were rated high in importance as major single causes of becoming homeless.

However, these factors may also be potential consequences of homelessness. Because life for homeless people is so stressful, being homeless can make even healthy people mentally or physically sick or lead to substance abuse. In extreme cases, homelessness may be a fatal condition. In any event, whatever the direction of cause and effect, homelessness enormously complicates the nurse's role in delivering adequate health care.

IMPACT OF HOMELESSNESS ON OLDER ADULTS

Many older homeless people may be seen as the victims of triple jeopardy. First, their early start in life was probably handicapped by unstable family situations and a variety of social problems such as poverty.[16] Second, their current circumstances necessitate a daily struggle to survive in a cruel, dangerous environment that lacks not only adequate shelter but also food, clothing, health-care services, social supports, and even the opportunity to keep clean. Third, homeless older people are at a point in their lives when their aging mind and body, already weakened by what may have been years of physical and mental privation, each day become increasingly vulnerable to current degradation as well as to normal age-related changes.

Defining Old Age in the Homeless

Life without a home may be prematurely aging; 50-year-old people who are homeless may physiologically resemble many 70-year-old adults in the housed population.[17] Thus, the category of older homeless person commonly starts at age 50.

What Percentage of the Homeless are Older Adults?

Researches have encountered difficulties in trying to estimate what percentage of homeless people are age 50 and older. For example, surveys that concentrate on public shelters probably underestimate the proportion of older adults because many of them avoid such places out of fear of violence, mistreatment, or institutionalization.[9]

In one of the few recent studies relevant to this issue, the authors of this chapter surveyed a random sample of long-term clients at an urban clinic for homeless people. Thirty of the clients surveyed (27 percent of the sample) were age 50 or over. The reader is cautioned against generalizing the results of a single study.

Roorda[18] concluded that the demographics of homelessness will inevitably change because the homeless population is aging along with the rest of America. Gerontologists agree that this burgeoning segment of the homeless population remains largely unrecognized. Vance[19] pointed out that this neglect of the importance of age differences in the homeless means there is a paucity of information for planning, program development, and service delivery. However, the limited available material on older homeless people convincingly demonstrates that their burdens are special and cumulative.[18]

Need for Specialized Services

Specialists in aging[17] emphasize the fact that homeless people 50 and over have health problems similar to those of much older housed members of the community. Homeless people between 50 and 62 may fall through the cracks when programs are restricted to those 62 and older.

Moreover, even homeless people aged 60 or older are probably not welcome in most existing Senior Centers and nutrition programs established for housed older adults. As discussed in the next section, there may be special need for age-segregated services provided for the homeless.

Violence and the Older Homeless Person

Being vulnerable and readily identifiable as such, the older homeless adult lives in fear of violence. (Indeed, open wounds and lacerations are common diagnoses in homeless people seeking health care.) Older homeless men are often verbally and physically abused by younger homeless men. For example, Doolin[16] reported that in Boston, older people felt crowded out by the younger clients in shelters open to all age groups. Some experts[16,20] therefore recommend an extra measure of support for older adults, which may require the provision of age-segregated services.

Rape is an act of violence that can happen to any woman, including older women in the general population. Older homeless women are particularly vulnerable because they live in such dangerous circumstances. Because many women do not report rape to the police, there are only rough estimates of the true extent of this crime. Estimates of sexual attacks on women over age 50 in the general population range from 2 to 35 per 1000.[21] Although no research on rape victims has focused on older adults, recovery from the trauma of rape is difficult at any age and may take a long time (e.g., years for many women). For the homeless older woman, the assault may intensify her feelings of vulnerability and helplessness. Moreover, fear of being infected by the acquired immunodeficiency syndrome (AIDS) virus intensifies the stress.

Detecting Alcoholism in the Homeless Older Adult

Curtis et al.[22] concluded that medical education is deficient in providing physicians with the skills to detect and treat older patients with alcoholism. Experts increasingly recognize alcoholism as the most pervasive health problem of homeless people of all ages.[23] When older people are involved, the problem is further complicated by the need for special criteria. Analogous to the effects of many prescribed medications in older adults, changes in body composition accompanying aging intensify blood alcohol concentration per volume ingested, and the aging central nervous system appears to become increasingly sensitive to alcohol.[24] Thus, the criterion for excessive alcohol intake must be lowered when older homeless people are involved. There is some evidence that alcohol abuse peaks between ages 30 and 64; moreover, some studies show a 3:1 ratio of men to women among homeless problem drinkers.[23]

How Homelessness Complicates Health Prevention and Health Protection.

Today's homeless people have the highest burden of untreated illness of any group in the United States.[25] Homelessness may present nursing's biggest challenge.

Homelessness is a level of existence that devours all one's time and energy to secure survival needs such as food, a bed for the night, and somewhere to clean up. There may be little or no margin to improve one's situation, seek necessary health care, or comply with a treatment regimen.

Koegel et al.[13] discussed this process in terms of the leveling effect of the conditions of homelessness. In other words, apart from any physical or mental disabilities a person has, homelessness itself is a sufficiently handicapping condition such that "each homeless person's adaptation suffers radically" (p. 104).[13] Cohen and Sokolovsky[20] discuss what has been called a homeless syndrome, a widespread condition among the homeless characterized by "depression, hopelessness, demoralization, and anxiety" (p. 62).

Barriers to Health Prevention and Health Protection

Despite difficulties in obtaining medical care, homeless people do seek health care. For example, Cohen and Sokolovsky,[20] in a survey of more than 250 older homeless men living in New York City, found that 77 percent had seen a physician in the past year and 38 percent had done so twice, primarily through hospitals (73 percent) or neighborhood clinics (26 percent). The number of visits was similar to that in a comparison sample of housed older men. However, because the homeless men reported more physical problems than did the housed sample, the homeless group may not have received all needed care.

Many deficiencies in the lives of the homeless complicate health promotion and health protection. Nurses with full awareness of these deficits may find it easier to be compassionate rather than angry or judgmental with homeless older adults. For example, a client may smell bad, be filthy, and be infested with lice because of lack of access to bathing facilities and living in a crowded, louse-ridden environment. Clients may fail to keep a follow-up appointment because watches and calendars are rare among the homeless. The client may even lack the price of public transportation to get to the appointment. Because vandalism and theft are so common, loss of prescribed medicines is also common. Even keeping a clean bandage on a wound may become an imposing task when the client lives in crowded, unclean surroundings with inadequate sanitary facilities.

Importance of the Nurse

Experts who have studied the homeless in depth[26] have concluded that health-care providers may be the only people willing to touch homeless people. Yet nurses and other care providers are human beings who may have many of the same fears and are repelled by many of the same things that repel nonprofessionals. Surveys have shown that about 20 percent of homeless people have an infectious or communicable disease; therefore, nurses must protect their own health while fulfilling the client's need for compassionate, competent care.

Nursing interventions with older adults may need to go beyond the multiple needs for physical and mental care and extend to assisting older homeless people in establishing entitlement to basic services and benefits. Special needs associated with being a homeless older person include support to help them negotiate access to basic needs and services, especially if senility is a problem; special protection from sexual and physical abuse on the streets and in shelters (for which older adults are seen as easy targets); special transportation to aid in the search for housing (which often presents formidable obstacles to older adults such as many stairs to climb); health care for multiple chronic diseases; and special eye and dental care to remedy years of neglect.[27]

Bowdler[25] emphasizes the need to be creative and flexible when caring for the homeless. It takes time to establish a trusting relationship to the extent that the client is willing to allow a complete history and physical examination. The nurse should also elicit the client's understanding of his or her own illness; many clients may verbalize bizarre body image and disease concepts. If substance abuse is an issue, Bowdler[25] advises:

> It is helpful to communicate the continuing option for substance abuse treatment while providing care for other health problems. . . . A therapeutic relationship can be developed through which the patient is encouraged to take responsibility for his/her health without enabling the patient to continue the substance-abusing lifestyle.

Remember that facilitating compliance and preventing noncompliance are part of the nurse's role. Boucher[28] and Damrosch[29] reviewed practical advice to achieve these goals. Easy tips to increase proper medication taking habits include giving the client a laminated, wallet-sized mediation card that lists the name, address, and telephone number of the health-care provider; providing pillboxes with separate slots for hours and days of the week; making the medication as simple and user-friendly as possible (e.g., when permissible, arrange for use of transdermal patches or other time-released medication instead of multiple daily doses); using weather-resistant packaging for medications or supplies; and having the client with special conditions such as diabetes wear a bracelet or necklace listing the disability.

To help clients keep appointments, supply the client with a photocopy of a page from a monthly calendar so the client can mark time until the next appointment. If the client can be reached by telephone or mail, a reminder of the appointment will be helpful.

The lifestyle of the homeless often results in fragmentation of care. Nichols et al.[30] developed a method for assisting a complex health-care system to coordinate the continuity of care and to track homeless clients; this method involves an instrument called the Tool for Referral Assessment of Continuity. Widespread implementation of this system is recommended to improve the quality of care provided to the homeless.

STUDENT EXPERIENCE WITH HOMELESS OLDER ADULTS

By working with older homeless adults, students become sensitized to their plight and to learn how to help them meet their health-care needs. McDonald[31] described a prototype community health experience designed for senior nursing students. The 14-week program involved each student in a case study involving a homeless client, who was contacted at least twice per month. Students kept logs of their visits, and group conferences provided support and problem solving. An especially rewarding experience was a health fair developed and run by the students. The fair included the distribution of free clothing, information on nutrition, an English and Spanish list of state resources, and a general health screening.

Anderson and Martaus[32] also provided a detailed description of a rewarding clinical experience with the homeless extending over two academic quarters. Senior nursing students gained experience at two church-affiliated sites, a community center, and a shelter for the homeless. An interesting feature of this teaching approach was the combination of community health and psychosocial nursing experiences. Although these two different clinical experiences involved homeless people of all ages, their methodologies could be applied to older homeless clients.

Value Orientations

Experts[33] have cited value differences between the homeless client and the health-care provider as a possible barrier to homeless people attempting to secure needed health services. Some nursing students, like students in all health-care disciplines, may need consciously to strive to overcome their middle-class bias. Two nurses, Downing and Cobb,[33] obtained evidence that a sample of homeless men had value orientations that might lead to conflict with the middle-class orientations of many health-care providers.

CLINICAL MANIFESTATIONS AMONG HOMELESS OLDER ADULTS

The clinical manifestations associated with homeless older adults are many and complex. Health deficits may have preceded or contributed to homelessness, or they may have resulted directly from the homelessness. Moreover, the social, physical, and spiritual aspects of homelessness may exacerbate illness and the normal problems of aging and may complicate medical and nursing access and treatment.

The Institute of Medicine[34] listed selected antecedents of homelessness, which include major mental illnesses, infections, debilitating diseases such as AIDS and tuberculosis, sequelae of accidents and injuries that leave people unable to work and without worker compensation, and the degenerative diseases that can accompany old age.

Health problems that occur as a result of homelessness include skin disorders, problems with extremities, trauma, malnutrition, parasite infestations, dental and periodontal disease, degenerative joint diseases, sexually transmitted disease, and infectious hepatitis and hepatic cirrhosis.[34]

Hazards of homelessness that can complicate care include difficulties with health-care access, continuity, and compliance with care. Aging further accelerates problems linked to increased fatigue or decreased mobility, diminished circulation, and increased susceptibility to infectious processes.

Health-care access decreases because of problems with both the homeless elderly person and the health-care delivery system. Older people who are extremely tired may not be able to make good decisions, may fall asleep on the way to a health-care appointment, may not have the means to make an appointment, may not hear his or her name called in the waiting room, and may appear noncompliant simply because of fatigue. Decreased mobility may make it impossible for the homeless older adults to use public transportation (even if he or she has the correct change and a senior citizen discount). A long walk may be out of the question.

Diminished circulation to the brain and extremities also contributes to impaired decision making and impaired mobility. The proximity to infectious agents, the stressed immune system, and the extremes of temperature to which homeless older adults are exposed increase their chances of contracting an infectious disease. Personal and environmental factors contribute to slow recovery as well as to added risks of opportunistic infections.

Environmental problems include difficult access to medication and a temperature-controlled place to store medicines, especially eyedrops, insulin, and antibiotics. Simultaneous access to clean water, a glass, and the medication may be difficult. Drugs, needles, and syringes are often stolen or lost.

Personal factors that can contribute to a slow recovery include a lack of time awareness, poor compliance patterns, fatigue or confusion, and limited functional ability.

GENERAL HEALTH HAZARDS OF HOMELESS OLDER ADULTS

Home provides safety and security from the physical and social hazards of the environment. As the length of time an older adult is homeless increases, so does the likelihood that he or she will fall prey to illness and accidental or deliberate trauma.

Health Care for the Homeless Clinics

The Robert Wood Johnson Foundation and the Pew Charitable Trusts in 1984 initiated a grant program to establish Health Care for the Homeless (HCH) clinics in 19 American cities. Current HCH programs provide services throughout the United States. For example, HCH in Maryland operates walk-in clinics in Baltimore and two outlying counties, providing comprehensive primary care, with referrals to hospital-based speciality clinics as needed. This organization also provides medical, social work, and mental health services on an outreach basis to 22 soup kitchens and shelter facilities in the state; outreach services to needy people on the street are also provided. A master's prepared nurse practitioner is the executive director of the organization, and nurses play a leading role in the success of the enterprise.[35]

In 1995, the authors surveyed a random sample of 110 long-term clients at an inner-city clinic providing health care for the homeless. Thirty (27 percent of the sample) had ages ranging from 50 to 68 (mean age 55). Twenty-six of the subjects were male. Most of these 30 inner-city residents were African-American, and 50 percent had completed high school. None of the 30 subjects was married, an indication of their relative social isolation.

Multiple diagnoses were the rule in this older subsample: 60 percent had three or more diagnoses involving serious or chronic conditions. The most common diagnoses were hypertension (found in 50 percent), alcohol abuse (40 percent), and psychiatric problems (27 percent). Although these data were obtained from a single homeless facility, the high level of morbidity found in these subjects is consistent with findings from previous studies.[17,18]

Management of Clinical Problems in Homeless Older Adults

In addressing the management of clinical nursing needs among homeless older adults, nurses should determine the appropriate levels of intervention and prevention, as well as the type of care delivery system. The nurse should establish a framework for intervention strategies.

Levels of intervention can include the nurse and an individual homeless person, the nurse and a group of homeless people, the nurse and a system, or the nurse with other care providers and an individual, group, or system. Each professional nurse must determine at which level his or her skills lie and should focus on approaches at this level of skill. Systems can include health-care delivery, housing, safety, transportation, church, or other systems that may affect the lives of homeless older adults.

For purposes of this chapter, the nurse working with an individual homeless person is the central focus for providing care. The nursing process (i.e., assessment, planning, implementation, and evaluation) is used to explain nursing actions, with nursing diagnosis as the end product of assessment.

1 *Primary Prevention*

Most health services for the homeless can be classified under secondary and tertiary prevention. As Berne et al.[36] pointed out, true primary prevention of homelessness demands changes in social policies that would grant such necessities as affordable housing, job training and guaranteed meaningful employment at an adequate wage for those who can still work, adequate levels of public assistance for those unable to work, access to health prevention and protection (including education about substance abuse and coping with stress), and drug treatment on demand.

Sortet[37] asserted that nurses in community health and other areas have a natural power base in their communities. There are many potential allies to join with nurses to achieve solutions to the problems of homelessness. Those who share responsibilities with nurses include other health-care experts; housing experts; job counselors; elected officials and members of public, private, and voluntary agencies; and people interested in older adults, families, abused people, the poor, the addicted and mentally ill, the unemployed and underemployed, and all the other underprivileged segments of our society.

Hodnicki[38] agrees that nurses need to serve as homeless advocates. She proposes that nurses act to coordinate the formation of coalitions of public and private agencies to assist homeless people and build support groups; increase public awareness of the problem via radio or television appeals, combining fundraising with information focusing on the problems of the homeless; write about homeless issues for the local newspaper; become members on community and hospital boards to help direct policy decisions; and engage in lobbying efforts to change policies at the local, state, and federal levels.

AIDS

The rate of AIDS infection among the homeless is estimated to be more than 10 times greater than in the general population.[11] Although adolescence and early adulthood encompass most AIDS cases, it is important to note that human immunodeficiency virus (HIV) can infect people at any age. Older homeless people may be at special risk for this infection, which is commonly transmitted by sharing of intravenous needles and through heterosexual or homosexual sexual activity.

With respect to sexual transmission, research indicates that older people have sex often enough to permit efficient HIV transmission. Moreover, older people may be more vulnerable to HIV infection via sex, probably because of age-related lowered immune system function and postmenopausal vaginal changes.[39]

Homeless older adults have special educational needs concerning safe-sex practices and the dangers of sharing needles. In many communities, free condoms are distributed by outreach workers to the homeless and other targeted populations. The nurse may want to secure a supply of condoms to distribute to sexually active homeless clients or inform the client about sources of free condoms in the community.

Education about contaminated needles is also important. Although distribution of clean needles to addicts is controversial and is illegal in some jurisdictions, providing the addict with equipment to clean needles with bleach is less problematic.

2 *Secondary Prevention*

The goal of secondary prevention is the early diagnosis and treatment of disorders and diseases. With regard to homeless older adults, the first step in secondary prevention is to find the people most at risk for these conditions, usually through community outreach services. Most older people are at risk for the health problems that come with aging. With advancing age and unprotected exposure to the physical and social environment comes the risk of additional and multiple ailments.

Once homeless older adults are located, assessment begins. Considerations that affect assessment include the availability of resources (people, equipment, and money) and the possibility of follow-up care. When an organized health-care program for the homeless is in place and when people and resources are available for follow-up, then assessment, planning, implementing, and evaluation can occur.

The first steps in the assessment process are keen observation and thorough history taking. Observation includes a head-to-toe view of the client while ambulating. A quick, thorough observation should address the areas on the observation checklist shown in Table 32–1. As the nurse works with this special population of homeless older adults additional items for the observation checklist should be added as needed.

History taking should occur in a location where the interviewer and the person interviewed are most comfortable and where privacy and safety are ensured. The purpose of history taking is to form a foundation for diagnosis, planning, implementation, and evaluation.[40] History taking helps the nurse categorize problems ac-

cording to priority, assess client potential and plan and predict the outcomes of nursing intervention.

The interview form of the history elicits subjective and historical data from the homeless person. The history also helps build a rapport between the nurse and the client and facilitate the sharing of information. When conducting the history-taking interview, the nurse's goal is to establish a quick link with the client and to develop a beginning level of trust and mutual respect.

Many agencies have printed health history forms, and agencies serving large numbers of homeless older people have adapted their forms to fit the needs of this population. The health history form usually contains the areas shown in Table 32–2.

Physical Findings

Physical findings are based on general assessment of functional ability by observing important aspects of functioning, sometimes with the help of an enhancing device (e.g., a stethoscope, blood pressure cuff, and monometer or thermometer). Functional abilities usually assessed are listed in Table 32–3.

Laboratory studies should screen for the major causes of death among homeless older adults and for infectious disease. Brickner et al.[41] reported that the major causes of death among homeless older adults are cancer, coronary artery disease, lung disease, and liver disease.

Therapeutic Management

Common disorders of homeless older adults, which are directly associated with homelessness, include peripheral vascular disease, infections, thermoregulatory

TABLE 32-1 OBSERVATION CHECKLIST

Observation	Checks
Overall appearance	Condition and amount of clothing (includes stains, cleanliness, appropriateness), general grooming; first impression, affect (sad, slow, quick, businesslike, happy, dazed)
Clearly observable health deficits	Draining sores; useless limbs; guarding (protecting a body part); swelling, bites; skin discoloration
Observable health aids	Bandages, crutches; canes; shopping cart; artificial limbs; eyeglasses
Head	Hair (amount and condition); head injuries; gross drainage from eyes, ears, nose; dentition; condition of eyes, nose
Trunk	Position (erect or bent); curvatures (neck and trunk)
Extremities	Swelling, guarding, exposed parts
Gait	Guarding; speed; ataxia; use of an appliance or aid; body mechanics
Visible possessions	Number of boxes, bags, walking aids
Odor	Odor of purulence; excreta; perspiration; vomitus; blood

TABLE 32–2 HEALTH HISTORY

Client Profile	Statement about the Client
Description of client	Age, gender, general characteristics
Chief complaint	Central problem(s) bothering the client
History of present illness	Client perceptions of the history of each complaint (health problem)
Medical history	Reported illnesses, surgery, hospitalizations, allergies, immunizations
Medication history	• List of all current medications (dosage, frequency, route of administration, how long the drug has been taken, the time the drug was last taken) • Past medications and adverse reactions • Use of alcohol, tobacco, and illicit and over-the-counter medications
Family history (depending on the homeless person, this area may be emotionally laden. Although the information may be valuable, the questioning may have to be omitted to preserve or attain trust)	Health trends in the family; illnesses and causes of death as remembered
Social history	Support system, sleeping and shelter arrangements, religion, work history
Patterns of daily living	Usual daily routine including sleep/rest, activity, diet (food and fluids), elimination, hygiene, shelter, storage of possessions, social interaction

TABLE 32–3 FUNCTIONAL ABILITIES

Functional Area	Physical Findings
Mobility	Ability to ambulate; transportation use and availability
Skin integrity	Color, temperature, dryness and moisture, rashes, ulcers, drainage, bruises, bites
Communication	Hearing, vision, speech
Circulation	Pulses (intensity and rhythm); chest, leg, or arm pain; blood pressure; edema, pain, or numbness of extremities
Oxygenation	Respiration quality; dyspnea, orthopnea, apnea; cough, sputum
Comfort	Pain; guarding; sleep difficulties
Nutrition	Teeth or dentures; chewing, swallowing; changes in appetite or weight; use and type of liquids (amount, time of day, and type of liquids consumed)
Elimination	*Bowel:* Constipation; diarrhea; character and color of bowel movement; colostomy *Bladder:* Hesitancy; urgency; frequency; amount; use of catheter *Skin:* Color, perspiration *Vomiting:* Type; amount
Sleep-wake pattern	Hours and location of sleep; sleep disruptions; sleep difficulties; sleep position
Management of health and illness	Ability to time and take medication; ability to comply with treatments; ability to keep appointments; access to pharmacy; ability to pay for liquids, food, medication, treatments
Activity, safety	Ability and resources to perform activities of daily living Safety of environment
Coping	Finances; health insurance

Laboratory results	Laboratory results should be within normal limits for the following:
	Blood studies
	    Electrolytes
	    Hemoglobin
	    White cell count
	    Enzymes
	Urinalysis
	Electrocardiogram
	Chest radiograph
	Stool (ova and parasites)
	Stool (occult blood)
	Mammogram
	Pap smear
	Testicular examination
	Venereal disease check
	AIDS check
	Tuberculosis check

TABLE 32–4 TEACHING GUIDE: MANAGEMENT FOR SCABIES AND LICE INFESTATION[42]

Scabies	• Dispose of old clothing or wash in water hotter than 120°F for >5 minutes; or set clothing aside for 3 days. • Avoid crowding, sleeping close to others. • Drug of choice is gamma benzene hexachloride. • Treat all contacts.
Lice	• Dispose of clothing, clean combs and brushes with boiling or very hot water (130°F). • Avoid close contact with others. • Drug of choice is gamma benzene hexachloride (as for scabies). • Treat all contacts.

disorders, trauma, infestations, hypertension, and nutritional disorders. Therapeutic management includes specific approaches to patient education related to the life condition of the client. Homelessness and old age are two variables that must be considered when teaching these clients. Therapeutic management for infestations,[42] is presented in Table 32–4. Scabies and lice infestation can lead to a fear of "bugs" and itching for up to 2 weeks after therapy.

Therapeutic management for nutritional disorders includes a thorough assessment of current dietary habits (all food and drinks) and recommendations for correcting the deficit or inappropriate diet. Homeless older adults are particularly prone to electrolyte imbalance from dehydration. Access to healthful liquids and bathroom facilities must be explored.

Table 32–5 provides a selected list of nutritional and vitamin deficiencies commonly found in older homeless people, along with an explanation of the possible con-

comitant state or harm.[43] Table 32–6 includes a list of select at-risk groups among older homeless people and an explanation of the possible concomitant state or harm.

Peripheral Vascular Disease

Peripheral vascular disease (PVD) is common among the homeless. PVD is a circulatory problem that results in increased incidence of death and of clinic visits for large numbers of homeless people, especially older adults. Chronic stasis ulcers of the lower extremities often occur after phlebitis or thrombosis. Gravitational flow to the lower extremities is interrupted by flexed sleeping positions. Being unable to elevate one's legs limits venous return and causes blood to pool, followed by edema, darkening of the skin, inflammation, and finally ulceration and infection. Once ulceration has occurred, treatment is more difficult because the environment does not foster the treatment plan, which includes elevating the extremities. Secondary infection can lead to septicemia and even death. Table 32–7 summarizes the recommended therapeutic management for PVD.

Nursing interventions take place at the direct care level and at the system level. Direct care needs of homeless older adults are the same as those of other people with adaptations for age and life situations. Teaching patients to care for themselves is vital, as is quick and expedited referral when additional care is required. The nurse must know where and how the patient rests and sleeps, what resources such as food and water are available, what social supports are available, and what tasks the patient is able (and willing) to perform.

At times the nurse may alert people in the patient's community to the conditions and needs of the individual. These people could include street vendors, soup kitchen workers, or security personnel. Often, these sup-

TABLE 32–5 SELECTED NUTRITIONAL AND VITAMIN DEFICIENCIES COMMONLY FOUND IN OLDER HOMELESS PEOPLE

Deficiency	Potential Concomitant State or Harm
Protein-calorie malnutrition	Depletion of fat and muscular tissue; water leaves body cells and accumulates between them; reductions in heart rate, blood pressure, and temperature; immune system is weakened. Client become apathetic, moves slowly. There is increased susceptibility to infections, which are widespread among the homeless.
B vitamins	Central nervous system is adversely affected.
Vitamin C	Wounds heal poorly. (Note that animal and insect bites and muggings, assaults, and other causes of bruises, lacerations, and broken bones are common among the homeless.)
Zinc	Lack of zinc can lead to skin rashes. Deficiency can blunt taste (which may lead to extremely high intake of salt or to other abnormal eating patterns).
Calcium	Calcium deficiency can cause osteoporosis (brittle bones), the 12th leading cause of death. Vertebral or hip fractures are common and are 10 times more common among women than men.
Thiamine	Beriberi can take two forms: Cardiovascular effects, which may culminate in heart failure Nervous system effects, which may result in weakened hands and feet (e.g., classic symptoms of wrist and foot drop)
Vitamin B_6	Deficiency can lead to depression.
Folic acid	Deficiency causes slower rate of cellular division. Bone marrow is especially vulnerable, leading to macrocytic anemia.
Folic acid/vitamin B_{12}/iron	Deficiency causes anemia.

Source: Adapted from Strasser et al.[43] p. 69, with permission.

TABLE 32–6   SELECTED AT-RISK GROUPS AMONG OLDER HOMELESS PEOPLE

Homeless Client's Status	Potential Concomitant State or Harm
Older	Specific nutritional needs and requirements are usually not met by diet available to the homeless; osteoporosis is a major problem.
Alcoholic	Deficiencies of water-soluble vitamins and certain minerals are likely. For example, alcohol interferes with absorption of thiamine, vitamin B_6, and folic acid (see Table 32–5).
Diabetic	Stress from instability of homelessness may aggravate glucose levels. Inability to coordinate scheduling of meals with insulin dosage may result in poor control of serum glucose. Renal and ocular damage, as well as increased susceptibility to infections, is possible.
Hypertensive	Salt, saturated fat, and cholesterol, which abound in food commonly available to the homeless, can exacerbate hypertension (or predispose the previously unaffected to the condition).
Menopausal	Special dangers of osteoporosis result from dramatic loss of calcium from bones (see Table 32–5).
Lactose intolerance	This is prevalent in adult African-Americans, Asians, and some Caucasians with Mediterranean backgrounds. Inactive lactase enzyme results in undigested lactose (from milk and dairy products), leading to diarrhea and gas pain. Foods rich in calcium must be found to replace milk and dairy foods.
Taking diuretics	This causes depletion of potassium reserves.
Taking antacids	This leads to imbalance in absorbed aluminum or magnesium.
Taking tranquilizers	Depressed appetite results.
Taking isoniazide	This drug (used to treat tuberculosis) interferes with vitamin B_6 metabolism.
Taking dilantin	This drug (used to treat epilepsy) interferes with folic acid metabolism.
Taking aspirin	Microscopic bleeding may lead to anemia.
Eating from garbage dumpsters or other sources of refuse	Food poisoning, food-borne parasites, and malnutrition can result.
Taking street drugs	Various interactions with the diet may lead to myriad nutritional deficiencies.

Source: Adapted from Strasser et al.[43] p. 71, with permission.

port people will do what they can to help the ill, older homeless person.

Nursing Care Plans

Many standardized nursing care plans are available in both hospitals and home care settings. Most clinical agencies have standardized plans and may now have problem-oriented medical records and nursing care plans on computer. Such standardized plans form a base that must be adapted for use with homeless older adults.

For example, sleep pattern disturbance in homeless older adults may be caused by an environment that is not conducive to sleeping, rather than by some physical or mental problem.[44] The outcome goals may be lower than those expected for the housed patient, and must consider the client's age, which alters many people's sleep-wake cycle. Nursing actions may include altering the environment as a central intervention strategy. Teaching homeless, sleep-deprived older adults how to adapt their medical and nursing care to life on the streets requires a keen understanding of the person's resources, mental ability, and motor skills.

Managing diagnostic monitoring poses additional problems related to the environment of the homeless. Money, transportation, and safety all play a part in the process. Dealing with prescription drugs, which can be stolen or mixed up when one is old, cold, and tired, requires conscientious supervision.

TABLE 32–7   NURSING CARE PLAN

Nursing Diagnosis: Impaired circulation	
Expected Outcomes	*Nursing Interventions*
Progression of the signs and symptoms will be prevented.	Reduce ambulatory venous pressure (elevate legs).
Wounds will remain clean without signs of infection.	Care for existing venous ulcer by means of an external compression device (e.g., compression stockings).
	Keep area clean with soap and water. Clean, dry socks can help protect the legs from trauma.
	Topical antibiotic ointments may be applied.
	Secondary infection requires bed rest, antibiotic therapy, and wound debridement.
	Skin grafts may be needed for people with chronic ulcers.

TABLE 32–8 RESOURCES

Coalition on Human Needs
1000 Wisconsin Avenue, NW
Washington, DC 20007
202-342-0726
Jennifer Vasiloff, executive director

Health Resources and Services Administration
5600 Fishers Lane
Rockville, MD 20857
301-443-0201
Ciro V. Sumaya, MD, administrator

Homelessness Information Exchange
1612 K Street NW, Room 1004
Washington, DC 20006
202-775-1322
Dana Harris, director

National Coalition for the Homeless
1612 K Street, NW, Suite 1004
Washington, DC 20006
202-775-1322
Fred Karnaf, executive director

3 Tertiary Prevention and Discharge Planning

Older people who are homeless must continue to be monitored after discharge. Homelessness alone implies too many risks from the environment, some of which the nurse can help correct. Being old exacerbates the problems of being homeless. Care for homeless older people must include outreach and on-site care. With minimal equipment, dressings can be changed even in crowded shelters. People can be taught in any setting, and a trusted nurse functioning as a primary provider or case manager can refer the homeless person for appropriate treatment.

Tertiary prevention in the form of rehabilitation and habilitation for homeless older adults can be carried out only after basic necessities such as food and shelter have been provided and only after the homeless person has reached a functional level of health.

The nurse's role in the discharge plan is to adapt nursing care to the reality of the streets and then to carefully monitor and refer the patient. Nurses and other professionals familiar with the plight of the homeless are working to eliminate the problem of homelessness, especially for the most vulnerable groups such as children and older people. Nurses who want additional information about homelessness issues and resources may contact the organizations listed in Table 32–8. A longer list of such organizations can be found in the reference handbook compiled by Hombs.[45]

Student Learning Activities

1 Arrange for the class to visit a local homeless shelter or invite the clinic nurse to meet with the class.

2 Discuss the most common health problems seen by the local homeless population.

3 What community resources are available to provide shelter and health care to the homeless?

REFERENCES

1 Pesznecker, BL: The poor: A population at risk. Public Health Nurs 4:237, 1984.
2 Select Committee on Hunger, US House of Representatives: Hunger among the homeless. US Government Printing Office, Washington, DC, March 1987, p 7.
3 Bassuk, EL, et al: Is homelessness a mental health problem? Am J Psychiatry 141:1549, 1984.
4 Bassuk, EL: The homelessness problem. Sci Am 251:43, 1984.
5 Bassuk, EL: Dilemmas in counting the homeless: Introduction. Am J Psychiatry 65(3):318, 1995.
6 Breakey, W, and Fischer, P: Homelessness: The extent of the problem. J Soc Issues 46(4):31, 1990.
7 Fischer, P, and Breakey, W: Homelessness and mental health: An overview. Int J Mental Health 14(4):6, 1986.
8 Struening, E, and Padgett, D: Physical health status, substance use and abuse, and mental disorders among homeless adults. J Soc Issues 46(4):66, 1990.
9 Zuk, IM: Mental health overview. In Rich, D, et al (eds): Old and Homeless: Double Jeopardy. Auburn, Westport, Conn, 1995.
10 Kanter, AS: Homeless but not helpless: Legal issues in the care of homeless people with mental illness. J Soc Issues 45(3):91, 1989.
11 Breakey, W, and Fischer, P: Down and out in the land of plenty. Johns Hopkins Magazine 37:16, 1985.
12 Wright, JD: Poor people, poor health: The health status of the homeless. J Soc Issues 46(4):49, 1990.
13 Koegel, P, et al: Subsistence adaptation among homeless adults in the inner city of Los Angeles. J Soc Issues 46(4):83, 1990.
14 Strasser, J: Urban transient women. Am J Nurs 78:2076, 1978.
15 Bassuk, E, et al: Characteristics of sheltered homeless families. Am J Public Health 76:1097, 1986.
16 Doolin, J: Planning for the special needs of the homeless elderly. Gerontologist 26:229, 1986.
17 Rich, DW: Labels and social context. In Rich, et al (eds): Old and Homeless: Double Jeopardy. Auburn, Westport, Conn, 1995.
18 Roorda, JR: Double jeopardy: Homeless and old. In Rich, D, et al (eds): Old and Homeless: Double Jeopardy. Auburn, Westport, Conn, 1985.
19 Vance, DE: A portrait of older homeless men: Identifying hopelessness and adaptation. J Soc Distress Homeless 4(1);57, 1995.
20 Cohen, C, and Sokolovsky, J: Old Men of the Bowery: Strategies for Survival. Guilford, New York, 1989.
21 Calhoun, K, and Atkeson, B: Treatment of Rape Victims. Pergamon, New York, 1991, p 115.
22 Curtis, JR, et al: Characteristics, diagnosis, and treatment of alcoholism in elderly patients. J Am Geriatr Soc 37:311, 989.
23 Boucher, LA: Substance abuse. In Rich, D, et al (eds): Old and Homeless: Double Jeopardy. Auburn, Westport, Conn, 1995.
24 Rains, V, et al: Recognition of alcohol dependence in the elderly. J Am Geriatr Soc 37:1204, 1989.
25 Bowdler, JE: Health problems of the homeless in America. Nurs Pract 14(7):44, 1989.
26 Baxter, E, and Hopper, K: The new mendicancy: Homeless in New York City. Am J Orthopsychiatry 52:393, 1982.
27 Damrosch, S, and Strasser, J: The homeless elderly in America. J Gerontol Nurs 14(10):28, 1988.
28 Boucher, LA: Medication: Overview and issues. In Rich, D, et al (eds): Old and Homeless: Double Jeopardy. Auburn, Westport, Conn, 1995.
29 Damrosch, S: Facilitating adherence to preventive and treatment regimens. In Wedding, D (ed): Behavior and Medicine, ed 2. Mosby, St Louis, 1995.
30 Nichols, J, et al: A proposal for tracking health care for the homeless. J Community Health 11:204, 1986.
31 McDonald, D: Health care and cost containment for the homeless: Curricular implications. J Nurs Educ 25:261, 1986.

32 Anderson, J, and Martaus, R: Combining community health and psychosocial nursing: A clinical experience with the homeless for generic baccalaureate students. J Nurs Educ 26:189, 1987.

33 Downing, C, and Cobb, A: Value orientations of homeless men. West J Nurs Res 12:619, 1990.

34 Institute of Medicine (Committee on Health Care for Homeless People): Homelessness, Health, and Human Needs. National Academy Press, Washington, DC, 1988.

35 Walsh Lopez, K: Personal communication, July 23, 1991.

36 Berne, AS, et al: A nursing model for addressing the health needs of homeless families. Image J Nurs Sch 22:8, 1990.

37 Sortet, J: Incompetency laws in need of review. J Community Health Nurs 7:37, 1990.

38 Hodnicki, D: Homelessness: Health-care implications. J Community Health Nurs 7:59, 1990.

39 Catania, J, et al: Older Americans and AIDS: Transmission risks and primary prevention needs. Gerontologist 29:373, 1989.

40 Iyer, P, et al: Nursing Process and Nursing Diagnosis. WB Saunders, Philadelphia, 1986.

41 Brickner, PW, et al (eds): Under the Safety Net. WW Norton, New York, 1990.

42 Brickner, PW, et al (eds): Health Care of Homeless People. Springer, New York, 1985.

43 Strasser, J, et al: Nutrition and the homeless person. J Community Health Nurs 8:65, 1991.

44 Gordon, M: Nursing Diagnosis: Process and Application. McGraw-Hill, New York, 1982.

45 Hombs, ME: American Homelessness. ABC-CLIO, Santa Barbara, Calif, 1990.

CHAPTER 33

Death and Dying

Donna Angelucci / Molly Lawrence

OBJECTIVES

Upon completion of this chapter, the reader will be able to:

- Describe pertinent demographic information pertaining to dying and aging
- Compare the frameworks of a variety of theorists
- Describe environmental options for the dying older adult
- Explain aging, dying, and their relevance to the normal life cycle
- Identify the parameters of a thorough nursing assessment for a dying patient
- Explain the three specific concerns inherent in caring for the dying older adult
- Delineate nursing directives in regard to the patient's right to self-determination
- Describe nursing care that fosters hope, trust, and dignity

Currently, most deaths occur in an institutional setting. As health-care professionals, nurses must assist older adults and their caregivers through the dying process and eventual death in a manner that is healing or health promoting for all involved. To accomplish this goal, nurses must learn to deal with death in such a way that allows the caregivers or family members to grow and allows the client to come to closure.

The dying process is as individual as each person is unique. The needs of the dying older adult are physical, social, and psychological. This chapter helps nurses develop a positive attitude toward dying and death and provides a knowledgeable basis for practice with older adults facing their final stage of life.

Theories of Death and Dying

The best known author in the field of death and dying is Elisabeth Kübler-Ross. Her work has sensitized nurses, health-care professionals, and consumers to the dying process and to the inherent needs of dying people. Her theory suggests that people who are dying experience five stages, beginning with the initial disclosure of terminality and ending with the final moments of life. Stage I, denial and isolation, usually represents a temporary defense that is replaced by partial acceptance. Denial should not be interpreted as a negative or derogatory adaptation. As a preliminary defense, denial assists the person by safeguarding him or her against perceived anxiety or threat. In stage II, anger, denial is replaced

with feelings of anger, rage, envy, and resentment. This is considered one of the most difficult stages for families and caregivers because these feelings are often directed at them. During stage III, bargaining, the dying person will try to postpone the inevitable by setting a self-imposed deadline for special family events such as weddings and religious functions. Bargains are often negotiated with God to procure additional time. Stage IV, depression, encompasses two types of losses: those that have occurred in the past and the imminent loss of life, which Kübler-Ross calls preparatory grief. Stage V, acceptance, is the final phase of the dying process.[1]

Lamberton[2] isolated four major coping strategies that a dying person may use: denial, dependence, transference, and regression. His theory emphasized a team approach in caring for the dying, with a focus on a palliative rather than curative approach to care. Consistent support by caregivers is needed as dying patients vacillate among the various modes of dependency and self-sufficiency. Dying people need to know they will not be abandoned or left alone.[2]

Pattison[3] disagrees with dividing the dying process into neat chronological stages. He identified a variety of ego-coping mechanisms that a dying person uses at different points during the life cycle. Older adults use altruism, humor, suppression, anticipatory thought, and sublimation to cope with terminal needs. Pattison refers to phases of the dying process: the acute phase, the chronic living phase, the dying phase, and the terminal phase. He notes that an array of psychological reactions surface during the living-dying interval. An individualized approach is necessary to respond to stresses and crises as they arise at any point in the dying process.

Weisman[4] suggests the possibility of phases with a continuous and fluid expression of emotional responses that occur during the dying process. He emphasizes a person's individuality rather than labeling according to an orderly succession of emotional reactions.

Kastenbaum[5] conducted a retrospective analysis called a psychological autopsy. He examined the dying person's reactions to determine appropriate interventions and determined that concepts of death change throughout life and in tandem with one's developmental level. He considers living and dying to be two phases of the same psychobiological process, which progresses until the termination of life.

Giacquinta[6] discusses stages and phases that families experience once the diagnosis of cancer is shared. The four stages include living with cancer, restructuring during the living-dying interval, bereavement, and re-establishment. Each stage consists of phases and specific hurdles such as despair, vulnerability, and helplessness. Fostering hope, security, and courage are just a few of the goals that guide nursing actions. The entire family rather than the person with cancer is considered to be the patient, and the principles can be applied to family units facing other life-threatening illnesses.

Normalcy of Death and Dying

Dying is a part of living. It is the process of coming to an end. Death is the permanent cessation of all vital functions, the end of human life. Birth, dying, and death are universal life events. Although unique to each individual, these events are normal and necessary life processes.

Attitudes toward death and dying have changed. In earlier days, people did not fear death. It was accepted as a natural progression of life. The process of dying took place in the presence of family, friends, neighbors, and children.

At the turn of the century, most deaths occurred in people under the age of 50 years. Today, most deaths occur in the older population. Eighty percent of deaths occur in an institutional setting. Therefore, children are not exposed to death during their formative years, when the support and security of their families could help them face this final life process. Nurses are present in various settings where the dying process occurs. Nurses need to feel comfortable with their own concerns and feelings about this process. Collegial support as nurses care for the dying is important to make this time a normal, growth-promoting experience.

The Dying Environment

ACUTE-CARE HOSPITALS

Even though most deaths occur in health-care institutions, the acute-care hospital or teaching hospital may be the least suitable place for the dying older adult. In the hospital setting, the disease process and diseased organ are the focus, with cure as the goal. Physicians and nurses often demonstrate discomfort and guilt when faced with those who are dying despite their efforts. Many health-care professionals have not been educated in the state-of-the-art care of the dying. Through education programs, physicians and nurses are learning how to deal with the care of dying older adults. The emphasis of education is to help health-care professionals face the issues of dying and death. Much can be done for the dying person beyond medical treatment. The dying process is the one during which emotional support becomes most important.

LONG-TERM CARE

Long-term care institutional settings provide health care for more than a million older adults in the United States. Decisions in the nursing home often include whether to withhold evaluation or treatment of medical problems as the patient faces death. Other decisions regularly faced as the end of life approaches involve resuscitation orders and considerations for transfer to an acute-care facility. Although there is a growing body of literature providing guidance for these decisions in clinical medicine, such guidance does not yet exist for long-term care. Many nursing home residents are unable to participate actively in making decisions about their personal health care. Anxiety can occur among families and health-care providers during attempts to make decisions regarding appropriate treatment as the patient approaches death.

Long-term care institutions serve older adults in need of treatment for chronic disease and disability when it is impossible or impractical to provide this care in the home or other setting. These institutions become home for many, although the major emphasis may be on the chronic illness or disability rather than on support of a lifestyle. The atmosphere of the long-term care setting is less critical than that of the acute-care setting. Often, because of this difference, the older person and family or caregivers can express and carry out their wishes regarding death in a relaxed, empathic setting. If previous decisions have been made regarding the dying process, death in a long-term care setting can occur in a calm, supportive atmosphere.

HOSPICE

A hospice is "a shelter or lodging for travelers, children, or the destitute, often maintained by a monastic order."[7] The contemporary use of the word identifies a program or institution specially designed to meet the needs of the dying. Emphasis is placed on the relief of both psychological and physical suffering, which includes pain relief.

The teamwork approach in hospice is a major focus. The core of the program is that members meet weekly to foster open communication and discussion of individual patients' needs. The interdisciplinary hospice care team, usually comprising a physician, nurses, social workers, psychiatrists, clergy, and volunteers, is the supportive connection between patient and services. This multidisciplinary approach lays the framework for the coordination of care, emphasizing the leadership and expertise of the members. Although each member has a different focus, the team is united in serving as the emotional care component for the dying.[8] The primary care unit is the patient and family. Services are available on a 24-hour basis. Programs vary but include inpatient or outpatient services. Bereavement follow-up is extended to family members after the death of the patient.

Hospices in the United States may follow any of a variety of protocols. There are inpatient hospice facilities in hospitals, in which patients may be designated to a specific unit or may be cared for on a "scatter beds" basis, with hospice patients occupying beds in various units. Outpatient and home care hospice services are often established through visiting nurse associations. Regardless of the setting, hospice care is deemed appropriate when a patient no longer responds to treatments, interventions for cure have been exhausted, and death is imminent.[9]

In many ways, a hospice is better understood as an attitude instead of a place, program, or unit. The dying person in a hospice setting is approached in a positive and growth-producing manner. The intent is to focus on the patient's courage and dignity rather than on dependence.[10] The inception of hospice care has sensitized humanity to the loving and coordinated palliative care of the dying person and his or her family. Its immeasurable rewards allude to the enrichment of life and living while dying.

HOME CARE

Another alternative may be to die at home. For this alternative, several factors must be considered because care of the dying at home imposes strain on the caregivers. If the patient's needs are greater than the available resources, both patient and caregiver may perceive the experience as negative. Many questions must be addressed: Who will provide the care? Will that person be able to maintain continuity of care? Are supportive resources, such as friends, social services, a nearby hospital, hospice services, and medical and financial assistance, available? Patient comfort and safety and caregiver support should receive equal attention.

Care at home depends heavily on the commitment and strength of several people to coordinate and provide care. Before becoming a caregiver, personal reflection is necessary. Good faith and intent are not the only character traits needed to take on this responsibility. Potential caregivers need to assess their own personal strengths, abilities, and limitations regarding the new role. A personal inventory includes an honest introspective survey on one's organizational skills, humor, health, energy level, flexibility, and problem-solving abilities. This type of self-examination will help the person identify attitudes and perspectives that will be brought to the caregiving situation.

The potential caregiver may feel ready for the responsibility. Once he or she is involved in the process,

however, difficulties may arise in providing proper physical and emotional care. These difficulties are expected and normal, and may warrant referral to an ancillary support system. Care of the dying can be a rewarding, fulfilling, yet exhausting experience. Honest ongoing reflection on the caregiver's limits, strengths, and needs is necessary to maintain a cohesive and respectful partnership with the dying patient.

Nursing Care and Support

Nursing the dying patient encompasses a holistic view of the person and includes the social, physical, and emotional environments. It promotes care of the whole person, with the dying patient in control of decision making. A model depicting the relationship between the nurse and the patient and caregiver is presented in Figure 33–1. This model can be used to guide nursing actions from a perspective of concerns: concerns of the nurse, concerns of the patient and caregiver, and those shared by both.

This model is based on the concept that an aura of openness, mutual trust, and truthfulness reigns within relationships. Interventions do not concern themselves with whether the patient should be told. The framework for this model is an honest, open-mindedness with roots in the open awareness theory. Open awareness, unlike closed awareness, lends itself to total honesty and meaningful communication with the older terminally ill patient.[11] It creates an ongoing atmosphere in which death is considered a natural and important process of life during which feelings must be shared with caregivers and loved ones. Open awareness helps dismantle the "conspiracy of silence" that may lead to an unhealthy approach toward care of the dying.

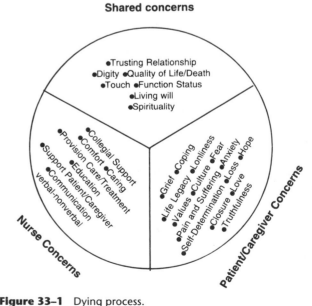

Figure 33–1 Dying process.

NURSING CONCERNS

As nurses work with older patients who are facing death, many issues arise that influence the nurse's ability to care competently for the older dying patient.

Collegial Support

Collegial support is crucial to nurses' well-being in today's complex health-care delivery system. This nursing concern is shown by being able to relieve a colleague of tasks when there is a need to spend time with a dying patient or distressed family; taking time to listen to coworkers without passing judgment or giving suggestions; offering words of encouragement or praise when needed; and providing a smile, touch, or other show of appreciation.

The support of colleagues builds strong bonds and allows each professional involved to grow. A mutuality develops with the increasing knowledge that colleagues will be reciprocal in their actions. These close collegial relationships allow for effective support and, thus, for high-quality care of the older patient who is dying.

Comfort

Giving comfort is a nurturing intervention used by nurses who care for the dying. Comforting actions relieve social, physical, and psychological discomfort; attempt to restore pleasure and a sense of well-being; and preserve dignity. Comfort measures may include sitting down with an older patient facing death, administering medication to relieve pain, or rubbing the patient's back.

Caring

Rather than calling on technical nursing skills, caring requires special attributes[9] of patience, honesty, trust, humility, hope, and courage. The most important attitude of caring is that each older person matters and that aging and facing death are as normal a part of life as any other developmental task.

Provision of Care and Treatment

It is essential for nurses to provide efficient technical care of the older patient who is dying. While providing physical care, the nurse continuously assesses the patient's cognitive-perceptual factors and helps him or her engage in growth-promoting behaviors until death.

Education

The goals of educating dying older adults to facilitate effective coping with their present health status, foster independent functioning as long as possible, and aid in maintaining an optimal level of health as these people approach the final stage of life.

SUPPORT OF PATIENT AND CAREGIVER

Kin caregivers who reported greater strain during caregiving were shown to have more difficulty adjusting to their relative's death.[12] The older adult confronting dying and death is believed to fear the events that surround the dying experience such as rejection, loneliness, loss of self-determination, and isolation more than the death itself. Often, the caregiver is hesitant to talk to the older adult about dying or death for fear of upsetting him or her. However, such discussion is usually not upsetting to the older adult. The nurse may need to arrange a family conference. Nurses must have courage and openness and be comfortable with their own feelings to be able to sit with people and just allow them to talk. Each patient and caregiver approaches this experience with unique expectations. With nursing support, all involved can grow and develop to promote life until death occurs.

Communication: Verbal and Nonverbal

Effective communication requires a repertoire of techniques and skills. Communication among the patient, caregiver, and nurse is critical to establish trusting relationships. Verbal communication techniques such as reflection, sensitive questioning, and answering direct and indirect questions with appropriate and honest information allow the nurse to enhance the nurse-patient-caregiver relationship.

Nonverbal communication is also essential. Smiling, touching, making eye contact, listening, and just being there are all nonverbal techniques that communicate concern and caring and aid in developing relationships. Nonverbal communication may be the most effective when physical changes have resulted in a loss of hearing, loss of vision, or neurological changes such as confusion.

PATIENT AND CAREGIVER CONCERNS

For each older patient and caregiver, the dying process is a unique and individualized experience involving many concerns. As these concerns are addressed, the patient can move on with his or her life tasks until the point of death.

Grief

Although no two people react to death and dying in exactly the same way, the physiological and psychological response to death, known as grief, has been described in stages by such notable people as Engel, Linderman, Parkes, Bolbey, and Kübler-Ross.

Grief is a normal and universal response to loss as it is experienced through feelings, behavior, and emotional suffering. It is a process of moving through the pain of loss. Losses of health, friends, relatives, jobs, and financial security are but a few of the cumulative losses that cause grief in the older person. The grieving period is a time for healing, adaptation, and growth.

Although many agree on the commonalities of grieving, there is also agreement that each person progresses through the grieving process differently. However, it is possible to describe clusters of phases characterizing grief reactions. These phases include initial shock and disbelief, which lead to awareness, and then protest, which eventually leads to reorganization and restitution.[13]

Nursing care for grieving patients and caregivers entails sensitive, caring, and emphatic exchange. Sharing of thoughts, feelings, and silence are appropriate nursing interventions. Anticipatory nursing guidance can help prepare dying people for both the pain and the naturalness of their feelings associated with the grief process.

Coping

Coping means contending successfully with a stressor.[14] The coping skills each person uses are unique to that person and vary in their effectiveness. Nursing interventions used to aid coping include social support, counseling, and acceptance. Counseling allows regular discussion to help the older patient and caregiver adjust. Accepting the patient and acknowledging his or her feelings enhance self-esteem and allow the older patient to maintain a self-concept as a unique individual.

Life Legacy

A legacy is a collection of one person's tangible and intangible assets that he or she transfers to another person to be treasured as a symbol of the bequeathor's immortality.[15] This process prepares the older patient for leaving the world with a sense of meaning. Legacies can be bequeathed in a variety of ways that allow the dying person to have a feeling of continuation and ties to those he or she leaves behind. For a discussion of assisting the older adult in preparing a life legacy, see Chapter 25.

Loneliness

Loneliness has a physical as well as an emotional component. Older adults experience multiple losses, which increase in number and significance as they near death. These losses send a signal of increasing dependency. Those who care for the older patient who is dying should be aware of the isolation and loneliness caused by the dying process.

Nurses decrease the loneliness that accompanies the dying process by spending time with the dying patient. Care should be focused on meeting the patient's physical needs such as pain relief and cleanliness and on his or her psychosocial needs such as talking, sharing, and being involved in life as much as possible. Brightening the environment can decrease the person's sense of aloneness. Objects that are familiar (e.g., a radio, flowers, cards) help keep the older adult in touch with life until the end of living. An intervention used in some settings is pet therapy. Studies have shown that pets can have positive effects on an older person's health.[16]

Values

A value is a quality that is intentionally desirable. People have ideological values, social values, and cultural values. It has been suggested that there are generational value differences and that values shift over the life span.[17] One's commitment to values seems to strengthen with age.

Nurses should be sensitive to the beliefs of the older patient who is approaching death. This sensitivity, combined with an attitude of caring, is helpful in showing acceptance of the older patient's values, even if they conflict with those of the nurse.

Culture

Culture provides people with an identity. *Culture* has been defined as the communicable knowledge for human coping within a particular environment that is passed on for the benefit of subsequent generations.[17]

Culture provides a sense of self, language and communication, dress, food, time and time consciousness, relationships, values, beliefs and attitudes, mental hang-ups and practice, work habits and practices, political systems, and beliefs about recreation and economics. Cultural beliefs also determine how the older adult defines health and illness and affect his or her approach to dying.

Lack of knowledge of cultural differences and variations can cause misunderstandings and misperceptions. It is important for nurses to be aware of and understand cultural factors that affect the older patient's behavior and attitudes about dying and death. Nurses need to take the necessary steps to enhance their knowledge of culture and its impact on the death process. Throughout this process of gaining knowledge and understanding, nurses are able to grow as individuals and provide a more individualized care for the older patient.[18] The nurse should be able to assist the older patient within cultural guidelines to accept the reality of death and continue a growth-promoting plan of care until the end of life. For an in-depth discussion of this topic, see Chapter 4.

Fear and Anxiety

A variety of fears are experienced by dying older adults from the time of the initial diagnosis until death. Fear of pain is the most common fear among these people. Other apprehensions include fears of abandonment, loss of independence, and the unknown. The fear of being abandoned has its roots in a societal portrait of the dying person who is alone, destitute, and deserted. Consistent human contact by both caregivers and family is of utmost importance when attempting to assuage the fear of abandonment. Emotional and physical presence will help develop the trust necessary to alleviate such fears. Older adults need to be told there will be someone with them when they are in need. When there are no known significant others or family, the nurse may need to be that consistent caregiver and support system.

As the dying patient continues to become weaker and more dependent on the caregivers and family, loss of function and independence becomes a major concern. To promote self-sufficiency as much as possible, the nurse needs to integrate the patient and family team into the daily care routine. This may include assisting with toileting, hygiene, and nutritional needs, as well as business and personal financial matters. Keeping the family system in control for as long as possible will help build self-esteem and alleviate feelings of inadequacy.

Anxiety is often affiliated with feelings of fear, worry, uneasiness, and apprehension. This distress is often associated with a fear of being a burden to others, being separated from loved ones, and enduring a painful death.[19]

Nurses need to identify the type and degree of fear and anxiety that dying patients may experience. Empathic care is the cornerstone to ameliorating the debilitating responses of the dying patient.

Pain and Suffering

A thorough pain assessment is needed. For the dying older adult, pain may also be accompanied by the distress of additional chronic illnesses such as arthritis and osteoporosis. It is important to remember that addiction to analgesic narcotics should not be a concern for the dying. The pain management goal should be to balance maintaining the patient in a pain-free state and controlling his or her sleepiness to permit participation in activities of daily living (see Chapter 22).

Suffering may involve myriad physical problems requiring nursing intervention. Providing basic supportive care measures such as range-of-motion exercises, turning and positioning, skin care, oral care, and dietary therapy is critical at this time. Other problems that can contribute to suffering include nausea, thirst, dyspnea, dysphagia, incontinence, alterations in mental functioning, and sensory changes.

Loss

Loss is a predominant theme characterizing many aspects of life for older adults. Losses may be experienced throughout the various stages of life, but their cumulative effect is felt acutely by older adults. Some older adults deal with losses better than others. For some, each loss represents a small death, bringing them closer to their own demise. Biological, psychological, personal, social, identity, functional, and philosophical losses can cause voids in one's life.

Nurses do not always realize the significance of losses that occur with older adults. Grief often follows loss. It is important for nurses to be able to discuss with an older patient and caregiver the significance of an impending loss of an event or person, or even of a title or idea. Acceptance of the inevitable losses associated with dying can lead to acceptance of the final life process.

Hope

Hope, trust, and quality of life are interrelated elements of productive coping. Hope is the intangible attitude designed to support people through adversity.[20] The intent of hope usually switches focus in the course of a terminal disease. Initially, when the diagnosis is first shared, hope focuses on treatment and successful cure. As treatment options become more limited or are unsuccessful, the patient begins to hope for palliation and comfort. Hope is nurtured through various avenues. Its underpinnings are of a spiritual nature and surface from a person's relationships with the world, family, and friends, as well as a feeling of self-worth and a sense that there is something in this world to attain.[21] Hopefulness is an active emotion that is necessary to making each day and situation the best it can be.

The nurse's role in inspiring hope in the dying older adult is multidimensional. Hope must be honest, real, and practical to the patient's needs. Examples of realistic hopes for a dying older adult include hoping to live one more comfortable week, yearning to see a garden grow, or hoping to welcome a grandchild into the world. The particular hopes the patient expresses provide essential clues to the nurse about the degree of the patient's hopefulness. According to Hickey,[22] approaches the nurse can use for enabling hope include helping the patient and family develop an awareness and appreciation of life, identifying reasons for living, and establishing support systems. The use of religion, humor, and realistic goal setting are also components of the nursing directives.[22] The nurse needs to sustain therapeutic communication and active listening skills. A realistically hopeful disposition can be nurtured by good nursing care, making possible the outcomes that a patient may desire and thus aiding in closure that is fulfilling and meaningful.

Closure

Closure encompasses a variety of tasks that are associated with arriving at a sense of finality in a positive, health-promoting way. It includes the need to say goodbye to neighbors, family, and friends and to make any legal and financial or religious arrangements desired. Closure often entails a life review to allow older patients and caregivers to feel that their death and dying will not result in untoward feeling about them or their life. (Refer to Chapter 25 for more information on the life review.) Often, older adults reconcile with an estranged relative or friend as they approach death. These tasks of closure help older patients and caregivers experience a finality and ultimate acceptance of the inevitable death.

Nurses can be an advocate for older patients and caregivers approaching the last developmental task. The nurse can support decisions that are made, maintain open communication so that the patients and caregivers can perform a life review and arrange family visits if necessary.

Love

Love must include a sense of belonging.[23] The dying process may create a sense of not being wanted or cared for. Through love, the patient and caregiver can grow and develop self-esteem.

Nurses are vital to fulfilling the need for love. The nurse's professional ability and concern for providing comfort to the dying patient meet the love needs of being cared for, belonging, and affiliation. The nurse's caring attitude also projects a sense of love. The patient's need for love is fulfilled by nurses' professional competence, giving of themselves, and meeting the patient's needs.

Truthfulness

The degree of truthfulness regarding illness, dying, and death should be in accordance with the patient's desires. A dying patient often has an awareness of his or her condition and may need only confirmation. Sometimes the caregiver does not want the patient to be told the truth because they fear this will cause the patient to give up. Counseling and understanding may be necessary to help the patient express his or her own desires.

SHARED CONCERNS

Shared concerns address the needs of both the nurse and the patient-caregiver team.

Trusting Relationship

A trusting relationship is the foundation for all interventions with the dying older adult. It is achieved through attitudes, behaviors, and value systems of the nurse and patient. Trust is the force that bonds the team members: "Trust is a belief that a person will respect another's needs and desires and will behave towards them in a responsible and predictable manner."[24] Developing a relationship on trust requires mutuality and confidence in the other person; it cannot be nurtured unless both parties trust each other.[24] The person who can trust is one who can "accept himself and others, and new experiences, who is capable of consistency and delayed gratification, can participate in relationships which are genuinely interdependent."[25] A trusting relationship with a dying patient is essential to open communication and increased effectiveness.

Dignity

Dignity is a right of every dying person, based on the fact that each person is a member of the human community. Dignity entails the understanding that the dying need personalized care, which includes active decision making and social control during the dying process.[26] The core of promoting dignity lies in the nurse's ability to enhance the patient's moral worth and self-determination. Benoliel[26] explains three goals relevant to the dying person's maintenance of dignity: to be informed about what is happening to him or her and then to have a caring person listen and discuss these concerns, to be part of the decision-making process, and to experience the multiple and conflicting responses to dying in an environment of openness and caring.

Quality of Life and Death

Quality of life is an intangible concept that is difficult to define. Weisman[20] classifies quality of life according to two major categories: societal factors pertaining to the environment and society at large (e.g., poverty, ignorance, fear) and individual factors pertaining to one's personal worth and welfare. It encompasses "options, respect, reasonable security and a sense of living up to potential."[20] The nurse's role in promoting quality of life involves maintaining the individuality of the older person, as reflected in his or her likes, dislikes, values, and philosophies of living.

Touch

Touch, one of the most important means of nonverbal communication, shows the nurse's caring, warmth, and sensitivity. In addition to its apparent emotional and psychological benefits, studies[27] have identified positive physiological response to touch: "The course and outcome of many an illness in the aged has been greatly influenced by the quality of tactile support the individual has received before and during illness."[27] Tenderly holding a patient's hand, warmly embracing a patient and giving a simple backrub are ways in which touch can enhance physical comfort and emotional support and can relieve anxiety.

Nurses need to examine their own feelings regarding use of appropriate touch as a means of aiding the dying patient. The professional should use this technique based on sound clinical judgments and patient- and family-generated clues. Both patient and nurse need to identify touch as a positive and mutually appealing intervention rather than an invasion of privacy. As with any form of communication, it is imperative that the nurse be sensitive to the patient's reactions to touch.[28]

Functional Status

The goal of maintaining function is another shared concern. The patient should be encouraged to do as much as possible for as long as possible. Family members can assist as function changes or diminishes. Involving the significant others in providing care such as bathing, feeding, and turning facilitates comfort for the patient, self-esteem for the caregivers, and an overall meaningful intervention.

Living Wills

The dying patient has many rights. The issue of advance directives involves the person's right to self-determination, of which the living will is one of the major instruments. Through its use, the patient, caregiver, and health-care team can enhance self-respect, trust, and quality of life for the dying patient. For a thorough discussion of this topic and a copy of a living will, see Chapter 5.

Spirituality

Meeting the spiritual needs of the dying patient should be of utmost concern for the nurse, patient, and family. Helping the patient to recognize and verbalize spiritual needs may help promote quality and meaning of life (see Chapter 29).

Summary

In today's world, care of the dying has taken on a new dimension. What was typically considered a taboo subject has risen to a level of increased sensitivity and awareness for the public and professionals alike. There has also been a societal change in recognizing the unique needs of older adults. Together, these two vital changes have had an impact on the nurse's role and responsibility in providing competent care to the older dying patient.

Student Learning Activities

1 Compare the needs of an older adult who is dying alone in an acute-care facility with those of one who is dying at home.

2 How would you address the needs of an older adult who expresses a fear of dying?

3 Interview a member of the chaplin service in your clinical agency regarding the services available to older adults and their family members when a death is expected.

REFERENCES

1 Kübler-Ross, E: On Death and Dying. Macmillan, New York, 1969.

2 Lamberton, R: Care of the Dying. Westport, Conn, 1973.

3 Pattison, EM: The Experience of Dying. Prentice-Hall, Englewood Cliffs, NJ, 1977, p 304.

4 Weissman, AD: The Realization of Death. Aronson, New York, 1974

5 Kastenbaum, R: Is death a life crisis? On the confrontation with death in theory and practice. In Datan, N, and Ginsberg, LH (eds): Life Span Developmental Psychology: Normative Life Crisis. Academic Press, New York, 1975, pp 15–50.

6 Giacquinta, B: Helping families face the crisis of cancer. AJN 10:1585, 1977.

7 Morris, W (ed): The American Heritage Dictionary of the English Language. Houghton-Mifflin, Boston, 1976, p 636.

8 Zimmerman, J: Hospice: Complete Care for the Terminally Ill. Urban & Schwarzenberg, Baltimore, 1981.

9 Munley, A: The Hospice Alternative: A New Context for Death and Dying. Basic Books, New York, 1983.

10 Saunders, C: The last stages of life. AJN 3:70, 1965.

11 Glasser, BG, and Strauss, AL: Awareness of Dying. Aldine-Atheton, Chicago, 1965, pp 119–121.

12 Bass, D, and Bowman, K: The transition from caregiving to bereavement: The relationship of care-related strain and adjustment to death. Gerontologist 30:35, 1990.

13 Engel, G: Grief and grieving. AJN 64:93, 1964.

14 Lazarus, R: Psychological stress and coping in adaptation and illness. Int J Psychiatr Med 5(4):329, 1975.

15 Haight, BK: The therapeutic role of a structured life review process in homebound elderly subjects. J Gerontol 43:40, 1988.

16 Harris, MD: Animal-assisted therapy for the homebound elderly. Holistic Nurs Pract 8:27, 1993.

17 Christenson, J: Generational value differences. Gerontologist 17:367, 1977.

18 Scholg, J: Cultural expressions affecting patient care. Dimensions Oncol Nurs 4(1):18, 1990.

19 Kübler-Ross, E: Death: The Final Stage of Growth. Prentice Hall, Englewood Cliffs, NJ, 1975, p 80.

20 Weisman, AD: Coping with Cancer. McGraw-Hill, New York, 1979.

21 Forbes, SB: Hope: an essential human need in the elderly. J Gerontol Nurs 20:5, 1994.

22 Hickey, SS: Enabling hope. Cancer Nurs 9:133, 1986.

23 Chipman, Y: Caring: Its meaning and place in the practice of nursing. J Nurs Educ 30:172, 1991.

24 Kreps, GL, and Thornton, BC: Health Communication: Theory and Practice. Longman, New York, 1984, p 104.

25 Thomas, MD: Trust in the nurse-patient relationship. In Carlson, C (ed): Behavior Concepts and Nursing Intervention. JB Lippincott, Philadelphia, 1970, p 119.

26 Benoliel, JQ: Care, communication and human dignity. In Garfield, C (ed): Psychosocial Care of the Dying Patient. McGraw-Hill, New York, 1978, p 39.

27 Montague, A: Touching: The Human Significance of the Skin. Harper & Row, New York, 1986, p 391.

28 Bradley, J, and Edenberg, MA: Communication in the Nursing Context. Appleton & Lange, Norwalk, Conn, 1990, p 37.

Alterations in Mental Processing

Sleep Disturbances

Sr. Rose Therese Bahr

OBJECTIVES

Upon completion of this chapter, the reader will be able to:

- Define sleep and sleep disturbances (e.g., insomnia, hypersomnia, sleep apnea)
- Identify the five stages of sleep patterns in terms of rapid eye movement and non–rapid eye movement sleep
- Describe the clinical manifestations of sleep disturbances in older adults
- Discuss the primary, secondary, and tertiary management of sleep disturbances in older adults by stating a nursing diagnosis with appropriate nursing interventions
- Analyze a research study conducted on sleep and wakefulness patterns in institutionalized older adults
- Implement teaching guides for health instruction of older adults and family members in maintenance of healthy sleep patterns

An area of great interest to older adults is that of health promotion. One major aspect of health promotion for the aging person is sleep maintenance to ensure restoration of bodily function to the optimal level of functioning and to ensure daytime alertness to accomplish tasks and enjoy a high quality of life.

Most older adults are at risk for sleep disturbance that may be caused by many factors (e.g., retirement and changes in social patterns, death of a spouse or close friend, increased use of medications, concurrent diseases, changes in circadian rhythms). Although changes in sleep patterns are viewed as part of the normal aging process, recent information indicates that many of these disturbances may be related to pathological processes that accompany aging.[1]

Before discussing the issue of sleep disorders in older adults, a brief overview of sleep as a normal, healthy function is necessary to appreciate how sleep changes may occur in older adults.

Sleep

A HEALTH PROMOTION ACTIVITY

Sleep is considered by Johnson[2] to be "one of the basic physiological needs experienced by human beings." Sleep occurs naturally, with inherent physiological and psychological functions that impart the restorative re-

pair processes of the body. Physiologically, when a person does not experience sufficient sleep to maintain a healthy body, effects such as forgetfulness, confusion, and disorientation may occur, particularly if sleep deprivation exists over a prolonged period.[3] Untoward effects of sleep deprivation on the already confused client, particularly one with Alzheimer's disease, include increased agitation, wandering behavior, restlessness, and sundown syndrome.[4-6]

Psychologically, sleep allows the person to experience a sense of well-being and psychic energy and alertness to accomplish tasks. Work performance, alertness, level of activity, and wellness are affected when sleep and wakefulness patterns are disrupted.[7,8] Snyder[9] suggests that the length of sleep periods may influence mortality rates. Data from a 6-year study[10] supported the hypothesis that people who have unusually long or short periods of sleep or who use sleeping pills have a significantly higher mortality rate than others. The lowest mortality rate from this study was found among those who slept 7 or 8 hours a night.

Sleep is a rhythmic and cyclical behavioral state that occurs in five stages (four non–rapid eye movement [NREM] and one rapid eye movement [REM]), as indicated by electroencephalogram (EEG) tracings, eye movements, and muscle movements.[11,12] In the awake stage, an EEG tracing is of low voltage, with random, fast waves, as noted in Figure 34–1. Stage 1 NREM sleep is identified by waves of low voltage, three to seven cycles

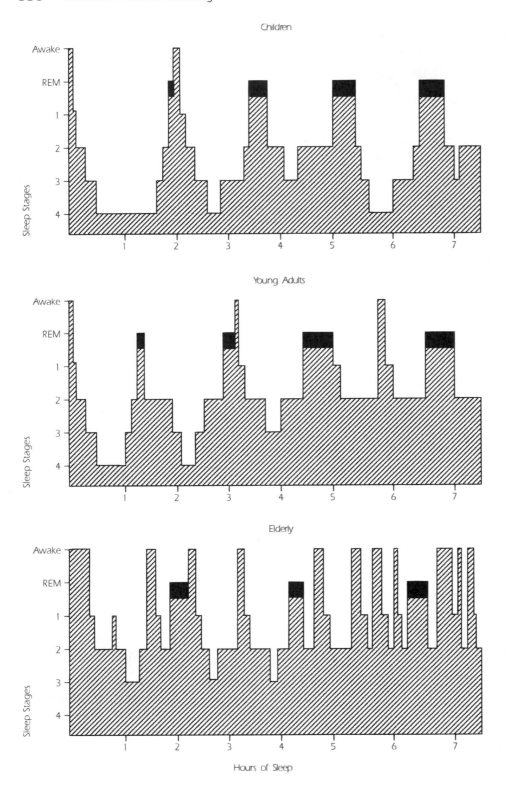

Figure 34–1   Human sleep stages. (From Hauri, P: The Sleep Disorders. Upjohn, Kalamazoo, MI, 1982, p 7, with permission.)

per second (cps), known as theta waves. Within a few seconds, stage 2 NREM sleep continues, characterized by 12 to 14 cps.

The EEG reveals sleep spindles and high-voltage spikes known as K complexes, described by Kleitman et al.[13] as well-delineated, slow, negative EEG deflections that are followed by a positive component. Stage 2 is

the first bona fide sleep stage, and mentation during this stage consists of short, mundane, and fragmented thoughts.[14] Stage 3 follows shortly thereafter and is the medium deep sleep stage. Stage 4 (delta) sleep is distinguished by slow delta waves, which characterize the deepest stage of sleep. REM sleep follows; at this stage, EEG tracings show low-voltage, random, fast movements of brain activity with sawtooth waves. REM sleep alternates with NREM sleep at about 90-minute intervals in adults.

About 80 percent of people awakened from REM sleep may recall dreams,[8] whereas only about 5 percent of NREM awakenings result in full-fledged dream reports. Between 60 and 80 percent of people awakened from NREM sleep can recall some fragments of thought (e.g., a line, a number, a face).[14,15]

SLEEP CYCLES

After going to bed, the person first passes through a stage of relaxed wakefulness characterized by alpha waves. The person then progresses through the stages of sleep in the following order: 1, 2, 3, 4, 3, 2, REM. Then stage 2 begins again unless the person wakes up. If the person awakens and then returns to sleep, which is common in older adults, stage 1 sleep begins again. In normal sleep patterns, about 70 to 90 minutes after sleep onset, the first REM period begins, alternating with NREM sleep in 90-minute cycles throughout the nocturnal sleep period.[3] The consequences of awakening, as occurs for nighttime toileting or nursing procedures, may

have detrimental effects on the older adult's physiological and mental functioning.[16,17]

Clinical Manifestations

SLEEP DISORDERS IN OLDER ADULTS

As mentioned earlier, a large proportion of older adults are at high risk for sleep disturbances as a result of various factors.[1] Pathological age-related processes may cause sleep pattern changes. Sleep disturbances affect 50 percent of people age 65 and older who live at home and 66 percent of those who live in long-term care facilities. Sleep disturbances and disorders affect the quality of life and have been associated with higher rates of mortality.[1]

During aging, sleep patterns undergo typical changes that distinguish them from those in earlier life (Fig. 34–2). These changes include increased sleep latency, early morning waking, and an increased number of daytime naps.[18] The amount of time spent in deeper levels of sleep diminishes. There is an associated increase in awakenings during sleep and in the total amount of time spent awake during the night. There appears to be a

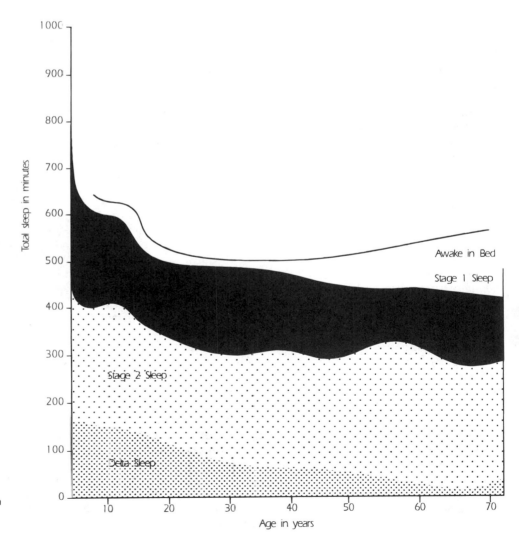

Figure 34–2 Development of sleep over a lifetime. (Adapted from Williams, RL, Karacan, I, and Hursch, CJ: Electroencephalography (EEG) of Human Sleep: Clinical Applications. John Wiley & Sons, New York, 1974, p. 490, with permission.)

RESEARCH BRIEF

Simpson, T, et al: Relationships among sleep dimensions and factors that impair sleep after cardiac surgery. Res Nurs Health 19(3):213, 1996.

A population of 97 cardiac surgery patients with the average age of 62 was studied several days before discharge to determine factors associated with the attempted length, effectiveness, disturbance, and nap supplementation of sleep. The group averaged little sleep with moderate disturbance and effectiveness and low nap supplementation. Factors influencing sleep included an inability to perform their usual routines before sleep, inability to get comfortable, noises, procedural care, pain, and an unfamiliar bed. Patients encounter sleep difficulties in this environment; consequently, nursing interventions are necessary to minimize these factors so that restorative powers of sleep might become a possibility for this aging population.

loss of effective circadian regulation of sleep ("Research Brief").

Among healthy older adults, few have symptoms related to changes in sleep and the distribution of sleep and waking behaviors.[1] However, many older people who have a variety of medical and psychosocial problems often have sleep disturbances. These conditions include the following:

- Psychiatric illnesses, particularly depression
- Alzheimer's disease and other neurodegenerative diseases
- Cardiovascular disease and cardiac surgery postoperative care[19,20]
- Upper airway incompetence
- Pulmonary disease
- Pain syndromes
- Prostatic disease
- Endocrinopathies

Three major complaints or disorders of initiating and maintaining sleep are prevalent among older adults.

Insomnia

Insomnia is an inability to sleep despite the desire to do so.[21] Older people are susceptible to insomnia as a result of changing sleep patterns, usually affecting stage 4 (deep sleep). Complaints of insomnia include the "inability to fall asleep, frequent awakenings, inability to return to sleep and early morning arousal."[10] Because insomnia is a symptom, attention must be given to contributing biological, emotional, and medical factors, as well as to poor sleeping habits. Insomnia may be of three types:

- *Short-term:* Lasts a few weeks and arises from temporary stressful experiences such as loss of a loved one, pressures at work, or fear of losing a job.

Usually this condition can be resolved without medical intervention as the person adapts to the stressor.
- *Transient:* Occasional episodes of restless nights caused by environmental changes such as jet lag, noisy construction near the person's home, or anxiety-producing experiences.
- *Chronic:* Lasts 3 weeks or throughout one's life. This condition can be caused by poor sleeping habits, psychological problems, extended use of sleep medication, excessive use of alcohol, disruptive sleep-wake schedules, and other health problems[6] Forty percent of chronic insomnia is caused by physical problems such as sleep apnea, restless leg syndrome, or chronic pain from arthritis.[21-23] Chronic insomnia usually requires psychiatric or medical intervention for its resolution.[10]

Hypersomnia

Hypersomnia is characterized by sleep times of more than 8 or 9 hours per 24-hour period, with complaints of sleep excessiveness. The causes of hypersomnia are speculative but may be related to inactivity, boring lifestyle, or depression.[15] The person may exhibit persistent daytime drowsiness, have "sleep attacks," appear to be drugged or comatose, or experience postencephalitic drowsiness.[15] Complaints of fatigue, weakness, and memory and learning difficulties are common.

Sleep Apnea

Sleep apnea is a cessation of breathing during sleep. This disorder is identified by symptoms of "snoring, interrupted breathing of at least 10 seconds, and unusual daytime sleepiness."[24] During sleep, breathing may be interrupted as many as 300 times, and apneic episodes may last from 10 to 90 seconds.[25] Adult men with a long history of loud, intermittent snoring who are obese with short, thick necks are usually at risk for sleep apnea. Symptoms of sleep apnea include the following[18,21]:

- Loud, periodic snoring
- Unusual nighttime activities such as sitting upright, sleep-walking, falling out of bed
- Broken sleep with frequent nocturnal waking
- Memory changes
- Depression
- Excessive daytime sleepiness
- Nocturia
- Morning headaches
- Orthopnea resulting from sleep apnea

Specific treatment of sleep apnea involves weight loss, with medical management or surgery to remove redundant tissue in the pharyngeal area. Patients may be advised to avoid alcohol and drugs that may interfere with the arousal response and to use extra pillows or to sleep in a chair.

All of these measures may help reduce the possibility of complications caused by sleep apnea. Table 34–1 lists several centers specializing in the diagnosis of sleep disorders.

TABLE 34–1   RESOURCES

Dartmouth-Hitchcock Sleep Disorders Center
Dartmouth Medical School
Hanover, NH 03756

Sleep Disorders Center
Boston City Hospital
808 Harrison Avenue
Boston, MA 02118

Sleep Disorders Center
Presbyterian Hospital
700 NE 13th Street
Oklahoma City, OK 73104

Sleep Disorders Center
Stanford University Medical Center
Stanford, CA 94305

Sleep Disorders Center
University of Cincinnati Hospital
234 Goodman Street
Cincinnati, OH 45267

Management of Sleep Disorders in Older Adults

1 Primary Prevention

Eleven rules for better sleep hygiene have been identified for primary prevention of sleep disturbances and disorders.

1 Sleep as much as needed, but not more, to feel refreshed and healthy the following day. Limiting the time in bed seems to solidify sleep; excessive time spent in bed seems to be related to fragmented and shallow sleep.

2 A regular arousal time in the morning strengthens circadian cycling and leads to regular times of sleep onset.

3 A steady daily amount of exercise probably deepens sleep; however, occasional exercise does not necessarily improve sleep the following night.

4 Occasional loud noises (e.g., aircraft flyovers) disturb sleep even in people who are not awakened by noise and cannot remember them in the morning. Sound-attenuated bedrooms may help those who must sleep close to noise.

5 Although excessively warm rooms disturb sleep, there is no evidence that an excessively cold room solidifies sleep.

6 Hunger may disturb sleep; a light snack may help sleep.

7 An occasional sleeping pill may be of some benefit, but their chronic use is ineffective in most insomniacs.

8 Caffeine in the evening disturbs sleep, even in those who think it does not.

9 Alcohol helps tense people to fall asleep more easily, but the ensuing sleep is then fragmented.

10 People who feel angry and frustrated because they cannot sleep should not try harder and

harder to fall asleep but should turn on the light and do something different.

11 The chronic use of tobacco disturbs sleep.[21]

Other primary preventive measures include the following[8,23]:

- A good mattress allows for proper alignment of the body.
- Temperature in bedroom should be cool enough (less than 75°F) to be comfortable.
- Caloric intake should be minimal at bedtime.
- Moderate exercise in the afternoon or early evening is advised.[13]

Table 34–2 provides a guide for patient teaching about sleeping disorders.

2 Secondary Prevention

Assessment by the nurse should include the following factors:

- How well the older person sleeps at home
- How many times the older person awakens at night
- What time the older person retires and arises
- What rituals occur at bedtime (e.g., bedtime snacks, watching television, listening to music, reading)
- What amount and type of exercise is performed on a daily basis
- What is the favorite position when in bed
- What kind of room environment is preferred (quiet, soft music, dim night-light, totally dark, door closed)

TABLE 34–2   TEACHING GUIDES: SLEEP AND WELLNESS

The older adult or family members should be taught about sleep as a wellness measure. Guidelines contributing to good-quality and adequate sleep, allowing the body to relax and be restored physically and mentally, include the following:

- Maintain an appropriate balance among rest, sleep, and activity.
- Manage the environmental factors to fall asleep in a manner that allows adequate restful sleep (lower volume on radio or television to reduce noise level).
- Reduce stress or tension of daily lifestyle to the degree possible to allow for adequate rest.
- Maintain comfort level in home and bedroom to ensure good-quality and adequate sleep.
- Ensure appropriate use of over-the-counter or prescribed medications that may affect sleep patterns (e.g., take drugs such as Lasix in the morning so that nightly sleep is not disturbed).
- Keep environmental stimuli to a minimum (e.g., dim night-light instead of high-intensity ceiling light in bathroom).
- Initiate safety precautions in sleep areas (e.g., move furniture out of pathway to bathroom).
- When usual sleep pattern is interrupted, stay calm and get up to read a book in another room until sleepiness occurs.
- Family or significant others must be supportive in helping to establish and maintain healthy sleep-rest patterns.

- What level of temperature is preferred
- How much ventilation is desired
- What activities are usually engaged in several hours before bedtime
- What sleep medications and other medications are ingested routinely
- How much time the person engages in hobbies
- The person's perception of his or her life satisfaction and health status[7]

As always, it is important to validate the assessment history with a family member or caregiver to ensure the accuracy of the assessment data if the patient is not considered competent to give a self-report.[10]

A sleep diary is an excellent mode of assessment for an older adult in his or her own home. This information provides an accurate record of any sleep problem. To obtain a true picture of sleep disturbances experienced by an older adult in the home setting or in a health facility, a diary should be kept for 3 to 4 weeks. A record should be kept of the following factors:

- How often assistance is needed for pain medication administration, inability to sleep, or bathroom use
- When the person is out of bed
- Number of times person is awake or asleep when observed by nurse or caregiver
- Occurrences of confusion or disorientation
- Use of sleep medication
- Approximate time the person awakens in the morning[10]

Therapeutic Management

Bootzin and Nicassio[26] suggest the following rules to maintain normalcy of sleep patterns:

- Go to bed only when sleepy.
- Use the bed only for sleeping; do not read, watch television, or eat in bed.
- If unable to sleep, get up and move to another room. Stay up until you are really sleepy, then return to bed. If sleep still does not come easily, get out of bed again. The goal is to associate bed with falling asleep quickly. Repeat this step as often as necessary throughout the night.
- Set the alarm and get up at the same time every morning regardless of how much you slept during the night. This helps the body acquire a constant sleep-wake rhythm.
- Do not nap during the day.[13]

Nursing Interventions

The following nursing interventions are recommended[21]:

- Maintain conditions conducive to sleep, which include attention to environmental factors and performance of bedtime rituals.
- Help the person relax at bedtime by giving a backrub, foot massage, or bedtime snack if desired. Passive exercise and stroking motions have a soporific effect.
- Proper positioning, alleviation of pain, and the provision of warmth with conventional blankets or an electric blanket is helpful.
- Do not permit caffeine (coffee, tea, chocolate) in the afternoon and evening.
- Use common-sense measures such as playing soft music on the radio and offering warm milk and other warm beverages or more substantial snacks to promote sleep in older adults without the use of hypnotics. At times, a nightcap of wine, sherry, brandy, or beer provides the internal warmth and relaxation the older person needs to fall asleep. However, the effects of one drink last for only two-thirds of the sleep cycle. Sedation wears off in the same amount of time, resulting in sleep fragmentation.
- Daytime napping is appropriate; however, total napping time should not exceed 2 hours.
- Daily exercise should be encouraged. It is one of the best promoters of sleep. Exercise should occur early in the day rather than close to bedtime because at that hour it may have an exhilarating rather than a soporific effect.
- Warm baths are sometimes relaxing for older adults but some dislike this intervention, complaining of dizziness when they emerge from the tub.

If these measures fail to improve the quality of sleep, drugs may be useful for a limited time, but only as a last resort. Ebersole and Hess[10] have identified various drugs as options for sleep inducement (Table 34–3).

The skillful nurse must be highly vigilant regarding the use of drugs and must assess the older adult frequently to ensure that excessive daytime drowsiness, confusion, and disorientation are not occurring. If evidence of any of these conditions appears, the drugs should be gradually withdrawn and nonpharmacological measures initiated.

3 Tertiary Prevention

If sleep disturbances such as life-threatening sleep apnea persist, the patient's condition may require rehabilitation through measures such as removal of obstructive tissue in the mouth that interfere with breathing passages. Many sleep disorder centers are now available around the country to evaluate sleep disturbances. These sleep centers, which are usually attached to research and clinical medical centers or universities, are equipped to detect brain electrical tracings and obstructed breathing through sophisticated medical devices. These data are helpful in determining the best treatment for correcting the difficulty and rehabilitating the older adult so that good-quality sleep can be enjoyed to the end of one's natural life.

TABLE 34–3 DRUGS AND OPTIONS FOR SLEEP INDUCEMENT

Choices	Dosage	Effect
L-Tryptophan	0.5–1 g just before bedtime	Converts to serotonin in brain; facilitates falling asleep sooner.
Sherry	Small glass at bedtime	Alcohol is a depressant; a small amount hastens sleep.
Antihistamine diphenhydramine (Benadryl)	25–50 mg	Produces drowsiness; some people become sensitized to muscle relaxant; relief of tension and anxiety.
Anxiolytic hydroxyzine (Vistaril)	50 mg	
Hypnotic chloral hydrate	250–500 mg	Produces drowsiness but may cause hyperstimulating effects.
Benzodiazepines		
Triazolam (Halcion)	0.125 mg	Hastens onset of sleep.
Temazepam (Restoril)	15–30 mg	Reduces sleep pattern distortion.

Student Learning Activities

1 Observe the routines on the evening and night shift in your clinical facility. How do these routines affect an older adult's ability to obtain needed hours of sleep?

2 Review the medication profile of an older adult. Which of these medications have intended effects or side effects that promote or disrupt sleep?

3 Develop a plan for the hospitalized older adult that includes health promotion activities related to sleep.

REFERENCES

1 National Institute of Health: The Treatment of Sleep Disorders of Older Adults. Consensus Development Conference, Washington, DC, March 26–28, 1990.

2 Johnson, J: Sleep and bedtime routines of noninstitutionalized aged women. J Commun Health Nurs 3(3):117, 1986.

3 Ancoli-Israel, S, and Kripke, D: Sleep and aging. In Calkins, E, et al (eds): The Practice of Geriatrics. WB Saunders, Philadelphia, 1986.

4 Hoch, CC, et al: Sleep patterns in depressed and healthy elderly. West J Nurs Res 10:239, 1988.

5 Evans, LK: Sundown syndrome in the elderly: A phenomenon in search of exploration. Journal of the University of Pennsylvania Center for Study of Aging 7:7, 1985.

6 Johnson, JE: Sleep problems and self care in the very old rural women: Nursing implications. Geriatr Nurs 17:2, 72, 1996.

7 Bahr, RT: Sleep-wake patterns in the aged. J Gerontol Nurs 9:534, 1983.

8 Bahr, RT, and Gress, L: The 24-hour cycle: Rhythms of healthy sleep. J Gerontol Nurs 8:323, 1985.

9 Snyder, F: Psychophysiology of human sleep. Clin Neurosurg 18:503, 1971.

10 Ebersole, P, and Hess, P: Life support needs. In Toward Healthy Aging: Human Needs and Nursing Responses, ed 3. CV Mosby, St Louis, 1990, p 187.

11 Lucas, EA, et al: The polysomnographic diagnoses of sleep disorders in elderly medical patients. Ala J Med Sci 10:239, 1988.

12 Prinz, PN, et al: Changes in the sleep and waking EEGs of nondemented and demented elderly subjects. J Am Geriatr Soc 30:86, 1982.

13 Kleitman, E, et al: Sleep Characteristics. University of Chicago Press, Chicago, 1937.

14 Foulkes, WD: Dream reports from different stages of sleep. J Abnorm Psychol 65:14, 1962.

15 Dement, WC, et al: White paper on sleep and aging. J Gerontol 30:25, 1982.

16 Lerner, R: Sleep loss in the aged: Implications for nursing research. J Gerontol Nurs 8:323, 1982.

17 Moffat, A: Immunity booster: "Get a good night's sleep." Am Health 7:54, 1986.

18 Hayter, J: To nap or not to nap. Geriatr Nurs 6:104, 1985.

19 Simpson, T, et al: Relationships among sleep dimensions and factors that impair sleep after cardiac surgery. Res Nurs Health 19(3):213, 1996.

20 Simpson, T, and Lee, ER: Individual factors that influence sleep after cardiac surgery. Am J Crit Care 5(3):173, 1996.

21 Snow, TL: Getting a good night's sleep: Sleep disturbances in the elderly. In Focus on Geriatric Care and Rehabilitation, 2(2), Aspen, Frederick, Md, 1988.

22 Houldin, AD, et al: Sleep-rest. In Nursing Diagnosis for Wellness: Supporting Strengths. JB Lippincott, Philadelphia, 1987, p 101.

23 Muncy, JH: Measures to rid sleeplessness. J Gerontol Nurs 12:6, 1986.

24 Kotagal, S, and Dement, W: Overview of sleep apnea and its prevalence in the elderly. Consultant 25:86, 1985.

25 Jaquis, J: Obstructive sleep apnea syndrome. Nurse Pract 12:50, 1987.

26 Bootzin, RR, and Nicassio, PN: Behavioral treatments for insomnia. In Hersen, M, et al (eds): Progress in Behavior Modifications. Academic Press, New York, 1978.

CHAPTER 35

Acute Confusion

Mickey Stanley

OBJECTIVES

Upon completion of this chapter, the reader will be able to:

- Define acute confusion
- Identify potential causes of acute confusion
- List signs and symptoms of acute confusion among older adults
- Discuss methods of primary, secondary, and tertiary prevention of acute confusion
- Describe the nurse's role in the management of acutely confused older adults
- Discuss the guidelines for the use of physical and chemical restraints in a confused older adult

Few problems associated with advanced age produce more fear in older adults and frustration among caregivers than acute confusion. The older adult fears loss of control over self and his or her destiny when the mind is no longer capable of its usual functions. Caregivers become frustrated when older adults lose their ability to reason, to communicate in previously established patterns, and to perform basic activities of daily living (ADLs).

Impact of Acute Confusion

The literature indicates that up to 50 percent of hospitalized older adults experience acute confusion.[1] However, only 3 of 10 confused older adults are diagnosed by their attending physician or nursing staff as experiencing acute confusion.[1] Reasons for this failure to recognize changes in mental status include the assumption that changes in cognition are a normal result of aging and a haphazard or incomplete assessment of cognitive function for acutely ill older adults.[1,2] The consequences of acute confusion can be devastating financially, physically, and emotionally. For example, confused patients require more intensive nursing services, require a longer hospitalization, and are more likely to need nursing home placement after discharge.[2] They are frightening to themselves, their families, and other patients. Unrecognized and untreated acute confusion may progress to chronic cerebral dysfunction resembling dementia.[3] In addition, studies have shown that as many as one-third of those affected will die.[1]

Nature of the Problem

Acute confusion can best be described as a poorly understood syndrome that results from a variety of mechanisms that produce brain dysfunction. Confusion is not a disease but rather a secondary response to a cause. The causes are considered to be either organic (i.e., hypoxia) or nonorganic (i.e., stress related).[4]

DEFINITION OF CONFUSION

Delirium is the medically correct term for the constellation of behaviors that represent what is called acute confusion in the nursing literature. Synonyms include *intensive care unit (ICU) psychosis, postcardiotomy delirium,* and *acute brain failure,* all of which refer to a syndrome characterized by a global cognitive impairment of abrupt onset.[3] The older person's ability to process incoming stimuli in a meaningful way is lost. The ability to reason, follow commands, attend to stimuli, and concentrate is altered.[2] The person's sleep-wake cycle is disrupted, recent memory is lost, and inappropriate verbal and motor behavior is experienced.[2,3] Older adults are often aware of these difficulties and can be frightened by the realization that they are "losing their minds."

Acute confusion or delirium is distinguished from dementia in terms of chronicity. Delirium has an abrupt onset and a usual duration of less than 1 month if the cause is recognized and treatment instituted.[2,4] Dementia is gradual in onset with progressive symptoms, lasts

RESEARCH BRIEF 1

Kroeger, LL: Critical care nurses' perceptions of confused elderly patients. Focus 18:295, 1991.

In this study, vignettes were used to determine critical care nurses' knowledge of the causes of and appropriate interventions for acute confusion among critically ill older adults. Although data were provided that indicated the patient in the vignette was hypoxic and had received a hypnotic, 78 percent of the nurses in the sample chose intensive care unit psychosis as the cause of the acute confusion.

for more than 3 months, and is irreversible. In practice, however, the two conditions are difficult to separate and the diagnosis is often made in retrospect. See Chapter 36 for a thorough discussion of dementia in older adults.

CAUSES OF CONFUSION

Two hypotheses currently exist about the causes of acute confusion. The first suggests that in response to a change in cerebral oxidative metabolism, there is a reduced synthesis or impaired release of one or more neurotransmitter substances (brain dopamine and acetylcholine).[5] An imbalance in the neurotransmitter substances interferes with the regulation of sleep, arousal, blood pressure, body temperature, learning, or affect.[4] This hypothesis is supported by the calming effect achieved with the antipsychotic agent haloperidol (Haldol), which antagonizes postsynaptic dopamine and re-establishes chemical equilibrium of the dopamine-acetylcholine system in the brain.[6] The second hypothesis suggests that acute confusion is a stress reaction mediated by the elevated plasma cortisol and its effect on the brain.[1]

A variety of conditions produce the symptoms of confusion. A representative list of organic causes of acute confusion can be found in Table 35–1. All of these conditions share the potential to disrupt the delicate balance required by the older brain for effective functioning. Previous literature has also identified environmental conditions such as sensory overload and sensory deprivation as causes of acute confusion.[1] Adams[6] suggests that sensory-induced psychosis is the result of the brain's failure to process information, rather than the cause of the failure. For example, sleep deprivation has been suggested as a cause of acute confusion. However, Adams[6] notes that, instead of being a cause of brain failure, sleep deprivation is a symptom of the condition resulting from an imbalance between brain dopamine and acetylcholine, which alters the sleep-wake cycle.

Although not considered causal in nature, personal and perceptual factors are important contributors to the development of acute confusion. Included in the personal factors are the concepts of exclusion and traumatic relocation. Exclusion is the practice of depersonal-

ization of older adults by caregivers. Drew[7] describes exclusion as the lack of emotional warmth by health-care personnel, citing as an example the nurse who is more interested in the bedside equipment than in the person lying in the bed. This care that is devoid of caring is called hollow expertise.[7] For patients who perceive themselves as a bother to the nurse, as many older patients do, this experience is stressful, requiring additional coping resources at a time when internal demands are high.

Traumatic relocation refers to the difficulties older adults experience in response to an abrupt or unplanned admission to an acute-care or long-term care facility.[2] Most adults, particularly older adults, gain a sense of who they are based on their perception of their life's accomplishments. Older adults often fill their personal space with reminders such as family pictures and mementos of the past. To be suddenly removed from their usual environment and routine and moved to a strange setting that is devoid of any personal effects is a disorienting experience leading to feelings of depersonalization and an altered self-concept.

Perceptual factors that promote the development of acute confusion include vision and hearing loss. Without these important senses, incoming stimuli are distorted or missed altogether. We all adapt to our environment through our senses, by using our intellectual senses and by moving around in our immediate environment. The way we code and make sense of the incoming stimuli is learned. For older adults, learning is slow and requires more frequent rehearsal of information. Learning is more effective when the content can be related to previously learned information. When the stimuli are foreign and distorted, the older adult may attempt to place this new information into a previously learned context. As a result, the older person may call out for a deceased loved one or behave as though he or she were in another setting.

Based on this information, consider the scenario of an older adult who is acutely ill and is transported to the

TABLE 35–1 ORGANIC CAUSES OF ACUTE CONFUSION

Acid-base imbalance	Electrolyte imbalance
Dehydration	Endocrine dysfunction
Drug withdrawal	Hypoglycemia
Barbiturates	Hypothyroidism and
Hypnotics	hyperthyroidism
Tranquilizers	Hepatic encephalopathy
Drugs	Hypotension and cerebral
Anticholinergics	ischemia
Anticonvulsants	Hypothermia and hyperthermia
Antidysrhythmics	Hypoxia
Antimicrobials	Infection and sepsis
Antiparkinsonism drugs	Upper respiratory tract
Bronchodilators	Urinary tract
Histamine blockers	Nutritional imbalances
Opiates and synthetic	Hypoproteinemia
narcotics	Vitamin deficiencies
Salicylates	
Tricyclic antidepressants	

Source: Adapted from Ludwig,[4] p 62.

TABLE 35–2 PRODROMAL SIGNS AND SYMPTOMS OF ACUTE CONFUSION

Insomnia	Vivid dreams or nightmares
Distractibility	Complaints of difficulty
Hypersensitivity to light	remembering
and sound	Excessive fatigue
Drowsiness	Short attention span
Anxiety	

acute-care facility via emergency medical services. The older person is abruptly removed from a familiar environment, hurried through multiple services such as the emergency and radiography departments, and admitted to the nursing unit. He or she is confined to bed with glasses and hearing aid removed, asked repeated questions, and given hurried explanations. Under these conditions, it is surprising that not all older adults become acutely confused.

Clinical Manifestations

Nurses and physicians often fail to recognize the early cues to acute confusion because the behavioral manifestations are often subtle and varied. Table 35–2 lists early or prodromal signs and symptoms of acute confusion.[4]

Three distinct forms of acute confusion have been recorded.[3] The most commonly recognized is the hyperactive form. The patient with this form of acute confusion may remove intravenous (IV) lines and dressings, pick at things in the air, climb over side rails, and call out for deceased loved ones. The autonomic nervous system response of tachycardia, dilated pupils, diaphoresis, and a flushed complexion may be seen.

In contrast to the hyperactive form, a hypoactive form has been noted. Older adults with this form of acute confusion are easily ignored and go undiagnosed because of their quiet, nondemanding behavior. Hypoactive confusion is characterized by excessive fatigue and hypersomnolence, progressing to loss of consciousness. This form may be misdiagnosed as depression.

However, most older adults fluctuate between hyperactive and hypoactive states, which constitutes the third form, mixed acute confusion. Agitation and hallucinations are often worse at night and alternate with lucid intervals during the daytime.

Nursing Management

1 Primary Prevention

Primary prevention for acute confusion begins with an understanding that it is not a normal consequence of aging. Rather, acute confusion has preventable causes. In general terms, the approach to primary prevention involves maintaining a homeostatic balance for the brain and limiting stressors that overtax the coping skills of older adults.

Nutrition and hydration programs are essential to the effective functioning of the brain. Conditions that produce confusion such as nutritional anemia, folic acid deficiency, and electrolyte imbalance (including magnesium) can be prevented through proper diet. Dehydration is common among older adults because of age-related changes in thirst sensation and frequent use of diuretics. A real challenge to nursing is to ensure that all older adults consume a balanced diet and approximately six 8-oz glasses of clear fluids daily, unless contraindicated by renal or heart failure. Community-dwelling and institutionalized older adults are at risk for nutritional and fluid imbalances and require nursing intervention through assessment, teaching, and program development.

A critical primary prevention measure for older adults in all settings is mental and physical activity. Case study reports have shown that older people who remain mentally alert and oriented well into the eighth and ninth decades are those who are interested and participate in life. For more on mental health, see Chapter 3.

The physical environment in the acute-care and long-term care setting must be structured to facilitate mental and physical activity. The client should have access to such sensory stimuli as radio or television. Programs such as old movies, local news broadcasts, and religious services that are chosen and attended to by the older adult have an orienting effect. However, when such stimuli are continuous, they become a source of disorientation and may trigger hallucinations. Inappropriate programs such as cartoons, continuous situation comedies, and violent programs may contribute to the older patient's confused state.

Appropriate use of color to aid the older adult's eye in discriminating between changing surfaces, use of nonglare lighting, removal of hallway clutter, and provision of a space for social interaction encourage older adults to be ambulatory. Remaining physically and socially active, even in the acute-care or long-term care setting, is key to maintaining cognitive function.

Because many episodes of acute confusion are attributed to the effects of drugs,[1,2] a primary prevention strategy is to avoid the use of drugs when possible. Table 35–1 lists the most common drugs known to produce confusion in this population. Using nonpharmacological approaches to induce sleep is an excellent example of this principle. If drugs are required, they should be started at the lowest possible dosage and increased to effect, or when one drug is added to the regimen, another should be deleted. For a more detailed discussion of this topic, see Chapter 8.

The older adult must not be infantilized or treated in a childlike manner. For example, calling adult incontinence pads "diapers" and the commode a "potty," as well as taking over decision making for older adults, strips them of their personal dignity and produces feelings of incompetence. All older adults should be assumed to be capable of participating in decisions regarding care and should not be forced into dependence out of convenience or expedience for the staff. Brannstrom et al.[8] found a higher incidence of confusion in task-

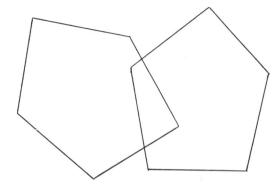

Figure 35–1 Intersecting pentagons.

oriented nursing units where ADLs were performed for older adults to get the work done on time ("Research Brief 2"). Caregivers must treat older adults as individuals and demonstrate a sense of caring and concern to avoid the problem of exclusion.

Additional primary prevention measures have been effective in reducing the incidence of confusion for older adults who have had surgery. These measures include continuous monitoring of oxygen saturation and blood pressure levels, with aggressive intervention to prevent hypoxia and episodes of hypotension, two factors that affect cerebral oxidative metabolism and produce confusion. The use of thermal head covers and limb drapes and the use of warmed IV fluids to prevent iatrogenic hypothermia have been found to decrease the incidence of postoperative confusion.[9]

2 Secondary Prevention

Assessment

Early and accurate assessment of changes in mental status is essential to preventing the devastating consequences of acute confusion. To obtain an accurate assessment, the caregiver must use a systematic approach and allow sufficient time for the person to respond. An older adult's cultural background and educational level must be considered when evaluating behavior, reasoning ability, and understanding of the current situation. Knowledge of the patient's usual personality and ability provides a basis for evaluation of cognitive abilities. Wolanin[10] states:

> Baseline information is important, and should be gathered on admission rather than after strange behavior forces the issue. Remember, there are people who have never expressed a coherent thought in their lives. It is their normal, natural state—normal for them.

Many nurses continue to rely solely on the components of orientation—person, place, and time—to determine whether mental status changes have occurred. However, research has demonstrated that these elements are the least sensitive markers of confusion. The cognitive aspects of attention and concentration are currently considered early markers of brain dysfunction.[2] These areas are easily assessed by asking the patient to count backward from 20 by threes or to draw something such as intersecting pentagons (Fig. 35–1).

Verbal and motor behavior is important to assess. Repeatedly asking the same question, changing the subject, or using sarcasm or witty remarks can signal faulty memory. Restlessness or excessive somnolence may be early warning signs. The inconsistent ability to perform ADLs is another possible early indicator of acute confusion. However, agitation is a late sign of acute confusion and is thought to occur in less than 30 percent of cases.[11]

The use of a standardized assessment tool to evaluate all aspects of cognitive function, such as the Short Portable Mental Status Questionnaire[12] (SPMSQ) is recommended (Table 35–3). This instrument provides a numerical score that can be monitored over time to aid in early recognition of subtle changes. However, to be of value, the tool must be used correctly on an ongoing basis.

Intervention for Physiological Etiologies

The nurse's role in treating acute confusion includes recognizing early indicators, aggressively searching for causal or associated factors (such as those presented in Table 35–1), and initiating treatment for any organic abnormalities. Organic causes have been noted in 80 to 90 percent of cases of older adults with diagnosed confusion.[2] However, the treatment of confusion is often delayed because of a lack of understanding of its significance or the belief that acute confusion in the acute-care setting is the result of environmental stressors that will resolve with transfer from the setting[13] (see "Research Brief 1").

Drug reactions or interactions and infection should be ruled out first as the precipitating cause of acute-onset confusion.[1,2] The nurse should examine the older

TABLE 35–3 SHORT PORTABLE MENTAL STATUS QUESTIONNAIRE

+	−		
		1	What is the date today?
		2	What day of the week is it?
		3	What is the name of this place?
		4	What is your telephone number?
		4a	What is your street address?
			(Ask only if patient does not have telephone.)
		5	How old are you?
		6	When were you born?
		7	Who is the president of the United States now?
		8	Who was the previous president?
		9	What was your mother's maiden name?
		10	Subtract 3 from 20, and keep subtracting 3 from each new number, all the way down.

Instructions for Completion of the SPMSQ

Ask the subject questions 1 through 10 in this list and record all answers. All responses to be scored correct must be given by the subject without reference to calendar, newspaper, or other aid to memory.
  Question 1 is scored correct only when the exact month, date, and year are given.
  Question 2 is self-explanatory.
  Question 3 is scored correct if any correct description of the location is given (i.e., name of city, state, or institution).
  Question 4 is scored correct when the telephone number can be verified or the patient can repeat the same number at another point in the questioning.
  Question 5 is scored correct when the stated age corresponds to the stated date of birth.
  Question 6 is scored correct when the month, exact date, and year are all given correctly.
  Question 7 requires only the last name of the president.
  Question 8 requires only the last name of the previous president.
  Question 9 is scored correct if a female first name plus a last name other than the subject's last name is given.
  Question 10 is scored correct if the entire series is given correctly. An error in the series or an unwillingness to attempt the series is scored as incorrect.

Scoring of the SPMSQ

Education and race are known to influence performance on mental status questionnaires. Thus, scoring of this instrument requires adjustment for these parameters. Three educational levels have been determined for this purpose:
  Patients with only a grade school education
  Patients with any high school education or who have completed high school
  Patients with any education beyond high school

0–2 Errors	Intact intellectual functioning
3–4 Errors	Mild intellectual impairment
5–7 Errors	Moderate intellectual impairment
8–10 Errors	Severe intellectual impairment

Allow one more error for only a grade school education.
Allow one fewer error for education beyond high school.
Allow one more error for black patients, with same educational criteria, to adjust for cultural language differences.

Source: Adapted from Pfeiffer,[12] p 433.

adult's medication profile. Have new drugs been added? Are any of the drugs listed in Table 35–1 present? If so, the need to discontinue the suspected offending drug should be discussed with the physician. Are therapeutic drug levels available for such common drugs as digoxin or theophylline? If not and if the patient has been receiving these drugs on an ongoing basis, the need for this laboratory test should be discussed with the attending physician.

The urinary and respiratory tracts are common sources of infection in older adults as a result of age-related changes. The patient's temperature must be monitored carefully. A body temperature of 97°F is common in older adults; thus, a temperature reading of 99°F is significant. See Chapters 15 and 17 for a review of these systems and the nursing management of these conditions.

Correction of underlying physiological problems must be accomplished slowly, with frequent monitoring of response. The older adult admitted with uncontrolled diabetes with a blood glucose level of 600 to 700 mg/dL needs careful insulin administration and fluid replacement. Overaggressive replacement of fluid in the hypotensive or dehydrated older adult often produces congestive heart failure, worsening the confused state. A useful method for evaluating the degree of total body water loss follows:

$$\text{Total body fluid} = 140 \text{ mmol/L} \times \text{Weight (kg)} \times 0.45 \text{ Serum Na (mmol/L)}$$

This value is then subtracted from the patient's estimated total body water (0.45 × weight) to determine the estimated water deficit. A condition of hyponatremia produces inaccurate results. A modest volume deficit

(1 to 2 L) can be corrected by oral rehydration therapy over 2 to 3 days.[14]

The older adult who returns from the operating room hypothermic should be warmed slowly, at a rate of approximately 1°F per hour. This is best accomplished by the use of warmed IV solutions, a head covering, and warm blankets. Conditions involving acid-base imbalance and hypoxemia usually respond to pulmonary hygiene and low levels of oxygen administration. The goal for therapy is restoration of a normal Pao_2 of about 80 mm Hg and a $Paco_2$ of 35 mm Hg.[9]

Supportive Interventions

A variety of nursing interventions have been shown to lessen the degree of confusion and restore cognitive function as soon as possible. These include reminiscence or life review, music therapy, reality orientation, activity programs, and restoration of a normal sleep pattern[15] (Table 35–4). Although recent memory is affected by an imbalance in neurotransmitter substances, long-term memory usually remains intact. By stimulating the use of this long-term memory, the nurse helps the older adult maintain a sense of self-worth and self-esteem. Music therapy has been shown to have a calming effect and may stimulate reminiscence for confused older adults.[15] It has also been used effectively as an adjunct to an activity program. A thorough discussion of these therapies is found in Chapter 25.

Reality orientation historically has focused on reminding older adults of the date, time, place, and person.[16] However, frequent questioning regarding these aspects of orientation produces anxiety and aggressive behavior in a confused person. A better approach is to engage the client in casual conversation that is focused on reality to the extent of his or her ability. For example, when an older adult calls out for someone, rather than reminding the older adult that the person is not present, it may be better to ask: "Were you thinking about (the person called)? Tell me about him or her." Discussions about what is happening to that person and what can be expected in the near future provide a frame of reference to interpret incoming stimuli. Families are usually an excellent source of reality for older adults.[17] Families should be encouraged to discuss news from home regarding what is happening with loved ones and those who are close to the client.

Families should be encouraged to bring photographs from home that can provide visual cues for the client and topics of conversation for nursing staff. Brannstrom et al.[18] found that nursing staff caring for confused older adults had difficulty relating to the person as a person, being much more inclined to take over daily tasks that the confused client was capable of performing and failing to talk to him or her. When a memorabilia board showing photographs of the client in previous years was placed at the bedside, the staff began to relate to the client in a more individualized manner. An improvement in cognition and functional abilities followed (see Table 35–4).

Additional issues regarding the nursing management of confusion involve how to approach the client, communication, and the use of restraints. The approach must be nonthreatening. Before touching a confused person, a nurse always should make eye contact first.[19] When the brain is not functioning normally, unexpected physical stimuli can be startling and may produce exaggerated responses. When attempting to remove the client from a situation, the nurse should offer his or her hand or arm, and then walk hand in hand to a

TABLE 35–4 NURSING CARE PLAN

Nursing Diagnosis: Alteration in thought processes related to stress of a strange environment and disrupted life pattern	
Expected Outcome	*Nursing Interventions*
Client experiences fewer episodes of acute confusion.	Provide orienting cues (day and night lighting, calendar and large-face clock, daily newspaper) and assist with selecting favorite radio or television program.
	Remove meaningless stimuli (get rid of unused equipment, turn off television when not attended to, keep conversation that does not include client out of hearing range).
	Introduce orientation cues with conversation. ("Good afternoon, Ms. Jones. It certainly is a rainy Thursday afternoon. Does it seem like you have been a patient in this unit for 3 days now?")
	Limit the number of staff involved in the client's care. Introduce yourself frequently. ("It's Jane, your nurse, again. I just came in to give you your medication.")
	Encourage the client to participate in controlling the environment (e.g., arranging personal effects, determining time for personal care and activities, adjusting room temperature and bed clothing).
	Respect the client's personal space and privacy. Call the client by his or her preferred name. Do not expose body parts without asking permission and explaining actions. Knock before entering room.
	Encourage family members to share personal news and participate in reminiscence or life review activities. Suggest that the family bring favorite photographs to serve as conversation items.

quiet or more appropriate setting. This allows the client some measure of control and may prevent an aggressive outburst.[15]

Communicate in a soft, soothing voice. The nurse must not respond to inappropriate language, keeping in mind that confusion is a symptom of brain failure. Because the confused older adult is incapable of reasoning and rational judgment, the nurse's attempts at rationalization will be ineffective. Trying to force the client to conform to expectations often aggravates the situation. A more effective approach is to make eye contact and address the person by name. By using slow deliberate actions, the nurse can reduce the pace of the situation. Short, simple sentences should be used, telling the client what is happening and what is going to be done.[20] If physical exercise is possible, walking may provide an outlet for pent-up energies. The nurse should stay with the client because these episodes are often frightening to the older adult, who may recognize that his or her behavior is out of control.

Physical restraints or chemical restraints are sometimes required to prevent confused older adults from injuring themselves or others. The most noted author on the medical management of delirium, Dr. Zbigniew Lipowski,[3] notes that as a short-term measure, haloperidol (Haldol) is the drug of choice for the acute management of hyperactive confusion. To achieve control of the agitated behavior, haloperidol is most effective when administered twice a day in small doses. Care must be taken not to oversedate the client. Haloperidol produces less daytime sedation and less orthostatic hypotension than other tranquilizing agents in older adults. However, extrapyramidal neurological effects such as shuffling gait, stooped posture, drooling, motor restlessness, and pacing are known to occur with prolonged use. If the agitation and restlessness increase with therapy, a drug reaction should be suspected and the drug discontinued.

Physical restraints must be used only on a temporary basis, after all other measures have been tried.[21] Nurses often cite inadequate staffing and prevention of falls as reasons for using restraints. However, studies[21] demonstrate that restraints do not prevent falls; moreover, restraints often increase the agitated behavior they were intended to control. As a result, the use of restraints increases the amount of nursing supervision required to ensure patient safety.

Based on these findings, the 1987 Omnibus Budget Reconciliation Act regulated the use of restraints in long-term care facilities. Physical and chemical restraints are allowed only with a physician's order indicating the reason for the restraint and length of time during which the restraint order is valid. The Food and Drug Administration (FDA) issued a warning in 1991 on the use of restraints in the acute-care facility. The FDA warning requires that institutions have, and communicate to all involved personnel, a policy for the use of restraints.[22] Table 35–5 lists the recommended components of such a policy. Nursing interventions that can be used instead of physical restraints include the following:

- Providing for direct supervision by a family member, support person, or nursing staff member

TABLE 35–5 GUIDELINES FOR RESTRAINT POLICY AND PROCEDURE[23]

Obtain physician's order for specific type of restraint. Order should indicate the reason for the restraint and length of time it is to be used.
Try all alternative methods to control behavior before selecting physical restraints.
Use the least restrictive restraint available for the problem behavior.
Restraint use for longer than 48 hours requires review and renewal by ordering physician.
Restraint use for longer than 14 days requires review by a committee.
Use restraints only according to manufacturer's guidelines.
When side rails are used to prevent client from getting out of bed, apply a vest restraint to prevent attempts to climb over the side rails.
When locked restraints are necessary, the key must be visible and available near the client's bed.
Document the following:
  Specific problematic behavior
  All efforts taken to control or eliminate the behavior
  Type of restraint used
  Times the restraint is removed (minimal every 2 hours)
  Condition of the skin under the restraint each time the restraint is removed
  Active and passive range of motion applied to the affected limb

- Keeping the immediate environment quiet with natural lighting
- Placing the client in a chair with removable lap tray or in a rocking chair close to the nurses' station
- Using pressure-sensitive alarms to alert the staff when the client attempts to get out of bed or chair
- Assessing for bladder distention or other noxious stimuli

When restraints are required, the least restrictive restraint that is specifically targeted to control the behavior in question should be used. For example, wrist restraints that restrict movement of limbs are excessive when the behavior in question is picking at IV sites or dressings. In this instance, padded mitts that limit dexterity will control the behavior for the length of time the IV or dressing is in place, without placing undue stress on fragile joints and skin. The nurse often requires creativity to discover behavior-specific alternatives. In addition, the source of the confusion must be actively searched out and attempts made to correct the underlying cause. Remember, physical and chemical restraints are a temporary measure only and cannot be used on an ongoing basis.

Key elements to record are serial assessments that allow evaluation of mental status changes over time. In the absence of a standardized measure of mental status (which is highly recommended), the components of attention and concentration, understanding of the current situation, appropriateness of behavior (both verbal and motor), and sleep-wake patterns must be recorded. An additional component to record is the client's response to nursing interventions, noting which interventions produce a calming effect. (For example, "When asked, patient selected an old movie to watch. She responded to the old cars and clothing in the movie by reminiscing about her childhood. She remained quiet throughout the movie, approximately 2 hours.")

Summary

Acute confusion is often a deciding factor for sending acutely ill older adults to long-term care facilities. Maintaining the safety of the older adult and of others is the primary purpose for this decision. Confused older people are at risk for falls, injury from fire, hypothermia and hyperthermia, malnutrition, and dehydration. Relocation to familiar surroundings can aid in re-establishing normal brain function when the cause of the acute confusion has been recognized and corrected. Discharge home can be a realistic goal if sufficient support is available to ensure the older adult's safety through the recovery period.[24] However, the needs of the entire family must be considered when deciding on the appropriate care for the confused older adult.

Student Learning Activities

1 Survey the nursing personnel in your clinical agency regarding their knowledge of the causes of acute confusional states. Discuss with the nursing staff the points presented in the debate regarding the use of soft restraints on a hospitalized older adult from Chapter 6.

2 How could the health promotion strategies from the chapter be implemented in your clinical facility?

3 Develop a pamphlet for families of confused older adults regarding the value of reminiscence, the presence of family, reflective listening, and a calm atmosphere in re-establishing normal mental functioning.

REFERENCES

1 St Pierre, MN: Delirium in hospitalized elderly patients: Off track. Crit Care Nurs Clin North Am 8(1):53, 1996.
2 Foreman, MD, and Zane, D: Nursing strategies for acute confusion in elders. Am J Nurs 96(4):44, 1996.
3 Lipowski, ZJ: Delirium: Acute Confusional States. Oxford Press, New York, 1990.
4 Ludwig, LM: Acute brain failure in the critically ill patient. Crit Care Nurse 9:62, 1990.
5 Rasin, JH: Confusion. Nurs Clin North Am 25:909, 1990.
6 Adams, F: Neuropsychiatric evaluation and treatment of delirium in the critically ill cancer patient. Cancer Bull 36:156, 1984.
7 Drew, N: Exclusion and confirmation: A phenomenology of patient's experiences with caregivers. Image 18:39, 1986.
8 Brannstrom, B, et al: ADL performance and dependency on nursing care in patients with hip fractures and acute confusion in a task allocation care system. Scand J Caring Sci 5:3, 1991.
9 Gustafson, Y, et al: A geriatric anesthesiologic program to reduce acute confusional states in elderly patients treated for femoral neck fractures. J Am Geriatr Soc 39:655, 1991.
10 Wolanin, MO: Physiologic aspects of confusion. J Gerontol Nurs 7:236, 1981.
11 Foreman, MD: Adverse psychological responses of the elderly to critical illness. AACN's Clin Issues Crit Care 3:64, 1992.
12 Pfeiffer, E: SPMSQ for the assessment of organic brain deficit in elderly patients. J Am Geriatr Soc 23:433, 1975.
13 Kroeger, LL: Critical care nurses' perceptions of the confused elderly patient. Focus 18:395, 1991.
14 Stanley, M: Caring for elders in critical care. AACN Clin Issues Crit Care 3:120, 1992.
15 Drury, J, and Akins, J: Sensory/perceptual alterations. In Maas, M, et al (eds): Nursing Diagnosis and Interventions for the Elderly. Addison-Wesley Nursing, Redwood City, Calif, 1991.
16 Hogstel, MO: Use of reality orientation with aging confused patients. Nurs Res 28:161, 1979.
17 Bay, EJ, et al: Effect of family visit on the patient's mental status. Focus 15:10, 1988.
18 Brannstrom, B, et al: Problems of basic nursing care in acutely confused and non-confused hip fracture patients. Scand J Caring Sci 3:27, 1989.
19 Montgomery, C: What you can do for the confused elderly. Nursing 21:55, 1987.
20 Struble, LM, and Sivertsen, L: Agitation: Behaviors in confused elderly patients. J Gerontol Nurs 13:40, 1987.
21 Wilson, EB: Physical restraint of elderly patients in critical care. Crit Care Nurs Clin North Am 8(1):61, 1996.
22 Tammelleo, DA: Restraints: A legal catch-22? RN 4:71, 1992.
23 Glickstein, JK: Suggested policies and procedures for the proper use of restraints. Focus on Geriatric Care and Rehabilitation 4:3, 1990.
24 Sullivan, EM, et al: Nursing assessment, management of delirium in the elderly. AORN J 53:820, 1991.

CHAPTER 36

Dementia in Older Adults

Christine R. Kovach / Sarah A. Wilson

OBJECTIVES

Upon completion of this chapter, the reader will be able to:

- Describe the signs and symptoms commonly observed during early-, mid-, and late-stage dementia
- Explain the screening procedures and assessments that are helpful in following and managing symptoms associated with illnesses that cause dementia
- Outline interventions that decrease environmental press coming from auditory, visual, tactile, and multiple competing stimuli
- Differentiate goals, care needs, and models of delivering care during early-, mid-, and late-stage dementia illness
- Describe nursing interventions that are useful when working with people who display behaviors associated with dementia

Dementia is a general term used to describe a global impairment in cognitive functioning that is usually progressive and interferes with normal social and occupational activities and activities of daily living (ADLs). The illnesses that give rise to dementia symptoms include Alzheimer's disease (AD), vascular problems such as multi-infarct dementia, normal pressure hydrocephalus, Parkinson's disease, chronic alcoholism, Pick's disease, Huntington's disease, and acquired immunodeficiency syndrome (AIDS). At least half of all nursing home residents have dementia.[1] It is estimated that 4 million Americans have AD and that by the year 2050, there will be 14 million people in the United States with the disease.[2]

AD alone costs the United States an estimated $90 billion per year in medical bills, long-term care costs, and lost productivity.[2] Dementia is a costly public health problem, but the challenges the dementing symptoms create in quality of life, caregiver stress, and maintenance of human dignity and personhood perhaps reflect a more significant human burden that nursing can work to ameliorate.

Pathology

AD accounts for at least two-thirds of dementia.[3] The specific causes of AD have not been established, although genetics appears to play a role. Other theories

that were once popular but are currently less supported include toxic effects of aluminum, a slow growing virus initiating an autoimmune response, or a biochemical deficiency.[4–6] Dr. Alois Alzheimer first described the two types of abnormal structures found postmortem in the brains of people with AD: amyloid plaques and neurofibrillary tangles. There also is a decrease in certain neurotransmitters, but particularly acetylcholine. The areas of the brain that are particularly affected by AD are the cerebral cortex and hippocampus, both of which are important in cognitive functions and memory.

Amyloid causes destruction of brain tissue. The amyloid plaques are derived from a larger protein, the amyloid precursor protein (APP). Families in which early-onset AD appears to be inherited have been studied, and some carry a mutation in the APP gene. Other APP gene mutations associated with later-onset AD and cerebrovascular disease have also been identified. There is an increased risk for late-onset AD with the inheritance of the apo E4 allele on chromosome 19.[7] Neurofibrillary tangles are collections of twisted nerve cell fibers, called paired helical filaments. The specific role these tangles play in the disease is under study. Acetylcholine and other neurotransmitters are chemicals needed for messages to be sent through the nervous system. A deficit of neurotransmitters leads to a breakdown in the complex process of communication between cells in the nervous system. Tau is a protein that is found in increased levels in the cerebrospinal fluid of people even in the earliest stages of AD. Findings suggest that AD may start at the cellular level, with tau being a molecular marker in the cell.[7]

Multi-infarct dementia is the second most common cause of dementia. These patients have cerebrovascular disease that, as the name implies, leads to multiple infarcts in the brain. However, not all people who have multiple cerebral infarcts have dementia. In comparison to people with AD, people with multi-infarct dementia have a more abrupt onset of illness, a stepwise rather than linear deterioration in cognition and function, and may show some improvements between cerebrovascular events.[8]

Most patients with Parkinson's disease who have a severe, lengthy course of illness develop dementia. In one study, patients were followed for 15 to 18 years after entering a levodopa treatment program and 80 percent were moderately or severely demented before they died.[9]

Stages of Dementia

AD and other illnesses that cause dementia are notable for the variability in the course, presentation, and progression of symptoms. Various classification systems exist for marking progression of the illness. Table 36–1 describes early-, mid-, and late-stage dementia symptoms. There is considerable overlap in symptoms between stages.

EARLY STAGE

Early AD has an insidious onset of symptoms, whereas the vascular dementias may present with more abrupt changes in cognition. Loss of recent memory leads to difficulty acquiring new information. The person may show poor judgment. For example, a woman may cook six chicken breasts for breakfast when chicken is not a traditional breakfast food and six would be too much food. There is difficulty with numbers; paying bills, balancing the checkbook, handling money, and making phone calls may be overwhelming. Problems with cognition and function are manifested, particularly when the person is in a new or stressful situation. Personality changes may be evident. For example, the industrious personality type may lack initiative and become more withdrawn. A calm person may begin to display temper outbursts and become anxious and restless. There may be confusion regarding time and spatial orientation; a person may arrive for an appointment at the wrong time or place or may drive to the neighborhood grocery store and be unable to find his or her way home. Anomia, or difficulty naming objects, is evident. For example, a person might say, "Give me the thing you write with" rather than ask for a pencil.

MIDSTAGE

Recent and remote memory worsen during midstage dementia and lack of judgment leads to concerns about safety. For example, the person generally cannot independently use a stove safely and may wander outside in cold weather without warm clothing. Apraxia, or inability to perform purposeful movements even though the sensory and motor systems are intact, will be evident. For example, a man will lose the ability to tie his shoes or necktie. Grooming will be poor, and the person will begin to need cuing and assistance with activities of daily living. Agnosia, or inability to recognize common objects, may be present. For example, if one hands the person a toothbrush or spoon, he or she may not know what should be done with the object. Urinary incontinence often becomes a problem in the latter part of this middle stage. In this midstage, a move to a supervised living situation often becomes necessary.

This is the stage in which, because of lack of impulse control, a decreased stress threshold, and difficulty making sense of the environment, challenging behavioral symptoms are a prominent part of daily life. Aggressiveness, anxiety, wandering and other activity distur-

TABLE 36–1 STAGES OF DEMENTIA SYMPTOMS

Early	Mild	Late
• Changes in mood or personality • Impaired judgment and problem solving • Confusion about place (gets lost driving to the store) • Confusion about time • Difficulty with numbers, money, bills • Mild anomia • Withdrawal or depression	• Impaired recent and remote memory • Anomia, agnosia, apraxia, aphasia • Severely impaired judgment and problem solving • Confusion about time and place worsen • Perceptual disturbances • Loss of impulse control • Anxiety, restlessness wandering, perseveration • Hyperorality • Possible suspiciousness, delusions, or hallucinations • Confabulation • Greatly impaired self-care abilities • Beginning of incontinence • Sleep-wake cycle disturbances	• Severe impairment of all cognitive abilities • Inability to recognize family and friends • Severely impaired communication (may grunt, moan, or mumble) • Little capacity for self-care • Bowel and bladder incontinence • Possibility of becoming hyperoral and having active hands • Decreased appetite; dysphasia and risk for aspiration • Immune system depression that leads to increased risk for infections • Impaired mobility with loss of ability to walk, rigid muscles, and paratonia • Sucking and grasp reflexes • Withdrawal • Disturbed sleep-wake cycle, with increased sleeping time

bances, socially inappropriate behavior, diurnal rhythm disturbances, perseverance (repetitive movements or vocalizations), delusions, paranoia, hallucinations, and attempts to leave the care setting are common.

Difficulty with language is present. The person may have receptive and expressive aphasia and, when unable to find the right word, may use illogical words or phrases to fill in the gaps (confabulation). The person may use a lot of words, but there is usually very little content in the message. There may be an increase in muscle tone, changes in gait and balance, and impaired depth perception, which all contribute to increased risk of falls. Appetite is generally good and the person may be hyperoral, wanting to put food and objects in his or her mouth.

LATE STAGE

During late-stage dementia, the person becomes more chairbound or bedbound. Muslces are rigid, contractures may develop, and primitive reflexes may be present. Paratonia is a primitive reflex and is manifested by the involuntary resistance in an extremity in response to sudden passive movement. Caregivers may inadvertently interpret this response as resistance to caregiving. Other primitive release signs such as sucking and grasp reflexes may return. The person may have very active hands and repetitive movements, grunting, or other vocalizations. There is depressed immune system function and this impairment coupled with immobility may lead to the development of pneumonia, urinary tract infections, sepsis, and pressure ulcers.

Appetite decreases and dysphagia is present; aspiration is common. Weight loss generally occurs. Speech and language are severely impaired, with greatly decreased verbal communication. The person may no longer recognize any family members. Bowel and bladder incontinence are present and caregivers need to complete most ADLs for the person. The sleep-wake cycle is greatly altered, and the person spends a lot of time dozing and appears socially withdrawn and more unaware of the environment or surroundings. Death may be caused by infection, sepsis, or aspiration, although there are not many studies examining cause of death.

1 *Primary Prevention*

Identification of characteristics of individual or environmental risks factors for AD could guide preventive interventions for the disease. The most consistent epidemiological finding associated with AD is the increase in prevalence and incidence associated with age.[10] People aged 75 to 85 years are more likely to develop dementia of the Alzheimer type (DAT) than to have a heart attack.[11] Incidence rates tend to be higher for women than for men in all age groups, although no biological explanation has been found to account for the sex difference. Other risk factors that have some association with AD are familial aggregation of Down's syndrome, familial aggregation of Parkinson's disease, late maternal age, head trauma, history of depression, and history of

hypothyroidism.[10] There are no major geographic differences in incidence or prevalence.

Education and occupation may compensate for neuropathological changes in AD and delay onset of symptoms.[12] Low attained education was also associated with a higher risk of AD and dementia in the nun study.[13] The nun study is a longitudinal epidemiological study of aging and AD in the School Sisters of Notre Dame, a religious congregation in the United States. The nuns are a unique group to study because they share the same adult history, including similar occupations, diet, socioeconomic status, home, and access to medical care. The nun study suggests that linguistic ability in early life may be a better marker than education of important aspects of cognitive ability in later life. Comparing autobiographies written at a mean age of 22 with cognitive function approximately 58 years later demonstrated that low linguistic ability in early life was a strong predictor of poor cognitive function and AD in later life.[14] Progression from low normal to impaired cognitive functioning was also associated with loss of independence in ADLs.[15] People with low scores on a cognitive examination should also have their physical function assessed. Secondary and tertiary preventive measures may be helpful in maintaining the current level of physical independence.[15]

A higher frequency of AD has been reported among relatives of people with AD than in the general population. Researchers have identified three different chromosomes that are associated in some families with AD.[16] The nurse should be careful when discussing inheritance with family members because presence of a genetic defect has been established only for a small group of families with autosomal-dominant AD. As more is learned about the role of genetics and AD, ethical questions about genetic testing will become more prominent.

Studies of AD-type brain alteration have taken advantage of the fact that nonhuman primates develop brain abnormalities similar to those in humans. The *Macaca multatta* is currently the best available model for age-associated behavioral and brain abnormalities that occur in older humans and those with AD.[17] The *Macaca* has a life span of more than 35 years. Older monkeys show alterations in neurotransmitter markers and amyloid that are similar to older humans and adults with AD. Researchers have identified a defective gene on chromosome 21 that appears to be the source of early-onset familial AD.[2] This mutation may be responsible for an accumulation of β-amyloid protein in the brains of patients with AD. The buildup of this protein may disrupt the transmission and reception of nerve signals in brain cells. Researchers plan to transfer this newly found gene into mice. The mice could then serve as animal models for further research.

2 *Secondary Prevention*

DIAGNOSIS AND SCREENING FOR DEMENTIA

Older adults often worry that they have beginning signs of dementia and query nurses and other health professionals in subtle ways regarding this fear. People who worry about having dementia almost always do not have true dementia but are experiencing age-associated memory changes, depression, or one of the reversible causes of memory impairment. Age-associated memory changes include increased forgetfulness, more difficulty learning new information, decreased retrieval ability, and decreased speed for encoding and retrieving information.[18]

A diagnosis of dementia should be made over time to distinguish the persistence or reversibility of symptoms. Many conditions, both physical and psychosocial, can cause temporary impairments in cognition. Common reversible causes of memory impairment include infection, thyroid abnormality, vitamin B_{12} and other nutritional deficiencies, drug toxicity or side effect, acute alcohol intake, anemia, tumor, or trauma. These causes of acute confusion and the associated treatment are discussed in Chapter 35.

A thorough history, physical examination, diagnostic workup, and neuropsychological testing are needed to arrive at a probable diagnosis of irreversible dementia. AD is still definitively diagnosed only on autopsy, but clinical diagnosis is usually accurate. DSM-IV criteria are used to establish a probable clinical diagnosis of dementia.[19] According to the DSM-IV criteria, there must be a decline in two or more areas of cognition significant enough to interfere with job or social functioning. Areas of decline may include memory, language, visual-spatial perception, construction, calculations, judgment, abstraction, and personality changes. Promising work is being done to develop definitive antemortem diagnostic tests through positive emission tomography scan procedures, blood testing, and other biochemical measurements. Computed tomography and magnetic resonance imaging scans are sometimes useful in delineating vascular problems as the causative factor for dementia.

Nurses should regularly perform assessments of cognition, behavior, and functional status with older adults who have suspected or confirmed dementia. These assessments are helpful in following the course of the illness and matching therapeutic interventions to level of ability. One of the keys to dementia care is to plan and organize activities the person can reasonably perform to avoid frustration, decreased self-esteem, and stress-related behavioral responses. If the person lives in a private residence, safety becomes an even greater concern. A home safety assessment can help identify potential safety hazards and preventive interventions can be instituted.

Many tools are available, and the best instrument varies based on stage of dementia, living situation, and presenting problems. Commonly used tools to assess cognition are the mini-mental state exam,[20] Clinical Dementia Rating,[21] and Short Portable Mental Status Questionnaire.[22] The KATZ ADL scales may be useful for assessing functional and instrumental ADLs early in the disease, but as functional status declines, a tool designed specifically for people with dementia is preferred. The Functional Behavior Profile is used to assess functional abilities in three domains: task performance, social interactions, and problem solving.[23] The Blessed Dementia Scale[24] assesses practical functions as well as mood and personality changes. Most of the instruments that assess behaviors associated with dementia were designed for research purposes.[25–28]

DECREASE ENVIRONMENTAL PRESS

The Progressively Lowered Stess Threshold model provides a useful framework for preventing many behaviors associated with dementia. Environmental press is the demand character of an environment. Environmental stressors require adjustments and adaptations from the person in the environment.[29] The person with dementia, because of impairments in ability to receive, process, and respond to stimuli, has a decreased threshold for tolerating and adapting to stresses from the environment.[30] Interventions that decrease environmental press and balance sensory calming experiences with sensory stimulating experiences are a hallmark of effective care for the person with dementia.

Nurses should conduct an assessment of environmental press in the living areas of the person with dementia and be alert for environmental press from auditory, visual, tactile, and multiple competing stimuli. Television sets are a particularly potent stressor because the person with dementia often cannot sort the sounds coming from the television from reality. The TV should be turned on only to watch a specific program and then turn it off. At home or in an institution, noisy cleaning should be done during one time of the day only.

Nurses should avoid overwhelming the person's ability to process stimuli by keeping verbal communication focused, deliberate, and simple. Words common to the patient's age and background should be used. The person should be approached calmly and cheerfully and spoken to in an adult, respectful fashion. Background conversations, too much decision making, and "why" questions should be avoided. For example, rather than asking, "What would you like for dessert?", nurses should ask "Would you like some ice cream?" The tone of voice should be calm and reassuring so that even if words are poorly understood, the person receives a message of calm, safety, and acceptance. If a message does not seem to have been received, the message should be repeated or another method of communication used. If possible, the conversation should remain on one topic unless the patient initiates a change. The nurse should use nonverbal communication and be alert for nonverbal cues from the resident that might indicate that his or her stress threshold is being reached or exceeded.

People with dementia have impaired depth perception and other visual changes. All glare from lighting should be eliminated. The nurse should keep lighting free of shadows during the daytime and use subdued lighting only during sleep. Dimmer switches that increase lighting as dusk approaches may be helpful in decreasing sundown syndrome (increased agitation commonly seen late in the day). Colors should be kept in the background, such as on walls, tables, and floor, subdued and monochrome; contrasting or brighter colors can be used to differentiate used items such as a cup, chair, or eating utensil. For example, if a dinner plate has a flow-

RESEARCH BRIEF 1

Synder, M, et al: Interventions for decreasing agitation behaviors in persons' dementia. J Gerontol Nurs 21(7):34–40, 1995.

The use of stress management techniques may be helpful in decreasing agitated behaviors in persons with dementia. This study used an experimental design to examine the effects of hand massage, therapeutic touch, and presence in promoting relaxation and decreasing agitation in nursing home residents with AD. Hand massage produced a greater relaxation response than therapeutic touch. No significant decrease in agitation behaviors was observed for any of the interventions.

ered pattern on it, the person with dementia may have difficulty distinguishing the flowers from the vegetables and other food on the plate. A better choice would be a solid light-colored plate with a brightly colored stripe to serve as a border and visual cue of where the plate ends. Spaces that are too big and filled with too many people and things tend to overwhelm the person. In general, room sizes should be small, well-organized, and well-lit. Dining rooms in long-term care facilities should ideally seat no more than 12 to 16 residents. Dividing large multipurpose rooms in long-term care facilities into smaller, more homelike activity and dining rooms benefits both the people with dementia and those who are cognitively intact.

Nurses should use slow, gentle, and reassuring touch. Some people with dementia are highly sensitive to touch and react negatively to invasion of personal body space, whereas others are very comforted by massage, hugs, and close contact with caregivers. Flannel sheets and silk pillowcases are comforting, and especially effective for residents who are anxious during the night and have difficulty sleeping. The person should be allowed a soft special pillow, plush pet animal, or doll if it is comforting. Hand massage has been shown to be effective in reducing agitation behavior among people with AD.

Nothing exceeds the stress threshold faster than multiple competing stimuli. Think about the multiple stimuli the person must process during bathtime: the sound of water running, the differing temperatures of the air and water, the feel of the soap and washcloth, the touch of the caregiver, the raising and lowering of arms and legs, and the movement of tactile stimulation from one part of the body to another. Stimulation should be kept as singular and focused as possible. For example, before the person enters the bathing room, the tub should be filled with water and all equipment organized. As the person is undressed, the nurse should cover each unclothed area with a bath blanket or towel. If comforting, the person may remain covered in this manner while in the tub, raising and lowering the linen only in the area being bathed.

OTHER INTERVENTIONS

To prevent deleterious effects of the illness, primary-self needs must be met. Primary-self needs are human beings' basic physical, comfort, and security needs. Because the person with dementia often cannot complete these tasks independently, the nurse should anticipate needs and assist the client. It is equally important that not too much is done for the person, or decline in functioning will be hastened. For example, rather than dress the person with midstage dementia, it may be sufficient for the nurse to set the clothes out in the order in which they should be donned. The nurse should give the person a toothbrush and use frequent verbal cues and reassurances to facilitate continued independence in oral care. Tasks should be divided into smaller steps, and step-by-step instructions should be given calmly, simply.

People with dementia often cannot articulate their discomfort (e.g., the feeling of full bladder, constipation, being too cold or too hot). Rather, when the person is experiencing some sort of discomfort, he or she may become anxious, wander, or withdraw. The nurse should help the person use the toilet regularly and have visual cues for locations of toilets. The protocol for conducting an assessment of a person with dementia who is experiencing behavior changes or agitation is presented in Table 36–2 and is particularly helpful as the illness progresses and verbal skills decline. If the physical assessment does not reveal an obvious source of discomfort and behavioral interventions are unsuccessful, a prescribed non-narcotic analgesic such as acetaminophen may be tried before giving a psychotropic drug. Perhaps the person is unable to indicate that a headache is present, or that an arthritic knee is aching. It is also important to check for side effects of drugs as a contributing factor in behavioral symptoms or functional decline.

DRUG THERAPY

Treatment for AD has been the focus of several investigations. The NIA Alzheimer's Disease Cooperative Study Unit has funded 23 study sites across the United States to determine whether deprenyl given in conjunction with vitamin E is beneficial for people with AD.[2] Deprenyl inhibits enzymes in the brain that impair certain neurotransmitter systems. It is thought that vitamin E counteracts destructive oxygen free radicals that break down cell membranes.

Tacrine (Cognex) is the first drug approved by the Food and Drug Administration (FDA) for the treatment of AD. It is a reversible inhibitor of cholinesterase, the enzyme that breaks down the neurotransmitter acetylcholine. Tacrine may benefit people with mild to moderate AD. High dosages of the drug cause liver transaminase elevations and gastrointestinal complaints.

Donepezil hydrochloride (Aricept) is a new drug that was approved in 1996 by the FDA for the symptomatic treatment of mild to moderate AD. Donepezil is also a reversible inhibitor of the enzyme that breaks down the neurotransmitter acetylcholine. This drug may allow a greater concentration of acetylcholine in the brain, thereby improving cholinergic function. Clin-

TABLE 36–2 PROTOCOL FOR BEHAVIORAL CHANGES OR AGITATION

1. Assessment:			Multistix (Urine)		
	+	**−**	**Test**	**Result**	**Adult Normal**
			Urinalysis		
Lungs			Leukocytes	_____	Negative
Eyes (drainage/irritation)			Nitrite	_____	Negative
Skin (rash, lesion, pressure)			Protein	_____	Negative
Rectal check			pH	_____	5–8.5
Multistix (see right)			Blood	_____	Negative
*If any of above are positive, chart and intervene as needed			Specific gravity	_____	1.000–1.030
2. If all of above are negative, try behavioral interventions (i.e., distraction, 1:1 activity, snacks, walking, audio/videotapes).	√if done		Ketones	_____	Negative
			Glucose	_____	Negative
3. If unsuccessful, medicate with nonnarcotic analgesic per physician order.					
4. If behavior still persists, medicate with PRN psych medication per physician order or call physician/psych consult, and chart in nurses' notes.			Signature: _____ Date: _____		

ical trials have shown that the drug is well-tolerated and effective in improving cognition, patient function, and quality of life scores in people with mild to moderate AD. There is no evidence that donepezil alters the course of the underlying dementing process.

The drug is well-tolerated. The most common signs and symptoms leading to discontinuation were nausea, diarrhea, and vomiting, occurring in 3 percent or fewer patients. As a cholinesterase inhibitor, donepezil may cause bradycardia, which could be problematic for people with sick sinus syndrome or other supraventricular cardiac conduction conditions. This once-daily oral medication does not require liver function monitoring.[31–33]

3 Tertiary Prevention

Families assume the greatest responsibility for caring for people with early and midstage dementia. More than 70 percent of people with AD are cared for at home by family members.[2] Many families experience social isolation, fatigue, and financial problems as caregiving activities consume more of their time and the family member exhibits more mental impairment. Most family caregivers are women, either spouses or daughters with their own life demands. Spouses are often older, with one or more chronic illnesses. They often neglect their own health needs as caregiving becomes more time-consuming. Home care has been described as a 36-hour-a-day responsibility with little relief for families.[34] Home health aides can assist with personal care, but these services are limited and are not covered by Medicare. Insti-

tutionalization often becomes the final alternative as families expend personal and economic resources.[35]

Adult day-care services provide families with some respite. Most offer some type of recreational and restorative activities. The person with severe or late-stage dementia may not be appropriate for adult day care. Transportation to the adult day care may be expensive and difficult to arrange.

Approximately 1 in 10 nursing homes has a special care unit (SCU) or program for people with dementia.[2] There is no agreed-on definition of an SCU, and some nursing homes may label a unit as an SCU if it provides minimal changes in environment or therapeutic activities.[36] Most SCUs charge more than regular units without the benefit of standards that would provide some means of evaluating resident outcomes.[37] Research on the effectiveness of SCUs is limited and often contradictory. There is considerable discussion about what makes a SCU "special." Five features have emerged as areas of agreement: Residents have a cognitive impairment usually caused by AD, activity programming is for the cognitively impaired, provisions are made for family programming and involvement, the physical and social environment is segregated and modified, and staff are selected for the unit and have special education.[38] The U.S. Office of Technology Assessment, a congressional research agency, released a report on SCUs in 1992. Six key principles emerged that identify the core of SCUs[1]:

1. Something can be done for people with dementia.
2. Many factors cause excess disability in people with dementia.
3. People with dementia have residual strength.

RESEARCH BRIEF 2

Kovach, CR, et al: The effects of hospice interventions on behaviors, discomfort, and physical complications of end-stage dementia nursing home residents. Am J Alzheimer Dis July/August:1–8, 1996.

The purpose of this study was to determine the effectiveness of hospice-oriented care on discomfort, physical complications, and behaviors associated with dementia for nursing home residents with an end-stage dementing illness. A pretest–post-test experimental design was used. Hospice households were created in three long-term care facilities. A multidisciplinary approach was used to design interventions focusing on comfort, quality of life, and dignity. Measurements were made of cognitive impairment, behaviors associated with dementia, and comfort. The study results show a significant difference in comfort levels in the treatment and control groups. The treatment group had less discomfort. The study supports the application of hospice concepts to care of nursing home residents with end-stage dementia.

4 The behavior of people with dementia represents understandable feelings and needs, even if the people are unable to express the feelings or moods.

5 Many aspects of the physical and social environment affect the functioning of people with dementia.

6 People with dementia and their families constitute an integral unit.

The purpose of most SCUs is to provide a low-stimulus environment that is safe and free from hazards and promotes quality of life. Most units have some type of environmental modifications and usually allow space for safe wandering. Activity programming and recreation are designed to meet the unique needs of residents and families. Facilities with SCUs report use of fewer physical and chemical restraints and a lower incidence of problem behaviors than traditional units.[37,39] The criteria for admission to an SCU usually include the person's cognitive status, behavioral manifestations of dementia, and functional ability. As a resident's functional status or physical condition deteriorates, the person is usually discharged from the SCU because of inability to participate in group programming and deterioration in physical status or increased physical care needs.[40]

The primary focus of providing care for a person with late-stage dementia is palliative: maintaining comfort, quality of life, human dignity, and personhood. The hospice movement has provided many strategies and interventions for people who are no longer candidates for curative or rehabilitative care. Traditionally, hospices have been associated with patients with a diagnosis of cancer. The application of hospice concepts in long-term care for people with late-stage dementia is a recent phenomenon.[39,41–43] Using the hospice concepts, staff in these agencies have enhanced physical and behavioral assessments skills to recognize when a resident is experiencing discomfort and to conduct routine risk assessments. Activity programming is individualized to meet each resident's specific needs. The staff recognize that families are an integral part of care and help families in maintaining hope and finding meaning. Home hospice services are becoming increasingly available in some areas for the person with end-stage dementia.

BEHAVIORS ASSOCIATED WITH DEMENTIA

Caregivers often speak of behaviors associated with dementia as problems. Reconceptualizing these behaviors as meaningful responses to events, stressors, or confusion arising from the environment is helpful in planning more appropriate nursing interventions. Many behaviors associated with dementia are actually attempts by the cognitively impaired person to cope with something that is difficult to understand and is perceived as threatening in some way. The person who is being transferred from the bed to the wheelchair may believe he or she is being harmed or will fall during the transfer. As an adaptive response, the person becomes resistive and begins hitting the caregiver. A person may hear a siren and a lot of commotion on the television. Unable to sort this noise from reality, the person may then attempt to exit the area in an attempt to find a calmer and safer place. Behaviors should be considered a problem only if the action interferes or potentially interferes with the health, rights, or safety of the person exhibiting the behavior or other people in the environment.

Many behaviors associated with dementia can be prevented by decreasing environmental press, carefully attending to primary-self needs, and balancing active times with quiet times.[39] Always note what triggers a behavioral response and see whether the triggering event can be eliminated. For example, if Mr. Cohen and Mr. Carter always argue when they are together, try to have them develop different social networks.

WANDERING AND NEED FOR MOVEMENT

Many people with dementia have the need to wander, move, or rock back and forth, or have very active, fidgeting hands. Research has shown that those who wander had more physical lifestyles in the past and that they used physical activity as a means of relieving and coping with stress.[44–46] This suggests that physical activity and wandering are coping tools that nurses should accommodate.

Perseverance is a term used to describe the repetitive movements and verbalizations commonly seen in this population. Perseverance may be classified as tense or calm. Calm perseverance is identified by the calm rhythm of the movements or verbalizations, relaxed facial expression, and relaxed muscles. Calm perseverance may be a coping mechanism and probably does not need to be treated if the behavior does not escalate and lasts no more than 30 minutes. If the person appears bored, getting him or her involved in a stimulating activity may be needed. Check to be sure the person will not sustain an abrasion from the movements and, if the behavior exceeds the stress threshold of others, move the person to an area where he or she can be observed but will not unduly increase environmental press. Tense perseveration, on the other hand, is often an indication of physical or psychological discomfort and is characterized by tense muscles and vocalizations and an escalation in the intensity of the perseverant behavior. Do an assessment for discomfort and check to be certain other primary-self needs have been met.

Rummaging through various items, drawers, and closets, as well as the need to keep hands active, is common during all stages of dementia, even though abilities and access to items decrease as the illness progresses. Interventions that may be helpful for all of the activity disturbances, including wandering, perseverance, rummaging, and active hands, are as follows:

- Move the person to a less stressful environment.
- Provide a safe wandering path and allow the person to wander. If the person is not independently ambulatory, help the person walk or engage in another physical activity several times a day.
- Use specially designed safe rockers as a means of providing for physical movement needs.
- Hold the person's upper body in your arms in a hugging fashion, and rock together with the person as a soothing movement.
- Look through activity therapy equipment catalogues and purchase puzzles, mobiles, handballs, cubes, and other items that are safe, adult-oriented, and stimulating.
- Fill a drawer or box with interesting textures and items such as Velcro, plush pets, and sandpaper. A theme could be used, such as baseball or baby clothes, for additional rummage boxes. Allow the person to rummage through these items at any time. On one end-stage dementia unit, every Monday an array of baby clothes come out of the dryer and residents delight in feeling the softness and warmth while folding the pretty baby items. Having a staff member reminisce with the residents about motherhood during this time makes the event social as well. Busy aprons and busy boxes can also be purchased or made and contain stimulating textures and adult-type activities for the hands. For example, a volunteer could secure to a board items that relate to auto mechanics or home repair.
- Give the person an activity to do that is not too difficult and optimally tied to the person's remembered past. The accountant may enjoy folding papers and attaching a paper clip to each. Using a calculator or typewriter is popular with people who formerly had clerical or bookkeeping jobs. Baking and gardening are popular activities. If people are severely demented, give each a portion of dough to knead in flour, while another loaf bakes in the oven. Everyone can feel a sense of accomplishment and enjoy eating fresh bread, even if the loaf that is baked is kept separate from the kneading activity.

- If the person touches or rubs his or her body excessively, be sure fingernails are clean and well-trimmed. Provide pants without a fly and zipper, and use shirts and dresses with fasteners in the back so that they are not easily removed. Provide other items to keep hands busy.

AGITATION AND AGGRESSION

Agitation tends to occur more often late in the day, and the term *sundown syndrome* has been coined to describe this phenomenon. Aggressive behavior may be physical or verbal and may be self-directed or directed toward others. Interventions that may be helpful include the following:

- Decrease the environmental press.
- Anticipate the person's needs to prevent frustration and discomfort.
- Keep lighting up to daytime levels until bedtime. Dimmer switches that increase lighting as the sun goes down are easily installed.
- Assess for hunger, thirst, and other primary-self needs.
- Increase feelings of security through verbal reassurance, nestling the person in a chair with bath blankets, or through the use of a soft pillow, plush pet animal, or doll.
- Increase feelings of familiarity through consistent staff and routines, friendly visiting, and keeping items tied to the familiar in visual range.
- Assess what triggers aggression and prevent the triggering event from occurring in the future.
- Use distraction and redirection to turn the person's attention to a more pleasurable event.
- Do not scold or try to teach the person. Both are ineffective because he or she lacks ability to learn.
- Speak to the person in a calm and reassuring voice at all times. Keep the message clear and simple.

DELUSIONS AND HALLUCINATIONS

Delusions and hallucinations are both common but not inevitable symptoms of dementia. Be certain the person's eyeglasses and hearing aid are in place and in good functioning order. If the delusion or hallucination is not upsetting to the person, no intervention is probably needed. If, as is often the case, the person becomes upset or fearful, the person should not be left in this state. Often, taking the person to another environment, turning on lights, and offering calm reassurance are all that is needed to provide comfort for this troubled state. If a person experiences persistent delusions or hallucinations, a psychotropic drug may be indicated. Do not tell the person that his or her thought or hallucination is incorrect or correct. Rather, validate the person's feelings through a comment such as, "I hear that you are upset. I am here to help you and I will keep you safe."

PLAN OF CARE

The nursing care plan in Table 36–3 is provided as an example using nursing diagnoses commonly

TABLE 36–3 CARE PLAN

Nursing Diagnosis: At risk for injury related to wandering	
Expected Outcome	*Nursing Actions*
Client does not become lost or sustain injury during wandering.	Avoid physical restraints. Provide safe area to wander. Clearly mark resident's room with picture or name and include familiar possessions in the room. Place alarms on all outside and hazardous exits. Ensure that resident wears appropriate clothing for the season. Assess for fall risk.

Nursing Diagnosis: Altered pattern of urinary elimination caused by perceptual alterations, nervous system damage, or frequent urinary tract infections	
Expected Outcome	*Nursing Actions*
Client maintains continence on four out of five voidings.	Mark bathrooms as "Men" and "Women," and use tape or arrows to indicate the way to the bathroom. Use prompted voiding based on individual pattern of voiding (e.g., taking to the bathroom every 2 or 3 hours, after meals, or before bedtime). Offer fluid every 2 hours during the day; restrict fluid after 6 PM. Use waterproof pants only if needed to prevent accidents and embarrassment. Use teaching devices to promote relearning feeling of bladder fullness if person is able to recognize the feeling. Supply a bedside commode or urinal if necessary and if person understands purpose. Assess whether person can manipulate clothing. Use Velcro closures to aid in easy removal or replacement.

Nursing Diagnosis: Impaired cognition related to disease process	
Expected Outcome	*Nursing Actions*
Client functions at the highest level possible.	Assist with sensory aids (i.e., hearing aids, eyeglasses). Use short, simple sentences. Do not give choices. Promote trust by use of touch (if appropriate) or unthreatening tone of voice. Praise desired behavior and ignore inappropriate behavior. Use large-lettered name tags for patients and staff (family may also need these). Label room, closet, and drawers with person's name (use name to which person usually responds). Use a calm, unhurried approach to care activities. Explain events as simply as possible just before they are to occur. Introduce yourself each time you come in contact with resident. Assign caregivers for continuity. Encourage use of familiar objects and reminiscence with photo albums.

Nursing Diagnosis: Altered nutrition; at risk for changing needs	
Expected Outcome	*Nursing Actions*
Client experiences no nutritional deficiencies.	Feed three balanced meals a day; increase complex carbohydrates. Limit extra salt and sugar if possible. Offer liquids every 2 hours, avoiding caffeine. Offer fruit and bran to help with elimination. Serve food that is easy to chew or use finger foods. Use finger foods or delay feeding if patient is upset. Assess for protein-calorie nutrition by daily weights. Offer snacks to maintain weight, especially if patient wanders.

TABLE 36–3   CARE PLAN *(Continued)*

Nursing Diagnosis: Altered sleep pattern	
Expected Outcome	*Nursing Actions*
Client sleeps through the night and stays awake most of the day.	Reduce naps during late afternoon; substitute morning naps to compensate for changes in sleep stages.
	Engage in daily activity such as exercise (sitting), walking, and games (ball toss).
	Carbohydrate snacks at bedtime may eliminate need for sleeping pills.
	Use nightlight to help in orientation.
	Assess for reactions of restlessness and insomnia that may occur in response to sedatives, hypnotics, or psychotropics.

applicable to a person with dementia. Potential nursing interventions are suggested. The reader is encouraged to expand on this plan of care using specific interventions based on data pertinent to the individual patient.

Table 36–4 gives a teaching guide for the families of patients with dementia. Table 36–5 lists some organizations that can be contacted for further information by the nurse or family members.

TABLE 36–4   TEACHING GUIDE: THE FAMILY

Provide information concerning dementia of the Alzheimer's type (or dementia generally).
  What is DAT?
    Describe pathology, stages or course of the disease, and outcome.
    Suggest readings.[34]
  Memory problems associated with the disease.
    Some long-term memory may remain intact, so give the person the opportunity to reminisce to integrate life experiences.
    Do not question the person.
  Combativeness.
    Remain calm and use diversionary measures.
    Teach communication techniques.
    Shouting may be misinterpreted as anger.
    People with DAT may think concretely.
      Example: Do not say "Jump in the shower now" because the person may respond with "I am afraid to jump."
  Problems in ADLs.
    Safety factors.
    Use handrails in the bathroom.
    Use nonskid rugs.
    Keep temperature control on water heaters.
    Install door devices that alert the caregiver when the person goes out.
    Keep controls on stoves and gas heaters.
    Consistent daily routine.
  Coping.
    Describe support groups available.
    Refer caregiver to community resources.
    Provide emotional support.
    Provide or encourage respite care; time away from the client (caregiving is difficult).
    Adult day-care centers.
    Vacations.
  Help the family identify stressors in caregiving.

Student Learning Activities

1 Contact the local Alzheimer's association to learn what services are available for people with AD and their families. Ask specifically about adult day care, nursing homes with specialized units, care at home, cost of services, available transportation, and reimbursement for services.

2 People with dementia and their families experience a number of losses. This activity will help you experience the kinds of feelings and thought that accompany many of these losses. Write down five of your most valuable possessions. Select one to give up. Imagine all your thoughts and feelings about giving up that valued possession. Repeat this process until you have one left. Share with your classmates why you kept this one until last and what it feels like to be without the other possessions.

3 You just came home from the doctor. You were told that you have Alzheimer's disease. Complete the following statements:

Right now I am feeling _____.

My primary concern is _____.

The most difficult thing about having this disease is _____.

_____ will take care of me.

Before the disease progresses, I want to _____.

I hope people will remember me as _____.

TABLE 36–5   RESOURCES: SUPPORT GROUPS FOR CAREGIVERS

Alzheimer's Association (formerly ADRDA)
National Headquarters
70 East Lake Street
Chicago, IL 60601
312-335-8882 or 800-272-3900
Familial Alzheimer's Disease Research Foundation
8177 South Harvard, Suite 114
Tulsa, OK 74137
918-493-8476

I hope that when someone else has to care for me, he or she will _____.

I wish I did not know I have this disease. (agree or disagree)

REFERENCES

1 Maslow, K: Current knowledge about special care units: Findings of a study by the U.S. Office of Technology Assessment. Alzheimer Dis Assoc Disord 8(1):14–39, 1994.

2 National Institute of Health: Progress report of Alzheimer's disease 1994. NIH, Bethesda, Md, 1995.

3 Grinspoon, L: Alzheimer's disease: Part I. Harvard Ment Health Lett 9(2):1–4, 1992.

4 Burns, EM, and Buckwalter, KC: Pathophysiology and etiology of Alzheimer disease. Nurs Clin North Am 23(1):11, 1988.

5 Katzman, R, and Jackson, J: Alzheimer's disease: Basic and clinical advances. J Am Geriatr Soc 39(5):516, 1991.

6 Timiras, PA: Physiological Basis of Aging and Geriatrics. Macmillan, New York, 1988.

7 National Institute of Health: Progress report of Alzheimer's disease 1996. NIH, Bethesda, Md, 1996.

8 Ham, RJ, and Sloang, PD: Primary care geriatrics: A case-based approach. Mosby, St Louis, 1992.

9 McDowell, FH, and Cedarbaum, FH: Natural history of dopa treated Parkinson's disease: 18 years follow-up. In Rose, FC (ed): Parkinson Disease Clinical and Experimental Advances. John Libby, London, 1987.

10 Rocca, WA: Frequency, distribution, and risk factors for Alzheimer's disease. Nurs Clin North Am 29(1):101–111, 1994.

11 La Rue, A: Aging and neurological assessment. Plenum, New York, 1992.

12 Stern, Y, et al: Influence of education and occupation on the incidence of Alzheimer's disease. JAMA 271:1004–1010, 1994.

13 Snowdon, DA, et al: Education, survival, and independence in elderly Catholic sisters, 1936–1988. Am J Epidemiol 130(5):999–1012, 1989.

14 Snowdon, DA, et al: Linguistic ability in early life and cognitive function in late life: Findings from the nun study. JAMA 275(7):528–535, 1996.

15 Greiner, PA, et al: The loss of independence in activities of daily living: The role of low normal cognitive function in elderly nuns. Am J Public Health 86(1):62–66, 1996.

16 Post, SG: Genetics, ethics, and Alzheimer disease. J Am Geriatr Soc 42:782–786, 1994.

17 Price, DL, and Sisodia, SS: Cellular and molecular biology of Alzheimer's disease and animal models. Ann Rev Med 45:435–446, 1994.

18 Yanagihara, T, and Petersen, RC: Memory disorders. Marcel Dekker, New York, 1991.

19 American Psychiatric Association: Diagnostic and Statistical Manual of Mental Disorders, ed 4. APA, Washington, DC, 1994.

20 Folstein, MF, et al: "Mini mental state": A practical method of grading the cognitive state of patients for the clinician. J Psychiatr Res 12:189–198, 1975.

21 Berg, L: Mild senile dementia of the Alzheimer type: Diagnostic criteria and natural history. Mt Sinai J Med 55:87–96, 1988.

22 Pfeiffer, A: A short portable mental status questionnaire for the assessment of organic brain deficit in elderly patients. J Am Geriatr Soc 23:433–441, 1975.

23 Baum, C, et al: Identification and measurement of productive behaviors in senile dementia of the Alzheimer type. Gerontologist 33(2):403–408, 1993.

24 Blessed, G, et al: The association between quantitative measures of dementia and of senile changes in the cerebral grey matter of elderly subjects. Br J Psychiatry 114:797–811, 1968.

25 Reisberg, B, et al: Behavioral symptoms in Alzheimer's disease: Phenomenology and treatment. J Clin Psychiatry (suppl)48:9–15, 1987.

26 Greene, JG, et al: Measuring behavioral disturbance of elderly demented patients in the community and its effects on relatives: A factor analytic study. Age Ageing 11:121–126, 1982.

27 Yudofsky, SC, et al: The overt aggression scale for the objective rating of verbal and physical aggression. Am J Psychiatry 143(1):35–39, 1986.

28 Drachman, DA, et al: The caretaker obstreperous-behavior rating assessment (COBRA) scale. J Am Geriatr Soc 40:463–470, 1992.

29 Lawton, MP: Environment and Aging. Center for the Study of Aging, Albany, NY, 1986.

30 Hall, GR, and Buckwalter, KC: Progressively lowered stress threshold: A conceptual model for care of adults with Alzheimer's disease. Arch Psychiatr Nurs 1:399–406, 1987.

31 Aricept package insert. Eisai Inc, November 25, 1996.

32 Eisai Press Release: Eisai receives FDA marketing clearance for Aricept (donepezil hydrochloride, a new treatment for Alzheimer's disease). Eisai Co, Ltd, November 25, 1996.

33 Rogers, SL, and Friedhoff, LT: The efficacy and safety of donepezil in patients with Alzheimer's disease: Results of a US multicentre, randomized, double-blind, placebo-controlled trial. Dementia 7:293–303, 1996.

34 Mace, NL, and Rabins, PV: The 36-hour day. Johns Hopkins University, Baltimore, 1991.

35 Paveza, GJ: Social services and the Alzheimer's disease patient: An overview. Neurology 43(4):11–15, 1993.

36 Ohta, RJ, and Ohta, BM: Special care units for Alzheimer's disease patients: A critical look. Gerontologist, 28(6):803–808, 1988.

37 Sand, BJ, et al: Alzheimer's disease: Special care units in long-term facilities. J Gerontol Nurs 18(3):28–34, 1992.

38 Maas, ML, et al: A nursing perspective on SCUs. Alzheimer Dis Assoc Disord 8(1):S417–424, 1994.

39 Kovach, CR, and Stearns, SA: DSCUs: A study of behavior before and after residence. J Gerontol Nurs 20:33–39, 1994.

40 Riter, RN, and Fries, BE: Predictors of the placement of cognitively impaired residents on special care units. Gerontologist 32:184–190, 1992.

41 Austin, B, and Melbourne, P: Hospice services for the terminal Alzheimer's patients. Caring November: 60–62, 1990.

42 Volicer, L, et al: Is hospice appropriate for Alzheimer patients? Caring November: 50–55, 1990.

43 Wilson, SA, et al: Hospice concepts in the care for end-stage dementia. Geriatr Nurs 17(1):6–10, 1996.

44 Cohen-Mansfield, J, et al: Two studies of pacing in the nursing home. J Gerontol 46:M77–M83, 1991.

45 Dawson, P, and Reid, DW: Behavioral dimensions of patients at risk for wandering. Gerontologist 27:104–107, 1987.

46 Thomas, D: The effect of premorbid personality characteristics and leisure preferences on wandering behavior among hospitalized patients with dementia. Unpublished doctoral dissertation, Temple University, Philadelphia, 1995.

SECTION VI

Epilogue

CHAPTER 37

The Future of Gerontological Nursing

Mickey Stanley

As we progress through the end of the twentieth century, all facets of the health-care professions are under intensive scrutiny. The continually rising cost of health care and our nation's inability to provide basic health and social care for all Americans are issues of great concern. People are living longer as a result of technological advances and lifestyle changes. Consequently, the predicted "graying of America" has arrived, with older adults constituting the fastest-growing segment of the population. By 2040, life expectancy is predicted to be 86 years for men and 91 years for women. In the next century, the health-care needs of this segment of the population, as well as those of the young and middle-aged, will be health promotion and health protection, housing, and social services.[1]

Nursing's Role

CLINICAL KNOWLEDGE AND SKILLS

Nursing's role in this evolutionary process begins with a thorough knowledge base of the aging process, both biophysical and sociological. Age-appropriate assessment skills and an ability to identify and plan for risk-factor reduction on primary, secondary, and tertiary levels will be essential. Balancing multiple chronic conditions, in both the acute and the stable states, will be a major challenge to older adults and to health-care professionals who serve as partners with older people in managing their care.

All Americans must put away ageist attitudes and begin to see all people, both young and old, as individuals with potential for successful aging. Nursing's advocacy role will be key to ensuring that older adults have an active voice in the decision making that affects them, as ethical issues cloud clinical decisions. Case management skills will be essential as the need for coordination of services increases to help older adults remain active and self-actualized throughout their lives.

The importance of health promotion and health protection must be emphasized during every encounter between older adults and health-care professionals. The critical aspects of health promotion include appropriate medication usage, healthy eating, appropriate physical and mental activity, stopping smoking, stress reduction, and the importance of staying actively engaged in life. The essential components of health protection involve risk factor identification and reduction, prompt detection and appropriate management of health problems, and an intentional focus on rehabilitation for all older adults. These elements apply to nurses in every role and practice setting.

NURSING RESEARCH

There is an urgent need for nursing research to guide practice in this area. To date, most research has excluded older adults as subjects because of the high-risk nature of this population. These barriers must be overcome and methods designed to ensure informed consent and appropriate access to representative populations of older adults that will allow rigorous study of critical questions regarding the health of this group. Nurses must participate on institutional review boards and review panels to ensure the protection of older adults' rights and the potential success of valuable studies.

Longitudinal studies are needed to determine the efficacy of health promotion activities and the most effective management, from both clinical and economic perspectives, of the major chronic disease states. The unique needs of frail older adults and of "young," healthy older adults require broad-based research programs. The impact of race and ethnicity on health-care practices and problems will be an important area of further study. In addition, the needs of special older populations such as the homeless, and those with acquired immunodeficiency syndrome and Alzheimer's disease will all benefit from additional research efforts.

Nurses in all roles and practice areas must consider nursing research a part of their practice. Nurses prepared with advanced degrees are needed to develop and direct worthwhile clinical studies. Nurses practicing with older adults in all settings are needed to provide insights into clinical issues and concerns, assist with data collection, and implement research findings. Nursing educators must instill a sense of appreciation for the research process and appropriate critique of research reports that will foster the development of future studies.

EDUCATION

Content on the unique aspects of nursing practice with older adults was rarely found in formal nursing education programs before the 1990s. Today an increasing number of undergraduate nursing programs offer course work and clinical experiences to prepare beginning practitioners with the knowledge and skills needed to practice in this emerging specialty. In addition, graduate programs in nursing are including gerontological nursing specialty tracts, and national continuing educational programs in gerontological nursing are increasing. As the specialty continues to grow along with the growth of this segment of the population, nurses will need to stay abreast of emerging trends and new information through continuing education programs and the printed literature.

CERTIFICATION

An increasing number of nurses are becoming certified in gerontological nursing through the American Nurses' Association each year. These newly certified experts can be expected to provide leadership at all levels of nursing practice and education. As they role model the value of appropriate nursing care for older adults through their own practice as well as through sharing their knowledge base in formal and informal teaching settings, the specialty of caring for the unique needs of older adults will continue to achieve the recognition it deserves.

Summary

This is an exciting time for those involved in providing high-quality health care for older adults. Knowledge to support the practice is growing daily. Opportunities to develop innovative practice models are limitless. The need for knowledgeable, committed nurses at all levels of practice has never been greater. The future of gerontological nursing is yours for the taking. Good luck!

REFERENCE
1 Alford, DM, and Futrell, M: Wellness and health promotion of the elderly. Nurs Outlook 40:5, 1992.

Index

Boxes are indicated with a *b* following the page number; tables are indicated with a *t* following the page number; figures are indicated with an *f* following the page number.